The Eagleton Reader

For *Oliver Francis Eagleton*
born in Dublin, 16 January 1997

The Eagleton Reader

Edited by Stephen Regan

BLACKWELL
Publishers

Copyright © Blackwell Publishers Ltd, 1998
Editorial apparatus, selection and arrangement copyright © Stephen Regan, 1998

First published 1998

2 4 6 8 10 9 7 5 3 1

Blackwell Publishers Ltd
108 Cowley Road
Oxford OX4 1JF
UK

Blackwell Publishers Inc.
350 Main Street
Malden, Massachusetts 02148
USA

British Library Cataloguing in Publication Data

A CIP catalogue record for this book is available from the British Library.

Library of Congress Cataloging-in-Publication Data
Eagleton, Terry, 1943–
    The Eagleton reader/edited by Stephen Regan.
        p.   cm.
    Includes bibliographical references and index.
    ISBN 0-631-20248-X. – ISBN 0-631-20249-8 (pbk.)
    1. Criticism.   2. Literature – History and criticism – Theory, etc.   3. English literature – History and criticism.   I. Regan, Stephen, 1957– .   II. Title.
    PN85.E34   1998
    809 – dc21   97-16433
                                                                                                CIP

Typeset in 10 on 12 pt Ehrhardt
by Best-set Typesetter Ltd., Hong Kong
Printed and bound in Great Britain by MPG Books Ltd, Bodmin, Cornwall

This book is printed on acid-free paper

Contents

Preface

In the summer of 1966 a highly provocative essay titled 'Politics and Benediction' appeared in *Slant*, the journal of the Catholic left. The essay proposed that the Catholic ceremony of benediction was complicit with the ways of capitalism in reducing the congregation to passive spectators and in treating the body of Christ as a commodity. In a later issue of *Slant*, 'Politics and Benediction' earned the severe rebuke of Edmund Hill OP for its intemperate politics and its abstruse phenomenology. The unrepentant author of this scurrilous piece of polemic was Terence Eagleton, a working-class radical from Salford in Lancashire, who had recently graduated from Cambridge University and taken up a fellowship in English at Jesus College. By his early twenties, he had already acquired a reputation as a combative, tenacious critic.

Sheer audacity, of a kind that frequently borders on self-parody, has been one of the most enduring and appealing qualities in Terry Eagleton's writings and lectures. It has helped to make him one of the most colourful and controversial figures in cultural politics today. The *Slant* story is more than a footnote in the history of the Catholic left. What it points to unmistakably is a convergence of cultural and political allegiances that even in the 1960s lifted Eagleton's interests well beyond the narrow confines of 'English'. Contrary to what his critics seem to think, Eagleton never abandoned 'English' for 'theory' or made some devious and suspect journey from literary studies to cultural politics: he was there from the start.

The extent to which Eagleton's theoretical preoccupations are rooted in radical theology is rarely acknowledged, but even now his essays are just as likely to appear in *New Blackfriars* as in *Diacritics* or *Textual Practice*. His early literary criticism enthusiastically embraces the writings of Gerard Manley Hopkins and Graham Greene, probing the metaphysics of sin and guilt with an ardent religious scholasticism. As a subtle defender of 'the word' and 'the truth', he later puts the brakes on the wilder flights of deconstruction. In his most recent critical engagement with postmodernism, he has turned to models of social justice and civic virtue that carry the imprint of radical Catholicism as well as revolutionary socialism. In his frequent forays into Irish cultural politics, from his early writings on Yeats to the massively ambitious *Heathcliff and the Great Hunger* in 1995, his instincts and sympathies have been those of a Catholic nationalist tradition. While it might be entirely feasible to take the boy out of the church, it is infinitely harder to take the church out of the boy.

Introducing a volume of critical writings by Terry Eagleton might seem a merely gratuitous exercise, since no one explains critical theory with greater clarity and cogency than he does. There are, however, significant aspects of his work, including its formative Catholic phase, that are often overlooked. There are vast swathes of his writing, in books such as *Exiles and Émigrés* and *The Rape of Clarissa* (both out of print), which deserve a broader readership; and there are dozens of journal articles from around the world which reveal a range and diversity of interests simply unknown to the vast majority of Eagleton's readers. The purpose of this book is to make a considerable part of that work more easily available, and to present it in a way that student readers, in particular, might find helpful. The arrangement of the book deliberately cuts against a simple chronological overview, pointing instead to particular cultural debates and significant moments of intervention and development within those debates. The headings attached to these distinctive projects or preoccupations are largely arbitrary ('Marxist critical theory' or 'cultural politics' might apply to all the essays printed here), but their purpose is to bring a diverse set of interests – literary, linguistic, theological, philosophical, political – into conjunction with each other, in a way that might illuminate the nature of Eagleton's critical achievements and those of Marxist criticism more generally.

To call Terry Eagleton the most gifted Marxist thinker of his generation is only a slender acknowledgement of his critical and creative achievements. There is simply no other cultural critic writing today who can match his popularity or his prolific output. His work has made an impact on the teaching of literary and cultural studies throughout Europe, and in almost every part of the world including China, Japan, India, Russia, Australia, Canada and the United States. For the post-1970s generation of students, researchers and teachers currently engaged in literary and cultural studies in Britain, Eagleton is the critic *par excellence*. The appeal of his work stems, in part, from the bold enquiry he has launched into the origins and aims of 'English studies', and from a closely related and equally relentless questioning of the function of 'criticism' today. Almost single-handedly he has transformed the very nature of critical discourse, breaking down distinctions between critical and creative writing, between academic seriousness and popular comedy, and generally making criticism a more companionable and hospitable domain.

A salient feature of his critical prose is its scintillating dialectical style, its shrewdly discerning grasp of social and cultural contradictions, and its hair-raising way of pushing conflicting arguments so forcefully into collision that they burst and suddenly reveal some unexpected insight or perspective. A favourite Swiftian technique is to construct some plausible, sophisticated argument with meticulous care, only to knock the skids from under it and watch it topple to oblivion.

Conversely, we are just as likely to be presented with a set of seemingly ridiculous, far-fetched assumptions, and then discover in the course of argument how just and reasonable they are. Such swift and agile reversals are the hallmark of his deft rhetorical style. Increasingly, his writing has adopted the deflationary humour, the epigrammatic wit and the delightful display of paradox that characterize the critical essays of Oscar Wilde. Eagleton has a repertoire of rhetorical ploys that effortlessly surpasses the skilful gambits of Roland Barthes and Jacques Derrida. While not being averse to the occasional deconstructive spin in his own writing, he has no truck with Derrida's evasion of political commitment.

Like Saint Oscar, Eagleton enjoys a fashionable flaunting of his dialectical tendencies, though strictly within the precincts of critical theory. At the same time, his fondness for ambivalence and disputation is not a merely academic inclination, but a way of articulating a deeply felt and lived response to the conflicts and injustices in class society. The early alignment of Marxist and Catholic beliefs produced an impressive series of books and essays, published in rapid succession between 1966 and 1970: *The New Left Church* (1966), *From Culture to Revolution* (1968), *Directions: Pointers for the Post-Conciliar Church* (1968) and *The Body as Language* (1970). From the outset, Eagleton's theoretical work has been in dialogue with various kinds of creative writing – poems, songs, fiction, plays – to the point where any neat distinction between the theoretical and the creative begins to blur. His essays and books have repeatedly acknowledged 'the end of English', and yet among his many publications, from *Shakespeare and Society* (1967) to *William Shakespeare* (1986), are some of the finest readings (and re-readings) of established authors on the English literary syllabus: Richardson, Dickens, Gaskell, the Brontës, Hardy and Lawrence. A dazzling exponent of deconstruction, he has also been one of its most scathing critics. English by nationality but Irish by descent, he has given himself the task of dismantling the various conflicting narratives that have shaped the literature and history of British–Irish relations in the past two hundred years.

If the essays gathered here show a remarkable agility of style and diversity of interest, they are also remarkably consistent; for while the method and the focus of the criticism might have shifted, sometimes dramatically, the political convictions have been unswerving and persistent. For over thirty years Eagleton has been steadfast in his commitment to the socialist transformation of class society, however outdated or obdurate that idea might seem amidst more fashionable postmodern pursuits. It is more than a shade ironic, therefore, that his critics seem to delight in the scandalous suggestion that 'Eagleton keeps changing his mind'. Another pervasive notion among his detractors is that of the adventurous Eagleton surfing wave after wave of cross-channel theory, enjoying the sport and merely adding to its popularity. While popularizing theory seems a wholly admirable activity, Eagleton's technique has never been one of simply encountering and responding to theory. If there is a single design in this *Reader*, it is to show how at every stage of engagement with theory, there is also a critical transformation of theory, an ability to use its insights and perspectives in the interest of a radical socialist politics.

From Culture to Revolution is the stirring title of a collection of papers from a *Slant* symposium held in 1967 to address 'the problems of a common culture'. While there is no doubt that Raymond Williams is the presiding spirit (his comments introduce and conclude the debate), there is no doubt either that Eagleton's concern is with the translation of cultural insights into political practice, and with giving the insights of Williams's *Culture and Society 1780–1950* a more revolutionary tenor. Eagleton's first full-length book of literary criticism, *Shakespeare and Society* (1967), is dedicated to Williams, and its concern with breaking down the settled distinction between individual and society, between spontaneous life and social structure, derives from his former teacher and colleague. The novelty of the book, however, is that it responds to Shakespeare's plays with an understanding of 'self' and 'society' that post-dates the Industrial Revolution and stems in part from a cultural analysis of its disruptive effects. In 1967 the book cut against established opinion by explicitly suggesting that 'What we judge in the plays as relevant, what we actually see, is shaped by what we see in our own culture, in ourselves' (p. 9). As the Conclusion to the book reveals, Eagleton is studiously extending the concerns of *Culture and Society* back into the work of Shakespeare, but his notable addition of Edward Carpenter to the cultural prophets of the late nineteenth century gives his argument about 'spontaneity' a valuable and original dimension.

Exiles and Émigrés (1970) turns to what was then the dominant European tradition of Marxist criticism, a tradition boldly led by Georg Lukács and shaped by his uncompromising belief in the efficacy of social realism. Eagleton subtly modifies and extends the argument that the realist novel reproduces the typical components of its history and functions as an 'intensive totality' of existing social relations. To anyone familiar with that tradition of Marxist literary theory, what is most striking is that Eagleton contradicts a fundamental tenet in the later writing of Lukács by giving a far more positive and appreciative response to 'the ideology of modernism' than the Hungarian Marxist would have countenanced. In this, he is already moving towards the more considered Marxist critique of modernism proposed by Theodor Adorno. Eagleton disputes the notion that modernist experimentalism necessarily involves an 'attenuation of actuality' and shows how D. H. Lawrence, for instance, achieves a marvellous 'totalization' of experience at the close of *The Rainbow*. By bringing colonialism, Englishness and exile to bear on the meanings and values of modernism, Eagleton enlarges and defines its possibilities as a subject of critical and cultural debate.

The methodological problem with which Eagleton grapples throughout the 1970s is how to root literature in its social conditions without reducing it to them. In his writings on Thomas Hardy and the Brontës, he turns increasingly to the Marxist structuralism of Lucien Goldmann. For Goldmann, what provides the mediating current between the organization or structure of history and the aesthetic structure of the text is the world view or mental structure of a particular social group or class. This structuralist method yields impressive results in Eagleton's *Myths of Power: A Marxist Study of the Brontës* (1975), especially in his reading of *Wuthering Heights*, but there remains some uncertainty about exactly how each order or level of the structural model – history, social consciousness, text – relates to the other. As the second edition of *Myths of Power* (1988) confirms, the book first appeared just as Marxist criticism (and literary theory generally) was about to undergo a dramatic transformation.

By 1976, Eagleton was already moving away from the Lukácsian idea of 'totalization' with its 'excessive pursuit of symmetry'. 'Marxist Literary Criticism', a key essay published in 1977, berates the neo-Hegelian Marxism of Lukács for its 'backward-looking, idealist notion of "wholeness"' and its 'stiff-necked, classicist contempt for modernist experiment'.[1] This was evidence of an increasing dissatisfaction with realist aesthetics. Even Goldmann's structuralism was posited on the idea that the text was 'expressive' of social consciousness, if not of social history. The leap from structuralism to post-structuralism was imminent. Even before *Myths of Power* was published, Eagleton was working on another way of considering the structural relations between literature and history. What this entailed was a radical epistemological break, whereby art came to be seen not as a reflex of social reality but as an active constituent of that reality. The focus now shifts to the idea of literature as a social practice and to ways of determining the ideological conditions under which the literary work is produced. This shift is powerfully evident in Eagleton's determination to establish a 'science of the text' in *Criticism and Ideology* and its popularizing 'primer', *Marxism and Literary Criticism*, both published in 1976.

Rather too much attention has been given to the impact of Louis Althusser on Eagleton's work at this time. Althusser's influential essay 'Ideology and Ideological State Apparatuses' – published in *Lenin and Philosophy and Other Essays* (1971) – undoubtedly informs the new systematic approach to ideological types and categories in *Criticism and Ideology*, but Eagleton's response to Althusser is by no means uncritical. The development of Eagleton's writings from 1975 onwards suggests that it was the writing of Althusser's colleague Pierre Macherey, especially *A Theory of Literary Production* (1966), that proved more influential and durable. Macherey's interest in the incompleteness of the text, in what the text does not and cannot say because of ideological constraints, connects his work with post-structuralist theories of textuality and provides a potent model for Marxist deconstruction.

Once again, what takes place is a complex engagement with a particular set of theoretical statements and positions, not a mere imitation but a careful deliberation over what might be adopted and refined, or otherwise discarded. While Macherey's theory of literary production shows ideology operating in the very material of the text – in its eloquent silences, its significant gaps and fissures – it overlooks the fact that texts are consumed as well as produced, and that the process of reading is historically mutable. In other words, Macherey presupposes an idealized, transcendental reader, whose response to the text is unvarying. In addition, Eagleton comes to see the Althusserian/Machereyan view of ideology drifting away from the problems of class struggle. In some respects, the theory of literary production that it underpins simply isn't materialist enough.

In what is probably the most decisive theoretical reorientation in his career, Eagleton turns back to the materialist aesthetics of Walter Benjamin and Bertolt Brecht, and reasserts the need for a more productive and effective cultural criticism. This new and fierce critical spirit is immediately evident in *Walter Benjamin or Towards a Revolutionary Criticism* (1981), a book still regarded by many of Eagleton's admirers as his finest achievement. The Preface to *Walter Benjamin* records the book's involvement in a more general shift in critical theory 'from narrowly textual or conceptual analysis to problems of cultural production and the political use of artefacts'.[2] The book also marks a stage of decisive rethinking within socialism itself: what relations exist between socialist cultural theory and cultural practice, and what bearing do these have on revolutionary politics? What political uses do theatre and comedy have? Benjamin's methods appear attractive, not least because they foreshadow some of the most striking features of post-structuralism, and so demonstrate how deconstruction might be put to use without abandoning a commitment to Marxism. At the same time, in a searching chapter titled 'Marxism and Deconstruction', the book launches into a sharp critique of the work of Jacques Derrida and his North American disciples, keeping the notion of any easy alliance firmly at bay.

Walter Benjamin also marks a clear recognition of the value and importance of feminist criticism, a theoretical perspective hardly entertained in works of literary criticism before the mid-1970s. Feminist criticism occupies many of the critical positions that Eagleton stakes out for a 'revolutionary literary criticism': it dismantles the dominant concepts of 'literature', returning literary texts to the broad field of actual practices; it interrogates established judgements and assumptions about particular authors and texts; it engages with the language and 'unconscious' of literary works; and it carries out its practice within a wide institutional and political context. In *The Rape of Clarissa*, published a year after *Walter Benjamin*, Eagleton draws extensively on the insights of feminist and psychoanalytic criticism in his study of language, sexuality and class struggle in the work of Samuel Richardson. Though not all feminist critics welcomed the potent blend of feminism, deconstruction and historical materialism, *The Rape of Clarissa* signalled a new eclecticism and openness to the vast proliferation of theory throughout the late 1970s and early 1980s. Such is the attitude of *Literary Theory* (1983), and one of the reasons for its enormous success and popularity is that it offers not just a survey but a provocative intervention within the history of theory, setting up a lively disputation with new criticism, structuralism, post-structuralism and psychoanalysis, and arguing the case for political criticism at every opportunity.

The Function of Criticism (1984) was the logical outcome of *Literary Theory* and a necessary companion to the earlier book. Going back to the opening chapter of

Literary Theory, 'The Rise of English', and picking up some of the rudiments of theory in eighteenth-century culture, *The Function of Criticism* looks at the history of critical practice in Britain since the Enlightenment. Criticism, it argues, was originally a political enterprise. 'born of a struggle against the absolutist state', and one which provided a space between state and civil society for 'rational judgement and enlightened critique'.[3] Arguing against the claim that literature and literary study have become contaminated by 'external' considerations, Eagleton proposes that 'criticism was only ever significant when it engaged with more than literary issues – when, for whatever historical reason, the "literary" was suddenly foregrounded as the medium of vital concerns deeply rooted in the general, intellectual, cultural and political life of an epoch.'[4] Unexpectedly, the book argues for the recovery of criticism's traditional role, as a way of redefining its present functions. Just as *The Function of Criticism* seeks to explain the current 'crisis in criticism' by pushing back to some fundamental moment, so *The Ideology of the Aesthetic* (1990), a much bigger and more ambitious book, seeks to illuminate the pre-history of theory in aesthetic philosophy. The book traces the complex relationship between aesthetics, ideology and political society, all the way from Immanuel Kant to Theodor Adorno.

The *Ideology of the Aesthetic* carries traces of two other cultural projects that were gathering pace at the outset of the 1990s. The Introduction to the book refers wistfully to what might have emerged if there had been space to review the progress of Irish cultural nationalism from Thomas Davis to Padraic Pearse in the light of European idealist thought. The closing chapter, meanwhile, takes a dim view of the current debates on ethics and aesthetics in the realm of post-structuralist and postmodernist theory. The first of these concerns finds ample realization in *Heathcliff and the Great Hunger* (1995), a book that flagrantly brings the language of contemporary cultural theory to bear on Irish literature and history, noting at the same time how the complexities and specificities of Irish experience reveal deficiencies in the theory. The second set of interests comes to fruition in *The Illusions of Postmodernism* (1996), the critical culmination of Eagleton's increasing unease with the evasions and obliquities of much postmodern cultural theory. What these books share is a deep and abiding concern with civic virtue and social justice. As Seamus Deane pointed out in his appreciative review of *Heathcliff and the Great Hunger*, the book's theme is 'the search for a foundation for moral and political principles that would secure a civil society'.[5] What generates Eagleton's compelling critique of theory in *The Illusions of Postmodernism* is a conviction that the old foundational discourses of reason, truth, freedom and subjectivity have been too easily and irresponsibly relinquished.

Both *Heathcliff and the Great Hunger* and *The Illusions of Postmodernism* traduce conventional academic discourse, one by wilfully transgressing established disciplines and the other by loading its criticism with a comic, but often caustic, irony. Traditional lines of division between seriousness and humour, and between creative and intellectual writing, are subtly erased. In an interview printed in *The*

Significance of Theory (1990) Eagleton suggests that feminist criticism has brought into play a more pleasurable style of writing, contesting the idea that pleasure is essentially frivolous and non-intellectual. At the same time, he attributes the wit and humour of his own increasingly relaxed and congenial style to the potent influence of Irish culture.

The growing convergence of intellectual and creative activities finds its apotheosis in *Saint Oscar and Other Plays* (1997). Eagleton's Introduction to the plays asserts, with the authority of Wilde himself, that there is no reason 'writing criticism or theory shouldn't be an art in itself, just as enthralling and fulfilling as fashioning fiction'.[6] The three Irish plays – *Saint Oscar, The White, the Gold and the Gangrene,* and *God's Locusts* – all transgress the jealously patrolled frontiers between 'art' and 'ideas'. *Saint Oscar and Other Plays* is a clear indication of Eagleton's continuing determination not to isolate 'theory' from other, popular kinds of cultural activity. It gives free rein to its author's penchant for satirical and political ballads. 'The Ballad of Marxist Criticism', which aptly closes *The Eagleton Reader,* is part of that venerable tradition, and a more entertaining introduction to his work than this one.

Notes

1 'Marxist Literary Criticism', in Hilda Schiff (ed.), *Contemporary Approaches to English Studies* (London: Heinemann, 1977), p. 99.
2 *Walter Benjamin or Towards a Revolutionary Criticism* (London and New York: Verso, 1981), p. xii.
3 *The Function of Criticism* (London and New York: Verso, 1984), p. 9.
4 Ibid., p. 107.
5 Seamus Deane, 'Soft Cop, Hard Cop' (review of *Heathcliff and the Great Hunger*), *London Review of Books* (19 Oct 1995), 28.
6 *Saint Oscar and Other Plays* (Oxford: Blackwell Publishers, 1997), p. 1.

Acknowledgements

I wish to thank those friends and colleagues who have shared my respect and enthusiasm for Terry Eagleton's work over many years, and who encouraged me to edit this *Reader*. I am especially grateful to Taieb Belghazi, Steven Connor, Adrian Cunningham, Ray Cunningham, Antony Easthope, Ken Hirschkop, Stephen Howe, Linda Hutcheon, Edward Larrissy, Willy Maley, Kate McGowan, Graham Martin, Don Milligan, Bernard O'Donoghue, Paul O'Flinn, Tony Pinkney, Stan Smith, Geoff Wade, Carol Watts and Patricia Waugh. The notes on Hardy, Wilde, Lawrence and Yeats owe a great deal to many discussions I have had with Ted Chamberlin, John Lavery, Brian Spittles, John Squires, Glyn Turton and John Unrau. The introductory material in the book was given a thorough overhaul by Stuart Sim and Kiernan Ryan, both of whom made very helpful comments. I should like to thank my colleagues at the Open University for their constant support and goodwill. I am deeply grateful to Lizbeth Goodman for her many valuable suggestions about the content and format of the book.

The selection of essays in this *Reader* was guided by numerous saints and scholars. Herbert McCabe OP (Blackfriars, Oxford) and Fergus Kerr OP (Blackfriars, Edinburgh) helped me to obtain material in early issues of *Slant* and *New Blackfriars*. David Cameron provided valuable information about the Oxford Amnesty Lectures. Tony Coulson, Liaison Librarian for Arts at the Open University, was immensely helpful with bibliographical matters. Jane de Gay very generously helped me in tracking down sources; Emily Spence assisted with proof reading; and Beata Piątek provided the image for the book cover. The preparation of the *Reader* was greatly eased by the excellent library facilities in Oxford, and I am grateful for the kind and friendly assistance I received from Helen Rogers, Tina King and Vera Ryhajlo in the Bodleian Library, from David and Val Horsfield at Ruskin College, and from Sue Usher and her colleagues in the English Faculty Library. I am deeply indebted to David Grylls, in the Department for Continuing Education, University of Oxford, for inviting me to teach on his Modern Critical Theory course. I have benefited greatly from his advice and support, and from the enthusiasm and commitment of the students we have taught together.

I am grateful to Terry Eagleton for responding so warmly and enthusiastically to the initial proposal for this *Reader* and for his close collaboration on its contents and design. Any spelling errors, stylistic infelicities or political misjudgements are, of course, entirely his. The inspiration behind *The Eagleton Reader* came from Andrew McNeillie, who not only commissioned the book but shaped and sustained it from the outset. I wish to thank him for his unstinting trust and encouragement.

Stephen Regan
Oxford, 1997

Part I Literary Criticism

Introduction

It seems fitting that this book should open with an early essay on D. H. Lawrence (Chapter 1), a writer whose exploration of the problems of social class and cultural identity has had a profound and lasting appeal for Marxist literary criticism. For Terry Eagleton, as for Raymond Williams, the novels of D. H. Lawrence show repeatedly how an instinctive allegiance to a working-class culture and a desire or determination to move beyond it can co-exist in painful and perpetual tension. The essay forms the closing chapter of *Exiles and Émigrés*, a formidable study of expatriatism in modern literature, which seeks to understand the dominance in early twentieth-century writing of such 'émigrés' as Joseph Conrad, Henry James, T. S. Eliot, Ezra Pound, W. B. Yeats and James Joyce. All of these authors were compelled to write about the seeming collapse and disintegration of Western civilization and all were able to draw on experiences and perspectives outside conventional English society. Lawrence, by contrast, was English, yet his working-class milieu afforded him a powerful critique of England that possessed both the distance and detachment of the outsider and the intimacy and inwardness of the native.

Exiles and Émigrés develops and extends the influential theories of realism proposed by the Hungarian Marxist critic Georg Lukács. Among the key terms in the book are 'totality' and 'totalization', with which Lukács described the capacity of literary works to embody a complete vision of society, bringing together both personal feeling and public event, both local insight and general understanding. Like Raymond Williams, whose study of realist fiction *The English Novel from Dickens to Lawrence* was published the same year (1970), Eagleton modifies the Lukácsian view of social realism, claiming that the process of grasping any culture as a whole becomes much more problematic in fiction from the mid-nineteenth century onwards. *Exiles and Émigrés* insists that the achievement of a comprehensive vision of society in nineteenth-century realism is decisively ruptured in the early twentieth century. In a social condition perceived as fragmentary and flawed, the common difficulty is that of discovering a vantage point from which a coherent vision might be possible. In this respect, the book is concerned not just with the perspectives of non-English writers but with the ways in which English writers such as George Orwell and Graham Greene were exiles within their own society, driven by the search for some point of transcendence from which their society might be explained and understood. It is here that the novels of D. H. Lawrence prove most revealing.

In some ways Lawrence appears to be the archetypal modern exile, a wanderer in Europe, America, Australia and New Mexico, but the concern in *Exiles and Émigrés* is with the nature of Lawrence's exile and estrangement within English culture. Adopting the vocabulary of Raymond Williams, Eagleton identifies pervasive 'structures of feeling' in Lawrence's novels, including the powerful pull between settlement and transcendence that characterizes *Sons and Lovers*. Ironically, Paul Morel moves beyond the boundaries of the family into a broader social sphere, but the force which impels him – his mother's influence – also brings him home. The recurrent rhythm of intimacy and estrangement, relatedness and autonomy, is played out over different generations in *The Rainbow*. One of the highlights of this essay is its superb analysis of the closing paragraph of *The Rainbow*, with its high praise for Lawrence's 'totalizing' achievement and his 'intensely persuasive vision of an entire culture'. *Women in Love* seems to reduce the complex social fabric of the earlier novels by focusing too intensely on a restricted set of relationships, while the relationships themselves have an 'attenuated' quality (a criticism Lukács frequently makes of modernist literature). In *Lady Chatterley's Lover* the conflict between Lawrence's increasing alienation from English society and his increasing determination to recover a lost sense of value in that society finally proves disabling. Even so, Lawrence is regarded as unusual among twentieth-century writers in presenting both an intimate understanding of English society and a comprehensive radical criticism of its forms and directions. It is well worth comparing this early essay on Lawrence with another study in *Criticism and Ideology* (pp. 157–61), in which a decisive break is made with the work of Georg Lukács. In the later book, Lawrence's 'vision' is reconfigured in terms of ideology and its complex relationship with literary form. A further study of Lawrence can be found in *Literary Theory* (pp. 151–5), where the ideas of Jacques Lacan are put to use in a psychoanalytical reading of *Sons and Lovers*.

Exiles and Émigrés was a bold and ambitious attempt to move beyond some of the limiting definitions of social realism in Marxist literary theory and to find a way of assessing those modern works of literature in which the possibility of a complete or 'total' vision of society is rendered problematic. Its method is tentative and exploratory, but its preoccupation with such issues as modernism, Englishness and cultural identity gives the book a continuing relevance. In addition, the book contains a brilliantly illuminating chapter, 'Reluctant Heroes: the Novels of Graham Greene' (first published in *Slant* in 1969), which demonstrates, among other things, that radical theology was a formative and distinctive component of Eagleton's critical thinking.

A radical Roman Catholic consciousness also permeates the early essay 'Nature and the Fall in Hopkins: A Reading of "God's Grandeur" ' (Chapter 2). A knowledge of theological debates on the Fall and the question of original sin is presented with casual ease – as the striking opening sentence of the essay demonstrates – but the complexity of these debates is thoroughly teased out in the reading of 'God's Grandeur' that follows. Like the essay on Yeats's 'Easter 1916' (pp. 350–8), this reading draws attention to fundamental ambiguities and complexities in the linguistic structure of the poem. In 'God's Grandeur', however, the central ambiguity is one that is already inherent in Roman Catholic doctrine, which leaves uncertain the issue of whether Nature after the Fall is innocent and sacramental or contaminated and debased by the consequences of sin. The essay challenges the argument that Hopkins held these opposing views consecutively and shows how a simple chronological account of the poet's ideas of Nature proves inadequate and misleading.

One way of reconciling Hopkins's seemingly conflicting views might be through a subtle distinction between the phenomenal and the noumenal: natural objects might on the surface be polluted, but their spiritual essences remain intact. There are further ambiguities, however, which complicate a reading of Hopkins's poem. 'God's Grandeur' deplores the consequences of human intervention in Nature and yet reveals a lack of confidence in Nature as an independent life-force. The meticulous attention to syntax and vocabulary in this essay are characteristic of 'practical criticism', though in many ways its style and technique are those of deconstruction. Instead of resolving and reconciling ambiguities in the conventional manner of practical criticism, the essay exploits intrinsic tensions and conflicts so that new possibilities of meaning emerge. In this respect, the method is one of 'dialectical' rather than 'practical' criticism.

The same dialectical tendency is evident in the provocative essay on Thomas Hardy's *Jude the Obscure* (Chapter 3), first printed in 1974 as the introduction to the New Wessex Edition of the novel. Here we are reminded of the fierce and persistent dialectic between idealism and harsh actuality that sustains so much of the novel's action. Idealism operates as a critique of reality, but is in turn exposed by that reality as hopelessly utopian. The more impoverished Jude's living conditions become, the more fantastic and grotesque are his illusions. In moving hopefully forward, Jude is, in effect, returning to the past. In foregrounding this dialectical process in *Jude the Obscure*, the essay quickly uncovers the novel's corrosive ironies and debilitating contradictions. Personal fulfilment for Jude can be achieved only by struggling for recognition within the very culture that denies and rejects him. Jude's dedicated work as a stonemason involves the repair and restoration of the structures that exclude him. The essay provides an excellent illustration of *materialist criticism* working adroitly and resourcefully on the fruitful territory of late nineteenth-century realist fiction. Like Raymond Williams, Eagleton briskly dismisses the facile myths about Hardy the pessimist, the fatalistic puppet master bemoaning the incursions of modernity and change into a previously stable rural world. Not content with those conventional accounts of Hardy's work that attribute its tragic vision to chance or heredity or some implacable cosmic force, he finds the roots of tragedy deeply embedded in material circumstances – in the social and economic inequalities of late nineteenth-century England. This method of historical materialism shows Eagleton rethinking the relationship between literature and history, and gradually turning to Marxist structuralism. It assumes that the structure of the novel, including characterization, dialogue and narrative events, corresponds closely to the actual social and cultural conditions of the day. The essay's confidence in this method rests on a belief in the efficacy of realism: its ability to render some truthful account of history. At the same time, however, Eagleton eschews any naive suggestion that realism works simply as 'reflection'. The argument, like that of Raymond Williams in *The English Novel from Dickens to Lawrence*, is that momentous social change produces new forms of consciousness which are registered in fiction. Sue Bridehead, for instance, is seen to dramatize the conflicts and evasions of a 'transitional form of consciousness, deadlocked between the old and the new'. She points 'beyond herself, to a confused, ambiguous structure of feeling which belongs to the period in general'.

The 'Postscript on Thomas Hardy' that follows is extracted from 'Liberality and Order: The Criticism of John Bayley', first printed in *New Left Review* in 1978 and collected with other essays in *Against the Grain* (1986). A slightly different version appears in *Walter Benjamin or Towards a Revolutionary Criticism* (1981). Eagleton's interest here is in the way Hardy's fiction has been 'produced' by criticism. Hardy continues to occupy a prominent but peculiar position in literary tradition: a writer widely acknowledged as a major realist, a creator of memorable landscapes and characters, yet fiercely castigated as the clumsy craftsman of wildly implausible events and coincidences. The essay demonstrates the extent to which criticism at different times has struggled to accommodate Hardy's fiction within existing standards of style and form, sometimes dismissing it (as F. R. Leavis does) from 'the great tradition' of the English novel. Since it was first published, Hardy's work has been criticized for both its rustic simplicity and its educated allusiveness. For Eagleton, however, the significance of Hardy's writing lies 'precisely in the *contradictory* constitution of his linguistic practice . . . in the ceaseless play and tension between the two modes'. Drawing on Renée Balibar's analysis of the ideological role of literature in the French education system, Eagleton proposes that what throws traditional criticism of Hardy's fiction into disarray is its undisguised linguistic class division. Raymond Williams is acknowledged as the only critic who detects in the language of Hardy's texts the social and ideological crisis of their times.

The publication of *Myths of Power: A Marxist Study of the Brontës* (1975) coincided with a turning point in contemporary literary theory. As the introduction to the second edition of *Myths of Power* (1988) points out, the book anticipated a resurgence of Marxist criticism but failed to reap the benefits of other powerful currents of thought, especially feminism, deconstruction and psychoanalysis, belatedly making an impact on literary criticism in Britain in the 1970s. As the chapter on *Wuthering Heights* (Chapter 4) makes clear, *Myths of Power* is a highly theorized account of the Brontë novels, yet there are times when the book's critical method seems close to conventional practical criticism, with its elaborate and detailed studies of character and incident. Theory and practice sit uneasily together at this stage.

The dominant theoretical influence in *Myths of Power* comes not so much from Georg Lukács as from the Romanian Marxist critic Lucien Goldmann, whose structuralist methodology provides the book with a way of mediating between different 'levels' of analysis, including text, author, ideology and social class. Goldmann detects a correlation between historical structures and mental structures, effectively shifting the focus of criticism to 'consciousness' and its manifestations in the structure of the text. The essay on *Wuthering Heights* opens with some reservations about Goldmann's methodology, but nevertheless accepts his notion that history manifests itself in the 'world view' of a particular social group or class. Although this potent Marxist structuralism represents a significant advance over the methods of Georg Lukács, it nevertheless remains indebted to traditional realist aesthetics. The fictional text is still regarded as 'expressive', even if what it expresses is class consciousness rather than social and historical events, and its power is seen to reside in its capacity to forge a coherent, unified vision out of conflict and contradiction. Both of these assumptions were severely questioned by Eagleton himself, just one year later, in *Criticism and Ideology*.

It should be immediately clear in the essay on *Wuthering Heights* that Emily Brontë's novel is being praised for its coherence of vision and its rigorous realist control, while the novels of Charlotte Brontë are seen, in contrast, to be fissured and flawed by the strains and pressures of their content. The 'consciousness' and the formal structure of *Wuthering Heights* are granted a validity and a value that Charlotte Brontë's novels fail to achieve. *Wuthering Heights* is presented as a novel that grapples honestly and openly with historical antagonisms, and its formal perfection is regarded as a measure of its authenticity. If, in the light of post-structuralist criticism, the essay too readily applauds the 'unified vision' of *Wuthering Heights* and downplays the significance of slippages and ruptures in the texts of Charlotte Brontë, it nevertheless goes a long way towards reversing an idealist trend in Brontë criticism that would render *Wuthering Heights* immune from all traces of historical and political conflict. The essay has lost none of its refreshing radicalism, and its way of positioning the novel within the power struggles of the landed gentry and the industrial bourgeoisie remains an exemplary instance of historicist enquiry. The love between Cathy and Heathcliff is seen as a paradigm of human possibilities in a world dominated by economic and cultural inequalities.

To move from *Myths of Power* (1975) to *William Shakespeare* (1986) is to encounter the dramatic shift from structuralism to post-structuralism that dominated and transformed critical theory in the intervening decade. Whereas *Myths of Power* was concerned with the expressive nature of the literary text and its capacity for registering the forms of consciousness within a particular social formation, *William Shakespeare* presents itself as 'an exercise in political semiotics, which tries to locate the relevant history in the very letter of the text'. The focus of interest is now shifted to the material nature of the text itself. The unruly and disruptive textual practices of Shakespeare's plays are not so much an expression as a physical symptom of the social order. It is here, in the materiality of the text itself, that 'the interrelations of language, desire, law, money and the body' can be seen to function in compelling and contradictory ways. Whereas the structuralist approach of *Myths of Power* stabilized such binary oppositions as nature and culture, body and soul, within the realm of a coherent, unified vision, the post–structuralist methodology of *William Shakespeare* delights in seeing such binaries constantly undoing and inverting themselves in a striking display of disunity.

One of the most potent deconstructive methods in *William Shakespeare* (well illustrated here in Chapter 5) is to establish a parallel between the paradoxes of language and the paradoxes of law, making the radical instabilities of one rebound upon the other. Language, like law, is seen as possessing both a general structure or set of rules and particular instances or events. Just as there are moments when language creatively surpasses the rules of the system, thus putting these rules into question, so there are moments when the interpretation of the law (particular verdicts and judgements) generously exceeds the law and threatens to undermine its structure. Eagleton's Shylock is a proto–deconstructionist, wilfully provoking Venetian law to the point where it risks undoing itself and exposing its contradictory nature. In both *The Merchant of Venice* and *Measure for Measure* the moral problem is that of discriminating between those occasions when it is proper to exceed the law and those when it is reprehensible to do so. Both plays are preoccupied with the politics of the body. In *The Merchant of Venice*, the dispute between Antonio and Shylock is one of flesh and blood: the bond between them both recognizes and perverts the common humanity invested in the body. In *Measure for Measure*, Angelo is seen to personify the contradictory relationship between law and desire in Vienna; the play exploits the problematic space between the abstract edicts of the law and the unpredictable claims and impulses of the body.

Eagleton's flair as a critic of contemporary poetry is briefly represented here by his incisive review of Tony Harrison's controversial poem *v.* (Chapter 6). The poem was published in 1985 and presented by Harrison on Channel 4 television in 1987. Eagleton's essay appeared in *Poetry Review* in June 1986. *v.* is an urban elegy, set in the graveyard where Harrison's parents are buried, on Beeston Hill in Leeds. Like Thomas Gray's celebrated 'Elegy in a Country Churchyard', on which it is loosely modelled, *v.* incorporates colloquial diction and classical allusion within its cumulative rhymed quatrains. The central dramatic incident in *v.* is the poet's confrontation with a skinhead football supporter who has vandalized the gravestones in the cemetery. The poem issues from Harrison's anger and disillusionment at the state of the nation (it was written during the miners' strike of 1984–5), but it also contains a powerful dialogue which ends with the poet's recognition of the skinhead as his alter ego.

Eagleton's review draws attention to what the Russian linguist Mikhail Bakhtin termed 'dialogism' – the multiplicity of contending voices in a literary work – hence the quip that 'Harrison is a natural Bakhtinian, even if he has never read a word of him'. The review gives high praise to Harrison's deft handling of the politics of language and also to the prevailing irony that distinguishes his treatment of social class and saves it from the kind of class sentiment that pervades the plays of Arnold Wesker. Harrison invokes self-criticism within the poem, though in Eagleton's opinion he doesn't go far enough. In a clever dialectical twist, the essay takes up the position of the skinhead and berates the poet for his dispirited political imagination. For all its linguistic vigour, the poem finally displaces its immediate social concerns by turning to metaphysical rather than political anxieties.

The closing essay on the novels of Milan Kundera (Chapter 7) was written in the late 1980s, shortly before the dramatic political transformation of Czechoslovakia and the rest of Eastern Europe. Acutely responsive to that tense, ambiguous moment, the essay contemplates 'the daily hermeneutics of suspicion . . . the compulsive reading of signs' which the state bureaucracy induces. The problem for Milan Kundera, as for Franz Kafka, is not just how to write, but how to read: 'How to read without overreading, avoid a naive empiricism without falling prey to semiological paranoia'. For Kundera, the novel is a place where the contingency of existence, the unbearable lightness of being, can be rediscovered. The essay pays tribute to the structural subversiveness of Kundera's anti-totalitarian fictions, seeing in these dislocated texts a seemingly effortless method that eschews both the outrage of modernism and the portentousness of postmodernism. There is also in Kundera's fiction a subversive sexual politics: a canny awareness of that transgressive celebration of the body that Mikhail Bakhtin termed 'the carnivalesque'.

1 The Novels of D. H. Lawrence

I

That D.H. Lawrence was an exile from his own culture – in some ways, indeed, the archetypal modern exile – is well enough known; the rootless, frustrated wanderings in Europe, America, Australia, New Mexico have been sufficiently documented for that image (translated, often enough, into the distorting terms of a Byronic Romanticism) to have established itself in the general consciousness. But the nature of Lawrence's exile from his own society runs deeper than this. In previous writers, we have seen forms of estrangement from English culture which arose from a simple externality, at crucial points, to the character of its common experience; we have also seen, most evidently in Orwell and Greene, the impotent passivity of the man trapped as a social exile within a culture which could not be escaped, a form of life too oppressively familiar to be surmounted. But neither description fits Lawrence at all exactly. Lawrence's achievement, as both man and writer, was to fight his way free from a repressive society by a route which, in his best work, involved no loss of inwardness with that determining social reality: it is in this that he is genuinely unique.

In his comment on Lawrence in *Culture and Society 1780–1950*, Raymond Williams has valuably emphasised the quality of his personal involvement, from the inside, with the culture he was to grasp, in his mature work, as a complete structure:

> . . . his first social responses were those, not of a man observing the processes of industrialism, but of one caught in them, at an exposed point, and destined, in the normal course, to be enlisted in their regiments. That he escaped enlistment is now so well known to us that it is difficult to realise the thing as it happened, in its living sequence. It is only by hard fighting, and further, by the fortune of fighting on a favourable front, that anyone born into the industrial working class escapes his function of replacement. Lawrence could not be certain, at the time when his fundamental social responses were forming, that he could so escape.[1]

Lawrence escaped enlistment, but not by the route which society conventionally offered men in his position: an extrication from the working class for the purposes of recruitment into the ranks of those who kept them in their place. This was not simply a matter of 'class-loyalty': it was that what Lawrence learnt from his childhood experience in a working-class family included, implicitly and persistently, an education in values and feelings which were themselves a continuous, often unconscious critique of that dominative middle-class mode. It was not that the working-class family provided a complete, alternative form of life to the orthodox society: not only because the ways of feeling it offered were always too close and immediate to be easily formulated into an alternative ethic, but because the home, and the whole working-class environment, had its share of a violence and domination which tied it to the entire society. The violence of Walter Morel in *Sons and Lovers* reproduces, clearly enough, the structure of the dominative society he serves: the imperious relation of the miner to his wife and children was for the young Lawrence the most evident point at which the harsh pressures of the working world entered, and disrupted, the family settlement. The angry, defensive gathering of the Morel children around the mother, in opposition to the brutality of the father, is not (as it might be in a middle-class setting) a matter of family temperaments or loyalties alone: it is a matter of a conflict and estrangement which reaches through the family context into the deeper alternatives of work and personal relationship, selfish individualism and solidarity, mechanical demand and moral sensitivity.

Yet Morel is not only seen as 'outside' the family context, as an alien intruder from the mines: he is also, and equally, a member of the family, who, both on human and economic terms, cannot be denied. It is this which is recognised by Mrs Morel, against her children's angry calls to shut the father out. The father cannot be shut out because he is the provider who holds the family physically together, the man whom Paul and the other children despise yet on whom they are radically dependent. It is for this reason that Paul's own childhood efforts to exclude the world of the father and centre instead on the mother imply a dividing of life and labour which is at once understandable and ultimately false: his hatred of the pit office where he has to collect Morel's wages must be rebuked by his mother, as a dangerously privileged hypersensitivity:

> 'They're hateful, and common, and hateful, they are, and I'm not going any more. Mr Braithwaite drops his "h's", an' Mr Winterbottom says "You was".'
> 'And is that why you won't go any more?' smiled Mrs Morel.
> The boy was silent for some time. His face was pale, his eyes dark and furious. His mother moved about at her work, taking no notice of him. . . . His ridiculous hypersensitivity made her heart ache.

Mrs Morel herself, the 'superior' daughter of an engineering foreman, has had to train herself to the adjustments of feeling which Paul experiences as degrading; and the adjustment is seen not only as a necessity, but as a whole and in some ways valuable way of living. The worlds of human relationship and industrial labour are separate and conflicting, but the separation must not simply be ratified: the conflicts must be fought out within a shared area of living – the family itself. It is within the family, where work and relationship converge, that the essential interactions of both structures of feeling must be seen: not as a simple alternative of colliery and home, but as an interrelation of elements within a single texture of life, where each acts on and modifies the other. Morel brings into the home the callous individualism of a wider society, but he also brings qualities which the mother cannot give: his quick, practical knowledge and vigour:

> The only times when he entered again into the life of his own people was when he worked, and was happy at work. Sometimes, in the evening, he cobbled the boots or mended the kettle of his pit-bottle. Then he always wanted several attendants, and the children enjoyed it. They united with him in the work, in the actual doing of something, when he was his real self again.
>
> He was a good workman, dexterous, and one who, when he was in a good humour, always sang. He had whole periods, months, almost years, of friction and nasty temper. Then sometimes he was jolly again. It was nice to see him run with a piece of red-hot iron into the scullery, crying:
>
> 'Out of my road – out of my road!'

When Morel can make living contact with his children, it is through this kind of immediate, material knowledge: through qualities directly connected with his life as a working man. And it is, to that extent, a fertilising contact – a bringing to bear of a range of experience beyond the home on the family relationships, which must be set against the losses of his selfishness and bad temper. It is not that Morel can be happy as a father and not as a workman, in some simple counterpoising of the two: the point, in a more subtle blending of home and work, is that his 'real', working self can come alive in a family context of free, rather than compulsory, labour.

Morel's selfishness is irresponsible; but it is also the stubborn resistance of a way of life able to exist on its own, immediately sensuous terms, to a kind of moral forcing:

> (Mrs Morel) fought to make him undertake his own responsibilities, to make him fulfil his obligations. But he was too different from her. His nature was purely sensuous, and she strove to make him moral, religious. She tried to force him to face things. He could not endure it – it drove him out of his mind.

It is the balance of sympathy which Lawrence is able to achieve between Morel and his wife which is most impressive. Morel's fecklessness is a serious defect: it is portrayed as an almost animal allegiance to the settled rhythms of an established

life-form which damagingly frustrates the possibility of transcendence: of extension, understanding, control. That transcendence, as usual in Lawrence, is
symbolised by the woman: but it is too close, as it is presented here, to aspects of an
essentially middle-class effort towards 'moral improvement' for it to be wholly
approved. Lawrence understands, as many middle-class observers would not, that
Morel's sullen obstinacy is more than animal stupidity: it is also the reflex habit of
a long defensive tradition, developed by the English working class as a protection
against patronage and manipulation from outside.

The strengths and weaknesses of that rooted tradition are, as a matter of general
history, almost inextricably linked, and there is a sense in which that inseparability,
understood as an experience rather than an analysis, is the subject-matter of *Sons
and Lovers*. What is most interesting about the novel is that settlement and transcendence – the instinctive allegiance to a working-class culture and the exploratory movement beyond it – are no more mechanically separable, despite their
evident conflict, than the equally conflicting priorities of work and home. Morel
moves within the close, restricted limits of a routine working life, instinctively
hostile to change and extension; yet that life traditionally includes a margin of free
autonomy which is jealously guarded: the right, after work, to the independence of
the pub or the day's outing with a mate. What thwarts that welcome release from
constraint is the family. The family, ideally a reserve of that freedom and permanent relationship absent at work (where labour is forced and relationships can be
broken at any point by dismissal or redundancy), is in fact experienced as a new set
of limiting duties and demanding pressures after the work-discipline has been
thankfully left behind. It is here that the abstract duality of compulsory labour and
free family leisure really breaks down, and the interpenetration of home and work
is felt at its most acute. For the working man, the most tangible relation between
work and home is the fact of poverty: poverty is the way in which the paucity of a
working life registers itself in the constraints of a family context. For the middle-
class man, there may be an escape from a demanding work-discipline to the relaxed
privacy of family life, but no such escape is open to a man like Morel. It is not only
that the work-discipline is harsher, and the energy for recreation therefore less
available, nor even that the boundaries between public work and private home-life
are less strict, in a community of families united by the same working experience;
it is that relaxation in a home permanently beset by human and financial anxieties
rooted in the character of the work itself is almost impossible. Lawrence understood this thoroughly, and it is on this basis, rather than on some patronising
admiration for 'animal vigour', that his sympathy with Morel rests. As the novel
progresses, Morel is reduced to a shrunken, almost broken man, and this is in part
a function of the novel's own shifting focus, as the immediate working environment
recedes into the background and Paul's own venture into consciousness begins to
predominate. Yet it is also important to see that what deprives Morel of manhood
is not only this changing perspective, and not primarily the brutal disciplines of

industrial capitalism, but the shaming consciousness of his failure to shoulder the burden of family life. Morel can survive the rigours of work, not only because he has the necessary physical strength, but because he clings to his narrow margin of freedom and retains from his youth a sensuous capacity to live for the present which inures him to the taxing demands of the pit. Yet these, precisely, are among the reasons which unfit him for family responsibility: the qualities essential to survive the world of work become the qualities which destroy his capacity for responsible relationship in the home. The fecklessness of Morel the miner, bred at least in part by a system of work which requires of him not human responsibility but mere physical expenditure, becomes the selfishness of Morel the husband and father, able to involve himself with his children only by his practical skills.

Morel, then, does not merely represent a narrow settlement which must be gone beyond: he symbolises also a stubbornly asserted independence of the ties of family which is in one sense destructive, in another sense an aspect of traditional masculinity which Paul himself is unable to achieve. There is a similar ambivalence in the portrayal of Mrs Morel. Mrs Morel is the central life-source of the family, and the bond which ties Paul to her, in an intense inwardness, ties him also to the working-class childhood culture of which she is symbol. But she is also, like the farmwomen of *The Rainbow*, the point which opens into a dimension beyond that immediate world: she represents an impulse within the traditional settlement for extension and transcendence. That transcendence, of course, will happen not through her own life but through Paul's, who is not to follow his father into the colliery. Yet the tension which this situation then involves is that the movement towards transcendence to a wider life springs from the very centre of the traditional culture: Mrs Morel is symbol both of that culture at its most positive, and of a striving towards the new. The result, in the relationship between her and Paul, is a complex irony. Paul, as his mother's child, moves beyond the boundaries of the family into a wider world; yet the force which impels him there – his mother's influence – is also the force which draws him irresistibly back home. For her part, Mrs Morel is determined that Paul should escape the colliery, but the love which motivates that choice is also unable to release him from its control into the desired life of developed consciousness and autonomous relationship. The result is then a deadlock: Paul can neither escape from his old environment into a new dimension nor re-enter its life on the old terms. He can reject Mrs Morel's possessiveness in the person of Miriam, yet the rejection of Miriam, paradoxically, is an option for his mother.

It is that option for his mother which inhibits Paul's independence; yet what independence he has is, ironically, an almost exact reproduction of the shifting instability of his father:

Morel sat down. Both the men seemed helpless, and each of them had a rather hunted look. But Dawes now carried himself quietly, seemed to yield himself, while Paul seemed to screw himself up. Clara thought she had never seen him look so small and mean. He was as if trying to get himself into the smallest possible compass. . . .

Watching him unknown, she said to herself there was no stability about him. He was fine in his way, passionate, and able to give her drinks of pure life when he was in one mood. And now he looked paltry and insignificant. There was nothing stable about him. Her husband had more manly dignity. At any rate *he* did not waft about with any wind. There was something evanescent about Morel, she thought, something shifting and false. He would never make sure ground for any woman to stand on.

The irony of Paul's condition is that freedom and rootedness are not really opposed feelings: on the contrary, it is because what rootedness he has known is so abnormally intense that the break beyond it can only take the form of an equally flawed restlessness. Paul's 'evanescent' mobility of spirit is not a clear alternative to the settled family culture, as his brother William's is; it is rather the reaction of a man who resents that culture's paralysing grip on his life but is unable to break free, the self-consuming motion of a man bound tight to what he struggles against.

Sons and Lovers is Lawrence's first major exploration of the problem of a man's relation to his own culture, and it is, of course, tentative and uncertain in its final attitude. At the level of explicit content, in the history of Paul Morel, it remains too deeply inward with the felt reality of working-class life for the movement beyond that world to be more than a confused sense of fumbling; yet it is precisely in the written depth and intricacy of that inwardness, in the marvellously rendered interior detail of family life, that Lawrence's own partial transcendence of the limits still constraining Paul reveals itself. It is not that Lawrence has moved beyond that life to a vantage-point from which it can be externally 'placed': for it was an aspect both of his integrity and his tragedy, as a man, that he recognised that, once that life was lost, there was nowhere else to move. The orthodox alternative – an enlistment in the middle class – hardly needed to be tried: for the sensitive working-class child, as Paul shows, can learn the essentials of that ideology, in the conditions of his own people, without moving from home. Nor is the 'placing' of those conditions achieved, in this novel, through 'ideas': Paul's irritation with Miriam's passionately abstract intensities springs in part from a sense that they falsify more tangible realities. The placing is achieved, not through 'spiritual' reflection, but through the qualities of writing in which the working-class world comes to life – qualities which contain their own organising evaluations:

> He jerked at the drawer in his excitement. It fell, cut sharply on his shin, and on the reflex he flung it at her.
>
> One of the corners caught her brow as the shallow drawer crashed into the fireplace. She swayed, almost fell stunned from her chair. To her very soul she was sick; she clasped the child tightly to her bosom. A few moments elapsed; then, with an effort, she brought herself to. The baby was crying plaintively. Her left brow was bleeding rather profusely. As she glanced down at the child, her brain reeling, some drops of blood soaked into its white shawl; but the baby was at least not hurt. She balanced her head to keep equilibrium, so that the blood ran into her eye.
>
> Walter Morel remained as he had stood, leaning on the table with one hand, looking blank. When he was sufficiently sure of his balance, he went across to her,

swayed, caught hold of the back of her rocking-chair, almost tipping her out; then, leaning forward over her, and swaying as he spoke, he said, in a tone of wondering concern:

'Did it catch thee?'

. . . 'Go away,' she said, struggling to keep her presence of mind.

He hiccoughed. 'Let's – let's look at it,' he said, hiccoughing again.

What is most impressive about this passage, enforcing as it does the unbalanced violence of Morel, is its refusal to surrender at any point to stock notions of lower-class brawling. The emotional crisis is acute, and the blood on the baby's shawl tactfully symbolic, but most of the attention is directed to the detail of bodily movement and the practical necessities of guarding the child from harm: of preserving physical, as much as personal, balance. It is through these quite physical terms that the essential judgements on both Morel and his wife are communicated: the father's fumbling, self-defeating, inarticulate uncertainty, which makes for both cruelty and tenderness; the mother's driving impulse to hold the family physically together, to subdue her own feeling to material necessity in a curt, practical coldness at once essential and estranging. It is in what is not said, by both Lawrence and his characters, and how it is not said, that the significance of the incident emerges.

In the pattern of *Sons and Lovers*, the rhythm of inwardness and externality to a culture expresses itself as a rhythm of successive generations. In the unfolding of a family history, each generation is tied by interior bonds to its parents and yet is external, even alien, to them; and it is this rich paradox which Lawrence exploits to furnish himself with a total structure for *The Rainbow*. Each settlement offers a source of life to its children, but in a continuity of conflict rather than of simple extension: the offered life must be accepted, but accepted in a way which, by gathering it into a movement of transcendence, seems also a denial of its terms. That sense of transcendence is the novel's opening emphasis, in the contrast between the men and women of a single generation:

But the woman wanted another form of life than this, something that was not blood-intimacy. Her house faced out from the farm-buildings and fields, looked out to the road and village with church and Hall and the world beyond. She stood to see the far-off world of cities and governments and the active scope of man, the magic land to her, where secrets were made known and desires fulfilled. She faced outwards to where men moved dominant and creative, having turned their back on the pulsing heat of creation, and with this behind them, were set out to discover what was beyond, to enlarge their own scope and range and freedom; whereas the Brangwen men faced inwards to the teeming life of creation, which poured unresolved into their veins.

The men who turn outwards to the beyond turn their backs on the rich fertility of the known life, but it is 'behind them' in a figurative as well as a literal sense: the old culture is broken with, but continues to sustain. In the early chapters of the novel, the sense of that transcendent realm enters Tom Brangwen's world: first through the foreigner he meets at Matlock, then through his wife Lydia. The foreigner rouses in Brangwen a radical discontent with his established life: 'He baulked the mean enclosure of reality, stood stubbornly like a bull at the gate, refusing to re-enter the well-known round of his own life. . . . He wanted to go away – right away. He dreamed of foreign parts. But somehow he had no contact with them. And it was a very strong root which held him to the Marsh, to his own house and land.' The tension here, between the tie to a traditional culture and a restlessness which impels Brangwen beyond its frontiers, is very close in quality to the problem which confronted Paul Morel; yet Brangwen's marriage to Lydia offers a kind of temporary solution. What is remarkable about *The Rainbow* is the way in which the question of balance between relatedness and autonomy, between the acceptance and surmounting of a particular context, is at once a cultural issue – the problem of attaining the right tension of intimacy and externality between generations, or between home and 'foreign' experience – and yet registers itself directly in the quality and movement of specific relationships. Those relationships emerge from, and help to shape, the deeper issues of cultural identity; and it is for this reason that Brangwen, in taking as his wife a woman who is at once mysteriously alien ('It was to him a profound satisfaction that she was a foreigner') and yet intuitively inward with the life of the Marsh, can reach a kind of fulfilment.

As the novel progresses, that kind of fulfilling balance becomes increasingly difficult to achieve. The 'mean enclosure' of quotidian reality can be re-created, for Brangwen, by the gathering of a transcendent mystery to its centre; but as the pressures of an impoverished society are taken, that movement towards transcendence, for want of an adequate cultural realisation, begins to turn in on itself, in an affirmation of passionate inwardness over against a public culture which now seems increasingly external. 'Transcendence' still finds a meaning within the unfolding, generational rhythm of an historical progress towards freedom, but its most obvious symbolism now carries a different reference, to a timeless moment of interior triumph over history and culture themselves:

> And yet, for his own part, for his private being, [Will] Brangwen felt that the whole of the man's world was exterior and extraneous to his own real life with Anna. Sweep away the whole monstrous superstructure of the world of today, cities and industries and civilisation, leave only the bare earth with plants growing and waters running, and he would not mind, so long as he were whole, had Anna and the child and the new, strange certainty in his soul.

This affirmative extrication from a public history repeats itself later, in Ursula's exultation with Skrebensky:

> During the next weeks, all the time she went about in the same dark richness, her eyes dilated and shining like the eyes of a wild animal, a curious half-smile which seemed to be gibing at the civic pretence of all the human life about her.

'What are you, you pale citizens?' her face seemed to say, gleaming. 'You subdued beast in sheep's clothing, you primeval darkness falsified to a social mechanism.'

She went about in the sensual sub-consciousness all the time, mocking at the ready-made, artificial day-light of the rest.

It is important to note this shift of meaning in 'transcendence' in *The Rainbow*, as it points forward to some of Lawrence's late attitudes, most evidently in *Women in Love*. Ursula's response is not wholly endorsed – it is described as a 'dark sensual arrogance', which cannot in any case be detached from its specific context in her spiritual history – but it is, nevertheless, a response which catches up, in its dualistic antitheses of passion and consciousness, authenticity and 'mere' social mechanism, person and public history, a significant range of Lawrence's own more questionable values. To say this is not merely to score a local point against Lawrence, but to notice what happens, almost inevitably, to the search for transcendence in a society which in practice denies its general and concrete realisation. *The Rainbow*, more obviously than *Sons and Lovers*, is able to grasp the interior connections between particular relationships and the shape of a common history: not only in the local context of the Marsh farm, where these are tangibly interwoven in the life of a working generation, but (a much more difficult recognition) in English society as a whole. In the development of Ursula – her teaching, her relations with Skrebensky and Winifred Inger – a whole social structure of feeling is projected, relating specific histories to the outlines of an entire culture in a way which was not on the whole possible in *Sons and Lovers*. A totalisation, of a kind, is achieved, without damage to the specificity of the inward and personal; yet it is important to see, as the above quotations indicate, that the relation of persons and society is as much one of contrast as of continuity. In one sense, of course, this is the whole of Lawrence's point: it is precisely in the telling opposition between the creative potency of individual lives, and the dehumanised mechanism of a dominative society, that the necessary social judgement is made to emerge. But his sensitive evaluation can be felt as interacting with a less flexibly intelligent model: the dualistic notion of an inwardly authentic spontaneity set over against a merely 'external' society which Lawrence inherited from nineteenth-century vitalism and idealism, and which was always deeply lodged in his thinking. When this model is dominant, it is not a particular society, but society itself, which deadens and falsifies; and the sense of a culture's externality to its members then becomes less the fruit of sensitive perception than the reflex response of a stereotype.

Yet it is a measure of *The Rainbow's* fine achievement that it does not, on the whole, surrender too readily to this stereotype in its actual writing. An interesting illustration is the encounter between Ursula and the family on the barge:

They had walked till they had reached a wharf, just above a lock. There an empty barge, painted with a red and yellow cabin hood, was lying moored. A man, lean and grimy, was sitting on a box against the cabin-side by the door, smoking, and nursing a baby that was wrapped in a drab shawl. . . .

'Good evening,' he called, half impudent, half attracted. He had blue eyes which glanced impudently from his grimy face. . . .

'May I look inside your barge?' asked Ursula.

'There's nobody to stop you; you come if you like. . . .'

Ursula peeped into the cabin, where saucepans were boiling and some dishes were on the table. It was very hot. Then she came out again. The man was talking to the baby. It was a blue-eyed, fresh-faced thing with floss of red-gold hair. . . .

Ursula, captivated by the child, offers the father her necklace to give to it:

The jewel swung from the baby's hand and fell in a little heap on the coal-dusty bottom of the barge. The man groped for it, with a kind of careful reverence. Ursula noticed the coarsened, blunted fingers groping at the little jewelled heap. The skin was red on the back of the hand, the fair hairs glistened stiffly. It was a thin, sinewy, capable hand nevertheless, and Ursula liked it. He took up the necklace, carefully, and blew the coal-dust from it, as it lay in the hollow of his hand. He seemed still and attentive. He held out his hand with the necklace shining small in its hard, black hollow.

'Take it back,' he said.

Ursula hardened with a kind of radiance.

'No,' she said. 'It belongs to little Ursula. . . .'

There was a moment of confusion, then the father bent over his child:

'What do you say?' he said. 'Do you say thank you? Do you say thank you, Ursula?'

'Her name's Ursula *now*,' said the mother, smiling a little bit ingratiatingly from the door. . . .

The father looked up at [Ursula] with an intimate, half-gallant, half-impudent, but wistful look. His captive soul loved her: but his soul was captive, he knew, always. . . .

Ursula joined Skrebensky. . . .

'I *loved* them,' she was saying. 'He was so gentle – oh, so gentle! And the baby was such a dear!'

'Was he gentle?' said Skrebensky. 'The woman had been a servant, I'm sure of that.'

There is enough externality in the passage's attitude to the working-class family to enforce a significant contrast with the treatment of the Morels: Ursula, ironically, is here in something like the position of Lily in *Sons and Lovers*, the refined young girl whom William brings home to survey the mysteries of working-class family-life. Lily's attitude was one of condescending amusement, which is not, of course, true of Ursula; yet there is a similarity of viewpoint, all the same, in this passing peep into an excitingly alien world. If Lily's response was one of amused patronage, Ursula's is one of amused admiration: both, essentially, suggest the attitude of an observer, briefly enjoying an environment which does not have to be permanently lived in, and no doubt enjoying it all the more for that. The texture of detailed description, in contrast with *Sons and Lovers*, is thin, and there is an alert awareness of 'impudence' and 'ingratiation', qualifying the vitality, which is again very much a middle-class attitude. Yet Lawrence's intimate feel for creative life is still sharp: the working man and his wife are hardly realised in any full way, but there is enough felt tenderness, even so, to show up the stiffness of Skrebensky, and the ideology he embodies, for what it is. That revelation is not simple: Ursula's action displays a generosity of spirit beyond Skrebensky, but a sense of its potential self-indulgence – its lavish offensiveness to the necessarily reserved and guarded thrift of the bargeman – is also communicated, to complicate judgement. The deepest moral insight is then the bargeman's capacity, in response to Ursula's openness, consciously to break with his settled habits, in a movement of reciprocation. Both he and Ursula, in contrast with Skrebensky, are able to recognise, and respond to, an event which transcends the limits of their habitual situations.

Ursula, then, has moved beyond her childhood culture, but she is still able to establish living connection with it; and it is this balance, between the more complete version of society possible to developed consciousness, and a preserved respect for its particular life, which is captured in the rhetoric of *The Rainbow*'s final passage:

> She saw the stiffened bodies of the colliers, which seemed already enclosed in a coffin, she saw their unchanging eyes, the eyes of those who are buried alive: she saw the hard, cutting edges of the new houses, which seemed to spread over the hill-side in insentient triumph, a triumph of horrible, amorphous angles and straight lines, the expression of corruption triumphant and unopposed, corruption so pure that it is hard and brittle: she saw the dun atmosphere over the blackened hills opposite, the dark blotches of houses, slate roofed and amorphous, the old church-tower standing up in hideous obsoleteness above raw new houses on the crest of the hill, the amorphous, brittle, hard edged new houses advancing from Beldover to meet the corrupt new houses from Lethley, the houses of Lethley advancing to mix with the houses of Hainor, a dry brittle, terrible corruption spreading over the face of the land, and she was sick with a nausea so deep that she perished as she sat. And then, in the blowing clouds, she saw a band of faint iridescence colouring in faint colours a portion of the hill. . . .
>
> And the rainbow stood on the earth. She knew that the sordid people who crept hard-scaled and separate on the face of the world's corruption were living still, that the rainbow was arched in their blood and would quiver to life in their spirit, that they would cast off their horny covering of disintegration, that new, clean, naked bodies would rise to a new germination, to a new growth, rising to the light and the wind and the clean rain of heaven. She saw in the rainbow the earth's new architecture, the old, brittle corruption of houses and factories swept away, the world built up in a living fabric of Truth, fitting to the over-arching heaven.

This, quite evidently, is a 'totalisation' of a direct and unflinchingly explicit kind: an intensely persuasive vision of an entire culture, sustained by the force of a controlled and intricately elaborated rhetoric. Yet it is clearly more than an abstract vision of collapse projected on to a selective pattern of local detail: the technique, in other words, is not Eliot's. At every point, generalising judgement is substantiated by the specific: not simply in the sense that particular perceptions exemplify an argument or are used to generate one, but in a highly complex blending and crossing of an actual and a moral landscape, where description and attitude continually combine. The 'brittleness' and 'hard cutting edges' of the new houses are both literal and figurative, and so is their uncontrolled sprawl over the hill-side: on the one hand a metaphor of spawning corruption, but also a particular network of 'amorphous angles and straight lines', clearly seen and registered. 'A dry, brittle, terrible corruption' is advancing across the land, but the terrain of its action is local geography: Beldover, Lethley, Hainor: 'advancing' is both factually exact, and charged with a menacing overtone of invasion. The vision is not 'inward', but neither is it Olympian: it totalises and elaborates, from the distancing standpoint of a solitary observer, a culture which is nevertheless intimately known. The image of the rainbow is visionary assertion rather than realistic assessment, and its specific point of purchase on the preceding description is disturbingly obscure; yet it captures, through an image of cultural death and re-creation, that fine tension of conflict and continuity which throughout the novel has characterised the interrelationships of persons and generations. The new creation which the rainbow prefigures is in one sense a decisive rupture with the diseased present, as the child ruptures the parental settlement; once contemporary society has been grasped with this degree of integral awareness, the solution can only be of such a total and revolutionary kind. Yet the rainbow is also symbol of what is 'living still', 'arched in the blood' of the corrupted present: to this extent it affirms both continuity and inwardness in the context of apocalyptic change. Society must be remade, with a completeness perceptible only to a man free from limiting investments in its present reality; yet it is *this* society which must be remade – these sordid, hard-scaled, separate people, known as they are from the inside. The form of contemporary culture is violently rejected, but within a continuing reverence for the still active energies of its people: and it is this fusion of uncompromising denial and persisting hope which is the passage's most striking quality. The novel's recurrent rhythm of intimacy and estrangement, settlement and transcendence, the spending and re-charging of energies, culminates here in an image of death and resurrection.

II

It is interesting to note the contrast between the stance of *The Rainbow*'s closing passage and the predominant tone of *Women in Love*:

'Not many people are anything at all,' [Birkin] answered, forced to go deeper than he wanted to. 'They jingle and giggle. It would be much better if they were just wiped out. Essentially, they don't exist, they aren't there.'

Birkin, of course, does not go entirely uncriticised: but it is significant that what qualifying judgements surround him concern not so much what he says, as the didactic manner in which he says it. If his position is not to be taken as wholly Lawrentian, it is not on account of other viewpoints in the novel which might challenge it: no such alternatives are available. So we are forced to conclude that Birkin's remarks merit serious attention, despite their flavour of contemptuous, neurotic externality posturing as reflective wisdom:

> 'We have an ideal of a perfect world, clean and straight and sufficient. So we cover the earth with foulness; life is a blotch of labour, like insects scurrying in filth, so that your collier can have a pianoforte in his parlour, and you can have a butler and a motor-car in your up-to-date house, and as a nation we can sport the Ritz, or the Empire, Gaby Deslys and the Sunday newspapers. It is very dreary.'

This is an extension, but also a vulgarisation, of *The Rainbow*'s final vision of decay: the generalised superficiality suggested by this lame collection of cant phrases is now much more a quality of the observer's standpoint than of what is observed. The world, in Birkin's own term, is 'extraneous' to creative individuality; and from this detached, disgusted viewpoint, society can be abstracted to 'mankind', and that in turn abstracted to a petty, ephemeral exhalation of a non-human creative urge:

> 'Let mankind pass away – time it did. The creative utterances will not cease, they will only be there. Humanity doesn't embody the utterance of the incomprehensible any more. Humanity is a dead letter. There will be a new embodiment, in a new way. Let humanity disappear as quickly as possible.'

A new creation is still desired, but it is no longer, as it was in *The Rainbow*, a re-creation. That revolutionary relationship to a culture which *The Rainbow* was able to define, grasping present and future in dialectical interrelation, overbalances here into a blank dislocation between actual and potential. The result is a curious deadlock: a new order must be achieved to replace the present, yet such an attitude already implies, if only negatively, a commitment to the present which is itself restrictive:

> 'I do think,' [Ursula said], 'that one can't have anything new whilst one cares for the old – do you know what I mean? – even fighting the old is belonging to it. I know, one is tempted to stop with the world, just to fight it. But then it isn't worth it.'
>   Gudrun considered herself.
>   'Yes,' she said. 'In a way, one is of the world if one lives in it. But isn't it really an illusion to think you can get out of it? After all, a cottage in the Abruzzi, or wherever it may be, isn't a new world. No, the only thing to do with the world, is to see it through.'

The offered alternatives are Ursula's refusal to be bound, even critically, to contemporary society – 'even fighting the old is belonging to it' – and Gudrun's tired option for compromise. The problem finds its fullest formulation in the issue of expatriatism:

> 'Oh, of course,' cried Gudrun, 'One could never feel like this in England, for the simple reason that the damper is *never* lifted off one, there. It is quite impossible really to let go, in England, of that I am assured . . . But wouldn't it be wonderful if all England *did* suddenly go off like a display of fireworks.'
> 'It couldn't,' said Ursula. 'They are all too damp, the powder is damp in them.'
> 'I'm not so sure of that,' said Gerald.
> 'Nor I,' said Birkin. 'When the English really begin to go off, *en masse*, it'll be time to shut your ears and run. . . .'
> 'Don't be too hard on poor old England,' said Gerald. 'Though we curse it, we love it really. . . .'
> 'We may,' said Birkin. 'But it's a damnably uncomfortable love: like a love for an aged parent who suffers horribly from a complication of diseases, for which there is no hope. . . .'
> 'Yes,' said Gudrun slowly, 'you love England immensely, *immensely*, Rupert.'

The relationship to England is still a complex fusion of commitment and rejection, but the complexity is now cerebral and asserted, reflected in the banal imagery and brittle feeling of the whole passage; if Birkin does 'love England immensely', it is nowhere shown in the novel. What *is* shown is the despairing vacuity of a particular group of bored middle-class intellectuals, hopelessly alienated from the concrete social realities they analyse at such length.

Gudrun's reaction to the mining community is a useful illustration of this changed relationship to English society:

> They were passing between blocks of miners' dwellings. In the back yards of several dwellings a miner could be seen washing himself in the open on this hot evening, naked down to the loins, his great trousers of moleskin slipping almost away. Miners already cleaned were sitting on their heels, with their backs near the walls, talking and silent in pure physical well-being, tired, and taking physical rest. Their voices sounded out with strong intonation, and the broad dialect was curiously caressing to the blood. It seemed to envelop Gudrun in a labourer's caress, there was in the whole atmosphere, a resonance of physical men, a glamorous thickness of labour and maleness, surcharged in the air. But it was universal in the district, and therefore unnoticed by the inhabitants.
>
> To Gudrun, however, it was potent and half-repulsive. She could never tell why Beldover was so utterly different from London and the south, why one's whole feelings were different, why one seemed to live in another sphere. Now she realised that this was the world of powerful, underworld men who spent most of their time in the darkness. In their voices she could hear the voluptuous resonance of darkness, the strong, dangerous underworld, mindless, inhuman. They sounded also like strange machines, heavy, oiled. The voluptuousness was like that of machinery, cold and iron.

It is the confusion of feeling here which is most interesting: the ambivalent blendings of fascination and disgust. The miners spread 'a glamorous thickness of labour and maleness' in the evening air, but their presence to Gudrun is precisely that: an atmosphere rather than a group of physical men, an hypnotic pattern of disembodied voices rather than a human conversation. The miners are mysterious, which is the source of both wonder and revulsion: they are potent and sensuous, but 'the voluptuousness was like that of machinery, cold and iron'. The simile is strikingly peculiar: how can a dark, sensual voluptuousness suggest the 'cold and iron' of machinery? The answer is that the passage is not really attending to the specific qualities of the miners: it is thinking of the 'dangerous underworld' they symbolise, which is literally mechanical but metaphorically dark and potent. Both meanings are forced together in the simile, but they are really irreconcilable images, springing from attitudes which conflict rather than interrelate: on the one hand, a revulsion from what the miners literally represent, but also an attempt, through metaphor, to endow them with a creative power alien to Gudrun herself. This forcing of images reveals the extent to which the whole passage, despite its effort to evoke a forceful physicality, operates in abstractions: the abstraction, for instance, of connecting the sound of dialect to a physical caress. Physical and moral meanings are subtly maladjusted: a fact which, as we shall see later, is indicative of a more general maladjustment, throughout the novel, between subjective feeling and objective life. The miners 'belong to another world': but while this is at one level part of their attraction for Gudrun, it is at another level what prevents their culture from engaging significantly with her own. The active tension of the earlier novels, between developed consciousness and a working environment, now appears as an unbridgeable rift.

That rift is perhaps most obvious in the scene where Birkin and Ursula give away a chair to a young working-class couple. The incident directly recalls the encounter with the family on the barge in *The Rainbow*, and so can be usefully compared with it:

> 'We wanted to *give* it to you,' explained Ursula, now overcome with confusion and dread of them. She was attracted by the young man. He was a still mindless creature, hardly a man at all, a creature that the towns have produced, strangely pure-bred and fine in one sense, furtive, quick, subtle. . . . His legs would be marvellously subtle and alive, under the shapeless trousers, he had some of the fineness and stillness and silkiness of a dark-eyed silent rat. . . .
>
> The man jerked his head a little on one side, indicating Ursula, and said, with curious amiable, jeering warmth:
>
> 'What she warnt? – eh?' An odd smile writhed his lips. . . . He was impassive, abstract, like some dark suggestive presence, a gutter presence. . . .
>
> 'Cawsts something to chynge your mind,' he said in an incredibly low accent.

Ursula finds the youth attractive, as she did the bargeman, but it is now the attractiveness of an animal. His 'dark suggestive presence' is associated, not with a human vitality, but with the 'gutter'; his slowness to respond to the gift is seen, not as the dignified independence of the bargeman, but as a vulgar and calculating suspicion.

It is difficult to see how a novel which supposedly elicits the pattern of feeling of a whole culture, and yet which is as external to its society as this, can really constitute a great achievement; and indeed *Women in Love* seems to me, for this reason, decidedly inferior to both *Sons and Lovers* and *The Rainbow*. It is not a question of 'social realism' against 'symbolism': it is that, whereas the unique strength of the earlier novels sprang in part from the immediate presence of a complex social fabric in which particular relationships were embedded, the narrowing evident in *Women in Love* – the intense focusing on a restricted set of relationships which seem to move in a vacuum – can be directly felt in the attenuated quality of the relationships themselves. There is, of course, a good deal of talk about 'society', but it is, precisely, talk: the vague, abstracted, flippant or earnest philosophising of a self-consciously lost generation. There is the social imagery of the mines; but the mines are not seen, as Ursula's school is seen in *The Rainbow*. And this pervasive thinness of social texture has an immediate effect upon the quality of personal life in the novel. Emotions in *Women in Love* have a curiously overwhelming intensity: there is this reaction of Gudrun's, for instance, to her first sight of Gerald –

> 'His totem is the wolf,' she repeated to herself.
> 'His mother is an old, unbroken wolf.' And then she experienced a keen paroxysm, a transport, as if she had made some incredible discovery, known to nobody else on earth. A strange transport took possession of her, all her veins were in a paroxysm of violent sensation.

– or Hermione's response to Birkin's absence at the church-altar:

> And then, he was not there. A terrible storm came over her, as if she were drowning. She was possessed by a devastating hopelessness. And she approached mechanically to the altar. Never had she known such a pang of utter and final hopelessness. It was beyond death, so utterly null, desert.

In each case (and these are only two, relatively minor instances) feeling becomes abnormally inflated because the capacity adequately to realise its 'objective correlative' in the public world has significantly diminished. The easy traffic between object and response which characterised *Sons and Lovers*, the sense of an objective world existing in its own substantial terms, is now almost entirely lacking. It is confined, essentially, to a few random passages of Nature description, where Lawrence's typifying genius comes momentarily through. The process which we observed in *The Rainbow*, of an inward, self-communing transcendence repelling the crude invasions of 'extraneous' society, culminates here in a dramatic and often wild disproportion between event and response, public culture and private experience.

Between *Women in Love* and *Lady Chatterley's Lover*, Lawrence travelled in Australia and New Mexico, driven from a collapsing England but unable to find an adequate foreign alternative. The effects of that frustrated exploration can be felt in *Lady Chatterley's Lover* in two, ironically conflicting ways: in an increased alienation from English society, and in an increased determination to salvage some positive value from it. Clifford Chatterley is 'frightened of middle and lower class humanity, and of foreigners not of his own class', and Connie can feel 'how little connection he really had with people':

> The miners were, in a sense, his own men; but he saw them as objects rather than men, parts of the pit rather than parts of life, crude raw phenomena rather human beings along with him.

It is against Clifford's 'nasty, sterile want of common sympathy', his incapacity to establish living relation with others, that Connie revolts; and in that revolt Lawrence's best self, with its memories of a past when miners were relatives and neighbours, can still be felt. But although Clifford's inhumanity is rejected, his actual judgements on the character of working people are still, paradoxically, half-endorsed:

> '. . . in your sense of the word, they are *not* men. They are animals you don't understand, and never could. Don't thrust your illusions on other people. The masses were always the same, and will always be the same. . . . The masses are unalterable. It is one of the most momentous facts of social science. *Panem et circenses*! Only today education is one of the bad substitutes for a circus. What is wrong today is that we've made a profound hash of the circuses part of the programme, and poisoned our masses with a little education.'
>
> When Clifford became really roused in his feelings about the common people, Connie was frightened. There was something devastatingly true in what he said. But it was truth that killed.

Clifford's position can be emotionally challenged, but not in a way which can question his intellectual argument. He has been satirised, early in the novel, for his fear of the lesser breeds, but Connie, too, is 'absolutely afraid of the industrial masses':

> Perhaps they were only weird fauna of the coal-seams. Creatures of another reality, they were elementals, serving the element of coal, as the metal-workers were elementals, serving the element of iron. Men not men, but animals of coal and iron and clay. Fauua of the elements, carbon, iron, silicon: elementals. . . . They belonged to the coal, the iron, the clay, as fish belong to the sea and worms to dead wood. The anima of mineral disintegration!

The deep alienation implicit in this unreal poetic musing is a constant element in the novel: it must be taken together with Connie's reflection that the affairs of nearby Tevershall 'sounded really more like a Central African jungle than an English village'.

Lawrence is still sufficiently intimate with English society to recognise, as Clifford cannot, that it has important sources of strength; but he is sufficiently exterior, as the returned exile, to share profoundly in Clifford's remote and dehumanising perspective. The problem which the novel poses, then, is how Chatterley's emotional frigidity towards those beyond his class is to be rejected without his particular judgements on their subhuman inferiority being called into radical question; and the answer, in a word, is Mellors. Mellors 'seemed so unlike a gamekeeper, so unlike a working-man . . . although he had something in common with the local people. But also something very uncommon.' Mellors, who is working-class Englishman, educated gentleman and mysterious foreigner (he has served in India), is thus the ideal formula for a 'solution': and much of the time, indeed, he is little more than that. Connie, tired of inadequate English lovers, desires a foreigner: 'not an Englishman, still less an Irishman. A real foreigner.' Mellors can fulfil this role, since he has lived abroad and is in any case of the alien working class; and since he has that English social background, Connie can satisfy her need for 'foreign' experience by a route which (we are supposed to believe) leads her to the heart of her own culture. In so far as Mellors is working class, Connie's relationship with him provides a living critique of Clifford's snobbery; but in so far as he has moved beyond that class, his behaviour does not disturb the novel's rigid preconceptions about the 'weird fauna' of the social underworld. Thus, Clifford's belief in dominative class-rule is satirically undermined in the scene where he is forced to accept Mellors's help with his wheel-chair; but since it is Mellors, rather than another, less 'uncommon' servant who is there to help, the satire goes against Clifford's personal impotence rather than his political ideology.

The achievement of *Lady Chatterley's Lover* lies in the fact that even here, at this late and radically disillusioned point of Lawrence's career, the sense of those creative potencies which can survive social disintegration is still quick and active. It is a measure of Lawrence's continuing genius that he is able, even at this sterile distance from an actual society, to recognise and re-create its most positive life. Yet this, in the context of the whole work, must be a marginal qualification rather than a general endorsement. As a complete novel, *Lady Chatterley's Lover* fails, and it fails because Lawrence, with his years of rootless exile behind him, is least in touch where he needs to be most incisive: in his feel for the tangible realities of his own society.

III

In a discussion with Ursula in *Women in Love*, Birkin voices a characteristic attitude towards their relationship:

'Don't you see that it's not a question of visual appreciation in the least,' he cried. 'I don't *want* to see you. I've seen plenty of women, I'm sick and weary of seeing them. I want a woman I don't see.'

Birkin's irritable rejection of Ursula's physical presence in his life is one symptom of the deadlock at which Lawrence himself, in his struggle with the problems of settlement and transcendence, finally arrived. Lawrence never relinquished his belief, inherited chiefly from his own working-class experience, that personal fulfilment could be found only in human relationship; but in his fight to break free of relationships which were in practice limiting and restrictive, human contact, and the very existence of others, could seem, at times, a thwarting bondage in itself. Birkin's search is for a relationship which has passed beyond relationship: for a rooted and permanent settlement which offers at the same time the ground of a limitless personal autonomy. *Women in Love* explores that paradox, and the deadlock to which it must inevitably lead, in terms of the relation between Birkin and Ursula; but that exploration is really only one expression of a more deep-seated cultural crisis in Lawrence's life and work. Lawrence lived the breakdown of an old community, and knew intimately both its positive and negative effects: in recognising the strengths of that childhood society, he could also feel, in the fabric of his own experience, the points where its established boundaries needed to be transformed into horizons. At the highpoint of his literary achievement, in *The Rainbow*, he exploited that relation of conflict with his own culture to create one of the greatest novels of the century, discovering, with admirable certainty, the balance-point at which the old world he had known could be both inhabited from within and grasped, as a totality, from without. The tragedy of Lawrence – and it is, in this sense, a representative tragedy – was that, once the boundaries were crossed, there was nowhere else to go. There was no protected area within his own culture to which he could turn, for the evaluation of his own early experience which he could achieve in *Sons and Lovers* was inevitably a critique, not merely of his own class, but of the total class-structure of which that working environment was an expression. He turned, for a while, to alternative cultures beyond England, but always in the final knowledge that the problem of his own life could never be genuinely solved on that ground. The problem lay in his own society, and while Australia and New Mexico could provide momentary release and experiment, they could offer no enduring solution. A third area of traditional refuge, one gratefully or desperately embraced by a good many of Lawrence's contemporaries and successors, was also vigorously denied: the refuge of art itself. In the face of often intolerable pressures, Lawrence continued to stand out against the flight into aestheticism; in *Women in Love*, indeed, the falseness of that solution is firmly linked, in the relation of Loerke and Gudrun, with the falseness of expatriate escape. In all these ways, Lawrence refused bad faith and betrayal, at the price of an isolation which came finally, in my view, to affect the quality of his art. His importance to the theme of this study can be seen to lie in a simple fact: if few twentieth-century writers have paralleled Lawrence in his uncompromisingly total and revolutionary critique of English society, few also have achieved his inward understanding of its character. It is a paradox and a relationship significantly uncommon in the history of contemporary English literature.

Note

1   Raymond Williams, *Culture and Society 1780–1950* (London, 1958), p. 202.

2 Nature and the Fall in Hopkins: A Reading of 'God's Grandeur'

Whether the Fall involves Nature as well as man is not a *de fide* matter in the Roman Catholic Church. As far as scholastic theology is concerned, the issue simply drops out of sight; the Fall is restricted to the issue of original sin, which is then, as at Trent, defined in human terms alone. Greek theology is, on the whole, more 'cosmically' framed and more insistent on the shared destiny of man and Nature; but a Roman Catholic is officially free to believe either that fallen man inhabits an innocent world, or that Nature itself is diseased and distorted as a consequence of sin. This ambiguity – the feeling that Nature is at once sacramental and radically vitiated – seems to me important for an understanding of the work of Gerard Manley Hopkins.

That Hopkins regarded the natural world as the object of divine grace is obvious enough from his poems; but it is also pretty clear that he thought Nature was sick and degenerate. One way of reconciling these apparently conflicting views is to suggest, as J. Hillis Miller does in his perceptive chapter in *The Disappearance of God*, that Hopkins held them more or less consecutively: the earlier Hopkins of 'God's Grandeur' and 'Hurrahing in Harvest' celebrated the innocence of Nature, while later in 'Spelt from Sibyl's Leaves' he was grimly alert to the facts of Nature's decay. It is possible to produce evidence from Hopkins's prose writings to support this interpretation. In 1866 Hopkins inserted in his Oxford notebook an extract from St. Bonaventure's *Life of St. Francis* that speaks of natural creation as a 'stairway which [leads] up towards Him who is the goal of all desires'. Celestial harmony is here the concord of all created beings. Fourteen years later, in one of his Liverpool sermons, Hopkins concedes that Nature is providentially planned for human use but lays a gloomy emphasis on its manifest imperfection: 'The sun shines too long and withers the harvest, the rain is too heavy and rots it or in floods spreading washes it away; the air and water carry in their currents the poison of disease . . . everything is full of fault, flaw, imperfection, shortcoming'.[1] This theme of natural perversity crops up again a year later in the Spiritual Writings, where Hopkins ponders the significance of the coil or spiral as a type of the Devil, seeing it as symbolic of 'motion lessening and at last ceasing', of Nature as caught up in a process of sickeningly entropic self-unravelling:

> God gave things a forward and perpetual motion; the Devil, that is/thrower of things off the track, upsetter, mischiefmaker, clashing one with another brought in the law of decay and consumption in inanimate nature, death in the vegetable and animal world, moral death and original sin in the world of man.[2]

Even so, a simple chronological account of Hopkins's view of Nature seems inadequate to the complexities of the poetry. A fairly early poem like 'In the Valley of the Elwy' may seem straightforward enough in its perception of a radical dissonance between sinful man and innocent Nature –

> Lovely the woods, waters, meadows, combes, vales,
> All the air things wear that build this world of Wales;
> Only the inmate does not correspond . . .[3]

– but 'Spring', written in the same month, is less unambiguous:

> What is all this juice and all this joy?
>   A strain of the earth's sweet being in the beginning
> In Eden garden. – Have, get, before it cloy,
>   Before it cloud, Christ, lord, and sour with sinning,
> Innocent mind and Mayday in girl and boy,
>   Most, O Maid's child, thy choice and worthy the winning.

Nature is juiced and vitalized by a dynamic 'strain' of prelapsarian innocence, but 'strain' suggests an elusive, precariously lingering survival from the past; the lines dexterously avoid equating Nature as it is with unfallenness, while at the same time contrasting it favourably with man's tendency to sin. Moreover, the sense of this strained, fragile survival within Nature then leads on to a suggestion of how likely the Eden of man's own past – his childhood – is to sour; and the imaginative logic of the imagery tempts us to read this feeling back into the previous lines about Nature, to wonder whether this too may not cloy. (The temptation is reinforced by the syntax, which makes us think at first that 'Have, get, before it cloy . . . and sour with sinning' applies to the 'strain of the earth's sweet being'.) A similar ambivalence crops up in 'The Sea and the Skylark', also written in the same month. In it the skylark's 'rash-fresh' song shames sordid man, who has 'lost that cheer and charm of earth's past prime', though any simple counterposing of human corruption and natural integrity is complicated by that 'past'. Nature may be holier than man, but there's a covert suggestion that its past may have been holier than its present.

Hopkins's later attitudes seem no less double-edged. 'Spring and Fall', for instance, sees Nature and man as bound together in decay; Goldengrove's 'unleaving' matches and symbolizes Margaret's own mortality. 'Ribblesdale', on the other hand, which was composed only two years later, lends a qualified support to Nature as against man – Nature 'canst but only be, but dost that long', happy in the sure, spontaneous enactment of its essences, whereas man lays waste his world.

The poem which seems to me to bring these ambivalences to a head is 'God's Grandeur', a poem that is cited by J. Hillis Miller in support of Hopkins's early view of Nature as innocent. To my mind it is a good deal more complex.

> The world is charged with the grandeur of God.
>   It will flame out, like shining from shook foil.
>   It gathers to a greatness, like the ooze of oil
> Crushed. Why do men then now not reck his rod?
>
> Generations have trod, have trod, have trod,
>   And all is seared with trade; bleared, smeared with toil;
>   And wears man's smudge and shares man's smell: the soil
> Is bare now, nor can foot feel, being shod.
>
> And for all this, nature is never spent;
>   There lives the dearest freshness deep down things;
> And though the last lights off the black West went
>   Oh, morning, at the brown brink eastward, springs –
> Because the Holy Ghost over the bent
>   World broods with warm breast and with ah! bright wings.

Here, as in some other Hopkins poems, one way in which the two responses to Nature I have discussed may be reconciled is by the skilful exploitation of a phenomenal/noumenal distinction. Even if natural objects are polluted, their spiritual essences remain intact because they are tucked away 'deep down' beneath Nature's smeared surface. But there seem at least two reasons why Hopkins is less sure about this resolution than might at first sight appear. In the first place, the celebratory optimism of the resolution seems to be qualified by a gloomier undertone which hints that Nature's infection may be more than superficial; in the second place, there is a problem about how grace, if it really is so deeply hidden, is to be freely and 'naturally' available to men. These problems reduce themselves to a single question: How far is Nature to be relied on as a source of grace?

The first problem is detectable in the shifting implications of lines 6–8. Granted that Nature's ultimate inexhaustible spiritual resources are located safely out of man's reach, how deeply into Nature does man's own disease in fact penetrate? 'Bleared' and 'smeared' suggest a merely surface damage, but 'seared' is arguably more serious; 'wears man's smudge' is again superficial, whereas 'shares man's smell' points perhaps to a less easily eradicable contamination. 'The soil is bare now' implies an objective impoverishment of Nature; human despoliation is no longer just a smearing and smudging which could be wiped clean, but a possibly irreversible plundering of natural life. That impression, however, is curiously qualified by the next image, that of the shod foot, which follows on with a deceptively unruffled air, concealing a shift of attitude beneath the coherence of tone. What's stressed now is a callousing of human sensuous perception. But if the soil *is* bare, what is there for man, shod or not, to feel? The opening lines of the stanza seem to suggest that Nature is 'objectively' fertile – charged with God's grace – but that man has destructively estranged himself from it; the closing lines project a bleaker image of alienated man in a withered and exhausted world.

A related ambivalence seems to lurk in the poem's opening images. In 'The Wreck of the Deutschland' Hopkins is explicit about the fact that a mere awareness of God's presence behind or beneath Nature isn't enough; some strenuously subjective, realizing response to that presence is also demanded:

> . . . tho' he is under the world's splendour and wonder,
>   His mystery must be instressed, stressed.

'God's Grandeur', on the other hand, appears considerably more reluctant to insist on that human reaction – not surprisingly, since its view of human agency ('trod') is fairly jaundiced. The poem's first two images prefer instead to present grace as spontaneously and independently at work in Nature, satisfyingly *there* despite men's blindness to it. There is, however, a slight but telling difference in these lines between two possible meanings of 'spontaneity': on the one hand, the sudden, marvellously unpredictable spontaneity of grace flaming out from Nature (when you least expect it, perhaps); on the other hand, the organic inevitability of 'It gathers to a greatness', where God's life is seen as coming to a head by an autonomous process of evolution. This second image implies a closer equation between grace and Nature than the first; it reveals a rather surer trust in the 'naturalness' and 'routineness' of the Spirit's activity in the world. And in this sense it qualifies the emphasis of the first image, which is concerned with the way grace flames *out* of Nature (how it's mysteriously released at Nature's points of self-transcendence). '*Will* flame out', rather like 'And yet you *will* weep' in 'Spring and Fall', is less a prediction about a process of natural growth than a stress on the sweet wilfulness of grace, its relative *independence* of routine process.

The question of how far Nature can be relied on in its quotidian processes to manifest the Spirit is further complicated by that 'shook'. 'Shook' suggests a feeling, common in Hopkins, that grace is in fact manifested much less in the 'phenomenal' presence of objects than in those points of crisis at which things are squeezed and pressurized into orgasmically releasing their divine 'juice'. And the way that happens, often enough, is by the human activity of instressing. (In 'Hurrahing in Harvest' it's the lack of a 'beholder' which leaves Nature's potencies implicit and incomplete.) 'Shook' suggests that instressing, but its implications are significantly muted. To spell them out would disturb the case that Nature can be trusted as an independent life-force *despite* man's relation to it. 'Shook', in fact, is too uneasily close to 'trod' to bear much weight. So the poem's opening lines hint at but pass over the issue of human agency. They proclaim a confidence in Nature's spontaneity, but they are ambivalent about how far this is, as it were, a 'natural' spontaneity; and they also imply that this dynamism has actually to be forced out from the surface of things, that it's less ordinarily available than might be thought. Its unpredictability is also a kind of elusiveness.

Similar problems emerge in the second stanza. The generousness of 'nature is never spent' is interestingly qualified by that '*dearest* freshness', which suggests (as elsewhere in Hopkins) rarity and expensiveness as well as lovableness. What the lines mean is that Nature's currency never runs out because it is backed by valuable capital reserves; but if 'dearest' and 'deep down' also suggest rare natural resources which are difficult to extract, 'never spent' comes oddly to carry a faint implication of hoarding. The image of the turning globe, however, undercuts any hint of miserliness; the freshness which we have just been told is 'deep down things', immune from man's grubby handling but therefore troublingly elusive, now becomes once more a matter of ordinary, automatic natural process. Grace, the image suggests, is as freely available as daylight – available on the surface rather than in the depths, as daylight bathes the surface of the globe. At the same time, of course, light is a source of life from *beyond* the world, 'natural' but springing from a cosmic depth; and to this extent the image successfully fuses the poem's two feelings about Nature and grace. 'Springing' does this too: it recalls the sudden, unpredictable flaming out of the foil simile, but within the context of predictable rhythmic process, of light gathering slowly to a greatness as the world turns.

Despite this skilful fusion of elements, however, the emphasis of these lines seems on the whole to fall on the naturalness of grace. This is why the final image is crucial. The spinning world has now become an egg over which the Holy Ghost broods. Daylight, after all, isn't a natural, organically inevitable event, but happens only because the Spirit constantly hatches it out of the darkness. If he stopped brooding, dawn would stop springing; the *bent* world is unable to renew itself out of its own natural resources.

Hopkins's poetry needs to reconcile a Christian humanist sense of man's superiority to natural things (man as 'Earth's eye, tongue, or heart', coaxing Nature to self-articulation) with an awareness of man's sinful dislocation from innocent creaturely life and his consequent despoliation of it. This tension seems to me clearly relevant to a poem like 'God's Grandeur', which appears at once to distrust man's intervention in Nature and yet to reveal a certain lack of confidence in the grace-giving capacity of a Nature which is 'un-instressed'. Ideally, then, Hopkins needs to construct an image which will protect Nature from human depredation while also leaving room for man's instressing activity. The danger is of maladjusting this tension – of protecting Nature from man only by removing its fundamental life so far from his violating grasp that the result, paradoxically, is an apparent endorsement of man's estrangement from the natural world. In its final world/egg imagery, 'God's Grandeur' may seem capable of achieving some state of balance between grace as on the one hand 'natural' and 'objective' and on the other hand special, as needing to be instressed, hatched out from a bent world; but the curious point is that it's the Holy Ghost, not man, who does this 'instressing'. The point of purchase of these images on the problems raised in the first stanza is in the end obscure. In what sense, if any, do they offer hope to alienated man in a withered world? Light and grace can be renewed, but can the soil? The resolution offered by the closing lines of 'The Windhover' – that man's plodding may energize rather than destroy the earth – isn't entertained here; instead the poem works with a dualistic image of man and Nature which permits hope precisely to the degree that it obscures the question of its realization.

Notes

1 *The Sermons and Devotional Writings of Gerard Manley Hopkins*, ed. Christopher Devlin, SJ (London, 1959), p. 90.
2 Ibid., p. 199.
3 It is interesting to compare these lines from 'In the Valley of the Elwy' with Hopkins's entry in his Journal for September 6th, 1874: 'Looking all round but most in looking far up the valley I felt an instress and charm of Wales. Indeed in coming here I began to feel a desire to do something for the conversion of Wales'. The apparent inconsequentiality of the second sentence in fact reveals how Hopkins's mind has moved unconsciously from a sense of natural beauty to a contrasting concern with human fallenness.

3 Thomas Hardy and *Jude the Obscure*

Jude the Obscure, Hardy's last novel, was first printed as a serial story in *Harper's New Monthly Magazine* from December 1894 to November 1895, and in November 1895 was published as a complete novel. In reply to a warning by Harper's that the novel should 'be in every respect suitable for a family magazine', Hardy had doggedly written 'that it would be a tale that could not offend the most fastidious maiden'; but Harper's ideal maiden was clearly more fastidious than Hardy's, and the serial version, like *Tess of the d'Urbervilles* before it, had to be heavily bowdlerised. When the novel was finally published as an unexpurgated whole, the critical comment it attracted was mean, bigoted and offensive. A bitter attack in the *New York World* led Hardy to urge Harper's to withdraw the book from circulation; Mrs Oliphant spearheaded the English onslaught with a review in *Blackwood's* entitled 'The Anti-Marriage League'; and the Bishop of Wakefield, disgusted with the novel's 'insolence and indecency', threw it into the fire. 'It is simply one of the most objectionable books that we have ever read in any language whatsoever,' commented the *New York Bookman*; and a reviewer in the *World*, betraying the characteristic Victorian middle-class opinion that gloom is somehow socially subversive, remarked that 'None but a writer of exceptional talent indeed could have produced so gruesome and gloomy a book.'

The effect of all this on Hardy was, in his own words, to cure him completely of further interest in novel-writing. But whether a major novelist really stops writing simply as a reaction to public opinion is surely doubtful. Hardy was certainly shaken by the mixture of panic, philistinism and hypocrisy his novel evoked, and saw exactly how that response ironically validated the book's case; but there were other reasons for his turning away from fiction. With *Tess of the d'Urbervilles* and *Jude the Obscure*, Hardy had brought his long exploration of the human condition of his society to a point of mature complexity; and, although it would be presumptuous to argue that, after that point, there was nowhere else for him to go, these two novels have a sense of imaginative resolution about them which makes their status as last novels logical rather than fortuitous – something more, anyway, than a submissive bowing to bad reviews. If 'resolution' in a different sense wasn't possible – resolution in the sense of providing formulated answers to the conflicts with which these novels deal – this was a mark of Hardy's realism about the limits of art rather than a symptom of despair.

Until quite recently, the story of Jude might have been summarised in a conventional critical account as the tragedy of a peasant boy who uproots himself from a settled and timeless rural community in the pursuit of learning, fails to achieve that worthy ideal through excessive sexual appetite, and in failing reveals the inexorable destiny of man himself, doomed to perpetual unfulfilment on a blighted planet. No part of that statement is in fact true, and to ask why not provides a starting point for a more accurate reading of the novel. Jude is neither a peasant nor particularly over-sexed; Marygreen, his childhood home, has nothing settled or timeless about it; the Christminster culture which attracts him is shoddy rather than worthy; and his failure to attain it has no 'cosmic' significance whatsoever. The novel goes out of its way to emphasise all these facts, and only a reading biased by ideological preconceptions about Hardy's fiction could fail to recognise them.

Jude is not a peasant: that class had long since been destroyed by changes in the social structure of the English countryside. He is the ward of a struggling shopkeeper who has herself declined from socially superior status, becomes a baker's delivery boy and later a stonemason. His place in Marygreen society, in other words, is with the semi-independent 'tradesman' class which, as Hardy points out in his essay 'The Dorsetshire Labourer' (in *Longman's Magazine*, July 1883), was being decimated by economic depression, increased social mobility and growing industrialisation. As a class, they offered a peculiarly intense focus for the disruptive social forces at work in the countryside, and so are almost always in the centreground of Hardy's fiction; it was the class into which he himself was born, as the son of a stonemason. As part of this class, Jude isn't 'uprooted' from Marygreen because there is nothing to be uprooted from. The fact that he doesn't belong to Marygreen in the first place, but was dumped there one dark night (as his own son is later unloaded in Aldbrickham), is significant: Jude's own lack of roots is symptomatic of the generally deracinated condition of the place. Marygreen is not timeless but stagnant, not settled but inert; it is a depressed and ugly enclave bypassed by history, stripped of its thatched and dormered dwelling-houses as the tradesmen, craftsmen and lifeholders move from the land. Like the five bottles of sweets and three buns behind the oxidised panes of Drusilla Fawley's shop-window, Marygreen is a stale remnant, a plundered landscape denuded of its historical traditions. What has ousted those traditions is utility:

> The fresh harrow-lines seemed to stretch like the channellings in a piece of new corduroy, lending a meanly utilitarian air to the expanse, taking away its gradations, and depriving it of all history beyond that of the few recent months, though to every clod and stone there really attached associations enough and to spare – echoes of songs from ancient harvest-days, of spoken words, and of sturdy deeds. (pp. 33–4)

The abstract imperatives of profit and utility have flattened and levelled all quali-
tative distinctions and concrete associations in Marygreen, superimposing their
directions on the place as rigidly as the harrow-lines do on the fields.

The boy Jude is himself a tool of those imperatives: as the harrow-lines dominate the arable land, so he is compelled for sixpence a day to impose his authority
on the birds in the fields by scaring them away with his clacker. Sorry for the birds,
Jude rebels against his slavish role and takes a redistribution of resources into his
hands: ' "Poor little dears!" said Jude, aloud. "You *shall* have some dinner – you
shall. There is enough for us all. Farmer Troutham can afford to let you have
some" ' (p. 34). This view isn't shared by Farmer Troutham, Jude's employer, who
assaults him with his own clacker. The punitive, profit-based relations of
Marygreen are in clear contradiction with the claims of cultured sensitivity: it is
Phillotson, the local representative of 'culture', who tells Jude to be kind to animals.
Yet, as always in the novel, the relation between ideals and harsh actuality is a
dialectical one: the ideal criticises the reality but is in turn exposed by it as limited
or utopian.[1] Jude's tender gesture prefigures his later courageous affirmations of
human solidarity (in the adoption of Father Time, for example), but it is also, of
course, amusingly sentimental. When it comes to food, men take priority over
birds. Later in the novel Jude is sickened by Arabella's pig-sticking, but her angry
comment, 'Poor folks must live', has a point, and Jude must learn it.

There is another important sense in which the relation between ideal and reality
in the novel is dialectical. The more starved and barren actual life is, the more the
ideals it generates will be twisted into bodiless illusions; Jude's 'dreams were as
gigantic as his surroundings were small' (p. 41). The most obvious instance of this
is Christminster. Christminster's phantasmal allure, glimpsed by Jude from the top
of his ladder, becomes after his arrival in the city the sinister phantasm of feeling
himself spectrally disembodied, stared through by passers-by when he is working
(again, with neat irony, on a ladder). If Marygreen is stripped of history,
Christminster is buried under it, a repressive rubble of crumbling masonry and
dead creeds. The two spots are ominously connected early in the novel, when the
man who points out Christminster to Jude gestures in the direction of the field
where the boy was beaten by Troutham. Just as Marygreen is swathed in deception
and superstition – Vilbert's quack medicine, Arabella's artificial hair, manufactured
dimples, false pregnancy and sexual trickery, the sham Gothic edifice which has
usurped the traditional church – so Christminster is a maze of false consciousness
and sham ceremony which imprisons Jude as effectively as Arabella's wiles. His
future turns out, precisely, to be a past; in moving hopefully forward he is rapidly
regressing.

The historical irony in which Jude is trapped is that personal fulfilment can be
achieved only by painfully appropriating the very culture which denies and rejects
him as a man. It is a contradiction in his relation with Christminster which is
focused most sharply in the issue of work – a central interest of Hardy's, in this and
other novels. As a stonemason trained in the countryside, and so relatively un-

scathed by an urban division of labour, Jude's work expresses a productive creativity which contrasts strongly with the sterility of the University. He works in direct, responsive relation to the material world; and as such his craft is an image of that attempt to subdue the 'insensate and stolid obstructiveness' of things to significant human purpose which is of wider importance in the novel. Craftsmanship, like authentic sexual relationship, mediates between the ideal and the actual. It is in the labour of the Christminster working class that Hardy discovers an alternative to the decayed world of the dons: 'For a moment there fell on Jude a true illumination; that here in the stone yard was a centre of effort as worthy as that dignified by the name of scholarly study within the noblest of the colleges. . . . He began to see that the town life was a book of humanity infinitely more palpitating, varied, and compendious than the gown life. These struggling men and women before him were the reality of Christminster, though they knew little of Christ or Minster' (pp. 104, 137). In examining the mouldings of the colleges, Jude discovers true historical continuity – not with the élitist University culture, but with 'the dead handicraftsmen whose muscles had actually executed those forms', men with whom he feels comradeship. On the basis of this sense of historical continuity, the identity he is seeking could be genuinely established.

Yet the irony, once again, is that Jude's labour-power is exploited literally to prop up the structures which exclude him. His work is restorative of the old world rather than productive of the new, devalued to 'copying, patching and imitating'. The dead, phantasmal past of Christminster sucks nutriment from the labour of the living, reducing them too to husks and corpses, spectres of their former selves. The true relations between labour and culture, conceived as simple opposites by the deluded Jude of Marygreen, are starkly disclosed in the divided world of Christminster: the cultural ideal is parasitic on working energies it ignores and represses, on labourers without whom 'the hard readers could not read nor the high thinkers live'.

Sue Bridehead has seen through the cultural idea, and emancipated herself from the stagnant medievalism of Christminster; but her emancipation is partial and in some ways false. She sees the University as a place 'full of fetichists and ghost-seers', but by the end of the novel she herself is both. If Jude can finally extricate himself from false consciousness through the painful process of experiencing the harsh conditions in which such illusions are needed in the first place, Sue's reaction against orthodoxy is idealist: the substitution of one spiritual ideology for another. She is still under the influence of idols: it is merely that statues of Greek deities replace statues of Christian saints on her mantelpiece. If Jude regresses in trying to move forward, so does she: she is 'more ancient than medievalism'. Jude lives a contradictory relationship with Christminster, strengthening the very walls which exclude him, and finally breaks with ecclesiastical art-work. Sue, the pagan designer of pious texts, lives out a similar conflict, and breaks free to become a teacher; but the deeper contradiction she incarnates is left relatively untouched by this act. Sue is Hardy's most masterly exploration of the limits of liberation in

Victorian society – more masterly by far than Angel Clare, who is an earlier experiment in the same mode. As both a chronically timid prisoner of convention and an impetuous rebel, Sue dramatises all the conflicts and evasions of what can best be termed a transitional form of consciousness, deadlocked between the old and the new. The psychological pattern to which that deadlock gives rise is one of masochism and self-torture – a continual process of acting impulsively and then punitively repressing herself for it.

This is most clear in her deep fear of sexuality. *Jude the Obscure* is a novel about passion – passion for human and sexual fulfilment, and its agonised frustration at the hands of a society which must everywhere deny it. Passion is a potentially liberating force in the novel, as Jude shows well enough. With 'a simple-minded man's ruling passion', Jude pursues his demand for recognition, refuses to back down from the question of his own identity, and is finally defeated and betrayed. But Jude is a genuinely tragic protagonist because the value released in that defeat, the insistence on a recognition of his total humanity, challenges, consciously or not, a society polarised between abstraction and appetite, labour and intellect. The problem is how to prevent that passion from being tamed and shackled by oppressive convention, and it is this which motivates Sue's rejection of marriage. But her rejection of marriage springs from the same source as her rejection of physical sexuality; in denying the false social embodiments of love, she denies the body itself. Her freedom, as a result, is in part negative and destructive – a self-possessive individualism which sees all permanent commitment as imprisoning, a fear of being possessed which involves a fear of giving. Her scorn for those whose 'philosophy only recognises relations based on animal desire' is genuinely progressive in its insistence on fully human relationship and conventionally Victorian in its belittling of physicality. Jude, fresh from the misery of a marriage with Arabella based 'on a temporary feeling which had no necessary connection with affinities that alone render a life-long comradeship tolerable' (p. 90), shares Sue's opinion; but, as that 'life-long' suggests, he is more inclined to welcome permanent and definitive commitments than she is, and less inclined to see sex as merely incidental to them.

There are other ways in which Jude and Sue differ. It isn't unimportant, for instance, that Sue's individualism springs in part from her reading of J. S. Mill, whose bourgeois notion of the autonomously developing self conflicts with Jude's own more communal and collectivist ethic. His membership of an Artizan's Mutual Improvement Society at Aldbrickham signifies his concern for the advancement of his class as a whole; and that concern for solidarity underlies his decision to adopt Father Time:

> 'What does it matter, when you come to think of it, whether a child is yours by blood or not? All the little ones of our time are collectively the children of us adults of the time, and entitled to our general care. That excessive regard of parents for their own children, and their dislike of other people's, is, like class-feeling, patriotism, save-your-own-soul-ism, and other virtues, a mean exclusiveness at bottom.' (p. 293)

Sue agrees that 'if [Father Time] isn't yours it makes it all the better', but for rather less altruistic reasons: she is reluctant to have his child by a previous marriage in the house. It is a difference between them which emerges again at the end of the book: Jude behaves 'honourably' towards Arabella because he is not 'a man who wants to save himself at the expense of the weaker among us' (pp. 401–2), whereas Sue, in her guilty return to Phillotson, is in the end such a woman. Even Jude can see this – can see that Sue has degenerated to a save-your-souler. 'I stuck to her, and she ought to have stuck to me. I'd have sold my soul for her sake, but she wouldn't risk hers a jot for me' (p. 394).

But this is to be too hard on Sue and not hard enough on Jude. Sue does, after all, give herself fully to Jude for a brief period of happiness, and the events which drive her back to Phillotson are horrific enough to make her betrayal understandable, if not excusable. And, if Sue is elusively unpossessable, Jude for his part is too ready to be appropriated, too uncritically willing to be the adopted son of the deathly lineage of Christminster. If Sue is finally enslaved by ghosts and fantasies, Jude has been so all along. It is a choice between that genuine disentanglement from delusion at which Jude must laboriously arrive, by which time his energies are spent, and the more rapid emancipation of Sue which, because it is ungrounded from the outset in much more than a mental conversion, is unable to withstand the buffetings of reality.

What is remarkable, in fact, is how Hardy retains some of our sympathy for Sue against all the odds. For there isn't, when one comes down to it, much to be said in her defence. Having speeded on the death of her first lover, Sue captivates Jude to enjoy the thrill of being loved, and then enters with dubious motives and curiously mechanical detachment into marriage with Phillotson, treating Jude with astounding callousness in the process. Having refused to sleep with Phillotson she abandons him for Jude, temporarily wrecking the schoolmaster's career, and refuses to sleep with Jude too. She then agrees to marry him out of jealousy of Arabella, changes her mind, and finally returns again to Phillotson, leaving Jude to die. It's clear that such an external account of Sue's behaviour is inadequate as a basis for total judgement, but it's also important not to slide too quickly over the incriminating facts. The problem is how we come to feel that Sue *is* more than just a perverse hussy, full of petty stratagems and provocative pouts; for that this is at one level an accurate description of her seems undeniable. One reason why we feel that she is more than this is, of course, because she is so deeply loved by Jude; but Jude's love of Sue, like his love of Christminster, is an authentic desire refracted through a flawed medium, and he himself comes at times as near as possible to seeing her in a much less attractive light. The answer to the enigma of Sue seems to lie, not in balancing her undoubtedly 'good' qualities against her more unpleasant characteristics, but in reconsidering the question of the 'level' at which Sue is finally to be evaluated. After Jude has complained that Sue wouldn't risk her soul for him, he adds that it wasn't her fault; and it is important to see here that Jude is both wrong (he is sentimentally idealising her, as he did before he had even met her), and in a different sense right. It isn't Sue's fault, not because she is morally innocent, but because Hardy, through his presentation of Sue, is evoking movements and forces which can't be exhaustively described or evaluated at a simply personal level. Sue, like Jude himself, is a 'representative' character, in the great tradition of nineteenth-century realism which Hardy inherited; and her elusive complexity stems in part from the fact that she points beyond herself, to a confused, ambiguous structure of feeling which belongs to the period in general. Her opaqueness and inconsistency as a character are thus neither merely personal attributes nor evidence of some failure of full realisation on Hardy's part; it is precisely in her opaqueness and inconsistency that she is at once most fully realised and most completely representative. If she were a 'fully rounded' character, as wholly knowable as, say, Eustacia Vye in *The Return of the Native*, it would be easier to treat her as an autonomous moral agent, meriting directly personal praise or blame; but she would be also to that extent narrowed, simplified, unrepresentative.

Hardy described the novel in his preface as dramatising 'a deadly war waged between flesh and spirit', and it seems worth trying to unpack some of the meanings of that phrase. It is tempting to think of it first of all in terms of a conflict between Arabella and Sue – or rather of those aspects of Jude which each woman is supposed to externalise. But to reduce the novel to an interior battle between appetite and ideal is surely to over-simplify. It isn't just that Sue can only in a very qualified sense be taken as some 'ideal'; it's also that Arabella is an equally unobvious candidate to fulfil the role of 'appetite'. The soft smack of the pig's pizzle which Arabella throws at Jude signifies, evidently enough, a materialist deflation of his priggish dreams of grandeur; but Arabella herself is far from symbolising the lure of some earthy sensuality which impedes Jude's striving for spiritual development. This is true at the level of plot – it isn't Arabella who prevents Jude from entering the University – and true also of the way she is characterised. What we remember about Arabella isn't her sensuality but her calculating acquisitiveness, her sharp, devious opportunism. She uses her sensual appeal twice to captivate Jude, but what she captivates him for is, in the end, economic security. Arabella is one of a financially insecure class who need to look sharp in a predatory society: 'Poor folks must live' is her watchword from beginning to end. The claim on Jude which she represents is less that of some symbolic abstraction like 'sensuality' or 'appetite' than the need for material provision in conditions of scarcity; she wants to utilise his labour to buy herself frocks and hats, as Christminster uses it to sustain its elaborate façades.

Whereas Jude and Sue struggle bravely against empty convention, Arabella recognises the artifice of those conventions but manipulates them pragmatically for her own advantage. 'Life with a man is more business-like after [marriage]', she tells Sue, 'and money matters work better' (p. 288). Fly and practical as she is in contrast with Sue, her investment in conventions which she basically scorns offers a parallel to Sue's position, and indeed the two women are alike in more than this. Both are individualists, and both exploit Jude: Arabella crudely and materially, Sue subtly and spiritually. (It is interesting that Jude's entry into relationship with Arabella is characterised less by the prodding of 'appetite' than by a sense of dreaming and drifting which resembles his first feelings about Sue.) Arabella, indeed, recognises the similarities between herself and Sue ('Bolted from your first, didn't you, like me?', p. 289), a parallel which Sue snobbishly refuses. In terms of the comparison, Arabella comes off in some ways rather better: there's a crude but candid authenticity about her desire for Jude ('I must have him. I can't do without him. He's the sort of man I long for', p. 69) which contrasts tellingly with the evasions of a woman who, as Jude complains, can never say directly whether she loves him or not. Arabella is able to throw over her false religious conversion and fatalistically acknowledge the thrust of her real feelings of Jude ('Feelings are feelings!'); Sue moves in precisely the opposite direction, disowning her true feelings for Jude for a fatalistic adherence to religious orthodoxy.

Sue's action in abandoning Jude for Phillotson is, in a precise, Sartrean sense of the term, one of bad faith. The attempt to live authentically in a false society collapses into guilty self-punishment, a flight from freedom into the consoling embrace of an impersonal system of authority which will relieve one of the burden of selfhood, and so of responsibility. Sue, the celebrator of a pagan joy in life, becomes the woman who is glad her children are dead, eager to flay her flesh and bring her body into corpse-like submission to a man she physically detests. There is no need for this society to crush those who make the break for freedom; the roots of its deathly ideology sink sufficiently deep in the mind for the self to act as its own censor, anxiously desiring its own extinction.

Jude fights hard against Sue's death–dealing fantasy. 'It is only [a fight] against man and senseless circumstance,' he argues, in response to her demands for conformity to 'the ancient wrath of the Power above us' (p. 362). His argument merely rehearses Sue's own earlier opinion that the roots of the tragedy are social – that 'the social moulds civilization fits us into have no more relation to our actual shapes than the conventional shapes of the constellations have to the real star-patterns' (p. 226). The deadly war between flesh and spirit is fundamentally a war between the spirit of man and the obstructive flesh of a recalcitrant society. Sue's attempt to absolutise a particular tragedy as an act of Providence is the most dangerous form of false consciousness, relieving of responsibility the true killer of her children – the society which turned the family from its lodging-houses. It is a mark of Jude's resilience and rationality that he refuses to make this error: absolute as the tragedy is for him, he sees it nonetheless as historically relative. He reflects that 'It takes two or three generations ·to do what I tried to do in one' (p. 345), and is interested to hear of schemes already afoot to help poor scholars into Christminster.

Two elements in the novel might seem to argue for Sue's fatalism. One is the emphasis on a hereditary curse in the Fawley family; the other is the role of Jude's son, Father Time. The factor of heredity certainly crops up from time to time, but in the end little is made of it, and it isn't an element in the final tragic catastrophe. It remains as an awkwardly unintegrated dimension of the novel, generating 'atmosphere' but not much else; and even if it is taken seriously it seems to amount to no more than Mrs Edlin's judgement that there is a temperamental instability in the family which unfits them for coping with difficulties ('But things happened to thwart 'em, and if everything wasn't vitty they were upset', p. 301). Then there is Father Time, who for so many critics has stood for an authentic authorial consciousness, gloomy, pessimistic and omniscient. But it isn't only that Father Time, for all the ponderous symbolism which surrounds him, has essentially the limited understanding of a child, killing himself and the other children on the basis of what is really a mistake – a breakdown of communication between himself and an adult. It's also that Father Time's pessimism springs from the weary passivity of a character who is outside history, unable to intervene constructively in it, condemned (like the naturalistic novelists of the period) to see things in a rounded, distanced, deterministic way. This is not, in fact, Hardy's way: Father Time is rather like the God in Hardy's poems who, precisely because of his transcendental, unhistorical status, is doomed to impotence and disillusion. Father Time can assume his omniscient, spectatorial stance only because his living will has been effectively destroyed; and in this he differs from his father, whose will does not consent to be beaten, and who continues to struggle almost until the end. *Jude the Obscure*, like all of Hardy's novels, proclaims no inexorable determinism, though anyone aware of the paltry percentage of working-class undergraduates now at Oxford might be forgiven for thinking differently.

Postscript on Thomas Hardy

The name 'Thomas Hardy', like that of any other literary producer, signifies a particular ideological and biographical formation; but it also signifies the process whereby a certain set of texts are grouped, constructed, and endowed with the 'coherency' of a 'readable' *oeuvre*. 'Thomas Hardy' denotes that set of ideological practices through which certain texts, by virtue of their changing, contradictory modes of insertion into the dominant 'cultural' and pedagogical apparatuses, are processed, 'corrected' and reconstituted so that a home may be found for them within a literary 'tradition' which is always the 'imaginary' unity of the present. But this, in Hardy's case, has been a process of struggle, outrage and exasperation. He is a major realist, the creator of 'memorable' scenes and characters; yet he can be scandalously nonchalant about the 'purity' of orthodox verisimilitude, risking 'coincidence' and 'improbability'. With blunt disregard for formal consistency, he is ready to articulate form upon form – to mingle realist narration, classical tragedy, folk-fable, melodrama, 'philosophical' discourse, social commentary, and by doing so to betray the laborious constructedness of literary production. He is, acceptably enough for a Victorian, something of a 'sage'; yet his fictional meditations assume the offensively palpable form of 'ideas', obtrusive notions too little 'naturalized' by fictional device. He seems, gratifyingly enough, a novelist of the 'human condition'; yet the supposedly dour, fatalistic bent of his art, its refusal to repress the tragic, has had a profoundly unnerving effect upon the dominant critical ideologies, and must be rationalized as 'temperamental gloom' or a home-spun *fin-de-siècle* pessimism. His 'clumsy' provincialism and 'bucolic' quaintness are tolerable features of a 'peasant' novelist; but these elements are too subtly intertwined with a more sophisticated artistry and lack of rustic 'geniality' to permit a confident placing of him as literary Hodge.

A predominant critical strategy has therefore been simply to write him out. Henry James's elegant patronage ('the good little Thomas Hardy') finds its echo in F. R. Leavis and *Scrutiny*, who expel Hardy from the 'great tradition' of nineteenth-century realism. More generally, Hardy criticism may be seen to have developed through four distinct stages, all of which may be permutated in the work of any particular critic. Hegemonic in Hardy's own lifetime was the image of him as anthropologist of Wessex – the charming supplier of rural idylls who sometimes grew a little too big for his literary boots. After the publication of *The Dynasts*, a new critical phase is initiated: Hardy is now, in G. K. Chesterton's notorious comment, 'the village atheist brooding and blaspheming over the village idiot', the melancholic purveyor of late nineteenth-century nihilism. It is this view, conveniently distancing as it is, which on the whole dominates the earlier decades of the century;[2] but throughout the 1940s and 1950s, Hardy's reputation is more or less in decline. An Anglo-Saxon criticism increasingly controlled by formalist, organicist and anti-theoretical assumptions ('New Criticism' in the United States, *Scrutiny* in England) can make no accommodation for Hardy's texts; R. P. Blackmur insisted in 1940 that Hardy's sensibility was irreparably violated by ideas.[3] From the late 1940s onwards, however, there is a notable shift towards a more 'sociological' reading of Hardy. In 1954, an influential study by Douglas Brown focused sentimentally upon the conflict between rural 'warmth' and urban invasion;[4] and four years later John Holloway was reflecting upon Hardy's 'vision of the passing of the old rhythmic order of rural England'.[5] Safely defused by such mythologies, Hardy could now for the first time merit the attention of critics more preoccupied with colour imagery than with the Corn Laws or the Immanent Will; and the 1960s and 1970s have witnessed a stealthy recuperation of his texts by formalist criticism.[6] In the year of the anniversary of his death, then, the critical floodgates stand wide open: he has been phenomenologized,[7] Freudianized,[8] biographized,[9] claimed as the true guardian of 'English' liberal-democratic decencies against the primitivist extremism of émigré modernists.[10]

The Scandal of Hardy's Language

From the beginning, however, the true scandal of Hardy has been his language. If there is one point on which bourgeois criticism has been virtually unanimous, it is that Hardy, regrettably, was really unable to *write*. Since this is rather a major disadvantage for a novelist, it is not surprising that criticism has found such difficulties with his work. Confronted with the 'unrealistic' utterances of his 'rustics' and his irritating 'oddities of style', criticism has been able to do little more than inscribe a 'Could do better' in the margins of Hardy's texts. The *Athenaeum* of 1874, reviewing *Far from the Madding Crowd*, complained that Hardy inserted into the mouths of his labourers 'expressions which we simply cannot believe possible from the illiterate clods whom he describes'. A reviewer of *The Return of the Native*, who protested *en passant* about the 'low social position of the characters', found that Hardy's characters talked as no people had ever talked before: 'The language of his peasants may be Elizabethan, but it can hardly be Victorian.' If the language of the 'peasants' was odd, that of their author was even odder. Again and again, Hardy is berated for his maladroit, 'pretentious' use of Latinisms, neologisms, 'clumsy and inelegant metaphors', technical 'jargon' and philosophical terms. On the one hand, criticism is exasperated by Hardy's apparent inability to write *properly*; on the other hand, it sneers at such attempts as the bumptiousness of a low-bred literary upstart. *Scrutiny* in 1934 bemoaned his 'clumsy aiming at impressiveness'; a doughty defender like Douglas Brown none the less finds his prose 'unserviceable, even shoddy'; and David Lodge informs us that 'we are, while reading him tantalized by a sense of greatness not quite achieved'.

The ideological secret of these irritabilities is clear. Early Hardy criticism passionately desires that he should be a categorizable chronicler of bumpkins, and protests when such 'rustic realism' is vitiated; later criticism desires to take Hardy seriously as a major novelist, but is forced to acknowledge that, as an 'autodidact', he was never quite up to it. What is repressed in both cases is the fact that the significance of Handy's writing lies precisely in the *contradictory* constitution of his linguistic practice. The ideological effectivity of his fiction inheres neither in 'rustic' nor 'educated' writing, but in the ceaseless play and tension between the two modes. In this sense, he is a peculiarly interesting illustration of that literary-ideological process which has been analysed in the work of Renée Balibar.[11] 'Literature', Balibar argues, is a crucial part of that process whereby, within the 'cultural' and pedagogical apparatuses, ideologically potent contradictions within a common language (in the case of post-revolutionary France, '*français ordinaire*' and '*français littéraire*') are constituted and reproduced. The 'literary' is an ensemble of linguistic practices, inscribed in certain institutions, which produce appropriate 'fictional' and ideological effects, and in doing so contribute to the maintenance of linguistic class divisions. Limited though such an analysis is by its residual 'sociologism', and fragile though it may be when exported from the specific pedagogical conditions of bourgeois France, it nevertheless has a marked applicability to Hardy. It is not a question of whether Hardy wrote 'well' or 'badly'; it is rather a question of the ideological disarray which his fictions, consciously or not, are bound to produce within a criticism implacably committed to the 'literary' as yardstick of maturely civilized consciousness. This is not to suggest that the question of the aesthetic effects of Hardy's texts can be reduced to the question of their ideological impact; that a text may embarrass a dominant ideology is by no means the criterion of its aesthetic effectivity, though it may be a component of it. But in Hardy's case, these two issues are imbricated with a peculiar closeness.

The only critic who has understood this fact is, characteristically, Raymond Williams, who finds in the very letter of Hardy's texts the social and ideological crisis which those texts are constructed to negotiate.[12] Williams, indeed, has been one of the most powerfully demystifying of Hardy critics, brilliantly demolishing the banal mythology of a 'timeless peasantry' dislocated by 'external' social change. But his text, symptomatically, has had little general influence; and the same may be said of Roy Morrell's masterly study,[13] which tackled and defeated several decades of belief that Hardy was a 'fatalist'. Despite these interventions, criticism remains worried by the precise status of Hardy's 'realism'; and it is not difficult to see why. For the contradictory nature of his textual practice cannot but throw into embarrassing relief those ideologically diverse constituents of fiction which it is precisely fiction's task to conceal; it is by 'not writing properly' that he lays bare the device.

John Bayley, however, is typically undisturbed by Hardy's 'disunity'; indeed it is precisely this, among other things, which attracts Bayley to him. In his introduction to the New Wessex edition of *Far from the Madding Crowd*, Bayley writes perceptively of that peculiarly Hardyesque diversity 'in which the separate ingredients seem quite unconscious of each other's presence', and recognizes the necessary recalcitrance of such fiction for the remorselessly 'organizing' intelligence of a Leavis or Trilling.[14] Pierre Macherey, however, has pointed out that the familiar bedfellow of 'normative' criticism is empiricism: the one seeks to 'correct' the text against a ghostly model of what it 'might have been', the other sinks itself tolerantly into the text 'as it is'. Neither method is thereby able to displace the work into its material determinants – to accomplish the difficult dialectical feat of 'refusing' the text's phenomenal presence while acknowledging that such a presence is *necessary* and *determinate*.

Notes

1   Thus the novel's original title, 'The Simpletons', is both an irony at the expense of the society and a comment on the nature of Jude and Sue's idealism.

2   See, for example, Helen Garwood, *Thomas Hardy: An Illustration of the Philosophy of Schopenhauer* (London, 1911); E. Brennecke, *Thomas Hardy's Universe* (London, 1924); A. P. Elliott, *Fatalism in the Works of Thomas Hardy* (London, 1935).

3   *The Southern Review* 6 (summer 1949).

4   Douglas Brown, *Thomas Hardy* (London, 1954).

5   John Holloway, *The Chartered Mirror* (London, 1960).

6   See, for example, David Lodge, *The Language of Fiction* (London, 1966); Tony Tanner, 'Colour and Movement in Hardy's *Tess of the d'Urbervilles*', *Critical Quarterly*

19 (1968); Ian Gregor, *The Great Web: The Form of Hardy's Major Fiction* (London, 1974).

7   See J. Hillis Miller, *Thomas Hardy: Distance and Desire* (Cambridge, Mass., 1970).

8   See Perry Meisel, *Thomas Hardy: The Return of the Repressed* (London, 1972).

9   See R. Gittings, *Young Thomas Hardy* (London, 1975).

10   See Donald Davie, *Thomas Hardy and British Poetry* (London, 1973).

11   See R. Balibar, G. Merlin and G. Tret, *Les français fictifs: le rapport des styles littéraires au français national* (Paris, 1974); and R. Balibar and D. Laporte, *Le français national: constitution de la langue nationale commune à l'époque de la révolution démocratique bourgeoise* (Paris, 1974).

12   Raymond Williams, *The English Novel from Dickens to Lawrence* (London, 1970), pp. 106ff.

13   Roy Morrell, *Thomas Hardy: The Will and the Way* (Oxford, 1965).

14   Thomas Hardy, *Far from the Madding Crowd* (London, 1975), p. 19.

4 Wuthering Heights

If it is a function of ideology to achieve an illusory resolution of real contradictions, then Charlotte Brontë's novels are ideological in a precise sense – myths. In the fabulous, fairy-tale ambience of a work like *Jane Eyre*, with its dramatic archetypes and magical devices, certain facets of the complex mythology which constitutes Victorian bourgeois consciousness find their aesthetically appropriate form. Yet 'myth' is, of course, a term more commonly used of *Wuthering Heights*; and we need therefore to discriminate between different meanings of the word.

For Lucien Goldmann, 'ideology' in literature is to be sharply distinguished from what he terms 'world-view'. Ideology signifies a false, distortive, partial consciousness; 'world-view' designates a true, total and coherent understanding of social relations. This seems to me a highly suspect formulation: nothing, surely, could be more ideological than the 'tragic vision' of Pascal and Racine which Goldmann examines in *The Hidden God*. Even so, Goldmann's questionable distinction can be used to illuminate a crucial difference between the work of Charlotte and Emily Brontë. Charlotte's fiction is 'mythical' in the exact ideological sense I have suggested: it welds together antagonistic forces, forging from them a pragmatic, precarious coherence of interests. *Wuthering Heights is* mythical in a more traditional sense of the term: an apparently timeless, highly integrated, mysteriously autonomous symbolic universe. Such a notion of myth is itself, of course, ideologically based, and much of this chapter will be an attempt to de-mystify it. The world of *Wuthering Heights* is neither eternal nor self-enclosed; nor is it in the least unriven by internal contradictions. But in the case of this work it does seem necessary to speak of a 'world-view', a unified vision of brilliant clarity and consistency, in contrast to the dominant consciousness of Charlotte's novels. Goldmann's distinction is valuable to that limited extent: it enforces an appropriate contrast between the elaborated impersonality of Emily's novel, the 'intensive totality' of its world,[1] and Charlotte's tendentious, occasionally opportunist manipulation of materials for ideological ends, her readiness to allow a set of practical interests to predominate over the demands of disinterested exploration. If *Wuthering Heights* generally transcends those limits, it is not in the least because its universe is any less ideological, or that conflictive pressures are absent from it. The difference lies in the paradoxical truth that *Wuthering Heights* achieves its coherence of vision from an exhausting confrontation of contending forces, whereas Charlotte's kind of totality depends upon a pragmatic integration of them. Both forms of consciousness are ideological; but in so far as Emily's represents a more penetrative, radical and honest enterprise, it provides the basis for a finer artistic achievement. *Wuthering Heights* remains formally unfissured by the conflicts it dramatises; it forges its unity of vision from the very imaginative heat those conflicts generate. The book's genealogical structure is relevant here: familial relations at once provide the substance of antagonism and mould that substance into intricate shape, precipitating a tightly integrated form from the very stuff of struggle and disintegration. The genealogical structure, moreover, allows for a sharply dialectical relation between the 'personal' and 'impersonal' of a sort rare in Charlotte: the family, at once social institution and domain of intensely interpersonal relationships, highlights the complex interplay between an evolving system of given unalterable relations and the creation of individual value.

One is tempted, then, to credit Goldmann's dubious dichotomy between ideology and world-view to this extent: that if 'ideology' is a coherence of antagonisms, 'world-view' is a coherent perception of them.[2] An instance of such coherent perception may be found in Emily Brontë's early essay 'The Butterfly':

> All creation is equally insane. There are those flies playing above the stream, swallows and fish diminishing their number each minute: these will become in their turn, the prey of some tyrant of air or water; and man for his amusement or his needs will kill their murderers. Nature is an inexplicable puzzle, life exists on a principle of destruction; every creature must be the relentless instrument of death to the others, or himself cease to live.[3]

This, clearly enough, is ideological to the point of prefiguring Social Darwinism; but it is difficult to imagine Charlotte having written with this degree of generalising impersonal poise, this fluent projection of fearful private vision into total, lucid statement. Charlotte, indeed, seems to have recognised something of this difference with her sister. 'In some points', she once wrote, 'I consider Emily somewhat of a theorist; now and then she broaches ideas which strike my sense as much more daring and original than practical.'[4] Defining the issue as a contrast between theory and practice seems significant: the cautious empiricist greets the totalising visionary with a mixture of respect and reservation. It certainly seems true of Charlotte that her *imaginative* daring is not coupled with any equivalent moral or intellectual boldness. Hunsden, Rochester, Shirley, Paul Emmanuel: all combine a civilised moderation with their Romantic radicalism, which could hardly be said of Heathcliff. Heathcliff, as Lockwood finds to his cost, is precisely *not* a rough diamond; he conceals no coy Hunsden-like affection beneath his barbarous behaviour.

The difference between Charlotte and Emily can be expressed another way. The spite, violence and bigotry which in *Wuthering Heights* are aspects of the narrative are in parts of Charlotte's fiction qualities of the narration. *Wuthering Heights* trades in spite and stiff-neckedness, but always 'objectively', as the power of its tenaciously detailed realism to survive unruffled even the gustiest of emotional crises would suggest. Malice and narrowness in Charlotte's work, by contrast, are occasionally authorial as well as thematic, so that characters and events are flushed with the novelist's ideological intentions, bear the imprint of her longings and anxieties. This, as I have argued, is less true of *Jane Eyre*, where a subtler epistomology grants the objective world its own relative solidity: we feel the menacingly autonomous existence of Brocklehurst, Mrs Reed, even Bertha, as we do not with Père Silas, Madame Walravens or Job Barraclough. Because these figures are so directly the spontaneous precipitates of authorial fantasy, they have both the vividness and the vacuity of Lucy Snowe's dazed perceptions. We are almost never at a loss what to think about a Charlotte character, which could hardly be said of *Wuthering Heights*. No mere critical hair-splitting can account for the protracted debate over whether Heathcliff is hero or demon, Catherine tragic heroine or spoilt brat, Nelly Dean shrewd or stupid. The narrative techniques of the novel are deliberately framed to preserve these ambivalences; those of Charlotte Brontë allow us fairly direct access to a single, transparent, controlling consciousness which maintains its dominance even when its bearer is in practice subdued and subordinated.

I have said that *Wuthering Heights* remains unriven by the conflicts it releases, and it contrasts as such with those Charlotte works which are formally flawed by the strains and frictions of their 'content'. Charlotte's fiction sets out to reconcile thematically what I have crudely termed 'Romance' and 'realism' but sometimes displays severe structural disjunctions between the two; *Wuthering Heights* fastens thematically on a near-absolute antagonism between these modes but achieves, structurally and stylistically, an astonishing unity between them. Single incidents are inseparably high drama and domestic farce, figures like Catherine Earnshaw contradictory amalgams of the passionate and the pettish. There seems to me an ideological basis to this paradoxical contrast between the two sisters' works. Charlotte's novels, as I have suggested, are ideological in that they exploit fiction and fable to smooth the jagged edges of real conflict, and the evasions which that entails emerge as aesthetic unevennesses – as slanting, overemphasis, idealisation, structural dissonance. *Wuthering Heights*, on the other hand, confronts the tragic truth that the passion and society it presents are not fundamentally reconcilable – that there remains at the deepest level an ineradicable contradiction between them which refuses to be unlocked, which obtrudes itself as the very stuff and secret of experience. It is, then, precisely the imagination capable of confronting this tragic duality which has the power to produce the aesthetically superior work – which can synchronise in its internal structures the most shattering passion with the most rigorous realist control. The more authentic social and moral recognitions of the book, in other words, generate a finer artistic control; the unflinchingness with which the novel penetrates into fundamental contradictions is realised in a range of richer imaginative perceptions.

The primary contradiction I have in mind is the choice posed for Catherine between Heathcliff and Edgar Linton. That choice seems to me the pivotal event of the novel, the decisive catalyst of the tragedy; and if this is so, then the crux of *Wuthering Heights* must be conceded by even the most remorselessly mythological and mystical of critics to be a social one. In a crucial act of self-betrayal and bad faith, Catherine rejects Heathcliff as a suitor because he is socially inferior to Linton; and it is from this that the train of destruction follows. Heathcliff's own view of the option is not, of course, to be wholly credited: he is clearly wrong to think that Edgar 'is scarcely a degree dearer [to Catherine] than her dog, or her horse'.[5] Linton lacks spirit, but he is, as Nelly says, kind, honourable and trustful, a loving husband to Catherine and utterly distraught at her loss. Even so, the perverse act of *mauvaise foi* by which Catherine trades her authentic selfhood for social privilege is rightly denounced by Heathcliff as spiritual suicide and murder:

> '*Why* did you betray your own heart, Cathy? I have not one word of comfort. You deserve this. You have killed yourself. Yes, you may kiss me, and cry; and ring out my kisses and tears: they'll blight you – they'll damn you. You loved me – then what *right* had you to leave me? What right – answer me – for the poor fancy you felt for Linton? Because misery and degradation, and death, and nothing that God or Satan could inflict would have parted us, *you*, of your own will, did it. I have not broken your heart – *you* have broken it; and in breaking it, you have broken mine.'[6]

Like Lucy Snowe, Catherine tries to lead two lives: she hopes to square authenticity with social convention, running in harness an ontological commitment to Heathcliff with a phenomenal relationship to Linton. 'I *am* Heathcliff!' is dramatically arresting, but it is also a way of keeping the outcast at arm's length, evading the challenge he offers. If Catherine is Heathcliff – if identity rather than relationship is in question – then their estrangement is inconceivable, and Catherine can therefore turn to others without violating the timeless metaphysical idea Heathcliff embodies. She finds in him an integrity of being denied or diluted in routine social relations; but to preserve that ideal means reifying him to a Hegelian essence, sublimely untainted by empirical fact. Heathcliff, understandably, refuses to settle for this: he would rather enact his essence in existence by becoming Catherine's lover. He can, it seems, be endowed with impressive ontological status only at the price of being nullified as a person.

The uneasy alliance of social conformity and personal fulfilment for which Charlotte's novels works is not, then, feasible in the world of *Wuthering Heights*; Catherine's attempt to compromise unleashes the contradictions which will drive both her and Heathcliff to their deaths. One such contradiction lies in the relation between Heathcliff and the Earnshaw family. As a waif and orphan, Heathcliff is inserted into the close-knit family structure as an alien; he emerges from that ambivalent domain of darkness which is the 'outside' of the tightly defined domestic system. That darkness is ambivalent because it is at once fearful and fertilising, as Heathcliff himself is both gift and threat. Earnshaw's first words about him make this clear: ' "See here, wife! I was never so beaten with anything in my life: but you must e'en take it as a gift of God; though it's as dark almost as if it came from the devil." '[7] Stripped as he is of determinate social relations, of a given function within the family, Heathcliff's presence is radically gratuitous; the arbitrary, unmotivated event of his arrival at the Heights offers its inhabitants a chance to transcend the constrictions of their self-enclosed social structure and gather him in. Because Heathcliff's circumstances are so obscure he is available to be accepted or rejected simply for himself, laying claim to no status other than a human one. He is, of course, proletarian in appearance, but the obscurity of his origins also frees him of any exact social role; as Nelly Dean muses later, he might equally be a prince. He is ushered into the Heights for no good reason other than to be arbitrarily loved; and in this sense he is a touchstone of others' responses, a liberating force for Cathy and a stumbling-block for others. Nelly hates him at first, unable to transcend her bigotry against the new and non-related; she puts him on the landing like a dog, hoping he will be gone by morning. Earnshaw pets and favours him, and in doing so creates fresh inequalities in the family hierarchy which become the source of Hindley's hatred. As heir to the Heights, Hindley understandably feels his social role subverted by this irrational, unpredictable intrusion.

Catherine, who does not expect to inherit, responds spontaneously to Heathcliff's presence; and because this antagonises Hindley she becomes after Earnshaw's death a spiritual orphan as Heathcliff is a literal one. Both are allowed to run wild; both become the 'outside' of the domestic structure. Because his birth is unknown, Heathcliff is a purely atomised individual, free of generational ties in a novel where genealogical relations are of crucial thematic and structural importance; and it is because he is an internal *émigré* within the Heights that he can lay claim to a relationship of direct personal equality with Catherine who, as the daughter of the family, is the least economically integral member. Heathcliff offers Catherine a friendship which opens fresh possibilities of freedom within the internal system of the Heights; in a situation where social determinants are insistent, freedom can mean only a relative independence of given blood-ties, of the settled, evolving, predictable structures of kinship. Whereas in Charlotte's fiction the severing or lapsing of such relations frees you for progress up the class-system, the freedom which Cathy achieves with Heathcliff takes her down that system, into consorting with a 'gypsy'. Yet 'down' is also 'outside', just as gypsy signifies 'lower class' but also asocial vagrant, classless natural life-form. As the eternal rocks beneath the woods, Heathcliff is both lowly and natural, enjoying the partial freedom from social pressures appropriate to those at the bottom of the class-structure, In loving Heathcliff, Catherine is taken outside the family and society into an opposing realm which can be adequately imaged only as 'Nature'.

The loving equality between Catherine and Heathcliff stands, then, as a paradigm of human possibilities which reach beyond, and might ideally unlock, the tightly dominative system of the Heights. Yet at the same time Heathcliff's mere presence fiercely intensifies that system's harshness, twisting all the Earnshaw relationships into bitter antagonism. He unwittingly sharpens a violence endemic to the Heights – a violence which springs both from the hard exigencies imposed by its struggle with the land, and from its social exclusiveness as a self-consciously ancient, respectable family. The violence which Heathcliff unwittingly triggers is turned against him: he is cast out by Hindley, culturally deprived, reduced to the status of farm-labourer. What Hindley does, in fact, is to invert the potential freedom symbolised by Heathcliff into a parody of itself, into the non-freedom of neglect. Heathcliff is robbed of liberty in two antithetical ways: exploited as a servant on the one hand, allowed to run wild on the other; and this contradiction is appropriate to childhood, which is a time of relative freedom from convention and yet, paradoxically, a phase of authoritarian repression. In this sense there is freedom for Heathcliff neither within society nor outside it; his two conditions are inverted mirror-images of one another. It is a contradiction which encapsulates a crucial truth about bourgeois society. If there is no genuine liberty on its 'inside' – Heathcliff is oppressed by work and the familial structure – neither is there more than a caricature of liberty on the 'outside', since the release of running wild is merely a function of cultural impoverishment. The friendship of Heathcliff and Cathy crystallises under the pressures of economic and cultural violence, so that the freedom it seems to signify ('half-savage and hardy, and free'[8]) is always the other face of oppression, always exists in its shadow. With Heathcliff and Catherine, as in Charlotte's fiction, bitter social reality breeds Romantic escapism; but whereas Charlotte's novels try to trim the balance between them, *Wuthering Heights* shows a more dialectical interrelation at work. Romantic intensity is locked in combat with society, but cannot wholly transcend it; your freedom is bred and deformed in the shadow of your oppression, just as, in the adult Heathcliff, oppression is the logical consequence of the exploiter's 'freedom'.

Just as Hindley withdraws culture from Heathcliff as a mode of domination, so Heathcliff acquires culture as a weapon. He amasses a certain amount of cultural capital in his two years' absence in order to shackle others more effectively, buying up the expensive commodity of gentility in order punitively to re-enter the society from which he was punitively expelled. This is liberty of a kind, in contrast with his previous condition; but the novel is insistent on its ultimately illusory nature. In oppressing others the exploiter imprisons himself; the adult Heathcliff's systematic tormenting is fed by his victims' pain but also drains him of blood, impels and possesses him as an external force. His alienation from Catherine estranges him from himself to the point where his brutalities become tediously perfunctory gestures, the mechanical motions of a man who is already withdrawing himself from his own body. Heathcliff moves from being Hindley's victim to becoming, like Catherine, his own executioner.

Throughout *Wuthering Heights*, labour and culture, bondage and freedom, Nature and artifice appear at once as each other's dialectical negations and as subtly matched, mutually reflective. Culture – gentility – is the opposite of labour for young Heathcliff and Hareton; but it is also a crucial economic weapon, as well as a product of work itself. The delicate spiritless Lintons in their crimson-carpeted drawing-room are radically severed from the labour which sustains them; gentility grows from the production of others, detaches itself from that work (as the Grange is separate from the Heights), and then comes to dominate the labour on which it is parasitic. In doing so, it becomes a form of self-bondage; if work is servitude, so in a subtler sense is civilisation. To some extent, these polarities are held together in the yeoman-farming structure of the Heights. Here labour and culture, freedom and necessity, Nature and society are roughly complementary. The Earnshaws are gentlemen yet they work the land; they enjoy the freedom of being their own masters, but that freedom moves within the tough discipline of labour; and because the social unit of the Heights – the family – is both 'natural' (biological) and an economic system, it acts to some degree as a mediation between Nature and artifice, naturalising property relations and socialising blood-ties. Relationships in this isolated world are turbulently face-to-face, but they are also impersonally mediated through a working relation with Nature. This is not to share Mrs Q. D. Leavis's view of the Heights as 'a wholesome primitive and natural unit of a healthy society';[9] there does not, for instance, seem much that is wholesome about Joseph. Joseph incarnates a grimness inherent in conditions of economic exigency, where relationships must be tightly ordered and are easily warped into violence. One of *Wuthering Heights*' more notable achievements is ruthlessly to de-mystify the Victorian notion of the family as a pious, pacific space within social conflict. Even so, the Heights does pin together contradictions which the entry of Heathcliff will break open. Heathcliff disturbs the Heights because he is simply superfluous: he has no defined place within its biological and economic system. (He may well be Catherine's illegitimate half-brother, just as he may well have passed his two-year absence in Tunbridge Wells.) The superfluity he embodies is that of a sheerly human demand for recognition; but since there is no space for such surplus within the terse economy of the Heights, it proves destructive rather than creative in effect, straining and overloading already taut relationships. Heathcliff catalyses an aggression intrinsic to Heights society; that sound blow Hindley hands out to Catherine on the evening of Heathcliff's first appearance is slight but significant evidence against the case that conflict starts only with Heathcliff's arrival.

The effect of Heathcliff is to explode those conflicts into antagonisms which finally rip the place apart. In particular, he marks the beginnings of that process whereby passion and personal intensity separate out from the social domain and offer an alternative commitment to it. For farming families like the Earnshaws, work and human relations are roughly coterminous: work is socialised, personal relations mediated through a context of labour. Heathcliff, however, is set to work meaninglessly, as a servant rather than a member of the family; and his fervent emotional life with Catherine is thus forced outside the working environment into the wild Nature of the heath, rather than Nature reclaimed and worked up into significant value in the social activity of labour. Heathcliff is stripped of culture in the sense of gentility, but the result is a paradoxical intensifying of his fertile imaginative liaison with Catherine. It is fitting, then, that their free, neglected wanderings lead them to their adventure at Thrushcross Grange. For if the Romantic childhood culture of Catherine and Heathcliff exists in a social limbo divorced from the minatory world of working relations, the same can be said in a different sense of the genteel culture of the Lintons, surviving as it does on the basis of material conditions it simultaneously conceals. As the children spy on the Linton family, that concealed brutality is unleashed in the shape of bulldogs brought to the defence of civility. The natural energy in which the Linton's culture is rooted bursts literally through to savage the 'savages' who appear to threaten property. The underlying truth of violence, continuously visible at the Heights, is momentarily exposed; old Linton thinks the intruders are after his rents. Culture draws a veil over such brute force but also sharpens it: the more property you have, the more ruthlessly you need to defend it. Indeed, Heathcliff himself seems dimly aware of how cultivation exacerbates 'natural' conflict, as we see in his scornful account of the Linton children's petulant squabbling; cultivation, by pampering and swaddling 'natural' drives, at once represses serious physical violence and breeds a neurasthenic sensitivity which allows selfish impulse free rein. 'Natural' aggression is nurtured both by an excess and an absence of culture – a paradox demonstrated by Catherine Earnshaw, who is at once wild and pettish, savage and spoilt. Nature and culture, then, are locked in a complex relation of antagonism and affinity: the Romantic fantasies of Heathcliff and Catherine, and the Romantic Linton drawing-room with its gold-bordered ceiling and shimmering chandelier, both bear the scars of the material conditions which produced them – scars visibly inscribed on Cathy's ankle. Yet to leave the matter there would be to draw a purely formal parallel. For what distinguishes the two forms of Romance is Heathcliff: his intense communion with Catherine is an uncompromising rejection of the Linton world.

The opposition, however, is not merely one between the values of personal relationship and those of conventional society. What prevents this is the curious impersonality of the relationship between Catherine and Heathcliff. Edgar Linton shows at his best a genuine capacity for tender, loving fidelity; but this thrives on obvious limits. The limits are those of the closed room into which the children peer – the glowing, sheltered space within which those close, immediate encounters which make for both tenderness and pettishness may be conducted. Linton is released from material pressures into such a civilised enclave; and in that sense his situation differs from that of the Heights, where personal relations are more intimately entwined with a working context. The relationship of Heathcliff and Catherine, however, provides a third term. It really is a personal relationship, yet seems also to transcend the personal into some region beyond it. Indeed, there is a sense in which the unity the couple briefly achieve is narrowed and degutted by being described as 'personal'. In so far as 'personal' suggests the liberal humanism of Edgar, with his concern (crudely despised by Heathcliff) for pity, charity and humanity, the word is clearly inapplicable to the fierce mutual tearings of Catherine and Heathcliff. Yet it is inadequate to the positive as well as the destructive aspects of their love. Their relationship is, we say, 'ontological' or 'metaphysical' because it opens out into the more-than-personal, enacts a style of being which is more than just the property of two individuals, which suggests in its impersonality something beyond a merely Romantic-individualist response to social oppression. Their relationship articulates a depth inexpressible in routine social practice, transcendent of available social languages. Its impersonality suggests both a savage depersonalising and a paradigmatic significance; and in neither sense is the relationship wholly within their conscious control. What Heathcliff offers Cathy is a non- or pre-social relationship, as the only authentic form of living in a world of exploitation and inequality, a world where one must refuse to measure oneself by the criteria of the class-structure and so must appear inevitably subversive. Whereas in Charlotte's novels the love-relationship takes you into society, in *Wuthering Heights* it drives you out of it. The love between Heathcliff and Catherine is an intuitive intimacy raised to cosmic status, by-passing the mediation of the 'social'; and this, indeed, is both its strength and its limit. Its non-sociality is on the one hand a revolutionary refusal of the given language of social roles and values; and if the relationship is to remain unabsorbed by society it must therefore appear as natural rather than social, since Nature is the 'outside' of society. On the other hand, the novel cannot realise the meaning of that revolutionary refusal in social terms; the most it can do is to *universalise* that meaning by intimating the mysteriously impersonal energies from which the relationship springs.

Catherine, of course, *is* absorbed: she enters the civilised world of the Lintons and leaves Heathcliff behind, to become a 'wolfish, pitiless' man. To avoid incorporation means remaining as unreclaimed as the wild furze: there is no way in this novel of temporising between conformity and rebellion. But there is equally no way for the revolutionary depth of relationship between Heathcliff and Catherine to realise itself as a historical force; instead, it becomes an elusive dream of absolute value, an incomparably more powerful version of Charlotte's myth of lost origins. Catherine and Heathcliff seek to preserve the primordial moment of pre-social harmony, before the fall into history and oppression. But it won't do to see them merely as children eternally fixated in some Edenic infancy: we do not see them merely as children, and in any case to be 'merely' a child is to endure the punitive pressures of an adult world. Moreover, it is none of Heathcliff's fault that the relationship remains 'metaphysical': it is Catherine who consigns it to unfulfilment. Their love remains an unhistorical essence which fails to enter into concrete existence and can do so, ironically, only in death. Death, indeed, as the ultimate outer limit of consciousness and society, is the locus of Catherine and Heathcliff's love, the horizon on which it moves. The absolutism of death is prefigured, echoed back, in the remorseless intensity with which their relationship is actually lived; yet their union can be achieved only in the act of abandoning the actual world.

Catherine and Heathcliff's love, then, is pushed to the periphery by society itself, projected into myth; yet the fact that it seems *inherently* convertible to myth spotlights the threshold of the novel's 'possible consciousness'. I take that phrase from Lukács and Goldmann to suggest those restrictions set on the consciousness of a historical period which only a transformation of real social relations could abolish – the point at which the most enterprising imagination presses against boundaries which signify not mere failures of personal perception but the limits of what can be historically said. The force Heathcliff symbolises can be truly realised only in some more than merely individualist form; *Wuthering Heights* has its roots not in that narrowed, simplified Romanticism which pits the lonely rebel against an anonymous order, but in that earlier, more authentic Romantic impulse which posits its own kind of 'transindividual' order of value, its own totality, against the order which forces it into exile. Heathcliff may be Byronic, but not in the way Rochester is: the novel counterposes social convention not merely with contrasting personal life-styles but with an alternative world of meaning. Yet it is here that the limits of 'possible consciousness' assert themselves: the offered totalities of Nature, myth and cosmic energy are forced to figure as asocial worlds unable to engage in more than idealist ways with the society they subject to judgement. The price of universality is to be fixed eternally at a point extrinsic to social life – fixed, indeed, at the moment of death, which both manifests a depth challengingly alien to the Lintons and withdraws the character from that conventional landscape into an isolated realm of his own.

Nature, in any case, is no true 'outside' to society, since its conflicts are transposed into the social arena. In one sense the novel sharply contrasts Nature and society; in another sense it grasps civilised life as a higher distillation of ferocious natural appetite. Nature, then, is a thoroughly ambiguous category, inside and outside society simultaneously. At one level it represents the unsalvaged region beyond the pale of culture; at another level it signifies the all-pervasive reality of which culture itself is a particular outcropping. It is, indeed, this ambiguity which supplies the vital link between the childhood and adult phases of Heathcliff's career. Heathcliff the child is 'natural' both because he is allowed to run wild and because he is reduced as Hindley's labourer to a mere physical instrument; Heathcliff the adult is 'natural' man in a Hobbesian sense: an appetitive exploiter to whom no tie or tradition is sacred, a callous predator violently sundering the bonds of custom and piety. If the first kind of 'naturalness' is anti-social in its estrangements from the norms of 'civilised' life, the second involves the unsociality of one set at the centre of a world whose social relations are inhuman. Heathcliff moves from being natural in the sense of an anarchic outsider to adopting the behaviour natural to an insider in a viciously competitive society. Of course, to be natural in both senses is at a different level to be unnatural. From the viewpoint of culture, it is unnatural that a child should be degraded to a savage, and unnatural too that a man should behave in the obscene way Heathcliff does. But culture in this novel is as problematical at Nature. There are no cool Arnoldian touchstones by which to take the measure of natural degeneracy, since the dialectical vision of *Wuthering Heights* puts culture into question in the very act of exploring the 'naturalness' which is its negation. Just as being natural involves being either completely outside or inside society, as roaming waif or manipulative landlord, so culture signifies either free-wheeling Romantic fantasy or that well-appointed Linton drawing-room. The adult Heathcliff is the focus of these contradictions: as he worms his way into the social structure he becomes progressively detached in spirit from all it holds dear. But *contradiction* is the essential emphasis. Heathcliff's schizophrenia is symptomatic of a world in which there can be no true dialectic between culture and Nature – a world in which culture is merely refuge from or reflex of material conditions, and so either too estranged from or entwined with those conditions to offer a viable alternative.

I take it that Heathcliff, up to the point at which Cathy rejects him, is in general an admirable character. His account of the Grange adventure, candid, satirical and self-aware as it is, might itself be enough to enforce this point; and we have in any case on the other side only the self-confessedly biased testimony of Nelly Dean. Even according to Nelly's grudging commentary, Heathcliff as a child is impressively patient and uncomplaining (although Nelly adds 'sullen' out of spite), and the heart-rending cry he raises when old Earnshaw dies is difficult to square with her implication that he felt no gratitude to his benefactor. He bears Hindley's vindictive treatment well, and tries pathetically to keep culturally abreast of Catherine despite it. The novel says quite explicitly that Hindley's systematic degradation of Heathcliff 'was enough to make a fiend of a saint';[10] and we should not therefore be surprised that what it does, more precisely, is to produce a pitiless capitalist landlord out of an oppressed child. Heathcliff the adult is in one sense an inversion, in another sense an organic outgrowth, of Heathcliff the child. Heathcliff the child was an isolated figure whose freedom from given genealogical ties offered, as I have argued, fresh possibilities of relationship; Heathcliff the adult is the atomic capitalist to whom relational bonds are nothing, whose individualism is now enslaving rather than liberating. The child knew the purely negative freedom of running wild; the adult, as a man vehemently pursuing ends progressively alien to him, knows only the delusory freedom of exploiting others. The point is that such freedom seems the only kind available in this society, once the relationship with Catherine has collapsed; the only mode of self-affirmation left to Heathcliff is that of oppression which, since it involves self-oppression, is no affirmation at all. Heathcliff is a self-tormentor, a man who is in hell because he can avenge himself on the system which has robbed him of his soul only by battling with it on its own hated terms. If as a child he was outside and inside that system simultaneously, wandering on the moors and working on the farm, he lives out a similar self-division as an adult, trapped in the grinding contradiction between a false social self and the true identity which lies with Catherine. The social self is false, not because Heathcliff is only apparently brutal – that he certainly is – but because it is contradictorily related to the authentic selfhood which is his passion for Catherine.

He installs himself at the centre of conventional society, but with wholly negative and inimical intent; his social role is a calculated self-contradiction, created first to further, and then fiercely displace, his asocial passion for Catherine.

Heathcliff's social relation to both Heights and Grange is one of the most complex issues in the novel. Lockwood remarks that he looks too genteel for the Heights; and indeed, in so far as he represents the victory of capitalist property-dealing over the traditional yeoman economy of the Earnshaws, he is inevitably aligned with the world of the Grange. Heathcliff is a dynamic force which seeks to destroy the old yeoman settlement by dispossessing Hareton; yet he does this partly to revenge himself on the very Linton world whose weapons (property deals, arranged marriages) he deploys so efficiently. He does this, moreover, with a crude intensity which is a quality of the Heights world; his roughness and resilience link him culturally to *Wuthering Heights*, and he exploits those qualities to destroy both it and the Grange. He is, then, a force which springs out of the Heights yet subverts it, breaking beyond its constrictions into a new, voracious acquisitiveness. His capitalist brutality is an extension as well as a negation of the Heights world he knew as a child; and to that extent there is continuity between his childhood and adult protests against Grange values, if not against Grange weapons. Heathcliff is subjectively a Heights figure opposing the Grange, and objectively a Grange figure undermining the Heights; he focuses acutely the contradictions between the two worlds. His rise to power symbolises at once the triumph of the oppressed over capitalism and the triumph of capitalism over the oppressed.

He is, indeed, contradiction incarnate – both progressive and outdated, at once caricature of and traditionalist protest against the agrarian capitalist forces of Thrushcross Grange. He harnesses those forces to worst the Grange, to beat it at its own game; but in doing so he parodies that property-system, operates against the Lintons with an unLinton-like explicitness and extremism. He behaves in this way because his 'soul' belongs not to that world but to Catherine; and in that sense his true commitment is an 'out-dated' one, to a past, increasingly mythical realm of absolute personal value which capitalist social relations cancel. He embodies a passionate human protest against the marriage-market values of both Grange and Heights at the same time as he callously images those values in caricatured form. Heathcliff exacts vengeance from that society precisely by extravagantly enacting its twisted priorities, becoming a darkly satirical commentary on conventional mores. If he is in one sense a progressive historical force, he belongs in another sense to the superseded world of the Heights, so that his death and the closing-up of the house seem logically related. In the end Heathcliff is defeated and the Heights restored to its rightful owner; yet at the same time the trends he epitomises triumph in the form of the Grange, to which Hareton and young Catherine move away. Hareton wins and loses the Heights simultaneously; dispossessed by Heathcliff, he repossesses the place only to be in that act assimilated by Thrushcross Grange. And if Hareton both wins and loses, then Heathcliff himself is both ousted and victorious.

Quite who has in fact won in the end is a matter of critical contention. Mrs Leavis and Tom Winnifrith both see the old world as having yielded to the new, in contrast to T. K. Meier, who reads the conclusion as 'the victory of tradition over innovation'.[11] The critical contention reflects a real ambiguity in the novel. In one sense, the old values have triumphed over the disruptive usurper: Hareton has wrested back his birthright, and the qualities he symbolises, while preserving their authentic vigour, will be fertilised by the civilising grace which the Grange, in the form of young Catherine, can bring. Heathcliff's career appears from his perspective as a shattering but short-lived interlude, after which true balance may be slowly recovered. In a more obvious sense, however, the Grange has won: the Heights is shut up and Hareton will become the new squire. Heathcliff, then, has been the blunt instrument by which the remnants of the Earnshaw world have been transformed into a fully-fledged capitalist class – the historical medium whereby that world is at once annihilated and elevated to the Grange. Thrushcross values have entered into productive dialogue with rough material reality and, by virtue of this spiritual transfusion, ensured their continuing survival; the Grange comes to the Heights and gathers back to itself what the Heights can yield it. This is why it will not do to read the novel's conclusion as some neatly reciprocal symbolic alliance between the two universes, a symmetrical symbiosis of bourgeois realism and upper-class cultivation. Whatever unity the book finally establishes, it is certainly not symmetrical: in a victory for the progressive forces of agrarian capitalism, Hareton, last survivor of the traditional order, is smoothly incorporated into the Grange.

There is another significant reason why the 'defeat' of Heathcliff cannot be read as the resilient recovery of a traditional world from the injuries it has suffered at his hands. As an extreme parody of capitalist activity, Heathcliff is also an untypical deviation from its norms; as a remorseless, crudely transparent revelation of the real historical character of the Grange, he stands askew to that reality in the very act of becoming its paradigm. It *is* true that Heathcliff, far from signifying some merely ephemeral intervention, is a type of the historically ascendant world of capital; but because he typifies it so 'unnaturally' the novel can move beyond him, into the gracefully gradualistic settlement symbolised by the union of Hareton and young Catherine. Heathcliff is finally fought off, while the social values he incarnates can be prised loose from the self-parodic mould in which he cast them and slowly accommodated. His undisguised violence, like the absolutism of his love, come to seem features of a past more brutal but also more heroic than the present; if the decorous, muted milieu of the Grange will not easily accommodate such passionate intensities, neither will it so readily reveal the more unpleasant face of its social and economic power. The 'defeat' of Heathcliff, then, is at once the transcending of such naked power and the collapse of that passionate protest against it which was the inner secret of Heathcliff's outrageous dealings.

We can now ask what these contradictions in the figure of Heathcliff actually amount to. It seems to me possible to decipher in the struggle between Heathcliff and the Grange an imaginatively transposed version of that contemporary conflict between bourgeoisie and landed gentry which I have argued is central to Charlotte's work. The relationship holds in no precise detail, since Heathcliff is not literally an industrial entrepreneur; but the double-edgedness of his relation with the Lintons, with its blend of antagonism and emulation, reproduces the complex structure of class-forces we found in Charlotte's fiction. Having mysteriously amassed capital outside agrarian society, Heathcliff forces his way into that society to expropriate the expropriators: and in this sense his machinations reflect the behaviour of a contemporary bourgeois class increasingly successful in its penetration of landed property. He belongs fully to neither Heights nor Grange, opposing them both; he embodies a force which at once destroys the traditional Earnshaw settlement and effectively confronts the power of the squirearchy. In its contradictory amalgam of 'Heights' and 'Grange', then, Heathcliff's career fleshes out a contemporary ideological dilemma which Charlotte also explores: the contradiction that the fortunes of the industrial bourgeoisie belong *economically* to an increasing extent with the landed gentry but that there can still exist between them, socially, culturally and personally, a profound hostility. If they are increasingly bound up objectively in a single power-bloc, there is still sharp subjective conflict between them. I take it that *Wuthering Heights*, like Charlotte's fiction, needs mythically to resolve this historical contradiction. If the exploitative adult Heathcliff belongs economically with the capitalist power of the Grange, he is culturally closer to the traditional world of the Heights; his contemptuous response to the Grange as a child, and later to Edgar, is of a piece with Joseph's scorn for the finicky Linton Heathcliff and the haughty young Catherine. If Heathcliff exploits Hareton culturally and economically, he nevertheless feels a certain rough-and-ready *rapport* with him. The contradiction Heathcliff embodies, then, is brought home in the fact that he combines Heights violence with Grange methods to gain power over both properties; and this means that while he is economically progressive he is culturally outdated. He represents a turbulent form of capitalist aggression which must historically be civilised – blended with spiritual values, as it will be in the case of his surrogate Hareton. The terms into which the novel casts this imperative are those of the need to refine, in the person of Hareton, the old yeoman class; but since Hareton's achievement of the Grange is an ironic consequence of Heathcliff's own activity, there is a sense in which it is the capitalist drive symbolised by Heathcliff which must submit to spiritual cultivation. It is worth recalling at this point the cultural affinities between the old yeoman and the new industrial classes touched on by David Wilson;[12] and F. M. L. Thompson comments that by the early 1830s a depleted yeomanry were often forced to sell their land either to a large landowner, or to a local tradesman who would put a tenant in.[13] On the other hand, as Mrs Gaskell notes, some landed yeomen turned to manufacture. Heathcliff the heartless capitalist and Hareton the lumpish yeoman thus have a real as well as an alliterative relation. In so far as Heathcliff symbolises the dispossessing bourgeoisie, he links hands with the large capitalist landowner Linton in common historical opposition to yeoman society; in so far as he himself has sprung from that society and turned to amassing capital outside it, still sharing its dour life-style, he joins spiritual forces with the uncouth Hareton against the pampered squirearchy.

In pitting himself against both yeomanry and large-scale agrarian capitalism, then, Heathcliff is an indirect symbol of the aggressive industrial bourgeoisie of Emily Brontë's own time, a social trend extrinsic to both classes but implicated in their fortunes. The contradiction of the *novel*, however, is that Heathcliff cannot represent at once an absolute metaphysical refusal of an inhuman society and a class which is intrinsically part of it. Heathcliff is both metaphysical hero, spiritually marooned from all material concern in his obsessional love for Catherine, and a skilful exploiter who cannily expropriates the wealth of others. It is a limit of the novel's 'possible consciousness' that its absolute metaphysical protest can be socially articulated only in such terms – that its 'outside' is in this sense an 'inside'. The industrial bourgeoisie is outside the farming world of both Earnshaws and Lintons; but it is no longer a *revolutionary* class, and so provides no sufficient social correlative for what Heathcliff 'metaphysically' represents. He can thus be presented only as a conflictive unity of spiritual rejection and social integration; and this, indeed, is his personal tragedy. With this in mind, we can understand why what he did in that two years' absence has to remain mysterious. The actual facts of his return, as an ambitious *parvenu* armed with presumably non-agrarian wealth and bent on penetrating agrarian society, speak eloquently enough of the real situation of the contemporary bourgeoisie; but it is clear that such social realities offer no adequate symbolism for Heathcliff's unswerving drive, which transcends all social determinants and has its end in Catherine alone. The novel, then, can dramatise its 'metaphysical' challenge to society only by refracting it through the distorting terms of existing social relations, while simultaneously, at a 'deeper' level, isolating that challenge in a realm eternally divorced from the actual.

It seems clear that the novel's sympathies lie on balance with the Heights rather than the Grange. As Tom Winnifrith points out, the Heights is the more homely, egalitarian place; Lockwood's inability at the beginning of the book to work out its social relationships (is Hareton a servant or not?) marks a significant contrast with the Grange. (Lockwood is here a kind of surrogate reader: we too are forestalled from 'reading off' the relationships at first glance, since they are historically moulded and so only historically intelligible.) The passing of the Heights, then, is regretted: it lingers on in the ghostly myth of Heathcliff and Catherine as an unbanishable intimation of a world of hungering absolution askew to the civilised present. Winnifrith declares himself puzzled by Mrs Leavis's point that the action of Hareton and Catherine in replacing the Heights' currant-bushes with flowers symbolises the victory of capitalist over yeoman, but Mrs Leavis is surely right: flowers are a form of 'surplus value', redundant luxuries in the spare Heights world which can accommodate the superfluous neither in its horticulture nor in its social network. But though the novel mourns the death of Wuthering Heights, it invests deeply in the new life which struggles out of it. In so far as Heathcliff signifies a demonic capitalist drive, his defeat is obviously approved; in so far as his passing marks the demise of a life-form rougher but also richer than the Grange, his death symbolises the fleeing of absolute value over the horizon of history into the sealed realm of myth. That death, however tragic, is essential: the future lies with a fusion rather than a confrontation of interests between gentry and bourgeoisie.

The novel's final settlement might seem to qualify what I have said earlier about its confronting of irreconcilable contradictions. *Wuthering Heights* does, after all, end on a note of tentative convergence between labour and culture, sinew and gentility. The culture which Catherine imparts to Hareton in teaching him to read promises equality rather than oppression, an unemasculating refinement of physical energy. But this is a consequence rather than a resolution of the novel's tragic action; it does nothing to dissolve the deadlock of Heathcliff's relationship with Catherine, as the language used to describe that cultural transfusion unconsciously suggests:

> 'Con-*trary*!' said a voice as sweet as a silver bell – 'That for the third time, you dunce! I'm not going to tell you again. Recollect or I'll pull your hair!'
>
> 'Contrary, then', answered another, in deep but softened tones. 'And now, kiss me, for minding so well.'
>
> 'No, read it over first correctly, without a single mistake.' The male speaker began to read; he was a young man, respectably dressed and seated at a table, having a book before him. His handsome features glowed with pleasure, and his eyes kept impatiently wandering from the page to a small white hand over his shoulder, which recalled him by a smart slap on the cheek, whenever its owner detected such signs of inattention. Its owner stood behind; her light, shining ringlets blending, at intervals, with his brown locks, as she bent to superintend his studies; and her face – it was lucky he could not see her face, or he would never have been so steady. I could; and I bit my lip in spite, at having thrown away the chance I might have had of doing something besides staring at its smiting beauty.[14]

The aesthetic false moves of this are transparently dictated by ideological compromise. 'Sweet as a silver bell', 'glowed with pleasure', 'shining ringlets', 'smiting beauty': there is a coy, beaming, sentimental self-indulgence about the whole passage which belongs more to Lockwood than to Emily Brontë, although her voice has clearly been confiscated by his. It is Jane and Rochester in a different key; yet the difference is as marked as the parallel. The conclusion, while in a sense symbolically resolving the tragic disjunctions which precede it, moves at a level sufficiently distanced from those disjunctions to preserve their significance intact. It is true that *Wuthering Heights* finally reveals the limits of its 'possible consciousness' by having recourse to a gradualist model of social change: the antinomies of passion and civility will be harmonised by the genetic fusion of both strains in the offspring of Catherine and Hareton, effecting an equable interchange of Nature and culture, biology and education. But those possibilities of growth are exploratory and undeveloped, darkened by the shadow of the tragic action. If it is not exactly true to say that Hareton and Catherine play Fortinbras to Heathcliff's Hamlet, since what they symbolise emerges from, rather than merely imposes itself upon, the narrative, there is none the less a kernel of truth in that proposition. Hareton and Catherine are the products of their history, but they cannot negate it; the quarrel between their sedate future at Thrushcross Grange and the spectre of Heathcliff and Catherine on the hills lives on, in a way alien to Charlotte's reconciliatory imagination.

There is another reason why the ending of *Wuthering Heights* differs from the ideological integration which concludes Charlotte's novels. I have argued that those novels aim for a balance or fusion of 'genteel' and bourgeois traits, enacting a growing convergence of interests between two powerful segments of a ruling social bloc. The union of Hareton and Catherine parallels this complex unity in obvious ways: the brash vigour of the petty-bourgeois yeoman is smoothed and sensitised by the cultivating grace of the squirearchy. But the crucial difference lies in the fact that the yeomanry of *Wuthering Heights* is no longer a significant class but a historically superannuated force. The transfusion of class-qualities in Charlotte's case rests on a real historical symbiosis; in *Wuthering Heights* that symbolic interchange has no such solid historical foundation. The world of the Heights is over, lingering on only in the figure of Hareton Earnshaw; and in that sense Hareton's marriage to Catherine signifies more at the level of symbolism than historical fact, as a salutary grafting of the values of a dying class on to a thriving, progressive one. If Hareton is thought of as a surrogate, symbolic Heathcliff, then the novel's ending suggests a rapprochement between gentry and capitalist akin to Charlotte's mythical resolutions; if he is taken literally, as a survivor of yeoman stock, then there can be no such historical balance of power. Literally, indeed, this is what finally happens: Hareton's social class is effectively swallowed up into the hegemony of the Grange. Symbolically, however, Hareton represents a Heathcliff-like robustness with which the Grange must come to terms. It is this tension between literal and symbolic meanings which makes the ending of *Wuthering Heights* considerably more complex than the conclusion of any Charlotte Brontë novel. Read symbolically, the ending of *Wuthering Heights* seems to echo the fusion of qualities found in Charlotte; but since the basis of that fusion is the absorption and effective disappearance of a class on which the novel places considerable value, Emily's conclusion is a good deal more subtly shaded than anything apparent in her sister's work.

Wuthering Heights has been alternately read as a social and a metaphysical novel – as a work rooted in a particular time and place, or as a novel preoccupied with the eternal grounds rather than the shifting conditions of human relationship. That critical conflict mirrors a crucial thematic dislocation in the novel itself. The social and metaphysical are indeed ripped rudely apart in the book: existences only feebly incarnate essences, the discourse of ethics makes little creative contact with that of ontology. So much is apparent in Heathcliff's scathing dismissal of Edgar Linton's compassion and moral concern: 'and that insipid, paltry creature attending her from *duty* and *humanity*! From *pity* and *charity*! He might as well plant an oak in a flower-pot, and expect it to thrive, as imagine he can restore her to vigour in the soil of his shallow cares!' The novel's dialectical vision proves Heathcliff both right and wrong. There *is* something insipid about Linton, but his concern for Catherine is not in the least shallow; if his pity and charity are less fertile than Heathcliff's passion, they are also less destructive. But if ethical and ontological idioms fail to mesh, if social existence negates rather than realises spiritual essence, this is itself a profoundly social fact. The novel projects a condition in which the available social languages are too warped and constrictive to be the bearers of love, freedom and equality; and it follows that in such a condition those values can be sustained only in the realms of myth and metaphysics. It is a function of the metaphysical to preserve those possibilities which a society cancels, to act as its reservoir of unrealised value. This is the history of Heathcliff and Catherine – the history of a wedge driven between the actual and the possible which, by estranging the ideal from concrete existence, twists that existence into violence and despair. The actual is denatured to a mere husk of the ideal, the empty shell of some tormentingly inaccessible truth. It is an index of the dialectical vision of *Wuthering Heights* that it shows at once the terror and the necessity of that denaturing, as it shows both the splendour and the impotence of the ideal.

Notes

1   See G. Lukács, *The Historical Novel* (London, 1962), especially chaps 1 and 2.
2   A coherence which is partial, limited, defined as much by its absences and exclusions as by its affirmations, and so (*pace* Goldmann) ideological.
3   Quoted by J. Hillis Miller, *The Disappearance of God* (Cambridge, Mass., 1963), p. 163.
4   Quoted in F. R. and Q. D. Leavis, *Lectures in America* (London, 1969), p. 127.
5   *Wuthering Heights*, ed. Ward and Shorter, ch. 14, p. 155.
6   Ibid., ch. 15, p. 168.
7   Ibid., ch. 4, p. 36.
8   Ibid., ch. 12, p. 130.
9   *Lectures in America*, p. 99.
10   *Wuthering Heights*, ch. 8, p. 66.
11   *Brontë Society Transactions* 78 (1968).
12   *Modern Quarterly Miscellany* 1 (1947).
13   F. M. L. Thompson, *English Landed Society in the Nineteenth Century* (London, 1963), p. 233.
14   *Wuthering Heights*, ch. 32, pp. 319–20.

5 Shakespeare and the Letter of the Law

I

It is a paradoxical fact about all language that it is at once entirely general and irreducibly particular. Any language can be viewed on the one hand as a system of relative regularities: we would not call a 'word' a mark which occurred only once. To be a word at all, it must have some given or potential location within the structure of language, some actual or possible place in the dictionary, which is independent of any single specific use of it. The same goes for the rules of language – syntax, semantics, and so on – which can be treated as purely formal conventions, independent of any concrete content. On the other hand, it is clear that all language is wholly particular, and that 'language in general' does not actually exist. Language is always this or that utterance in this or that situation. The paradox, then, is that actual speech or writing subverts the very generality of the structure which brings it into being.[1] What structural linguistics terms *parole*, the particular concrete utterance, in this sense trangresses the very *langue* (or general linguistic structure) which produces it. There is, in other words, something about language which always 'goes beyond': all discourse reveals a kind of self-surpassing dynamic, as though it were part of its very nature to be and do more than the dictionary can formulate. This is perhaps most evident in a poem, which deploys words usually to be found in the lexicon, but by combining and condensing them generates an irreducible specificity of force and meaning. A literary text is in one sense constrained by the formal principles of *langue*, but at any moment it can also put these principles into question. Language is a specific *event*, which cannot simply be read off from the formal structures which generate it.

If this is true of language, it is also true of law. For law to be law its decrees must be general and impartial, quite independent of and indifferent to any concrete situation. If this were not so we might end up with as many laws as there are situations, which would defeat the whole idea of law by violating its *comparative* nature, its attempt to apply the same general principles to widely different conditions. One law for one group and another law for another is commonly felt to be objectionable: it can lead to privilege, which literally means 'private law'. Yet the law, like language, 'lives' only in specific human contexts, all of which are unique. The gap between the general character of law and these unique individual contexts is bridged by the law's 'application'; but this, as with language, can never be a simple matter of reading off the rights and wrongs of a given action from the formal abstract tenets laid down in the statute book. Such application involves the creative *interpretation* of those tenets, and may well result in modifying or transforming them. As with language, the formal structure of the law generates certain events (verdicts, legal judgements, and the like) which may end up by undermining that structure. Legal case-history is not just a record of past 'applications' of the law, but a tradition of continuous reinterpretation of it which bears in forcibly on any current act of legal judgement.

In interpreting the law creatively, it is usually felt that one should have due regard to its 'spirit': judgements should be realistic and commonsensical, not narrowly technical or pedantic. Thus, in *The Merchant of Venice*, it is Shylock who has respect for the spirit of the law and Portia who does not. Shylock's bond does not actually state in writing that he is allowed to take some of Antonio's blood along with a pound of his flesh, but this is a reasonable inference from the text, as any real court would recognize. No piece of writing can exhaustively enumerate all conceivable aspects of the situation to which it refers: one might just as well claim that Shylock's bond is deficient because it does not actually mention the use of a knife, or specify whether Antonio should be sitting down, suspended from the ceiling or dressed in frilly knickerbockers at the time of cutting. Any text, that is to say, can be understood only by going beyond its letter, referring it to the material contexts in which it is operative and the generally accepted meanings which inform and surround it. Portia's reading of the bond, by contrast, is 'true to the text' but therefore lamentably false to its meaning. There is nothing 'false' about her reading in itself, which the text, taken in isolation, will certainly bear out; it is just that her interpretation is *too* true, too crassly literal, and so ironically a flagrant distortion. Portia's ingenious quibbling would be ruled out of order in a modern court, and Shylock (given that his bond were legal in the first place) would win his case.

The paradox, then, is that to preserve the structure of the law you must transgress what it actually says. By failing to do this, Portia threatens to bring the law into disrepute, skating perilously close to promoting 'private law' by a reading which is aberrant because too faithful. There is a ruthless precision about her sense of the text which exactly parallels Shylock's relentless insistence on having his bond. In this sense, one might claim, Shylock is triumphantly vindicated even though he loses the case: he has forced the Christians into outdoing his own 'inhuman' legalism. Indeed it is tempting to speculate that Shylock never really expected to win in the first place; he is hardly well placed to do so, as a solitary, despised outsider confronting a powerful, clubbish ruling class. One can imagine him waiting with a certain academic interest to see what dodge the Christians will devise to let one of their own kind off the hook. Perhaps he throws the audience a knowing wink when Portia produces her knockdown argument. Shylock's curious reluctance to specify his motive in pursuing his suit, the oddly gratuitous quality of his vengeance, might be construed as evidence for this, as might one of his most crucially revealing declarations:

> The pound of flesh which I demand of him
> Is dearly bought, 'tis mine, and I will have it.
> If you deny me, fie upon your law!
> There is no force in the decrees of Venice.
>
> (IV.i.99–102)

It is almost as though Shylock is defying the court to deny him in order to expose its own hollowness. Either way he will win: by killing Antonio, or by unmasking Christian justice as a mockery. If the decrees of Venice were shown to be worthless, troubling political consequences might be in store for the state. To catch the Christians out in a *particular* juridical shuffle is of course to discredit the law in general, just as to lend out money gratis *à la* Antonio is to affect the general rate of exchange in the city. What is at stake in the courtroom, then, is less Shylock's personal desire to carve up Antonio than the law of Venice itself: will it maintain its proper indifference to individuals, penalize one of its own wealthy adherents at the behest of an odious Jew? The answer, of course, is that it will not; but in order to avoid doing so it must risk deconstructing itself, deploying exactly the kind of subjective paltering it exists to spurn. To protect itself, the law is forced into a hermeneutical errancy, the final consequence of which might be political anarchy. Shylock thus induces the Venetian law partly to undo itself, entering that alien system from the inside and operating its rules in a style which presses them towards self-contradiction. He takes 'for real' the dramatic charade of a system in which he has little faith, in order to uncover the genuine illusions at its heart.

That it should be the Christians who deny the spirit of the law is, of course, deeply ironic, since they see themselves precisely as resisting Shylock's own hard-hearted legalism in the name of the 'human'. The 'human' is that which escapes the tyrannical precision of writing, the living voice of Portia's eloquence rather than the steely fixity of print. But this is absurd, since writing (legal bonds, commercial contracts, state decrees, marriage agreements) is of the very essence of Venetian society. In such a social order, who buys, eats, rules or cohabits is inescapably a question of script: there can be no appeal to some realm of purely 'human' values which lies quite beyond the letter. The human is not that which goes beyond writing, but the way in which writing, or language, goes beyond itself; writing itself is a matter of flesh and blood, as Antonio learns to his discomfort. One of the problems the play faces, then, is how to distinguish this positive mutual involvement of language and the body from that tyranny of the letter which destroys the body's substance. In one sense, written letters would seem more real than airy speech because they are material, and so rather like the physical body. The meaning or 'spirit' of such script then becomes analogous to the soul or consciousness, and like consciousness can enter into conflict with its material medium. In another sense it is 'breath' or living speech which is more aptly symbolic of the body, being a direct product of it. Speech, however, is passing and perishable, unfixed in contrast with script; and this unfixedness can cause it to deceive more readily than writing, which can always be used in evidence against you. Unlike Antonio's pledge, the lovers' vows to safeguard their mistresses' rings are not made in writing, and so may the more easily be broken; written contracts may oppress one in the lethal immutability of their letter, but by the same token they can protect you more efficiently against others' infidelity. In any case, as we have seen already, the immutability of print can be much exaggerated. The difficulty, then, would seem to be one of reconciling the warm yet perishable substance of breath with the necessary permanence and generality of a writing which constantly threatens to stifle it. Shylock warns Antonio that 'I'll have my bond, I will not hear thee *speak*'; Portia, by contrast, is all passionate eloquence. Any assumption that the latter is 'truer' than the former, however, is thrown into question by the fact that Portia is in disguise, considerably less disinterested than she appears, and intent on rescuing her lover's best friend by a quibble. Eloquence is never, it would seem, pure authentic presence; there is always an element of rhetorical artifice inseparable from it. The more intense their emotions, the more intricately florid the diction of Shakespeare's characters tends to grow.

Portia's courtroom speech in defence of Antonio is metaphorical excess in the service of crabbed literalness; and how to attain an acceptable measure between these two extremes is one of the play's preoccupations. The norm is defined by Nerissa, when she remarks to her mistress that 'they are as sick that surfeit with too much as they that starve with nothing' (I.ii.). Gratiano, who believes that 'silence is only commendable/In a neat's tongue dried, and a maid not vendible', speaks 'an infinite deal of nothing', in marked contrast to the glum taciturnity of Antonio, whose melancholy is (like unrequited love) the very image of an 'all' based on a negation. Melancholy, as Freud wrote, is mourning without an object: founded on some lack or loss, it pervades the whole of one's experience but, because apparently causeless, seems at the same time a pure void:

> In sooth, I know not why I am so sad.
> It wearies me; you say it wearies you;
> But how I caught it, found it, or came by it,
> What stuff 'tis made of, whereof it is born,
> I am to learn;
> And such a want-wit sadness makes of me
> That I have much ado to know myself.
>   (I.i.1–7)

Melancholy is much ado about nothing, a blank, motiveless devaluation of the world. The less its cause can be identified the more acute the condition grows, feeding on its own indeterminacy; and the more acute the condition, the less definable its grounds. We have already seen such paradoxes of 'all' and 'nothing' associated in Shakespeare with money, and it is thus not accidental that Antonio is not only melancholic but a merchant – indeed *the* Merchant – of Venice. Melancholia is an appropriate neurosis for a profit-based society, discarding the use values of objects in order to plunder them for substance with which to nourish itself. Jaques in *As You Like It* can 'suck melancholy out of a song, as a weasel sucks eggs', reducing reality to empty husks to feed his gloomy narcissism.

Melancholy, then, overrides measure, but does so destructively. The play's more creative metaphor of such surplus value is mercy, which disregards the precise exchanges of credit and debt, crime and punishment, in a lavishly gratuitous (grace-like) gesture. This, of course, is what Portia requests of Shylock, who is sensible to be rather wary. For such gratuitousness is a deeply ambivalent quality: if it can creatively short-circuit the harsh equivalences of justice (an eye for an eye and a tooth for a tooth), it is also, one might claim, all very well for some. Those who wield power can afford to dispense with exact justice from time to time, since they, after all, control the rules of the game. It is less easy or intelligent for outcasts like Shylock, whose sole protection lies in the law, to conjure it away so cavalierly. The victimized need a fixed contract, however hard-hearted that may seem, precisely because they would be foolish to rely on the generosity of their oppressors, who are even more hard-hearted than print. If mercy is gratuitous, then the dispossessed can never quite know when their superiors are likely to be seized with a spontaneous bout of geniality. Gratuitousness, moreover, has a hint of Portia's perverse reading of the bond, an act which equally threatens to erode the essential impartiality of law.

The problem would seem to be that the formal, abstract character of the law is both necessary and reifying. It is necessary if social cohesion is to be sustained, since the law mediates diverse situations to each other by subsuming them under stable principles. Yet in doing so it threatens to erase what is specific about those situations, homogenizing vital differences as an inflexibly levelling force. The alternative to this would seem to be purely *ad hoc*, context-bound judgements of the Portia kind, bending general norms to fit particular instances. But this approach lands you in a kind of indifferentism ironically close to the one you were seeking to escape: by giving free rein to the signifier it would appear to license any interpretation you like, processing and permutating the evidence to confirm a given theory. Anarchy and authoritarianism are not, after all, the binary opposites they seem: each returns a partial response to the problem of how to hold to consistent criteria while recognizing that they are likely to be transformed and transgressed. The hermeneutical dilemma posed by *The Merchant of Venice* could be seen as a conflict between licence and constraint. A true reading is at once constrained by the text and transgressive of it, neither flatly literal nor fancifully metaphorical. To interpret is to activate a set of codes; but part of what those codes will sometimes tell you is when to throw them aside and go beyond them, like ladders kicked away once mounted. Yet how does one discriminate between a productive 'going beyond' and a purely whimsical one? Where does one draw the dividing-line between a surplus which is fruitful and one which is mere inflation?

Some of the meaning of the play's curiously sharp focusing on the bond may be found in Shylock's magnificent protest against anti-semitism:

> I am a Jew. Hath not a Jew eyes? Hath not a Jew hands, organs, dimensions, senses, affections, passions, fed with the same food, hurt with the same weapons, subject to the same diseases, healed by the same means, warmed and cooled by the same winter and summer, as a Christian is? If you prick us, do we not bleed? If you tickle us, do we not laugh? If you poison us, do we not die? And if you wrong us, shall we not revenge? If we are like you in the rest, we will resemble you in that.
>
> (III.i.)

What individuals share most vitally in common is the body: it is by virtue of our bodies that we belong to each other, and no cultural or linguistic community which is not somehow founded upon this fact is likely to survive. For the texts in which Shylock trusts – the Old Testament – the body is not in the first place a physical object but a form of relationship, a principle of unity with others.[2] Shylock's ferocious insistence on having Antonio's flesh must be read in the light of his sufferings at the hands of anti-semites; not just as revenge for them – though this is no doubt one of his motives – but as a scandalous exposure of that which Antonio owes him – his body, an acknowledgement of common humanity with Shylock – and arrogantly denies. It is a matter of flesh and blood between the two men in every sense: the ritual carving up of Antonio, coolly appropriating part of his body, is a kind of black mass or grotesque parody of eucharistic fellowship. Shylock claims Antonio's flesh as his own, which indeed, in a sense which cuts below mere legal rights, it is; and the bond looms as large as it does because it becomes symbolic of this more fundamental affinity. To refuse Shylock his bond means denying him his flesh and blood, and so denying *his* flesh and blood, his right to human recognition. The bond, in one sense destructive of human relations, is also, perversely, a sign of them; the whole death-dealing conflict between the two men is a dark, bitter inversion of the true comradeship Shylock desires, the only form of it now available to him. The impersonal absolutism of his pursuit of the bond parodies the absoluteness and impersonality of the bonds which link us to a common humanity, and which no mere subjective whim can set aside. Shylock makes out his deal with Antonio to be a friendly one ('this is kind I offer'), an assessment not entirely tongue-in-cheek: the usurer, astonishingly, is setting aside his customary credit and debt calculations for an object which is literally worthless, not even as profitable as mutton. There is a bizarre gratuitousness about Shylock's bargain, which demands both more and less than he would normally ask in such matters; indeed Antonio himself thinks the deal a generous one, though Bassiano doesn't share his opinion. Shylock breaks with his usual business code to give Antonio special treatment: he demonstrates favouritism and partiality, risking a bad exchange. It may seem perverse to 'favour' someone by having him pledge his life to you, but the alternative to this 'all' is nothing, since Antonio may well go scot-free. The bond is a 'merry sport', a pointless jape or exuberant fiction so monstrous in its implications that it is hard to take it seriously, so excessive of all customary measure as to mean nothing.

Like jesting, the bonds of human solidarity are beyond all reason. There is no reason of a calculative kind why human beings should respond to each other's needs: it is just part of their 'nature', constitutive of their shared physical humanity, that they should do so. Shylock implicitly makes this point before the Venetian court when he stubbornly refuses to provide a rationale for his apparently inhuman behaviour:

> As there is no firm reason to be rend'red
> Why he cannot abide a gaping pig;
> Why he, a harmless necessary cat;
> Why he, a woollen bagpipe, but of force
> Must yield to such inevitable shame
> As to offend, himself being offended;
> So can I give no reason, nor I will not,
> More than a lodg'd hate and a certain loathing
> I bear Antonio, that I follow thus
> A losing suit against him. Are you answered?
>
> (IV.i.53–62)

The closest analogy to the 'inexplicable' demands of our common physical humanity is, ironically, the pure subjectivism of 'taste' or prejudice. 'Human nature', in the sense of the mutual needs and responsibilities which spring from our sharing in the same material life, is for Shakespeare the measure of all significant language and action, but itself escapes such measure; it is the 'ground' of our social life which cannot itself be grounded. It is thus both 'objectively' determining and, paradoxically, as resistant to rational enquiry as a merry sport or a fear of cats. Shylock values Antonio's worthless flesh immeasurably more than the sum Antonio has pledged, and refuses to be bribed by Portia; and he is, of course, right to believe that human flesh and blood cannot be quantified. That which is nugatory, beyond all measure, is also that which is most precious, as the ambiguous term 'invaluable' would suggest. It is Antonio himself who is the quantifying bourgeois, and Shylock who stands up for a more traditional conception of bonds and values.[3] Shylock's action cuts against bourgeois Venice in two opposed ways. On the one hand, it manifests a 'gratuitousness', with its special regard for an individual and its partiality in hatred, which defies the abstract quantifications of both law and money. On the other hand, it is performed in the name of an impersonal human bonding which makes no whimsical dispensations for individuals. Shylock thus behaves in an apparently capricious way to reveal the absolutely binding nature of a common humanity: Portia acts with parallel whimsicality to ward off such a recognition.

For the worthless to become most precious is also the point of the casket scenes at Belmont, where the relative values of lead and gold are inverted. If Shylock refuses gold, so does Bassanio; both prefer flesh and blood – in Bassanio's case, Portia's. But for Bassanio to obtain Portia is also of course for him to grow rich. Having improvidently thrown his money around, Bassanio has come to Belmont to buy up the well-heeled Portia with the aid of Antonio's loan, rashly jeopardizing his friend's life in the process; but there is nothing surprising in the way this self-loving parasite then elevates love over riches in the very act of purchasing a woman. Such romanticism, with its sanctimonious talk of the inestimability of love, is just the other side of the commercial coin: the bourgeoisie have always pretended that sex transcends utility, at the very moment they debase it to a commodity. The Romantic is in this respect just the flipside of the Utilitarian, fetishizing a realm (the love of a good woman) supposedly free of his own squalid transactions. 'The bourgeois viewpoint,' Marx comments, 'has never advanced beyond this antithesis between itself and this romantic viewpoint, and therefore the latter will accompany it as its legitimate antithesis up to its blessed end.'[4] The irony of this is that the very qualities in which love is thought to transcend money – its measurelessness, transmutability, inexplicable mystery – are the very characteristics of money itself. Money is less the opposite of erotic desire than its very image. Indeed Bassanio makes this point himself when he compares love to an inflated language, a phenomenon which, as we have seen, is for Shakespeare akin to commercial dealings:

> Madam, you have bereft me of all words;
> Only my blood speaks to you in my veins;
> And there is such confusion in my powers
> As, after some oration fairly spoke
> By a beloved prince, there doth appear
> Among the buzzing pleased multitude,
> Where every something, being blent together,
> Turns to a wild of nothing, save of joy
> Express'd and not express'd. . . .
>
> (III.ii.176–84)

A man in debt, like Bassanio, is actually 'worse than nothing'; has, as it were, a negative value. But the magic of capital investment can transfigure such nothing into everything.

The casket scenes, then, represent the acceptably idealist face of mercantile society, with their naive contrasts of appearance and reality. Shakespeare rejects any simple counterpointing of the two, believing in what Lenin once called the 'reality of appearances'. In this society, flesh and blood are inescapably bound up with profit and loss, in the selling of a daughter as much as in the maiming of Antonio. At Belmont, money is a question of measure, whereas love is 'free'. Shylock does not share this false consciousness: for him, love is not the subjectivist whims of Eros but the ruthlessly impersonal requirements of *agape* (charity), which demands precise services, obligations and recognitions. These properly impersonal constraints allow no room for 'freedom': the racist Antonio is not in fact free to kick Shylock around like a dog, since all individuals have an equal claim on one's humanity regardless of their race or other distinguishing features. There is something necessarily abstract about charity, just as there is about the law. Portia thinks that mercy is free, 'not strained' (constrained), but this is surely dubious: mercy must not, for example, be allowed to make a mockery of justice. It belongs to justice to make recompense for injuring another, which mercy may temper but cannot cavalierly wish away. Would it have been admirably merciful, or an obscene insult to the dead, to have allowed a later anti-semite, Adolf Eichmann, to go free? Should one cease to press for justice even though one's actions unavoidably injure one's oppressors?

The impartiality of law, then, must act as a symbolic embodiment of the impersonal claims of human justice and charity. The law of Venice, of course, does nothing of the kind, even before Shylock intervenes to deconstruct it: it is class law, as Shylock himself makes brutally clear:

> You have among you many a purchas'd slave,
> Which, like your asses and your dogs and mules,
> You use in abject and in slavish parts,
> Because you bought them; shall I say to you
> 'Let them be free, marry them to your heirs –
> Why sweat they under burdens? – let their beds
> Be made as soft as yours, and let their palates
> Be season'd with such viands'?
>
> (IV.i.90–7)

If the Duke is worried about refusing Shylock his pound of flesh, it is because, as Antonio comments, the thing will look bad in the eyes of foreign businessmen. The problem, however, is that the law would seem able to sustain its proper impartiality, and so buttress social order, only at the cost of a frigid indifference to particular cases which estranges it from common humanity and so paradoxically risks a *collapse* of social order. There would appear in this sense to be something self-deconstructive about the law, which tends to frustrate its own ends in the very act of trying to promote them. The law necessarily abstracts and equalizes, and so tyrannizes over 'flesh and blood' in the sense of concrete human situations, even as, at another level, it embodies the 'bonds' of that humanity. But if this uniformity is thrown aside for purely *ad hoc* or *ad hominem* judgements, then each situation becomes autonomous (literally, a 'law unto itself') and so just as absolute in its own way as the law it sought to replace. What is lost by this move is the comparative evaluation of different conditions, which then become as tautological as the self-referring sign. Indeed logically speaking we would then not even be able to speak of a 'condition', for one condition is identifiable only if it can be roughly demarcated from another. True law is, so to speak, metaphorical, seeking a balance of similarities and differences; but this fine tension, as with all metaphor, can always split apart in either direction, reducing unique situations to singular identity or fostering – what is strictly unthinkable – a cult of pure difference. Angelo in *Measure for Measure* goes for the former option; Lucio for the latter.

II

That anarchy and authoritarianism are not quite the contraries they seem is made dramatically obvious in *Measure for Measure* by Angelo's sudden about-turn from repressive legalist to rampant lecher. But this *volte face* is not as mysteriously inexplicable as it may seem. For one thing, a purely abstract or formal law, unresponsive to the claims and impulses of the body, becomes detached from desire, including its own, and such desire may consequently run unchecked. In this sense Angelo enacts in his own person the rift between law and desire in Vienna as a whole: frigidly unyielding to flesh and blood, the law he incarnates is unconstrained by sensuous needs and so a blank space open to being inscribed by the body, captivated by Isabella's sexual attractiveness, in the most negative way. For another thing, law and desire share a similar quality of indifference: Angelo's lust for Isabella's body is as ruthlessly impersonal as the levelling categories of law, for which bodies are also in a certain sense interchangeable. Moreover, the play makes it clear that law actually *breeds* desire as well as blocks it.[5] The law is not simply repressive, a negative prohibition placed upon the will; what is desired is precisely what is most strictly tabooed, and the taboo perversely intensifies the yearning. It is Isabella's chaste untouchability which fuels Angelo's passion, so that desire and prohibition become mutually ensnared, apparent opposites which are in truth secret conditions of one another:

>   . . . it is I
> That, lying by the violet in the sun,
> Do as the carrion does, not as the flow'r,
> Corrupt with virtuous season. Can it be
> That modesty may more betray our sense
> Than woman's lightness? Having waste ground enough,
> Shall we desire to raze the sanctuary,
> And pitch our evils there? O, fie, fie, fie!
> What dost thou, or what art thou, Angelo?
> Dost thou desire her foully for those things
> That make her good?
>
>   (II.ii.165–75)

Excessive restraint breeds libertinism, just as a glut of liberty leads to restraint:

> *Lucio*   Why, how now, Claudio, whence comes this restraint?
> *Claudio*   From too much liberty, my Lucio, liberty;
>   As surfeit is the father of much fast,
>   So every scope by the immoderate use
>   Turns to restraint. Our natures do pursue,
>   Like rats that ravin down their proper bane,
>   A thirsty evil; and when we drink we die.
>
> (I.ii.118–24)

There is another important sense in the play in which law and flesh and blood are not simply to be counterpointed. In refusing to sacrifice her chastity for her brother's life, Isabella would seem to elevate an abstract moral absolute over the immediate claims of humanity. Critics have accordingly complained about the prudishness with which she is prepared to exchange Claudio's head for an intact hymen. But this is to misunderstand the subtle relations between the essential generality of law and its particular instances. If you compromise a principle in one pressing situation for the sake of flesh and blood, then you ineluctably compromise the security of all the flesh and blood which takes shelter beneath that principle. If Angelo is allowed to get away with his sexual schemings in this instance, what woman in Vienna is safe? Then indeed the ruling class may be permitted to treat all women's bodies as their private possessions. Just as a particular commercial bargain may alter the general rates of exchange which govern it, so more than one woman's virginity is at stake in turning down Angelo's deal.

As its title suggests, *Measure for Measure* is much concerned with the question of exchange values, epitomized in the strict interchanges of an impersonal justice which disregards particular qualities. The law must lay aside specific bonds of friendship or favouritism:

> It is the law, not I, condemn your brother.
> Were he my kinsman, brother, or my son,
> It should be thus with him.
>
> (II.ii.80–2)

Isabella's response to the 'precise' Angelo's stern impartiality is to point out that all human beings are sinful:

> If he had been as you, and you as he,
> You would have slipp'd like him; but he, like you,
> Would not have been so stern.
>
> (II.ii.76–8)

This is hardly a knockdown argument: all Isabella claims, in a useless tautology, is that if Angelo had been Claudio he would have behaved like him. To reason in this way is to retreat to the autonomous individualism and self-referentiality of 'private law' – which is no law at all, and which, as we have seen, is just as absolute and self-grounding in its own way as autocratic legalism. The law then becomes a kind of private language, which is a contradiction in terms. Even Elbow's crashing mala-propisms ('respected' for 'suspected', and so on) gather a clear enough public meaning from their contextual consistency, tracing within themselves the shadow of the 'normative' social term from which they deviate. The case Isabella is fumbling for is not the vacuously self-evident point that if Angelo was Claudio he would be Claudio, but that all individuals, because of their shared moral frailty, are in some fundamental sense equal and interchangeable: because we all sin we should be ready to forgive sin in others. Angelo rejects this plea out of hand:

> You may not so extenuate his offence
> For I have had such faults; but rather tell me,
> When I, that censure him, do so offend,
> Let mine own judgement pattern out my death,
> And nothing come in partial.
>
> (II.i.27–31)

What Angelo fails to see here is that this closed circuit of mutual recriminations could be made to cancel itself out: why not flip this vicious circle over at a stroke and transform it into a virtuous circle of mutual forgiveness? Why should not a negative reciprocity of values be inverted into an affirmative one, two negatives make a positive, our common weakness become the ground of mercy rather than censure? If everyone condemns everyone else because they may be arraigned themselves, then this pointlessly self-supporting structure could be turned inside out, and everyone exculpate each other in just as groundlessly ritual a way. For Angelo, however, this would make a mockery of justice. The fact that I am morally weak is no logical bar to my judging such weakness in others, just as the fact that I am a hopeless football player does not prevent my appreciating fine or foul play as a spectator. It is an individualist mistake, a Romantic fetishizing of 'private' experience, to believe that we can only judge accurately of that of which we have direct inward knowledge. Besides, the fact that I am in principle capable of the crimes of those I accuse does not mean to say that I have actually committed them, and so disenfranchised myself from judgement; mercy would seem rather too abstract in this respect, too inattentive to the faults which the judge actually has. Angelo, who is by no means a straw target as a moral theorist, believes that if we simply forgave each other all the time we would be allowing the 'inherent' meaning and value of particular actions to be smothered in a sentimental subjectivism which attended less to what was materially 'there' than to the quality of our response to it. And this would just be a more subtle form of abstraction than the relentlessly impersonal operations of justice.

The ironic flaw in Angelo's position, however, is that if we were really to attend to 'inherent' values and meanings, to see things as they really are without the subjectivist squint of mercy, we would actually be compelled to forgive each other all the time. This, indeed, is the best card Isabella plays:

> Alas! alas!
> Why, all the souls that were were forfeit once;
> And He that might the vantage best have took
> Found out the remedy. How would you be
> If He, which is the top of judgement, should
> But judge you as you are?
>
> (II.ii.73–8)

If you do in fact estimate individuals as they truly are, then nobody would ever get off at all; 'use every man after his desert,' Hamlet comments, 'and who shall scape whipping?' Christ, it would seem, is clement only by a calculated moral squint, systematically refusing to judge us as we are. To treat someone 'as they are' may be at the deepest level to treat them as representative, just as the law does, but in this case representative of the moral fragility of humankind in general, and so conveniently combining the law's abstract generality with a sympathetic understanding of particular flesh and blood. In this way one might hope to avoid both legalistic and partial judgements at a stroke. The harsh indifference of the law might be made to work against itself without lapsing into mere merciful whimsy, for mercy, properly understood, is just as remorselessly impersonal a claim on our humanity as is justice. Indeed, in one sense it is more abstract than justice as it actually *overlooks* particularities, pretends that they are not there.

The problem, however, is how this global undercutting of exact exchanges is to be distinguished from indifference in its most negative, Lucio-like sense. Lucio is an ethical naturalist whose complacent appeal to the body cynically subverts all values. 'Flesh and blood' can mean the body as biological given, whose appetites may be endorsed simply because they are there. Or it can be a normative rather than a descriptive term, meaning a solidarity with human infirmities which none the less, through the discriminations of justice, acknowledges them as such rather than, like Lucio, nonchalantly turning a blind eye. Forgiveness is valuable precisely because it is difficult: it means bearing with others *despite* a recognition of the injuries they have done you. Lucio's man-about-town cockiness is thus a caricature of the virtue, valueless because it does not have to pay for its tolerance. There can be a worthless sort of mercy: as the Duke comments, 'When vice makes mercy, mercy's so extended/That for the fault's love is th'offender friended' (IV.ii.107–8). In a similar way, Isabella distinguishes 'lawful mercy' from the 'ignominy in ransom' or 'foul redemption', which is Angelo's distortion of it. Mercy is not mere gratuitousness: to be *too* free, as with Lucio's abusive tongue, is to wound and constrain others. Justice and mercy must be blended together rather like precision and creativity in language: to be too precise like Anglelo is to reify law and language to a fixed transcendental sense, ignoring the creative 'surplus' or surpassing of the norm which all actual speech and judgement involves. But that surplus must not be allowed to exceed the measure to the point where it undercuts it entirely, for then there would be no finely discriminated situations to be forgiving *about*.

Lucio's cynical indifference is paralleled in the play by the astonishing moral inertia of Barnadine, a Musil-like psychopath so careless of life that he objects to being executed only because it interrupts his sleep. Death, in a familiar cliché, is the great leveller, reducing all exact values and distinctions to nothing, and Barnadine gains a curiously enviable freedom by appropriating this future state into the present, as an image of living death. If he is unperturbed by the thought of execution, it is in a sense because he is dead already, living at that end-point where all odds are struck even. The state must defer his dying until he has been persuaded to accept it willingly, otherwise the punishment will have no point. Unless Barnadine somehow 'performs' his own death, it will not consitute an event in his life and so will discredit the law that has inflicted it upon him. There is no more effective resistance to power than genuinely not caring about it, since power only lives in exacting a response of obedience from its victims. The play distinguishes this biological indifference from what it sees as an authentic living towards death, of the kind Claudio finally comes to embrace: 'If I must die,/I will encounter darkness as a bride/And hug it in my arms' (III.i.). The suicide and the martyr look alike, but are in fact opposites: the one throws away his life because he judges it worthless, the other surrenders his most valuable possession. The martyr becomes something by actively embracing nothing; the suicide simply substitutes one negativity for another. Though death finally erases all measure and distinction, you must cling provisionally to those values while you live, just as mercy ultimately undercuts the tit for tat of justice but must not be permitted to undo those mutualities completely.

The chief form of tit for tat in the play is a ceaseless exchange and circulation of bodies: Angelo's for the Duke's, Isabella's (so Angelo hopes) for Claudio's, Barnadine's for Claudio's, Mariana's for Isabella's. Bodies are a kind of language, which can either falsify (as in the bed trick with Mariana) or involve a just and proper correspondence. The final distribution of bodies to their appropriate positions is the event of marriage, with which the play concludes. Yet no unblemished justice can ever quite be achieved, since no two things are exactly identical and so can never effect a purely equitable exchange. If x is equivalent to y, then we have proclaimed in the same breath that x is not in fact y, superimposed similitude on difference. No one term can fully represent another, just as Angelo cannot entirely incarnate the absent Duke, since a total identity of both terms would spell the death of representation itself. There is always, in other words, some residue of difference, dislocation or disparity in any proper exchange which threatens to undo it; and something of the play's notoriously factitious conclusion may well spring from this fact.

But there are also other senses in which *Measure for Measure* can never quite attain the ideal towards which it strives: a judicious balance of justice and mercy, precision and superfluity, equivalence and unique identity, general and particular, inherent and imputed values. The law must be above sin; yet since no human being is without sin it would seem inherently estranged from flesh and blood. The law tends naturally towards reification, caught in a cleft stick between its abstract edicts and its particular objects. To uphold its generality you must treat particular cases as exemplary; but this means punishing Claudio for a vice which 'all ages smack of'. Isabella, who represents a general principle to Angelo in her own person, finds that she has seduced him by her person rather than by the principle. One individual may justifiably penalize another if he is himself guiltless of that particular offence; but taken as a whole the human race cannot pass judgement on itself, since this would be as pointlessly tautological as someone placing himself under arrest. The rigorously impersonal transactions of justice must be maintained, if social order is not to crumble; but the mercy which is officially 'supplementary' to that justice threatens to erode it from the inside, and it is within this irresolvable tension that humanity must live. They must cling to the centrality of measure and normativity, while recognizing in a difficult double optic that these things are ultimately groundless. Forgiveness – the active forgoing of exact equivalences, the gratuitous rupture of the circuit – is the trace of this final groundlessness (which is also the future levelling of death) within the regulated symmetries of the present. The most effective spur to being sinless oneself, it might be cynically considered, is that it grants you a title to pass judgement on others; virtue in oneself would thus seem linked to vice in others, just as mercy would seem to flourish on sin (since one's own immorality is the offender's hope for forgiveness). A thoroughly vicious ruler who acknowledged his own moral turpitude would appear to be the criminal class's best guarantee for a troublefree life. The choice would seem to be between this politically undesirable solution, a relatively sinless ruler who none the less exercised clemency, and a prince who did not regard his own moral laxity as any obstacle to executing the law. The latter solution divorces the general and particular too sharply, resulting in a reified authority which is bad for social harmony; the second possibility is the ideal one, but frustratingly difficult to achieve precisely because mercifulness springs from an inward sympathy with sin, and a virtuous exponent of it thus begins to sound like a contradiction in terms. Shakespeare's quandary is a version of Bertolt Brecht's, who once remarked wryly that only somebody inside a situation could judge it, and he was the last person who could judge. It is all very well to speak of a prudent balance of justice and mercy; but how is the necessarily transcendental principle of the law to avoid being corroded and contaminated by the specific perplexities it has to sort out? How is mercy to break the vicious circle of prosecutions when it must somehow spring from inside that circle, from a humble solidarity with vice? If that censorious circularity is indeed transformable into a community of mutual acceptance, from what vantage-point – inside or beyond the circuit, or at its very edge – can this be effected? These are not, finally, questions which the play can satisfactorily answer. Instead, we are told that people get married, even though marriage, which as we have seen already is an undecidable merging of gratuitous affection and inherent propriety, is part of the very problem to which it is being proposed as a solution.

III

Perhaps one of the central puzzles confronting *Measure for Measure* can be summarized in this way. In order to preserve political stability, you need that fine mutuality of values which is justice; yet to achieve this mutuality requires an abstract, overarching structure (law), and the very abstractness of this structure tends to strip situations of their determinate qualities, rendering them arbitrarily interchangeable with each other, and thus fostering a mutability which helps to undermine political order. In this sense law operates rather like money, language and desire: all of these systems involve exchange and equivalence, which is in itself a stabilizing factor; but because they are necessarily indifferent as systems to particular objects or uses, they tend to breed an anarchic state of affairs in which everything blurs indiscriminately into everything else, and the system appears to be engaging in transactions for its own sake. There is, in other words, something in the very structures of stability themselves which offers to subvert them, something in the very fact of being 'precise' which leads, as in Angelo's case, to manic disorder.

In seeking to oppose Angelo's absolutism, Isabella, despite her belief that 'truth is truth to the end of reckoning', draws at one point on a linguistic analogy: 'That in the captain's but a choleric word/Which in the soldier is flat blasphemy' (II.ii.130–1). Context, in short, defines meaning: the meaning of a word is not some fixed, inherent property, but simply its various uses in particular situations. Shakespeare himself by no means entirely endorses Isabella's case, however, for good reasons of his own. For his work makes it clear that such a 'contextualism' of meaning, pressed to a logical extreme, would result in just the kind of relativism he sees as inimical to political cohesion. Take Isabella's point a few steps further and we might all end up as Elbows, privately legislating Humpty Dumpty-wise the meaning of our own words. For Shakespeare, it is the consistency or self-identity of a term from context to context which determines its proper meaning, just as it is consistency which is usually in his plays the most suggestive index of human sanity. (It is the 'dependency of thing on thing' in Isabella's discourse which, the Duke says, persuades him that she is not mad). This is not to say that Shakespeare ignores the plurality of contexts in which a word can be used; it is just that he believes that any actual use of it must be consistent with a more general context even if it goes beyond it, just as any specific application of the law must balance a respect for general principles with sensitivity to a particular state of affairs. There seems little doubt that in *Troilus and Cressida* Shakespeare sides with Hector against Troilus in their heated exchange over the question of Helen's value:

> *Hector*   Brother, she is not worth what she doth cost
> The keeping.
> *Troilus*   What's aught but as 'tis valued?
> *Hector*   But value dwells not in particular will:

> It holds his estimate and dignity
> As well wherein 'tis precious of itself
> As in the prizer . . .
>
> (II.ii.51–7)

Hector wants a fusion of intrinsic and assigned values, so that he can use the 'given' qualities of things as a norm for assessing other people's value-judgements. This, at least, is what Ulysses does later in the play:

> Nature, what things there are
> Most abject in regard and dear in use!
> What things again most dear in the esteem
> And poor in worth!
>
> (III.iii.127–30)

Troilus, by contrast, holds to an existentialist rather than essentialist theory of value, as is clear from his hot retort when Helen's worth is questioned:

> Is she worth keeping? Why, she is a pearl
> Whose price hath launch'd above a thousand ships,
> And turn'd crown'd kings to merchants.
>
> (I.ii.)

Troilus means formally that Helen has launched a thousand ships because she is a pearl, but there is an implication that she is a pearl *because* she has done so; it is the activity she has given rise to which confers value upon her, not her inherent value which justifies that activity. Pearls, after all, are valuable because their rarity involves a good deal of labour in obtaining them, not because they have (like, say, water) some intrinsic property beneficial to humanity. But if Helen is precious because she is the focus of such admirable strivings, must not Troilus be implicitly invoking certain 'objective' standards of value to decide that such strivings are admirable in the first place? The question of value, in short, is merely pushed one stage back, and nothing is actually resolved.

If this is a difficulty with appeals to merely 'conjunctural' value – that they would always seem implicitly to evoke more general norms even in the act of denying them – there would seem another kind of problem with the absolute standards of Hector and Ulysses. For these standards, by which particular situations can be judged, always turn out to be no more than the distilled experience of previous situations. To claim that the use of a word in a specific context must be governed by its 'inherent' meaning is just to say that this particular context must be related to others. Any general principle can thus be deconstructed into an accumulated set of discrete particulars. A 'given' or 'inherent' value simply means what others – perhaps in the past – have held to be precious, and thus risks losing its transcendental authority. To state what something 'really' means is just to report on the ways other people have happened to use the word; all meaning is in this sense dialogic or 'intertextual'. If this is so, then the well-ordered norms which Shakespeare would seem to desire merely push the problem of relativism back a stage. All that can be appealed to against the subjectivism of a Troilus is simply a wider intersubjectivity, which cannot be anchored in anything beyond itself.

The paradigm of a fixed value would seem to be a thing's absolute identity with itself, as in this bantering exchange between Pandarus and Cressida:

> *Pandarus*   Well, I say Troilus is Troilus.
> *Pandarus*   Then you say as I say, for I am sure he is not Hector.
> *Pandarus*   No, nor Hector is not Troilus in some degree.
> *Cressida*   'Tis just to each of them: he is himself.
>
> (I.ii.65–8)

This is hardly Shakespeare's most richly exploratory piece of dialogue. To describe what something 'really' is inevitably involves you in contextualizing comparisons; simply to call something an apple is already to have assigned it to a general class of objects, which are what they are because they are not, say, bananas. Troilus, who disdains comparisons and holds romantically to the unique quality of things, replies to Aeneas's enquiry, 'Wherefore not afield?' with the profoundly informative, 'Because not there' (I.i.). Achilles' stiff-necked pride is a refusal to define himself in any terms beyond his own being, the futile circularity of self-conferred, publicly unwarranted value: 'He that is proud eats up himself' as Agamemnon remarks (II.iii.). Achilles' privatized, grossly inflated scale of values ('Things small as nothing, for request's sake only,/He makes important' (II.iii.)) may be contrasted with Diomed's shrewdly measured estimation of Helen, a most untypical burst of judiciousness for this play:

> For every false drop in her bawdy veins
> A Grecian's life has sunk; for every scruple
> Of her contaminated carrion weight
> A Troyan hath been slain.
>
> (IV.i.71–4)

Once you begin weighing and comparing, however, the object whose value you sought to determine is no longer identical with itself: it is 'differed' by your speech, inscribed within a context of otherness, and the danger is that there is in principle no end to such differencing. What then becomes of the integrity of the very thing you seek to judge? If Agamemnon is Achilles' commander, Achilles Thersites' lord, Thersites Patroclus's knower and so on, then where does the metaphorical chain of mutually definitive items stop? Ulysses warns the languidly *dégagé* Achilles that 'no man is the lord of anything,/Though in and of himself there be much consisting,/Till he communicate his parts to others' (III.iii.116–17). Social relations are not simply the medium within which an individual may choose to express his already well-formed identity, but the very discourse which constitutes that self. Others are, so to speak, the signifiers which produce the signified of oneself. But if this social emphasis guards against the tautology of possessive individualism, it does so only at the cost of dividing and destabilizing identity, dwindling it to a mere effect of the Other. It would appear that the self, like signs and values, has no choice between being fully, autonomously itself, which is a kind of nothing, and being a shifting cypher wholly dependent on context, which is another kind of nothing.

This is also a dilemma in respect of the self's history. If history furnishes you with a norm or standard beyond the existential moment, it also tends to dissolve on closer inspection into no more than a cumulative series of such fleeting instants. This is the point of Ulysses' great speech on time, which reduces history to so much dead weight to be shucked off at each new moment:

> Time hath, my lord, a wallet at his back,
> Wherein he puts alms for oblivion,
> A great-siz'd monster of ingratitudes.
> Those scraps are good deeds past, which are devour'd
> As fast as they are made, forgot as soon
> As done. Perseverance, dear my lord,
> Keeps honour bright. To have done is to hang
> Quite out of fashion, like a rusty nail
> In monumental mock'ry.
>
> (III.iii.)

The logical strain of this is apparent: Ulysses urges perseverance – pursuing a consistent project over time – in the very act of deconstructing such continuities into an eternal present. If the past is oblivion, what are you persevering *in*, and who is doing the persevering? The ideal way to live, in a familiar Romantic paradox, would be constantly to teeter on the brink of achievement without actually doing anything: 'Things won are done, joy's soul lies in the doing' (I.ii.279–80). For once you have acted, your act may be confiscated by others, reinscribed in their own contexts and so struck worthless, as easily as Cressida is translated to the Greek camp. What the shattered Troilus finds to say of his unfaithful mistress ('this is, and is not, Cressid') could in fact be said of any word, deed or value, which is always ambiguously yours and not yours, private property and an effect of the Other. Troilus knows that 'the desire is boundless, and the act a slave to limit' (III.ii.), and that such desire breeds 'monstruosity': 'something', any particular action, is nothing, drawn into the past as soon as performed, and only desire, which is lack, is ironically something. This barren history is the narrative *Troilus and Cressida* has to deliver, as both sides struggle to remember what it is they are fighting about, and as, beyond the dramatic conclusion, the war drags on.

Notes

For theoretical background, see Ferdinand de Saussure, *Course in General Linguistics* (London, 1978); V. N. Voloshinov, *Marxism and the Philosophy of Language* (New York, 1973); Ludwig Wittgenstein, *Philosophical Investigations* (Oxford, 1953); Jacques Derrida, *Of Grammatology* (Baltimore, 1976) and *Writing and Difference* (London, 1978); and Jonathan Culler, *On Deconstruction* (London, 1983).

1   See Paul de Man, *Allegories of Reading* (New Haven and London, 1979), pp. 268ff.
2   For a modern view of this belief, see Maurice Merleau-Ponty, *The Phenomenology of Perception* (London, 1962), Part 1.
3   See Walter Cohen, '*The Merchant of Venice* and the Possibilities of Historical Criticism', *English Literary History*, 49 (1982), for an excellent discussion of the 'archaic' or residual character of Shylock.
4   Karl Marx, *Grundrisse* (London, 1973), p. 162.
5   See Jonathan Dollimore, 'Transgression and Surveillance in *Measure for Measure*', in Jonathan Dollimore and Alan Sinfield (eds), *Political Shakespeare* (Manchester, 1985), for an illuminating treatment of the dialectic between law and desire in the play.

6 Tony Harrison's *v.*

v. stands for *versus*, hence conflict, division, the struggle between classes (this poem was written during the Miners' Strike) and between the sexes (V with a slash down the middle was sexist graffito), and of course stands also for aggression of the V-sign; but if the two fingers are turned round they come to signify a nation united rather than fissured, and the two meanings are yoked contradictorily together in the football graffito 'UNITED *v*', perhaps with the depressing implication that we only find community in antagonism to others. Some drunken skinhead shortcutting his way through Beeston Hill graveyard in Leeds after Leeds United have lost yet another match relieves his wrath by aerosolling UNITED on the tombstone of Harrison's parents, an act which divides the poet himself between scandalised burgher/dutiful son whose impulse is to rub it off, and the writer with a quick eye for the serendipitous symbol who is tempted to let it stand as

> an accident of meaning to redeem
> an act intended as mere desecration
> and make the thoughtless spraying of his team
> apply to higher things, and to the nation.

The self-division is in fact tripartite, since a deeper proletarian part of Harrison neither bridles at the skin's act nor seeks sentimentally to appropriate it but thoroughly empathises. If the bosses splash their own logos around the place, and if Harrison's own name has been up in Broadway lights, why not allow this graveyard artist a little self-advertising?:

> Some, where kids use aerosols, use giant signs
> to let the people know who's forged their fetters
> like PRI CE O WALES above West Yorkshire mines
> (no prizes for who nicked the missing letters!).
> . . .
> Letters of transparent tubes and gas
> in Düsseldorf are blue and flash out KRUPP.

Arms are hoisted for the British ruling class
and clandestine, genteel aggro keeps them up.

Speculating whether taking it out on tombstones is 'just a *cri-de-coeur* because man dies', Harrison is roughly taken to task for his lah-di-dah frenchifying by the offending skinhead himself, who in a redundant moment of drama (redundant because we didn't need to be explicitly told) is revealed as his own *Doppelgänger* (though we're spared the lah-di-dah German):

So what's cri-de-coeur, *cunt? Can't you speak*
the language that yer mam spoke. Think of 'er!
Can yer only get yer tongue round fucking Greek?
Go and fuck yerself with cri-de-coeur!

At this point the dialogism, in Bakhtinian terms, becomes positively polyphonic, a multiplicity of contending voices: Harrison's mother didn't in fact like 'the language he spoke', or at least wrote, finding it as obscene as she would the skinhead's. The more the poet is irked by the yob's taunts, the more his own idiom merges with his ('You piss-artist skinhead cunt'), and the youth in his turn comes up with the odd scriptural allusion which belongs to Harrison's culture, not his own.

Harrison is a natural Bakhtinian, even if he has never read a word of him. No modern English poet has shown more finely how the sign is a terrain of struggle where opposing accents intersect, how in a class-divided society language is cultural warfare and every nuance a political valuation. As in Harrison's own translations, one tongue inheres parasitically within another, now clashing, now complicitous; culture is ambivalently wealth and deprivation, self-exploration and self-exile. You don't need to tell Tony Harrison that Rambo is a French poet only for a dwindling rump of us. The deeply ironic structure of all this is part of what saves him from Weskerian sentiment, and the irony is inscribed in the very form of his verses, where the excitement is always a question of how he will once more pull off the precarious trick of just subduing colloquial raw materials to some semblance of iambic order without civilising them out of sight. The verse-forms really have to flail around to hold together, and their ironic awareness of this, magnificent in *v.*, is part of their meaning.

Even so, one worries a bit about those Broadway lights. The churchyard vandal stands to the left of the poet: in fact he's less a vandal than a kind of political *avant-gardist* of a vaguely Futurist kind, liberating art onto the streets (his work is strewn all over Leeds), the kind of man you feel Mayakovsky would have got on with. He disfigures tombstones not just for kicks but on more reflective and defensible political grounds:

Ah'll tell yer then what really riles a bloke.
It's reading on their graves the jobs they did –
butcher, publican and baker. Me, I'll croak
doing t'same nowt ah do now as a kid.

If the tone here is shaky, the idea is brilliant: it's the employed the kid resents, not the dead. Harrison too is worried by worked-out pits: in a fine symbolic stroke, Beeston Hill cemetery actually stands above one, which is why its obelisks list, one vacuity underlying and threatening to drag down another. But the poet's anxieties are less short-term social than long-term geological, metaphysical rather than political, the drained undermining pit as symbolic of some impending inner subsidence. The inconceivable age of a geological seam makes any personal life appear sickeningly frail:

> Listening to *Lulu*, in our hearth we burn,
> as we hear the high Cs rise in stereo,
> what was lush swamp club-moss and tree-fern
> at least 300 million years ago.

The actual Miners' Strike impinges on *v.* hardly at all, other than in a moving epigraph taken from Arthur Scargill which might have been spoken with Tony Harrison specially in mind: '*My father still reads the dictionary every day. He says your life depends on your power to master words.*' Harrison's own dispirited political imagination, which belongs in this sense to the 1980s, is curiously at odds with the volume's linguistic vigour and technical high-jinks, as he approaches a cross-roads within himself in middle life between angry proletarian and bruised metaphysician. The choice is between being pained primarily by oppression, and being pained primarily by division and disunity – the difference, roughly, between radical and liberal. Harrison's young skinhead knows well enough that the talk of 'peace' and 'unity' which so haunts his creator is in present political conditions an insulting mystification. He needs to harangue his author a little further, reminding him that the solace and unity *v.* finally seeks in sexual relationship isn't abstractable from the destiny of nations, and that it is out of conflict and division, not peace, that Harrison has over the years produced the poetry for which we so much admire him.

7 Estrangement and Irony in the Fiction of Milan Kundera

Milan Kundera tells the story in *The Book of Laughter and Forgetting* of a Czech being sick in the middle of Prague, not long after the Soviet invasion of the country. Another Czech wanders up to him, shakes his head and says: 'I know exactly what you mean'.

The joke here, of course, is that the second Czech reads as *significant* what is in fact just a random event. In the post-capitalist bureaucracies, even vomiting is made to assume some kind of instant symbolic meaning. Nothing in Eastern Europe can happen by accident. The logical extreme of this attitude is paranoia, a condition in which reality becomes so pervasively, oppressively meaningful that its slightest fragments operate as minatory signs in some utterly coherent text. Once the political state extends its empire over the whole of civil society, social reality becomes so densely systematized and rigorously coded that one is always being caught out in a kind of pathological 'overreading', a compulsive semiosis which eradicates all contingency. 'No symbol where none intended', Samuel Beckett once remarked; but in 'totalitarian' societies, monolithic structures of meaning, one can never be quite certain what's intended and what isn't – whether there is ominous meaning or not in the delayed arrival of your spouse, the boss's failure to say good morning, that car which has been behind your own for the past ten miles. Tereza in *The Unbearable Lightness of Being* makes love with an engineer in his flat, but later she will wonder about the drabness of the place compared to his elegance, that edition of Sophocles on the shelf, the few moments he was away making the coffee. Is it the abandoned apartment of an imprisoned intellectual? Is the engineer a police agent, and was he turning on the ciné camera while supposedly making the coffee?

Survival in Eastern Europe demands an awareness of this possible sub-text, a daily hermeneutics of suspicion; but then how, in behaving with such vigilance, is one to avoid becoming collusive with a power for which no event can be accidental, no gesture innocent? How to read without overreading, avoid a naive empiricism without falling prey to semiological paranoia? The most celebrated of all modern Czech writers, Franz Kafka, suspends his readers between narrative and sub-text, the bald appearance of events and the ceaselessly elusive truth of which they might just be dimly allegorical. Such truth is never totalisable, shifting its ground each time one approaches it; there is, perhaps, a metanarrative which rigorously determines the slightest detail of quotidian life but which is always elsewhere. If this is an allegory of the disappeared God, it is also one of the post-capitalist state, a paradoxical condition in which everything is at once compulsively legible, locking smoothly into some univocal story, and yet where history is awash with secrets, whispered treacheries, tell-tale traces. In this drably positivist world, everything lies on the one hand drearily open to view, tediously repetitive and flatly two-dimensional, the mysterious depths of subjectivity drained off from a world which becomes brutely self-identical. On the other hand, nothing is ever quite what it seems; so that a 'postmodernist' eradication of depth, mystery, subjectivity co-exists strangely with a persistent 'modernist' impulse to decipher and decode, a sense of concealment and duplicity.

Kundera's fiction opposes to the sealed-off metanarrative of post-capitalist bureaucracy a set of notably dislocated texts, although not at all in the manner of some sophisticated Western deconstruction. The structural subversiveness of his novels lies simply in the loose capaciousness whereby they encompass *different stories*, sometimes to the point of appearing like a set of *nouvelles* within the same covers. This is not the modernist undermining of narrative realism of a Beckett, for whom one arbitrary story generates another equally gratuitous and then another, until the whole text becomes no more than a machine for pumping out tall groundless tales in an honorable Irish tradition. Each of Kundera's stories has a 'sense' to it, and interacts with the others; but it must be allowed to exist in its own narrative space free from metanarrational closure, absolved from the authoritarianism of the 'closed book'. Kundera constantly interrupts himself in order to give the slip to the totalitarian drive of literary fiction, breaking off the narrative to deliver his latest ontological musings, inserting a sheaf of brief philosophical reflections between episodes, airily abandoning the fictional pretence in the interests of historical documentation. All of this is done casually, apparently spontaneously, without modernist outrage or obtrusiveness, utterly bereft of any intense aesthetic self-consciousness or portentous experimentalism. There is no sense of shock or rupture in his texts, no heavily calculated violations of plausibility or deftly engineered incongruities, no calculated cacophony of discourses. For this to happen would suggest that one was still in thrall to some literary orthodoxy one was grimly or scandalously intent on discrediting, whereas Kundera conveys the rather more shocking sense of *unconcern*, a writer who has, so to speak, just not been told that you shouldn't hold up the narrative with metaphysical speculations about angels and devils, and who would not understand what you were talking about if you were to tell him so. He treats the novel as a place where you can write anything you like, anything, as it were, that has just come into your head, as a *genre* released from constraint rather in the manner of a diary. No doubt, psychobiographically speaking, this artlessness is the effect of a finely conscious art, but his writing bears none of its traces and communicates instead a quite astonishing 'naturalness', a stunning off-handedness and laid-back companionability which forces the reader genuinely to doubt whether it is in the least aware of its own brilliance. Nothing could be more suspect for the *avant-garde* West than this spurious naturalisation of the sign, this cavalier lucidity and apparently effortless transparency, which could only for us be yet another craftily contrived style, a cultural sign every bit as eloquent and flamboyant as the laboriously constructed 'degree zero' writing of a Camus or a Hemingway. But our own suspicion of the natural springs from the conditions of a late bourgeois society in which ideology has had several centuries to disseminate itself into the textures of lived experience, crystallizing its devious impulses as the self-evident or commonsensical; in this sense we suspect the 'natural' exactly because ideology has succeeded in its historic task, requiring a violent demystification in fictions which ironise their every proposition. This is not the situation in Eastern Europe, whose political hegemony was only recently installed, moreover, from the outside, and which has therefore had little time or opportunity to flesh itself into a full-blooded phenomenology of everyday life. In such societies, given the grotesque discrepancy between material hardship and the idealising claims of the state, it is ideology which is transparently fictional, portentously self-conscious, the very reverse of spontaneous or self-evident; and the 'naturalness' of the Kundera style, its easy, intimate relation with the experiential, is thus as politically significant as is its conversion of the novel into a space of free-floating discourses in a rigorously codified society. Kundera's relaxed, unfussy lucidity is postmodernist in a genuine sense of the word, an art which becomes possible only when all the heart-burnings and agonisings of modernism proper, its heady trans-gressions and self-important experiments, can now at last be taken for granted, put quietly to use once shorn of their portentousness. For it is exactly that portentous-ness which links them, in sensibility if not in doctrine, with the histrionic posturings of the ideological.

'The only thing we *can* do', comments one of Kundera's characters about the writing of fiction, 'is to give an account of our own selves. Anything else is an abuse of power. Anything else is a lie.' The paradox of such liberalism for Kundera is that it keels over inexorably into a kind of totalitarianism. The narrative of just one individual becomes a closed book, a sealed, autonomous world every bit as absolute and author-itarian as the absolutist state. Such solipsism is the mere flipside of Stalinism, sucking reality into its own self-regulating logic with all the imperious-ness of the central committee. Difference and uniqueness are no salvation in themselves from the dreary self-identity of the post-capitalist state; the unique has an unbearable lightness and frailty about it, as though anything which happens only once might as well not have happened at all. *Einmal ist keinmal.* If history can be dissolved into pure difference, then the result is a massive haemorrhage of mean-ing: because past events only happen once they fail to take firm root and can be expunged from memory, having about them the ineradicable aura of pure accident. The past thus perpetually threatens to dissolve beneath the heel of the present, and this plays straight into the hands of the absolutist state, devoted as it is to airbrushing disgraced politicians out of ceremonial photographs. What imbues persons and events with unique value, then, is precisely what renders them insubstantial, and Kundera's writing is deeply gripped by this sickening ontological precariousness. Pure difference cannot be valuable, for value is a relational term; but repetition is an enemy of value too, because the more something is repeated the more its meaning tends to fade. Kundera's fiction, both formally and thematically, is given over to examining this contradiction: it must keep different stories structurally separate, exploring the distinctiveness of particular relationships and identities, but always with a profoundly ironic sense of what they share in common, a suspicion that they are in some covert way variations upon a single theme.

The point where difference and identity undecidably converge for Kundera is above all sexuality, linking as it does the unrepeatable quality of a particular love-relationship with the ceaselessly repetitive, tediously predictable character of the bodily drives. What might be thought to be most deviant, stimulating, shockingly unconventional – a sexual orgy – turns out to be hilariously comic in its endless mechanical repetitions, the supposed singularity of erotic love uproariously repeated in a wilderness of mirrors, each individuated body mockingly mimicking the next. Kundera recognizes the profound comedy of repetition, which is one reason why sex is usually the funniest part of his novels: his laughter is that release of libidinal energy which comes from momentarily decathecting the utterly self-identical love-object, the magnificent *non-pareil*, in the moment of wry recognition that we all share a common biology. The traditional name of this moment is, of course, the carnivalesque, that aggressive onslaught on the fetishism of difference which ruthlessly, liberatingly reduces back all such metaphysical singularity to the solidarities of the flesh. *The Farewell Party* in particular centres upon fertility, child-bearing, procreation, and like several of Kundera's texts is particularly interested in animals.

The political problem of all this is apparent: how is one to use the fleshly solidarity of the human species as a powerfully demystifying force while avoiding that brutal erasure of differences which is Stalinist uniformity? Kundera's anti-Stalinism is interesting precisely because it refuses to fall back upon an unquestioning romantic idealism of the individual; indeed its carnivalesque impulse presses any such romantic idealism to the point of absurdity. The problem is how to stay faithful to that recognition without lapsing into biologistic cynicism, or, as Kundera might himself put it, crossing over that hairthin border which distinguishes 'angelic' meaning from the demonic cackle of meaninglessness. Reproduction, in every sense of the word, may be a source of emancipatory humour, which is one thing Marx meant by suggesting that all tragic events repeated themselves as farce; but the farce in question is destructive as well as redemptive, which was another of Marx's meanings. The bureaucratic state is itself a contradictory amalgam of romantic idealism and cynical materialism: its discourse is the undiluted *kitsch* of high-sounding sentiment, whereas its practice renders individual bodies and events indifferently exchangeable. It is difficult, then, to subvert its romantic idealism without lapsing into a version of its own lethal levelling. The image of ungainly naked bodies crowded into a single space stirs Kundera to debunking laughter, but it is also for him the image of the concentration camp.

Every time something is repeated, it loses part of its meaning; the unique, however, is a romantic illusion. This is the contradiction within which Kundera struggles, which can be rephrased as an unrelaxable tension between too much meaning and too little. An order in which everything is oppressively meaningful buckles under its own weight: this is the realm of what Kundera names the 'angelic', which the demonic exists to puncture. The demonic is the laughter which arises from things being suddenly deprived of their familiar meanings, a kind of estrangement effect akin to Heidegger's broken hammer, and which a monstrous proliferation of the supposedly singular can bring about. Meaninglessness can be a blessed moment of release, a lost innocent domain for which we are all nostalgic, a temporary respite from the world's tyrannical legibility in which we slip into the abyss of silence. The demonic is thus closely associated in Kundera's fiction with the death drive, a spasm of deconstructive mockery which, like carnival, is never far from the cemetery. It is a dangerous force, by no means to be euphorically, unqualifiedly celebrated as in the naiveties of some Western deconstruction: it has a malicious, implacable violence about it, the pure negativity of a Satanic cynicism. It is therefore, as Kundera well sees, a tempting lure for the opponents of angelic-authoritarian order, who will be led by it to their doom. The savage irony of the demonic is that it finally dismantles the antithesis of the angels only to conflate the whole of reality indifferently together in a levelling not far from the angels' own. Bodies are interchangeable for both Stalinism and carnival, transgression prized by both revolutionary and cynic. Just as we are precariously positioned by our very bodiliness on an indeterminate frontier between sameness and difference, biology and history, so we must seek to situate ourselves on some almost invisible border between meaning and meaninglessness, embracing all that the angels reject ('shit' is the blunt term Kundera gives to the angelically unacceptable) without settling for that shitlike amorphousness which is Stalinism or nihilism. Happiness is the yearning for repetition, but repetition is what erodes it; the male sexual drive, rather like the authoritarian state, is cripplingly divided between a romantic idealism of the particular (the wife, the permanent mistress) and a promiscuous exchangeability of bodies. The novel records these truths, but is itself an image of them: to write is to cross a border where one's own ego ends, creating characters who are neither imaginary self-identifications nor opaquely alien, but who repeat the self with a difference.

The novel has its inward necessity, its specific structural logic, but it is also a place where the contingency of existence, the unbearable lightness of being, can be reinvented and to some degree redeemed. When Beethoven, as Kundera reminds us, based a quartet on the words *Es muss sein*, he weaved an idea of destiny out of what had in fact been a casual joke between himself and a friend. Metaphysical truth was born of playfulness; as in Kundera's *The Joke* a whole metaphysical politics is set in motion by a piece of wit. Human beings, unable to tolerate the frail contingency of their being, must for Kundera rewrite their chance histories as necessity; and this, precisely, is what the novel itself continually does, endowing the accidental with a determinate form. But it is also the characteristic strategy of Stalinism, for which nothing is allowed to escape into pure randomness; and Kundera must therefore write *lightly* as well as lucidly, bathing what is in the aura of what might not have been. It is for this reason, perhaps, that his narratives are as spare and uncluttered as they are, eschewing the ponderousness of the metaphysical. His cavalier way with them reminds us of their frailness as fictional inventions; and when he speaks in his own voice, the philosophical wisdom he communicates is more the auratic, Benjaminesque 'experience' of the traditional tale-teller than the speculations of a theoretically minded modernist. What intensities there are in Kundera's work belong, as it were, to the subject-matter rather than to the mode of conveying it, hedged round continually with an irony which represents the borderline between too much meaning and too little, the portentous solemnity of the ideological and the bland dissociation of the cynic.

The dissonance in Kundera between a conventionally romantic subject-matter and a decidedly non-romantic handling of it has itself a political root. For if on the one hand his astonishingly subtle explorations of personal relationships redeem that which Stalinism expels, the ironic pathos with which such relationships are invested is just the reverse of that triumphalistic sentimentality which is Stalinism's ideological stock-in-trade. *Kitsch* is the name Kundera gives to all such 'shitless' discourse, all such idealising disavowal of the unacceptable; and in the realm of *kitsch*, the dictatorship of the heart reigns supreme. Totalitarian *kitsch* is that discourse which banishes all doubt and irony, but it is not a grim-faced, life-denying speech: on the contrary, it is all smiles and cheers, beaming and euphoric, marching merrily onwards to the future shouting 'Long live life!' The Gulag, as Kundera comments, is the septic tank used by *kitsch* to dispose of its refuse. If Stalinism cannot be opposed by romanticism it is precisely because it has a monopoly of it; and this is one reason why Kundera's own critique is bent inevitably towards the materialism of the body, whose joyous affirmations must always be radically double-edged, which knows shit and ecstasy together. Carnival generates a collective imagery which can undermine ideological *kitsch*; but in the end Kundera is unable to accept this, precisely because he comes to define kitsch as any *collective* imagery whatsoever. His critique of oppressive ideologies is at root curiously formalistic: what seems wrong with *kitsch* is finally not this or that enunciation or emotion, but the bare fact that it must be a commonly shareable discourse. This is not simply individualist dissent, of a familiarly Eastern European kind: it is that Kundera seems genuinely unable to imagine any universally shared emotion which would not, by definition, be intolerably banal. It is this which leads him to write that 'The brotherhood of man on earth will be possible only on a base of kitsch.' The best response to this is not to produce the kinds of political argument with which Kundera is doubtless all too familiar; it is simply to point out that any such formulation is untrue to the power of his own fiction. For it is exactly from the irresolvable conflict between the unique and the necessarily repeatable, the fragility of the particular and the comedy of the collective, that his fiction draws part of its formidable strength. To collapse that tension on either side is the real banality; and if Kundera's writing is valuable, it is among other reasons because he makes any such erasure of conflict harder to effect.

Part II   Cultural Politics/Sexual Politics

Introduction

Terry Eagleton's interests and commitments as a critic have never been narrowly confined to 'literature'. Unlike some of his contemporaries who made the journey from 'literary studies' to 'cultural studies', what he practised from the outset was cultural politics. His literary criticism has sometimes drawn very potently on the insights of feminist and psychoanalytic theory, transmuting itself into the discourse of sexual politics. The essays in this section have been selected for their clear and consistent focus on cultural politics and sexual politics.

'The Idea of a Common Culture' (Chapter 8) is a key chapter in the book *From Culture to Revolution*, edited by Terry Eagleton and Brian Wicker. The book draws on the proceedings of a 1967 symposium organised by *Slant*, the journal of the Catholic left, to address 'the problems of a common culture'. In promoting a fruitful dialogue between Catholic radicals and 'the New Left' regrouping of socialist thinkers in the mid 1960s, the symposium was closely identified with the religious and political idealism of the New Left Church. Raymond Williams and Stuart Hall are notable contributors, and Williams both introduces and closes the debate on culture and revolution. Eagleton's contribution, and indeed the entire book, bears the palpable imprint of Williams's formidable *Culture and Society 1780–1950*, first published in 1958 but widely popularized in several Penguin paperback reprintings from the 1960s onwards.

Culture and Society surveys an English tradition of radical dissent from industrial capitalism, especially as it manifests itself in the semantic history of the word 'culture' in the writings of authors as various as William Cobbett, Matthew Arnold, John Ruskin and William Morris; but it also establishes a powerful critique of the political and economic structures which help to perpetuate cultural inequality in postwar society. The *Slant* symposium acknowledges Williams's ideal of a common culture as 'an intricate and sophisticated formula', and one deserving 'further analysis and extension'.[1] Its principal aim, according to the editors of *From Culture to Revolution*, is to explore the problems of achieving a common culture, from philosophical, literary, theological and sociological angles. At the same time, there is a common desire among contributors (including Williams) to bring the tradition of radical humanism in *Culture and Society* into closer contact with 'a socialist theory and practice more immediately preoccupied with the realities of struggle, conflict and power'.[2]

Like Williams, Eagleton establishes the broad diversity of meanings that 'culture' signifies, ranging from a body of intellectual and artistic work to a whole way of life. He finds in romanticism an important clarification and interrelation of these different meanings and a strong sense of continuity between culture as imaginative creativity and culture as lived experience. In the early nineteenth century, however, the romantic conception of culture shows signs of a growing rift: culture as the embodiment of ideal human values becomes steadily dissociated from social reality. This loss of connection between cultural meanings becomes a central dilemma for mid-Victorian liberalism: how is culture as fine living and fine art to be disseminated widely throughout culture as a whole, rapidly changing society? While Matthew Arnold seems to epitomize the liberal predicament, only William Morris comes anywhere near to providing a theoretical resolution. Eagleton then turns to the work of T. S. Eliot, F. R. Leavis and Raymond Williams for their respective conservative, liberal and radical socialist perspectives on culture and society. The critical distinction between Williams and Eliot is that for Williams a culture is common not just when it is commonly shared but when it is commonly made. Williams's ideal of culture is not a static one in which existing values and meanings are transferred across classes, but one of shared responsibility, participation and control. 'The Idea of a Common Culture' is not just an impressive articulation of the culture and society debate, but a vigorous attempt to give the terms of that debate a more explicitly socialist and revolutionary inflection. The problem of a common culture is the problem of revolutionary socialism.

The essay on politics and sexuality in the poetry of Alfred Tennyson (Chapter 9) was delivered as a lecture at the now legendary '1848: Sociology of Literature' conference at Essex University. Taking its bearings from Antonio Gramsci's Marxist theory of political hegemony and Jacques Lacan's psychoanalytic theory of language and subjectivity, the essay proposes that the struggle of the nineteenth-century bourgeois state to secure political dominance might be likened to the working out of the Freudian Oedipal complex. The emergence and settlement of state power during the transitional crisis occasioned by class struggle in the 1840s and the spectre of revolution in Europe is seen to parallel the emergence of the human subject, swayed by the masculine and feminine imperatives of its parents. The essay finds in Tennyson's poetry an imaginary resolution of this crisis, and one which intriguingly relates the production of political power to the production of sexual identity.

Both *The Princess* and *In Memoriam* are seen to be implicated in what Lacan describes as the passage from the 'mirror phase' of life (when the child experiences an imaginary sense of 'fullness' in the womb of its mother) to the dubious 'symbolic order' (following birth) in which the self's relationship with the world has to be refashioned and identity reconstituted. The ideological function of *The Princess* is to show that process of reconsolidation through a working out of the Oedipal problems of the Prince. The ending of the poem, however, is seen as contradictory, in that the Prince both transcends and preserves the Oedipal complex, achieving his manhood in love and in battle, yet remaining in childlike dependence on the maternal Ida. The essay turns to a deconstructive reading of *In Memoriam* posited on the powerful absence of Tennyson's beloved Arthur Hallam. The death of his friend is 'nothing less than the striking from the world of the "transcendental signified"' and a decentring of the self from its imaginary relation of unity with the world.

The potent theoretical *mélange* at work in the Tennyson essay is given extensive scope in a remarkable book-length study of a single novel: *The Rape of Clarissa: Writing, Sexuality and Class Struggle in Samuel Richardson* (1982). As its subtitle suggests, the book draws on three principal developments in modern critical theory: post-structuralist theories of textuality; feminist and psychoanalytic perspectives on gender and sexuality; and Marxist theories of historical materialism. Eagleton's reading of Richardson's novel (extracted here as Chapter 10) approaches the letters of Lovelace and Clarissa as semiotic scripts replete with ideological significance. While the act of writing for both correspondents is a sublimation of sexual desire, there are telling differences in their epistolary styles. Lovelace is 'a post-structuralist precursor . . . a pathological spinner of groundless narratives', whereas Clarissa strives for stable representation, exerting the fullest possible control over her meanings: 'Lovelace's writing is mercurial, diffuse, exuberant. Clarissa's letters are signs of a unified self, orderly regimes of sense that brook no contradiction'.[3]

While Eagleton's critical prose indulges in the covert pleasures of *écriture* with all the seemingly effortless *brio* of Roland Barthes or Jacques Derrida, his political sensibility is closer to that of Antonio Gramsci and Walter Benjamin. It is Benjamin, above all, who provides the inspiration and critical assurance that informs the introduction to *The Rape of Clarissa*. The task of criticism, then, lies not in some self-serving post-structuralist *jouissance*, but in 'forging conjunctures between our own moment and a redeemed bit of the past, imbuing works with retroactive significance so that in them we may better read the signs of our own times'.[4] In the extract printed here, Eagleton rounds on that species of fashionable deconstruction that would seek to 'vilify Clarissa and sing the virtues of her rapist'. Such criticism is as obdurately unhistorical as the liberal humanism that would sentimentalize Clarissa and celebrate the inviolable mystery of the individual. Cutting against both orthodoxies, Eagleton argues that Clarissa exposes the rift between the piety and the practice of the middle class. Clarissa's death signifies 'an absolute refusal' of 'sexual oppression, bourgeois patriarchy and libertine aristocracy together'.

'The Crisis of Contemporary Culture' (Chapter 11) was Terry Eagleton's inaugural lecture as Warton Professor of English, delivered before the University of Oxford on 27 November 1992. The lecture is a sparkling performance piece, packed with comic irony. Although he repeatedly insists that he will not be talking about critical theory, Eagleton's obvious target is the resistance to theory in Oxford itself. Adopting the devious Swiftian manoeuvre of occupying the discourse of the opposition, he exposes the facile and commonplace caricaturing of theory and popular culture: 'I will not speak much of theory because it is in any case the mere tip of a much bulkier iceberg, one element of a project which is out to liquidate meaning, destroy standards, replace *Beowulf* with the *Beano Annual* and compose a syllabus consisting of nothing but Geordie folk-songs and gay graffiti.' Quoting Walter Benjamin, he suggests that the crisis of contemporary culture might reside in the fact that 'everything just goes on'. There is, however, a more specific crisis, which has to do with national identity and with the fate of a traditionalist, post-imperial culture in an era of multinational capitalism and rapid geopolitical transformation. The relevance of this to literary theory and the study of English is that English has always been preoccupied with the legitimacy of national origins.

From the beginning, English had a significant role in a broader cultural project directed at national unity and social cohesion. The current crisis involves a recognition that culture is increasingly unable to fulfil its classical role as a reconciling, harmonizing agent. Postmodern culture is 'a more fragmentary, eclectic, demotic, cosmopolitan culture than anything dreamt of by Matthew Arnold', a culture that bears the imprint of the rampant consumerism and commodification of late capitalism. With characteristic bathos, Eagleton suggests that one manifestation of the current crisis is an increasing cultural rift between mystification and disenchantment: 'Shakespeare still embodies timeless value; it's just that you can't produce his stuff without the sponsorship of Prudential Insurance'. If culture once provided the balm for social conflict, it is now itself the site of a general struggle of values and meanings.

Notably free of the blandishments that customarily inform inaugural lectures, Eagleton's performance is as forthright and uncompromising as ever. He chastises the university in which he works for providing 'a milieu which appears congenitally suspicious of adventurous thought', and if sometimes he adopts the mantle of the nineteenth-century sage, sounding oddly like Ruskin or Arnold, he also delivers those shafts of alliterative wit that are unmistakably his own: 'what is common sense in Christ Church is not necessarily common sense in the Caribbean; and the way you read Yeats in Belfast bears only a dim resemblance to the way you read him in Balliol.' As well as a shrewd and discerning analysis of the signs of the times, 'The Crisis of Contemporary Culture' is a staunch defence of theory as 'a systematic reflection on literary writing' and as 'a fundamental challenge to our current division of academic labour'.

The essay that closes this section (Chapter 12) is an entertaining and informative review of Peter Brooks's *Body Work* (1993). Eagleton sees the fashionable preoccupation with the body in contemporary theory as an extension of radical politics into sexual politics that began in the late 1960s. In the process, however, some of the most vital concerns in radical politics have been displaced by the glamour of sexuality. In the current critical climate of 'the new somatics', labouring bodies and undernourished bodies are distinctly unappealing. The old 'humanist sense of the body as practice and project' is now thoroughly *passé*.

In citing Maurice Merleau-Ponty's *Phenomenology of Perception* as 'the finest body book of our era', Eagleton returns to his own little-known body work within an earlier generation of somatic studies. *The Body as Language* appeared in 1970, long before such notable theorists of the body as Julia Kristeva and Jacques Lacan began to make an impact on British post-structuralist thought. Eagleton's body book is a heady brew of linguistics, theology and philosophy, drawing in equal measure on the writings of Merleau-Ponty, Wittgenstein and Marx. What Eagleton adopts most tellingly from Merleau-Ponty is the suggestion that 'authentic human-ity' is constituted through 'bodiliness': through a physical dialogue with other bodies and objects which establishes a world of common meanings. Capitalism is then seen as a form of alienation that intrudes between subjectivity and sensuous life, inducing chronic estrangement. It is the abrogation of this position and its insistence on the 'incarnate nature of being' that Eagleton objects to in postmodern theories of the body. The new somatics reconstitutes the relationship between language and the body in such a way that it threatens to dispel subjectivity alto-gether, and along with it any grounds for a radical social critique. While generally praising Brooks's *Body Work*, the essay is sceptical of those body books that seem to exist largely because 'the body' is all the rage.

Notes

1 *From Culture to Revolution* (London and Sydney: Sheed & Ward, 1968), p. 3.
2 *From Culture to Revolution*, p. 4.
3 *The Rape of Clarissa* (Oxford: Blackwell, 1982), pp. 46, 53.
4 *The Rape of Clarissa*, p. vii.

8 The Idea of a Common Culture

The difficulties involved in talking about culture in relation to a whole social reality often seem to unravel back to the problem of which meaning of 'culture' is being focused upon. There seem to be three major contemporary uses of the term 'culture', and it is the interconnections between these meanings which seem most significant. Culture can mean, first, a body of artistic and intellectual work of agreed value, and the processes of making and sharing in this work; secondly, extending outwards from this, it can mean what could be called a society's 'structure of feeling', the shifting, intangible complex of its lived manners, habits, morals, values, the pervasive atmosphere of its learnt behaviour and belief, as this registers itself in fairly inarticulate ways in the social consciousness: registers itself, that is, obliquely and dialectically, in what could be called (adapting a phrase used by Perry Anderson in a different context) 'the invisible colour of daily life itself'. And thirdly, extending even further outwards, culture can of course mean a society's whole way of life in an institutional sense, the totality of interacting artistic, economic, social, political, ideological elements which composes its total lived experience and which defines it as *this* society and not as some other.

The first point to be made is that we don't have to choose between these alternative versions: 'culture' can be legitimately used to mean any of these things. But the 'culture and society' debate began, in the late eighteenth and early nineteenth centuries, with the recognition that all these versions of culture were deeply interrelated. It began, that is to say, when, under new kinds of severe social pressure, the connections between art, value, habit, belief on the one hand, and specific forms of economic and socio-political life on the other, began to coalesce in new ways in the consciousness of certain thinkers. The term 'culture' became a new way of relating the texture of lived experience to a recognition of social change, a language in which both could be discussed simultaneously; it offered a range of insight into the reciprocal mediations between a personal structure of feeling, a social structure of feeling, and a complex of changing social institutions. These relationships became galvanised to an intense point, forming the essential structure of what we have come to call romanticism. The romantic belief, which the English romantics inherited from Europe, that man was caught up dialectically as a creative agent in the complex movement of his history, became in the English context a way of connecting a crisis of personal value to the general crisis of society; it also allowed access to the realities of institutional change through the focus of the ways that change had registered itself phenomenologically, in style, tone, quality, habit.

We can bring this abstraction to bear on particular cases. Wordsworth and Coleridge inherited the term 'cultivation' from the eighteenth century, but gave it a radically new emphasis: what they did, put crudely, was to shift its meaning from a wholly personal context – the cultivated individual, embodying a sensitive and discriminating code – to the quality of life of a whole society. This shift in emphasis can be understood only in terms of the actual changes which English society was undergoing – the changes which Blake, Burke, Cobbett and Carlyle register and evaluate directly. There was an awareness, in these writers, that the growth of industrialism, the destruction of traditional forms of agrarian life, the rise of a new, mechanistic philosophy and practice and of the idea of political democracy, were linked in complicated ways to a new insistence on terms like art, spontaneity, imaginative creativity, cultivation. Art and society, cultivation and civilisation, poetic art and utilitarian practice, begin to form new contrasts and connections; English society was felt to be undergoing a whole series of changes – in feeling, social relationship, physical landscape, artistic forms, economic organisation – which were finally parts of a single process, and the term 'culture' seemed to crystallise these complex interrelations. Through this term a writer could grasp the active relations between, to give some random but central instances, new theories of imaginative creativity and the enclosure of the common land, new metrical experiments in poetry and new versions of man as self-creating, self-liberating agent, the release of new areas of experience into language, and the French and American revolutions. The language of culture became, for a single moment at the peak of early romanticism, the terms for a totalisation of social experience into a fresh intelligibility.

The contrasts and connections of art and society – 'culture' and 'culture' – sometimes expressed themselves in an appeal which to us defines the most obvious aspect of romanticism: the artist's cry against a decreative and mechanistic society which was actively cancelling his own values and the critical response to them. Typical of this is Wordsworth's recognition, in the preface to *Lyrical Ballads*, that a new combination of forces, amongst them the massing of men in industrial towns and their imaginative impoverishment by a new, cheap, commodity-literature, was conspiring to blunt general participation in the values and relationships which great art embodies. Blake, as well, is a characteristic figure in this tradition: the romantic artist, freshly conscious of his work as incarnating a spontaneous and transcendent creativity at odds with the utilitarian theory and practice of his time, protests against the reduction of his own faculties to the status of market commodities. But the romantic artist wasn't merely fighting a rearguard action against the rise of industrial capitalism: he was also actively offering his art as the expressive symbol of human energies, values and capacities which that society needed to suppress, and which could in some way regenerate it. The connections of art, industry, class and politics – connections knotted in the term 'culture' or 'cultivation' – meant that for the romantic artist there was no hard line between a poetic and a political insight, as the unselfconsciousness with which Shelley can talk about 'poetic institutions' makes clear. Society must be changed, human energies released from the oppressive disciplines of mechanical working and feeling, so that the artist may have an audience, may draw on a general community of sensibility; yet art itself will be a powerful agent in that change, communicating the values of relationship and creativity to a society which, in Carlyle's phrase, has become 'mechanical in head and hand'. The relation between art and society, that is to say, is dialectical, and it is this tradition which Ruskin, William Morris and D. H. Lawrence inherit directly. Ruskin and Morris, both of whom begin from the impossibility of art in a divided and alienated society, develop into a recognition of the role of art in the achievement of social change; and because the arts which concerned them were intrinsically social, they focus the earlier romantic abstraction into a contrast between the qualities of life available in significant work and the impoverishment of meanings inherent in a society which can offer, in Cobbett's and Carlyle's phrase, only a 'cash-nexus' relation between men, a utilitarian calculus of self-interest. Lawrence receives the full pressure of this tradition, locating in art and sexuality an authenticity which provides the touchstone by which the quality and structure of industrial capitalism can be measured. At every point in this tradition, the three major meanings of culture – as art, as lived experience, as social structure – are linked and interwoven into a new social critique. The style of Cobbett's *Rural Rides*, with its fluent totalisation of observed physical landscape, economic analysis, social documentation, personal biography and recorded qualities of life into a complex whole, is the style of a new social response, forging revolutionary yet organic connections from the heart of new social pressures.

Already, in the later generations of romantic poets and in the final developments of the earlier writers, this totalisation can be felt to be fragmenting, and a new kind of art being created out of that experience. Where the early Wordsworth could grasp the continuity between imaginative creativity and forms of radical social change, the mature Keats can explore only the hiatus between poetry and philosophy, fantasy and social reality. Shelley's *Defence of Poetry* recaptures, for a moment, the connection of artist and society, but now in the different, more self-consciously rhetorical and individualist language of later romanticism. The process of disintegration is actually incarnated in the development of Carlyle, perhaps the single most important thinker in this early tradition. The causes of the painful decline from the fine penetration of early essays like *Signs of the Times* and *Chartism* to the strident posturing of *Latter-Day Pamphlets* lie, not in the history of Carlyle's personal psychology, but in the opening of what felt like an unbridgeable rift between two meanings of 'culture': culture as the direct, dialectical embodiment of ideal human value, and culture as the negotiation of this value into social reality. As the mechanical habits of English society consolidate themselves after the reform bill, Carlyle is driven back on his values in a vacuum, until he comes instinctively to lash out at any means of their social realisation as part of the mechanism he attacks. His values – the humane rejection of a 'cash-nexus' society, the inferiority of false social forms to a kind of cosmic authenticity discernible in genuine community – remain intact on the surface, but precisely because the hardening of an atomistic society cuts them adrift from social effectiveness, they become subtly undermined from within. (We can see the process happening again in our own century, in aspects of D. H. Lawrence.)

It is this rift in the early romantic conception of culture (and 'romantic' here is taken to include Hegel and Marx, as well as Wordsworth and Coleridge) – a rift between what can be grasped in theory as the fulfilling of human potential and what is negotiable in practice – which permeates the texture of mid-Victorian society. Dickens, George Eliot, Mill, Arnold, Mrs Gaskell, Disraeli, Charles Kingsley (to name only some obvious figures) all reveal, in one way or another, this loss of connection between cultural meanings. Mill struggles to relate Bentham and Coleridge – utilitarian practice and ideal cultivation – and in doing so reduces Coleridge to a kind of gloss on Benthamism, an additional category of feeling tacked onto an essentially bourgeois ethic. The cultivation which Coleridge grasped as a dialectical unity of personal value and social structure is reduced, in Mill's *Autobiography*, to a matter of inward, private feeling, a protected refuge from the necessarily neutral world of external political activity. The sharp sense of self-determining individual creativity, of the unfolding of authentic personal meanings, which Mill can touch on in *On Liberty*, resists translation into social terms; Mill, the sensitive individualist *and* the rationalist, pragmatic reformer of the social machine (the term fits his view), reflects that dualism which was to pass into such diverse places as *Fabian Essays* and the novels of Henry James. Mrs Gaskell, in *Mary Barton* and *North and South*, can handle both the flow of humane feeling and the detailed fact of the capitalist system, but not to the point where the first can engage with and challenge the second; the system is finally accepted, the personal values cultivated precariously within its limits. Disraeli, in the *Coningsby* trilogy, can bring inherited cultural values into relation with a contemporary social condition only by forcing both into caricature and deploying literary devices; Kingsley, in *Alton Locke* and *Yeast*, struggles painfully for a point of contact between imaginative fantasy, social documentary, political manifesto, traditional narrative-structures and absolute religious truth: the structural disintegration of his novels reveals a deeper, social and intellectual, loss of control. No one is more successful than Dickens and George Eliot in incarnating the actual processes by which personal feeling, physical environment and social structure interlock into a total cultural statement: the major realist novel, in its complex orchestration of value, event, relationship and institution into a consistent whole, is itself a direct reflection of the theme which concerns us here. Yet Dickens, in *Hard Times*, can nurture spontaneous-creative life only outside the industrial system, in the circus-image, or, in other novels, in the single authentic relationship which can be salvaged from general falsity. Eliot, in *Felix Holt*, finds it increasingly difficult to employ in her account of political experience the subtle and delicate methods used to evoke the complexity of the novel's personal relationships; in *Daniel Deronda*, the realist focus of *Middlemarch* has shifted into a concern with aesthetic experience, intense personal inwardness, society with a capital 'S', and a vision of human potential which is only incidentally social.

These are inevitably crude, short-hand critical comments, which don't pretend to do full justice to the specific writers in question. I particularly don't want to be understood as advancing these points as moral or aesthetic condemnations of these writers, in any simple way. In some, but not all of them, the moral dilemma does embody itself as an aesthetic flaw, but it is, in any case, a dilemma which can't be dealt with in terms of mere condemnation. What I am trying to pinpoint is a disintegration of the romantic idea of culture, when it is brought through art into close relation with society, and one way of presenting this dilemma, as it can be traced through the work of George Eliot, Mrs Gaskell, Mill and Arnold, is to say that it is the dilemma of liberalism. It is here, more than at any other point, that the nineteenth-century experience can be related to the 'culture and society' debate today.

Liberalism, in fact, reveals a series of paradoxes which relate closely to the problem of culture and social change. It exhibits an active and sometimes agonised concern with humane value, community, personal fulfilment, yet stops short at the precarious frontier where such a critique of value and relationship passes over into a critique of the concrete socio-economic structures in which the values are rooted. This paradox is itself motivated by a more fundamental one: that the very values of openness, tolerance, variousness and flexibility which liberalism displays are themselves wrestled historically from a point of privilege within the system to which the values are critically applied. In this sense, liberalism is peculiarly self-cancelling: to press through its humanist critique to the limit would be, inevitably, to destroy a total social system, and with it its own vantage-point. Liberalism can reflect critically on everything but the socio-economic basis of its own values: the very tone and texture of its criticism evokes the ethos of the society it criticises, and the supple, many-faceted quality of its approach – its resolution to see all aspects of a case, to take nothing for granted, to work pragmatically and follow the argument wherever it leads – is itself, partially, a function of its effective impotence, its abstraction from a real political world, its rootless and privileged isolation. Because of this fact, liberalism actually helps to sustain, by a further paradox, the system it critically opposes: it provides the essential margin of self-questioning but finally absorbable anxiety which furnishes society with a humanitarian safety-valve, renders society properly vulnerable to criticism, but criticism couched in its own language and so controllable. Finally, since intelligent liberalism includes within itself, by definition, the ever-open possibility of self-criticism, it can accommodate radical assaults on its own stand-point while remaining effectively unaltered: it is, in this sense, self-regulating, and so in a way impregnable.

In Mill, Eliot, Arnold and Mrs Gaskell, we can watch this liberal humanism in action, at different levels of sensitivity and intelligence. The problem which dominates the nineteenth-century liberal mind is really this: how is culture (fine living, fine art) to be disseminated widely throughout culture (a whole, rapidly-changing society) without the values themselves undergoing radical re-definition, and so challenging the very structures through which they are transmitted? The liberal *Angst* is here at its acutest: the values, as they are currently available, are in a sense absolute, but so also is the imperative (partly moral, partly self-preservative) that they should be extended to new social groups. If extension inevitably involves corruption, what is to be done? The contradiction is at its sharpest when traditional cultural values are thought of, not only as judgements about art, but formulations derived from the way of life of a specific ruling-class: culture as cherished manners, habits, social values. Culture in *this* sense would clearly not be inherently available for wider extension without undergoing fundamental change: attempts by some liberal thinkers (Matthew Arnold in his essay *Democracy*, for instance) to resolve the contradiction by imagining a new society into which older values could be artificially transplanted simply underline the sense of deadlock. The conservative answer, that the values should not be extended, is rejected by the liberal; but so also is the radical response (the response, notably, of William Morris) that the inherited values are absolute only in the sense of being formulations rooted in a particular historical experience, and so open to change, and enrichment, once they are offered for general re-definition.

It is here that we can see the significance of Matthew Arnold. Arnold illustrates almost all the liberal paradoxes we have described, in his attitudes to culture and society: he is the well-bred aesthete committed to culture as (in his own phrase) 'absolute and eternal', yet also the radical reformer engaged in culture as a concrete, historical and common process; he is a liberal, yet castigates the fundamental forms of a liberal society; he can make illuminating connections between the quality of literature and the quality of social life, yet can also exploit literary technique, in his social writing, for caricature, emotive persuasion and over-neat rhetorical generalisation; he can commit himself to social equality on one page and to putting down the workers by force on the next. He can explode, in *Culture and Anarchy*, a sacred tenet of liberalism by insisting that freedom is not an end in itself but a means to common moral improvement, while in *The Function of Criticism at the Present Time* he can dismiss the practical man as inherently crude and inferior, and posit a supple and varied consciousness as his deepest value. He was deeply concerned, in his actual professional work, for the quality of common experience; he was also concerned, in some of his writing, to caricature and debase the lives of ordinary people by an external and satirical treatment. One instance of this ambiguity in Arnold will have to suffice: after arguing in his essay *Equality* for an egalitarian society, he continues by describing equality in these terms: 'Whether he mix with high or low, the gentleman feels himself in a world not alien or repulsive, but a world where people make the same sort of demands on life . . . as he himself does.' In a couple of sentences, an argument which the chartists would have recognised as their own is reduced to the traditional imagery of the English gentleman at ease in his club.

One could go on describing this tension in Arnold's thinking at much greater length – in terms of his Hegelianism, of his emphasis on social tone and style rather than social content, and the relations of this to his literary criticism – but enough has been said to make the essential point. Arnold epitomises one aspect of the later, Victorian stages of the 'culture and society' debate: the point at which two meanings of the original term – culture as ideal value and culture as a whole, realisable way of life – can no longer be easily connected. The other major aspect, which Ruskin and Disraeli reflect, is one in which ideal values and social forms *can* be related, but only at the cost of a massive oversimplification of society itself, of a utopian medievalism. It is not until William Morris, who connected the values of the tradition to a viable political force – the organised labour movement – that the problem comes anywhere near theoretical resolution.

One of the crucial new developments of the 'culture and society' debate, in our own century, was the increasing centrality of a new meaning: the idea of a common culture. To understand the continuity of the nineteenth-century debate with contemporary cultural argument involves some grasp of the range of meanings which this new phrase has crystallised, and such an analysis can be best pursued by an examination of three pivotal modern figures: T. S. Eliot, F. R. Leavis and Raymond Williams. These figures represent respectively what could be termed the conservative, liberal, and radical socialist perspectives on culture and society, a fact which provides a wider framework for the comparison.

First of all, as an essential preliminary, we can draw a distinction between the work of Eliot and Leavis. Leavis's position (and of course it extends well beyond Leavis himself) is that art and the common life were related in a past, 'organic' society, but that their present relationship, in the context of a commercialist and philistine culture, can only primarily be one of a mutually defining hostility. Culture (art) is related to culture (society) by an aware and vigorous effort to keep free of its debasing influence, and so to make what creative inroads it can into the consciousness and behaviour of what can only, in such a society, be a minority – inroads which demand the nurturing of a finely sensitive but trenchantly defensive élite. The continuity of this with nineteenth-century liberal humanism is clear: there are certain preserved and defined values to which individuals may be admitted, but which cannot, without grave loss, be extended to society as a whole; the definition and transmission of the values will always be the province of, to use an Arnoldian term, the 'remnant', the few sensitive and decent individuals who can avoid both the decreative influence of contemporary culture and the callousing of a formulated commitment to change it. Although the values are themselves social, concerned with the quality of human relationship and moral vitality, the energy which goes into their definition is liberal-individualist: it is preoccupied, that is, with exploring the possibilities of *personal* living, in what is seen as an impossibly brutalised and impersonal society, rather than with connecting these values to the kinds of socio-political agencies which could ensure their general embodiment in the common life. Politics, technology, ideology, institutions, even democracy, are part of what threatens this essentially personal spontaneity, and any contemporary political engagement – even an engagement devoted to changing the criticised society in the direction of vitality and sensitivity – is contemptuously written off. Instead, the values will be insinuated gradually, by the processes of education and individual growth.

Eliot shares Leavis's nostalgia for an 'organic' society (a nostalgia which links Burke, Cobbett, Coleridge, Carlyle, Pugin, Ruskin and many others, and is notably qualified or rejected by George Eliot, Dickens and Lawrence); he also shares his belief that fully conscious culture can only be the property of an élite, although he differs radically about the nature of that élite. But Eliot is in the radical conservative tradition of Burke, Coleridge and Disraeli, rather than in the liberal tradition of Mill and Arnold; he believes, that is, not in a continuing and ineradicable tension between a finely aware élite and a philistine mass, but in the possibility of a commonly shared cultivation, and this is what he calls a 'common culture': a society of shared belief, meaning, value and behaviour. Eliot's faith in a common culture of shared belief, however, is somewhat hampered by his conservative assumption that most people are incapable either of conscious culture or conscious belief, and his work in *The Idea of a Christian Society* and *Notes Towards a Definition of Culture* is directed to resolving this problem. The term which gives a clue to his method of resolution is *conscious* culture and belief: Eliot thinks, to put it bluntly, that most people are too stupid to have beliefs or sensibilities, but they can embody, in the unconscious texture and rhythm of their narrow, habitual lives, an oblique and distilled version of those values which are fostered by the consciously aware élite – an élite which in Eliot's case correlates rather conveniently with the traditional ruling English class of which he was a member. In this sense Eliot can argue for a common culture (in his case, a common Christian culture), although one in which participation is stratified by stable levels of consciousness – levels which correspond, more or less, to the contours of the existing class-system. The role of the ruling élite will be to distil its values into the unconscious reaches of society, whose mindless, habitual enactment of them will in turn sustain and enrich cultural consciousness; society is seen, as it was seen in the tradition of conservative social thought which Eliot inherited, as a self-nourishing, organic cycle of rigidly stratified classes, who share at different levels in a single culture, and contribute, in their structured inequality, to a harmonious whole. There can certainly be no question of any direct offering of the values of high culture to what Eliot calls the 'lower orders', since this will be merely to adulterate what is offered; but by stressing that a culture is for the most part unconscious, and that its values can be unconsciously

transmitted, Eliot escapes from the liberal tension between extension and preserva-
tion which we have described above. If culture can be unconsciously disseminated,
then the 'masses' can be mindlessly incorporated into what can then be called a
'common' culture, without being integrated to the point where they can share in
shaping its values; Eliot thus manages to have his common culture and his political
conservatism simultaneously, rejecting the cultural forms of a liberal bourgeois
society while clinging to an extreme version of its political and socio-economic
assumptions.

Eliot's emphasis on the unconscious nature of a lived culture is crucial to his
argument: a culture, precisely because it is the whole way of life of a people, can
never be fully brought to consciousness, and the culture of which we are conscious
is never the whole of culture. It is this point which links Eliot's argument to the
third perspective on culture and society, that of Raymond Williams and the radical
socialist case with which he is connected. In the Conclusion to his *Culture and
Society 1780–1950*, Williams places a similar stress on the unconsciousness of a
lived culture, but links it to a different structure of values:

> A culture, while it is being lived, is always in part unknown, in part unrealised. The
> making of a community is always an exploration, for consciousness cannot precede
> creation, and there is no formula for unknown experience. A good community, a
> living culture, will, because of this, not only make room for but actively encourage
> all and any who can contribute to the advance in consciousness which is the
> common need. . . . We need to consider every attachment, every value, with our
> whole attention; for we do not know the future, we can never be certain of what may
> enrich it.

For Williams, a culture's unconsciousness, its lack of availability as a whole to any
one point within it, is a consequence of its openness to every offered contribution;
the culture can never be brought fully to consciousness because it is never fully
finished. The making of a common culture is a continual exchange of meanings,
actions and descriptions, never self-conscious or totalisable as a whole, but growing
towards the advance in consciousness, and thus in full humanity, of all its members.
The crucial distinction between Williams and Eliot is that for Williams a culture is
common not only when it is commonly shared but when it is commonly *made*: when
common sharing is mediated by collaborative participation. A common culture, for
the radical socialist, is a culture which engages, in the creation and sustaining of all
its forms – artistic, political, moral, economic – the fullest collaborative participation of all its members. For Eliot a culture is common when commonly shared, at
different, fixed levels of participation and response: the conscious defining and
nourishing remains the preserve of the few. The full meaning of the socialist idea
of a common culture is not that the ready-made meanings and values of others
should be taken over and lived passively by a whole people, but that a whole way of
life should be continually re-made and re-defined in that people's collective praxis.

It is for this reason that Williams, like William Morris, links a moral and artistic meaning of culture – community of meaning, sensibility and belief – to a political meaning: community of institution and material life. The making of a common culture, radically conceived, implies the rule of common responsibility, participation and control – 'the full democratic process' – in every structure of the culture itself. The problem of a common culture is the problem of revolutionary socialism.

One can put the difference between Williams and Eliot in another way. In Williams's version of a common culture, the conscious and unconscious life which for Eliot are characteristic of different social classes are aspects of a single process. Williams's common culture is at once more and less conscious than Eliot's: more conscious, because it engages the active participation of all its members; less conscious, because what will then be created according to this rule can be neither prescribed in advance nor fully known in the making. Williams makes this point explicitly, in relation to the meaning of the term 'culture':

> We have to plan what can be planned, according to our common decision. But the emphasis of the idea of culture is right when it reminds us that a culture, essentially, is unplannable. We have to ensure the means of life, and the means of community. But what will then, by these means, be lived, we cannot know or say. The idea of culture rests on a metaphor: the tending of natural growth. And indeed it is on growth, as metaphor and fact, that the ultimate emphasis must be placed.
>
> (*Culture and Society 1780–1950*, conclusion)

The idea of culture as the conscious tending of spontaneous growth holds both elements in fusion: a truly common culture, precisely because it engages the fullest conscious collaboration of all its members, can never be wholly self-transparent, wholly described. Eliot's idea of culture, by contrast, forces a wedge between these aspects: the minority foster meanings and values and then transmit them to the unconscious majority. It follows that for Eliot the values *can* be to some extent prescribed in advance: the essentials of the culture already exist in the minds of the few, and Eliot can say now, roughly, what the values are. They are, moreover, values which ultimately transcend temporal existence itself, and as such cannot be radically modified by the history into which they are inserted. Both Williams and Eliot point to the values of an existing social class as the creative symbol of a new society: for Eliot, the traditional sanctities of the ruling élite, for Williams the values of common responsibility and cooperative equality of the working-class movement. But whereas Williams imagines these values, once extended to new groups, as undergoing radical re-working, rejecting any simple panacea of 'proletarian' culture, Eliot anticipates no such re-creation. It is precisely because Eliot's idea of culture involves unconsciousness in the majority that he can consciously prescribe the values: since the people are excluded from active re-definition, the culture can be said to exist, in idea, already. Eliot does not have to wait and see what will emerge from common collaboration, since on his model there will be no such collaboration.

What is perhaps most striking about Eliot's model of a common culture is its static quality, and it is this which Williams criticises. Both writers are concerned to contrast a *common* with a *uniform* culture: both stress the unevenness and variety of any collectively lived experience. But for Eliot the variety springs, ironically, from a quite rigid structure of levels: all will not experience alike because all will not participate alike. Williams, while agreeing that full participation in the whole culture will be impossible, locates the essential variety of experience in the content, rather than simply in the form, of a common culture: the culture, precisely because it demands complex and collaborative participation in the shaping of its structures and meanings, will be infinitely richer, more various, open, supple, free – in a sense more dislocated, although within a sustaining unity – than the supposedly common culture we have at present. A common culture is so far from being uniform that it views our present society, not as pluralist and open but as oppressively restricting, by its political structures and assumptions, the energies of most of its members. What we can expect, Williams says, 'is not a simple equality (in the sense of identity) of culture; but rather a very complex system of specialised developments – the whole of which will form the whole culture, but which will not be available or conscious, as a whole, to any one group or individual living within it' (*Culture and Society*, Pelican edn, 234). Eliot avoids the assumption that a common culture implies uniformity, but not the Leavisite myth of an 'organic' society: when he imagines a common culture, he needs, in Williams's words, to imagine 'a society which is at once more stable and more simple than any to which his discussion is likely to be relevant' (232). The judgement seems particularly just, on a thinker who can at one point in *The Idea of a Christian Society* gravely announce that 'On the whole, it would seem preferable for most people to continue living in the places in which they were born'.

The radical idea of a common culture, then, will be 'inorganic' from Eliot's viewpoint precisely because of its openness to common definition and thus to specialised complexity; its unity, as opposed to uniformity, will rest in the general recognition and enactment of the rule of common participation. A common culture cannot be prescribed in advance, and one kind of liberal is likely to seize enthusiastically on this point; but that is not to say that it is built on nothingness, on a mere dynamic openness to each and every version of experience. To achieve a common culture, as Williams reminds us, we need first to achieve the *means* of community at every level of the common life, and it is from this controlling rule that the experience of the culture will be extrapolated: the lived experience of a common culture will be related to this practical basis of political, social and economic community as spoken language is related to its grammatical structure. (Wittgenstein's discussion of what is involved in following a rule, rather than in obeying a law, is directly relevant to this model.) Assent to the creation of a genuinely 'open' society implies, first of all, assent to a 'closed' value-judgement:

the judgement that collective responsibility and cooperative equality, rather than possessive individualism and competitive inequality, is the ground of a good society. To assent to this, Williams is saying, is to be driven beyond a liberal or conservative faith in community of meaning, belief and sensibility to a faith in such forms as authentic only when mediated by community of material life: to, in short, a revolutionary socialism. Eliot, as Williams sees it, is forced contradictorily to demand a community of meaning and belief in the context of a commitment to political and economic structures deeply atomistic in their effect: the moral and artistic versions of culture refuse to enter into significant relationship with culture in its widest sense. Eliot dissolves the praxis inherent in the idea of culture: he fails to see, to quote Peter Winch in his *The Idea of a Social Science*, that 'social relations between men and the ideas which men's actions embody are really the same thing considered from different points of view'.

For the socialist, belief in the possibility of a common culture is belief in the capacity of 'high' culture, when shared and re-made by a whole community, to be enriched rather than destroyed; it is also a belief that sharing at *this* level of cultural meaning can make sense only within the admission of the people as a whole to controlling participation in the making of culture as a whole way of life, and that this operation, on any realistic estimate, will mean a revolutionary politics. The conservative, of course, sees the whole enterprise as disastrous, at both levels; the liberal will recognise the need for community of access to the values of culture, but will reject or qualify the practical agencies created to ensure that access. Part of the difference, perhaps, lies in whether society is seen as static or moving, as a finished structure or an ongoing human creation. The socialist belief in the possibility of a common culture is grounded in a recognition that the growth of literacy, industrialism and democracy in Britain has been a growth towards total control by a whole society over its own experience, a reaching for full collective responsibility through the struggles of a long revolution still far from finished. The process has been faced at many points by the kind of conservative response which Eliot has epitomised for us: the urge to erect barriers, to draw the line in front of one's own feet and place literacy, culture, education on this, not that side, has been a recurrent reaction, and Burke's rejection of the 'swinish multitude' has taken a good many subsequent forms, even in the most enlightened of social thinkers. Each time, however, the revolution for wider participation has continued; each grudgingly lowered barrier, each new form of incorporation, has been the cue for a further integration, until the whole process can only be halted or denied by replacing the images of growth with those of stasis. The conservative version of a stable and stratified society, with given degrees and relations of culture, and the liberal version of the few just men sustaining a developing personal tradition within an unchanging, impersonal society, both end by doing this. They are both versions which have to be encountered and understood, if a common culture in its fullest sense is to exist.

9 Tennyson: Politics and Sexuality in *The Princess* and *In Memoriam*

Perhaps I could begin by suggesting, rather frivolously, that the mid-nineteenth-century bourgeois state had problems in resolving its Oedipus complex. In striving to achieve its manhood – that is to say, to secure that full political dominance which I will designate as 'masculine' – it needed to settle a certain envying hostility towards its own repressive 'father' – towards that other form of state power figured in Tennyson's *The Princess* by the hermaphroditic Prince's own father, the barbaric, nakedly militaristic, blatantly sexist king. Such iron political repression continues, of course, to be a necessity for the mid-nineteenth-century state; but in so far as this brutally explicit *dominance* fails to secure the conditions of ruling–class *hegemony*, the admiring identification with the strong father must be tempered and complicated by a sustained Oedipal allegiance to the 'mother' – that is to say, to those 'civilizing' values of 'sweetness' and 'moral nobility' which are paradigmatically 'feminine'. There is, however, an additional contradiction here. For if sexual reproduction is to be continued, and the social relations of capitalist production correspondingly perpetuated, the Oedipal relation to the mother must be repressed and transcended; yet how is this then to avoid the irruption into the social formation of that heterogeneous flux, process and production of sexual *desire* which is potentially subversive of the social order? If this threat is to be avoided, the woman must naturally be desexualized: all women must become 'mothers'. (I shall suggest later that, in marrying Ida, the protagonist of *The Princess* is among other things marrying his mother.) But if the woman is desexualized, how is the bourgeois social formation to survive by the progenitive reproduction of its individual agents?

I read the ideological project of *The Princess* as an imaginary 'resolution' of these contradictions by a re-fashioning of what we may call, after Lacan, the 'symbolic order'. And although I am far from suggesting that the sexual 'code' of the text is purely phenomenal – that the poem is not 'really' about sexuality – I want to argue that this dominant semiotic code does indeed, in its turn, encode other ideological motifs, one of which I have already adumbrated – the question of a certain transitional crisis in the nature of state power, occasioned most directly by the sharpening of the class struggle in the 1840s, by the stage of development of the productive forces, and by the minatory spectre of the events in France. As what we may risk calling a 'psychoanalysis of the bourgeois state', the text subtly imbricates the questions of the production of sexuality and the production of political power – the reshaping of the symbolic order and the qualified recasting of the structures of bourgeois dominance. (And there are other codes also, as I will show later – most notably, the problem of the nature of literary production itself, of which the text's strikingly bizarre *form* is at once index and attempted resolution.)

That *The Princess* concerns a severe disturbance in the symbolic order – that is to say, in that distribution and stabilization of sexual roles which rests upon the post-Oedipal acceptance of difference, opposition and exclusion – is obvious enough on even the most cursory reading. The bare bones of its narrative, after all, concern a 'feminine' male assuming female disguise in order to woo a 'masculine' female to whom he plays the roles of both child and lover. The poem's ideological project will then be to 'resolve' this socially subversive androgyny by re-establishing that 'otherness' of sexual roles essential for socio-sexual reproduction, while simultaneously effecting that controlled *transference* and reciprocity of sexual characteristics (power and gentleness, knowledge and wisdom, etc.) essential for the 'humanization', and so consolidated hegemony, of the bourgeois state. To put the matter another way: the ceaselessly heterogeneous, polyvalent flux of *desire* must be caught up, trapped and stabilized in a regulated symbolic exchange of discrete, reified 'sexual characteristics'.

A good many Tennysonian texts are marked by a notably ambivalent attitude towards the 'otherness' of the woman. That the woman should be 'other' is, as I have argued, naturally essential for socio-sexual reproduction; but it is precisely this 'otherness' which is also at the root of Tennyson's profound fear of the woman. (And 'Tennyson' here is no more than a name for the mid-Victorian ideological formation, whatever pathological problems he may himself have endured.) Sexuality is commonly associated in Tennyson with violence and death; the sexual strife between the Prince and Ida triggers off a war, and inscribed on the gate of Ida's feminist college is the motto: 'Let no man enter in on pain of death'. To penetrate the mysterious female stronghold, to enter the *vagina dentata* of the woman, is to risk that symbolic death which is castration. Tennyson fears women because they signify the potentially subversive flux of desire, and so unmask the guilty secret of the sublimated allegiance to the mother; but he fears them also because they represent the repressed 'female' in himself – the erotic, privatized, psychically 'estranged' literary producer impermissably at odds with the 'masculine' state ideologue, the poet whose texts must ceaselessly displace their sensuality into sensuousness. The distance between, say, 'Mariana' and the 'Ode on the Death of the Duke of Wellington' is an exact measure of this 'feminine'/'masculine' contradiction, which is no mere question of clinical biography, but an objective contradiction traversing the places of the mid-Victorian poet within the social formation. For on the one hand, given the necessary marginalization of poetic production within

Victorian ideological production as a whole, the poetic text becomes the repository of those 'feminine' elements expelled by the crass 'masculinity' of the dominant utilitarian ideology – becomes, in a phrase, the locus of 'lyrical sensibility'. Yet on the other hand, the poetic producer must necessarily remain bound by the 'masculine' propositional discourses of that ideology. Alfred Lord Tennyson, private lyricist and Poet Laureate, is a name which marks one particular nexus of this contradiction within aesthetic ideology. Indeed it is a striking index of that fact that the 'public', 'masculine' text which unquestionably confirms his function as literary state-lackey (*In Memoriam*) is no more than a restless congeries of private ('feminine') lyrics.

It is as an attempted resolution of this (and other) contradictions that I read *The Princess*. For if it is faintly frivolous to suggest that the Victorian state had Oedipal problems, it is flagrantly obvious to point out that the Prince in this poem does so. Overshadowed by his ravingly sexist father, and devoted to the image of his mother ('No Angel, but a dearer being, all dipt / In Angel instincts, breathing Paradise'), the sexually indeterminate Prince ('blue-eyed, and fair in face . . . With lengths of yellow ringlet, like a girl') has yet to achieve his manhood; his tediously frequent hallucinations, in which reality dissolves into mocking illusion, signify, in Lacanian terms, his inability properly to enter into the symbolic order. They involve a 'swooning' which is, symbolically, sexual impotence and castration; and to overcome this symbolic impotence (which is, as we shall see, 'ideological' as well as sexual), the Prince must confront, in displaced and mystified form, the repressed 'femininity' in his personality. The way he achieves this in the first place is by assuming female dress and personality – that is to say, by symbolically castrating himself, and so acting out in fiction and charade his actual, symbolically castrated condition. In thus 'fictionalizing' and 'mythifying' that condition, the assumption of female dress and voice has, one might say, something of the structure of the neurotic symptom: it allows the Prince at once to express his psychological disturbance and yet to conceal it (since it is farcically obvious that he is in fact a man). The disguise, as it were, reinforces his maleness in the very act of dissembling and displacing it.

But the Prince's true fulfilment of his manhood is, of course, his winning of the Princess Ida, for which the female disguise is merely instrumental. If the Prince is a feminine male, Ida is a masculine female; and one might write the ideological equation of the poem thus: feminine male × masculine female = masculine male + feminine female. (Although this, given the ideologically essential transference of 'sexual characteristics' which I have already discussed, will do only as a partial, provisional formulation.) As a 'masculine' woman, Ida symbolizes for the Prince the fearfully emasculating power of female sexuality; this, indeed, is one of the text's multiple sexual ambiguities, since although Ida's feminism in one sense 'desexualizes' her (thus rendering her less of a sexual threat to the Prince), that feminism also signifies the full achievement of her womanhood. If the Prince can 'feminize' a 'masculine' woman, then he can gain his own manhood by having confronted, and conquered, the fearful 'masculine' power of female sexuality. In this sense, Ida is the Prince's own alienated masculinity, the 'ideal ego' (in Lacan's term) to which his relationship is the 'imaginary' one of simultaneous identification/estrangement. But at the same time, since this 'ideal ego' is in fact a woman, the Prince, in winning her ('Lay thy sweet hands in mine and trust in me'), is, so to speak, incorporating the female into himself, and thus coming to terms with the 'feminine' aspects of himself in ways fully acceptable to the symbolic order (i.e. in marriage).

The text, then, has fulfilled its ideological function. The symbolic order has been re-consolidated, although in suitably refurbished form. The ideologically unacceptable sexist coerciveness of the Prince's father ('Man with the head and woman with the heart, / Man to command and woman to obey') has been qualified by a judicious incorporation of certain 'feminine' qualities into the sexist bourgeois state, for the purpose of buttressing its hegemony. For if women are excessively subjugated, the genetic effects of this upon their sons, and the 'spiritual' effects of it upon their husbands, may well prove socially and politically disastrous. 'If she be small, slight-natured, miserable, / How shall men grow?' Women should not be excessively subjugated, then, in order that their sons and husbands, as members of the hegemonic class, may be better equipped to subjugate them more efficiently. Part of the apparatus of that repression is, of course, the ideological practice of 'literature' itself, which includes *The Princess*. I do not mean by this merely that the poem's blatantly sexist 'content' reinforces the oppression of women; I am referring also to what the poem achieves in *the material practice of its writing*. For we must remember that Ida is a '*Poet*-Princess', who recognizes that a crucial condition of women's liberation consists in the wresting of the educational and 'cultural' apparatuses from male domination. She and her comrades have conquered, and transmuted, the 'masculine' discourses of science, learning, history, mythology – in brief, those discourses which Tennyson himself, as 'feminine' poet, finds so difficult to introduce, other than nervously and obliquely, into his own poetic production. (One might say of his texts that their 'thought' consists at best of feelings tremulously tinged with concepts.) In appropriating Ida, Tennyson/the Prince have recovered their aesthetic-ideological, as well as sexual, potency, united with their poetic, as well as 'masculine', ideal-ego. That recovery *is* the textual practice known as *The Princess*; in expropriating the women of their learning and smashing up their college, the Poet Laureate has provided himself with the materials for a 'masculine', 'public' poem.

It would be mistaken, however, to conclude that *The Princess* triumphantly resolves the contradictions which are the very process of its constitution. It is true that the text transforms the college into a hospital, thus returning its inmates to their proper roles of ministering tenderly to fevered males; it is true also, in a crucial symbolic act, that Ida is persuaded to return Psyche's child to her, thus confirming the sacredness of maternity and the priorities of familial sexual reproduction. Yet for all that, the Prince himself remains locked to the end in his Oedipal problems in a way which profoundly disturbs and interrogates the poem's attempt to re-constitute the symbolic order. For one of the text's deepest ironies is that the Prince finally wins Ida, and so achieves full manhood, only by a process which involves his regression to a childlike dependence on her 'maternal' ministrations, when he lies, injured after battle, in that state of 'psychotic' hallucination which signifies his inability fully to enter the symbolic order. It is no accident that the hymn of praise to his mother I quoted previously occurs just before he successfully concludes his wooing; the Oedipus complex has, so to speak, merely been transferred. Or perhaps it would be more accurate to say that the true contradiction lies in the fact that the complex has been at once transcended and preserved; the Prince has achieved his manhood in love and battle, yet remains tied as a child to his maternal mistress.

It is the necessity of this contradiction which it is important to emphasize. If the social relations of production are to be perpetuated, the Oedipus complex must be overcome in the name of a mature sexuality; but if the disruptiveness of desire is to be curtailed, the woman must be 'desexualized' to a mother-image which will then induce impotence in the male. The poem is scored through by this contradiction, as it is by the related one I have described: that, precisely at the point where the capitalist social formation needs to assert the stringent discipline of the 'masculine' principle, it needs also to qualify that principle with the virtues of 'femininity'. This, indeed, is the note of compromise on which the poem ends, in its explicitly political comments on the upheavals in Europe. The Tory member's son makes his chuckle-headed chauvinist contrast between British stability and European turmoil, and there is no doubt that the comments are textually endorsed; yet the author's persona then instantly inserts his tempering, reformist, 'feminine' caveat, recalling the 'social wrong' of Britain itself and the need for political patience.

Formally speaking, *The Princess* is, of course, a narrative within a narrative – a mythical tale concocted by seven mindless Oxford undergraduates lolling indolently within an aristocratic country seat. The entire poem, in other words, is precisely a sport, an idle frivolity, a distracting device, a light-hearted piece of ritualized upper-class self-indulgence. The whole text is officially no more than a verbal game, uncertain how seriously to take itself; and it is important to register the ideological necessity of this fact. For if the Prince himself, in his hallucinatory fits, is unable to 'know the shadow from the substance', finding reality a 'mockery' and 'hollow show', exactly the same is true of the poem itself. Indeed one of its most curious features is its constant undertone of farce – a farce which seems to consist in nothing less than the poem's sporadically sending itself up. I am thinking, for example, of the absurdity of the disguised Prince's piping up in a female treble, or of that strikingly dissonant moment when, fleeing for his life from an enraged bunch of feminists, he tells us that 'secret laughter tickled all [his] soul'. It seems to me difficult to see these devices as anything other than 'defence' and 'displacement' mechanisms, analogous to the Freudian joke, whereby disturbing material almost too painful to be admitted into consciousness is allowed through only in 'emasculated' form. The poem, in short, can 'succeed' (not that it does) only partly, cancelling and 'castrating' its own serious, 'masculine' substance – repressing its own material reality as a writing practice, as sober Victorian epic, and displacing itself instead into the 'feminine' modality of frivolous sport.

Yet there is an additional contradiction here, for if it is true that the poem casts itself into such 'feminine' modality, it is nonetheless imperative that the 'masculine' voice maintains its dominance – that, within the interplay of voices which speak or sing the text, the women are subordinated to the lowly status of intermittent lyrical 'punctuations' of the men's narrative ('To give us breathing space', as the authorial persona generously remarks). So that while the formal frame of the text is 'femi- nine' sport, and the 'feminine' thus 'officially' dominant, this frame is in fact no more than the support of 'masculine' discursive dominance. It is, however, in any case somewhat misleading to speak of the poem as characterized by an 'interplay of voices'. For what is most graphically evident is that the poem displays no *dialectic* of discourses whatsoever; the seven male voices are in no sense differentiated, rigorously subjected as they are to a single, dominant narrative discourse whose only alterity is 'feminine' lyrical interlude. There is no sense in which one discourse inheres within, contradicts, interrogates or 'de-centres' another, as there is with both Clough and Browning. So if the ideological motifs of *The Princess* concern, in the Lacanian sense, the 'symbolic', the sealed closure of its inexorably 'centred' form is, again in Lacan's sense, classically 'imaginary'. Which is no more than to remind ourselves that the substance of the poem is *myth* – for myth is precisely that self-enclosed order of plenitude whose opposite is the open dialectic of history. Myth, one might argue, is 'metaphorical', in that it represents a substitute structure of significations for the historical; and the deepest formal irony of the poem is then that, myth though it is, its actual 'content' is *metonymic*, concerned with the movements and displacements of narrative/desire. This metonymic movement is enclosed, stabilized within the metaphorical; and one index of this stabilization is precisely the regular recurrence of the 'feminine' lyrics within the narrative. For if narrative is predominantly metonymic, lyric is predominantly metaphorical. The 'metaphorical' females are thus allowed from time to time gently to supervene on the 'metonymic' males, to recall and recuperate their turbulent narrative into the securing, anchoring, 'timeless' mythological themes of love, sorrow, parting, re- union and so on.

If *The Princess* is a 'full' poem, constituted by a highly wrought, gorgeous density of language, *In Memoriam* is a notably 'empty' one, whose language seems listlessly to turn around some central elusive negativity. That negativity, formally speaking, is the absence created by the death of Hallam – a death which for Tennyson is nothing less than the striking from the world of the 'transcendental signified'. Emptied of this ideological bedrock of senses, all that *In Memoriam's* own signifiers can do is set up subliminal resonances between each other, in order to generate some mood or context which might capture some substantive signified which forever evades them. The text's language thus involves a constant displacement of meaning: it becomes a kind of narcotic or masturbatory act, a melancholic self-drugging:

> In words like weeds I'll wrap me o'er
> Like coarsest clothes against the cold,
> But that large grief which these enfold
> Is given in outline and no more.

But it is not quite the conventional proposition that the poem has a meaning but cannot express it: the 'grief' the text speaks of is no less than the *grief of a whole crisis of language*, which is in turn the grief of a whole crisis of mid-nineteenth-century bourgeois ideology. For Hallam, as I have argued in *Criticism and Ideology*, is nothing less than the empty space congregated by a whole set of ideological anxieties concerned with science, religion, the class struggle, in short with the 'revolutionary' de-centring of 'man' from his 'imaginary' relation of unity with his world. Tennyson's relation with Hallam was of this classically 'imaginary' kind (he describes the relation at one point as that of mother and child); but Hallam's death has dislodged the poet from that 'imaginary' narcissistic plenitude of identity and left him dolefully stranded in the 'symbolic order', marooned in that ceaseless play of difference, loss, absence and exclusion which is part of the very linguistic form of the text. To enter the symbolic order is to recognize that the world is independent of one's consciousness, that its continued existence does not depend upon oneself, and thus that one can die. Indeed as Tennyson writes, in a passage which unquestionably proves that he had read Lacan's *Ecrits*:

> The baby new to earth and sky,
> What time his tender palm is pressed
> Against the circle of the breast,
> Has never thought that 'this is I':
>
> But as he grows he gathers much,
> And learns the use of 'I' and 'me',
> And finds 'I am not what I see,
> And other than the things I touch'.

The contradiction of *In Memoriam*, however, is that while Hallam's death has forced it into this consciousness of differentiation and opposition (and evolutionary science has, of course, demonstrated 'man's' contingency to the universe), the text also finds it ideologically impermissible to accept this shattering of 'man's' metaphysical centredness. If the baby of the above stanzas is slowly emerging from the 'mirror-phrase', Tennyson himself is still trapped within it, or is even prior to it:

> So runs my dream: but what am I?
> An infant crying in the night:

> An infant crying for the light:
> And with no language but a cry.

In Lacan's parlance, 'demand' has not yet been mediated through language into 'desire'. The poem's ideological strategy, then, must be to come gradually to terms with the loss of Hallam, but then mythically to reconstruct the symbolic order into a 'higher' version of the lost 'imaginary'.

As the 'transcendental signifier' of *all* losses, Hallam, in Lacanian terms, represents the phallus for Tennyson. In order to 'enter into its manhood' – that is to say, to overcome its 'feminine' and 'infantile' grief and grow into a 'masculine', affirmative and thus ideologically efficacious text – the poem must recognize the necessity of the absence and opposition which the phallus signifies. But this recognition is constantly forestalled by the fact that the text's relation to Hallam is not only 'imaginary', but also Oedipal, fraternal and homosexual. Indeed, in a bafflingly complex series of slippages, Hallam figures for the text at various times as mother, brother, lover, wife and husband. The significant missing term is, of course, 'father'. If the poem can give up wishing to marry Hallam (either as mother, wife or husband) and establish him instead as the type of 'masculine' authority, then it can establish its own sexual identity as his admiring yet strong and separate son, or younger brother. The determinants which effect this transposition in the text are political ones. Given the threat of revolutionary upheaval, the poem must transcend its private 'feminine' melancholy and turn instead to the problem of 'masculine' political dominance:

> . . . Is this an hour
> For private sorrow's barren song,
> When more and more the people throng
> The chairs and thrones of civil power?

Hallam, had he lived, would have become a good counter-revolutionary politician,

> . . . A potent voice of Parliament,
> A pillar steadfast in the storm,
>
> Should licensed boldness gather force,
> Becoming, when the time has birth,
> A lever to uplift the earth
> And roll it in another course . . .

But even as a corpse he remains a powerful symbol of bourgeois hegemony: 'A deeper voice across the storm',

> Proclaiming social truth shall spread,
> And justice, ev'n tho' thrice again
> The red fool-fury of the Seine
> Should pile her barricades with dead.

To put the matter a little crudely: what has enabled the text to overcome its Oedipus complex is 1848.

It is in this way, then, that *In Memoriam* is finally able to enter the symbolic order – to become itself the ideologically potent, fully-sexed son of its dead father. Instead of wishing to marry Hallam, it celebrates the marriage of Tennyson's own younger sister, in a triumphant reaffirmation of bourgeois sexual reproduction. And yet for all that, the poem does not abandon the 'imaginary'. I argued earlier that the poem's language partook of the 'symbolic'; but it does not, naturally, press that all the way into the full-bloodedly *symboliste* discourse of a Mallarmé, where the evaporation of the signified into an infinite play of signifiers becomes the basis for a radically new poetic. *In Memoriam* is still ideologically constrained by the demand to produce a coherent propositional realism; so that while the bond between signifier and signified has certainly loosened, a 'mirror-relation' between 'word' and 'thing' is nevertheless preserved. And if the poem sustains the 'imaginary' at its linguistic level, it does so also, in the end, at the level of 'content'. Hallam is finally elevated to a cosmic type of some future human unity, reverently installed as a privileged subject within the life of that divine Subject of subjects on which the whole of creation centres. The closing stanzas of *In Memoriam* would seem powerfully to validate Louis Althusser's claim that the 'model' for all ideology is fundamentally theological.

I want to end on what the liberal critics call a 'personal note'. Given the ideological conditions within which this paper is produced, it would be surprising, since I am male, if it did not contain residual elements of sexism. One such element I thought I had spotted, in re-reading what I have written – that I give a good deal more attention to the Prince in *The Princess* than to Ida herself. But this seems to me to reflect a significant fact about the poem. The poem is mistitled: ostensibly 'about' Ida, it in fact concerns problems of 'masculine' hegemony. There is a revealing discrepancy between the poem's title (which, as with all literary texts, is part of its meaning) and the substance of the poem itself, which the title displaces. In this case, at least, it would seem that the sexism is the text's, rather than my own.

10 The Rape of Clarissa

Clarissa is the story of a young woman of outstanding kindness, virtue and intelligence who is made to suffer under a violently oppressive family, is tricked away from home by a notorious sexual predator, deceived, imprisoned, persecuted, drugged and raped, and finally impelled to her death. What have the critics made of this narrative?

Dorothy van Ghent's classic essay on the novel begins by noting that its central action, the rape, 'might have assumed a position of minor importance among Moll [Flanders]'s adventures in adultery, bigamy and incest – conceivably an incident that Moll might even have forgotten to make a "memorandum" of'.[1] Considered in the abstract, van Ghent comments, 'the deflowering of a young lady' represents 'a singularly thin and unrewarding piece of action . . . and one which scarcely seems to deserve the universal uproar which it provokes in the book'.[2] Van Ghent has great fun with Clarissa's torture at the hands of Lovelace – 'Clarissa on her knees in prayer in miraculously dirt-resistant white garments, or Clarissa in torn clothes and with streaming eyes, prostrated at the feet of her demon-lover' – and manages to imply that she deserves what she gets: 'The womanly quality which Richardson has made attractive in these images is that of an erotically tinged debility which offers, masochistically, a ripe temptation to violence.'[3] Pausing to compare the image of Clarissa with a *Vogue* cover-girl ('a wraith of clothes, debile and expensive, irrelevant to sense-life or affectional life'),[4] or 'the many-breasted woman with torn dishabille and rolling eyeballs' on the cover of detective stories ('she is to be vicariously ripped and murdered'), van Ghent goes on to scoff at 'virginal, high-minded, helpless womanhood' and remarks, falsely, that chastity in *Clarissa* is a physical attribute.[5] *Clarissa* is not a tragedy, she considers, because it ends happily in the heroine's attainment of heaven. Clarissa 'goes off' with Lovelace as an act of daughterly rebellion (she is in fact *tricked* into elopement, a fact which Ian Watt also obscures), and the novel finally endorses the values of 'parental authoritarianism in the family, and the cash nexus as the only binding tie for society at large'.[6] Clarissa herself is an image of 'perverted sexuality' and 'the sterilization of instinct': her death is a macabre ritual, a 'common orgy' in which 'she performs her [death throes] charmingly'. Van Ghent quotes approvingly V. S. Pritchett's comment in *The Living Novel* that Clarissa 'represents that extreme of puritanism which desires to be raped. Like Lovelace's her sexuality is really violent, insatiable in its wish for destruction.'[7] The whole novel is no more than a rapist's wish-fulfilment, the fascinating motif of 'the carnal assault on a virgin'; its imagery renders 'defloration exciting and attractive'. The essay's final gesture, unsurprisingly, is to put in a word for the squirearchy: Lovelace is the work's 'whipping boy' for its own hypocritically disowned indulgences.

Most literary critics, Raymond Williams once remarked, are natural cavaliers;[8] but even van Ghent's hard-boiled scepticism appears pious when placed beside William Beatty Warner's *Reading Clarissa*, a fashionably deconstructionist piece out to vilify Clarissa and sing the virtues of her rapist. Clarissa, as we have seen, holds to a severely representational ideology of writing, trusts in the stable sign and the unitary self, and subscribes to the values of truth, coherence and causality; Lovelace, by contrast, is a proto-Nietzschean who celebrates plurality, groundlessness and *jouissance*. It seems logical, then, that a contemporary deconstructionist should find Lovelace the hero and Clarissa the villain, without allowing a little matter like rape to modify his judgement. 'By winning our laughter and giving us pleasure, Lovelace helps to undo the matrix of truth and value through which Clarissa would have us see, know and judge.'[9] The rapist is merely a Derridean jester misunderstood: 'There is an artistry and economy in Lovelace's use of the lie. But beyond this, the lie has a peculiar aptness for use in an assault on Clarissa. If Lovelace can get Clarissa to live within an acknowledged lie at Sinclair's – like the notion that she is his wife – he can disrupt the ground of her self-complacence.'[10] It is difficult to see what 'lie' signifies for Warner in the first place, since he does not of course subscribe to the boring old metaphysical bugbear of 'truth'; but it certainly serves to excuse Lovelace's action of imprisoning Clarissa in a brothel once we realize that this is a salutary deconstruction of her metaphysical delusions, a radical, perhaps even comradely, gesture. Warner, who finds Clarissa's sisterly friendship with Anna Howe 'chill and uninteresting',[11] regards Lovelace as 'defer[ring] any drastic step, like rape or marriage, that might simplify their relationship',[12] though he does not develop this intriguingly original ground for objecting to rape. He concedes that Clarissa in the brothel is 'imprisoned, surrounded by evil, and in danger of violation',[13] but judiciously mutes these realities to an 'image of virtue in distress', which sounds less unpleasant. The best way to deconstruct Clarissa's tediously unified self is, in fact, to rape her: 'rape is the most cogent response to Clarissa's fictional projection of herself as a whole unified body "full of light". [Lovelace] can subvert this fiction by introducing a small part of himself *into* Clarissa. Thus the rape, like all Lovelace's displacements, will seek to induce the slight difference that will make all the difference.'[14] Lovelace, whom Warner finds 'charming', moves towards the rape 'with an inexorable necessity': what else can the poor fellow do if he is out to deconstruct her? His deceptive enticing of Clarissa from her home is just 'Lovelace's joke'; the violence of his rape is less 'insidious' than the 'will to power' which compels Clarissa herself to write her story, enamoured as she is of old-style ontological claptrap like truth, meaning, narrative and causality. Lovelace's 'shortcomings', Warner writes, 'are not held against him by the lover of comedy';[15] Clarissa, presumably, couldn't take a joke, although Warner does generously acknowledge that 'something genuinely arresting' happened to her when she was drugged and raped, and informs us that, having been raped, she 'feels used'. It is not, however, that she has been used by a sexual oppressor, but by 'Lovelace's fictional machinery'. Warner greatly relishes Lovelace's unspeakably cynical defence of the rape of his 'pretty little miss', and regards most critics as conspiring with the prim Clarissa to judge Lovelace in such shabbily undeconstructed terms as 'seriousness, consistency, sympathy, maturity, a full deep heart, and belief in the "real"'.[16] His book is an ominous exposé of the truly reactionary nature of much deconstructionist 'radicalism', once divorced from the social and political contexts it so characteristically finds hard to handle.

Not all critics, gratifyingly, have been as flagrantly prejudiced or obtusely unhistorical as Warner and van Ghent. But even as judicious and illuminating a study of the novel as Ian Watt's is not without its symptomatic blind spots. Watt, at least, sees that Clarissa's virginity is in no sense a commodity, for if it were then Lovelace would have been right to believe that 'once overcome [is] for ever overcome', and, as he discovers to his cost, this is not so. He is also right to point out, as most critics do, that Clarissa is dangerously unclear and to some degree self-deceiving about her initial feelings for Lovelace: 'we are fully entitled to suspect Clarissa herself of not knowing her own feelings; and Lovelace is not altogether wrong in suspecting her of the "female affectation of denying [her] love".'[17] Not *altogether* wrong; but within a few pages this emotional *ambiguity* in Clarissa has unquestioningly become her 'unconscious love' for Lovelace,[18] and on the following page, with gathering dogmatic certainty, Clarissa's utterly well-grounded doubts about her seducer have become spuriously equated with his own 'false sexual ideology'. Once this move has been made, the ground is cleared for a reckless comparison of what are now the 'star-crossed lovers' Clarissa and Lovelace to the great romantic tragedies of Romeo and Juliet or Tristan and Isolde. The implication is clear, and common: Clarissa and Lovelace are equally cocooned in false consciousness, mutually thwarting and travestying; how tragic that they were unable to liberate one another's real selves. This, to be sure, contains a seed of truth; but it obscures the fact that Lovelace, far from figuring as some Romeo in wolf's clothing, is for the most part simply a wolf, and is perceived by Clarissa to be so. To suggest a symmetry between Clarissa's partial, understandable self-deceptions and Lovelace's unremitting schizoid fantasies is to cast a slur upon Clarissa.

In support of his attempt to convict Clarissa of collusion in the rape, Watt predictably quotes her delirious ramblings after the event:

A lady took a great fancy to a young lion, or a bear, I forget which – but of a bear, or a tiger, I believe it was. It was made her a present of when a whelp. She fed it with her own hand: she nursed up the wicked cub with great tenderness; and would play with it without fear or apprehension of danger . . . But mind what followed: at last, somehow, neglecting to satisfy its hungry maw, or having otherwise disobliged it on some occasion, it resumed its nature; and on a sudden fell upon her, and tore her in pieces. And who was most to blame, I pray? The brute, or the lady? The lady, surely! for what *she* did was *out* of nature, *out* of character, at least: what it did was *in* its own nature.[19]

This, written directly after the rape has occurred, must of course be read in the light of the irrational guilt women commonly experience after such violations. Even then, however, it will hardly bear close scrutiny. Lovelace was not made a present of Clarissa's 'when a whelp', if this means that she originally thought him innocuous; on the contrary, her suspicions of him date back to their earliest encounters. She never 'nursed him up with great tenderness', or 'play[ed] with [him] without fear or apprehension of danger': she treated him with proper vigilance from the outset. The lady was not in fact to blame; Clarissa's self-castigation is quite unjustified. The passage commonly quoted to demonstrate a rare moment of self-insight on her part in fact reveals a self-lacerating mystification. The rape has simply thrust her more deeply into ideological submission. If Watt's judgement, generally so exact, is inaccurate here, it is equally so in his assertion that 'Clarissa dies rather than recognize the flesh.'[20] On the contrary, she dies because she has recognized it all too well.

The view of Clarissa as neurotic prude has become the merest commonplace of Richardson criticism. Irwin Gopnik can write *en passant*, unarguedly, of her 'naïve, adolescent, morbidly self-pitying, sublime idealism',[21] and Leslie Fiedler writes airily of the book's 'pornographic' aspects. Eaves and Kimpel rightly retort that anybody reading *Clarissa* for this reason is in for a disappointment: 'We see very little sex in it, surprisingly little considering the story.'[22] 'One cannot but sympathize with [Clarissa's] demand [to be treated as a person],' they write, adding with remarkable liberality of spirit that 'even today, a young girl who does not want to be raped ought not to be raped.'[23] (The implications of that 'even today' are interesting: even in these permissive times when young girls may well not care whether they are raped or not, it is obligatory to abstain.) Eaves and Kimpel's moral generosity does not, however, stretch to sympathy with the important, largely suppressed current of women's writing which was influenced by Richardson: 'We are not much concerned,' they announce, 'with his influence on a few second-rate sentimental females.'[24]

It is now possible to see why *Clarissa* has proved such a scandalous text for modern criticism. It deeply offends the fashionable liberal assumption that virtue is boring, the banality that the devil has all the best tunes. For here is a novel whose protagonist is not only kind, chaste and conscientious but also embarrassingly rich and real. Lovelace is also, of course, a magnificently realized character; but the devil-worshipping critics have to struggle hard to suppress the fact that, as Eaves and Kimpel argue, 'Whatever of himself Richardson put into Lovelace, he rejected, and not merely in a conventional moralistic way, but with a side of his mind as deep and at least as important as the side which was able to realize Lovelace.'[25] Effectively ignored throughout the nineteenth century, Richardson stages a come-back when a more sophisticated criticism comes to discern that Clarissa is not all she is cracked up to be. Suavely 'knowing' analyses become possible once Clarissa's faults are triumphantly unmasked – once it is seen that she is after all spiritually proud, dangerously unclear about her own deeper feelings, prey to a certain moral *hauteur* and self-admiration, irritatingly inflexible at unpropitious moments and prone to masochistic self-abasement. Once the spicy news is out that the madonna has feet of clay – that she is, after all, a woman, with sexual impulses and moral failings – an avenging male iconoclasm moves in. The way is then clear for the cavaliers, deconstructionists and debunking liberals to insinuate that Clarissa is only a little less reprehensible than Roxana. In this, as usual, Richardson had pre-empted his critics: he writes that he had deliberately given his heroine moral defects to make her more convincing.[26] Clarissa is indeed far from a madonna: her treat-ment of Lovelace can be exasperatingly perverse, her moral self-assurance repel-lent, her denial of her own sexual instincts seriously damaging. But even when the most damning evidence has been gleefully summoned for the prosecution, it re-mains, on balance, remarkably feeble. 'The minor reticences and confusions re-vealed in the feminine correspondence,' writes Ian Watt, 'are insignificant compared to the much grosser discrepancies between Lovelace's pretended atti-tude to Clarissa and the falsehoods and trickeries which his letters reveal.'[27] The ideological benefits to be reaped from discrediting Clarissa are considerable. For it allows criticism to fend off the sheer radicalism of this astonishing text, and whole generations of students to believe, amazingly, that 'one of the greatest of the unread novels' (Christopher Hill) is not only unendurably long but priggish, preachy and pornographic to boot.

Some of the charges against Clarissa – that she is prudish, dull, naïve, chroni-cally idealizing or tediously meek seem to me merely false. Other accusations – that she is responsible for her own rape, or that she is fit meat for voyeurs – are not only false but, so to speak, slanderous. Still other criticisms – that she is morbid, masochistic and narcissistic – are true in a sense, but rarely in the sense in which they are intended. Such upbraidings are in any case typically exaggerated: they apply more to the protracted scenes of Clarissa's dying than to her earlier career. And it is of course just these amazing scenes – in which Clarissa holds public audience on her death bed, orders her coffin and writes letters upon it, attends with quiet efficiency to the last detail of her testament and interment – which have provoked the mocking incredulity of the critical cavaliers. That tell-tale device on Clarissa's coffin – a serpent with its tail in its mouth – has been busily enough annotated, as 'emblem of an endlessly self-consuming sexual desire' (Watt), sign of a sterile narcissism. But narcissism, as Lear remarked about low voices, is an excellent thing in a woman. What struck the patriarchal Freud as particularly regressive in women – their 'cat-like' proneness to sensual self-delight, their cool, self-fulfilling independence of male desire – are precisely the qualities which patriarchy is unable to countenance.[28] Female narcissism is not only scandalous but fearful: it allows men a glimpse of that terrifying condition in which woman might be independent of them. It is by virtue of her profound narcissism, not by dint of being fetishized to the phallus, that Clarissa is finally able to slip through the net of male desire and leave the hands of Lovelace and her family empty. Her elaborate dying is a ritual of deliberate disengagement from patriarchal and class society, a calculated 'decathecting' of that world whereby libidinal energy is gradually withdrawn from its fruitless social investments into her own self. Dorothy van Ghent, predictably, finds this farcically distasteful: 'The scene in the death room is an astonishing one. The room is crowded with people, all pressing around the dying woman to obtain her blessing. The mourning is as public as possible; every sigh, every groan, every tear is recorded. One is given to understand that nothing could be a greater social good than Clarissa's death, nothing could be more enjoyable than to watch her in her death throes (she performs them charmingly), nothing a greater privilege than to be present at this festival of death and to weep and sniffle in the common orgy.'[29] Twentieth-century academics do not of course commonly die in public, and so may be forgiven for finding this spectacle indecorous. Van Ghent would presumably have Clarissa a Little Nell, expiring in decent privacy. But the public nature of Clarissa's death is the whole point: her dying is in a profound sense a political gesture, a shocking, surreal act of resignation from a society whose power system she has seen in part for what it is.[30] It would be considerably too convenient for the ruling class to make of her death a hole-in-the-corner affair. The death is a properly collective event, a complex, material business, a negation of society which is also, curiously, a living part of it. Clarissa is no Lady of Shallot but a saint and martyr – that is to say, one whose life has been lifted out of the merely private arena into the public sphere, in an exemplary liturgical action whose end is to involve and transform others. Richardson is not to be contrasted as a novelist of the 'personal' with his 'social' rival Henry Fielding.[31] Every sigh, groan and tear must indeed be duly recorded, taken down in writing and used as damning documentary evidence against a society where the rape of a Clarissa is possible. That scrupulous record is, of course, the novel *Clarissa* itself. Clarissa's death is indeed intended as a 'great social good', tragic though it remains, and there is certainly both pleasure and privilege in being allowed to participate in it. But the pleasure is less that of a morbid voyeurism than of an appropriate sadism: every symptom of Clarissa's saintliness, every sign that she is intelligently in command of her dying and utterly autonomous of others, is a nail, not in her own coffin, but in that of the society which has driven her to her death and must now stand by, guilty, horror-stricken and ineffectually repentant. Who indeed would not find these scenes deeply enjoyable, with an eye to their devastating effects on Lovelace and the Harlowes? Clarissa, to adopt van Ghent's sarcastic term, does indeed 'perform' her death; that, precisely, is the point.

That which is purely itself, like the self-gratifying narcissist, cannot be represented. For representation involves spacing, division, an articulation of signs, and it is this which Clarissa finally denies. Brooding upon her own being, rapt in an 'imaginary' relationship to her own death, she refuses incorporation into social discourse and transforms herself instead into a pure self-referential sign. Her death is thus the consummation of her ideology of writing: in dying, she achieves that pure transparency of signifier to signified which she seeks in the integrity of her script. Such transparency – the baffling enigma of that which is merely itself – is bound to appear socially opaque, a worthless tautology or resounding silence. There is nothing to be done with it, as the patriarchs can finally do nothing with Clarissa, the stubborn little minx who perversely insists upon dying and leaving them with blood on their hands. When all the voices are crying for compromise, Clarissa moves steadfastly into her death, as courteously unheeding of this clamouring as her author was of those readers who begged for a marriage to Lovelace and a happy ending. In refusing this compromise, Richardson cunningly pressed the Christian ideology of his audience to its intolerable limits: if you really believe a heavenly reward is the ultimate good, why would you have Clarissa live? The more transparent Clarissa becomes, the less legible she is, for such an unbroken identity of purpose must in the end have the inscrutability of a cypher. Her 'morbid' death wish remains unswerving, for in this society death is indeed the only place of inviolable security. Her 'masochism' is complete, for she has understood well enough that this is no society for a woman to live in. It is no accident that the liberal critics, who find such masochism and morbidity a little unhealthy, should be equally blind to the radicalism of that political insight.

What Clarissa's death signifies, in fact, is an absolute refusal of political society: sexual oppression, bourgeois patriarchy and libertine aristocracy together.[32] If Lovelace is unable fully to enter the symbolic order in the first place, Clarissa is the 'transcendental signifier' who ends up by opting out of it. She is not, needless to say, some feminist or historical materialist *avant la lettre*: nobody could be more submissive to patriarchal order, more eloquent an ideologue of bourgeois pieties, than Clarissa Harlowe. It is hard for the modern reader to hear the litany of posthumous praises sung to her unbelievably upright existence without feeling a wild surge of iconoclasm. Yet each item of that litany, each tedious piece of testimony to Clarissa's impeccable moralism and conformism, simply twists the dagger a little deeper in the very social order of which she was so fine a flower. The more the novel underwrites those values, the more it exposes the Harlowes; the more meekly bourgeois Clarissa is revealed to be, the more devastating grows the critique of those who did her to death. There seems little doubt that in the prolonged detail of the death scenes the text unleashes upon Clarissa a sadistic violence which belongs with its Lovelacian unconscious. But the more it punishes her, the more virtuous she is made to appear, and so the more savage becomes the indictment of Lovelace and the Harlowes. The death scenes become the medium whereby Lovelace's sadism may be turned against himself, and harnessed to bring low the bourgeoisie into the bargain. Bourgeois ideology is made to stand shame-faced and threadbare in the light of its own doctrines. The impossibly ideal nature of Clarissa's virtue is indeed beyond realism, a kind of grave parody of official moral ideology which, by pressing it to an intolerable extreme, begins to betray something of its corrupt reality.

It is not only that Clarissa exposes the rift between bourgeois pieties and bourgeois practice; it is also that those pieties themselves, once submitted to the pressures of fictional form, begin to crack open. 'It is Richardson's greatness,' writes Christopher Hill, '. . . that his respect for Clarissa's integrity led him to push the Puritan code forward to the point at which its flaw was completely revealed, at which it broke down as a standard for conduct for this world. His *conscious* desire in writing the novel was to assert the bourgeois and Puritan conception of marriage against the feudal-cavalier standards of Lovelace and the Harlowes emphasis on concentration of property. But the contradictions of subordination in equality which were inherent in the Puritan view of women were too strong for him.'[33] Richardson, who in private life argued against full sexual equality and thought polygamy a possible option, is constrained by the logic of his own fiction to throw that whole ideology into radical question. Like Clarissa, his pen exceeds his inten-tions, conjuring a levelling sub-text from beneath the carefully policed script of his novel. Standard Christian values are pitted against 'parental authoritarianism and the cash-nexus', which van Ghent absurdly takes to be the novel's positive values; but then, in a further antithesis concealed within this opposition, those values of female subordination are themselves interrogated by an altogether more subversive voice. It is a voice most evident in the comradely correspondence between Clarissa and Anna Howe. Anna is no feminist paradigm – she believes, for example, that 'our sex are best dealt with by boisterous and unruly spirits' – but she is perhaps one of the nearest things to a militant separatist that the eighteenth-century novel has to offer:

> Upon my word, I most heartily despise that sex! I wish they would let our fathers and mothers alone; teasing *them* to tease *us* with their golden promises, and protestations, and settlements, and the rest of their ostentatious nonsense. How charmingly might you and I live together, and despise them all! But to be cajoled, wire-drawn, and ensnared, like silly birds into a state of bondage or vile subordination: to be courted as princesses for a few weeks, in order to be treated as slaves for the rest of our lives. Indeed, my dear, as you say of Solmes, I cannot endure them![34]

Caustic, humorous and debunking, unswerving in sisterly solidarity yet astrin-gently critical, Anna is part of Clarissa's own unconscious, able to articulate that which it would be improper for the heroine herself to voice.

Clarissa is mildly scandalized by Anna's high-handed treatment of her suitor Mr Hickman, and gently reproves her for this injuriousness. Hickman is a good man, and in this sense Anna's behaviour is certainly unwarranted; but there is more at stake in the sexual power struggle than one man's sensibilities, and to this extent Anna's lack of charity is politically justified. Clarissa, typically, adheres to absolute standards of truth and justice; Anna shrewdly recognizes that such values are indissociable from the shifting power strategies in which they are embedded. To be false or unjust, in conditions where the other has the power advantage, may be a productive error, as near to 'genuine' truth and justice as one can get. Clarissa's 'representational' model of truth, as fixed correspondence between discourse and reality, overlooks the fact that truth is always a matter of power and position, a function of social relations, an effect of particular discourses in particular conditions. How are women to live by truth and justice in a society where the very criteria for defining what counts as such are already in the hands of patriarchy? What is the value of truth when like the confessional letter it merely delivers you over to oppression and so perpetuates a pervasive falsity? *Clarissa* implicitly poses to political society a question which shakes it to the roots: can truth and power be compatible? Can one trust simply to the 'literal' truth of one's discourse and discount its mystifying effects? Or can one falsehood be countered only by another more fruitful falsehood, which in shifting the balance of power in one's favour may bring a deeper demystification to birth? Can those who are stripped of power from the outset, excluded by the rules of discourse from full subjecthood, enter the power game at all without being instantly falsified? And is it any less misinterpretable to stay silent?

The great warring of discourses that is *Clarissa*, in which statements are minefields and paragraphs political tactics, turns upon such fundamental questions. It is as a struggle over meanings, a wary negotiating of nuances and implications, that the battle between the classes and the sexes is conducted. There is hardly a proposition in the book that is not refracted through the play of power interests, saturated to its roots by strategic considerations, bristling with tactical manoeuvres. To write is to gain a toe-hold in the power struggle, a continual skirmishing and out-flanking. In this, Richardson resembles no writer quite so much as his admirer Henry James. For those who enter upon this dangerous game with a handicap – their sex – nothing is more important than the code of propriety, which is at once something less than the whole truth and an indispensable set of defences without which no truth could survive. In modern parlance, the code serves as a kind of 'problematic', the shared invisible underside of all utterances, the matrix which determines their status as acceptable discourse. Alan McKillop writes of Clarissa's 'excessive propriety',[35] but the short answer to that is Ian Watt's: 'As a result of these revelations [Lovelace's trickeries], we realize that the code which might seem to make Clarissa too prudent is not prudent enough when measured against the outrageous means which men allow themselves to gain their ends.'[36] When Mark Kinkead-Weekes complains with some justice that Clarissa is at certain times too undiplomatic, too stiffly unyielding in her dealings with Lovelace, we feel entitled to ask what could possibly count as excessive vigilance in addressing a man who has just raped you? Indeed, one of the novel's strengths is that it seems ready to risk the charge of 'overniceness' in Clarissa, even to the point of her becoming unsympathetic – that it accepts this as an unavoidable 'bind', an untenable but essential position into which vice manipulates virtue.

Clarissa's own faith is that truth and propriety are not fundamentally at odds. As in the Janus-faced letter, at once nature and artifice, it is the code itself which should determine how 'free' you can be. Clarissa's letters are for the most part political gestures in just this sense, scrupulous alignments of tactics and truthfulness. If Belford admires her as a 'lady scrupulously strict to *her* word, incapable of art or design',[37] this indifferent novelist is also after all the woman capable of penning on her death-bed the most Lovelacian *double entendre* of all, in her true but grossly misleading comment that she is about to depart for her 'Father's house'. This blending of sincerity and deception is a necessity for the oppressed: Anna Howe remarks on the dangers of a woman writing her heart to a man practised in deceit. Truth may not be compatible with virtue: it is virtuous to forgive another's faults, but Clarissa's excuses for her vicious bully of a brother ('. . . really a worthy young man, but perhaps a little too headstrong in his first resentments and conceptions of things'[38]) amount to wholesale distortion. It is equally virtuous to be humble, but humility for Clarissa often enough means false self-accusation. It is by trusting to the possibility of disinterested truth that she falls foul of Lovelace in the first place. Lovelace has been maligned by the Harlowes, so Clarissa feels compelled to speak up for him in the name of an objective justice: 'It is then the call of justice, as I may say, to speak a little in favour of a man, who, although provoked by my brother, did not do him all the mischief he could have done him, and which my brother had endeavoured to do *him*.'[39] This is in any case rationalizing, as Clarissa already finds Lovelace sexually attractive: her impartial intervention is considerably more interested than she admits. Once victimized by her family and abducted by Lovelace, she will soon discover that enunciations of truth and justice are not to be so easily disengaged from the power interests and social relations which frame them. As with Richardson's own struggles with literary form, she will see the problem of reconciling such judicious metalanguage with the passions and prejudices of the moment.

What Clarissa will discover in particular is the most demoralizing double bind of all: the truth that it is not so easy to distinguish resistance to power from collusion with it. There is no way she can escape from Lovelace without talking to him, and to talk is to create a certain complicity. If Clarissa negotiates she is guilty of compromise; if she refuses to bargain her position becomes even more untenable. Power reproduces itself by engendering in its victims a collusion which is the very condition of their survival. Few people are likely to bulk larger in a woman's life than the man who has raped her: even the ruthlessly impersonal act of rape cannot help generating between Clarissa and Lovelace something that might genuinely be called a bond. This is not to lend credence to the offensive suggestion that Clarissa desires her own violation; it is simply to question the sentimental, characteristically male notion that women are the mere passive victims of men's power. As Michèle

Barrett has written: 'An analysis of gender ideology in which women are always innocent, always passive victims of patriarchal power, is patently not satisfactory.'[40] Lovelace's exercise of power is bound to evoke countervailing tactics in Clarissa, if she is to survive at all; she is thus drawn onto the terrain of a conflict in which she will always be the loser because the rules disadvantage her from the outset. To protect her own position means submitting to a struggle which jeopardizes it at every step. What critics have read, often rightly, as her pride, self-will, artfulness or inflexibility are inseparable from this fact. The novel sees well enough that if virtue is necessary it is also an encumbrance, since to behave well in a predatory society is the surest way to unleash its violence.

What will finally strike Lovelace impotent, however, is the fact that he cannot secure Clarissa's collusion. His own tactics are parasitic on Clarissa's counter-moves: it is the thrill of the chase he finds most erotic, a sadistic delight in the prey whose very pain forces her to respond. Clarissa's pleadings thus fuel the very force they are intended to check. But once Lovelace is reduced to the humiliating gesture of having to drug his victim in order to rape her, he has lost the war even before he has performed the act. A forced victory is no victory at all: Lovelace can hardly demonstrate that all women are secretly lecherous if Clarissa is unconscious at the crucial moment. In a sense nobody experiences the rape: not the reader, not the comatose Clarissa, not even Lovelace, for whom the act is purely empty. As in Hegel's great myth of master and slave, Lovelace requires from Clarissa the very autonomy he finds unbearable; to quell her freedom is to undermine himself. To recognize that master and victim are always somehow complicit may induce a certain political pessimism, but it may also do the opposite: the fact that the dependence is not all one way is, in this novel at least, what will bring the ruling class low.

Clarissa's 'representational' model of truth, which abstracts truth from its strategic contexts, is exposed by the novel as severely limited. Yet if it is not simply discarded, it is because the alternative – a 'conjunctural' view of truth as pragmatist and provisional, a mere cluster of passing interests – is too close to Lovelace for comfort. For there is no doubt that his political violence is intimately linked to his epistemological scepticism and 'deconstructive' style. Linguistic lawlessness is the other face of his sexual libertinism: a writing which brooks no closure is a desire which knows no mercy. His fertile productivity as author, conjuring fiction out of fiction with effortless *brio*, is the barren epistemology of one for whom truth is whatever instruments of oppression he can breezily assemble, whatever profitable mystification he can momentarily improvise. Lovelace can unfix a sign as deftly as he can break a hymen, 'differencing' with all the delight of one to whom any woman's identity is purely indifferent. It falls to the bourgeoisie, then, to stem the profligate force of the aristocratic pen and penis by effecting a moral closure. It must deploy its own countervailing ideologies of truth, representation and the unitary subject against this deathly dissemination. No reading of the novel which ignores this historical necessity in the name of *écriture* can fail to be moralistic. But though Lovelace is not allowed to deconstruct that bourgeois ideology, he does, after all, powerfully challenge it. Two centuries or so before our current altercations over 'transcendental' and 'deconstructed' subjects, stable sign and floating signifier, Richardson had cast a critical eye on both sides of the argument. If he plumped firmly for one, it was not without awareness of what sacrifices of *jouissance* that option entailed, what rich reaches of subversive wit it excluded. There is no way in which the creator of Lovelace could have felt other than deeply ambiguous about the sober Clarissa, lovingly though he endorsed her. It seems unthinkable that Richardson could have fashioned Lovelace without considerable unconscious guilt: the very fact that he could think his thoughts put him beyond the ideological closure that is Clarissa. His affirmation of Clarissa's world may thus be in part expiatory. Of course Lovelace is only a fiction – indeed trebly so, a literary character who sometimes sees himself as such and is a gripping story-teller in his own right. The novel exploits this fictional status, allowing us to enjoy him as a character while rejecting him as a 'real' man. But that Lovelace is fictional is no true expiation of guilt, for fiction is itself a guilty enough affair. Lovelace worries his author not only because he is a dissolute aristocrat but because he is a type of the writer, and the two figures are disturbingly interrelated. Richardson's own plots, after all, have no more substance behind them than Lovelace's fantasies: his narratives are as arbitrarily self-generating as Lovelace's sexual devices. Indeed it is possible to read Lovelace's pathological pursuit of the 'real' of Clarissa as an allegory of the writer's hunt for an essential truth – a truth which fragments with each new paragraph. 'The real is not representable,' writes Roland Barthes, 'and it is because men ceaselessly try to represent it by words that there is a history of literature . . . literature is categorically realist, in that it never has anything but the real as its object of desire; and I shall say now, without contradicting myself . . . that literature is quite as stubbornly unrealistic: it considers sane its desire for the impossible.'[41] What Richardson needs, to ground his writing in truth and purpose, is the closure of Clarissa; but at the level of narrative it is just this closure – Clarissa's refusal to be seduced – which keeps Lovelace as a character in business, providing the generative mechanism of the entire text. The novel's 'guilt', then, is that the more it protects its heroine's virtue, the longer it is able to indulge its 'hero'. Lovelace and Clarissa are complicit as units of textual 'grammar', however 'semantically' antithetical they may be.

   Lovelace, however, cannot ultimately be indulged: the political price is too high. Richardson does not allow the unconscious to seduce him from the primacy of class struggle. The coherent bourgeois subject must be affirmed, and *jouissance* consciously sacrificed, if ruling-class rapacity is to be defeated. The tragic irony of the text is that it can ensure the victory of Clarissa only by fetishizing her, as Lovelace does, to the miraculously integral phallus. Only by aggressively repressing the woman can it aggressively cut down the man; woman as madonna is the only response to woman as whore. Anagrammatically, it is possible to produce either 'a whole' or 'a whore' from 'Harlowe', but neither without leaving an excess. If the aristocracy cannot be opposed by a call for sexual emancipation, it is not only because such a call would be anathema to bourgeois puritanism; it is also because the aristocracy has itself parodied and discredited that solution. Its crime is not only that it oppresses women, but that in doing so it practises a debased version of a *jouissance* which some have argued is properly their own. The 'feminine' excess, fluidity and bodiliness of Lovelacian writing forces femininity itself into the protective enclosure of the masculine. It forces it, that is to say, into the equally intolerable clutches of middle-class patriarchy, in a contradiction at once deadlocked and symbolically defeated in the dying body of Clarissa. There can be no intercourse between Clarissa and Lovelace, no relaxing of this historically vital opposition between fetishism and fluidity, the impossibly self-identical and dangerously diffusive self. They exchange only in the very letter of Richardson's text – that seamless fetish of a novel alive with subversive force.

Whatever the ideological option of a Richardson, *Clarissa* still poses an acute problem for us. Not a problem *consciously* posed by the text, but one that it can be persuaded to raise by a certain reading. For we can surely accept neither the 'imaginary' selfhood of a Clarissa nor the oppressive opportunism of a Lovelace. Put another way, we can endorse neither the deconstructive reading of a Warner nor the liberal humanism of a Kinkead-Weekes. For Kinkead-Weekes, whose love for Clarissa seems to fall not far short of Richardson's own, what the novel finally vindicates is the inviolable mystery of the individual. It is not only that this reading is unhistorical, abstracting some changeless pith of selfhood from the variable historical ways in which subjects are constructed; it is also that it fails to note the irony that such spiritual individualism is the acceptable face of the very system which kills Clarissa. In this sense the novel sees further than its critic: it certainly sees that such individualism is no *answer* to social contradictions. For Kinkead-Weekes, writing at a later stage of class society where such spiritual individualism has successfully identified itself with the 'human' as such, social contradictions would seem no more than the setting for some timeless moral drama. In the world of *Clarissa*, the final exercise of 'free' individual choice is in fact a tragic option for self-extinction. Clarissa is a living contemporary for Kinkead-Weekes, but only because he has abolished history altogether. He is as unable to historicize his liberal humanism as Warner is to distance his deconstructionism. Kinkead-Weekes is right to see that the novel affirms the 'inviolability of personality', but uncritically assimilates that concern to the ephemeral pieties of twentieth-century liberalism. (The fact that he would no doubt be concerned to learn that his book was 'ideological', as Warner no doubt would not, simply testifies to the difference between long-established prejudices and brashly emergent ones.) The 'integrity of the human person' is indeed preserved, but, as Raymond Williams adds, 'fanatically' so; the unflawed identity which Kinkead-Weekes applauds is a fetish. Warner certainly sees this, and with a vengeance; but he is blind in his turn to the necessities of eighteenth-century class struggle. What Kinkead-Weekes fails to recognize is that there are more ways than one of imagining the 'inviolable' self.

His own image is unreservedly essentialist: the immaculate mystery beneath the skin. But the 'inviolable' is also that which slips through the net of signification: that desire which never achieves final definition, not because it is magically at one with itself but because it is always self-divided. *Clarissa* shows us that there is no way of thinking the unity of the self without reckoning into account the unconscious. This is not to belittle 'humanism': it is merely to recognize that it is a project still to be constructed, not a received set of liberal shibboleths. For those today concerned as Richardson was with social transformation, there can be no cavalier dismissal of the 'human', 'closure' or the 'unified self', to be dispersed at a touch of deconstruction. Such notions remain as politically vital for us as they were for Samuel Richardson. What is *Clarissa* but a warning that the trading of such imperatives for the short change of eroticism and *écriture* delivers you to the political enemy? Yet Clarissa is sacrificed anyway, inviolable or not; and this in turn should expose the political defects of a theory of the subject which rests content with coherence and closure, refusing that satirical question mark that is Lovelace.

Richardson's 'fanaticism', according to Williams, is a matter of abstracting sexuality from the whole social process. This, for so finely Lukácsian a critic, is a curious judgement on *Clarissa*, whatever its relevance to *Pamela*. For *Clarissa* superbly 'totalizes' the sexual and the social, conscious of what we might today call the 'relative autonomy' of sexual oppression while materialist enough to discern its economic basis. Sexuality, far from being some displacement of class conflict, is the very medium in which it is conducted. In one sense, the novel does indeed sharply counterpose social relations and sexuality: Clarissa has the unenviable choice of becoming a pawn in the Harlowes' property game or Lovelace's erotic object. Yet this contradiction between bourgeois property and aristocratic anarchy conceals a deeper complicity. Both display a form of possessive individualism. If Lovelace and the Harlowes are ideological antagonists, they are nevertheless part of the same ruling-class power bloc; the Harlowes object to Lovelace not primarily because he is sexually immoral but because he threatens the marriage deal which might elevate them to the nobility. In material terms, the tragedy of Clarissa is not 'world-historical' but a storm in a teacup; it dramatizes a collision between two wings of the eighteenth-century ruling class whose true destiny lay not in conflict but in alliance. In ideological terms, however, the tragedy is indeed of 'world-historical' proportions, a key phase of English class history. Lovelace is a reactionary throwback, an old-style libertine or Restoration relic who resists a proper 'embourgeoisement'; the future of the English aristocracy lies not with him but with the impeccably middle-class Sir Charles Grandison. The death of Clarissa is the mechanism of his downfall, and in that sense the triumph of bourgeois patriarchy. Yet the death, as we have seen, is a two-edged sword: it cannot cut down Lovelace without mutilating the Harlowes too. No Harlowe-like critique of Lovelace is fully possible, for it was they who forced their daughter into his arms in the first place. It is for this reason, not on account of an undue specializing of class crisis to virginity, that the novel has finally nowhere to turn but to Clarissa herself. Her dying encompasses both aristocracy and bourgeoisie, revealing their true unity of interests. Lovelace, as Jean H. Hagstrum has suggested, represents a cynical Hobbesian deflation of middle-class sentimental hypocrisy; but having used him to discredit that ideology, the novel will then use Clarissa in turn to discredit him.

The death of Clarissa is, of course, a deeply ambiguous affair. On the one hand, as Williams rightly argues, its utter refusal of compromise is 'the reverse of consolidation, of the necessary settlement, the striking of a bargain between advantage and value'.[42] It is thus a death against the grain of history, an inversion of *Pamela*, an implacable negation of property and progress. Indeed, writing *Clarissa* seems to have retrospectively revised Richardson's views of his earlier novel: 'It is apparent by the whole tremor of Mr B.'s behaviour,' he writes in a letter of 1749, 'that nothing but such an implicit obedience, and slavish submission, as Pamela shewed to all his injunctions and dictates, could have made her *tolerably* happy, even with a *reformed* rake.'[43] On the other hand, nothing could be more meekly masochistic than this aggressive onslaught on the whole social system, nothing more pacific than Clarissa's resolute turning of her face to the wall. It is by forgiving the aristocrat that she vanquishes him: her victory takes the form of a spiritual submission of which he himself is incapable. The death is a kind of psychical device whereby the novel throttles back its own social aggression, turns it around and lets it lash itself quiet on the body of Clarissa herself. If the bourgeoisie are to attain spiritual hegemony over the squirearchy, this is an essential inversion: you must not fight the class enemy with his own weapons, and the fact that the bourgeoisie are in practice indistinguishable from their superiors on this score counts heavily against them. Clarissa's forgiveness of Lovelace thus reflects something of the bourgeoisie's impulse to make peace with the traditional ruling class; but it also of course frustrates it, since, given her death, no actual alliance will ensue. There is a similar ambivalence in her relationship to bourgeois patriarchy. On the one hand, her death is the strongest conceivable affirmation of that ideology: it is less Lovelace's rape, than the melancholy into which she is plunged by her father's curse, which causes her to die. Clinically speaking, Clarissa dies of depression: unable to live in the knowledge that her obnoxious family have cast her out, she sinks into profoundly masochistic guilt.[44] But her every refusal to condemn the Harlowes, her saintly internalizing of such aggression, blackens them a little deeper in the reader's eyes. If they execrated a daughter as merciful as this, their chances of heaven must indeed be slim. In this sense, the more Clarissa slips into false consciousness, the more admirable she becomes; Richardson is able to let us see that she is both lovable and mistaken, playing off her lowly self image against her objective significance. The 'objective guilt' of the raped woman merges with the 'objective guilt' of the traditional tragic scapegoat, who though innocent assumes the sins of the community. The more virtue is at odds with truth in humbly maligning itself, the more it shames its oppressors. The two uneasily coexisting aspects of Richardson's own sensibility – his Christian piety and social aggressiveness – are brought into devastating interaction.

Perhaps the critics have disliked Clarissa's 'unconscionable time a-dying' (Johnson) because it is not really very realistic. (One might, incidentally, counter Johnson's jeer by pointing out that Clarissa is most impressive not for her protracted death but for the fact that she survives as long as she does.) Mark Kinkead-Weekes has no particular objection to the death on this score, but the title of his study – *Samuel Richardson, Dramatic Novelist* – is nevertheless significant. Post-Leavisite criticism likes its fictional 'ideas' to come in subtly dramatized, psychologically plausible form; whatever is not instantly soluble in the textures of 'lived experience' is suspect as dryly theoretic. From this viewpoint, however, *Clarissa* appears less and less realist the further one steps back from its relentless detail, in a reversal of those representational canvases which dissolve as you approach them into streaks and blurs. In fact the more scrupulous the realism grows the less realist it is, since the more ludicrous it becomes that anybody could have written so many letters and still found time to eat. (Lovelace has been estimated to have written 14,000 words in a single day.) 'Did I, my dear, in what I have repeated, and I think they are the very words, reflect upon my father?' asks Clarissa anxiously of Anna Howe.[45] Representational writing must brim itself full of another's 'very words' if it is to avoid deception, and so simply veers into an alternative fiction: how could Clarissa have possibly recalled her father's discourse *verbatim*? The problem of *Clarissa* in this sense is the problem of how not to become *Tristram Shandy*. How is it to sustain its dogged faith in the representational sign through all that welter of detail, subduing such material to shapely narrative and causal coherence? It is because the ideology of realism never falters that the text is as inconveniently long as it is: the reader must not be shamelessly manipulated *à la* Sterne, cheated by authorial whim or elision, forced to complain that this is anything less than the authorized blow-by-blow account. Yet viewed from a long way off, the very disproportion of this discourse to what it is 'about' – the rape of Clarissa – has a sort of modernist smack about it, as language is unleashed in pursuit of a truth for which it is at once excessive and too meagre. It is, to adopt Clarissa's own word, a text about 'nothing' – about a female body which, for all one's painstaking rhetoric, can never be represented. Neither the cause nor the object of this discourse can be inscribed within it, for both lead us back to an unconscious on the repression of which the whole top-heavy textual business thrives. Without the repressions of Clarissa and the neuroses of Lovelace there would be no novel at all. *Clarissa* as a text would not need to exist if its author were able to 'know' these submerged realities, rather than be constrained to pursue them in the very act of writing.

The death of Clarissa – that Samson-like act of self-immolation by which she brings her enemies toppling to the ground – is certainly resistant to any purely realist reading. Unswerving in its local verisimilitude, the novel coolly throws to the winds any plausibility of the whole. The apotheosis of Clarissa is a brazenly didactic, allegorical gesture, as unpalatable to narrowly realist taste as *Paradise Lost* or Brecht's *Lehrstücke*. It is a death as scandalous in literary form as in ideological content. At this historical point, there is no 'realist' way in which the deathly contradictions of patriarchy and class society may be resolved; what we are offered instead is a tragic negation which is, inseparably, utopian transcendence, cutting the knot of all those thwarting realist complexities in a boldly gratuitous gesture which trusts in heaven alone. Raymond Williams sees this as a false displacement, an abstracting of actual history to a 'fallen world' which must be virtuously spurned. Yet if this is doubtless how Richardson and Clarissa view the matter, theirs is not necessarily the last or most authoritative word. What societies cannot yet accomplish historically, they often enough nurture in the realm of myth; and this seems to me the most relevant contemporary reading of Clarissa's religious faith. Williams recognizes that 'there was not, as yet, any available and adequate social response' to this 'basically ruthless social order',[46] but he fails to relate this political insight to Clarissa's supreme trust in God. In the England of 1748, an 'adequate social response' to human exploitation may be as remote as Clarissa's God, but it will also need to be as absolute and all-encompassing. Certainly no mere reformism will suffice to uproot the Harlowes and Lovelaces of history, as the novel plainly enough implies. Clarissa is not, after all, purely narcissistic. As far as she is concerned, she relies not upon her own powers but upon heaven: 'God Almighty would not let me depend for comfort on any but himself.'[47] There is a source of power and solace beyond Clarissa, for which her dying is no merely individualist act but a sign of human solidarity. If for Richardson and his heroine that absent dimension has the name of God, we ourselves, reading the novel after the advent of the women's movement, may perhaps give a more precise name to those sources of power and solace, with the historical emergence of which a modern Clarissa would not need to die.

Notes

1   *The English Novel: Form and Function* (New York, 1961), p. 45.
2   Ibid., p. 47.
3   Ibid., p. 49.
4   Ibid., p. 51.
5   This is a common error of critics: Leslie Fiedler believes that 'Clarissa is, indeed, indistinguishable from her virginity' (*Love and Death in the American Novel*, p. 64), and David Daiches, who thinks Clarissa is 'silly', holds that 'Richardson had a purely technical view of chastity.' (*Literary Essays* (London, 1956), p. 47).
6   *The English Novel*, p. 61.
7   Ibid.
8   *The Long Revolution* (London, 1961), p. 256.
9   *Reading Clarissa*, p. 30.
10 Ibid., p. 32.

11   Ibid., p. 39.
12   Ibid.
13   Ibid., p. 42.
14   Ibid., p. 49.
15   Ibid., p. 80.
16   Ibid., p. 268.
17   *The Rise of the Novel*, p. 238.
18   Cynthia Griffin Wolff, in her highly interesting study, speaks of Clarissa's 'adoration' of Lovelace, a strange hyperbole (*Samuel Richardson and the Eighteenth Century Puritan Character*, p. 96).
19   Vol. 3, p. 206.
20   *The Rise of the Novel*, p. 247.
21   *A Theory of Style and Richardson's 'Clarissa'*, p. 90.
22   *Samuel Richardson*, p. 258.
23   Ibid., p. 105.
24   Ibid., p. 611.
25   Ibid., p. 260.
26   *Selected Letters*, p. 101.
27   *The Rise of the Novel*, p. 239.
28   See Freud, 'On Narcissism: An Introduction', *Standard Edition*, vol. XIV. But see also, for a feminist valorizing of female narcissism, Ulrike Prokop, *Weiblichen Lebenszusammenhäng* (Frankfurt am Main, 1976), Sarah Kofman, *L'Énigme de la femme* (Paris, 1981), and Janine Chasseguet-Smirgel, 'Feminine Guilt and the Oedipus Complex', in *Female Sexuality*, ed. Chasseguet-Smirgel (Ann Arbor, Mich., 1970).
29   *The English Novel*, p. 60.
30   'Clarissa is a champion of the downtrodden woman of her day and all days' (Jean H. Hagstrum, *Sex and Sensibility*, p. 206). This – a note rarely struck in Richardson criticism – comes within what is in general one of the finest recent accounts of the novel.
31   A commonplace of Richardson criticism: see Leo Braudy's extraordinary claim that 'In *Clarissa* society has effectively vanished and the battleground is inside the self' ('Penetration and Impenetrability in *Clarissa*', in *New Aspects of the Eighteenth Century*, ed. Philip Harth (New York and London, 1974), p. 186).
32   I use the term 'bourgeois' here in a broad sense: strictly speaking, the Harlowes are gentry, as indeed is Lovelace. But Lovelace has close aristocratic connections and lives an aristocratic ideology, whereas the Harlowes, although in no sense social upstarts, are closer ideologically to the middle class.
33   'Clarissa Harlowe and her Times', *Essays in Criticism* 5 (1955), pp. 334–5.
34   Vol. 1, p. 131.
35   *The Early Masters of English Fiction* (London, 1962), p. 73.
36   *The Rise of the Novel*, p. 239.
37   Vol. 2, p. 159.
38   Vol. 4, p. 354.
39   Vol. 1, p. 136.
40   *Women's Oppression Today* (London, 1980), p. 110.
41   Lecture in Inauguration of the Chair of Literary Semiology, Collège de France, *Oxford Literary Review* (autumn 1979), p. 36.
42   *The Country and the City*, p. 65.

43   *Selected Letters*, p. 124.
44   Otto Rank has suggested that if Don Juan's infantile sexual regressiveness is forever frustrated in its search for the mother's body, the more successful form of regression in the legend is death itself, which has a similar goal: 'The devouring animals of the underworld, the grave, and the coffin are clearly unambiguous mother symbols' (*The Don Juan Legend*, p. 96). It would seem, then, that *Clarissa* 'splits' these two forms of regressiveness between its two protagonists. Rank's remarks on the ambivalent attitude of the daughter to the murderer of her father are also perhaps relevant to Clarissa's attitude to Lovelace: the daughter 'partly welcomes the murderer as a liberator and a new beloved, and partly scorns and persecutes him as a weaker substitute for the lost primal object' (p. 101).
45   Vol. 1, p. 102.
46   *The Country and the City*, p. 65.
47   Vol. 4, p. 339.

11 The Crisis of Contemporary Culture

St Catherine's, the college to which I've just migrated, got its name by a mistake. The college began life in the nineteenth century as a society for matriculating students too poor to gain entry to the University, which is not least of the reasons why I am honoured to be associated with it. For their social centre, the early students used St Catherine's dining rooms, so-called because they were situated on Catte Street, and 'Catte' was mistakenly thought to be an abbreviation of 'Catherine'. Hence the name of the modern college. There can't be many Oxford colleges named after a café, though the name of my old college, Wadham, smacks a little of a department store. There is rich material here for theoretical reflection, on catechresis and the floating signifier; on the mimicry and self-masking of the oppressed; on the parodic process, noted in Marx's *Eighteenth Brumaire*, whereby an impoverished present decks itself out in the alluring insignia of a sacred past; on the appropriation of a woman's name, and the name of a martyr at that, by a group of dispossessed men; and on the Nietzschean notion of genealogy, that tangle of crimes, blunders, oversights and off-chances which for the more conventionally minded goes by the name of tradition. I raise these suggestive topics only to send them packing, since I don't intend to devote a lecture to the name of my new college. Suffice it to say that when I reflect on my own dubious genealogy and penchant for mimicry, I can't avoid the overpowering feeling, not least in the small hours of the morning, that I have become Warton Professor by a kind of mistake. But since being a professor is better than having a job, I don't intend to look a gift horse in the mouth.

I don't in fact intend to say much at all about critical theory – the intellectual equivalent of crack, as Geoffrey Elton has called it – since I find myself increasingly restive with a discourse which obtrudes its ungainly bulk between reader and text. You may have noticed that some critical languages do this more than others. Terms such as symbol, spondee, organic unity and wonderfully tactile draw the literary work closer to us, while words like gender, signifier, subtext and ideology simply push it away. It is helpful on the whole to speak of cosmic vision but not of colonialism, of beauty but not the bourgeoisie. We may talk of the oppressiveness of the human condition, but to mention the oppressiveness of any particular group of people within it is to stray out of literature into sociology. 'Richly metaphorical' is ordinary language, readily understood from Bali to the Bronx; 'radically masculinist' is just the barbarous jargon of those who, unlike C. S. Lewis and E. M. W. Tillyard, insist on importing their tiresome ideological preoccupations into properly aesthetic matters. But I will not speak much of theory because it is in any case the mere tip of a much bulkier iceberg, one element of a project which is out to liquidate meaning, destroy standards, replace *Beowulf* with the *Beano Annual* and compose a syllabus consisting of nothing but Geordie folk songs and gay graffiti. What is at stake, in other words, is nothing less than a pervasive crisis of Western culture itself; and though this epochal upheaval is not everywhere dramatically apparent, and certainly not in the Oxford Examination Schools, we should remind ourselves of Walter Benjamin's dictum that the fact that 'everything just goes on' *is* the crisis.

What is the nature of this upheaval? It is surely coupled with a crisis of nationhood, for what after all holds the nation together but culture? Not geography, to be sure: you can be British in Hong Kong or Gibraltar; and not just the political state either, since that somewhat anaemic unity has to be fleshed out in the lived experience of a corporate form of life. But that corporate national identity has now been thrown into question by a number of factors: by the advent of a multinational capitalism which traverses national frontiers as casually as *The Waste Land*; by the geopolitical transformations through which the advanced nations are now swinging their guns from facing eastwards to train them on the south; by the impact of revolutionary nationalism on the metropolitan centres; by the arrival, in the shape of postmodernism, of a thoroughly cosmopolitan culture; and by the presence of ethnic diversity in a deeply racist society. In much of this, there is for shamelessly unreconstructed Marxists like myself an intellectually pleasing contradiction to be noted between base and superstructure, as the logic of immigrant labour and global capitalist integration finds itself at odds with the spiritual imperatives of a traditionalist, parochial, post-imperial national culture.

None of this is irrelevant to the study of English, as Sir Arthur Quiller-Couch well knew. 'Few in this room', he remarked in Cambridge in 1916, 'are old enough to remember the shock of awed surmise which fell on young minds presented, in the late 70s or early 80s of the last century, with Freeman's *Norman Conquest* or Green's *Short History of the English People*, in which, as though parting clouds of darkness, we beheld our ancestry, literary as well as political, radiantly legitimised.'[1] The study of English was from the outset all about the legitimacy of national origins, all to do with the unspeakable anxiety that you might turn out as a nation to be something of a bastard. Hitching the study of modern English to the rude manly vigour of the Anglo-Saxons was one way of laying claim to such a suitably authorizing heritage, though it posed a problem too: did we really want to be as rude, hairy and vigorous as all that? As one early opponent of English at Oxford put it: 'An English school will grow up, nourishing our language not from the humanity of the Greeks and Romans but from the savagery of the Goths and Anglo-Saxons. We are about to reverse the Renaissance.'[2] 'Ethnicity' was not drafted into English studies by the polytechnics; it was of the essence from the beginning. English first germinates in Victorian England as part of a deeply racialized ethnology, and its immediate forebear is a comparative philology which seeks in language the evolutionary laws of racial or national *Geist*. If, for Oxford students today, so-called Old English is compulsory but a systematic reflection on what it means to read is not, this is a direct consequence of the racism and chauvinism of our forefathers. 'I would like to get up a team of a hundred professors', commented Oxford's Sir Walter Raleigh, with the civilized humanism which was to become the hallmark of his subject, 'and challenge a hundred Boche professors. Their deaths would be a benefit to the human race.'[3] And Raleigh was a good deal more liberal-minded than almost any of his colleagues.

Confronted in the early decades of this century by the challenge of a cosmopolitan modernism, English responded with the *ersatz* internationalism of Empire, at once global in reach and securely nation-centred. The writ of the English language ran all the way from Kerry to Kuala Lumpur; yet this confident hegemony contained the seeds of its own deconstruction. For it was characteristic of the Leavisian ideology of English, at least, to discern a peculiarly intimate relation between a certain richly resourceful use of the national language, and a certain uniquely English mode of experiencing; and from this viewpoint *Finnegans Wake* was entirely unthinkable even though it actually happened. (I speak, incidentally, as one who hails from a nation which was charitable enough to write most of your great literature for you.) Such colonial or post-colonial writing drives a dangerous wedge between signifier and signified, dislocating the nation's speech from its identity. You can, of course, try to take care of all this by some such absurdity as 'Commonwealth literature', or by its later, theoretically more sophisticated mutation, 'Third World studies', which is today not even arithmetically accurate; but the embarrassing truth remains that there is now apparently a plurality of discourses of the human, and since the human is by definition a singular essence this cannot actually be so. It is surely for this reason that literature – that esoteric pursuit of a few thousand not politically very important people like ourselves – has become in our time so curiously politicized. For there is no doubt that for the first time since the late 1960s, the so-called humanities, of which literary studies have been traditionally the flagship, have come in the West to provide an arena of intensive political contestation; and though this is in part a discursive displacement depressingly typical of our times, it is none the less testimony to the truth that the crisis which we are enduring is of a peculiarly cultural kind. Nobody out there beyond academia cares very much whether we talk about signifiers rather than symbols, or codes rather than conventions; it is not for these sorts of reasons that literature has become important, or that there has been so much blood on the Senior Common Room floors. If literature is important today, it is because it is held to incarnate, in peculiarly graphic and sensuous form, the fundamental, universal language of humanity, at a moment when the regimes under which we live have need of that notion but have themselves rendered it profoundly problematic. Literature provides our most intimate, subtly affective acquaintance with that tongue, and so is the concrete correlate of that abstract political unity which we share as formally equal citizens of the state. I should confess in parenthesis here that I too believe in a common humanity, but that as a socialist I regard it less as an intuitive given than as a political task still to be undertaken. But for those who do not hold that view, the current challenge to this particular ideology of literature is understandably alarming. For many of them have long ceased to identify much of value in social life in general; and if the aesthetic cannot articulate that value, then where else, in a progressively degraded society, is there to go? If the materialists can get their grubby paws even on that, then the game is surely up. It is no doubt for this reason that the in-fighting over something as apparently abstruse as literary theory has been so symptomatically virulent; for what we are really speaking of here is the death of civilization as we know it. What is at stake in these contentions is nothing less than the devastating historical irony by which the advanced capitalist system has come steadily to undermine its own metaphysical rationales. And this is a good deal more serious than the question of whether *jouissance* or utter tedium is the most appropriate way to describe our response to *The Battle of Maldon*.

Like many human societies to date, capitalist regimes need to underwrite their activities by some appeal to transcendental value, but as Jürgen Habermas has argued it is in the nature of such rationalizing, secularizing social orders to bring their own metaphysical foundations into increasing discredit, disenchanting with the one hand what they mystify with the other. In this sense too, base and superstructure, commodity production and spiritual legitimation, are embarrassingly at odds. Shakespeare still embodies timeless value; it's just that you can't produce his stuff without the sponsorship of Prudential Insurance. Postmodernism, taking its cue from its mentor Friedrich Nietzsche, offers an audacious way out of this impasse: forget about ontological grounds and metaphysical sanctions, acknowledge that God – or the superstructure – is dead, and simply generate up your values from what you actually do, from that infinitely proliferating network of conflict and domination to which Nietzsche gives the name of will to power. Such a strategy promises to overcome the performative contradictions of advanced capitalism – the disabling discrepancies between fact and value, rhetoric and reality, what we actually do and what we say that we do, which are themselves a source of ideological instability. But it exacts an enormous cost, which these social orders are quite properly too prudent to pay: it asks them to forget that the role of culture is not only to *reflect* social practice, but to *legitimate* it. Culture must not simply generate itself up from what we do, for if it does we will end up with all the worst kinds of values. It must also idealize those practices, lend them some metaphysical support; but the more the commodity form levels all hierarchies of value, mixes diverse life-forms promiscuously together and strikes all transcendence empty, the more these societies will come to deplete the very symbolic resources necessary for their own ideological authority.

This contradiction can be seen at almost every level of contemporary social life. If you erode people's sense of corporate identity, reducing their common history to the eternal now of consumerist desire, they will simply cease to operate effectively as responsible citizens; and so you will have to manufacture that corporate identity synthetically, in the shape of the heritage industry or imperial war. If you allow education to be invaded by the levelling, fragmenting commodity form, you will need all the more stridently to insist on basics, fixed canons, immutable standards. The more you commercialize the media, the more you will feel the need for poems that rhyme and say nice things about Lord Nelson. The more cheap black labour-power you exploit, the more you will feel inspired to preserve the unity and purity of the national culture. In all these ways, anarchy and autocracy, money and metaphysics, exchange value and absolute value are both strangers and brothers, sworn foes and intimate bedfellows. So it is that the intellectuals of the New Right, having actively colluded with forms of politics which drain purpose and value from social life, then turn their horror-stricken countenances on the very devastated social landscape they themselves have helped to create, and mourn the loss of absolute value. It would help in this respect of course if they could surmount their clerkly scepticism long enough to get to the baptismal font; but since most of them cannot, whatever their secret hankerings, they must make do instead with that familiar surrogate for religion known as culture.

What has happened is that culture is less and less able to fulfil its classical role of reconciliation – a role, indeed, on which English studies in this society were actually founded. And this is so for a quite evident reason. For as long as the conflicts which such a notion of culture sought to mediate were of a material kind – wars, class struggle, social inequities – the concept of culture as a higher harmonization of our sublunary squabbles could just retain some thin plausibility. But as soon as such contentions become themselves of a cultural kind, this project becomes much less persuasive. For culture is now palpably part of the problem rather than the solution; it is the very medium in which battle is engaged, rather than some Olympian terrain on which our differences can be recomposed. It is bad news for this traditional concept of culture that the conflicts which have dominated the political agenda for the past couple of decades – ethnic, sexual, revolutionary nationalist – have been precisely ones in which questions of language, value, identity, and experience have been to the fore. For these political currents, culture is that which refuses or reinforces, celebrates or intimidates, defines or denies; it is brandished as precious weapon or spurned as insolent imposition, cherished as a badge of identity or resisted as that which can do no more than tell you that you don't belong, never did and never will. And all this is surely strange, because culture is not only supposed to be innocent of power: it is the very antithesis of it. Somewhere between Shelley and Tennyson, the poetic and the political, the aesthetic and the institutional, were reconstituted as one another's opposites, as the intimate affective depths of the former became intuitively hostile to the rebarbative abstractions of the latter. Which is to say that one way of theoretically constructing literature came to be at odds with another. In the altercations between Burke and Paine, critics and intellectuals, Englishness and Continentality, the lyrical Donne and the revolutionary Milton, sensuous intuition and a central human wisdom won the day; and this thoroughly alienated theory of writing, now styled as the spontaneous certainties of the human heart, was then ready to do battle with an antagonist known as Theory, which like all such oppositional creeds lacked the conservative's privilege of not having to name himself.

What is subverting traditional culture, however, is not the Left but the Right – not the critics of the system, but the custodians of it. As Bertolt Brecht once remarked, it is capitalism that is radical, not communism. Revolution, his colleague Walter Benjamin added, is not a runaway train but the application of the emergency brake. It is capitalism which pitches every value into question, dissolves familiar life-forms, melts all that is solid into air or soap opera; but it cannot easily withstand the human anxiety, nostalgia and deracination which such perpetual revolution brings in its wake, and has need of something called culture, which it has just been busy undermining, to take care of it. It is in the logic of late capitalism to breed a more fragmentary, eclectic, demotic, cosmopolitan culture than anything dreamt of by Matthew Arnold – a culture which is then a living scandal to its own firmly Arnoldian premisses. Postmodernism then simply inverts this contradiction, seeking to undo the metaphysical, monological aspects of the system with something of its own heterogeneity. At its most callow, such theories complacently underwrite the commodity form, and do so in the name of an opposition to élitism. Nothing could in fact be more offensively élitist, more aloofly academicist, than this cynical celebration of the market-place, which for ordinary men and women has meant homelessness and unemployment rather than random libidinal intensities, and which globally speaking means war as well as cosmopolitan cuisine. Such 'radicalism', one might claim, deserves the reactionaries it drives to apoplexy, the one engendering the other in some stalled dialectic. What concerns the reactionaries is not random libidinal intensities, which they wouldn't recognize at a distance of ten yards, but the supposed erosion of cultural standards; and nowhere is that assumed declension more evident than in language, which is another reason why literary studies have shifted to the eye of the political storm. 'Language is fascist', remarked Roland Barthes, in one of those extravagant hyperboles for which we all loved him; and though it isn't of course true, what is undoubtedly true is that linguistic purity is the last refuge of the paranoid and pathological, the visceral, proto-fascist fantasy of those who feel undermined in their very being by the polyglot social order they themselves have helped to fashion. For language lies at the root of human identity, and to tamper with that is either poetry or treason.

The presumed decline in cultural standards can of course be traced back at least as far as Samuel Johnson, and perhaps to the Book of Exodus. No doubt the Assyrians worried about the brevity of their adolescents' attention span, and the

Phoenicians lost sleep over poor spelling. We should, I think, give no comfort to those who in the name of a fashionable anti-élitism would ignore real evidence of cultural deprivation; though we should remember of course that there is no single index of cultural flourishing or decline. But the present Government's plans for remedying what it sees as the inadequate state of English studies in our schools rest on a drastically mechanistic understanding of the subject, and if implemented will do serious damage to the moral and social development of school students. If the Government goes ahead with its philistine, ill-informed proposals, it will produce a generation of grammatically competent children without a creative idea in their heads. We are dealing here with ideologues for whom language is essentially an elocutionary affair, poetry a kind of metrical patriotism and English literature a semantic Stonehenge. Indeed one wonders why they don't surrender the teaching of English wholesale into the hands of the National Trust. Grammar and spelling are of course part of the material groundwork of social communication, and I know of no English schoolteacher who would disagree; but it is one thing to insist on competence in these areas, and quite another thing to betray a marked hostility to regional, ethnic, and working-class forms of speech, which can only injure the self-esteem of children who already feel rejected. All bureaucrats fear creativity, which is why the Government wants to police and centralize the teaching of a subject vitally concerned with exploration; and if we allow them to succeed, they will simply clone our children in their own bloodless and boring image.

English studies in this country emerged at the same moment as so-called mass culture, and fought from the first a rearguard action against it. But there is another, somewhat more positive story to tell. We think of deconstruction today as a particular way of talking about texts; but when English first saw the light of day in British academia, it represented a deconstruction all in itself. It was the inscription of a certain tentative otherness at the heart of the academic Establishment, and that otherness was a question of both class and gender. English was a popular subject at the time with the ordinary men and women who filled the extra-mural classes up and down the country; but since the university professors of Anglo-Saxon could hardly fill their own classrooms (a defect which I'm sure has been remedied today), these people had hardly anyone to teach them. This was one reason why university English got started, and one reason why it was so ferociously opposed. It represented a link or hinge between academia and the common life, which was not much to the taste of the former. As for gender, women made up two-thirds of the Modern Languages school at Cambridge from which Cambridge English finally evolved, and the first five years of Oxford English saw sixty-nine women students and only eighteen men. It was clearly a problematic, androgynous, cissy sort of thing to read, neither fish nor fowl, an undisciplinable discipline too pleasurable and subjective to be properly examinable; and perhaps the greatest act of institutional violence in the entire history of this non-subject was the abrupt repression of this whole gendered dimension of it as soon as the discipline achieved a modicum of respectability. In post-First World War Cambridge, this inherently deconstructive, dangerously feminized project was recast in the language of muscularity and robustness, of the sinewy and the vigorous, of moral maturity and phallocentric fullness, all of which were found exemplified in perhaps the most pathologically sexist author that the modern English canon – no slouch at such selections – has managed to produce. It is only in recent decades that the literary repressed has returned with a vengeance – that we have begun to register the fact that if literature is centrally concerned with anything, it is not truth or morality but fantasy and desire, and that these perilous forces can no longer be defused by the language of an anodyne romantic idealism, which is never far from the language of male domination. Thomas Warton, first historian of English poetry, knew this in his own way, in his enlightened efforts to salvage from the enormous condescension of classicism that scenario of desire we know as the Gothic.

While others have been busy drafting their film or science fiction courses, or exploring Kant and Kristeva, Oxford has been cautiously reconsidering the question of compulsory Anglo-Saxon. It has, of course, some historical excuse for its belatedness in these affairs – I mean the fact that for a long time it was not only pre-theoretical, but pre-critical too. Leavis never hit it, let alone Derrida, judging at least from some circumspect glances I received when I arrived here over twenty years ago from Leavisian Cambridge. And I am not one of those on the Left who would wish to suppress the more radical aspects of that breathtakingly bold venture for the sake of some reach-me-down caricature of liberal humanism. But it is never too late to mend, and I want to suggest some of the ways in which we might do so. It is, to begin with, no use perpetuating the illusion that the feminist approach to literature can remain equivalent in status to the study of medieval Welsh. If we do not set literary works in their multiple dimensions of desire, if we fail to attend centrally to the motions of sexual power and the unconscious within them, then we can abandon any pretence that we are attending to the words on the page. Something similar goes for literary theory, which means no more than a systematic reflection on literary writing. At present, we have a handful of freaks and fanatics who perversely prefer to know what they are up to when they are reading, as opposed to those normal decent God-fearing folk who don't need to bother. That such reflection should be a purely optional matter, that students should not receive some intensive preliminary training in the history and methodology of their trade, is plainly absurd, and we should be grateful that the medics and aeronautical engineers don't follow our example. Oxford English prides itself on its historical approach to literature – by which it usually means, in an intriguing tautology, the history of literature. But works of art are not born of previous works of art; they have a much less distinguished parentage, which like the Oedipal child they would often enough seek to disavow, and that is material history. To study such works in the material conditions of their production and reception: this, I take it, is what my friend and comrade Raymond Williams meant by cultural materialism, and it would prove a valuable antidote to the chronically idealist assumptions which mark so much of this Faculty's way of doing things.

But which works should we be studying in any case? Not, I think, English literature, but writing in English, which is quite a different matter. The English language is now homeless and centreless, and our syllabus, which by and large stops short at Dover, has dismally failed to register the fact. The centre can no longer hold – which is to say that it won't do to supplement a body of metropolitan work with an exotic neo-colonial fringe. I am afraid that in this respect we are going to have to rethink our assumptions from the ground up – just as we are in respect of the study of popular culture. For it is idle to imagine that a literature which now moves so wholly in the context of film, television, video, and journalism can remain self-identical – can signify exactly what it used to signify, sublimely unblemished by its altered cultural environs. This is not to license some naïvely indiscriminate celebration of such culture, or to suggest that there is anything particularly radical in itself about studying it. An English Faculty replete with doctoral theses on *Neighbours* rather than Nashe may just mean that we've succeeded in killing that too. But why don't we study popular culture? Because it isn't valuable? Well, even by the constrained criteria of the canon, much work in this area, not least in film, would make the grade – and, one might add, some work within the canon only just scrapes in. Objections to such study have little to do with aesthetic value, and everything to do with ideological prejudice.

There is, you may be thinking, something of a utopian smack to these proposals. Will they really get through the next meeting of the Faculty Board? (A body to which I am delighted to say I have finally been appointed, after a mere twenty-three-year probationary period.) They would demand a good deal of energy; but there is plenty of energy about, though much of it is currently confiscated by that perverse misapplication of time and effort we know as the doctoral thesis. And the stakes, after all, really couldn't be higher. For we live, culturally speaking, at a moment of considerable danger, when a particularly virulent brand of humanism poses an insistent threat to civility. In the name of decency, good sense, the richly individual and irreducibly specific, this militant ideology strives to disseminate a version of the human which is culpably blind to all the most powerful determinants of our common life, and to which, it appears, no women, working people, or men and women of colour need apply. It will take more than a few meetings of the Faculty Board to send it packing; but nothing less is surely worthy of our intellectual endeavours.

The English, wrote a nineteenth-century commentator, have little capacity for abstract thought, but a great genius for poetry. It is remarkable how much of our social and intellectual history is crystallized in this simplistic opposition. We can feel, but we can't think – or rather we are wary of those modes of speculative thought which would seek to put a whole form of life into critical question. The opposite of poetry in England is not prose but Jacobinism; and if the phrase literary theory seems to some an oxymoron, it is because literature for the English is an alternative to systematic enquiry, not an object of it. How often are students of literature urged to eschew abstraction and attend to the particular (I was about to say 'concrete', but that's a Cambridge word, not an Oxford one), as though this poor tattered particular, violently ripped from its informing cultural context, were not the most meagre abstraction of all. It is not too much to claim that this whole ideology of the literary work is a traumatized response to the French revolution, which is still alive and kicking in the political unconscious of the nation, and with which English literary criticism conducts a ghostly, interminable dialogue. It is not for nothing that English studies were born at a stroke with that wayward child of Jacobinism known as the theory and practice of Bolshevism. If literary criticism has been so curiously to the fore in English culture, then it is largely because some of the academic disciplines which surround it have disowned their own intellectual responsibilities. For the great speculative questions of truth and justice, of freedom and happiness, have to find a home somewhere; and if an aridly technical philosophy, or a drearily positivist sociology, are no hospitable media for such explorations, then they will be displaced on to a criticism which is simply not intellectually equipped to take this strain. Cultural theory (I will say two words about it at last) is then to be understood as a response to this historical emergency — as an attempt to take up, from within the literary field itself, the questions which cognate disciplines have largely evaded, but to bring something of their own rigour to bear on them. It is born, then, of a double refusal: on the one hand, of the reduction of such questions to mere pseudo-problems or technical exercises which has so marked English philosophy and social science; on the other hand, of that moralistic displacement of them which has been, on the whole, the most that criticism has been able to offer by way of reaction.

To this extent, cultural theory represents a fundamental challenge to our current division of academic labour, which is not least of the reasons why the Establishment finds it such a nuisance. And one does not need to look far beyond Oxford to observe this process at work. For much of the most interesting postgraduate work in the humanities now being carried out here is departmentally vagrant, constantly transgressing the frontiers between traditional subject-areas and in perpetual danger of disappearing down the cracks between them. Where exactly do you go in this place if you wish to work on Jacques Lacan? Hardly to English, since he laboured under the disadvantage of being French; surely not to Modern Languages, since he wasn't much of a literary theorist; not to Philosophy, to be sure, since the Ecrits read rather differently from David Hume. Perhaps you would be sent up the hill to the Warneford psychiatric hospital, and I don't mean to find a supervisor. Of course it is possible to claim that if these fancy foreigners can't find a niche on our syllabus, then this is their look-out rather than ours; but the truth is that the traditional structure of our knowledge is now in the melting-pot, and Oxford has been complacently blind to the fact.

Perhaps the University believes that it can afford such complacency, given its continuing pulling power with students. But in my own Faculty at least, it has been resting on its tarnished laurels a little too long. For it is no good pulling in bright students only to frustrate them; and many of those students are indeed baffled and thwarted by a milieu which appears congenitally suspicious of adventurous thought. It is not long before they learn that the accuracy of their spelling is held in at least as much regard as the subtlety of their insights. If Oxford is not concerned about the growing discrepancy between its own ideological values and those of some of its most promising students, then it ought to be; for its whole pedagogical method is based on the assumption that teacher and student speak fundamentally the same language. What holds the institution together is not bureaucracy or canons or course work, but a consensus so deep that like all such consensuses it is always already in place, the invisible stage-setting of any particular encounter, and will always survive such confrontations intact. But that consensus has in fact been fraying at the edges for some time; and if some of my colleagues have been a little slow to wake up to the fact, it is because it has done its work too well and persuaded them too that it is no more than common sense. But what is common sense in Christ Church is not necessarily common sense in the Caribbean; and the way you read Yeats in Belfast bears only a dim resemblance to the way you read him in Balliol.

Perhaps English studies in this society are gradually changing their spots. Perhaps even Oxford has been brought grudgingly to recognize that it is not only socialists and feminists who read other than disinterestedly. Perhaps the astonishing arrogance of believing that it is others who have political assumptions, while you just take the stuff straight, has been somewhat eroded. One would like to think so, though the fact that three years ago the English Faculty established a post in critical theory and has just seen fit to abolish it might qualify one's optimism somewhat. English in some form or other will of course carry on; and if it succeeds in carrying on as it is at present it will have conveniently evaded a number of uncomfortable challenges. But it will also have paid an enormous price for this conservatism. For if, in Benjamin's phrase, everything just goes on as it is, English studies can abandon an illusion that they have anything of significance to say to those outside the charmed circle of academia. And if this comes about, then it will represent a profound betrayal of their own finest traditions. For all the greatest moments of English criticism, from the Enlightenment to *Scrutiny*, have been points at which, in speaking of the literary work, criticism has found itself unavoidably speaking of more than it – found itself, indeed, mapping the deep structures and central directions of an entire culture. It is not difficult to judge which forms of criticism today are true to that honourable tradition, and which represent a drastic impoverishment of it.

I have spoken of a crisis of culture; but the dangers we confront run a good deal deeper. For men and women do not live by culture alone; and in the narrower sense of the term the great majority of them do not live by it at all. Radical cultural theorists have many faults, but megalomania is unlikely to be among them: it belongs to our very materialism to believe that, in any profound process of social change, we are not likely to be positioned at the centre. It is not the question of whether Alice Walker is greater than Thomas Mann which Washington is weighing up; it is weighing up whether the devastation wreaked by the collapse of the Soviet bloc will permit it easy pickings, or unleash forces which might dangerously destabilize its global rule. It is also watching to see whether the erstwhile post-capitalist nations will prove in the long run reliable partners in the enterprise of subjugating the south, or whether their traumatic insertion into world capitalism will prove so disruptive that they too must be kept constantly under the gun. None of this has much to do with the literary canon; but though culture is by no means central to these matters, it is not simply peripheral either. For the study of human culture addresses itself to the question of how these world-historical issues shape up in lived experience, how they pass through the defiles of the signifier to emerge as symbolic meaning; and to this extent the study of culture concerns itself with what is most distinctive about humanity, if not with what is most crucial to its survival and well-being. Culture can be defined in one sense as that which is surplus, excessive, beyond the strict material measure; but that capacity for self-transgression and self-transcendence is precisely the measure of our humanity.

This is not, curiously enough, how they view the matter in Downing Street. The problem for them is not, as they like to proclaim, that there is too little culture around, but that there is a risk of there being too much. There is a real danger, in short, of producing a population with reasonably high cultural expectations in a society which cannot even provide them with employment. And since this is a classic recipe for political disaffection, we may be sure that the Government's more clairvoyant commissars are already bending its ear about the undesirability of educating the young beyond their station. No government can afford its people to be at once idle and well-educated; and if it can do little about the former, given a grave economic crisis of the system under which we live, then it is highly probable that it will try even more strenuously than it has already to do something about the latter. We will be thrown back to that condition, elegiacally recollected by our reactionaries, in which culture will once again be the preserve of the élite, while a vocationalism without vocations will be the destiny of the people.

But it is the past, as well as the future, which radicals seek to protect; for, as Walter Benjamin remarked, not even that will be safe from the enemy if he wins. Benjamin's habit was to look backwards rather than forwards, finding a desirable future already dimly adumbrated in the hopes of those oppressed ancestors whose projects of emancipation had been crushed in their own time. 'It is not', as he comments, 'dreams of liberated grandchildren which stir men and women to revolt, but memories of enslaved ancestors.' And those who do not remember are, as Freud warned us, compelled to repeat. If radicals do not succeed in their current endeavours, then it is not only our progeny who will suffer the consequences; it is also the Jude Fawleys and the early students of St Catherine's College, those men and women who stood for generations outside the locked gates of this University, and dreamed fruitlessly of a condition in which culture might be available for all. If we fail, then we fail them too, freezing them in eternal unfulfilment. Looking backwards is second nature to Oxford; it is about time that it found a way of doing so, examining the exclusions on which it was historically built, which would be a way of moving towards a more just and rational future.

Notes

1   Quoted by Stefan Collini, 'Genealogies of Englishness: Literary History and Cultural Criticism in Modern Britain', in Ciaran Brady (ed.), *Ideology and the Historians* (Dublin, 1991), p. 247.
2   Quoted by Chris Baldick, *The Social Mission of English Criticism* (Oxford, 1983), p. 74.
3   Quoted by Baldick, *Social Mission*, pp. 88–9.

12 Body Work

There will soon be more bodies in contemporary criticism than on the fields of Waterloo. Mangled members, tormented torsos, bodies emblazoned or incarcerated, disciplined or desirous: it is becoming harder, given this fashionable turn to the somatic, to distinguish the literary theory section of the local bookshop from the soft porn shelves, sort out the latest Jackie Collins from the later Roland Barthes. Many an eager masturbator must have borne away some sexy-looking tome only to find himself reading up on the floating signifier.

Sexuality began in the late Sixties, as an extension of radical politics into regions it had lamentably neglected. But as revolutionary energies were gradually rolled back, an increased concern with the body came to take their place. In the Seventies we had class struggle and sexuality; in the Eighties we had sexuality. Erstwhile Leninists were now card-carrying Lacanians, and everyone shifted over from production to perversion. The socialism of Guevara gave way to the somatics of Foucault and Fonda. As usual, this happened on the most spectacular scale in the United States, which had never had much grasp of socialism to begin with, and where the Left could find in the high Gallic pessimism of Foucault a sophisticated rationale for their own political paralysis. The fetish, for Freud, is that which plugs an intolerable gap; and sexuality itself has now become the greatest fetish of all. In classrooms from Berkeley to the Bronx, there's nothing more sexy than sex; and a concern with physical health has now escalated into an American national sickness.

The body, then, has been at once the focus for a vital deepening of radical politics, and a desperate displacement of them. There is a glamorous kind of materialism about body talk, which compensates for certain more classical strains of materialism now in dire trouble. As a stubbornly local phenomenon, the body fits well enough with the postmodernist nervousness of grand narratives; as well as with American pragmatism's love affair with the concrete. Since I know where my left foot is at any particular moment without needing to use a compass, the body offers a mode of cognition more intimate and internal than a now much scorned Enlightenment rationality. In this sense, a theory of the body runs the risk of self-contradiction, recovering for the mind just what was meant to deflate it; but if the body provides us with a little sensuous certitude in a progressively abstract world, it is also an elaborately coded affair, and so caters to the intellectual's passion for complexity. It is the hinge between Nature and Culture, offering surety and subtlety in equal measure. Indeed what else is psychoanalysis but the thinking person's horror fiction, a discourse which wonderfully combines the cerebral and the sensational?

For the philosophers and psychologists, 'mind' is still a sexy notion; but literary critics have always been wary of the unhoused intellect, preferring their concepts to come fleshed and incarnate. To this extent, the new somatics is simply the return in a more sophisticated register of the old organicism. Instead of poems as plump as an apple, we have texts as material as an armpit. The turn to the body sprang first from a structuralist hostility to consciousness, and represents the final expulsion of the ghost from the machine. Bodies are ways of talking about human subjects without going all sloppily humanist, avoiding that messy interiority which drove Michel Foucault up the wall. For all its carnivalesque cavortings, body talk is thus our latest brand of repression; and the postmodern cult of pleasure, not least in its Parisian variants, is a very solemn, high-toned affair. Either, like Peter Brooks in *Body Work*, you write about this bizarre stuff in an impeccably academic idiom, thus risking an incongruous clash of form and content; or, like some of his American colleagues, you let the body take over your script and risk disappearing up your own pretentious wordplay and idle anecdotalism.

For the new somatics, not any old body will do. If the libidinal body is in, the labouring body is out. There are mutilated bodies galore, but few malnourished ones, belonging as they do to bits of the globe beyond the purview of Yale. The finest body book of our era is Maurice Merleau-Ponty's *Phenomenology of Perception*; but this, with its humanist sense of the body as practice and project, is now distinctly *passé*. The shift from Merleau-Ponty to Foucault is one from the body as relation to the body as object. For Merleau-Ponty, the body is 'where there is something to be done'; for the new somatics, the body is where something – gazing, imprinting, regimenting – is being done to you. It used to be called alienation, but that implies the existence of an interiority to be alienated – a proposition of which somatic criticism is deeply sceptical.

It is part of the damage done by a Cartesian tradition that one of the first images the word 'body' brings to mind is that of a corpse. To announce the presence of a body in the library is by no means to allude to an industrious reader. Thomas Aquinas thought that there was no such thing as a dead body, only the remains of a living one. Christianity pins its faith to the resurrection of the body, not to the immortality of the soul; and this is just a way of saying that if the afterlife doesn't somehow involve my body, it doesn't involve me. The Christian faith has, of course, much to say of the soul too; but for Aquinas the soul is the 'form' of the body, as wedded to it as a meaning to a word. It was a point taken up by the later Wittgenstein, who once remarked that the body was the best image we had of the human soul. Soul talk was necessary for those confronted with a mechanical materialism which saw no real distinction between the human body and a banana. Both, after all, were material objects. In this context, you needed a language which sought to capture what differentiates the human body from the things around it. Soul talk at its best was a way of doing this. It easily backfired, though, since it is wellnigh impossible not to picture the soul as a ghostly sort of body, and so find yourself simply slipping a fuzzy object inside a grosser one as a way of accounting for the latter's uniqueness. But the human body does not differ from jam jars and elastic bands because it secretes a special entity they lack. it differs from them because it is a point from which they can be organised into significant projects. Unlike them, it is creative; and if we had had a language which adequately captured the human body's creativity we would perhaps never have needed soul talk in the first place.

What is special about the human body, then, is just its capacity to transform itself in the process of transforming the material bodies which surround it. It is in this sense that it is anterior to those bodies, a kind of 'surplus' over and above them, rather than an object to be reckoned up alongside them. But if the body is a self-transformative practice, then it is not identical with itself in the manner of corpses and dustbins; and this is a claim that soul language is also trying to make. It is just that it locates that non–self-identity in the body's having some invisible extra which is really me, rather than seeing the real me as a creative interaction with my world – a creative interaction made possible and necessary by the peculiar sort of body I have. Badgers and squirrels can't be said to have souls, however winsome they may be, because their bodies are not the kind that can work on the world and so necessarily enter into linguistic communion with those of their kind. Soulless bodies are those which do not speak. The human body is that which is able to make something of what makes it; and in this sense its paradigm is language, a given which continually generates the unpredictable.

One can see the point, then, of dropping talk of having a body and substituting talk of being one. If my body is something I use or possess, then it might be thought that I would need another body inside this one to do the possessing, and so on *ad infinitum*. But this resolute anti-dualism, though salutary enough in its way, is untrue to a lot of our intuitions about the lump of flesh we lug around. It makes perfect sense to speak of using my body, as when I suspend it courageously across a crevice so that my companions can scramble to safety across my spine. Nothing is more fashionable in modern cultural theory than talk of objectifying the body, feeling somehow that it is not my own; but though plenty of objectionable objectification goes on, not least in sexual conduct, the fact remains that the human body is indeed a material object, and that this is an essential component of anything more creative we get up to. Unless you can objectify me, there can be no question of relationship between us. The body which lays me open to exploitation is also the ground of all possible communication. It was Marx who ticked off Hegel for equating objectification with alienation, and the rampant culturalism which marks today's avant-garde theory needs to learn the lesson anew.

Merleau-Ponty recalls us to the fleshly self, to the situated, somatic, incarnate nature of being. His colleague Sartre has a somewhat less upbeat narrative to tell of the body as that 'outside' of ourselves we can never quite get a fix on, that otherness which threatens to deliver us to the petrifying gaze of the observer. Sartre is anti-Cartesian enough in his notion of consciousness as mere hankering vacancy, but sufficiently Cartesian in his sense of the nameless gap which separates mind from members. The truth does not, as the liberals say, lie somewhere in between, but in the impossible tension between these two versions of bodiliness, both of which are phenomenologically just. It is not quite true that I have a body, and not quite true that I am one either. This deadlock runs all the way through psychoanalysis, which recognises that the body is constructed in language, and knows too that it will never entirely be at home there. For Jacques Lacan, the body articulates itself in signs only to find itself betrayed by them. The transcendental signifier which would say it all, wrap up my demand and deliver it whole and entire to you, is that imposture known as the phallus; and since the phallus does not exist, my bodily desire is condemned to grope its laborious way from partial sign to partial sign, diffusing and fragmenting as it goes. It is no doubt for this reason that Romanticism has dreamt of the word of words, of a discourse as firm as flesh, or of a body which has all the universal availability of a language while sacrificing none of its sensuous substance. And there is a sense in which contemporary literary theory, with its excited talk of the materiality of the text, its constant interchanges of the somatic and semiotic, is the latest version of this dream, in suitably sceptical postmodernist style. 'Material' is one of the great buzz-words of such thinking, a sound at which all progressive heads reverently bow; but it has been stretched beyond all feasible sense. For if even meaning is material, then there is probably nothing which is not, and the term simply cancels all the way through. The new somatics restores us to the creaturely in an abstract world; but in banishing the ghost from the machine, it risks dispelling subjectivity itself as no more than a humanist myth.

Body Work is one of the more distinguished products of a rather suspect genre. Peter Brooks ranges with admirable acuity from Sophocles to scopophilia, the novel to the visual arts. The book is lavishly furnished with plates of the naked female form, so that male readers can gaze upon the way they gaze upon them. Brooks is one of our best Freudian critics, and here brings a wealth of psychoanalytic insight to bear on the body in Balzac and Rousseau, James and Zola, Gauguin and Mary Shelley. If there is a unifying theme in this impressively diverse exploration, it is the way the body must be somehow marked or signed in order to enter narrative, pass from brute fact to active meaning. 'Signing the body,' Brooks writes, 'indicates its recovery for the realm of the semiotic'; and from Oedipus to Hans Castorp he maps this recurrent conversion of flesh into text.

This is a fertile notion; but it has to be said that it is one of the few genuinely original bits of conceptualisation in an oddly predictable book. There is the sense of a rather conventional mind at work on unconventional materials; and few of its manoeuvres are as arresting as Brooks's earlier reflections on the unconscious dynamics of narrative in *Reading for the Plot*. The orthodox heterodoxy of the new somatics remains firmly in place, determining each critical move; and though this results in some brilliant local readings, the book never offers to press beyond a now familiar set of motifs. Thus, Brooks has some excellent comments on the relations between privacy, the novel and an increasing attention to the body. The rise of the novel, he points out, is closely tied to the emergence of a private sphere of domestic relations, and the theme of the private body rudely invaded is central to writers like Richardson and Madame de Lafayette. It is also a vital concern in Rousseau, with his tiresome compulsion to bare his behind, and Brooks has a good deal to say of the *Confessions* and *La Nouvelle Héloise*. But what he has to tell us, in effect, is that the body in Rousseau is a place 'where scenarios of desire, fulfilment, censorship, and repression are played out'; and this is hardly world-shaking news.

There are some genuinely original insights about the staging of the body in the French Revolution, which Brooks, who in a previous work pulled off the improbable trick of making the topic of melodrama theoretically exciting, sees as a melodramatising of it. But he then turns to Balzac and spends a good deal of time meticulously hunting down semiotic markings of the body in his work. This is a fresh way of reading the texts, but it does little to elaborate the 'marking' theory itself, beyond offering yet more exotic instances of it. There is an equally scrupulous account of the fetishisation of Emma Bovary's body, which, so Brooks deftly demonstrates, is always perceived in bits and pieces; but while this illuminates Flaubert interestingly enough, it fails to push forward a reach-me-down psychoanalytic discourse of metonymies and objectifying gazes, desiring subjects and recalcitrant objects, exhibitionism and epistemophilia. Zola's *Nana* is seen as engaged in a fruitless pursuit of the truly naked body, the real material thing, as it strips its heroine bare; but we are still caught here within a constricted language of concealing and revealing, nudity as culture and nakedness as nature. A chapter on Gauguin deals with the primitivist, exoticised body – a way of seeing which Brooks considers is not just stereotypically objectionable but actually turned by the artist to some productive uses. This is an unpredictable move to make; but it is made within a still rather predictable set of critical strategies.

It has been apparent for some time that literary theory is in something of a cul-de-sac. Derrida has written little of substance for years; de Man produced his most stunning effects by dying and leaving an unsavoury past to be unearthed; Marxism is licking its wounds after the collapse of the post-capitalist bureaucracies. The pathbreaking epoch of Greimas and the early Kristeva, the Althusserians and avant-garde film theorists, radical Barthes and reader-response theory, now lies a couple of decades behind us. Few truly innovative theoretical moves have been made since; the new historicism, for all its occasional brilliance, is theoretically speaking a set of footnotes to Foucault. It is as though the theory is all in place, and all that remains to be done is run yet more texts through it. This, in effect, is what

Body Work does; but Peter Brooks has proved himself capable in the past of generating genuinely new ideas, and it is an ominous sign of the critical times that this latest book never offers to transfigure the concepts on which it relies. Caught in its modish conceptual universe, *Body Work* is quite incapable of rounding upon itself to inquire into its own historical conditions of existence. Why produce three hundred pages on the body in the first place? Well, it's all the rage at the Modern Language Association. But to produce a less banal response to that question would require a rather grander narrative than American criticism, for entirely understandable reasons, is at present prepared to deliver.

Part III   Marxism and Critical Theory

Introduction

In 1976 any critic working in England and attempting to formulate a systematic Marxist theory of literature was likely to feel 'acutely bereft of a tradition'.[1] Yet *Criticism and Ideology*, which sets out to do just that, is a bold and brilliant book. The task it sets itself is hugely ambitious. It begins with a consideration of the ideological factors which have shaped literary criticism, including the interests of the influential *Scrutiny* group in Cambridge. It then proposes a Marxist critical method capable of dealing with both general (economic) and literary modes of production, as well as with a range of ideological components (general, authorial and aesthetic). Subtly reworking some of the most recent theories of ideology in the work of Louis Althusser and Pierre Macherey, Eagleton offers a sophisticated 'science of the text' which integrates a semiotic approach to language and a materialist conception of history. The closing chapters of the book discuss the relations between text and ideology, and consider the problem of aesthetic value.

'Ideology and Literary Form' (only part of which is reprinted here as Chapter 13) was the first section of the book to be written. By Eagleton's own admission, the section is 'excessively cryptic and elliptical' in style and 'partial and reductive' in some of its readings of literary texts.[2] Its importance, however, lies in its conceptualization of the relations between literature and the changing ideological formations in which it is produced. Its underlying purpose is a critique of the social and aesthetic 'organicism' with which certain writers, especially in the nineteenth century, seek to conceal or resolve historical conflict.

In some ways, 'Ideology and Literary Form' is a reworking of the earlier 'Culture and Society' arguments advanced by Raymond Williams and by Eagleton himself (see Chapter 8). 'Organicism', in this respect, is ideologically consistent with the Romantic idealism and liberal humanism that informs some of the most influential definitions of culture from the late eighteenth century onwards. This time, however, Eagleton employs a much more dynamic model of ideology, one which is vitally connected to class power and dominance through Antonio Gramsci's fertile conception of 'hegemony'. Like Gramsci, Eagleton insists that culture, as well as politics and economics, has a crucial role in attaining and preserving class dominance.

Gramsci's point is well illustrated in the efforts of Matthew Arnold to bring about a radical realignment of class forces in Victorian Britain. Whatever altruism it possesses, Arnold's social criticism is aimed primarily at converting a materialistic, philistine middle class into 'a truly *hegemonic* class – a class with cultural resources adequate to the predicament it has come to hold in history'. The moral and intellectual leadership that Gramsci demands for the modern proletariat is sought by Arnold on behalf of the Victorian middle class. As Victorian capitalism assumes a more corporate form through increasing centralization in all areas – industry, agriculture, the railways, education, public health – it turns to culture and other organic ideals as justification and compensation for the political inequalities and divisions it creates.

The notion of organic form finds a parallel in the aesthetics of nineteenth-century fiction, as George Eliot's novels clearly testify. Eagleton discovers in these novels a potentially tragic collision between two forms of mid-Victorian ideology: the Romantic individualism of an earlier generation and the growing 'corporatism' of a later phase of social and cultural history. The novels of Dickens, like those of Eliot, seek to resolve ideological conflicts through literary devices, but Dickens's fiction shows more explicitly how conflict inscribes itself in the ruptures and fissures of the text and in a self-contradictory mixing of fictional modes and genres: gothic, romance, moral fable, popular theatre, journalism and didacticism.

A critique of organicist ideology is carried through to *Walter Benjamin or Towards a Revolutionary Criticism* (1981), a book that seems in its very style and structure to be a flagrant disavowal of organic unity. *Walter Benjamin* wilfully eschews the niceties and proprieties of conventional academic discourse. It is neither an introduction to Benjamin's writing nor a summary of his principal works. Instead, it adopts a typical device from Benjamin in blasting his work out of the continuum of history, so that it might illuminate the problems facing a revolutionary criticism in the present. In the period between *Criticism and Ideology* and *Walter Benjamin*, socialism was itself undergoing transformation on a global scale, and Marxist literary theory was shifting its attention from textual politics to problems of cultural production. At the same time, Eagleton was experimenting with Brechtian political drama and poetry, rethinking the relations between socialist theory and cultural practice, and increasingly turning his attention to the political uses of theatre and comedy.

The opening section of *Walter Benjamin* (reprinted here as Chapter 14) shows how Benjamin's work anticipates many of the preoccupations of post-structuralism, and yet does so in a way that reinforces, rather than undermines, its author's political commitments. Characteristic of the book is the way in which Eagleton brings the writings of Benjamin to bear on English literary criticism, simultaneously allowing that conjuncture of ideas to illuminate Benjamin's own revolutionary procedures. Benjamin's interest in the seventeenth-century *Trauerspiel* or baroque allegory in *The Origin of German Tragic Drama* is brought into critical alignment with the interests of T. S. Eliot and F. R. Leavis in seventeenth-century poetry. Eagleton argues that what Eliot and Leavis object to in the language of Milton is that 'surplus of signification' that post-structuralism knows as *écriture*. This is also what Benjamin discovers in the *Trauerspiel*, but the profound gulf between materiality and meaning earns his fullest critical enquiry rather than his critical disdain. What Eliot and Leavis regard as a 'dissociation of sensibility' betrays a fetishism of the organic and a particular ideological construction of seventeenth-century England.

Benjamin's reading of the *Trauerspiel* suggests an approach to *Paradise Lost* that moves beyond the formalism of Eliot and Leavis, and locates its revolutionary origins in its radically unstable signification. What surprises Eagleton is that Milton's critics should have sought a harmonious resolution of form and content, words and objects, in a poem so 'massively and self-consciously "literary"', so 'scarred and contorted by the labour of its own production'. The privileged status of *script* and the significance of *the word* in the English puritan tradition raise questions about the problematic nature of fiction in the eighteenth century, briefly diverting the essay into a scintillating deconstruction of *Tristram Shandy* and *Gulliver's Travels*. As well as informing a new, productive reading of Milton's revolutionary epic, *The Origin of German Tragic Drama* is seen to prefigure Benjamin's later defence of Brechtian drama, which like the *Trauerspiel* lays bare its own devices and switches ostentatiously between them.

'Deconstruction and Human Rights' (Chapter 15) was written for the Oxford Amnesty Lectures in 1992. As part of a fund-raising initiative for Amnesty International, a number of speakers of international reputation, including Hélène Cixous, Julia Kristeva, Edward Said and Jacques Derrida, were invited to lecture in Oxford on a subject related to human rights. Lecturers were asked to consider 'the consequences of the deconstruction of the self for the liberal tradition. Does the self as constructed by the liberal tradition still exist? If not, whose human rights are we defending?'[3] As Barbara Johnson points out in her introduction to the published lectures in *Freedom and Interpretation*, the critique of the subject is one of the most controversial aspects of a thoroughgoing deconstruction of the foundational ideals of Western civilization. It proposes that 'the self' or 'the subject' is not a free, rational, autonomous entity, but one shaped and disciplined, as Michel Foucault argues, by the institutional constraints of family, school, the factories, the police and the prisons. In the psychoanalytic writings of Jacques Lacan, the notion of a stable, unified self is an imaginary or illusory condition.

Eagleton detects 'an ethical turn' in deconstruction, but one that shifts the whole question of ethics from a subjective to a linguistic register. Ethical matters are then reconstructed as functions of linguistic predicaments rather than the exercise of the individual will. He notes in the work of Jacques Derrida a certain embarrassment with political ethics that manifests itself in a 'finespun obliquity on issues of central political importance'. In this respect, neither liberal nor post-structuralist theory seems able to countenance the fact that there are 'key political struggles that someone is going to have to win and someone will have to lose'. In an effort to find a more productive theory of ethical and political responsibility, the essay turns to the ancient moral tradition of republican virtue in which free and equal citizens devoted themselves to the public realm. In the eighteenth century this dispensation yielded to the modern world of commerce, and 'virtue' gave way to 'manners' and economic privileges. Eagleton sees Marxism as 'a strikingly original combination of these two modes of thought and practice', a bold synthesis of civic humanism and commercial humanism. The essay welcomes the opportunity for Marxism and deconstruction to join hands in transgressing 'the strict economy' of bourgeois morality.

One of the salient characteristics of Eagleton's work to date is the increasingly sharp focus it has given to the concept of ideology. Among his most ambitious projects in the 1990s has been the attempt to clarify and refine the notion of ideology at a time when 'the end of ideology' is being declared in some theoretical circles. *Ideology*, a rich and expansive study of the subject published in 1991, acknowledges the pressing contradiction that, in a world so obviously racked by ideological conflict, the very concept of ideology seems to have been rendered obsolete in postmodern and post-structuralist thinking. Eagleton surmises that the explanation for this demoting of ideology has much to do with a postmodern scepticism about truth and representation, and with a general reformation of the relations between rationality, interests and power.

The great value of *Ideology* is its exhaustive coverage of the different lineages in the history of the concept. In the opening chapter of the book, Eagleton presents no fewer than sixteen definitions of ideology, ranging from 'the process of production of meanings, signs and values in social life' to 'the process whereby social life is converted to a natural reality'.[4] The book proceeds to examine some of the central contradictions surrounding ideology. Is ideology *any* set of beliefs motivated by social interests or does it pertain to the *dominant* forms of thought in society? Can it be both illusion *and* the medium in which we make sense of the world? Is ideology a pejorative or a neutral term? Is its function epistemological (to do with true or false cognition) or sociological (to do with the function of ideas within social life rather than their reality or unreality)? Eagleton notes that some of the most productive currents in Marxist theory have straddled the epistemological and sociological definitions of ideology. He suggests that both the wider and the narrower senses of ideology have their uses, despite their mutual incompatibility. His own response to this vast array of meanings and definitions is the candidly Brechtian one of 'use what you can'.

The study of ideology printed here as Chapter 16 is the introduction to the Longman Critical Reader on ideology (1994), the purpose of which is to make available some of the classic texts on ideology and to illustrate the variety of modern debate on the topic. Eagleton begins by contrasting some of the negative definitions of ideology as false consciousness or fanaticism with its more positive eighteenth-century Enlightenment definition as the study of knowledge or ideas. How was it, he asks, that a term synonymous with scientific rationalism should end up denoting idle abstraction and illusion? His investigation into this instability of meanings takes him into some of the prominent debates within the Marxist heritage, from Marx and Engels to Lukács, Gramsci and Althusser. He ventures a plausible definition of ideolog, based on Michel Foucault's notion of competing and conflicting discourses: 'ideologies are sets of discursive strategies for displacing, recasting or spuriously accounting for realities which prove embarrassing to a ruling power; and in doing so, they contribute to that power's self-legitimation'. Even so, he concedes that this formulation doesn't cover those instances in which ideology is used as a positive description of radical or oppositional ideas – feminist ideology or republican ideology, for instance. It is reassuring in the midst of his vigorous debate to be reminded that nobody has yet come up with a single adequate definition of ideology.

The introduction to *Marxist Literary Theory* (Chapter 17) confronts the crisis in Marxism as it turns in the 1990s to consider the question of its own survival. Was Marxism totally discredited, it asks, by the overthrow of the ruling bureaucracies in Eastern Europe? 'Did the fall of the Berlin Wall mean that Georg Lukács's remarks on Balzac were now valueless?' While accepting that theory and practice don't always function harmoniously together, Eagleton nevertheless dismisses the position that would pronounce Marxism politically bankrupt and yet still regard it as a valid tool of intellectual analysis. Marxism, he claims, is not in crisis on account of a disabling political disillusionment over the disintegration of the Soviet Union and its influence in Eastern Europe, but as the consequence of a more general sense of impotence and frustration as capitalism proceeds without an effective political opposition. The essay steps back from the prevailing crisis and adopts a more hopeful position, acknowledging socialism as one of the greatest reform movements in the history of humanity and one accustomed to serious set-backs.

The purpose of the essay is not to dwell on the seeming decline of Marxism but to offer an assessment of its contribution to cultural theory. Eagleton outlines four principal kinds of Marxist criticism, each corresponding to a particular set of interests or concerns, and also to particular historical phases. What he terms *anthropological* criticism is that current of Marxist cultural enquiry that asks how art relates to myth, ritual, religion and language. It asks about the function of art within social evolution and about the nature of aesthetic response. Anthropological criticism belongs to the period of the Second International (1889–1914), and establishes a line of thought that extends to Ernst Fischer's *The Necessity of Art* (1959). In contrast, *political* criticism is a more explicitly polemical and interventionist mode of enquiry, represented by Lenin's pamphlets on Tolstoy and by Trotsky's *Literature and Revolution*. It belongs to the years of the Russian revolution and has its triumph in socialist realism.

The third wave of Marxist criticism is *ideological*; it attends to the ideology of form and considers the nature of social consciousness in literary works. Among other things, it asks if art is a reflection, displacement, transformation or reproduction of its social conditions. This is the tradition of Lukács, Gramsci, Bloch, Adorno, Goldmann and Althusser. The final mode of criticism is *economic* and concerns itself with modes of cultural production, including the institutions of patronage and the social contexts of producers and recipients. This tradition has its roots in Brecht's epic theatre and in Walter Benjamin's seminal essay 'The Author as Producer'. In Britain it is well represented by what Raymond Williams came to describe as 'cultural materialism'. What the essay ultimately presents is not just a well-informed survey of Marxist cultural debate, but a political intervention at a critical moment in that debate. Some of the most impressive Marxist criticism, it reveals, has been 'the product of a cultural displacement occasioned by political deadlock'. While this hardly helps to reunite theory and practice in the present, it nevertheless suggests the need to keep alive the various strands of Marxist cultural criticism as important resources of hope for the future.

'Marxism without Marxism' (Chapter 18) offers another perspective on the evasive and ambiguous politics of deconstruction. Jacques Derrida's *Specters of Marx* (1995) seems to presage a new post-structuralist alignment with Marxism, but Eagleton remains deeply unimpressed. While not wishing to be unwelcoming towards such a renowned fellow-traveller, he cannot help but suspect that Derrida has turned to Marxism at a time when its marginality makes it all the more alluring for post-structuralist practice. Derrida's revisionist account of deconstruction as a radical creed 'in the spirit of Marxism' sits oddly alongside what passes for deconstruction in North America, where deconstruction has functioned mainly as a substitute politics or displaced dissent.

Eagleton detects in *Specters of Marx* a genuine outrage at the late capitalist world order, but also an opportunistic move in which Marxism is adopted as an instrument of critique but never seriously entertained as an effective and organized socialist politics. Derrida's 'Marxism without Marxism' is one in which the spirit of Marxism prevails but its actual historical progression is treated with supreme indifference. His 'New International' without name and without party is given recognition in this essay only as 'the ultimate post-structuralist fantasy'.

Notes

1 *Criticism and Ideology* (London: New Left Books, 1976; Verso, 1978), p. 7.
2 *Criticism and Ideology*, p. 7.
3 Barbara Johnson (ed.), *Freedom and Interpretation* (New York: Basic Books, 1993), p. 2.
4 *Ideology: An Introduction* (London and New York: Verso), pp. 1–2.

13 Ideology and Literary Form

Bourgeois ideology in nineteenth-century England confronted a severe problem. Nurtured in the sparse soil of Utilitarianism, it was unable to produce a set of potently affective mythologies which might permeate the texture of lived experience of English society. It needed, therefore, to have constant resort to the Romantic humanist heritage – to that nebulous compound of Burkean conservatism and German idealism, transmitted by the later Coleridge to Carlyle, Disraeli, Arnold and Ruskin, which has become known as the 'Culture and Society' tradition. It was a tradition which offered an idealist critique of bourgeois social relations, coupled with a consecration of the rights of capital. The peculiar complexity of English nineteenth-century ideology, founded on a complex conjuncture of bourgeois and aristocratic classes within the dominant bloc, lies in part in this contradictory unity between what Antonio Gramsci refers to as 'organic' and 'traditional' elements.[1] An impoverished empiricism, unable to rise to the level of an ideology proper, is driven to exploit the fertile symbolic resources of Romantic humanism, drawing on its metaphysical sanctions and quasi-feudalist social models to ratify bourgeois property relations. The 'Culture and Society' tradition is the literary record of this ideological conjuncture; John Stuart Mill, mechanistically harnessing Coleridge to Bentham in the late eighteen-thirties, provides one of its more palpable instances.[2]

Gramsci, indeed, has commented directly on this ideological formation in nineteenth-century England. 'There is a very extensive category of organic intellectuals – those, that is, who come into existence on the same industrial terrain as the economic group – but in the higher sphere we find that the old land-owning class preserves its position of virtual monopoly. It loses its economic supremacy and is assimilated as "traditional intellectuals" and as directive (*dirigente*) group by the new group in power. The old land-owning aristocracy is joined to the industrialists by a kind of suture which is precisely that which in other countries unites the traditional intellectuals with the new dominant classes.'[3]

One aspect of this assimilation can be seen in bourgeois ideology's growing dependence on 'organicist' concepts of society.[4] As Victorian capitalism assumes increasingly corporate forms, it turns to the social and aesthetic organicism of the Romantic humanist tradition, discovering in art models of totality and affectivity relevant to its ideological requirements. During the second half of the century, the initially poetic notion of 'organic form' becomes progressively extended to the dominant literary mode of the time, fiction. A serious aesthetics of fiction consequently develops, to discover its major ideologue at the end of the century in Henry James.[5] This essay will survey, in skeletal and schematic form, some relations between a sector of the major literature of the last century and the ideological formations in which it is set; it will do so by taking the concept of 'organic form' as one crucial nexus between history and literary production.[6]

1 Matthew Arnold

The assimilation of 'traditional' to 'organic' intellectuals of which Gramsci speaks is the key to the historic significance of that powerful Victorian poet, critic and ideologue, Matthew Arnold. Arnold, apostle of Culture and scourge of bourgeois philistinism, has always exercised a potent influence on modern liberals and even on socialists; did he not claim, after all, that Culture 'seeks to do away with classes', that 'the men of culture are the true apostles of equality'?[7] Yet Arnold's project is not, need one say, the revolutionary abolition of class-society. Quite the reverse: it is to effect a radical realignment of class-forces within the ruling bloc of Victorian England, so as more effectively to incorporate the proletariat. The thrust of Arnold's social criticism is to convert a visionless, sectarian bourgeoisie, pragmatically sunk in its own material interests, into a truly *hegemonic* class – a class with cultural resources adequate to the predominance it has come to hold in history. For Arnold, the aristocracy is rapidly losing political hegemony, but its historical successor, the bourgeoisie, is disastrously unprepared to assume it.[8] He insists, accordingly, on the need for the middle class to attain to more corporate, cultivated forms, and to do so by enshrining itself in a civilising state educational system. What Antonio Gramsci demands for the modern proletariat – that it should achieve 'moral and intellectual leadership' as well as material power – Matthew Arnold seeks for the Victorian bourgeoisie. The proletariat, Gramsci argues in *The Modern Prince*, 'alongside the problem of the conquest of political power and of economic power must, just as it has thought about organising itself for politics and for economics, think also about organising itself for culture'.[9] Arnold's own programme could hardly be more deftly formulated.

It is this ideological necessity which underlies Arnold's apparently altruistic efforts to 'Hellenise' his stiff-necked fellow-bourgeois. State-established schools, by linking the middle class to 'the best culture of their nation', will confer on them 'a greatness and a noble spirit, which the tone of these classes is not of itself at present adequate to impart'.[10] Such an enterprise, Arnold claims, 'would really augment their self-respect and moral force; it would truly fuse them with the class above, and tend to bring about for them the equality which they are entitled to desire'.[11] The bourgeoisie is bereft of that pervasive spiritual predominance which has ratified aristocratic rule; unless it can rapidly achieve such cultural supremacy, installing itself as a truly national class at the 'intellectual centre' of society, it will fail in its historical mission of politically incorporating the class it exploits:

> It is of itself a serious calamity for a nation that its tone of feeling and grandeur of spirit should be lowered or dulled. But the calamity appears far more serious still when we consider that the middle classes, remaining as they are now, with their narrow, harsh, unintelligent, and unattractive spirit and culture, will almost certainly fail to mould or assimilate the masses below them, whose sympathies are at the present moment actually wider and more liberal than theirs. They arrive, these masses, eager to enter into possession of the world, to gain a more vivid sense of their own life and activity. In this their irrepressible development, their natural educators and initiators are those immediately above them, the middle classes. If these classes cannot win their sympathy or give them their direction, society is in danger of falling into anarchy.[12]

The bourgeoisie, then, must appropriate the civilised aesthetic heritage of a failing aristocracy in order to equip itself with an ideology (Culture) capable of penetrating the masses. In a 'cultured, liberalised, ennobled, transformed middle class', the proletariat will have 'a point towards which it may with joy direct its aspirations'.[13]

Arnold's notion of class hegemony, it should be noted at once, is theoretically invalid. It is, indeed, a classic illustration of that historicist error which grasps ideology as the 'world view' of a 'class-subject', a spiritual vision imposed by that class on society as a whole.[14] Yet Arnold's argument as a whole marks a significant mutation in nineteenth-century liberalism. As Victorian capitalism is driven to transcend its earlier individualist phase and organise itself into more corporate forms, so the classical liberalism which finds a late, defeated expression in John Stuart Mill's *On Liberty* (1859) suffers a parallel transformation. Arnold believes that 'all tendencies of human nature are in themselves vital and profitable';[15] but it is now imperative to harmonise them within a cohesive, conflict-free order – within, in a word, Culture. Spiritual *laissez-faire* is historically obsolete; it must yield to a faith in 'the nation in its collective and corporate character, entrusted with stringent powers for the general advantage, and controlling individual wills in the name of an interest wider than that of individuals'.[16] A bourgeoisie sunk in individualist dogmatism must now consider whether state action, 'which was once dangerous, may [not] become, not only without danger in itself, but the means of helping us against dangers from another quarter'.[17]

The corporate state, then, is the social locus of Culture – of that symmetrical totality of impulses which is the organic form of a civilisation. Yet if Arnold is in this sense in advance of his age, a 'Liberal of the future'[18] bearing the new needs of the bourgeois state, he can be so precisely because he is in another sense reactionary. If his critique of bourgeois pragmatism stems from the sensed need for a more richly elaborated ideology, it springs also from a traditionalist conception of culture as 'an inward condition of the mind and spirit . . . at variance with the mechanical and material civilisation in esteem with us'.[19] The 'progressive' Inspector of Schools, and the patrician Professor of Poetry, both stand in conflict with conventional bourgeois liberalism; they meet in the aestheticised sociology of *Culture and Anarchy*.

Arnold's concern for the aesthetic meanings of Culture is both productive and disabling for the ideological ends he serves. Productive, in that art offers a prototype of how human subjects are spontaneously, subconsciously *affected*, and thus is relevant to the problem of ideology in general. Disabling, in that the consequence of such an intuitive aesthetics is a politically catastrophic vagueness. Arnold correctly perceives that ideologies establish themselves chiefly through image and representation rather than through systems of doctrine: Culture, in contrast with 'Jacobinism', is eternally dissatisfied with 'the men of a system, of disciples, of a school; with men like Comte, or the late Mr. Buckle, or Mr. Mill'.[20] Indeed it is precisely divisive rationalist debate over 'doctrines' which threatens to destroy those instinctual pieties and spiritual allegiances which ideology must nurture. Doctrine, then, must yield to poetry, literature must oust dogma:

> The future of poetry is immense, because in poetry, where it is worthy of its highest destinies, our race, as time goes on, will find an ever surer and surer stay. There is not a creed which is not shaken, not an accredited dogma which is not shown to be questionable, not a received tradition which does not threaten to dissolve. . . . More and more mankind will discover that we have to turn to poetry to interpret life for us, to console us, to sustain us. Without poetry, our science will appear incomplete; and most of what now passes for religion and philosophy will be replaced by poetry. . . . The day will come when we shall wonder at ourselves for having trusted to them, for having taken them seriously; and the more we perceive their hollowness, the more we shall prize 'the breath and finer spirit of knowledge' offered to us by poetry.[21]

'Poetry', that is to say, is the final resort of a society in dire ideological crisis, replacing criticism with consolation, the analytic with the affective, the subversive with the sustaining. As such, it comes to denote less a particular literary practice than the mode of operation of ideology in general. Yet Poetry, like Culture, is thereby emptied of content in direct proportion to its all-pervasiveness, as Frederic Harrison perceived in his devastating parody of *Culture and Anarchy*:

There is harmony, but no system; instinct, but no logic; eternal growth, and no
maturity; everlasting movement, and nothing acquiesced in; perpetual opening of all
questions, and answering of none; infinite possibilities of everything; the becoming all
things, the being nothing.[22]

It is a theoretical nullity obvious enough in Arnold's 'touchstones' concept
of criticism, in which an entirely intuitive response to some ghostly resonance
supposedly common to a handful of poetic images ripped from their aesthetic
and historical contexts is solemnly elevated into an absolute measure of literary
evaluation.

Culture and Anarchy opposed the claims of 'Hellenism' to 'Hebraism', liberal
cultivation to moral commitment, in a drive to deepen the spiritual hegemony of
the middle class, Yet in doing so it risked liberalising out of existence the very
'absolute' moral values which in practice sustained bourgeois hegemony. In the
'theological' works which follow *Culture and Anarchy*, then, Arnold needs to
counterbalance Hellenism with the Hebraistic virtues of duty, obedience and
submission – virtues whereby a dangerously rationalistic working class may be
ideologically integrated into political society. Many of the masses, Arnold complains in *God and the Bible*, have espoused a sort of revolutionary deism, based on
the supposed 'rights of man' and hostile to all traditional culture. The essential
corrective is Christianity: man in Christ knows duties rather than rights, surrender-
ing himself to the 'sweet reasonableness' of a corporate order of divine law. Yet if
the masses are to be reclaimed from 'Jacobinism', much unacceptable religious
doctrine will need to be poeticised away. The proletariat have turned from the
Bible, Arnold remarks in *Literature and Dogma*, because of the spurious theological
categories in which it is tricked out. A wholesale demythologisation is therefore
crucial: the scriptures must be stripped to a suggestive poetic structure for shoring
up a conservative social morality. A Hellenised religion must become the
handmaiden of a Hebraistic ethics.

One of the more discreditable facts about Matthew Arnold was his refusal to
support an authentic demythologiser of his own day, Bishop John William Colenso.
Arnold criticised Colenso, as Lionel Trilling has pointed out, because he believed
that 'the factory operatives whom Colenso had in mind could not possibly be
edified-that is, their spirits could not be raised, their moral sense heightened
nor their religious faith strengthened – by this work'.[23] Colenso's scriptural
questionings are ideologically damaging: 'The great mass of the human race have to
be softened and humanised through their heart and imagination, before any soil can
be found in them where knowledge may strike living roots . . . only when [ideas]
reach them in this manner do they adjust themselves to their practice without
convulsing it.'[24] Colenso, in short, is unpoetical and so politically dangerous: his
rationalist critique of the Bible checks that dissolution of dogma to image which
alone can infiltrate proletarian sensibilities, assuring rather than disrupting, sooth-
ing rather than subverting. If Culture is too elusive and élitist an instrument for this

pressing task, then religion – traditionally one of the most potent and pervasive modes of ideological control – must be refurbished and transformed for this end. Arnold's anxieties over Colenso recall his fears, recorded in the Preface to his *Poems* of 1853, about the spiritually undermining effects of his own earlier poetry. He rejects *Empedocles on Etna* from that volume because it seems calculated to depress rather than to elevate the reader; true poetry must dispense 'disinterested objectivity' rather than gloom and neurosis, appealing to 'those elementary feelings which subsist permanently in the race, and which are independent of time'.[25] 'Moral grandeur' must combat 'spiritual discomfort': poetry must become the ideological resolution of real contradictions.

2   George Eliot

To turn from Matthew Arnold to George Eliot is to see in peculiarly complex form some of the ideological conflicts which Arnold's idea of Culture is intended to resolve. Eliot's literary career, from her translation of Strauss's *Das Leben Jesu* (1846) to *Daniel Deronda* (1876), is almost exactly coterminous with the period of Victorian prosperity which follows the severe depression and fierce class-struggles of the eighteen-thirties and forties. During this period productive output increased spectacularly, Britain's volume of world trade grew rapidly, and money-wages probably rose by at least a third between 1850 and 1870. A familiar political consequence of this prosperity was a partial though marked incorporation of the working class. From the mid-century onwards, until the resurgence of proletarian militancy in the depressed eighties, corporatism becomes a prominent characteristic of wide areas of the working-class movement.[26] Having defeated the first wave of working-class militancy, the industrial bourgeoisie had begun by 1850 to consolidate its victory. Sections of the working class advanced economically, only to become at each stage politically incorporated. On the eve of the second Reform Bill, R. H. Hutton argued in *Essays in Reform* (1867) that the trade unions had taught the workers the value of cooperation, sacrifice and solidarity, and that this principle might be usefully integrated into society as a whole. Through the unions, the working class had come to appreciate the value of true government and to distrust 'mere scattered energies'. This 'class-patriotism' must at all costs be channelled to national account; the spirit of trade unionism must be grafted 'into the richer growth of our national politics'.[27]

The ideological matrix of George Eliot's fiction is set by the increasingly corporate character of Victorian capitalism and its political apparatus. Eliot's work attempts to resolve a structural conflict between two forms of mid-Victorian ideology: between a progressively muted Romantic individualism, concerned with the untrammelled evolution of the 'free spirit', and certain 'higher', corporate ideological modes. These higher modes (essentially, Feuerbachian humanism and scientific rationalism) seek to identify the immutable social laws to which Romantic individualism, if it is to avoid both ethical anarchy and social disruption, must conform. In principle, it is possible for Romantic individualism to do so without betraying its own values. For if it is true on the one hand that scientific rationalism, in judiciously curbing the disruptive tendencies of Benthamite egoism, also obstructs Romantic self-expression, it is also true that it reveals certain historically progressive laws with which the developing individual may imaginatively unite. Moreover, the Religion of Humanity imbues scientific law with Romantic humanist spirit, discovering that law inscribed in the very passions and pieties of men. Unlike the obsessively abstract, systemic symbology of Comtism, it can offer itself as a totalising doctrine without detriment to the 'personal' – to a lived relation with immediate experience. The Religion of Humanity protects Romantic values against an aggressive rationalism; but by rooting those values in the human collective, it defends them equally against an unbridled individualism. By virtue of this ideological conjuncture, the Romantic individualist may submit to the social totality without sacrifice to personal self-fulfilment.

In principle, that is; in practice, a potentially tragic collision between 'corporate' and 'individualist' ideologies is consistently defused and repressed by the forms of Eliot's fiction. As the daughter of a farm-agent, the social locus of corporate value for Eliot is rural society; it is here, most obviously in *Adam Bede* and *Silas Marner*, that the cluster of traditionalist practices and 'organic' affiliations imputed to the English provincial countryside is 'selected' by the national ideology as paradigmatic, at a point where that ideology demands precisely such images of social incorporation. Rural society in *Adam Bede*, as John Goode has commented,[28] is chosen as a literary subject not for its cloistered idiosyncratic charm but as a simplifying model of the whole social formation – a formation whose determining laws may be focused there in purer, more diagrammatic form. The function of the framing, externalising forms of Eliot's rural novels – pastoral myth, moral fable – is to allow for such 'transparency', but in doing so to recast the historical contradictions at the heart of Eliot's fiction into ideologically resolvable terms.

It is not, naturally, that the organicist modes of Eliot's novels are the 'expression' of her authorial ideology. As a literary producer, George Eliot delineates a 'space' constituted by the insertion of 'pastoral', religious and Romantic ideological sub-ensembles into an ideological formation dominated by liberalism, scientific rationalism and empiricism. This conjuncture is overdetermined in her case by elements of sexual ideology, which both reinforce the drive to individual emancipation and ratify the 'feminine' values (compassion, tolerance, passive resignation) called upon to forestall it. There is no question of reducing the metropolitan rationalist intellectual George Eliot to the 'subject' of a provincial, petty-bourgeois 'class-ideology'. The phrase 'George Eliot' signifies nothing more than the insertion of certain specific ideological determinations – Evangelical Christianity, rural organicism, incipient feminism, petty-bourgeois moralism – into a hegemonic ideological formation which is partly supported, partly embarrassed by their presence. This contradictory unity of ideological structures provides the productive matrix of her fiction; yet the ideology of her texts is not, of course, reducible to it. For Eliot's literary production must be situated, not only at the level of 'general' ideology, but also at the relatively autonomous level of the mutation of literary forms. For each of her texts displays a complex amalgam of fictional devices appropriate to distinct generic modes: 'pastoral', historical realism, fable, mythopoeic and didactic discourse, even (with *Daniel Deronda*) elements of utopian fantasy. None of these discourses can be placed in any simple expressive relation to ideological forms; on the contrary, it is the mutual articulation of these discourses within the text which *produces* those ideological forms as literary signification. Two examples of this process will have to suffice. The biographical mode of *The Mill on the Floss* encompasses at least two distinct forms of literary discourse: a kind of descriptive 'pastoral' (the Dodsons, Maggie's early life at the mill), and the complex psychological drama of Maggie's subjective development. It is the interplay of these mutually conflictual modes which produces the ideological contention between 'tradition' and 'progress' inscribed in the figures of Tom and Maggie Tulliver. But it is a contention which the novel's 'pastoral' devices simultaneously resolve. For just as the text's synthetic closure simplifies Tom to a type of eternal childhood, so the image of the river – symbol of moral drifting and wayward desire – naturalises and thus deforms the values of liberal individualism, figuring them as a mindless yielding to natural appetite rather than as positive growth. An opposition between 'natural' and 'cultural' discourses is transformed into a polarity between two modes of 'natural' signification: Nature as positive (pastoral), and Nature as negative (appetitive). Again, it is not difficult to see how in *Middlemarch* the realist form itself determines a certain 'ideology of the text'. In the earlier 'pastoral' novels, Eliot's realism is partly signified by her apologetic engagement with socially obscure destinies; yet that engagement does not necessarily extend to a fully 'internal' mode of characterisation. Once it does so, however, the novel-form is instantly decentred: since every destiny is significant, each is consequently relativised. Realism, as Eliot conceives of it, involves the tactful unravelling of interlaced processes, the equable distribution of authorial sympathies, the holding of competing values in precarious equipoise. The 'general' ideological correlative of this textual ideology is, naturally, liberal reformism; no other ideological effect could conceivably be produced by such an assemblage of fictional devices.

That Eliot's fiction recasts historical contradictions into ideologically resolvable form is evident enough in the case of *Adam Bede*. Adam himself, with his Carlylean gospel of work and stiff-necked moralism, is an 'organic' type – a petty-bourgeois pragmatist who 'had no theories about setting the world to rights', and who thus functions as a reliable agent of the ruling class. Yet these 'organic' values are forbidden by the novel's form from entering into significant deadlock with any 'authentic' liberal individualism. Such individualism figures in the text only in the debased and trivialised form of a hedonistic egoism (the anarchic sexual appetite of Arthur Donnithorne and Hetty Sorrel), which the stable structures of rural society can expel or absorb without notable self-disruption. Hetty has unwittingly ruptured the class-collaboration between squire and artisan, turning Adam against Arthur; but once she is, so to speak, deported from the novel, that organic allegiance can be gradually reaffirmed. Moreover, the morally intransigent Adam has been humanised by his trials to the point where he is now spiritually prepared to wed the 'higher' working-class girl, Dinah Morris, whose Evangelical fervour for duteous self-sacrifice matches his own doggedly anti–intellectual conformism. Adam is thus allowed to advance into more richly individualised consciousness (he ends up owning a timber-yard) without damage to his mythological status as organic type, an admirable amalgam of naturalised culture and cultivated nature.

In choosing rural petty-bourgeois life as a 'paradigmatic' region, Eliot betrays towards it an ambiguous attitude which reveals, in turn, her problematic relationship to her readership. She extends the conventions of literary realism to a sensitive treatment of socially obscure figures; but while she insists on the latent significance of the apparently peripheral lives she presents, she also apologises, with a blend of genial patronage and tentative irony, for choosing such an unenlightened enclave as the subject-matter of serious fiction. That hesitancy of tone focuses an ideological conflict. It exposes the contradiction between a rationalist critique of rural philistinism (one coupled with a Romantic individualist striving beyond those stifling limits), and a deep-seated imperative to celebrate the value of such bigoted, inert traditionalism, as the humble yet nourishing soil which feeds the flower of higher individual achievement. *Adam Bede* tries for a partial solution of this dilemma by romantically idealising the common life in the figures of Adam and Dinah, fusing the intense with the ordinary. In *The Mill on the Floss*, however, such a synthesis calls for a considerably more obtrusive manipulation of literary devices.

The rural society of the *Mill* – one of struggling tenant farmers becoming enmortgaged and forced to ruin by the pressures of urban banking and agricultural industry – is less easily idealised than the society of *Adam Bede*. As urban capital penetrates into the countryside, those conflicts in rural society suggested yet suppressed in *Adam Bede* erupt to provide one of the *Mill*'s central images – the financial collapse of Dorlcote Mill itself. Moreover, if Hetty Sorrel can be effectively externalised as a socially disruptive egoist, Maggie Tulliver of the *Mill* is a bearer of authentic liberal values who is by no means so easily dislodged. Whereas *Adam Bede* divided moral fervour and restless individualism between Dinah and Hetty, Maggie Tulliver combines both; and this forestalls the simple resolution available to the earlier novel. Allured by a liberal individualism which decisively breaks with the stagnant oppressiveness of the rural petty bourgeoisie, Maggie must none the less refuse that ethic in the name of a commitment to the traditionalist social milieu of her childhood. In this way, nostalgia for an idealised upbringing at the mill becomes translated into a defence of clannish, claustrophobic *mores* against the Romantic spontaneity of the self, treacherously entwined as it is with appetitive egoism. The claustrophobia, and the snare of self-sacrifice, are clearly registered by the novel; yet one reason why they cannot be decisively rejected is because the only alternative commitment which the book allows Maggie is Stephen Guest. Guest cannot represent a true fulfilment for her: his personal flaws are subtly related to his class position, as an overbred product of the predatory capitalism which is ousting the old rural world of her father. In grasping this connection, the novel at once shows a complex historical sense beyond the range of *Adam Bede*, and conveniently renders Maggie's return to St Oggs more palatable. In a parallel way, the career of Tom Tulliver strikingly renders the contradictions of rural society: Tom strives to help his ruined father by prospering within the very urban capitalism which has brought about the mill's collapse. Yet it is not this historically complex and self-divided Tom with whom Maggie finally unites. The novel's transparently engineered conclusion – Maggie's self-sacrificial drowning with her brother – suppresses ideological conflict by the magical stratagem of a literary device. Maggie's death is at once guilty expiation and affirmative self-fulfilment; in uniting with her brother, object of romantic love and bigoted type of organic community, she achieves and abnegates herself in the same act, endorsing the imperatives of 'organic' morality while attaining to a fulfilling individual transcendence of them.

That the nostalgic organicism of Eliot's historically backdated rural fiction is determined in the last instance by the exigencies of the present is evident enough in *Felix Holt, The Radical*, written about the first Reform Bill on the eve of the second. Felix is essentially an urban version of Adam Bede, a petty-bourgeois craftsman no more representative of the proletariat in whose name he speaks than his pre-industrial predecessor. His 'radicalism', accordingly, consists in a reformist trust in moral education and a positivist suspicion of political change – a combination heroically opposed by the text to an unsavoury alliance of opportunist Radical politics with the insensate irrationality of the masses. Felix's *Address to Working Men*, with its call for a conversion of class interests into class duties, its apologia for cultural privilege and fear of mass action, merely projects the novel's sustaining ideology of 'organic' change into more crudely explicit terms. In this sense, *Felix Holt* highlights the ideological impotence of those 'pastoral' images which persist within Eliot's realist fictional mode. It is a self-contradictory work because it insists (as its self-consciously assertive title would suggest) on 'centring' such an image – Felix himself – in an urban context which can only enforce its effective displacement, transplanting a marooned, moralising Adam Bede to the town. The novel's 'official' project is in conflict with what it reveals: Felix's 'progressive' political critique is no more than the idealist protest of traditionalist values against the political itself. What the book wishes to assert of its protagonist – that he is more radical than the Radicals – simply cannot be reconciled with what it shows of him, as a doughty defender of landed property. The solution to this contradiction lies in the 'personalisation' of Felix himself, as a forcefully charismatic hero compensating in physical presence for what he politically lacks.

If Felix is in this sense a 'false' centre, the novel has a real but displaced centre in Mrs Transome. Both characters are historically obsolete; Mrs Transome is presented as a pathetically outdated feudalist whose pieties are ridden over roughshod by her Radical son. Yet if the novel mourns in her the death of tradi- tional society, that mourning must be refracted in the case of the equally obsoles- cent Holt to a 'progressive' position. The Mrs Transome scenes are nothing less than the aesthetic betrayal of this ideological contradiction at the novel's heart – the unabsorbed region of bleakness, nostalgia and frustration with which nothing can be politically done, which is thereby forced to the work's ideological margins, but which protests by its sheer artistry against such relegation. Mrs Transome is an implicit refutation of Felix and contemporary history, even as Felix himself is fundamentally a refusal of that world; there is thus a double displacement at work in the text. *Felix Holt* betrays in its formal structure – in the disjunction between its political region and its Mrs Transome episodes – a self-division which fails to achieve thematic articulation. The artistic power of the Mrs Transome scenes suggests the residual presence of an ineradicable 'personal' disillusionment which refuses to be totalised and absorbed by the novel's official progressivist ideology. Liberalism, raised by the quasi-positivist Holt to more corporate and 'scientific' forms, at the same time disengages itself from such potentially tyrannic totalities to defend the 'personal' values they threaten. The structural dislocations of the text are produced by that ideological dissonance; but that dissonance is equally the product of the interplay between the three distinct 'texts' which struggle for dominance within the novel as a whole. For *Felix Holt* is a contradictory amalgam of organicist myth (Felix), psychological drama (Mrs Transome) and political fiction; its discourse is the product of a series of slippages or mutations from each of these traditional forms to the other. It is in the hiatuses produced by these partial, ineffective transformations of mode that the ideology of the text inheres.

Eliot's fiction, indeed, displays from the outset a conflict between ideological totalities which outstrip classical liberalism, and a fear of the disruptive effect of such totalities on the 'personal' values bred by that liberal lineage. (It is a conflict revealed in her ambiguous fellow-travelling relations with the English Positivists, whom she supported but could not bring herself to join.) Fiction is organic totality, but *phenomenological* totality; its creation of seamless, symmetrical wholes must be achieved without damage to the integrity of immediate experience.[29] That problem is thematically evident in *Romola*, where Savonarola's 'passionate sense of the infinite', his seductively corporate vision, is entwined with a moral despotism which violates liberal sanctities. Yet those sanctities are in themselves insufficient: 'tender fellow-feeling for the nearest has its danger too, and is apt to be timid and sceptical towards the larger aims without which life cannot rise to religion'.[30] In Arnold's terms, it is a conflict between a dangerously decentred Hellenism and an oppressively sectarian Hebraism.

Liberal-minded working men like Felix Holt seem to propose one answer to that problem, blending 'culture' with moral discipline; yet after *Felix Holt* Eliot did not repeat the doomed experiment of centring such 'pastoral' figures within urban landscapes. The Bede–Holt character in *Middlemarch* is Caleb Garth, stock type of rural organicism, but decidedly muted and marginal within the novel's structure. As such figures decline in ideological impact, value shifts to an alternative opposi-tional standpoint: in the case of *Middlemarch*, to the cosmopolitan artist Will Ladislaw. If the traditionalist craftsman forms a pocket of spiritual resistance within bourgeois society, the cosmopolitan artist inhabits such a dissentient space outside it. He is, however, no complete compensation for the outmoded organicist type: if Ladislaw has the edge over Garth in liberal culture it is because he lacks his social rootedness. It is only with Daniel Deronda, who combines synoptic vision with settled allegiance, that this ideological dilemma can be finally dissolved.

This is not to say, however, that Garth's values do not finally triumph in *Middlemarch*. They do, but in the 'higher' mode of a wide-eyed liberal disillusion-ment which, with the collapse of more ambitious commitments, is compelled to find solace in the humble reformist tasks nearest to hand. The irony of *Middlemarch* is that it is a triumph of aesthetic totalisation deeply suspicious of ideological totali-ties. Each of the novel's four central characters represents such an historically typical totalisation: Casaubon idealism, Lydgate scientific rationalism, Bulstrode Evangelical Christianity, Dorothea Brooke Romantic self-achievement through a unifying principle of action. Each of these totalities crumbles, ensnared in the quotidian; and that ensnarement can be read in two ways. It is in part a salutary empiricist check to the tyranny of theoreticism; but it also signifies the bleak victory of an entrenched provincial consciousness over rationalist or Romantic drives to transcend it. That stalemate, the novel's title suggests, springs from a transitional phase of rural society at the time of the first Reform Bill; yet there is no doubt that the novel's judiciously muted disillusion, its 'end-of-ideologies' ambience, belongs to its post-second Reform Bill present. The problem which *Middlemarch* objec-tively poses, and fails to resolve, is how ideology is to be conceptually elaborate yet emotionally affective – how it is to nurture 'irrational' personal pieties while cohering them into a structure which surpasses mere empiricism and Romantic spontaneity. What is needed, according to Ladislaw, is 'a soul in which knowledge passes instantaneously into feeling, and feeling flashes back as a new organ of knowledge' – a question to which we have seen Matthew Arnold address himself. Confronted with the aggressive modes of working-class consciousness caricatured in *Felix Holt*, the cautious empiricism of the bourgeois liberal tradition must be reaffirmed; yet that empiricism is in itself an ideologically inadequate response to the historical moment of post-Reform Bill England, with its demand for a more intensively incorporating ideology.

This dilemma is figured in *Middlemarch* in one of its key images: that of the *web* as image of the social formation. The web is a *derivative* organic image, a mid-point between the animal imagery of *Adam Bede* and some more developed theoretical concept of *structure*. The complexity of the web, its subtle interlacing of relatively autonomous strands, its predatory overtones, the possibilities of local complication it permits, accommodate forms of conflict excluded by the more thoroughgoing organicist imagery of *Adam Bede*. But at the same time the web's symmetry, its 'spatial' dehistoricising of the social process, its exclusion of levels of contradiction, preserve the essential unity of the organic mode. The web's complex fragility impels a prudent political conservatism: the more delicately interlaced its strands, the more the disruptive consequences of action can multiply, and so the more circumspect one must be in launching ambitiously totalising projects. Yet conversely, if action at any point in the web will vibrate through its filaments to affect the whole formation, a semi-mystical relationship to the totality is nevertheless preserved. Here, as in the novel's closing trope of the river, which in diffusing its force to tributaries intensifies its total impact, natural imagery is exploited to signify how a fulfilling relation to the social totality can be achieved, not by ideological abstraction, but by pragmatic, apparently peripheral work. And if *Middlemarch*'s natural metaphors perform this function, so does its aesthetic imagery. As Ladislaw remarks to Dorothea: 'It is no use to try and take care of all the world; that is being taken care of when you feel delight – in art or in anything else.' The problem of totality within the novel is effectively displaced to the question of aesthetic form itself, which gives structure to its materials without violating their empirical richness. The novel, in other words, formally answers the problem it thematically poses. Only the novelist can be the centred subject of her own decentred fiction, the privileged consciousness which at once supervenes on the whole as its source, and enters into empathetic relation with each part.

Middlemarch, one might say, is an historical novel in form with little substantive historical content. The Reform Bill, the railways, cholera, machine-breaking: these 'real' historical forces do no more than impinge on the novel's margins. The mediation between the text and the 'real' history to which it alludes is notably dense; and the effect of this is to transplant the novel from the 'historical' to the 'ethical'. *Middlemarch* works in terms of egoism and sympathy, 'head' and 'heart', self-fulfilment and self-surrender; and this predominance of the ethical at once points to an historical impasse and provides the means of ideologically overcoming it. History in the novel is officially in a state of transition; yet to read the text is to conclude that 'suspension' is the more appropriate term. What is officially offered as an ambivalent, intermediate era leading eventually to the 'growing good of the world' is in fact more of an historical vacuum; the benighted, traditionalist-minded Middlemarch seems little more responsive to historical development than does the Hayslope of *Adam Bede*. There is, then, a discrepancy between what the novel claims and what it shows: in aesthetically 'producing' the melioristic ideology intimated by its title, it betrays a considerably less sanguine view of historical progress. It reveals, in fact, an image of the early eighteen-thirties which belongs to the jaundiced viewpoint of where they actually led to – the early eighteen-seventies, where Will Ladislaw's pioneering reformist zeal 'has been much checked'.

Middlemarch projects back onto the past its sense of contemporary stalemate; and since the upshot of this is a radical distrust of 'real' history, that history is effectively displaced into ethical, and so 'timeless', terms. Yet such displacement thereby provides Eliot with an ideological solution: for what cannot be resolved in 'historical' terms can be accommodated by a moralising of the issues at stake. This, indeed, is a mystification inherent in the very forms of realist fiction, which by casting objective social relations into interpersonal terms, constantly hold open the possibility of reducing the one to the other.[31] In *Middlemarch*, such an ethical reduction of history is achieved in the 'solution' of self-sacrifice, to which, in their various ways, Dorothea, Lydgate and (in a sense) Bulstrode struggle through. The suffering abnegation of the ego offers itself as the answer to the riddle of history.

Yet such a solution is ideologically insufficient, as Will Ladislaw's presence in the novel would suggest. For Ladislaw, while consenting to the course of social evolution, also retains an individualist verve which challenges such mature resignation. As a politically reforming artist, he suggests that empirical labour and Romantic self-affirmation need not be incompatible; in Mr Brooke's words, he is 'a sort of Burke with a leaven of Shelley'. The novel's difficulty in 'realising' him springs from its incapacity to see how this desirable ideological conjuncture, yoking prudent gradualism to visionary Romanticism, can be achieved in the historical conditions it describes. At this point, therefore, a different kind of history becomes necessary. What cannot be effectively achieved in Ladislaw can be re-attempted on more propitious terms in that later amalgam of Romantic prophet and reformist politician, Daniel Deronda.

What is demanded, in fact, is a 'totalising' vision which binds the individual to the laws of a social formation, preserves the 'personal' pieties violated by such visions in *Romola* and *Middlemarch*, and romantically liberates the self. The answer to this problem is *Daniel Deronda*. In that novel, Eliot finds a magical solution to her ideological dilemma in Deronda's Jewishness, which provides him with a fulfilling romantic identity while incorporating him into the complex totality of a corporate historical culture. Deronda's early liberalism is fruitlessly Hellenistic, a decentred spreading of sympathies which erodes his capacity for principled action: 'a too reflective and diffuse sympathy was in danger of paralysing in him that indignation against wrong and selectness of fellowship which are the conditions of moral force'. Hebraism provides the essential corrective – a faith which involves 'the blending of a complete personal love in one current with a larger duty' through an obedient 'submission of the soul to the Highest'. Such submission, however, leaves the 'personal' values of liberalism intact: Deronda's vision is of 'a mind consciously, energetically moving with the larger march of human destinies, but not the less full of conscience and tender heart for the footsteps that tread near and need leaning-place (*sic*)'.

The problem, in other words, can be 'solved' only by the invention of a *displaced* totality outside the sterile detotalisation of post-Reform Bill England – a totality which is then, as it were, instantly exported, as Deronda leaves to discover his destiny in the Middle East. The difficulty then is to bring this factitious totality into regenerative relation with bourgeois England – a difficulty 'solved' by Deronda's redemptive influence on the broken, dispirited victim of that society, Gwendolen Harleth. But in attempting this solution the novel splits into self-contradiction – splits, indeed, down the middle. For Daniel can only fulfil his destiny by withdrawing from Gwendolen to the Middle East, abandoning her to a nebulous Arnoldian trust in some ideal goodness. The formal dislocations of *Daniel Deronda* are the product of its attempt to overcome the ideological contradictions from which it emerges; it is in the silence between its 'Gwendolen' and 'Daniel' episodes that the truth of those contradictions speaks most eloquently.

Middlemarch's relative obliquity to 'real' history is in part a consequence of Eliot's belief (compounded of positivism and idealism) in the power of ideas to shape social existence. Yet what the novel manifests is precisely the fatal disjunction between notion and fact, rendering the one emptily utopian and the other banally empirical. If Deronda's visions are to assume historical flesh, the possibility of such contradiction must be eradicated. The novel therefore presses Eliot's trust in the determining force of ideas to a mystical extreme: dreams, desires, shadowy impulses are now grasped as proleptic symbols of what is actually to be. Such dreams effectively conspire in creating the future: Daniel muses that Mordecai's nature may be one of those in which 'a wise estimate of consequences is fused in the fire of the passionate belief which determines the consequences it believes in'. History becomes the phenomenal expression of spiritual forces at work within it; and there can thus be no essential contradiction between what the imagination seizes as true and what historically transpires. The novel, in other words, is driven to the desperate recourse of adopting a mystical epistemology to resolve its problems, and so is effectively forced beyond the bounds of realism. The whole implausible structure of coincidence and hidden kinship which props up the narrative suggests a significant transmutation of the realism of *Middlemarch*, where such devices are sparingly used.

In this sense, *Daniel Deronda* marks one major terminus of nineteenth-century realism – a realism now buckling under ideological pressures it is unable to withstand. But it is not merely a question of the 'aesthetic' being rudely invaded by the 'ideological'. For *Daniel Deronda* also signifies a crisis-point in the relatively autonomous evolution of realist forms – a point at which the problematic *fictionality* of those stolidly self-confident forms is becoming incorporated as a level of signification within the text itself. The novel's notable preoccupation with art is in one sense a displaced desire for the organicist ideal: art liberates the individual subject but exacts submission to an impersonal order, incarnates an ideal excellence but demands much humble labour, elicits an ascetic Hebraism but calls forth a devotion akin to sexual love. Yet it also signifies the text's constant oblique meditation on its own fictive status – on that circular movement whereby 'real' events within the fiction are themselves in some sense 'fictions' which prefigure a 'reality' of illusory proportions. That there could be no Mordecai outside the limits of fictional discourse (as there could indeed be a Bulstrode) is the true index of the novel's ideological dilemma – a dilemma which is nothing less than the crisis of realist signification itself. *Daniel Deronda* is itself a proleptic sign of a desired social reality; but since that social reality is a fictional construct, unable to project itself beyond the bounds of aesthetic discourse, the text can in the end only signify itself. What it discloses, in that process of self-signification, is an absence which must necessarily evade its aesthetic constructions – the suppressed blankness of the abandoned Gwendolen Harleth, sign of the 'real' ideological paucity to which the novel is a mythological riposte.

Eliot's fiction, then, represents an attempt to integrate liberal ideology, in both its Romantic and empiricist forms, with certain pre-industrial, idealist or positivist organic models. It is an enterprise determined in the last instance by the increasingly corporate character of nineteenth-century capitalism during the period of her literary production. Yet this is not to argue for a simple homology between literary and historical systems, or for a reductively diachronic reading of Eliot's *oeuvre*. It is not a question of Eliot's work evolving from pre-industrial 'pastoral' to fully-fledged realism in response to some linear development of bourgeois ideology. On the contrary, it is a question of grasping at once the ideological synchronies and formal discontinuities of her texts – of theorising the set of disjunctures whereby distinct literary discourses produce a corporatist ideology which is present from the outset. The *differences* of Eliot's fiction are the effect of a continual repermutation of the literary forms into which it is inserted – a repermutation which in each of her texts 'privileges' a particular, dominant discourse which 'places' and deforms the others. Within this synchronic practice a significant development can be discerned: one from an essentially *metaphorical* closure of ideological conflict (social history as analogous to natural evolution) towards an essentially *metonymic* resolution of such issues ('personal' values, visions and relations as the solution to social ills).[32] The naturalising, moralising and mythifying devices of the novels effect such closures, but in the act of doing so lay bare the imprint of the ideological struggles which beset the texts. It is in the irregular transmutation of one fictional code into another, the series of formal displacements whereby turbulent issues are marginalised yet remain querulously present, that Eliot's organic closures betray their *constructing* functions. What threatens to subvert them is not a suppressed 'outside', but the absences and dislocations they internally produce.

As Victorian capitalism moves into its imperialist stage, the true historical basis of the 'idyllic' rural organicism *of Adam Bede* becomes progressively exposed. *Impressions of Theophrastus Such* (1879) places its plea for 'corporate existence' in the context of nationalist rhetoric and a warning of the dangers involved in undergoing 'a premature fusion with immigrants of alien blood'. 'The pride which identifies us with a great historic body', Eliot writes, 'is a humanising, elevating habit of mind, inspiring sacrifices of individual comfort, gain, or other selfish ambition, for the sake of that ideal whole; and no man swayed by such a sentiment can become completely abject.' The corporate society which in *Daniel Deronda* remained a goal to be realised, and so an idealist critique of contemporary England, has now become an effusive celebration of the *status quo*. The voice of liberal humanism has become the voice of jingoist reaction.

3 Charles Dickens

The major fiction of Victorian society was the product of the petty bourgeoisie. The Brontës, Dickens, Eliot, Hardy: it is with them, rather than with Thackeray, Trollope, Disraeli, Bulwer Lytton, that the finest achievements of nineteenth-century realism are to be found. Ambiguously placed within the social formation, the petty bourgeoisie was able on the whole to encompass a richer, more significant range of experience than those writers securely lodged within a single class. But it was also able to find epitomised in its own condition some of the most typical contradictions of bourgeois society as a whole. Indeed, 'conventional' bourgeois experience in England proved remarkably unpropitious for the production of major fiction.[33] Only writers with an ambivalent class-relation to the society could, it seemed, be open to the contradictions from which major literary art was produced. (This is true, earlier in the century, of Jane Austen, in whose work the situation of the minor gentry offers a peculiarly privileged focus for examining the conflicts and alliances between aristocracy and bourgeoisie.) As the petty-bourgeois realist tradition declines towards the end of the century into naturalism (Gissing, Wells, Bennett), its fraught, problematic relation to the society is, so to speak, confiscated by the *émigré* writers – James and Conrad, and later Eliot and Pound. A similarly ambiguous relationship occurs in twentieth-century Irish society, to produce the major art of Yeats and Joyce.

This is not to argue, however, that major nineteenth-century realism was the product of the 'class-ideology' of the petty bourgeoisie. For there is, strictly speaking, no such ideological sub-formation: 'petty-bourgeois ideology' exists as a strikingly pure and contradictory unity of elements drawn from the ideological realms of both dominant and dominated classes in the social formation. What is in question with all of these texts is the peculiarly complex, over-determined character of their mode of insertion into the hegemonic ideological forms – a complexity which is in part the product of literary 'realism' itself. For realism, as we have seen in the case of George Eliot, produces in one of its currents a 'democratic' ideology – one progressively responsive to suppressed social experience and humbly quotidian destinies. Yet its aesthetic ideology of 'type' and 'totality' (and we should be in no doubt as to the *ideological* character of such notions) insists on the integration of these elements into a unitary 'world view'. The ideology of the realist text resides not in this dominant 'world view', but in the formal mutations and displacements which signify its attempts to subordinate other modes of discourse. In the case of the earlier Charles Dickens, for example, each text is a veritable traffic-jam of competing fictional modes – Gothic, Romance, moral fable, 'social problem' novel, popular theatre, 'short story', journalism, episodic 'entertainment' – which permits 'realism' no privileged status. The later 'realism' of Dickens is thus of a notably impure kind – a question, often enough, of 'totalising' forms englobing non-realist 'contents', of dispersed, conflictual discourses which ceaselessly offer to displace the securely 'over-viewing' eye of classical realism. If Dickens's movement towards such realism produces a 'totalising' ideology, it is one constantly deconstructed from within by the 'scattering' effect of quite contrary literary devices. In the end, Dickens's novels present symbols of contradictory unity (Chancery Court, Circumlocution Office) which are the very principles of the novel's own construction. Only these symbolic discourses can finally provide an 'over-view'; but precisely because their coherence is nothing less than one of systematic contradiction, such an over-view is merely the absent space within which disparate rhetorics are articulated.

The fact that Charles Dickens was an urban rather than rural petty bourgeois marks a significant distinction between his fiction and that of George Eliot. Of all the major English writers of the past century and a half, Dickens is perhaps the least contaminated by organicist ideologies. With him, the Romantic humanist critique of industrial capitalism remains strikingly 'spontaneous', with none of the elaborate ideological realisation it receives in the work of Carlyle or D. H. Lawrence. Dickens treats the most available contemporary forms of organicism – Young England, medievalism, the cult of Nature, the Oxford movement – with the contempt of an *urban* petty-bourgeois writer, one for whom there is no satisfactory withdrawal into the mystifications of pastoral. The retreat to Nature in Dickens is for the most part a negative gesture, associated with death and regression to childhood, social disengagement rather than social paradigm. If Nature for George Eliot suggests the socially structured world of rural England, it is for Dickens a locus of sentimental moralism rather than of sociological law. Little Nell is a symbol of natural value expelled from the predatory city, but it is the archetypally urban Quilp who engages his author's imagination. The spontaneous, empiricist character of Dickens's Romantic humanism, evident in the 'Christmas spirit' and the vulgar vitalism of *Hard Times*, emerges as a significant aesthetic and ideological weakness. Yet in the mature work that very weakness productively deprives him of a ready-fashioned organicist ideology, *à la Daniel Deronda*, by which to mediate and 're-solve' the conflicts in question. In a transitional work like *Dombey and Son*, the absence of such an ideology results in a text twisted and self-divided by the very contradictions it vulnerably reproduces. The famous railways scene, for example, exhilaratedly affirms bourgeois industrial progress at the same time as it protests gloomily against it on behalf of the petty bourgeoisie it dooms to obsolescence. Yet although that protest is partly couched in natural imagery, Dickens has no organicist ideology like Eliot by which to aesthetically integrate his conflicting symbols, no ideological resources by which to secure a reconciliation of 'tradition' and 'progress'. The contradictions remain visibly inscribed in the text, to enrich and enliven its dramatically irregular development.

A central symbol of Dickens's Romantic humanism is childhood innocence, which the novels bring into a series of complex structural relations with adult experience. Since the child is isolated, victimised and unable to totalise his perceptually fragmented world, the positive value he incarnates figures effectively as a negation. Such negativity clearly reflects the theoretical limitations of Dickens's moralistic critique of bourgeois society: the child's passivity is a dramatic index of his oppression, but also removes him from the world into a realm of untaintable goodness. On the other hand, the child's very blankness brings into dramatic focus the social forces which dominate him; he becomes, in a Brechtian metaphor, the empty stage on which these historically typical forces contend. Oliver Twist is such a negative centre, whose effective absence from his own narrative allows him passively to focus the socially significant; yet his nullity is also determined by the novel's ideological inability to show him as social *product*. To do that, indeed, would be to undercut the very unhinging of Oliver from history which finally ensures his fabular triumph. The novel argues at once that Oliver is and is not the product of bourgeois oppression, just as the 'real' world of bourgeois social relations into which he is magically rescued is endorsed against the 'unreal' underworld of poverty and crime, while simultaneously being shown up by that underworld as illusory.

Dickens's fiction thus reveals a contradiction between the social reality mediated by childhood innocence, and the transcendental moral values which that innocence embodies. It is a contradiction intrinsic to petty-bourgeois consciousness, which needs to embrace conventional bourgeois ethics in an undermining awareness of the harsh social realities they suppress. One effect of this is a set of formal dissonances in the novels themselves. *Pickwick Papers*, for example, cannot really be a *novel* in the traditional sense, since Pickwick's complacent innocence renders him incapable of any significantly interconnected experience beyond the merely episodic. The book consequently needs a supplementary centre in Sam Weller, who, though officially subordinate (Pickwick's servant), is in fact the master. In a double displacement of the text's bourgeois blandness, the unpalatable experience it expels from its official narrative erupts elsewhere, in the grotesquely violent, death-obsessed tales by which that narrative is regularly interrupted. In a somewhat parallel way, Quilp in *The Old Curiosity Shop* symbolises the smouldering, anarchic vengeance which the novel wreaks on its own decorous, sentimental story-line.[34]

Dickens's fiction, like Eliot's, deploys literary devices to 'resolve' ideological conflict; but his novels are more remarkable than Eliot's for the clarity with which those conflicts inscribe themselves in the fissures and hiatuses of the texts, in their mixed structures and disjunct meanings. It is not that Eliot's work does not also reveal such formal dislocations, as I have suggested; it is rather that Eliot's writing, sustained by an aesthetic as well as social ideology of organic form, strives for such organic closure more consciously and consistently than does Dickens's. His novels, by contrast, offer their self-contradictory forms and internal inconsistencies as part of their historical meaning. Dickens's mature work certainly achieves aesthetic integration, but it is of a significantly different kind from Eliot's. Whereas Eliot's organicist ideology provides a structure for social totalisation, Dickens is forced in his later fiction to use as aesthetically unifying images the very social institutions (the Chancery Court of *Bleak House*, the Circumlocution Office of *Little Dorrit*) which are the object of his criticism. It is, ironically, these very systems of conflict, division and contradiction which provide Dickens with a principle of symbolic coherence. In this sense, the aesthetic unity of his mature work is founded, not on a mythology of 'organic community', but on exactly the opposite: on the historical self-divisions of bourgeois society. It is not that the early Dickens's perception of character as idiosyncratic and non-relational yields to a vision of social unity; it is rather that such non-relationship is now shown to be *systemic* – the function of decentred structures like Chancery, finance capitalism and the Circumlocution Office, elusive centres which seem all-pervasive yet everywhere absent.[35] Characters in later Dickens remain individually graphic and grotesque, but are now increasingly grasped as the bearers of these structures, which act as the true protagonists of the later fiction.

What Eliot's writing attempts to resolve *synchronically* – a conflict between two phases of bourgeois ideology, determined by certain mutations in the historical nature of English capitalism – Dickens's fiction moves through *diachronically*. The anarchic, decentred, fragmentary forms of the early novels correspond in general to an earlier, less organised phase of industrial capitalism; the unified structures of the mature fiction allude to a more intensively coordinated capitalism, with its complex networks of finance capitalism (Merdle in *Little Dorrit*), its progressively centralised state bureaucracy (the Circumlocution Office) and its increasingly monolithic ideological apparatuses (the educational system of *Hard Times*, the juridical structures of *Bleak House*).[36] (The railways of *Dombey and Son* mark a transitional stage in this development – a visibly unifying network which none the less, in the entrepreneurial 'spontaneity' of their creation and the heterogeneous quality of experience to which they give rise, recall the arbitrary, explosive energies of the early novels.) Yet this diachronic movement is not one from 'individualism' to 'community'. It is a movement from the novel of the absent centre (innocent child, blankly conventional adult) around which certain contradictions knot themselves, to the novel of the decentred totality – a novel which mimes, in its integrated symbolism, a set of conflicts and non-relations now grasped as systemic.

Notes

1   For Gramsci, 'organic' intellectuals are those who come into existence on the basis of an emergent social class, but who then confront – and need to vanquish and assimilate

– those 'traditional' intellectual categories which survive from previous social conditions. Gramsci argues, significantly enough for the English tradition, that 'The popularised traditional type of intellectual is represented by the literary man, the philosopher, the artist' (*Selections from the Prison Notebooks*, p. 9). It is important to distinguish Gramsci's use of the term 'organic' from the meaning I assign to it in this essay.

2   See F. R. Leavis (ed.), *Mill on Bentham and Coleridge* (London, 1950). Eric Hobsbawm has noted the ideological limitations of 'pure' Utilitarianism – how its demystification of 'natural rights' could seriously weaken the force of 'metaphysical' sanctions in the defence of property, substituting for them the considerably less powerful, politically more volatile category of 'utility'. (*The Age of Revolution: Europe 1789–1848*, London, 1964, p. 236.)

3   *Selections from the Prison Notebooks*, ed. Quintin Hoare and Geoffrey Nowell Smith (London, 1971), p. 18.

4   I use 'organic' and 'organicism' to signify social and aesthetic formations with the supposedly spontaneous unity of natural life-forms, and more generally to denote symmetrically integrated systems characterised by the harmonious interdependence of their component elements.

5   The notion of fiction as organic form is not, however, a merely 'superstructural' matter. By the time of James, changes in the material mode of literary production meant a shift from the densely populated 'three-decker' novel, with its diffuse, multiple plots, to the more 'organic' single volume. We have here, indeed, a singularly complex instance of the conjuncture between the capitalist mode of production in general, the literary mode of production, 'aesthetic' ideology, and the demands of the dominant ideology.

6   I must apologise for the somewhat heterogeneous quality of the materials examined in this chapter, embracing as they do social criticism, fiction and poetry, as well as writers whose relation to English society may well seem highly tangential. Yet that tangentiality, as I hope will become apparent, is part of my point; and the unity of the materials studied here lies primarily in the *theme* of organicism.

7   *Culture and Anarchy, ed.* Ian Gregor (Indianapolis and New York, 1971), p. 56.

8   Arnold is in fact significantly inconsistent about which class actually exercises political hegemony in England. His usual position – the result of an inability to distinguish real hegemony from the administration of the state apparatus – is that the aristocracy are still the dominant class. Indeed as late as 1879 he is writing that 'The middle classes cannot assume rule as they are at present – it is impossible' ('Ecce, Convertimur ad Gentes', *Matthew Arnold: English Literature and Irish Plitics*, ed. R. H. Super (Ann Arbor, Mich., 1973), p. 17). In *Friendship's Garland*, on the other hand, he remarks that the aristocracy administer and the middle class govern.

9   *Selections from the Prison Notebooks.*

10   *The Popular Education of France*, in *Democratic Education*, ed. R. H. Super (Ann Arbor, 1962), p. 22

11   Ibid., p. 23.

12   Ibid., p. 26.

13   Ibid., pp. 322, 324

14   For a criticism of this conception of ideology, see Nicos Poulantzas, *Political Power and Social Classes* (London, 1973), pp. 195–224.

15   *The Study of Celtic Literature*, in *Lectures and Essays in Criticism*, ed. R. H. Super (Ann Arbor, 1962), p. 348.

16   *Culture and Anarchy*, p. 60.

17   *Democratic Education*, p. 4.

18   His own description of himself in 'The Future of Liberalism', *English Literature and Irish Politics*, p. 138.

19   *Culture and Anarchy*, p. 38. Arnold's description of the English class-structure – Barbarians, Philistines, Populace – itself rests on an essentially aristocratic notion of 'rank'; he has no concept of social class as an inherently *relational* reality.

20   *Culture and Anarchy*, p. 54.

21   'The Study of Poetry', *English Literature and Irish Politics*, pp. 161–2.

22   'Culture: A Dialogue', *Fortnightly Review* (Nov 1867).

23   *Matthew Arnold* (New York, 1949), p. 211.

24   'The Bishop and the Philosopher', *Macmillan's Magazine* (Jan 1863).

25   *On The Classical Tradition*, ed. R. H. Super (Ann Arbor, 1960), p. 4.

26   The forms of that increasing corporatism from the mid-century onwards are familiar: the large-scale expansion of industrial units and the advent of the 'high farming' period of extensive organised agriculture, the growth of capitalist partnerships and joint-stock enterprises, the railway amalgamations, the gradual emergence of an increasingly centralised state bureaucracy in such spheres as education and public health. Corresponding to these developments are the corporatist forms assumed by bourgeois ideology (Positivism, Christian socialism, neo-feudalism, neo-Hegelianism and so on), and by wide sections of the working-class movement: conciliatory trade unionism, cooperative and friendly societies, saving banks etc.

27   There is an untypically close correlation between this transition in the class-struggle and a particular literary development: the distance which separates the ideology of Mrs Gaskell's *Mary Barton* (1848) from her *North and South* (1855). It is a distance in which the very moment of historical mutation is disclosed.

28   *Critical Essays on George Eliot*, ed. Barbara Hardy (London, 1970), p. 20.

29   It is significant that Eliot's well-known dictum that art, although the highest form of teaching, should never lapse from the 'picture' to the 'diagram' occurs in a letter to Frederic Harrison in which she refuses his suggestion that she should produce a full-blooded positivist novel (George Eliot, *Letters*, ed. Gordon S. Haight (London, 1956), vol. 4, p. 300).

30   *Romola* (London, 1883), vol. 2, pp. 332–3.

31   A point made by Francis Mulhern in 'Ideology and Literary Form – a comment', *New Left Review* 91 (May/June 1975).

32   For this general distinction in fiction, see Francis Mulhern, 'Ideology and Literary Form'.

33   This is one reason for the structural dissonances of some of Dickens's early fiction. Novels like *Nicholas Nickleby* and *Martin Chuzzlewit* present a blankly absent centre in the figure of the conventional, bourgeois-minded protagonist; the true life of the novels is to be found in the nooks and peripheries, swirling around this absent centre.

34   A point made by John Carey in *The Violent Effigy: A Study of Dickens' Imagination* (London, 1974), p. 26.

35   These complex totalities may be contrasted with the monistic industrial system presented by the sealed and static *Hard Times*, with its crude binary opposition between

that system and 'life'. *Hard Times* can be seen in this sense as a false, premature over-totalisation.

36   It is not, naturally, a question of simple homology between literary and historical systems, as this formulation might seem to suggest. What is at issue, rather, is the difference between an earlier 'impure' articulation of discourses ideologically overdetermined by a relatively unsystematic Romantic humanism, and the *relatively* more coherent codes of the later fiction, overdetermined by the increasing predominance of corporatist ideological elements.

14 Walter Benjamin: Towards a Revolutionary Criticism

Walter Benjamin found it demeaning
To leave more than fragments for gleaning;
His Ursprung *explains*
That God gave us brains
To deem meaning itself overweaning
ALAN WALL

The progressive discovery of Walter Benjamin that has marked the past two decades is not really very surprising. For who could be more appealing to Western Marxists than a writer who manages marvellously to combine all the vigorous iconoclasm of a materialist 'production aesthetics' with the entrancing esotericism of the Kabbala? Who indeed could speak to us more persuasively, torn as we are between media technology and idealist meditation? In the doomed, poignant figure of a Benjamin we find reflected back to us something of our own contradictory desire for some undreamt-of emancipation and persistent delight in the contingent. *The Origin of German Tragic Drama* stands at the confluence of these impulses – for nothing could be at once more boldly dialectical and more intriguingly arcane than the seventeenth-century *Trauerspiel*.

For an English critic in particular, Benjamin's return to the seventeenth century inevitably recalls the apparently similar gestures of T. S. Eliot and F. R. Leavis. Restless with an eighteenth century that it has already rewritten as 'Augustan', thwarted by its own ideological creations, twentieth-century English criticism peers back beyond that artificially pacified epoch to glimpse in its turbulent prede-cessor an image it can call its own. Far from merely paralleling that project, however, Benjamin's recourse to the *Trauerspiel* neatly exposes its ideological basis. Writing of John Donne in *Revaluation*, F. R. Leavis suggests that his 'utterance, movement and intonation are those of the talking voice . . . [exhibiting] a natural speaking stress and intonation and an economy that is the privilege of speech . . .'.[1] Pope's verse is similarly expressive: 'above every line of Pope we can imagine a tensely flexible and complex curve, representing the modulation, emphasis and changing tone and tempo of the voice in reading . . .'.[2] It is this trace within script of the living voice that the linguistic disaster of Milton has fatally erased. Milton's language 'has no particular expressive work to do, but functions by rote, of its own momentum, in the manner of a ritual'; his diction at its worst is a 'laboured, pedantic artifice', in which the obtrusive sign draws imperiously onto itself that attention to 'perceptions, sensations or things' that it is its business to foster.[3] Milton's arid, factitious discourse suggests a medium 'cut off from speech – speech that belongs to the emotional and sensory texture of actual living and is in resonance with the nervous system'.[4] What is 'natural' about Donne, by contrast, is precisely his subtle rootedness in 'idiomatic speech'. Eliot, who is similarly in pursuit of a poetry that infiltrates 'the cerebral cortex, the nervous system, and the digestive tracts',[5] also finds such a bodily semiotic in Donne rather than in Milton, whose 'remoteness . . . from ordinary speech'[6] is for the early Eliot grievously disabling.

For both critics, the contrast between Donne and Milton is cast in terms of the 'visual' versus the 'auditory' imagination. What both in fact find corrupting in Milton is an irreducible surplus of signification that deflects the sign from its truly representational role – and reveals, in Leavis's phrase, 'a feeling *for* words rather than a capacity for feeling *through* words'.[7] That surplus of signification we can designate as *écriture*; and for Benjamin it lies at the heart of the *Trauerspiel*. Seventeenth-century allegory, obsessed as it is by emblem and hieroglyph, is a profoundly visual form; but what swims into visibility is nothing less than the materiality of the letter itself. It is not that the letter flexes and effaces itself to become the bearer of 'perceptions, sensations or things', as Leavis would have us believe of Donne; it is rather that 'at one stroke the profound vision of allegory transforms things and works into stirring writing'.[8] The allegorical signifier is 'not merely a sign of what is to be known but it is in itself an object worthy of knowledge':[9] its denotative force is inseparable from its complex carnality. The writing of *Trauerspiel*, Benjamin remarks, 'does not achieve transcendence by being voiced; rather does the world of written language remain self-sufficient and intent on the display of its own substance'.[10]

This is not to say that such writing is not 'voiced' at all – that sound is merely quelled by its material thickness. On the contrary, the baroque signifier displays a dialectical structure in which sound and script 'confront each other in tense polarity',[11] forcing a division within discourse that impels the gaze into its very depths. That division, for Benjamin, is ontological: spoken language signifies the 'free, spontaneous utterance of the creature',[12] an expressive ecstasy at odds with that fateful enslavement to meaning which the language of allegory entails. What escapes such enslavement is shape and sound, which figure for the baroque allegorist as a self-delighting, purely sensuous residue over and above the meaning with which all written language is inexorably contaminated (and here, of course, 'written language' can mean nothing less than 'language as such'). Seeking in the fullness of sound to assert its creaturely rights, language is nonetheless grimly subdued to significance; the 'semiotic', in the Kristevan sense of that babble or prattle of loosely articulated impulses below the threshold of meaning, enters the constraints of the 'symbolic' but just manages to remain heterogeneous in relation to it.[13] No finer image of such constraint can be found than in the baroque echo-game, in which the echo, itself quite literally a free play of sound, is harnessed to dramatic meaning as answer, warning, prophecy or the like, violently subordinated to a domain of significance that its empty resonance nonetheless threatens to dissolve.

What Benjamin discovers in the *Trauerspiel*, then, is a profound gulf between materiality and meaning – a gulf across which the contention between the two nevertheless persists. It is precisely this which Eliot detects in Milton: 'to extract everything possible from *Paradise Lost*', he comments, 'it would seem necessary to read it in two different ways, first solely for the sound, and second for the sense'.[14] The semiotic contradiction that Benjamin singles out is resolved into separate readings. For Leavis, the 'Miltonic music' is little more than an external embellishment, clumsily at odds with the springs of sense. That this should be scandalous for both critics is hardly surprising, given their commitment to the very aesthetic ideology that Benjamin so ruthlessly demystifies: that of the *symbol*. Ineluctably idealizing, the symbol subdues the material object to a surge of spirit that illuminates and redeems it from within. In a transfigurative flash, meaning and materiality are reconciled into one; for a fragile, irrationalist instant, being and signification become harmoniously totalized. It is impossible that allegory should not appear prolix, mechanical and uncouth in the light of such glamorous notions, and indeed Benjamin is only too aware of the fact; what else is his entire book but an effort to salvage allegory from the 'enormous condescension' of history, as allegory's whole striving is itself for the painful salvaging of truth? Symbolism has denigrated allegory as thoroughly as the ideology of the speaking voice has humiliated script; and though Benjamin himself does not fully develop the connection, it is surely a relevant one. For the allegorical object has undergone a kind of haemorrhage of spirit: drained of all immanent meaning, it lies as a pure facticity under the manipulative hand of the allegorist, awaiting such meaning as he or she may imbue it with. Nothing could more aptly exemplify such a condition than the practice of writing itself, which draws its atomized material fragments into endless, unmotivated constellations of meaning. In the baroque allegory, a jagged line of demarcation is scored between theatrical object and meaning, signifier and signified – a line that for Benjamin traces between the two the dark shadow of that ultimate disjoining of consciousness and physical nature which is death. But if death is in this sense the final devastation of the sign, the utter disruption of its imaginary coherence, so too is writing itself, which happens at the sliding hinge between signifier and signified, and with which, as we shall see later, death itself is intimately associated.

Since Benjamin, like Bertolt Brecht, believes in starting not from the good old things but from the bad new ones,[15] he does not mourn the bereft condition of the baroque world, sundered as it is from all transcendence. It is true, as we shall see, that he considers such barrenness to contain the seeds of its own redemption; but even so he welcomes the *Trauerspiel* as figuring the real, demystified form of 'man's subjection to nature'.[16] For Eliot and Leavis, on the other hand, this drastic disso-ciation of sensibility – for that, after all, is another jargon for what we are discussing – is an ideological menace. The world of the *Trauerspiel* is not one in which characters feel their thought as immediately as the odour of a rose; and even if the typewriter had been invented they would hardly have combined hearing the noise of it with the experience of reading Spinoza. The *Trauerspiel*, with its habitual disarticulation of elements, knows nothing of that fetishism of the 'organic' which haunts an Eliot or Leavis, and which informs the German Romantic criticism Benjamin so courageously challenged. In the baroque, 'the false appearance of totality is extinguished',[17] even if it then yields grounds to a fetishism of the fragment. Eliot and Leavis, gripped by the good old things, return wistfully to the time when the intellect was at the tip of the senses and the social relations of exploited farm-labourers constituted a 'right and inevitable' human en-vironment.[18] Indeed what is the Metaphysical conceit but the organic society in miniature, a *Gemeinschaft* of senses and intellect, a transfiguring flash in which the material object is rescued from its facticity and offered up to the ephemeral embrace of spirit? It is no wonder that the criticism of Eliot and Leavis betrays such a deep 'phonocentric' prejudice – in favour of what Jacques Derrida has described as an 'absolute proximity of voice and being, of voice and the meaning of being, of voice and the ideality of meaning'.[19] For if poetry is to slide into the cerebral cortex, nervous system and digestive tracts to perform its ideological labour, it must free itself from the thwarting materiality of the signifier to become the subtilized medium of the living body itself, of which nothing is more symbolically expressive than the 'spontaneous' speaking voice. Unless the 'thing' is ripely, unmediatedly present within the word, it will fail to be borne subliminally to that realm which for both Eliot and Leavis is the very heartland of 'human experience', and which historical materialism knows to be the very terrain of the ideological.

Benjamin, by contrast, does not fall prey to the illusion that the voice is any more spontaneous or immaterial than script. 'That inward connection of word and script', he quotes Johann Wilhelm Ritter as reflecting, 'so powerful that we write when we speak . . . has long interested me. . . . Their original, and absolute, simul-taneity was rooted in the fact that the organ of speech itself writes in order to speak. The letter alone speaks, or rather: word and script are, at source, one, and neither is possible without the other. . . . Every sound pattern is an electric pattern, and every electric pattern is a sound pattern.'[20] In the *Trauerspiel*, Benjamin continues, 'there is nothing subordinate about written script; it is not cast away in reading, like dross. It is absorbed along with what is read, as its "pattern".'[21]

That Leavis should manifest such hostility to Milton is itself a profound historical irony. For his animus against Milton is among other things the irritation of a
petty-bourgeois radical with a thoroughly 'Establishment' figure – a poet solemnly
venerated for his rhetorical grandeur by generations of patrician academics. But
with the exception of William Blake, English literature has produced no finer petty-
bourgeois radical than John Milton.[22] Leavis's own signal virtues – his unswerving
seriousness and nonconformist courage, his coupling of trenchant individualism
and social conscience – would not have been historically possible, in the precise
configurations they display, without the revolutionary lineage of which Milton was
such an heroic architect. Leavis cannot perceive this grotesque irony, partly because the Milton he assails remains the construct of the ideological enemy, partly
because his formalism necessarily blinds him to the 'content' of Milton's work. In
this, Leavis and Eliot are at one: the former is largely indifferent to the theological
and political substance of Milton's texts, while the latter, in so far as such substance
concerns him at all, finds it 'repellent'. Such resistance to 'ideas' stems logically
from the empiricism and irrationalism that both critics variously championed
throughout their careers; few critics have betrayed such programmatic anti-
intellectualism as the formidably erudite Eliot. But it also has a more particular root
in their ideological construction of seventeenth-century England. For their shared
linguistic idealism impels them to locate the mourned *Gemeinschaft* primarily in
language itself. Not entirely, to be sure: 'health' of language must signify cultural
sanity, and Leavis, rather more than Eliot, is concerned to give such sanity a social
habitation. But both are forced to 'bracket' the ideological content of the texts they
admire to an astonishing degree: the desirable wedlock of being and meaning
manifest in the verbal form of a Donne poem or Webster tragedy must be celebrated in systematic inattention to the flagrant dislocations of their content. If the
Donne of *Songs and Sonnets* centres himself as a dramatic voice, a colloquially
expressive subject, it is not least because he is concerned to construct a defiant
'imaginary' coherence across a decentred, Copernican world of 'symbolic' differences. His mechanism of sensibility may indeed be capable of devouring any
experience, but usually only to spew it back again as an inferior metaphor of the
imaginary subject-position he can achieve with his mistress. Both Eliot and Leavis,
it is true, discern in such seventeenth-century *Weltanschauungen* relevant paradigms for contemporary experience; but this is not the most typical focus of their
interest. Eliot may draw upon such paradigms in *The Waste Land*, but his criticism
is remarkable for its almost comic lack of interest in what a poet actually has to 'say'.
Such formalism is the concomitant of a necessary depoliticizing, as Raymond
Williams has shrewdly noted:

> let me take a case which was very important in clarifying my attitude to Leavis. I said
> to people here at Cambridge: in the thirties you were passing severely limiting
> judgments on Milton and relatively favourable judgments on the metaphysical poets,
> which in effect redrew the map of seventeenth-century literature in England. Now

you were, of course, making literary judgments – your supporting quotations and analysis prove it, but you were also asking about ways of living through a political and cultural crisis of national dimensions. On the one side, you have a man who totally committed himself to a particular side and cause, who temporarily suspended what you call literature, but in fact not writing, in that conflict. On the other, you have a kind of writing which is highly intelligent and elaborate, that is a way of holding divergent attitudes towards struggle or towards experience together in the mind at the same time. These are two possibilities for any highly conscious person in a period of crisis – a kind of commitment which involves certain difficulties, certain naïvetés, certain styles; and another kind of consciousness, whose complexities are a way of living with the crisis without being openly part of it. I said that when you were making your judgments about these poets, you were not only arguing about their literary practice, you were arguing about your own at that time.[23]

The triumph of Benjamin's text, by contrast, lies in its subtle imbrication of form and motif. In the jaded, secularized world of the *Trauerspiel*, rife as it is with sluggish melancholy and pure intrigue, the leakage of meaning from objects, the unhinging of signifiers from signifieds, is at once a matter of *énoncé* and *énonciation*, as the features of an already petrified, primordial landscape undergo a kind of secondary reification at the hands of the 'fixing' hieroglyph. Those features, indeed, include 'psychology' itself, which, elaborately encoded as it is, attains to a kind of dense objectivity in which 'the passions themselves take on the nature of stage-properties'.[24] Signifieds metonymically displace themselves onto their signifiers, so that jealousy becomes as sharp and functional as the dagger with which it is associated. If this domain of thickly reified signs is predominantly spatial, it is nevertheless propelled slowly forward by an ineluctable temporality; for allegory, as Fredric Jameson has remarked of the *Trauerspiel*, is 'the privileged mode of our own life in time, a clumsy deciphering of meaning from moment to moment, the painful attempt to restore a continuity to heterogeneous, disconnected instants'.[25] Benjamin distinguishes three kinds of temporality: the 'empirical' time of empty repetition, which belongs to the *Trauerspiel* and, as we shall see later, to the commodity; 'heroic' time, centred upon the individual tragic protagonist; and 'historical' time, which is neither 'spatial' as in the *Trauerspiel* nor individual as in tragedy, but which prefigures his later concerns with the '*nunc stans*' or *Jetztzeit*, in which time receives its collective fullness. The freezing of time achieved by the *Trauerspiel* signifies the need of the absolutist state to bring history to an end; the absolutist monarch himself becomes the primary source of signification in a world drained of historical dynamic. This theme, too, will find a later echo in Benjamin, in that ultimate abolition of history which is fascism. Such significant temporality as there is, however, belongs more to hermeneutic practice itself than to its objects; the time of the *Trauerspiel* is as empty as its *realia*, the negation of that teleological vision which Benjamin will later denounce as 'historicism', listlessly open to the *Jetztzeit* – the totalizing, transfiguring moment – that never comes. As the petrified stage-properties are ritually shuffled, time is almost folded back into space, dwindled to a recurrence so agonizingly empty that some salvific epiphany might indeed just be conceived to tremble on its brink. If there is a moment in the *Trauerspiel* that resembles the *Jetztzeit* – the apocalyptic point at which time stands still to receive the plenitude of hitherto dismembered meaning – it resembles it only as caricature: 'the narrow frame of midnight, an opening in the passage of time, in which the same ghostly image constantly reappears'.[26]

Benjamin's treatment of the *Trauerspiel* might suggest, in contrast to Leavis and Eliot, an approach to *Paradise Lost* that has moved beyond formalism. For Milton's text too, remote as it is from those that Benjamin examines, is the drama of a jagged line scored by some primordial catastrophe between *physis* and meaning, the plot of a history reduced by God's apparent withdrawal to certain signs and fragments urgently in need of decipherment. The withdrawal *is*, of course, merely apparent: an eschatology unknown to the baroque is still active, and will finally usher into history the transcendental signifier that already lies concealed in its midst. But for all that, the transcendental signifier *is* concealed, and to justify its dealings with humankind demands an awkwardly discursive hermeneutic that is the precise reverse of the conceit. The conceit 'naturalizes' its incongruous couplings, amazing us with a 'spontaneity' that we appreciate all the more because its artifice is kept cunningly in view; wit is intellect without labour. Milton's God is equally unlaborious, pure symbolicity whose 'material' acts have the immediacy of spirit; but he is so only from the standpoint of eternity. Viewed from the fallen realm of a revolutionary history gone awry, those acts must be painfully decoded, elaborated and reassembled, in a narrative that can expose their logic only at the cost of laying bare its own devices.

The slippages and lacunae entailed by such a practice are precisely what Milton's critics have denounced. The poem is not really very realistic: at one moment Satan is chained to the burning lake, and before you can look again he is making his way towards the shore. George Eliot would have handled the whole thing incomparably better. Leavis, significantly, is much preoccupied with such Waldockian points,[27] upbraiding the poem for its lapses of consistency. It is not fortuitous that a phonocentric criticism, concerned to chart the very anatomy of feeling in the sinuous flexings of speech, should pull a naive representationalism in its wake: for both ideologies, the signifier lives only in the moment of its demise. What is fascinating about *Paradise Lost* is precisely its necessary lack of self-identity – the persistent mutual interferences of what is stated and what is shown, the contradictory entanglements of 'epic' immediacy and hermeneutic discourse, the fixing of significations at one level that produces a sliding of them at another. All of this, for Leavis, is simply offensive: he cannot see that it possesses that quality of *provocative* offensiveness which Benjamin discerns in the baroque, any more than he can read the harsh laboriousness of some of the poem's language as anything but a violation of sensuous immediacy. In fact, the language of *Paradise Lost* is a labour that works athwart the 'natural' texture of the senses, failing or refusing (it is immaterial which) to repress its own artifice. Nothing could be further from the swift fusion of the conceit than the calculated self-conscious unfurling of the epic simile, with all its whirring machinery of production unashamedly on show. And nothing could be closer to one aspect of Benjamin's *Trauerspiel*, in which 'the writer must not conceal the fact that his activity is one of arranging'.[28] What is perhaps most surprising about Leavis's attitude to *Paradise Lost* is his failure to be surprised by it. For few English literary works could surely be more bizarre, more boldly exotic, more massively and self-consciously 'literary'. The poem is so defiantly resistant to a merely realist reading, so scarred and contorted by the labour of its own production, that this very form becomes its most crucial signified.

Leavis's response to this weird phenomenon is to complain that the sound distracts him from seeing what is going on. Fredric Jameson has suggested another way of viewing this form of artifice:

> unlike prose narrative, artificial epic takes as its object of representation not events and actions themselves but rather the describing of them: the process whereby such narrative raw materials are fixed and immobilized in the heightened and embellished speech of verse. There is thus already present in epic discourse a basic and constitutive rift between form and content, between the words and their objects. . . . It can therefore be asserted that the poet of artificial epic does not compose immediately with words, but rather works, as with his most fundamental raw materials and building blocks, with just such perceptual or gestural signifiers, juxtaposing and reunifying them into the sensuous continuity of the verse paragraph.[29]

What is true of 'artificial epic' is true also of the *Trauerspiel*. There too the relative fixity of the component parts – which as Benjamin points out 'lack all "symbolic" freedom of expression',[30] belonging as they do to some great storehouse of subjectless script – compels attention, in a way equivalent to the phenomenological bracketing, to the act of interpretation itself. Milton's resounding litanies of proper names have the effect of Jameson's pre-fashioned blocks; and Benjamin himself comments how the baroque uses the capital letter so as to break up language and charge its fragments with intensified meaning. 'With the baroque the place of the capital letter was established in German orthography.'[31] Milton's sonorous names, aimed at the impressionable ear, might still of course be claimed as part of a phonocentric strategy. Yet what we have in effect is an ear without a voice: what speaks is the names themselves, discrete and monumental, uninflected by the tones of a punctual subject and grandly excessive of any strict regime of sense.

This is not a common occurrence in the literature of the time. We have become accustomed since Derrida to associating a Western prejudice for 'living speech' as against script with a metaphysic of the human subject, centred in the plenitude of its linguistic presence, the fount and origin of all sense. It is in this refusal of the materiality of the sign, this ineradicable nostalgia for a transcendental source of meaning anterior to and constitutive of all sign-systems, that Derrida finds the Western tradition most deeply marked by idealism. The speaking voice, obliterating its own materiality in the 'naturalness' of its self-production, opens a passage to the equivalent 'naturalness' of its *signata* – a passage blocked by the materiality of script, which (for this lineage) is thus destined to remain external to the spontaneous springs of meaning.

It could then hardly be otherwise than that the dense corpus of *writing* we know as the eighteenth-century English novel should find itself plunged into a severe dilemma, given the influence upon it of that ideological discourse we loosely term 'puritanism'. For installed at the very centre of puritanism is the living word – the word preached, proclaimed, consumed, obeyed and violated, the word valorized by its roots in the authentic experience of a subject, and radiant with the full presence of the divine Subject of subjects. The living Word of God, the pure expressivity of the Father, creates that sacred space in which speaking and listening persons are constituted as pure subjects for themselves and others, in a ceaseless redoubling of that transcendental intersubjectivity which is the Trinity. Of course, for the puritan tradition, *script* has a privileged status. But that is no more than to say that the enigmatic materiality of the biblical text must be dispersed by the power of grace, so that the living speech of its Author may be freed from its earthly encasement. *Texts* become *voices*, for the anguished John Bunyan of *Grace Abounding*: writing itself becomes a Subject, to be 'heard' rather than 'read', a living flesh to be cherished as the presence among men and women of the Word of words. The Word is fully present within all his words, as the principle of their unity; yet for individuals struggling in the opaqueness of history, the primordial Word is refracted amongst his various texts, which thus demand scrupulous decodement for the life-giving discourse of their Author to sound through. The meaning of that vast, cryptic sign-system which is history must be constantly displaced to be discovered – ceaselessly referred to a supportive system of transcendental *signata*, in an act whose literary name is allegory. In a double hermeneutic, historical significations must first be referred to the privileged signs of scripture, which must then be themselves disencumbered of their polyvalence to reveal a unitary Truth.

It is not surprising, then, that what strikes us most about the 'puritan' fiction of Defoe is precisely the weightlessness of its signifiers, which efface themselves in a potentially infinite metonymic chain to yield up all the material immediacy of their signifieds. Yet this instantly involves us in a contradiction at the very heart of the puritan ideology. For if the 'innocence' of Defoe's dematerialized writing marks the presence of a privileged autobiographical subject, a lonely Cartesian ego radically anterior to its material embodiments, the same device so foregrounds the material world itself as to threaten constantly to reduce the subject to no more than a reflex or support of it. The subject's epistemological security of position is in contradiction with its 'real' precariousness and contingency; safely lodged in its *retrospective* account of its turbulent experiences, it nonetheless dwindles more than once within its own narration to a cypher as empty as its signs, a mere formal motivation of plot, a perfunctory 'suturing' of heterogeneous material events. An idealism of the literary sign fatally inverts itself into a mechanical materialism of the subject: Defoe's 'degree zero' writing clears a space for that subject's expressivity, only to find that space then crammed with material *signata* which threaten to engulf and confiscate subjectivity itself.

It is this contradiction within puritan ideology, between the privilege and precariousness simultaneously assigned to the subject, that finds a different form in the novels of Samuel Richardson. For what could serve as a more dramatic image of that duality than the sight of the puritan serving-maid Pamela, cowering in her bedchamber before the rapacious advances of Mr B, yet at that very moment *writing it out*, scribbling a desperate letter, centring herself in the expressive plenitude of 'written speech' at the very instant her subordinate petty-bourgeois status is about to be sexually exploited? Fascinated by print, yet deeply embroiled in the ideological modes of the 'living', evangelizing word, Richardson discovers in the epistolary novel a breathtakingly ingenious 'solution' to his dilemma – a literary form in which 'writing' and 'experience' are absolutely synchronous, given spontaneously together, in which the act of script can become exactly contemporaneous with the very point and genesis of experience itself. For Richardson, there is nothing that cannot be *written*; but this is the precise opposite of that deconstruction of the subject into the play of *écriture* with which Derrida's work concerns itself. On the contrary, it is nothing less than the wholesale dissolution of script into the originating subject – a triumphant victory over the 'alienations' of writing, which are ceaselessly recuperated in that unity of subject and object which is the identity between Pamela as writing subject and the 'I' of whom she writes.

Except, of course, that such an identity, constituted as it is by that 'mirror relation' of Pamela to herself which is writing, is merely imaginary, as Henry Fielding in *Shamela* was the first to see. There *is* no such unity between the Pamela who writes and the Pamela whom she reveals; and it is part of the interest of Richardson's psychologism, which stakes all signification in the living subject, that when produced in fictional form it cannot help but betray those material determinants of the subject's construction that the subject speaks only to deny. For nothing could be more flagrant than what Fielding, in his own way, saw – that if we submit the epistolary texts of a Pamela or a Clarissa to a symptomatic reading, alert to their palpable absences and resonating silences, then we can begin to construct alongside the cohesive 'phenomenal' text the 'latent', mutilated text that forms the very matrix of its production. Indeed nothing could be easier to hear than the ideological and psychoanalytic discourses that truly 'write' Pamela and Clarissa, discourses that resound scandalously through the cohering letter of the subject. The phenomenal text exists to 'write out' (cancel) those discourses – to displace the guilty, inarticulable contradiction between the petty bourgeoisie's simultaneous desire for and aversion to the fertilizing embrace of the aristocracy. It is the subject constituted by the repression of that contradiction (and of others) which figures for Henry Fielding as the very mark of ideological degeneracy – Fielding, whose own fictions install the reader in the gap between their 'latent' and 'phenomenal' levels, baring the mechanisms by which a resolution of contradictions may be *arbitrarily* achieved by the forms of fictive discourse.

It is an index of the reversibility between the subject Pamela and her 'expressive' account that the very text of *Pamela* assumes the status of a subject within the novel itself – a 'character' of mystery, scandal and intrigue that at one point is actually lost. But this confrontation of the text with itself does not assume the form of an inquiry into the conditions of its own possibility, as it does, most notably, with Sterne's *Tristram Shandy*. That the famous 'rise of the novel' in England should produce almost instantaneously the greatest 'anti-novel' of all time should not seem fortuitous, in the light of what has been said: for Sterne's fiction is nothing less than a flamboyant exposé of the impossible contradictions inherent in a representational writing that can fulfil its function only by abolishing itself. *Tristram Shandy* centres itself in a benevolistic (rather than puritan) ideology of the subject, fighting the anonymity of script to invest all in expressivity, in the search for which even typography itself must be wrenched into submission. Bemused as it is by the problematic relations between matter and spirit, the novel finds the major trope of that dilemma in itself: by what Cartesian miracle can black marks on white sheets become the bearers of meaning? How can there conceivably be a passage from 'book' to 'text'? How can the materiality of language and the 'artifice' of aesthetic device hope to leave unimpaired the full presence of the author to his readers? Inexorably 'alienated' by the 'externality' of *écriture*, the reader must be ceaselessly re-centred, so that Tristram's project of self-recuperation through some form of infinite autobiography is at the same time the reader's continuously re-totalized possession of the materials. Yet this, of course, is the sign of an enormous irony, for this potentially boundless plethora of signification in fact produces an endless deconstruction of the fiction, jamming the narrative and radically decentring the reader. To pursue the logic of 'representation', to insure against the problematic bond between 'ideal' signifier and 'material' signified by anxiously explicating every iota of possible meaning and forestalling every conceivable misreading, is to load representational discourse with a weight under which it buckles and all but collapses. And this movement of construction/deconstruction is nothing less than the process by which Tristram produces himself as a 'writing subject' by a constant decomposition of himself into the material determinants that went into his making, thus undermining his security of position as subject with every step he takes to consolidate it. Every taking up of position involves both Tristram and the reader in an instant displacement, just as every attempt at representation dissolves into a spawning infinity of significations. It is this uncontrollable discourse – the endless, sprawling mesh of possible other words that each of Tristram's enunciations drags fatally in its wake – that constitutes the 'unconsciousness' that deconstructs his efforts to centre himself in speech. The 'imaginary' relation between the Tristram who writes, and the Tristram he writes of, is ruptured and confounded with every proposition; there is no way in which his writing can round on itself, *à la* Pamela, in a moment of total self-recuperation, no way in which the discourse of the writing subject can inscribe within itself the lost, secret mechanisms of that subject's process of construction. The desperate hunt for the moment of genesis of all

meaning – Tristram's attempts to isolate the inner structure of his psychic wound-
ing, Uncle Toby's physical reconstructions of the very instant of his impotency –
is a mere hurtling from one signifier to another, a ceaseless spiralling within
language that can never emerge into some transcendental sense. The privileged
mechanisms of production evade exposure, dissolved as they are in the endless play
of signs mobilized in their pursuit. They must of necessity be absent, for *writing
itself* is the very sign of their repression – the displaced potency and *ersatz* manhood
produced by some primordial sexual crippling that resists reconstruction. The
moment of Tristram's entry into the symbolic order – into language – cannot be
reproduced *within* that order, any more than the eye can reproduce itself within the
field of vision; it can be alluded to only in the *form* of the symbolic, in its infinite
play of difference and absence. The castrated narrative of *Tristram Shandy* is the
sign of its castrated author, but – since it *is* his impotency – can tell him nothing of
the 'real' causes of that lack. The novel's discourse thus installs itself in the space
of a primordial absence – a bodily mutilation – which is nothing less than the *nature
of literary discourse itself*, and which can consequently never quite round on its
repressed origins.

For Sterne, then, the problematical structure of the sign itself – how can it be
both meaning and materiality? – opens out into another question, that of the
structure of the subject. It is a question posed on the terrain of that immense irony
which is autobiography: how can the subject's discourse signify his material determinants when it is itself the product of their repression? Or – to re-pose the
question as the problem of literary representation – how can the signified be
captured other than in an infinite chain of signifiers within which it will itself
assume the status of one more signifier? To turn back from Sterne to Swift is to see
how, in *A Tale of a Tub*, all of these problems are already adumbrated – how,
indeed, they thrust themselves forward as inescapable corollaries of that new,
obsessionally subject-centred literary *genre* which, much to Swift's ideological
disgust, was in process of arising. *Gulliver's Travels* is Swift's major riposte to that
genre – a work which, tempting the reader into its space with the bait of the
'coherent subject' Gulliver, does so only to reveal Gulliver as an area traversed and
devastated by intolerable contradiction. Like Sterne, Swift locates the material/
ideal contradiction of his theological problematic in the sign itself, which seems to
recognize no middle ground between elaborating its referent out of sight, and
evaporating into it (those Laputans who hold up material objects to one another
rather than exchange words). It is these material/ideal contradictions that the
fourth book of *Gulliver's Travels* detonates within the reader, ruthlessly dispersing
him or her amidst mutually incompatible discourses. Gulliver despises men as
Yahoos and identifies with the Houyhnhnms; the Houyhnhnms despise the Yahoos
and regard Gulliver as one of them; we are amused by the Houyhnhnms and by
Gulliver's delusions, but are close enough to the Yahoos for the amusement to be
uneasy; and to cap it all there are some respects in which the Yahoos *are* superior
to humans. There is no way for the reader to 'totalize' these contradictions, which

the text so adroitly springs upon him or her; he or she is merely caught in their dialectical interplay, rendered as eccentric to himself as the lunatic Gulliver, unable to turn to the refuge of an assuring authorial voice. To deconstruct the reader, reducing him or her from positioned subject to a function of polyphonic discourses: this is the *ideological* intervention accomplished by all of Swift's writing. And it is here that a discourse concerned with Derrida circles to the name of Brecht.

There is no doubt that when Benjamin writes of the doleful tainting of language by meaning, its leashing to logicality, he betrays a nostalgia for the pure, prelapsarian word.[32] But this is not quite Eliot's 'dissociation of sensibility' or Leavis's organicist delusions. For Eliot and Leavis, a 'prelapsarian' language is one transparent to the body: it is thus 'material' only by derivation. In the postlapsarian Miltonic era, language disentwines itself from the digestive tracts and falls into its own clogging material mode. For Benjamin, the Edenic word is likewise bodily, expressive and mimetic; but it never ceases to manifest a materiality of its own. 'Language communicates the linguistic being of things. The clearest manifestation of this being, however, is language itself. The answer to the question "*What* does language communicate?" is therefore "All language communicates itself".'[33] Ironically, this materialism of the word is nowhere more evident than in the 'postlapsarian' language of baroque. The more things and meanings disengage, the more obvious become the material operations of the allegories that fumble to reunite them. Such unity, to be sure, can be won only at the cost of a grievous reification: emblem and hieroglyph paralyse history to print, and the body achieves its deepest signification as corpse. But if experience is in this way converted to a stilted, repetitive text, it is only the more dramatically to reveal that it is, in some sense, 'text' in the first place. The lumbering action of the *Trauerspiel* writes large or plays through in slow motion something of the nature of language 'as such'. The matter-laden letters of such drama press an Edenic materiality of the word to a point of grisly caricature; and this differs sharply from a Leavisian view of the relations between Donne and Milton.

It is certainly true that we cannot imagine the shattered world of the *Trauerspiel* without itching to construct some pre-given unity from which it has lapsed away; in this sense Benjamin's text confronts us with the familiar problem of trying to think difference without positing the unity it denies. But if allegory 'enslaves objects in the eccentric embrace of meaning',[34] that meaning is irreducibly multiple. The very arbitrariness of the relations between signifier and signified in allegorical thought encourages 'the exploitation of ever remoter characteristics of the representative objects as symbols, so as to surpass even the Egyptians with new subtleties. In addition to this there was the dogmatic power of the meanings handed down from the ancients, so that one and the same object can just as easily signify a virtue as a vice, and therefore more or less anything'.[35] In an astounding circulation of signifiers, 'any person, any object, any relationship can mean absolutely anything else'.[36] The immanent meaning that ebbs from the object under the transfixing gaze of melancholy leaves it a pure signifier, a rune or fragment retrieved from the clutches of a univocal sense and surrendered unconditionally into the allegorist's power. If it has become in one sense embalmed, it has also been liberated into polyvalence: it is in this that for Benjamin the profoundly dialectical nature of allegory lies. Allegorical discourse has the doubleness of the death's head: 'total expressionlessness – the black of the eye-sockets – coupled to the most unbridled expression – the grinning rows of teeth'.[37] The mortified landscape of history is redeemed, not by being recuperated into spirit, but by being raised, so to speak, to the second power – converted into a formal repertoire, fashioned into certain enigmatic emblems which then hold the promise of knowledge and possession.

History, then, as always for Benjamin, progresses by its bad side. If there is a route beyond reification, it is through and not around it; if even apparently dead objects, in the sepulchral splendour of the *Trauerspiel*, secure tyrannical power over the human, it remains true that the tenacious self-absorption of melancholy, brooding upon such husks, embraces them in order to redeem them. For Benjamin, such redemption is finally Messianic; but even his Messianism has a kind of dialectical structure. The baroque renounces eschatology: it shows no immanent mechanism whereby earthly things are even now being gathered in and exalted. Instead, the rich profusion of mundane objects is seen as a kind of plundering of the hereafter: the more history is thoroughly secularized, the less possible it is to characterize heaven in its terms. Heaven, accordingly, is reduced to a pure signifier, an empty space, but this vacuum will one day engulf the world with catastrophic violence.[38] If this apocalypticism is for us one of the least palatable elements of Benjamin's thought, it nonetheless marks a kind of 'negative dialectics' that, for all its idealism, comes close to the productively pessimistic side of historical materialism. Indeed to 'begin from the bad side' is a methodological premise for Benjamin, as is clear enough from his study of Baudelaire: 'sundering truth from falsehood is the goal of the materialist method, not its point of departure. In other words, its point of departure is the object riddled with error, with *doxa*.'[39] It is by submitting itself to the mixed substance of the empirical object, not by transfiguring that object at a stroke into its appearance 'in truth', that the progressively discriminative movement of inquiry proceeds. It is not always easy, admittedly, to distinguish this clearly from the positivist tendency for which Adorno chides Benjamin, the 'wide-eyed presentation of mere facts'[40] that in the very density of its description seems to pass right through the object and emerge on the other side as a sort of ghosted theorizing of it. 'There is a delicate empiricism', Benjamin quotes Goethe as writing, 'which so intimately involves itself with the object that it becomes true theory.'[41] Whatever the limits of this emphasis, it belongs with the Benjamin who acknowledged the mixed substance of his own political situation, stranded between Communists and bourgeoisie – who recognized that 'right' in such a condition could only mean 'necessarily, symptomatically, productively false'.[42] To begin from the bad side is to reckon loss, ambiguity and *mauvaise foi* into the calculation; and Benjamin began his own writing career with a book that turned such things to productive use.

What Benjamin asserts of the allegorical object – that at its nadir of blank inertia, purged of all mystified immanence, it can be liberated into multiple uses – has more than an echo of Georg Lukács's *History and Class Consciousness*, which in similar idealist fashion sees the reduction of the proletariat to the paradigmatic commodity as the prelude to its emancipation. The *Trauerspiel* ransacks heaven and ruins all transcendence, marooning its characters in a world of paranoid, patriarchal power; but by the same token it disowns all facile teleologies, ruptures the imaginary relations of myth and scatters free those symbolic fragments from which the emblem may forge fresh correspondences. Released from the ideological tyrannies of Nature, the subject can find no consolation in a compensatory myth of history, for that too has shrunk to sheer ritual repetition. If discourse has been similarly debased to a mere permutation of properties, an arbitrary *bricolage* of elements, this itself subverts the logocentrism of the symbol and unmasks the speaking voice as yet another inscription. The more the signifier becomes fetishized in the ceaseless pedantries of emblematic correspondence, the more suggestively arbitrary it comes to seem: the very laborious effort expended on asserting its iconic or 'motivated' relations with the signified comes curiously to demystify itself, revealing how usably unmotivated it actually is. The enigmas of history force the techniques of their decipherment into peculiar self-consciousness, so that concealment on one level produces exposure on another: a fetishized reality gives birth to a fetishized hermeneutic, but one so palpably so that it lays bare its own devices. And trembling on the brink of this historical collapse, waiting in the wings for its redemptive entry, is, precisely – nothing: the pure signifier of a paradise that never comes, an utterly destructive apocalypse that is at once everything and nothing, a spasm of empty space that consummates all those deaths and absences that are language itself.

The truly materialist version of Benjamin's redemptive hope will come not through his mentor Lukács but through his friend Bertolt Brecht. For nothing is quite so striking as the way in which the *Origin* recapitulates, even before they had been properly initiated, all the major themes of Benjamin's later championship of Brechtian drama. Baroque allegory lays bare the device, posing motto and caption in blunt, obtrusive relation to the visual figure, defeating the mystifications of symbolism. In the dense hieroglyphics of this genre, *writing* comes to receive all its material weight – but this in a dialectical way, since as we have seen any figure or object can come to mean absolutely anything else. Objects in such spectacles are always strictly coded, in a discourse as far as Jacques Derrida himself would wish from the speaking voice; and images, far from being hierarchically ranked, are piled in a seemingly haphazard way one on the other, with no 'totalizing' aim in mind. Yet for all that the drama is ostentatiously a construction, though of a notably decentred kind: its diverse, elaborate features submit inexorably to a structure that yet forever refuses to unite them, allowing them their jarring particularity and glittering ornamentation. 'Shock' is thus an essential quality of such texts: the baroque, for Benjamin, is nothing if not provocative and offensive. The allegorist is spontaneously anti-Hegelian: the 'essence', rather than lurking behind the object as its repressed secret, is dragged into the open, hounded into the brazen status of a caption. The relation between object and essence is metonymic rather than metaphorical: 'in the context of allegory the image is only a signature, only the monogram of essence, not the essence itself in a mask'.[43]

If it is true that the action of such melancholic dramas moves with a certain heavy-handed slowness, it is also true that situations can change in a flash. Objects in such texts are fanatically collected, but then slackly and indifferently dispersed in their arrangements; and the very form of the *Trauerspiel* reproduces this irregular impulse, since it builds act upon act in the 'manner of terraces', repulsing any suave linearity of presentation for a syncopated rhythm that oscillates endlessly between swift switches of direction and consolidations into rigidity. The imagery of the *Trauerspiel* rudely dismembers the human body in order to allegorize its discrete parts, sundering its organic unity (in a manner analogous, perhaps, to Freud's) so that some meaning may be rescued from its parcelled fragments. Like Benjamin's own later philosophy of history, the *Trauerspiel*, obsessed with the transience of the present and the need to redeem it for eternity, blasts coherences apart in order to salvage them in their primordial givenness.

It is surely clear that what we have here are all the seeds of Benjamin's later defence of Brecht. The drama as fragmented, device-baring, non-hierarchical, shock-producing; theatre as dispersed, gear-switching and dialectical, ostentatious and arbitrary yet densely encoded: what Benjamin discovered in Brecht was precisely how you might do all this and be non-melancholic into the bargain.[44] And the secret of the *Origin* is not merely that it speaks of these qualities; it is that it is itself constituted by them. For there is hardly an epithet used by Benjamin to describe his object of study that does not glance sideways at his own critical method. That this is so, yet that he succeeds in displacing rather than reproducing the texts in question, is surely one of the book's most remarkable triumphs. Since the text believes that the task of philosophy is to divest phenomena of their empirical trappings so that they may be lifted into a realm of essences whose mutual interrelations constitute truth, this is a triumph it doubtless needs; though even this epistemology, as we shall see later, has a materialist seed.

Notes

1   (London, 1949), pp. 11, 13.
2   *Revaluation*, p. 31.
3   Ibid., p. 49.
4   Ibid., p. 51.
5   'The Metaphysical Poets', *Selected Essays* (London, 1963), p. 290.
6   *Selected Prose of T. S. Eliot*, ed. Frank Kermode (London, 1975), p. 268.
7   *Revaluation*, p. 50.

8   *The Origin of German Tragic Drama*, trans. John Osborne (London: New Left Books, 1977), p. 176.
9   Ibid., p. 184.
10 Ibid., p. 201.
11 Ibid., p. 201.
12 Ibid., p. 202.
13 See *La Révolution du langage poétique* (Paris, 1974).
14 *Selected Prose of T. S. Eliot*, p. 263.
15 See *Understanding Brecht*, trans. Anna Bostock, with an introduction by Stanley Mitchell (London: New Left Books, 1973), p. 121.
16 *The Origin of German Tragic Drama*, p. 166.
17 Ibid., p. 176.
18 F. R. Leavis and Denys Thompson, *Culture and Environment* (London, 1933), p. 87.
19 *Of Grammatology*, trans. Gayatri Chakravorty Spivak (Baltimore and London, 1976), p. 12.
20 *The Origin of German Tragic Drama*, pp. 213–14. Cf. Marx and Engels: 'from the start the "spirit" is affected with the curse of being "burdened" with matter, which here makes its appearance in the form of agitated layers of air, sounds, in short, of language' (*The German Ideology*, London, 1965, p. 41). In a conversation recorded by Gershom Scholem, Benjamin sharply rejected a distinction between writing and the voice, 'with such animosity as if someone had touched a wound' (Preface to *Briefe*, ed. Gershom Scholem and T. W. Adorno, 2 vols. (Frankfurt am Main, 1966), 1, p. 16). Scholem comments elsewhere that Benjamin spoke as though he were writing.
21 *The Origin of German Tragic Drama*, p. 215.
22 A fact in some sense obvious to the soldiers of the first Russian revolution of 1905, who carried copies of *Paradise Lost* with them and read it enthusiastically as a libertarian text.
23 *Politics and Letters* (London: New Left Books, 1979), pp. 335–6.
24 *The Origin of German Tragic Drama*, p. 133.
25 *Marxism and Form* (Princeton, 1971), p. 72.
26 *The Origin of German Tragic Drama*, p. 135.
27 See A. J. A. Waldock, *Paradise Lost and Its Critics* (Cambridge, 1947), for a characteristically 'realist' reading of the poem. Waldock's book, however, shows in unconsciously Machereyan style how the official ideology of Milton's poem is ruptured and embarrassed by the formal figurations (narrative, character and so on) it is constrained to assume.
28 *The Origin of German Tragic Drama*, p. 179.
29 *Fables of Aggression: Wyndham Lewis, the Modernist as Fascist* (Berkeley, Los Angeles and London), 1979, pp. 76, 78.
30 *The Origin of German Tragic Drama*, p. 166.
31 Ibid., p. 208.
32 See 'On Language as Such and on the Language of Man', *One-Way Street and Other Writings*, trans. Edmund Jephcott and Kingsley Shorter (London: New Left Books, 1979), pp. 107–23.
33 Ibid., p. 109.
34 *The Origin of German Tragic Drama*, p. 202.
35 Ibid., p. 174.

36 Ibid., p. 175.
37 *One-Way Street and Other Writings*, p. 70.
38 See 'Theologico-Political Fragment', Ibid., pp. 155–6.
39 *Charles Baudelaire: A Lyric Poet in the Era of High Capitalism*, trans. Harry Zohn (London: New Left Books, 1973), p. 103.
40 *Aesthetics and Politics* (London: New Left Books, 1977), p. 129.
41 'A Small History of Photography', *One-Way Street and Other Writings*, p. 252.
42 *Briefe*, 2, p. 530.
43 *The Origin of German Tragic Drama*, p. 214.
44 What Angus Fletcher has to say of allegory in his unsurpassed study is particularly appropriate to Brechtian theatre: 'the price of a lack of mimetic naturalness is what the allegorist, like the Metaphysical poet, must pay in order to force his reader into an analytic frame of mind. . . . The silences in allegory mean as much as the filled-in spaces, because by bridging the silent gaps between oddly unrelated images we reach the sunken understructure of thought . . .' (*Allegory: The Theory of a Symbolic Mode* (Ithaca, NY, 1964), p. 107). The whole cluster of concerns that Fletcher delineates – allegory, multiple meaning, didacticism, montage, surrealistic surface textures – is of the closest relevance to Benjamin's cultural interests.

15 Deconstruction and Human Rights

Deconstruction has two embarrassments with the phrase 'human rights', one with each word. In deconstructive eyes, the whole notion surely belongs to a discreditable metaphysical humanism – which is not to say that it is strategically unusable, just ontologically baseless. To what sort of subject could such rights conceivably attach themselves? 'Ethics', writes Paul de Man in *Allegories of Reading*, 'has nothing to do with the will (thwarted or free) of a subject, nor *a fortiori* with a relationship between subjects.'[1] De Man will accordingly shift the whole question of ethics from a subjective to a linguistic register – which is to say that moral imperatives share in the aberrational nature of all language when it strives, hopelessly yet ineluctably, to *refer*. The implacability of such imperatives becomes merely one not particularly privileged instance of the fatality of language itself, which imposes its august law upon us with all the blind determinism of an Aeschylean drama. The ethical, in this bleak scenario, has nothing to do with human decision; it is that which, like language, we cannot help feeling the force of, a set of groundless edicts in the face of which the subject would seem entirely passive. To dissolve the humanist subject to sheer randomness, or to the effect of an iron determinism, are equally effective ways of disposing of it. Like the Habermasians with whom deconstruction is so deeply at odds, de Man has come up here with a kind of linguistic neo-Kantianism[2] – with this difference, that the law to which we cannot help conforming clearly has no truck with value. It is hard to see how one can speak of moral value when one has no choice but to obey, just as it was hard for Nietzsche to work out what exactly was valuable about giving expression to the will to power, since we articulate it anyway just by virtue of what we are. In his foreword to Carol Jacobs's *The Dissimulating Harmony*, de Man argues that 'what makes a reading more or less true is simply the predictability, the necessity of its occurrence, regardless of the reader or of the author's wishes.'[3] J. Hillis Miller in his *The Ethics of Reading* sees this necessity as the very model of the ethical; but if de Man means what he says literally – that we *really* can't help reading the text this way – then this is a mistaken view of the nature of moral absolutes, which can of course always be disobeyed, and which would not be in business if they could not be. To model moral imperatives on literally unavoidable readings, like modelling them on the laws of nature, is simply to confuse the moral and phenomenal realms in a most un-deManian fashion. In a notable shuffle, Miller goes on to speak of the way that we can't avoid making judgments or issuing commands; but this is by no means the same thing as being unable to avoid obeying such commands or accepting such judgments. 'Ethical' deconstruction, then, delivers us a neo–Kantianism shorn of both subject and value; and it is not easy to see how this is going to form the most reliable basis for our deliberations over what to do about the boat people.

Deconstruction's embarrassment with ethics is, more precisely, an embarrassment with *political* ethics. There is a good deal in the recent Derrida about gift and promise, obligation and responsibility; but it is hard to see how this might be brought to bear on the nature of neo-Stalinism or the oppression of women. Indeed, Derrida himself seems to have grown increasingly restive with such humdrum political matters, as when he asserts in a recent interview that deconstruction is neither conservative nor revolutionary, and that this is what gets on its opponents' nerves.[4] We have become accustomed of late to hearing from Derrida such statements as (I parody a little): 'I am not *for* socialism; but I am not *against* it either. Neither am I *neither* for nor against it, nor simply for or against the whole opposition of "for" and "against".' Equivocation and ambiguity are not always moral virtues; and there seems no doubt that such finespun obliquity on issues of central political importance has done much to disillusion those erstwhile enthusiasts for deconstruction who somewhat gullibly credited its promissory note to deliver some political goods. In its finely drawn distaste for 'categories', deconstruction is merely the mirror image of the banal liberal humanism it seeks to subvert. If it acknowledges in a notional sort of way that closure – a certain provisional naming and identifying – may be enabling as well as unproductive, its sensibilities are nevertheless wounded by such crudely one-sided commitments. The truth that neither liberal nor post-structuralist seems able to countenance is that there are certain key political struggles that someone is going to have to win and someone will have to lose. To deconstruct *these* binary oppositions is to be complicit with the political status quo, as with that fashionable brand of neocolonialist theory for which colonialist and colonized would seem mere mirror images of each other in their ambivalences and self-divisions. It is an affront to intellectuals, whose work must necessarily negotiate complexity and indeterminacy, that all the most important political conflicts are in this sense essentially *simple* – not, naturally, in their character, but from the standpoint of whose cause is essentially just.

Even so, deconstruction has made a tentative turn to the ethical, in part under the pressure of the de Man affair; and Hillis Miller's *The Ethics of Reading* is exemplary in this respect. The first note Miller strikes is an ominous separation of the ethical and political: 'No doubt the political and the ethical are always intimately intertwined, but an ethical act that is fully determined by political considerations or responsibilities is no longer ethical. It could even in a certain sense be said to be amoral.'[5] As with many non-radical uses of the term, 'political' here has an inescapable ring of expediency and opportunism; tell me your definition of politics, as they say, and I will tell you your politics. A 'fully political' act, whatever that is, can only count as non-ethical if, in a pointless circularity, the political has been voided of ethical content in the first place, covertly downgraded to sheerly pragmatic status. The more full-bloodedly political our actions, the less they have moral value – a point that might have come as a surprise to Dr Martin Luther King, Jr. The ethical is intertwined with the political, but, in a gesture of exclusion and separation, must finally stand puristically alone. This is an odd move for a deconstructionist to make, and one which Aristotle, among others, would have found unintelligible.[6] For how could one judge qualities of character and action in isolation from the *polis* that produces them? How could there be a non-political virtue? There is a science that inquires into the nature of the good life, Aristotle remarks towards the beginning of the *Nicomachean Ethics*, and its name is – politics. The modern reader flicks back bemusedly to the title page, wondering whether she has picked up the wrong volume. In traditional Marxist parlance, it is moralism, not true moral judgment, that artificially detaches an action from its determining historical context and seeks to examine it in isolation. The ethical and the political are not, *pace* Miller, ultimately separate realms but different viewpoints on the same object – the one assessing such matters as desires, virtues, and so forth, the other, more capacious, discourse reflecting on the matrix of practices, institutions, social relations, and the rest within which such things are alone intelligible. It is in this sense that for Aristotle ethics is a kind of sub-branch of politics, a particular dimension within its general enquiry. The ethical judgment Miller delivers on the relations between the ethical and political is itself only fully intelligible within a certain political history, for which the political has indeed become a degraded domain. There is nothing surprising in believing after Irangate that our actions shed their ethical content the more closely they approximate the 'fully political'. But if Miller's ethical judgment is indeed unwittingly conditioned by such a political history, then it merely deconstructs itself.

Like de Man, Miller is an unconfessed neo-Kantian who thinks of ethics primarily in terms of absolute imperatives and categorical necessities for which, as he remarks, 'there is absolutely no foundation in knowledge, that is in the epistemological realm governed by the category of truth and falsehood.'[7] Like de Man too, Miller offers us this version of the ethical as though it were timeless and universal, rather than the fruit of a quite recent, deeply controversial history. There is no reason to assume that ethics is primarily a matter of absolute imperatives or necessities. Absolutes are not necessarily all that interesting: Aquinas, for example, believed that lying was absolutely wrong, but he did not mean by this that it was necessarily *very very* wrong, wrong in some dramatically illuminating way, and he certainly thought it less important than actions such as killing, which he held could be in some circumstances justified. Not all moral prescriptives weigh in on us with the inexorable force of some Sophoclean fate; in fact, Bernard Williams has enforced an interesting distinction between the 'moral' and the 'ethical' which is relevant to this point.[8]

The assumption that the ethical consists chiefly in imperatives, prescriptives, prohibitions, and the like is a convenient one for post-structuralists, since it promises to reduce the whole question to that discursive or performative realm where they feel most at home – indeed, which is for them, in a certain sense, all there is. If the ethical cannot be dissolved to the discursive, then this most vital of problems threatens to elude their grasp; but in a striking irony, this reduction can take place only by defining ethics in terms of mysteriously ungrounded utterances, and so entering into an unholy alliance with a tradition of moral thought – Kantianism which is in other ways quite rebarbative to the deconstructive mind. If the work of Paul de Man has a repressive austerity about it that makes even the sage of Königsberg look a bit of a libertine, the same cannot be claimed of the deconstructive sensibility in general, whose sportive, hedonistic, aleatory bias would, one might have thought, run directly contrary to a world of unconditional decrees and dire necessities. By what strange paradox or inversion does deconstruction, that most iconoclastic, libertarian of projects, come to find itself intoning absolute commands? Can it be serious?

The answer lies partly in the fact that such absolutes, as we shall see in a moment, are not really absolutes at all, and partly in the attractiveness for deconstruction of Kant's separation of pure and practical reason. For Kant, the kind of knowledge we can have of the world is not adequate to ground our moral projects; for deconstruction, knowledge is just too precarious and bedevilled a business to ground anything at all. It is on this terrain that puritan and libertarian, the deontological and the deconstructive, Stoicism and skepticism effect their unpredictable encounter. Miller, as we have seen, writes of the 'uttering of ethical commands and promises ("You should do so and so; You will be happy if you do so and so") for which there is absolutely no foundation in knowledge'. It depends, of course, on what is meant by 'foundation'; but if Miller means, as he sometimes seems to, that ethical utterances have no relation whatsoever to the cognitive, then the case is clearly false. ('You will be happy if you do so because scientific research reveals that if you do not then your belly will burst in a most unpleasant manner.') This may not be, in one sense of the term, a way of *founding* right conduct on knowledge of what is the case, since it implies a value judgment ('having your belly burst is a bad thing'); but it certainly couples the two realms in ways that Miller would appear at times to ignore.

Ethical judgments thus become, in Miller's terms, 'a baseless positing, always unjust and unjustified, therefore always likely to be displaced by another momentarily stronger or more persuasive but equally baseless positing of a different code of ethics.'[9] In this Darwinian struggle between moral codes, an absolute is absolute until it ceases to be so, in which case it is not absolute at all. Such judgments for deconstruction are 'absolute' not because they are unquestionably well founded, but precisely because they are not. If there is no good reason to obey them, then there is no good reason to disobey them either. They are 'absolute' in proportion to their utter gratuitousness, their very groundlessness a kind of ground in itself. And it is in this sense that the Kantian turn finally leads deconstruction back to its home ground. For the moral law, which would appear in its implacable absolutism to transcend the shifting vagaries of the signifier, and so lend deconstruction a moral urgency and engagement it might otherwise seem to lack, is simply another instance of that supreme discursive fiction which is the world itself, its very rhetorical authority necessarily betraying its linguistic arbitrariness. The unconditioned nature of an *acte gratuit* is mistaken for the unconditional nature of an absolute moral command. Deconstruction, in a most unKantian move, does indeed in a sense unite pure and practical reason, since both are unmasked as baseless fictions; but it separates them at the same time, since the very baseless fictionality of the world is what prevents the moral law from being anchored there. It must, therefore, as with Kant, be founded in itself – the absolutism of which allows it to rise above the world and issue its unquestionable edicts, the arbitrariness of which means that it has secretly never left that realm at all. The Kantian 'giving of the law to oneself' becomes just another instance of the self-referential signifier, so that the law sits in august judgment on that of which it is part. Moreover, the *enigma* of this Kantian law, which seems to hail from nowhere, has a powerful appeal to the quasi-mystical side of the deconstructive sensibility, its fascination with the elusive and ineffable.

What happens, in short, is an aestheticizing of the ethical, which, like the work of art, is absolute and arbitrary, lawful and lawless together. It is significant in this respect that the later work of Jean-François Lyotard should attempt to derive a political ethics not from Kant's second *Critique*, but from his third.[10] Kant himself, of course, wished to distinguish moral and aesthetic questions, but the alternative source of a deconstructive ethics – Friedrich Nietzsche – saw no such necessity. Miller's and de Man's 'baseless positing' is purely Nietzschean, and the whole of this deconstructive ethics a curious amalgam of his influence and Kant's. Deconstruction inherits from Kant the notion of a self-grounding moral law that must be unconditionally obeyed; but in a Nietzschean move this law is no longer to be located in a community of autotelic subjects, or in the moral nature of humanity, but in sheer arbitrary rhetorical force. The law is rewritten as language; and since language for deconstruction is at once arbitrary in its workings and absolute in its claims, this conveniently draws together Nietzsche and Kant. In Nietzsche himself, this rhetorical force is sometimes purely decisionistic: 'Genuine philosophers . . . are commanders and legislators: they say: *thus* shall it be!'[11] This supposed source of moral judgments is thus itself open to moral judgment, in its authoritarian elitism. But what 'posits' for Nietzsche is less the subject than the will to power, of which it is composed; and for 'will to power' in the case of deconstruction one can read, simply, 'language'. Language for Paul de Man is that blind, mechanistic phenomenon, aleatory and inexorable, which is at once the 'subject' of ethical imperatives and, like the will to power, beyond ethical reach itself, utterly neutral as regards value, as blankly inhuman as that Kantian law which issues its edicts in icy disregard of whether its flesh-and-blood subjects can actually live up to them.

This whole conception of the law is thus politically sterile. For, as Schiller was not slow to recognize, no authority as indifferent to the question of *hegemony* as this could possibly hope to secure its subjects' allegiance. The account of the law delivered by Miller and de Man cannot possibly make sense of how the law operates politically, which is one reason among several why this brand of deconstructive ethics cannot provide us with an adequate politics. In Gramscian terms, the deManian model of the law at once overemphasizes its coerciveness and drastically underrates its consensual strategies. In one sense, the law can dispense with such strategies because it imposes itself absolutely; in another sense, as a sheer baseless fiction, it would seem to be badly in need of them. Unless, that is, there is a covert elitism at work here: intellectuals like Miller and de Man will obey the law despite having blown its rhetorical cover, while the masses will obey it precisely because they have not.

Some Marxist theoreticians of the Second International period had incongruous recourse to Kantian ethics because their positivist view of history could yield them no answers as to what was valuable or desirable. That socialism is historically inevitable in no sense entails that it will be particularly pleasant. Deconstruction has turned to Kant to fill a somewhat similar gap; but it might have been well advised to turn elsewhere. An ethics of a kind can be generated up from the theoretical notions of deconstruction itself, in the sense that (for example) there is a political ethics implicit in its concern with the otherness and partial opacity of human subjects, or in the project of emancipating the signifier from its enthrall-ment to violently stabilized meaning. The problem with the former path, however, is that it lands you up with little more than a conventional liberal pluralism, which hardly matches up to the radicalism of deconstruction's more mind-shaking, un-nerving insights. The problem with the latter route is that it threatens to deliver you a naïve romantic libertarianism. This is *too* radical for the deconstructionists, whose more sceptical, pessimistic, equivocatory post-1968 personae will tirelessly insist on the inescapability of the logocentric, the inevitable imbrication of law with desire, the metaphysical nature of revolution, and the fractured, fragile quality of the subjects who might be called upon to be its agents. The 'libertarianism' of post-structuralism is calculatedly self-baffling and self-undoing, and as such no sure basis for a politics. But the recourse to Kant will furnish you no politics beyond an orthodox liberalism; and it will deflect your ethical thought in the direction of a peculiarly anaemic discourse of law, rights, and duties, which not only sits uncom-fortably with deconstruction's deep suspicion of all forms of normativity but, more significantly, represents an undue narrowing of another, much richer and more fertile, tradition of moral thought.

It is that alternative discourse that J. G. A. Pocock has dubbed 'civic human-ism'.[12] This more ancient moral heritage is concerned not primarily with rights but with virtues; and far from elevating the ethical over the political *à la* Miller, it regards human beings as naturally political animals and views their moral qualities within this context. The virtuous man, for this strenuously masculinist style of thought, is one who has enough property, preferably of a landed kind, to be released from economic preoccupations into the business of exerting his personal capacities for the good of the *polis* or *res publica*. Republican virtue of this kind takes the form of a community of free, equal, self-governing citizens whose ethical ideal consists in developing their autonomous personalities through a devotion to the public realm. Such a conception involves notions of distributive justice or *suum cuique*, since each citizen must contribute to the common good in a style proper to his own personal talents; but this republican model of virtue, in Pocock's words, 'exceeded the limits of jurisprudence and therefore of justice as a jurist conceived it'. Virtue cannot be reduced to a matter of right; rather, the laws of a republic 'were the formal structure within which political nature developed to its inherent end'.[13]

It is this tradition of republican virtue that Pocock sees as entering into conflict with a more narrowly framed juristic conception of political morality. In ancient society, law is of the empire rather than the republic, and its attention is fixed on *commercium* rather than *politicum*. 'As the *polis* and *res publica* declined towards the level of municipality, two things happened: the universe became pervaded by law, the locus of whose sovereignty was extra-civic, and the citizen came to be defined not by his actions and virtues, but by his rights to and in things.' Jurisprudence, which deals in such relations to things, shifts emphasis from the purely political realm to what Pocock describes as 'the thick layers of social and material reality by which the *animale politicum* is surrounded'. It is thus predominantly social rather than political, concerned with 'the administration of things and with human relations conducted through the mediation of things, as opposed to a civic vocabulary of the purely political, concerned with the unmediated personal relations entailed by equality and by ruling and being ruled.'[14] Civil law, so Pocock argues, thus presents us with a species of possessive individualism that long predates early modern capitalism; the citizen is now defined as right-bearer and proprietor rather than by his participation in the political sphere. What we are examining, in short, is the root of what the modern period will term liberalism, which characterizes morality in a discourse of law and right, rather than in terms of the virtuous personality. Political sovereignty is alienated from the public sphere into the possession of the prince or magistrate, and exists to safeguard the rights of citizens who have now become depoliticized. The political now denotes less a system of relations between citizens than a set of law-governed relations between authorities and subjects.

For the virtuous citizen of civic humanism to become entangled in exchange relations would be to court the danger of dependence on the favours of the state, and so of corruption. Virtue and commerce are thus irreconcilable – which is to say that virtue in an increasingly commercialized social order cannot truly be exercised in the social, only the political, sphere, and so is at risk of appearing restricted and archaic. The possession of property, for civic humanism, is simply a material prerequisite for the exercise of one's political personality; for the juristic conception, property becomes a system of legally defined relations between persons and things, or between persons through things, and the good life can now be characterized in these terms. It is this eighteenth-century ideology, at odds with the values of civic humanism, which Pocock calls 'commercial humanism', and which, having abandoned the hard road of republican virtue, must seek out another route to the moral good. In the new, modern world of commerce and the arts, the old amateur political activist must yield ground to the private, specialized individual, whose interactions with other social beings and their products become increasingly complex and differentiated, developing and refining his personality by modulating barbarous passion into the subtleties of sympathetic social intercourse. If this subject has delegated his political power to a professional caste of specialized representatives, he is more than compensated for this loss of antique virtue by the infinite enrichment of his personality through his proliferating relationships with people and things. Virtue, an essentially political notion, thus yields ground to the alternative social conception of 'manners', which it is the function of commerce to nurture; and the unified, vigorously autonomous personality of the *res publica* is cheerfully surrendered for the more specialized, differentiated, decentred subject of a commercial dispensation.

In the light of this complex, contentious history, it is possible to register the narrow one-sidedness of a post-structuralist ethics that appears to take the Kantian, liberal, juridical conception of morality as a self-evident starting point. For if that thoroughly ideological formation finally prevailed in modern society, it did so only in the teeth of radically alternative images of the good life that never quite faded from view. What happened, then, to the civic humanist lineage? I want to argue that one of its major inheritors is, in fact, Marxism; and though Pocock himself has little enough to say about this doctrine, other than assuring us more than once that he doesn't subscribe to it, there are nevertheless some instructive parallels to be drawn.

Marx's general debt to the history that Pocock records is fairly obvious: he was, broadly speaking, an Aristotelian who held that the end of history was happiness, that the nature of humanity was political, and that the good life consisted in developing and exercising one's capacities in sustaining and reproducing the common weal. Marxism falls squarely within the ethical tradition of 'virtue' rather than 'right', concerned as it is with the creative unfolding of the individual personality in its social interactions with others. But if Marxism is thus an extension of the civic humanist tradition, it is also a critical transformation of it; and to launch this critique, it has recourse, ironically enough, to the commercial humanist inheritance that for Pocock is the antithesis of classical republican virtue. Indeed, Marxism is a strikingly original *combination* of these two modes of thought and practice, pitting the one against the other in order to achieve some novel synthesis that finally transcends both.

Civic humanism, despite its inflatedly idealist vision of the good life, is materialist in a roughly Marxian sense: it has grasped the truth that to be good you have to be well-heeled. This is not, of course, to claim that the poor are morally shabby, simply that for there to be general well-being as the 'virtue' tradition sees it – for every human personality to flourish in the richness of its creative powers – certain material preconditions must be in place. Individuals cannot thrive in this way if they are forced to lead a life of wretched toil, which is why for Marx socialism depends upon a high level of development of the productive forces. The point of this development is to release men and women as far as is feasible from the exigencies of the labour process, so that they may be free for politics. Socialist republicanism – the active participation of all individuals in their own self-government – takes a lot of time; and such socialist democracy will prove impossible if you bring off a 'socialist' revolution in desperately backward economic conditions without international support. In such a situation, men and women are likely to find themselves coerced by an authoritarian state into developing the forces of production as rapidly as possible; and this will prove inimical to the construction of the socialist res publica. The effort to lay the economic basis for the political institutions of socialism will itself break them steadily down. This, in effect, is the historical-materialist critique of Stalinism; and it involves the tragic irony that socialism is least possible where it is most urgently necessary. As Marx puts the point in Capital: work will remain a necessity under socialism, but beyond that horizon, with the advent of full communism, will begin 'that development of human energy which is an end in itself, the true realm of freedom, which, however, can blossom forth only with this realm of necessity as its basis'. Marx adds, with what one likes to think of as calculated bathos: 'The shortening of the working day is its basic prerequisite.'[15] Without such a material base, the only socialism possible would be what Marx scathingly describes as 'generalized scarcity'.

It is clear, then, that Marxism and civic humanism are at one in their acknowledgment of the material conditions of virtue, and both to this extent are profoundly at odds with the formal ethical idealism of a Kant. For civic humanism, as Pocock comments, 'property was both an extension and a prerequisite of personality'; to be in possession of independent landed property was to have a chance of virtue, both in the positive sense that it freed you from the economic preoccupations of the merchant to engage in republican politics, and in the negative sense that it thereby protected you from the moral corruption consequent on depending for handouts on the men in government. 'The moral personality', so Pocock writes, 'in this sense is possible only upon a foundation of real property, since the possession of land brings with it unspecialized leisure and the opportunity to virtue, while the production and exchange of goods entails activities too specialized to be compatible with citizenship.'[16] But if Marxism is, to this extent, in alignment with civic humanism, it also puts it into radical question. For what that humanism aloofly excludes, in its wholehearted dedication to the political realm, is precisely what Pocock calls the 'thick layers of social and material reality by which the animale politicum is surrounded'; and this, in effect, is the kernel of Marx's *Critique of Hegel's Doctrine of the State*. Hegel's political idealism leads him to elevate the state over the civil society in which, for the materialist Marx, it has its roots, an artificial dissociation of the political and socio-economic spheres that for Marx can only be a source of profound mystification. It is here, then, that Marx turns, as it were, to Pocock's alternative tradition of commercial humanism, which views the unfolding and enrichment of the human subject in social and economic, rather than narrowly political, terms. The language in which Pocock describes that ideology – the refinement and diversification of human potentialities through increasingly specialized capacities to produce and distribute – is very close to Marx's unceasing hymn of praise to the more progressive dimensions of capitalism. Socialism builds on the commercial humanist as well as civic humanist lineage, acknowledging that its own project depends upon the bourgeoisie having charitably and conveniently developed the forces of production to the highest degree known to history, and along with them, inseparably, those refined human skills, powers, and forms of association essential to a socialist polity. It is just that Marxism notes, as commercial humanism does not, that this exhilarated unfolding of human wealth, in both moral and material senses, is also the narrative of an unspeakable tragedy, occurring as it does under the sign of scarcity, violence, and exploitation.

How, then, does Marxism seek to repair that tragedy in the future? In Pocockian terms, it is by projecting the political values of civic humanism into the socio-economic sphere of commercial humanism. Economic life, rather than furnishing a mere private prerequisite for politics (civic humanism), or providing the forum for essentially private, depoliticized relations (commercial humanism), must itself be transformed into an arena of freedom, autonomy, equality, and democratic rule by the socialization of industry. Civic humanism must be reconstructed on the basis of commercial humanism, and both historical practices thereby sublated and surpassed. The economy must itself become a field for the flourishing of public virtue, not just a private occasion or opportunity for it, and virtue and commerce thus cease to be antithetical. If civic humanism relegates the economic to a mere precondition, commercial humanism delegates the political to oligarchy and absolutism; Marxism, by contrast, seeks to undo both projects by deploying the one against the other.

The Marxist tradition has itself been divided over whether the good life finally consists in an emancipation from labour or in its conversion into a locus of human creativity. If William Morris took the latter view, it is arguable that Marx himself espoused the former: full communism would mean the automation of the labour process and the consequent freeing of human energies into extra-economic activities (though Marx seems also to have acknowledged that a certain residual drudgery would probably prove inescapable). To this extent, in a curious irony, Marx's ultimate political vision would seem to rejoin the doctrines of civic humanism: the economic is just a means for getting you beyond it. In the precommunist realm of socialism, however, labour would remain a necessity; and it is here that

Marx's projecting of republican virtue into the commercial field comes most evidently into play.

Such a projection, one might claim, brings with it a certain deconstruction of sexual oppositions. If the civic humanist ideology is vigorously masculine in its military, heroic values, commercial humanism, with its emphasis on the tempering and refining of disruptive passion through sympathetic social intercourse, is stereotypically feminine. Marx's dismantling of the distinction between state and civil society, public and private, political and social, thus throws both sexual stereotypes into question. For the state to wither away in its present form, and for civil society to become fully publicized, is for the privileged sphere of 'masculinity' to yield to a 'femininity' which, having now fully entered the public realm, is no longer identical with itself, no longer recognizable in its familiar ideological guises. It is a question of deconstruction rather than synthesis: for Marx, the false autonomous state is an outgrowth of civil society, parasitic on the very basis it spurns, and will disappear when that civil society comes into its political own. If civic humanism suppresses the 'feminine', commercial humanism celebrates a false ideological version of it; both creeds are, to that extent, caught within the same problematic. To deconstruct the boundaries between public and private is not to incorporate the one terrain into the other while preserving their given identities, but to strike the whole opposition as it stands quite meaningless. It is only on this basis that other, less disabling distinctions between public and private might then be able to emerge.

If Pocock has little to say of Marxism, much the same can be said of the erstwhile Marxist Alasdair MacIntyre, in his engaging polemic *After Virtue*. In Pocockian parlance, MacIntyre is a latter-day civic humanist who wishes to reinvent the Aristotelian tradition of virtue in the teeth of an Enlightenment liberal individualism, with its vacuous talk of universal rights and its damaging dislocation of fact and value. 'What is central to [the republican] tradition', MacIntyre suggests, 'is the notion of a public good which is prior to and characterizable independently of the summing of individual desires and interests. Virtue in the individual is nothing more than allowing the public good to provide the standard for individual behaviour.'[17] There can be no virtue outside the individual's active sharing in a concretely particular form of social life, or outside his or her adherence to a specific historical tradition. MacIntyre's historicism allows him to deliver an illuminating exposé of the particular social conditions that breed moral doctrines of a Kantian kind; he is shrewdly alert to the historical circumstances in which facts and values fall apart, leaving moral imperatives, from Kant to emotivism, hanging in their own mysteriously autonomous space, to be seized on by a Miller or de Man for their deconstructive ends. But this very historicist strength is also the source of MacIntyre's theoretical weakness. For what he offers in opposition to Enlightenment universalism is the claim of one's particular historical tradition; and it is hard to see how this can avoid relativism. 'What the good life is for a fifth-century Athenian general will not be the same as what it was for a medieval nun or a seventeenth-century farmer.' Are all these forms of life, then, to be indifferently endorsed? MacIntyre would seem to assume, rather like Matthew Arnold, that belonging to a tradition is a good in itself; in Wittgensteinian or postmodernist fashion, there is apparently no possibility of subjecting a whole form of life to moral scrutiny. 'I am a citizen of this or that city, a member of this or that guild or profession; I belong to this clan, this tribe, this nation. Hence what is good for me has to be the good for one who inhabits these roles.'[18] (I belong to the clan known as the SS, the nation known as Nazi Germany, the profession of pornographer. . .)

Marxism for MacIntyre can offer no authentic alternative to Enlightenment individualism, since it is essentially an offspring of it. What he fails to see is that Marxism is indeed a child of the Enlightenment insofar as it adopts a universalist perspective but that what it universalizes is precisely a version of MacIntyre's own cherished republican virtue. It is true that Marxism has an absolute, universal ethic: the unquestionable value of the free, all-around realization of human powers and capacities. 'True wealth', Marx writes in the *Grundrisse*, consists in 'the absolute working-out of (human) creative potentialities, with no presupposition other than the previous historical development, which makes this totality of development, i.e. the development of all human powers as such, the end in itself, not as measured on a *predetermined* yardstick.'[19] MacIntyre would doubtless find this a good deal too romantic, as perhaps I do myself; but there is no doubt that Marx speaks here in the tradition of Aristotelian and Hegelian virtue. He speaks, moreover, as a historicist; for the whole of Marxism is an inquiry into the concrete historical conditions that would allow such potentialities to be realized, and which would define what would count as such realization in particular social conditions. There is no need, then, for MacIntyre to view Marxism as wholly inimical to the moral lineage he himself embraces; it is just that for Marx such an 'absolute working-out of creative potentialities' must become available for everyone, rather than remain the prerogative of nineteenth-century Welsh attorneys or *fin de siècle* Mexican dentists. It *must* be universalized because capitalism has ensured that it *can* be. If Marx is an Enlightenment universalist, then, it is not primarily (if at all) because he promotes the abstract human rights that MacIntyre regards as so much hot air, but because he sees the historical possibility of the practice of virtue being brought within the reach of all men and women.

Not that Marx would have had much truck with phrases like 'the practice of virtue'. In a letter to Engels in 1864, he complains that the Mazzinists have forced him to throw into his Preamble to the Statutes of the International one or two phrases about duty, right, truth, justice, and morality. But don't worry, he reassures his collaborator: they aren't likely to do much damage. He also protests in a letter of 1877 against those who want to replace the materialist basis of socialism by 'modern mythology, with its goddesses of Justice, Liberty, Equality, and Fraternity'.[20] Marx must preserve his materialist manhood in the face of these female deities, and there is no doubt that he finally escaped unscathed.

In the light of such comments, it may seem peculiarly disingenuous for a Marxist to accuse deconstruction of experiencing embarrassment over such phrases as 'human rights'. For the Marxist tradition has betrayed an at least equal embarrassment with ethical concepts, to the point where commentators have wondered whether Marx credited such notions at all. There is more than enough in Marx's own writings to suggest that morality is just class ideology; but those writings are also suffused with sufficient moral zeal and indignation to make us wonder how Marx could have been so blinded to the basis of his own social critique. It is still a matter of controversy among Marxist scholars whether Marx believed that capitalist exploitation was a matter of injustice. On the one hand, he seems to deny that the wage relation is unjust; on the other hand, he talks of the capitalist actually stealing from the worker. So either for some strange reason he did not regard stealing as a question of injustice, or he was simply confused. Norman Geras has offered an attractively ingenious solution to this problem, which is that Marx did, in fact, think capitalism was unjust but did not think that he did.[21] He did not think that he did because he wrongly subscribed to a narrowly juridical conception of justice, which he then quite understandably rejected. Geras's point can perhaps be amplified: Marx did, in fact, believe in morality, but he did not know that he did, because he identified moral discourse with the impoverished juridical notions of the bourgeois liberal tradition, which he quite properly regarded as ideological. Deconstruction, on the whole, makes the same mistake, but sees nothing ideological about what it is doing. Marx did not seem to realize that what he himself was engaged upon *was* morality, in a richer, more ancient sense of the term than the one he recognized – that an inquiry into the material conditions of free self-development *is* a moral project, and a far more productive one than Kantian or deconstructive talk of absolute imperatives. Marx habitually counterposes the 'materialist' to the 'moral': but this is only because he too readily surrenders the whole category of morality into the hands of the bourgeois idealists.

As I have argued elsewhere, the truth is that Marx does not so much reject morality as translate it in large part from 'superstructure' to 'base'.[22] The moral then becomes identical with the dynamic self-realization of human powers and capacities – projected into the productive process itself, in the broadest sense of that term, rather than narrowly identified with certain superstructural ideologies and institutions. But if Marx considered that this then took care of such notions as justice and right, he was, in fact, mistaken. For the 'dynamic self-realization of human powers and capacities' is a highly abstract formulation, which leaves open the question of by what criteria we should assess, in any concrete situation, which and whose powers are to be actualized, and which and whose curtailed. When Marx writes, in the passage from the *Grundrisse* quoted above, of 'the development of all human powers as such', he seems to assume that all human powers are beneficent. But we know from the rest of his work that he did not actually assume this; so we are left with the problem of what criteria he would employ to distinguish between more and less beneficial powers. One such criterion can be inferred from his writings: you should realize only those powers and capacities that will allow for the free, all-around development of the capacities of others. A condition, in short, in which 'the free development of each is the condition for the free development of all', as the *Communist Manifesto* famously puts it. If it is of the essence of human beings, as the *Economic and Philosophical Manuscripts* argue, that they can so objectify their own 'species being' as to produce their own life freely and consciously, and if it is in the nature of their material and biological conditions that they must do this not in isolation but in mutual association, then it follows that happiness, or well-being, can consist only in each individual realizing her productive 'species being' in and through the equivalent self-realization of every other. It is this that distinguishes a communist from a liberal ethics; but it will tell you nothing as it stands about what is to count as all this in any specific historical situation. For that purpose, 'superstructural' discourses and institutions of justice and morality would remain essential.

J. G. A. Pocock reminds us that there is no simple opposition between the tradition of civic humanism and a more juristic style of moral thought. On the contrary, the former, while resisting the ideological *dominance* of the latter, nevertheless implicates it. As Pocock writes: 'Virtue as devotion to the public good approached identification with a concept of justice; if the citizens were to practice a common good, they must distribute its components among themselves . . . [and] a particular mode of participation might be seen as appropriate to the specialized social individual: to be proper to him, to be his propriety or property. Ideas of *suum cuique*, of distribution and of justice were therefore inherent in the civic republican tradition.'[23] Just the same, in fact, can be asserted of Marx. Marx's ideals of freedom, community, and self-actualization inevitably entail notions of distributive justice, since the whole point of Marxism is to bring about a condition in which these goods can be distributed to everyone. 'From each according to their ability, to each according to their needs', the celebrated slogan of the *Critique of the Gotha Programme*, is a principle of distributive justice; but it is one that has broken beyond the falsely equivalencing or homogenizing principles of bourgeois justice in general, since individual needs are, of course, unique, specific, and unequal. Full communism will not be, as some commentators have considered, a society beyond justice, but a society in which justice is practised otherwise. And it is here, finally, that Marxism may be said to join hands with deconstruction. For the notion of exceeding or transgressing some strict economy in the name of that which eludes its spuriously equivalencing principle is at once typically deconstructionist and a way of characterizing the transition, as Marxism conceives it, from bourgeois to socialist morality, and from exchange-value to use-value. It is just that, for Marxism at least, this move transforms the question of human rights, rather than simply disposing of it. The rights that now matter have become the equal rights of men and women to access to the means of their uniquely individual self-realization; and to this extent, the civic humanist and juristic conceptions of morality are no longer so evidently in conflict.

Deconstruction is wary of Enlightenment universalism, but then, in an apparently paradoxical move, turns to Kant, or some suitably Nietzscheanized version of him, for some of its ethical insights. In doing so, I have argued, it implicitly subscribes to a peculiarly unproductive starting point for ethical enquiry in general, and ignores some more promising styles of moral discourse. It does so, one imagines, because the 'virtue' tradition is far too humanistic for deconstructive taste. Nothing could be more distressing to the deconstructive sensibility than the vision of these repellently replete subjects, securely centred in their autonomous being, strenuously realizing a wealth of vital powers. It is not the kind of prospect likely to enthrall an admirer of Mallarmé or an apologist for *aporia*. The 'virtue' tradition is indeed vulnerable to a deconstructive critique, as its inherent masculinism and productivism are to a feminist one. But it is not, after all, quite as full of itself as all that. For the Marx of the *Economic and Philosophical Manuscripts*, the human subject is extrinsic to itself; and what endows it with its essence – its 'species being' – is exactly what renders it non-identical to itself. It belongs to human species being that it can objectify it own determinations, thus opening up a fissure within itself from which that ceaseless self-transgression known as history can flow. It is because the human animal is not identical with its own determinations that it is a historical and linguistic being. This surplus over itself is for Marx what gives it its value; but 'surplus', for Marxism as for *King Lear*, is an ambivalent term. The lack of self-identity that allows the human animal freely and consciously to produce its own life is also what allows it to objectify and exploit the productive species being of others for its own self-aggrandizing ends. For Marx, it is in the nature of human nature to be in excess of itself, but that excess can prove destructive if it is not justly distributed. Creatively exceeding the norm is a fine thing for both Marxism and deconstruction, certainly finer than the rigorous equivalences of justice. But it must not be allowed to make a mockery of them either.

Notes

1   Paul de Man, *Allegories of Reading* (New Haven and London: Yale University Press, 1979), p. 206.
2   For an illuminating critique of the Kantian basis of Habermasian 'discourse ethics', see Albrecht Wellmer, *The Persistence of Modernity* (Cambridge, Mass.: MIT Press, 1991), chapter 4.
3   Foreword to Carol Jacobs, *The Dissimulating Harmony* (Baltimore and London: Johns Hopkins University Press, 1978), p. xi.
4   Afterword to G. Graff, ed., *Limited Inc* (Evanston, Ill.: Northwestern University Press, 1988), p. 43.
5   J. Hillis Miller, *The Ethics of Reading* (New York: Columbia University Press, 1987), p. 4.

6   For a useful account of Aristotle's ethical thought, see Jonathan Lear, *Aristotle: The Desire to Understand* (Cambridge: Cambridge University Press, 1988), chapter 5.

7   Miller, *The Ethics of Reading*, p. 48.

8   Williams draws a distinction in his *Ethics and the Limits of Philosophy* (London and Cambridge, Mass.: Harvard University Press, 1985) between a narrowly 'moral' concern with questions of obligation, and the wider field of ethical inquiry.

9   Miller, *The Ethics of Reading*, p. 55.

10 See in particular Jean-François Lyotard and Jean-Loup Thébaud, *Just Gaming* (Minneapolis: University of Minnesota Press, 1985).

11 Friedrich Nietzsche, *Beyond Good and Evil*, in W. Kaufmann (ed.), *Basic Writings of Nietzsche* (New York: Modern Library, 1968), p. 326.

12 See J. G. A. Pocock, *Virtue, Commerce, and History* (Cambridge: Cambridge University Press, 1985), and *The Machiavellian Moment: Florentine Political Thought and the Atlantic Republican Tradition* (Princeton: Princeton University Press, 1975).

13 Pocock, *Virtue, Commerce, and History*, pp. 42, 43.

14 Ibid., pp. 43, 44.

15 Karl Marx, *Capital*, vol. 2 (New York: International Publishers, 1967), p. 820.

16 Pocock, *Virtue, Commerce, and History*, pp. 103, 110.

17 Alasdair MacIntyre, *After Virtue* (London: Duckworth, 1981), p. 220.

18 Ibid., pp. 204–5.

19 Karl Marx, *Grundrisse* (Harmondsworth: Penguin, 1973), p. 488 (emphasis in the original).

20 Quoted in Svetozar Stojanovic, 'The Ethical Potential of Marx's Thought', in Tom Bottomore (ed.), *Interpretations of Marx* (Oxford: Blackwell, 1988), p. 178.

21 See Norman Geras, 'The Controversy about Marx and Justice', *New Left Review* 150 (March/April 1985).

22 See Terry Eagleton, *The Ideology of the Aesthetic* (Oxford: Blackwell, 1990), p. 223.

23 Pocock, *Virtue, Commerce, and History*, p. 42.

16 Ideology

1 Ideology and Enlightenment

Like much else in the modern world, the concept of ideology is a child of the Enlightenment. For most of us nowadays 'ideology' has something of a pejorative ring to it, evoking as it does a whole array of negative notions from false consciousness to fanaticism, mental blockage to mystification. In ordinary conversation, to claim that someone is thinking or speaking 'ideologically' is usually to suggest that their view of things is skewed by a set of rigid preconceptions. If only they were to shuck off this conceptual straitjacket, they might begin to see the world as it truly is. But this is not at all how the term 'ideology' started life. 'Ideology' means, literally, the study or knowledge of ideas; and as such it belongs to the great dream of the eighteenth-century Enlightenment that it might somehow be possible to chart the human mind with the sort of delicate precision with which we can map the motions of the body. What if that most obscure and elusive of realities, consciousness itself, could be *scientifically* known? What if it were possible to demonstrate a certain lawful regularity in its operations – in the way we generate ideas from sensations, in the manner in which those ideas are permutated, and so on all the way up to our loftiest spiritual conceptions? Can there be a materialism of the mind – of that which seems the very opposite of matter?

In this sense, the nearest modern equivalent to the classical notion of ideology would be the science of psychology. But there is an important difference between the two. Ideology, in its Enlightenment sense, is concerned with ideas as *social* phenomena, as modern-day psychology is usually not. Its aim is not just to map some abstraction known as 'consciousness', but (at least for some Enlightenment theorists) to uncover the laws of a system of social thought. And to this extent it hovers ambiguously between what we know as psychology, and what nowadays would be termed the 'sociology of knowledge'. Ideologists believed that particular social ideas could be traced back to certain universal operations of the mind; but the point of doing this was to give them the capacity to alter men's and women's ways of thinking. If, for example, we could show that the mind worked by certain principles of association, then it might be possible to alter our social environment so that we associated x with y rather than a with b, and so developed ideas which were conducive to human dignity, freedom and justice rather than to superstition and oppression. All this, to be sure, has something of a quaint ring for us today; but it reflects the naive utopianism of a revolutionary age, which was busy sweeping away idols and fetishes of various kinds, and which did not hesitate to carry this campaign into the very inner sanctum of humanity. Ideology, then, begins life as nothing less than an ambitious project of mental engineering, which will sweep clean the Augean stables of mind and society together, and in doing so free men and women from the taboos and mystifications under which they have languished. The hardest form of emancipation is always self-emancipation; and the science of ideology, flushed with all the euphoria of an age of Reason, believes that the revolution against false gods must be carried into the inmost recesses of consciousness itself.

What this amounts to is that ideology is the equivalent in the mental realm of the overthrow of priest and king in the political one. And to this extent, ironically enough, the science of ideology is itself ideological – a reflex in the sphere of consciousness of real material conditions. The man who actually coined the term, the French revolutionary aristocrat Destutt de Tracy, did so in a prison cell during the Reign of Terror, firm in his belief that reason, not violence, was the key to social reconstruction. Reason must replace religion: which is to say that custodianship of the mind and soul must be wrested from the priests and invested instead in an élite of scientific specialists who would be, so to speak, technicians of social consciousness. As Antonio Gramsci recognised in his celebrated concept of 'hegemony', no successful transformation in the sphere of politics can neglect the business of influencing hearts and minds; and the science of ideology, born in the blood and turmoil of the French revolution, was the first attempt to systematise this project in the modern age. Ideology, then, belongs to modernity – to the brave new epoch of secular, scientific rationality which aims to liberate men and women from their mystifications and irrationalisms, their false reverence for God, aristocrat and absolute monarch, and restore to them instead their dignity as fully rational, self-determining beings. It is the bourgeois revolution at the level of the mind itself; and its ambition is nothing less than to reconstruct that mind from the ground up, dissecting the ways we receive and combine our sense-data so as to intervene in this process and deflect it to desirable political ends.

If this bold enterprise scandalised the reactionaries, it was because it represented an impious meddling with sacred mysteries. For surely the mind is the one place where we are free – free of the drearily determining laws which govern our physiological life, and perhaps our social existence as well. Ideology for its opponents is a form of vulgar reductionism, seeking to model the very pith of our dignity and autonomy – consciousness itself – on all that threatens to enslave it. Intoxicated with a mythology of pure reason, it sets out to purge humanity of its essential mystery, converting the mind itself into a sort of material object as mechanically predictable as the circulation of the blood. It is, in short, a kind of madness of Reason – a hubristic campaign to blueprint our elusive spiritual being, and to do so, moreover, for the purposes of controlling and manipulating it. Those traditional guardians of the human psyche – the priests – knew at least that it was inviolable and irreducible, as the inscription of God himself in humanity; now this last bastion of our freedom is to be rudely invaded by the same grubby hands which broke open the Bastille. In its own day, then, the new science of ideology attracted all the virulent opposition which has been reserved in our own time for psychoanalysis. For the scandal of Freud is not finally his embarrassing revelations about infantile sexuality or the precariousness of gender; it is the fact that the human psyche itself can now, apparently, be scientifically dissected like a muscle, and this not just in its topmost, more socially obvious layer ('consciousness') but in its murkiest unconscious depths.

The conflict in our own time between 'theorists' and 'humanists' is a legacy of these eighteenth-century quarrels. 'System', Roland Barthes once commented, 'is the enemy of Man' – meaning that the 'Man' of the humanist is all that cannot be analysed and tabulated, all that slips through the net of theoretical enquiry. In late eighteenth-century England, the names for this running battle were Paine and Burke: Thomas Paine, with his revolutionary fervour and serene confidence in reason; Edmund Burke, for whom the whole notion that the social order can be submitted to rational critique is a kind of blasphemy. For Burke, human affairs are too intricate, intuitive and opaque, too much the product of immemorial custom and spontaneous habit, to be charted with any certainty; and this belief is inevitably coupled with a conservative politics. For if the skein of social life is so elusively tangled, then only those delicate refurbishings and readjustments we know as reform can avoid shearing brutally through it. For this standpoint, we cannot put our social life into radical question precisely because we are the products of it, because we bear in our bones and fibres the very traditions we are foolishly seeking to objectify. Radical critique would thus involve some impossible hauling of ourselves up by our own bootstraps, some doomed attempt to examine ourselves as though we were not present on the scene of enquiry. And where exactly would we have to be standing to perform such an operation? A rejection of ideology is thus an endorsement of the political status quo, just as the opponents of 'theory' today tend to be conservative. In modern English history, 'ideologists' have generally been known as 'intellectuals', and the term carries a significantly disparaging resonance. Intellectuals are bloodless, clinical creatures bereft of the ordinary human affections, crushing spontaneity and intuition with their cerebral convolutions. They are *alien* animals because they strive to 'estrange' our familiar forms of life, casting upon them the coldly critical eye of a Martian or a visiting anthropologist. Like the early French ideologues, they try to uncover the laws or 'deep structures' by which our most taken-for-granted institutions work; and this might only succeed in disabling those institutions, exposing them to a rigorous scepticism under whose baleful glare they might wilt and wither. The traditional quarrel between ideologue and conservative is being rehearsed today in the battle between those radical theorists who believe that a fundamental critique of a particular social order is both possible and necessary, and those pragmatist descendants of Nietzsche or Heidegger or Wittgenstein or John Dewey for whom this is mere intellectualist fantasy.[1] For if human beings are actually constituted to their roots by their social practices, how could they ever hope to leap out of them in imagination and subject them to thoroughgoing critical analysis? Would this not be like the eye trying to catch itself seeing something, or trying to shin up a rope you are yourself holding?

The pragmatist case against the 'ideologist' is that to do what she aims to do, she would have to be standing at some Archimedean point outside the culture she hopes to criticise. Not only does no such point exist, but even if it did it would be far too remote from our form of life to gain any effective hold upon it. This, in my view, is a misguided notion: it is perfectly possible, as with the Marxist concept of an 'immanent' critique, to launch a radical critique of a culture from somewhere inside it, not least from those internal fissures or fault-lines which betray its underlying contradictions. But if the pragmatist charge is not generally valid, it would certainly seem to apply to the early French ideologues. These men sought to submit their societies to the gaze of Reason; but whose reason, and reason of what kind? For them reason really was a 'transcendental' faculty, sublimely untainted by social factors. Yet this, ironically, contradicts the whole spirit of their project, which sets out precisely to examine how the human mind is conditioned by its social and material environment. How come that *their* minds – their notions of reason – are so immune from their own doctrine? What if the grand science of ideology was no more than a socially conditioned reflex in the head of its founder? If everything is to be exposed to the clear light of reason, must this not include reason itself? And would we not then discover that this supposedly timeless, transcendental faculty was no more than the style of rationality of a particular, newly dominant social class at a specific historical time? What we might find, in short, is that ideology in the classical sense of the word is ideology in one contemporary sense: the partisan perspective of a social group or class, which then mistakes itself as universal and eternal.

For some theorists of our time, notably the Marxist philosopher Louis Althusser and his progeny, ideology is the opposite of science; so it is ironic that the concept was born precisely as an exciting new science. For some other thinkers, notably the early Marx and Engels of *The German Ideology*, ideology means ideas which have floated free of their material foundation and deny its existence; so it is a further irony that ideology in its infancy was part of a more general materialist enquiry into society as a whole. Indeed for the founder of the discipline, Destutt de Tracy, it was part of 'zoology': of a science of humanity in general. How then did it come about that, not long after its inception, 'ideology' came to mean idle abstractions, illusions and chimeras with no root in the real world? The answer, in a word, may be Napoleon. As Napoleon tightened his authoritarian political control, the French ideologues rapidly became his *bêtes noires*; and the concept of ideology itself entered the field of ideological struggle. Tracy and his kind, so he complained, were 'dreamers' and 'windbags', intent on destroying the consoling illusions by which men and women lived. Before long he was seeing ideologues under every bed, and even blamed them for his defeat in Russia. The ideologues, he charged, had substituted a 'diffuse metaphysics' for a 'knowledge of the human heart and of the lessons of history' – an ironic enough accusation, since it was precisely 'metaphysics' that the materialistically minded ideologues were out to combat. The confrontation between Napoleon and Tracy, then, is an early instance of the conflict between the pragmatist who appeals to custom, piety, intuition and concrete experience, and the sinister 'intellectual' who puts all of this in brackets in his remorseless rationalism. The French exponents of ideology were not in fact metaphysicians; as we have seen, they believed in a close interrelation between ideas and material circumstances. But they did believe that ideas were at the very foundation of social life, and so were an odd mixture of materialist and idealist. It is this belief in the primacy of ideas which Napoleon, who claimed to have invented the term 'ideologue' himself as a derogatory label for his opponents, seized on in his campaign to discredit them. The kernel of his accusation is that there is something irrational about excessive rationalism. In his eyes, these thinkers have pursued their enquiry into the laws of reason to the point where they have become locked within their own abstract space, as divorced from material reality as a psychotic. So it is that the term ideology veers on its axis, as a word originally synonymous with scientific rationalism ends up denoting an idle and speculative idealism.

2   The Marxist Heritage

The belief that ideas are socially conditioned is now so obvious to us that it requires a leap of imagination to envisage how anyone might think differently. But the belief is not of course obvious at all, not least for those brands of philosophical dualism or idealism for which consciousness is one thing and the material world quite another. Before the French ideologues, a good many thinkers had speculated in a rather crudely materialist vein on the influence on our minds of climate, or physiology, or national character; and for English empiricism it is sense-perception which lies at the source of all our concepts. But none of this is quite what the modern sense of the term 'ideology' is trying to capture. The study of ideology is more than just some sociology of ideas; more particularly, it claims to show how ideas are related to real material conditions by masking or dissembling them, displacing them into other terms, speciously resolving their conflicts and contradictions, converting these situations into apparently natural, immutable, universal ones. Ideas, in short, are here granted an active political force, rather than being grasped as mere reflections of their world; and in its day the Marxist tradition has sought to describe ideology in terms of any or all of these various strategies. The source text for this tradition is Marx and Engels's *The German Ideology*, in which the authors see ideology as essentially an inversion of the relation between consciousness and reality as they themselves conceive it. For a materialist like Marx, consciousness is inseparably bound up with social practice, and is secondary to it; for the Hegelian philosophers whom they oppose, ideas are thought to be both autonomous of such practice and the root cause of social existence. By granting such primacy to ideas, Marx's antagonists would seem to suggest that if you change people's minds, you change their conditions of life. Marx himself wants to insist that you could only transform human consciousness by transforming the material conditions which create it. A materialist analysis, in short, goes hand in hand with a revolutionary politics. The rationalist creed that one should combat false ideas with true ones is decisively rejected; and so is the related idealist doctrine that consciousness is the key to social reality. In a pathbreaking move, then, *The German Ideology* rejects rationalism, idealism and any mere 'sociology of knowledge'; instead, in an audacious reformulation, it insists that consciousness is essentially *practical*, and that one of its practical uses is to distract men and women from their oppression and exploitation by generating illusions and mystifications. Paradoxically, then, ideas *are* practically related to real life; but that relation takes the mystifying form of a non-relation, in the shape of the idealist fantasy that consciousness is grandly independent of all material determinants. To put the point another way: there is an apparent non-correspondence between ideas and reality in class society, but this non-correspondence is structural to that form of life, and fulfils an important function within it.

It would appear, then, that to dub an idea 'ideological' is not just to call it false or deceptive, but to claim that it fulfils a particular kind of deceptive or mystifying function within social life as a whole. And as far as that goes, it might be thought that true ideas might do just as well as false ones. In the end, for this style of thought, an ideological notion is one which is somehow convenient for our rulers – one which conceals or naturalises or otherwise legitimates an unjust form of power. And in *The German Ideology*, given the thinkers the authors are out to assail, these ideas are most often metaphysical fantasies and chimeras of various sorts which downgrade the importance of material struggle. But this means that there is, from the outset, a tension in Marx's thought between two rather different senses of the term ideology. On the one hand, ideology has a point, a function, a practical political force; on the other hand it would seem a mere set of illusions, a set of ideas which have come unstuck from reality and now conduct an apparently autonomous life in isolation from it. This tension is not exactly a contradiction: one can see well enough how encouraging certain religious or metaphysical illusions may serve to mystify men and women as to their real material interests, and so have some practical force. But to see ideology just as 'illusion' has seemed to many later thinkers to deny its materiality, as well as to overlook the fact that many of the notions which we call ideological may succeed as well as they do precisely because they are true. People who enjoy dwelling upon Winston Churchill's dogged resilience and powers of leadership are probably speaking ideologically, but they are not thereby lying. *The German Ideology* makes it sound as though all ideology is idealist; but this is plainly not the case. The thought of the French ideologues or English empiricists is certainly in some sense materialist, but it is not hard to point out its ideological functions. So, at the very origin of the tradition we are examining, there is a revealing ambiguity: is ideology primarily an *epistemological* affair, concerned with what Theodor Adorno once termed 'socially necessary illusion', or is it a *sociological* matter, insisting on the way certain ideas intersect with power? Can thought have a firm anchorage in material life and still be ideological? And if ideology, as with the early Marx and Engels, means ideas independent of that life, how can this be so if all consciousness is in truth practical consciousness?

Whatever these difficulties, the early Marxian claim that 'the ideas of the ruling class are in every epoch the ruling ideas' is a remarkably bold and original formulation. For this is to assert a startlingly direct hook-up between consciousness and power, which goes far beyond any mere insistence that ideas are socially conditioned. We are moving instead towards the proposition, more fully elaborated by later Marxists, that ideas are weapons in a field of struggle – that an 'ideological' discourse, properly understood, means one which, deciphered and decoded in certain ways, will betray in its limits and emphases, its silences, gaps and internal contradictions, the imprint of real material conflicts. On this view, ideology is a form of thought generated or skewed out of shape by the exigencies of power; but if it is therefore traced through with significant tensions and inconsistencies, it also represents an attempt to mask the very conflicts from which it springs, either by denying that they exist, or by asserting their unimportance or inevitability. Ideologies are sets of discursive strategies for displacing, recasting or spuriously accounting for realities which prove embarrassing to a ruling power; and in doing so, they contribute to that power's self-legitimation.

Such, at least, is one strong contemporary understanding of ideology. It is not one without its problems, as we shall see in this book. For some thinkers, like the later Karl Marx, ideology is less a matter of thought or discourse than of the very objective structure of class society itself. For others like Althusser, it is less consciousness than unconsciousness; for others again, ideology is less a 'tool' of a ruling power than an effect of a social and political situation as a whole, a complex field in which different groups and classes ceaselessly negotiate their relations rather than a well-bounded form of consciousness which can be neatly assigned to this group or the other. There are difficulties, too, about the fact that 'ideology' is sometimes used to cover radical or oppositional ideas: if ideology means the ideas of the ruling class, why does Lenin speak approvingly of 'socialist ideology', and why would many people want to claim that feminism or anarchism or republicanism were 'ideological'? For the moment, however, we can stay with the conception of ideology as a set of discursive strategies for legitimating a dominant power, and enquire more precisely into what these strategies consist in. We should note before we do, however, that the concept of a 'dominant ideology', as a coherent bloc of ideas which effectively secures the power of a governing group, has been greeted with scepticism in certain quarters, a view made plain by the work of Nicholas Abercrombie and his colleagues.[2]

Ideologies are often seen as *rationalisations* of a set of (normally unjust) social interests. I say 'normally unjust', because one would think that a set of just social interests would hardly need rationalising. But some plainly unjust views do not need rationalising either: ancient society saw nothing reprehensible in slave-owning, and felt no need to dress it up in some plausible apologia as we would have to do today. For one extreme sort of contemporary free marketeer, there is no reason to justify the suffering that *laissez-faire* generates: for him, the weak can simply go to the wall. But much ideological rationalisation does of course go on; and rationalisation, which is essentially a psychoanalytic category, can be defined as 'a procedure whereby the subject attempts to present an explanation that is either logically consistent or ethically acceptable for attitudes, ideas, feelings, etc., whose true motives are not perceived'.[3] Whether all ruling powers fail to perceive how discreditable their true motives really are is in fact questionable. Someone who behaves disreputably but conceals the fact from himself is known as self-deceived – a concept which is of vital importance in the study of ideology. And it is true that ruling powers are often enough engaged in what the linguisticians would call a 'performative contradiction' between what they say they are doing and what they are actually doing – a contradiction which it may be part of the function of their discourse to mask even from themselves. But we should beware of excessive charity here: dominant groups and classes are quite frequently well aware of how shabby their conduct is, and simply seek to hide this from their subordinates rather than from themselves. Some such groups feel no urge to rationalise their motives, either because they do not regard them as shameful or because they are not in fact so; but others will engage in more or less systematic attempts to provide plausible justifications for conduct that might otherwise be the object of criticism. For some sociologists of a Nietzschean bent, notably Vilfedo Pareto in his *Treatise of General Sociology* (1916), all social interests are in fact irrational, so that the whole of our social discourse is in effect ideological, substituting apparently rational belief for affective or instinctual motives. Rationalisation may involve trying to square a discrepancy between conscious belief and unconscious motivation; or it may involve trying to square the circle between two sets of contradictory beliefs. (Whether it is in fact possible for us to hold contradictory beliefs simultaneously, and how this might come about, is a fascinating aspect of the theory of ideology.) Rationalising our beliefs in this way may help to promote and legitimate them; but there is the occasional case of interests which get promoted precisely because they do not rationalise themselves, as in the case of a self-confessed hedonist who wins our sympathy by his or her disarming candour. A stoical or fatalistic world-view may rationalise the wretchedness of some oppressed group's conditions of life; but it will not necessarily serve to advance their interests, other than in the sense of supplying them with an opiate. In this situation, it is not simply a question of the group's beliefs being at odds with its interests, but of its having conflicting kinds of interests. Indeed we should note here that oppressed groups may engage in rationalisation just as full-bloodedly as their masters, persuading themselves that their misery is inevitable, or that they deserve to suffer, or that everyone else does too, or that the alternative might be a good deal worse. Such rationalisations on the part of the oppressed may not promote their interests; but they may certainly advance those of their rulers.

Ideologies are commonly felt to be both *naturalising* and *universalising*. By a set of complex discursive devices, they project what are in fact partisan, controversial, historically specific values as true of all times and all places, and so as natural, inevitable and unchangeable. That much of the language we dub ideological engages in such manoeuvres is undoubted; but we should hesitate before viewing this as characteristic of all ideology without exception. Ideology very often presents itself as obvious – as an 'Of course!' or 'That goes without saying.' But not all ideological doctrines appear obvious, even to their most ardent adherents: think of the Roman Catholic dogma of the Assumption of the Blessed Virgin, which is hardly a matter of plain common sense even for a devout Catholic. Many people revere the monarchy, or are enthusiasts for multinational capitalism; but they are not always obtuse enough to believe that the world would simply grind to a halt without these institutions, or that they have existed from time immemorial. The case that ideology always and everywhere dehistoricises the world, making it appear natural and ineluctable, is based on the dubious assumption that ideology is never able to reflect upon itself – that, as Louis Althusser observes, it is never able to announce 'I am ideological'. But 'never' is surely too strong. 'I know I'm a terrible reactionary, but I just can't see that women are equal to men'; 'I'm a racist and proud of it'; 'Sorry to be so disgustingly bourgeois, but would you mind removing that pig from the drawing room?': all of these statements may serve as coy or defiant self-rationalisations, but they reveal in ideology a limited degree of self-awareness which any full-blooded 'naturalisation' thesis perilously overlooks. For the 'naturalising thesis, ideologies are sealed universes which curve back on themselves rather like the cosmos, and admit of no outside or alternative. They can also acknowledge no origin, since that which was born can always die. Ideologies, on this view, are thus parentless and without siblings. But many apologists for capitalism or patriarchy are well aware that alternatives to them exist; it is just that they do not agree with them. And hardly any devotees of parliamentary democracy are dim-witted enough to believe that it flourished among the ancient Druids. Besides, not everything which is natural is ideological. It is natural to human beings – proper to their material constitution – to be born, eat, engage in sexual activity, associate with one another, suffer from time to time, laugh, labour and die. The fact that all of these activities assume different cultural forms is no argument against their naturalness, however nervous of the term a certain fashionable culturalism may be. Any society which legislated against our laughing would be unnatural, and could be opposed on those grounds. When the rulers of the *ancien régimes* of eighteenth-century Europe heard the word 'Nature', they reached for their traditional privileges.

Just as some human practices are natural, so some are genuinely universal. Ideologies do often enough deceptively generalise their own highly particular beliefs to global or transhistorical status; but sometimes – as, for instance, with the liberal doctrine that all human beings should be equally accorded justice and dignity – they are quite right to do so. Marx and Engels believed that new social movements or classes, on their first revolutionary emergence, quite often present themselves as representing the interests of all; but while this is sometimes mystifying, it is also sometimes true. It would indeed be ultimately in the interests of everybody, even of men, if patriarchy were to be brought low.

Many theories of ideology regard it as a kind of screen or blockage which intervenes between us and the real world. If only we could nip around this screen, we would see reality aright. But there is, of course, no way of viewing reality except from a particular perspective, within the frame of specific interests or assumptions, which is one reason why some people have considered that all of our thought and perception is in fact ideological. But this is surely to widen the term to the point of uselessness. Any term which tries to cover too much threatens to cancel all the way through and end up signifying nothing. 'Ideological' is not synonymous with 'cultural': it denotes, more precisely, the points at which our cultural practices are interwoven with political power. Whether this is always a *dominant* power, or whether it always and everywhere involves naturalising, falsity, mystification, the masking or rationalising of injustice or the spurious resolution of social contradictions, are controversial issues in the theory of ideology; but if ideology just means something like 'a specific way of seeing', or even 'a set of doctrinal beliefs' then it rapidly dwindles in interest. We would not usually call a set of beliefs about whether lamb is tastier than haddock ideological, even though it is true that there is no belief which *could* not be ideological, given the appropriate circumstances. It all depends on who is saying what to whom, with what intentions and with what effects. Ideology, in short, is a matter of *discourse* – of practical communication between historically situated subjects – rather than just of *language* (of the kinds of propositions we utter). And it is not just a matter of discourse which is slanted or prejudiced or partisan, since there is no human discourse which is not.

Let us return, however, to the notion of ideology as a kind of screen or blockage between us and the world – one thrown up, perhaps, by social interests or 'false consciousness'. The model depends on a distinction between appearance and reality: there is a real state of affairs out there, but we represent it to ourselves or others in distorting or obscuring ways. A psychological analogy might be appropriate here: over there is reality, and over here the fantasies we entertain about it. But it is part of Freud's enterprise to deconstruct this duality: for him, what we term 'reality' is itself shot through with psychical fantasy, as much a construct of our unconscious desires as of our conscious perception. There is some sense in which the appearances are here actually part of the reality, not a mere screen which we could slide aside to see things as they really are. Much the same is true of Marx's later theory of ideology, as it can be pieced together from his economic studies in *Capital*. What Marx argues here is that our ideological misperceptions are not just the upshot of distorted ideas or 'false consciousness', but somehow inherent in the material structure of capitalist society itself. It is just in the nature of that society that it presents itself to our consciousness other than how it is; and this dislocation between appearance and reality is structural to it, an unavoidable effect of its routine operations. Thus, the wage contract for Marx involves exploitation, but it presents itself spontaneously as an equal exchange. Competition operates to obscure the ways in which value under capitalism is determined by labour-time. And the real social relations between men and women are concealed by the celebrated 'fetishism of commodities', in which what are actually social interchanges take the form of interactions between commodities. Ideology, which for the younger Marx was a matter of illusions and chimeras, is now folded into the material world itself, anchored no longer in consciousness but in the day-to-day workings of the capitalist system. There is a kind of dissembling or duplicity built into the very economic structures of capitalism, such that it simply cannot help appearing to us in ways at odds with what it is.

This is a deeply suggestive theory; but it hardly covers all of what we mean by ideology, and (along with certain dubious epistemological assumptions) it runs the risk of reducing ideology to the economic. The great tradition of Western Marxism, from Georg Lukács to Louis Althusser, has in general reacted sharply against economic reductionism, seeking to restore to Marxist theory the centrality of culture, practice and consciousness. Perhaps the key text in this lineage is Lukács's *History and Class Consciousness* (1923), a bold and brilliant attempt to reintroduce the importance of social consciousness to a Marxism previously afflicted by economic determinism. For Lukács, social consciousness – in particular the class consciousness of the proletariat – is not just a reflection of social conditions, but a transformative force within them. Thought and reality are part of the same dialectical process; and if a particular social class is able to dominate others, it is because it has managed to impose its own peculiar consciousness or world-view upon them. Capitalist society in general is ridden with reification, experienced as a set of discrete, isolated entities whose connections have been hidden from view; but it is in the interests of a subject class – in this case, the proletariat – to grasp that social order in its dynamic totality, and in doing so it becomes conscious of its own commodified status within it. The self-consciousness of the working class, then, is the transformative moment in which it grasps itself as a subject rather than an object, recognising that it is itself through its labour the author of this society which appears to it as alien and opaque, and reclaiming that alienated product through revolutionary action.

In a breathtakingly original move, Lukács has here rewritten Marxist theory in terms of Hegel's philosophy of the subject; and no subsequent Marxist thinking about ideology was to be immune from its effects. There is, nevertheless, much in Lukács's doctrine which is open to criticism. For one thing, in the typically 'historicist' style of Western Marxism, he assumes that social classes can best be seen as 'subjects', each equipped with a distinctive and cohesive form of consciousness. It is doubtful, though, that any 'class consciousness' is that pure and unified: ideology is perhaps best seen as a field of struggle and negotiation between various social groups and classes, not as some world-view intrinsic to each of them. For another thing, Lukács assigns too high an importance to 'consciousness' within social life as a whole. Ideology may be an indispensable part of political rule; but it is surely not what *centrally* secures such government, which is normally a question of much more material techniques. What is especially interesting in Lukács, however, is his supposed theory of 'false consciousness', which raises some difficult epistemological issues. In reaction to the scientistic conceptions of truth and falsehood typical of so much of the Marxism he inherited, Lukács locates truth instead in the fullest possible consciousness of an historically 'progressive' class. Truth is no longer an abstract, contemplative affair, but a function of the practical coming to consciousness of a class which must in its own interests grasp more of the dynamic totality of society than those which have come before it. Among other problems, there is a real danger here of relativism: what is true or false is tied to the historical situation of a specific social class, rather than being (as we might think of many propositions) true or false regardless of who is uttering them. But this does not mean that Lukács holds that the consciousness of non-progressive classes is therefore false, in the sense of giving a distorting image of reality as it is. On the contrary, he believes that the consciousness of the bourgeoisie truthfully reflects the reified, atomised social conditions in which they find themselves – so that, intriguingly, 'false consciousness' means less a view of things which is false to the true situation, than a view of things which is true to a false situation. Quite what is meant by a 'false situation' is a thorny issue; but Lukács is working here with the interesting notion of a social consciousness which is, so to speak, true as far as it goes, but structurally bound and limited by the historical situation which produced it. On this view, an ideological discourse is not just false or mystificatory; it is rather that in delivering some undoubted truths, it continually finds itself pressing up against certain limits or frontiers inherent in its style of thought, which are the inscription within it of certain 'limits' in historical reality itself. This, in effect, is what Marx thought was ideological about the discourse of the bourgeois political economist with whom he did battle; and it descends to modern 'structuralist' Marxists as the concept of a 'problematic'.

Another of the great Western Marxists – Antonio Gramsci – had rather little of originality to say of the concept of ideology, since it is subsumed for him under the more encompassing notion of 'hegemony'. Hegemony for Gramsci suggests the varied techniques by which ruling classes secure the consent of their subordinates to be ruled; and though ideology is certainly part of this process, it includes a great many other measures too. Indeed Gramsci develops his idea of hegemony partly because the theories of ideology of the 'orthodox' Marxism of his day had grown dismally impoverished, reducing social consciousness for the most part to a mere reflex of economic conditions. It was left to the French Marxist philosopher Louis Althusser to incorporate some aspects of Gramsci's concept of hegemony into a strikingly novel theoretical synthesis, which along with Gramsci drew heavily on structuralism and psychoanalysis. For Althusser, ideology works primarily at the level of the unconscious; its function is to constitute us as historical subjects equipped for certain tasks in society; and it does this by drawing us into an 'imaginary' relation with the social order which persuades us that we and it are centred on and indispensable to one another. Ideology is not thereby false, since, first of all, this relation is more a matter of unconscious feelings and images than of falsifiable propositions, and secondly because all of this goes on within certain material practices and institutions – 'ideological state apparatuses', as Althusser calls them – which are indubitably real. An 'ideological' problematic for Althusser is in effect a closed universe which continually returns us to the same starting-point; and science, or Marxist theory, is to be sharply counterposed to it. Ideology 'subjects' us in a double sense, constructing our subjectivity by persuading us into internalising an oppressive Law; but since it is thus at the very root of what it is to be a subject, inseparable from our lived experience itself, it is an essential dimension of any society whatsoever, even a communist one. With several of his challenging theses – that ideology has nothing to with falsehood, that it is more unconscious than conscious, that it is the medium of our very subjectivity, that it is more a question of ritual practice than conscious doctrine, that it is 'eternal' in its duration and immutable in its structure – Althusser at once returned the whole topic of ideology to a central place in radical thinking, and sought to overturn many of that thinking's presuppositions.

3 Ideology and Irrationalism

No single conception of ideology – least of all Althusser's, with its many questionable assumptions – has commanded universal assent from those at work in this field. Indeed it is hardly an exaggeration to claim that there are almost as many theories of ideology as there are theorists of it. For Theodor Adorno, ideology is essentially a kind of 'identity thinking', erasing difference and otherness at the level of the mind as remorselessly as commodity exchange does at the level of the material. For the American sociologist Martin Seliger, ideology is best seen as a set of action-oriented beliefs, whose truth or falsehood, conservatism or radicalism, is quite irrelevant.[4] A whole span of thinkers – Jürgen Habermas, Nicos Poulantzas and Alvin Gouldner among them – take ideology to be a wholly modern, secular, quasi-scientific phenomenon, in contrast to earlier brands of mythical, religious or metaphysical thought. Karl Mannheim, by contrast, sees ideology as essentially antiquated forms of thought out of sync with what the age demands. Definitions of ideology range from 'systematically distorted communication' (Habermas) to 'semiotic closure' (post-structuralism), from 'the confusion of linguistic and phe-nomenal reality' (Paul de Man) to a discourse marked by certain significant ab-sences and elisions (Pierre Macherey). For those like Lukács and his disciple Lucien Goldmann, ideology is a 'genetic' affair, its truth to be located in the historical class or situation from which it springs; for others, ideology is a functional matter, a question of the effects of certain utterances whatever their source. Many theorists now consider the truth-value of ideological statements to be irrelevant to the business of classifying them as ideological in the first place; others hold that ideology may indeed contain important truths, but ones deformed by the impact of social interests or the exigencies of action. A history of the concept of ideology could be written in terms of what is taken as its opposite, all the way from 'seeing reality as it is' (the early Marx and Engels) and 'a consciousness of totality' (Lukács) to 'science' (Althusser) and 'a recognition of difference' (Adorno). Ideology can be theoretically elaborate (Thomism, Social Darwinism) or a set of spontaneous, automated habits (what the French sociologist Pierre Bourdieu calls *habitus*). It can mean, too vaguely, 'socially conditioned or socially interested thought' or, too narrowly, 'false ideas which help to legitimate an unjust political power'. The term may be pejorative, as with Marx or Mannheim; positive, as (sometimes) with Lenin; or neutral, as with Althusser. There are those like Lucien Goldmann for whom ideologies are highly structured, internally coherent formations, and others like Pierre Macherey for whom they are amorphous and diffuse.[5] Whereas Adorno sees ideology as falsely homogenising, Fredric Jameson views its essential gesture as an absolute binary opposition.[6] And there is the odd right-wing academic like Kenneth Minoghue for whom left-wingers have ideology while conservatives see things as they really are.[7]

Theories of ideology are, among other things, attempts to explain why it is that men and women come to hold certain views; and to this extent they examine the relation between thought and social reality. However that relation is conceived – as reflection or contradiction, correspondence or dislocation, inversion or imaginary construction – these theories assume that there are specific historical reasons why people come to feel, reason, desire and imagine as they do. It may be because they are in the grip of embattled sectional interests, or because they are hoodwinked by the false forms in which the social world presents itself, or because a screen of fantasy interposes itself between that world and themselves. With Louis Althusser, however, we touch on the rather more alarming claim that some kind of imaginary misperception of both self and world is actually latent in the very structure of human subjectivity. Without this misperception, human beings for Althusser would simply not be able to function as their societies require them to; so that this flaw or misconception is absolutely necessary to what we are, structurally indis-pensable to the human animal. Sectional interests might be abolished, screens of fantasy removed and social structures transformed; but if ideology lies at the very root of our being, then a much gloomier picture begins to emerge. Behind Althusser's claim, whether consciously or not, lies the thought of Friedrich Nietzsche, for whom all purposive action depends on the consoling fiction that we are unified selves, and on a necessary oblivion of the random, ineffably complex and shameful determinants of our actual human existence. For Althusser, the 'imaginary' self of ideology is a coherent one, which is why it is able to undertake socially essential action; but 'theory' is grimly aware that such unity is in fact a myth, that the human subject – like the social order itself – is no more than a decentred assemblage of elements. The paradox emerges, then, that we become subjects only by a repression of the determinants which go into our making; and this is precisely the major insight of Sigmund Freud. We become subjects for Freud by passing more or less successfully through the Oedipal trauma; but to operate effectively we must repress that hideous drama, and we do so by opening up within us the place known as the unconscious, driving our insatiable desire underground. Forgetting is then for Freud our 'normal' condition, and remembering is simply forgetting to forget. For these thinkers, then, there is something chronically askew about human beings, a kind of original sin by which all perception includes misperception, all action involves incapacity, all cognition is inseparable from error. One name for this line of thought in our own time has been post-structuralism; but that particular discourse is just the latest phase of a long post-Romantic tradition, which stretches from the German philosopher Arthur Schopenhauer to his disciple Nietzsche and on to Freud and a whole host of twentieth-century thinkers. For this lineage, one cannot really speak of false consciousness because now *all* consciousness is inherently false; whoever says 'consciousness' says delusion, distortion, estrangement. Reason is just a blundering instrument in the service of Will (Schopenhauer), power (Nietzsche) or desire (Freud); and it is in the nature of this accidental spin-off of evolution to miss the mark, to be self-deceived, to be tragically blinded to its own deeper determinations. Freud, to be sure, inherits much of the Enlightenment tradition too, with his courageous belief in the 'talking cure', in the power of analysis to set right some of our discontents; but for this 'irrationalist' heritage in general, ideology is a useless notion since it covers more or less all we know as the conscious mind. Consciousness is now itself a monstrous aberration, and is divided by some unspannable abyss from the reality it vainly seeks to embrace.

There seems little doubt that this powerful philosophical tradition captures some of the way the human mind is. But if the Enlightenment errs on the side of a hubristic rationalism, this current of thought is too ready to sweep aside as so much trivia those *particular* social mechanisms which cause men and women to languish in the grip of oppressive ideas, and so to collude in their own wretchedness. To this extent, one could view the 'irrationalist' tradition as at once an essential corrective to some vulgar notion that we could emancipate our minds simply by rationally reorganising our society, and as an ideology in exactly the Marxist sense, naturalising and universalising specific forms of irrationality to the structure of human consciousness as such. If all consciousness is false consciousness, then the term covers too much and drops out of sight; and this is one major reason why there has been so little talk of ideology in a postmodern age. For the relativist climate of postmodernism is in general wary of concepts of truth, suspecting them to be absolutist and authoritarian; and if one cannot speak of truth, then one cannot logically speak of falsehood either. To identify an ideological view, so the argument goes, you would need to be in secure possession of the truth, to see things precisely as they are; but since any such claim is epistemologically overweening, there is no point in speaking of ideology. To which the first response is that ideology, as we have seen, is at least as much concerned with the functions, effects and motivations of discourses as with their truth-value; and the second response is that it is plainly false to imagine that, in order to spot a falsehood, distortion or deception, you must have some access to absolute truth. Those postmodernists who assert that this last statement is untrue have just undermined their own case. The notion of absolute truth is simply a bugbear here; we do not need intuitive access to the Platonic Forms to be aware that apartheid is a social system which leaves something to be desired. What most theories of ideology assert is that for oppressed and exploited peoples to emancipate themselves, a knowledge of how the social system works, and how they stand within it, is essential to their project; so that the opposite of ideology here would be less 'science' or 'totality' than 'emancipatory knowledge'. The theory of ideology claims further that it is in the interests of the system in question to forestall such accurate knowledge of its workings, and that fetishism, mystification, naturalisation and the rest are among the devices by which it achieves these ends. There are those for whom accurate knowledge is vital, just because they need urgently to change their situations; and there are others (postmodernist academics among them) who can afford their cognitive indeterminacy. Because seeking a true self-understanding, in conditions of illusion and obscurantism, involves certain virtues (of honesty, realism, tenacity and so forth), emancipatory knowledge is at once cognitive and ethical, bridging a gap which Immanuel Kant declared unspannable.

Postmodernism is an 'end of ideology' world, just as it has been declared to be the end of history. But this, of course, is true only for postmodern theorists. It is hardly true for American Evangelicals, Egyptian fundamentalists, Ulster Unionists or British fascists. Some ideologies (those of neo-Stalinism, for instance) may have crumbled, while others (patriarchy, racism, neo-colonialism, free-marketeering) remain as virulent as ever. We must ponder, then, the extraordinary irony that, in a world gripped by powerful, sometimes death-dealing ideologies, the intellectuals have decided that the ideological party is over. In part, of course, this merely reflects their customary distance from the world in which most people have to live; in part, it reflects their mistaking the media and the shopping mall for the rest of social reality. It is also the consequence of a fashionable cult of neo-Nietzscheanism: if power, desire and sectional interests are the very stuff of reality, why bother to speak of ideologies as though there was anything beyond them, or as though they could ever be changed? But it springs also from certain alterations in the nature of capitalism, which in its more classical period sought to justify itself by rhetorical appeals to moral value, but is nowadays often enough content to appeal to self-interest and consumerist hedonism. An 'end to ideology' is in this sense an ideology all in itself: what it recommends is that we forget about moral justifications altogether and simply concentrate on enjoying ourselves. In this sense, our present end-of-ideology climate differs from the 'end of ideology' current during the Cold War. What this came down to, in effect, was that while the Soviet Union was in the grip of ideology, the United States saw things as they really were. Sending one's tanks into Hungary is an instance of ideological fanaticism; subverting the democratically elected government of Chile is a matter of adapting realistically to the facts.

There is a common dystopian fantasy of a world so thoroughly ideologised that all dissent has been contained, all conflicts papered over, all rebellion rendered unthinkable. For some, this fantasy is not so distant: we live, so the argument goes, in a world of doped telly-viewers who have long since been cowed into apathetic conformity. In this dark vision, the powers which rule our lives have now become thoroughly internalised; and it is true that any dominant ideology which wishes to succeed must aim precisely at this. For it is not enough to win the mere outward obedience of men and women; ideally, they should come to identify that power with their own inward being, so that to rebel against it would be a form of self-transgression. Power must become at one with the very form of our subjectivity; indeed for a political pessimist like Michel Foucault, it is power which actually produces that subjectivity in the first place. The Law must be inscribed on our hearts and bodies, since it demands of us not simply a passive tolerance but an ardent embrace. Its ultimate aim is not simply to induce us to accept oppression, but cheerfully to collude in it; women under patriarchy are kept in place not primarily by coercion, but by guilt, low self-esteem, a misplaced sense of duty, feelings of powerlessness, fear of alienating the love and approval of others, anxieties about appearing unfeminine, a feeling of solidarity with similarly placed women, and so on. The Law is not satisfied with a mere ritual obedience; it wants us instead to look it in the eyes and whisper that we have understood. And if this were indeed our situation, then the dystopian cynics would be right. But there are excellent psychoanalytic reasons for believing that this all-powerful authority is itself a psychological fantasy. First, not all power or authority is of course oppressive: deployed by the right hands in the right ways, it can be a source of human benefit. Secondly, the ego's relationship to the superego (or internalised source of authority) will never cease to be ambivalent, torn as it is between fear and affection, duty and dissent, guilty acquiescence and smouldering resentment. Every oppressive form of rule harbours the secret knowledge that it lives only in the active consent of those it subjugates, and that were this consent to be withdrawn on any major scale, it would be struck powerless. If an unjust authority cannot secure such widespread consent, then it will be often enough forced to resort to coercion; but in doing so it will tend to suffer a massive loss of credibility, alienating its subjects even more thoroughly. Every such authority knows also that men and women will only grant it their consent if there is something in it for them – if that authority is capable of yielding them, however meagrely, some gratification to be going on with. If it is able to do this, then individuals will quite often put up heroically with various kinds of misery; but the moment it ceases to grant them any such fulfilments, they will rebel against it as surely as night follows day. The dystopian vision is wrong on this account; but it is wrong also to imagine that what keeps us in our allotted places is mainly some omnipotent ideology. For there is no reason to suppose that people who meekly acquiesce in some unjust social order do so because they have obediently internalised its values. Many of the British people accepted the government of Margaret Thatcher; but it appears that only a minority of them actually endorsed her values. There are much more humdrum reasons why people will fall into line: because they can see no workable alternative to what they have, because they are too busy caring for their children and worrying about their jobs, because they are frightened of the consequences of opposing a particular regime. Ideology plays a part in persuading people to tolerate unjust situations; but it is probably not the major part, and it almost never does so without a struggle.

Notes

1   For an excellent analysis of some of these arguments, see Christopher Norris, *Deconstruction and the Interests of Theory* (London: Routledge, 1989).
2   See N. Abercrombie et al., *The Dominant Ideology Thesis* (London: Allen & Unwin, 1980).
3   J. Laplanche and J. B. Pontalis, *The Language of Psycho-Analysis* (London: Hogarth Press, 1980), p. 375.
4   See Martin Seliger, *The Marxist Conception of Ideology* (Cambridge: Cambridge University Press, 1977).
5   See Pierre Macherey, *A Theory of Literary Production* (London: Routledge, 1978), Part 1.
6   See Theodor Adorno, *Negative Dialectics* (London: Routledge, 1973), Introduction, and Fredric Jameson, *The Political Unconscious* (London: Methuen, 1981), pp. 115ff.
7   See Kenneth Minoghue, *Alien Powers* (London: Weidenfeld & Nicolson, 1985), p. 5.

17 Marxist Literary Theory

It is no longer possible, if it ever really was, to take the word 'Marxist' in the phrase 'Marxist criticism' for granted, and turn instead to the critical issues at stake. For Marxism is at present enduring the most grievous crisis of its fraught career – a crisis which involves nothing less than the question of its very survival. If this has never quite been true before, the fact is not necessarily to Marxism's credit. The long night of Stalinism did more to discredit the doctrine, not least in the eyes of those working people in the West who might have stood to gain something by it, than all the polemics of the right-wing intelligentsia put together; but at least Stalinism and its progeny seemed to mean that Marxism of some species was here to stay, as a fact if not as a value. Ironically, what discredited it at one level served to entrench it at another. It may not have been to one's taste, but one couldn't ignore it – whereas today, in the turbulent aftermath of all that, it is possible for some to find virtue in Marxist thought exactly because it can be easily enough sidelined in political reality.

But it was not the collapse of neo-Stalinism, or however the political taxonomists choose to label whatever was under way in Eastern Europe, which first plunged Marxism into crisis. The chronology here is simply false, for Marxism was already in deep trouble before the first brick of the Berlin wall had been loosened. It was not the implosion of the Soviet world, but the quickening contradictions of the Western one, which first began to undermine historical materialism. If, as Fredric Jameson has maintained, the 1960s came to an end in 1973–4 with the international oil crisis, then the heady Althusserian heyday of the early and mid-1970s, when something like a Marxist *culture* last existed in the West, was already, unbeknown to itself, the beginnings of a political downturn. The same period witnessed the end of the great wave of national liberation movements throughout the world, movements which had dealt international capitalism a series of staggering rebuffs. A few years later, high Althusserianism had veered on its axis and worked its way through to so-called post-Marxism, as the ice age of Reagan–Thatcherism set in. Under mounting economic pressure, the political regimes of the West shifted sharply to the right, and Marxism was one casualty of this carnival of reaction.

In what exact sense, though? For it is not as though anyone actually *disproved* the doctrine. It is not as though they needed to. In the new ambience of political cynicism, cultural philistinism and economic self-interest, Marxism was less and less even *in question*, as quaintly antiquarian a pursuit for some as Ptolemaic cosmology or the scholasticism of Duns Scotus. One no more needed to refute it than one would waste time refuting a fakir or a flat-earther. For many, Marxism, in Foucauldian phrase, was less and less 'in the truth', no longer quite the kind of epistemic object which might seriously qualify for debate as to its truth-value. It was becoming less false than irrelevant, a question on which it was no more necessary to have a firm opinion than it was on crop circles or poltergeists. One might have thought that if Marxism was true in 1975, as many then claimed it was, then – short of some immense sea-change in the world itself – it would also have been true in 1985. But in 1985 it was mattering less whether it was true or not, just as the existence of God was a burning issue in 1860 but hardly so one century later. Marxism was now less a discomforting challenge than the irritating or endearing idiosyncrasy of those unable to relinquish an imaginary selfhood inherited from the past. It belonged irrevocably to the great epoch of modernity, within which, whether true or false, it figured as an entirely intelligible project. Once that age had passed into a different problematic, Marxism could be seen as at best a set of valid responses to a set of questions which were no longer on the agenda. It thus crossed over, in the eyes of some, from being false but relevant, to true but superfluous. And the line between claiming that it was superfluous because capitalism *should* not be defeated, and asserting that it was redundant because the system *could* not be defeated, became easy enough to cross.

Marxism, then, was taken to be less disproved than discredited, out of the question rather than out of arguments. But quite *what* had been discredited was not entirely clear. Did the fall of the Berlin wall mean that Georg Lukács's remarks on Balzac were now valueless? Did the rise of market relations in Poland mean that nobody involved in the celebrated 'transition from feudalism to capitalism' debate had uttered a single illuminating word? This, indeed, would be the unity of theory and practice with a vengeance, outMarxizing the Marxists themselves! It would, to be sure, be singularly unMarxist to regard Marxism itself as politically bankrupt while still a useful tool of intellectual analysis. The American professor who re-marked of Marxism in my hearing that of course the economics were up the spout but it could still throw a lot of light on Chaucer was not just being a selective Marxist, he was being no sort of Marxist at all. For whatever else Marxists may disagree upon, they are agreed that the term 'Marxist' functions more like the word 'carpenter' than it does like the word 'Cartesian'. But this is not to claim, even so, that theory and practice always dance harmoniously together. Marxist theory may be ultimately for the sake of political practice; but it would be a brand of Marxist pragmatism (commonly known as Stalinism or historicism) to hold that the truth-value of the theory is determined by its success in a particular political conjuncture. For one thing, it is not easy to know whether it was the theory which brought about the success; perhaps the very fact that you were in error allowed you to achieve what you wanted. For another thing, Marxist theory itself contains explanations of why theory and practice do not always slide together quite so symmetrically. And if theory exists now for the sake of practice, that practice exists for the sake of some future condition in which we would not need to rationalize the pleasures of thought at the tribunal of some instrumental reason.

But there is another consideration at stake here. Part of the crisis of Marxism would seem to be that it is no longer easy to say what *counts* as being a Marxist, if indeed it ever was. In our own time, it has proved possible for individuals to discount many of the classical doctrines of the creed – the labour theory of value, the notion of historical laws, the contradiction between the forces and relations of production, the model of base and superstructure, the idea of 'class identity', the supposedly scientific basis of Marxist epistemology, the concept of false consciousness, the philosophy of 'dialectical materialism' – and still lay claim to the name of Marxist. Whether it is possible for someone to renounce *all* of these tenets and still remain in some meaningful sense a Marxist is rather less obvious; but it has certainly become less clear just how many of the 39 articles, so to speak, one needs to subscribe to in order to lay claim to the title. There are 'Marxists' these days – to continue the ecclesiastical analogy – who resemble the kind of extreme-liberal Anglican who has no time for the doctrines of the existence of God, the divinity of Christ, heaven and hell, the sacraments, the Ten Commandments or the resurrection. Such a faith is not even precise enough to be wrong. Of course, if the word 'Marxist' is to have meaning, then there must logically be something which is incompatible with it – just as one can find all kinds of feminists, but not feminists who think male dominance of women an excellent thing. But it is likely, even so, that the word 'Marxist' works to denote a set of family resemblances rather than some immutable essence. Certainly Marx and Engels themselves repudiated the idea that social class, or even class struggle, was original to their way of thinking. What they considered innovative about their theory was the claim that the rise and fall of social classes is bound up with the rise and fall of historical modes of production. There seems no epistemological doctrine which Marxism does not share with a host of other realisms, so that those unwary Marxists who believe they are unique in holding to the objective independent existence of the material world have obviously not been chatting to conservative middle-class philosophers. The 'last-instance' determination of the economic would appear a peculiarly Marxist claim, but it is one that Freud, no particular friend of Marxism, subscribed to himself, when he remarked that the motive of all social life was finally an economic one. As for more narrowly political beliefs – equality, common ownership, self-government and the rest – it is hard to think of any which Marxists do not share in common with other types of radicals or revolutionaries. And this has a bearing on the issue of validation. For the *distinctive* focus of Marxism, as opposed to some other styles of socialism, is not the 'political conjuncture', but the *longues durées* of – for example – the conflict between the forces and relations of material production.

The validity or otherwise of its claims about such epochal questions cannot be decided by the political short term, which is not to say that they cannot be determined at all – that Marxism is, as Popper would have it, inherently unfalsifiable and so intrinsically unscientific. It is just that you cannot determine the truth of such broad claims in the same way as you can the truth of the charge that Stalin murdered kulaks.

But surely, it will be objected, almost a century of botched Marxist experiment is *longue durée* enough. If *that* isn't enough to demonstrate that the theory simply doesn't work in practice, then what would conceivably count as conclusive evidence? But assessing the success of a theory involves taking into account what *it* would count as success; we do not upbraid Einstein for failing to find a cure for cancer. And none of the founding theorists of Marxism imagined for a moment that it could provide the means by which desperately backward societies could throw off their oppressors, catapult themselves single-handed into the twentieth century and construct socialism in a besieged and isolated state. This would involve the back-breaking task of developing the productive forces from a very low level – a task which capitalism had cannily entrusted to individual self-interest, and so had magnificently accomplished. But if men and women in post-capitalist conditions proved understandably reluctant to submit themselves freely to such a dispiriting labour, then an authoritarian state would have to step in and do it on their behalf, thus undermining the political content of socialism (popular participatory democracy) in the very process of striving to lay down its economic base. Building socialism takes time – time for the complex business of democratic self-management; and this in turn requires a shortening of the working day impossible if people have no food or shoes. It also helps if you inherit a wealth of cultural resources, sophisticated institutions of civil society and a flourishing tradition of bourgeois liberalism, for socialism is of course the 'sublation' of such a precious liberal humanist heritage and not simply its antithesis. But these resources, not to speak of the basic educational skills essential for socialist democracy, are scarcely likely to thrive in conditions of economic backwardness. One of the tragic ironies of the twentieth century, then, is that socialism has proved least possible where it has been most urgently necessary. It was this, no doubt, that Lenin had in mind when he remarked with dialectical deftness that it was the relative absence of culture (in the sense of an elaborate realm of 'civil society') which had made the revolution in Russia possible to achieve, but the very same absence of culture (in the sense of spiritual and material resources) which had made it so hard to sustain.

Is this to claim, then, that only the well-heeled can go socialist, abandoning the Third World to its fate? Not at all; it is to claim rather, as did the Bolsheviks, that socialist change can surely be initiated in such conditions, but that unless the richer nations come to its aid it is very likely to be forced down the Stalinist path. There can be no socialism in one country in an interdependent world, even if the process has to start somewhere. All this has long been understood by the Marxist tradition itself. If one wants a critique of neo-Stalinism which is materially based, historically rooted and implacably critical, then one has to turn to key aspects of the Marxist heritage, rather than to the middle-class liberal one. Liberalism has properly defended civil liberties in the neo-Stalinist societies, but this, for a Marxist, was never really radical enough. What happened in Eastern Europe a few years ago – the overthrow of the ruling bureaucracies by popular power, in a gratifyingly bloodless series of revolutions – was what many currents of Marxism had been calling for for well over half a century. If it arrived a little later than, say, the incurably hopeful Trotsky had expected, it was better late than never. It also took place, by a pleasing irony, at just the historical point when sophisticated Western leftists everywhere had abandoned the whole notion of popular revolution as incorrigibly naïve. And what happened in the wake of those revolutions – a reversion to, or inauguration of, capitalist social relations – was a development which key currents of modern Marxism had also for a long time foreseen as an ominous possibility. The downfall of the ruling bureaucracies was a necessary, but by no means sufficient, condition of constructing democratic socialism.

If Marxism is in crisis, then, it is not on account of some pervasive left disillusionment over the disintegration of the post-capitalist countries. You can, after all, suffer disillusion only if you were illusioned in the first place; and the last time that the Western left harboured widespread illusions about the Soviet Union was the 1930s. If the left is in some disarray, it is not in the first place to do with Marxism, but with a far more general sense of impotence and frustration consequent on the fact that capitalism for the moment lacks an effective, concerted political challenge. In that sense, the system can be said so be currently victorious – but the very word has something of a grotesque ring to it. For how can a global system which is at once the most productive history has ever witnessed, yet which needs to keep the great majority of men and women in a state of spiritual and material deprivation, possibly be described as successful? To this extent, the rancour of the socialist contains an implicit hope: what is so bad about this system is exactly the fact that it doesn't and can't work. Socialism may be pitched into crisis for this or that reason from time to time; but capitalism exists in a state of chronic neurosis, and could not do otherwise.

It is typical of Marxism, as opposed to other styles of socialist belief, to have paid special attention to the *contradictions* of capitalism – to the ways that it can't help producing wealth and poverty at a stroke, as material conditions of one another. And this, in turn, lends it a peculiar stance towards the question of modernity. Modern radicalisms have tended on the whole to divide between nostalgic-regressive and progressive-technological strains: between romantic anti-capitalism and Fabianism, the potter's wheel and the Futurist machine, Lukács and Brecht. Marxism, however, at once outdoes the Futurists in its praise for the mighty achievements of modernity, and outflanks the romantic anti-capitalists in its remorseless denunciation of the very same era. As both the offspring of Enlightenment and its immanent critique, it cannot be readily categorized in the facile pro- and anti-modernist terms now fashionable in Western cultural debate. Whereas modernism proper was really just confused on this score, never really able to square its revolt against modernity with its dependence upon it, and whereas postmodernism either commodifies the past or erases it, Marxism alone has sustained the eminently dialectical belief, inimical at once to romantic nostalgia and modernizing triumphalism, that modern history has been inseparably civilization and barbarism. This dialectical view can in turn be rephrased as another. Marxism gives immense weight to culture, social construction, historical change, sceptical as it is of the supposedly natural and immutable; and to this extent it has something in common with postmodernism. Unlike postmodernism, however, it is at the same time deeply suspicious of the cultural, which it views as in the end the offspring of labour, as well as, often enough, a disownment of it; and since the historical narrative it has to deliver is one of recurrent struggle, scarcity and suffering, as well as of dynamism, open-endedness and variety, it is less likely to be seduced by some modish notion of an endlessly pluralist history. The story which Marxism has to tell is more tedious, but also more true to the humdrum, vulnerable nature of humanity, than exotic tales of difference, multiplicity and mutability. It is not that Marxism does not *wish* such fables to be true; it is rather that they can only be true of some transformed future, when History (or, as Marx puts it, pre-history) would be thankfully over, and real histories might consequently begin. Marxism is all about how to get from the kingdom of identity to the realm of difference; it is just that it is wary of the kind of callow idealism that believes you can do this by studying Derrida rather than Aristotle, or more generally by adopting a different outlook on life.

If socialism were just an outlook on life, then one might well expect it to go under, disabled by its Stalinist distortions and crippled by the onslaughts of the free marketeers. But socialism is more than just a good idea, like brushing one's teeth or wrapping Westminster bridge in crêpe paper; it is arguably the greatest reform movement in the history of humanity, and one well accustomed to serious setbacks. If it is aware of the formidable power of what it opposes, it is equally conscious of how quickly and unpredictably history can alter. And even if it does not do so – even if 'late' capitalism turns out to mean a long way from the beginning rather than anywhere near the end – there is no reason why this sobering thought should change what one strives for, which remains true and valuable whether or not it can be realized in the here and now.

Culture for Marxism is at once absolutely vital and distinctly secondary: the place where power is crystallized and submission bred, but also somehow 'superstructural', something which in its more narrow sense of specialized artistic institutions can only be fashioned out of a certain economic surplus and division of labour, and which even in its more generous anthropological sense of a 'form of life' risks papering over certain important conflicts and distinctions. Culture is more than just ideology, but it is not a neutral or transcendent entity either; and any Marxist criticism worth the name must thus adopt a well-nigh impossible double optic, seeking on the one hand to take the full pressure of a cultural artefact while striving at the same time to displace it into its enabling material conditions and set it within a complex field of social power. What this means in effect is that one will find oneself bending the stick too far towards formalism and then too far towards contextualism, in search of that ever-receding discourse which would in allegorical manner speak simultaneously of an artistic device and a whole material history, of a turn of narrative and a style of social consciousness.

Very schematically, it is possible to distinguish four broad kinds of Marxist criticism, each of which corresponds to a certain 'region' within Marxist theory, and also (very roughly speaking) to a particular historical period. These are the *anthropological, political, ideological* and *economic* – modes which in their various intricate permutations go to make up the corpus of criticism recorded in this book. '*Anthropological*' criticism (the term needs its qualifying quotation marks) is the most ambitious and far-reaching of all four approaches, seeking as it does to raise some awesomely fundamental questions. What is the function of art within social evolution? What are the material and biological bases of 'aesthetic' capacities? What are the relations between art and human labour? How does art relate to myth, ritual, religion and language, and what are its social functions? These and cognate questions are not on the whole ones with which we feel terribly comfortable today, smacking as they do of the compulsively synthetic vision of the late nineteenth-century human sciences. The postmodern sensibility is allergic to such embarrassingly large issues, which stride briskly across epochs and civilizations, assume certain abiding identities ('art', 'labour'), and tend to substitute evolution for history. But from G. V. Plekhanov to Christopher Caudwell, and with the odd late flowering like Ernst Fischer's *The Necessity of Art*, this has formed one important current of Marxist cultural enquiry. It represents a materialism of a somewhat fundamentalist but none the less interesting kind – an attempt to demystify idealist notions of art by situating it in the context of what the young Marx himself called our 'species being', of the natural history, so to speak, of the species. Positivist, functionalist and biologistic in bent, it nevertheless contrasts tellingly in its scope and intellectual energy with the dwindled vistas of contemporary left-historicism, for which phenomena would seem to live and die in their punctual historical moments, reducing all generality or persisting identity to so much metaphysical or ideological baggage. But as Francis Mulhern has well argued, this is to reduce *history* to *change*, whereas history 'is also – and decisively, for its greater part – *continuity*. The historical process is differential: it is patterned by a plurality of rhythms and tempos, some highly variable, some very little so, some measured by clocks and calendars, others belonging to the practical eternity of "deep time".'[1] The time of a literary work is not the time of the human body, which has altered very little in the course of evolution; but neither is it the time of an ephemeral event like a handshake. Texts persist as well as mutate, strike correspondences as well as enforce differences, 'constellate' distinct historical moments as well as measure their mutual estrangement. The brand of extreme historicism which imprisons works within their historical context, or the kind of new historicism which incarcerates them in our own, are then perpetually liable to raise a set of problems which are in part pseudo-problems, such as 'how come that I, a twentieth-century non-believer in the Furies with liberal views on incest, can respond as I do to ancient Greek tragedy?' It is, famously, the kind of question which lost Karl Marx some sleep as well. But Marxism is not just an historicism, and neither should one assume that all historicisms are radical. Many of them are anything but. Transhistorical concepts have their place in historical materialism, since transhistorical activities play a key role in human history. And it is one of the virtues of 'anthropological' Marxist criticism, for all its limitations, to remind us of the fact. The realm of culture is changing, whereas that of the biological species is a good deal more stable; but this antithesis obscures as much as it illuminates. For culture, in the broadest sense of the term, is also a permanent necessity of our material being, without which we would quickly die. Our 'species being' brings with it a kind of structural gap or absence where culture of some kind must be implanted if we are to survive and flourish; and though *what* kind of culture is of course highly variable, the *necessity* of culture is not. It is not so much, then, the culturalist doctrine that 'the nature of humanity is culture' as the rather more dialectical point that we are cultural beings of our very nature.

Anthropological criticism belongs above all to the period of the Second International, with its encyclopaedic scholarship and confidently totalizing vision, its positivist assurance of certain progressive historical laws which render socialism inevitable, its curious blending of mechanical materialism and neo-Kantianism which allows it to speak in one breath of the opposing thumb and in the next of the faculty for appreciating beauty. From the time of the Bolsheviks, however, a *political* criticism comes to the fore, which addresses a quite different set of issues. With Plekhanov and his colleagues, Marxist criticism had been a contemplative, largely academic affair; now, from Lenin's pamphlets on Tolstoy to Trotsky's *Literature and Revolution*, criticism becomes a matter of polemic and intervention, of seeking to shape state cultural policy or confound some opposing cultural-political tendency, of winning over the fellow travellers or fighting off the Mensheviks. Cultural questions become, in part, code for much deeper political matters; where you stand on art reflects your position on the working class, on bourgeois democracy, on socialism in one country or the relative importance of peasant and urban proletariat. What is at stake is no longer the biological basis of the aesthetic faculty but whether art should be openly tendentious or 'objectively' partisan, whether avant-garde experiment is a way of figuring the revolutionary future or merely of alienating the unsophisticated masses, whether art should tell it as it is or as it should be, whether it should be mirror or hammer, cognitive or affective, beamed in unabashed class terms at the proletariat or imaging forth the 'universal' socialist being already in the making. Should the literature of class society be dumped, re-fashioned or disseminated amongst the people in cheap popular editions? Was a bad poem by a worker better than a good one by a bourgeois? Should art be scaled down to the present level of the masses, or the masses elevated to the current level of art? Was it elitist to use pen and paper rather than scribbling your poems on people's shirt-fronts in the street? Was any literary form compatible with a committed art, or was realism to be given a special privilege?

All of these issues belonged to the great ferment of activity around the years of the Russian revolution, when an entirely new cultural project, apparently without precedent, was in train, when it was as though the whole of familiar history had gone into the melting pot and the answers to some urgent questions had to be improvised as one went along. If it is impossible for us now to recapture that vertiginous mixture of anxiety and euphoria, it is nevertheless possible to trace the marks of it in the critical debates of the time, which still resound today with a vigour and audaciousness we have yet to reattain. And these great electrifying currents of energy, as new critical concepts are invented on the wing and as theory must hobble hard to keep up with artistic practice, belong not just to the world's first workers' state but to the wider context of radical European modernism, to the world of Dada, Surrealism, Brecht and Weimar. The role of culture is now nothing less than to fashion the forms of subjectivity appropriate to a revolutionized reality. It is not, as in our own time, that a radical culture overshoots a conservative reality; on the contrary, the problem is that reality is shifting before one's eyes but human consciousness is unable or unwilling to keep pace with it. Just as industrial capitalism required a whole new human sensorium, so industrial socialism is in hot pursuit of a subjectivity adequate to its new social relations, and it is to this task, rather than to the annotation of colour symbolism in Pushkin, that the Soviet critic is dedicated. Literary critic and literary practitioner will hammer out a new relationship, as in the liaison between the Formalist Osip Brik and the Futurist Mayakovsky, or later between Benjamin and Brecht – a relationship in which the critic is, as it were, tester, analyst and supplier of linguistic techniques and materials to the artist himself. And we are speaking in any case not of isolated academic critics but of movements, journals, collectives: of agit-prop and the Left Front in Art, Proletkult and RAPP.

The triumph of the doctrine of so-called socialist realism, and the rolling back of the more militant artistic projects, will finally put paid to this great epoch of cultural experiment, as a Soviet Union confronted by the rise of fascism feels the need to downplay an aggressive cultural proletarianism for the sake of an alliance with the progressive bourgeoisie of other nations. With the exception of the school of Bakhtin, which is itself forced underground, all the most creative developments in Marxist criticism will then shift elsewhere – to the so-called Western Marxist lineage of Lukács, Gramsci, Bloch, Adorno, Brecht, Benjamin, Marcuse, Caudwell, Sartre, Goldmann, Althusser. Most of these theorists are either quite outside official Soviet ideology or in some notably oblique relationship with it – relentless critics of orthodox Marxism, maverick fellow-travellers like Benjamin or Sartre, or (like Lukács and Althusser) party members whose cultural or theoretical work runs implicitly against the grain of the political establishment. All of them, as supposedly materialist thinkers, grant a remarkably high priority to culture and philosophy, and do so in part as a substitute for a politics that has failed.[2] For Georg Lukács, a dialectical totality which refuses to be realized in political reality is kept alive instead in the realist work of art. For Ernst Bloch, aesthetic utopia keeps open a perspective which Stalinism has closed off, whereas for Adorno and Marcuse 'high' culture, for all its objectionable privilege and anodyne harmonies, lingers on as the best that we can now do by way of political critique. Gramsci will harness culture to a resourceful new theory of power ('hegemony'), while Sartre will discover in the very act of writing a mode of freedom which implicitly rebukes Soviet as well as capitalist reality. Meanwhile, with Benjamin, Adorno and others of the Frankfurt school, a new and momentous field is delineated, that of popular culture in its structural opposition to high modernism.

Criticism, in other words, is now politics by other means, encompassing as it does questions of mass culture, literacy, popular education, power formations and forms of subjectivity as well as, more narrowly, the artistic text. But if this third wave of Marxist criticism can best be dubbed *ideological*, it is because its theoretical strengths lie above all in exploring what might be called the *ideology of form*, and so avoiding at once a mere formalism of the literary work and a vulgar sociologism of it. The wager here is that it is possible to find the material history which produces a work of art somehow inscribed in its very texture and structure, in the shape of its sentences or its play of narrative viewpoints, in its choice of a metrical scheme or its rhetorical devices. So it is that Lukács will trace the bourgeoisie's loss of historical direction in the disintegration of its narrative methods, or Walter Benjamin will detect the invisible presence of the Parisian crowd in the very perceptual strategies of Baudelaire's poetry. Lucien Goldmann will unearth from the work of Racine and Pascal an abiding structure of categories which binds them to the fortunes of an ousted social class, while Theodor Adorno detects in the conflictive, fragmentary nature of the modernist work of art an ultimately self-thwarting attempt to hold out against the miseries of ideological closure and economic commodification.

This studied avoidance of mere 'content analysis' reaches a point of self-parody in the work of the Althusserian critic Pierre Macherey, for whom what a literary work does *not* say – its eloquent silences, significant elisions, half-muttered ambiguities – are far more revealing of its relation to social ideologies than anything it may happen to utter. All of this intense preoccupation with literary form is not much remembered about Marxist criticism by its political opponents, who find it on the whole more convenient to believe that Marxist critics are only bothered about whether the author was progressive or reactionary, how many copies the novel sold and whether it mentions the working class. It is as though one were to judge the rich inheritance of psychoanalytic criticism by its speculations about phallic symbolism. Critics of Marxism still regularly accuse Marxist critics of paying scant attention to the 'words on the page' in their rush to read some ulterior political meaning into them. They cannot have read Trotsky's *Literature and Revolution*, Adorno's literary essays, Bakhtin's reflections on Dostoevsky, Benjamin's work on Baudelaire, Della Volpe's Marxist-semiotic studies of poetry, Sartre's writings on Flaubert, Fredric Jameson on Balzac or Conrad, or a host of similar studies. In general, the charge that Marxist criticism deals for the most part in unwieldy generalities is quite insupportable. And it is worth remembering in any case that not to attend to a work's historical range of reference is hardly to do justice to the 'words on the page'.

'Ideological' criticism has busied itself in the main with the relation between literary works and forms of social consciousness. It has also involved some subtle epistemological reflections: is art reflection, displacement, projection, refraction, transformation, reproduction, production? Is it an embodiment of social ideology or a critique of it? Or does it, as the Althusserians thought, critically 'distantiate' that ideology while remaining caught up in its logic? Would a 'revolutionary' artwork be one which had risen above ideology altogether, or one which transformed its readers' relations to that ideology? And which of the twenty different meanings of the term 'ideology' is at stake here? These and parallel questions have been the occasion for some of the most *intellectually* resourceful work in Marxist criticism; but it has not on the whole been the most *politically* productive. Indeed one might almost risk the formulation that the theoretical strengths of Marxist criticism have been more or less proportionate to its political weaknesses. The claim requires instant qualification: it is hardly true of the Left Front in Art, André Breton, Bertolt Brecht, Christopher Caudwell. But it remains true that much of the best Marxist criticism has been the product of a cultural displacement occasioned by political deadlock. Georg Lukács's turning from direct political engagement to literary criticism, under the shadow of Stalinism, is an exemplary moment here, as are Gramsci's reflections on language and philosophy in a fascist prison cell, or Benjamin's esoteric researches on Baudelaire in political exile. The fluctuating interests of the Frankfurt school, as it veers from the political-economic to the cultural-philosophical during the long freeze of fascism, world war and cold war, is another case in point. And the Althusserian concern for culture springs from a belief in the 'relative autonomy' of such areas which forms part of a critique of a repressive Marxist orthodoxy. It may well be, then, by a choice historical irony, that one effect of political downturn for the left was to concentrate wonderfully the critical mind, or at least to deflect it creatively.

Yet this deflection was not without its penalties. It is hard to concern yourself with ideologies, even from a materialist standpoint, without slipping unconsciously into the idealist faith that ideas are what finally count. It is a fallacy to which academics, even radical ones, are an easy prey by virtue of their profession; and part of what we observe happening in this third great wave of Marxist critical writing, roughly from Lukács's studies of the novel to, say, the contemporary work of a Williams or a Jameson, is the steady academicization of what for Trotsky, Breton,

Caudwell and Brecht had been a mode of political intervention. This is not a cheap gibe at 'armchair Marxists': it is not the fault of the left that it has been deprived of political outlets, and it is preferable for radical ideas to survive in an armchair than to go under altogether. Part of the task of socialist intellectuals is to preserve precious traditions, which is for the most part more a matter of reflection than of action. Even so, the intellectual apogee of Marxist criticism corresponded with a certain political declension, and a preoccupation with 'marginal' areas like literature and philosophy reflected in part the social marginality of radical thinkers themselves. Marxist criticism was now an isolated theoretical enquiry rather than part of a political or institutional process, a fact which reflected the dwindling of a left 'public sphere' in society as a whole.

There had always been, however, a counter-movement to this trend, one which constitutes our fourth, *economic* (the term is grossly inadequate) dimension of Marxist criticism. Unlike the previous currents, this one is much harder to periodize: it has cropped up in one guise or another throughout the history of Marxist cultural theory, weaving its way in and out of other kinds of approach. Its topic is what might be called *modes of cultural production*: its primary concern is neither with the concrete literary work, nor with the abstractions of a social formation, but with that whole intermediary space which is the material apparatuses of cultural production, all the way from theatres and printing presses to literary coteries and institutions of patronage, from rehearsing and reviewing to the social context of producers and recipients. Described in this way, the area is hard to distinguish from the so-called sociology of literature, and indeed is often distinctive only by virtue of its political assumptions and anti-empiricist methods. As with any major shift of theoretical interest, this one had its material conditions: the fact that what was emerging from the high-modernist period onwards, but at greatly accelerated speed in the post-war decades, was a new form of culture whose material apparatuses (film, radio, television, sound recording) were not only the most striking and novel thing about them, but had as media of communication an obvious and intimate relation to their 'content'. Much the same might be said about books, which are of course quite as much material media, social institutions and nodes of social relations as television; but all of this had been long since 'naturalized', as we came to stare through the stubborn material fact of a book to its etherial sense, no longer intrigued by the mystery of how these little black marks on the page could actually be meanings. It was then as though modern cultural technology violently estranged these familiar perceptions, forcing us once again to register the way a particular medium generates specific sorts of meanings, confronting us once more with the social or collective nature of a long-privatized 'art' in the form of (say) cinema audiences, and making dramatically clear the interpenetration between these cultural institutions and the power of capital itself. In other words, one no longer had to argue so strenuously for the material nature of culture when it leapt out at you on the flick of a switch, or for its economic basis when it came wrapped in advertising.

Much of this was already obvious to the early revolutionary avant-garde, the Futurists, Constructivists and Surrealists who recognized that a revolutionary culture could not consist of pumping different materials down the same channels but meant a transformation in the means of communication themselves. Brecht's so-called epic theatre is an inheritor of this lineage, and its major theorist is his colleague Walter Benjamin, not least in his seminal essay 'The Author as Producer'. In Britain, it was a form of criticism already adumbrated in the early 1960s in Raymond Williams's *The Long Revolution*, a work which can now be seen as laying the ground for what the later Williams will come to describe as 'cultural materialism'. The phrase offers to resolve the paradox we have touched on before – that culture for Marxism is at once central and secondary. On the one hand, culture is no more than a sector of the wider field of materialism in general; on the other hand, by being thus 'materialized', it comes to assume a force and reality of which aesthetic idealism had deprived it. What is now at stake, in other words, is not just an alternative reading of literary works but a materialist re-reading of the culture of which they are part; and this allows the 'economic' approach to art to draw together something of the other procedures we have outlined. For cultural materialism depends to some extent on certain broader 'anthropological' categories of labour, production, communication and so on; it examines the relations between material media and meaning, and thus learns from the formal concerns of ideological criticism; and by carrying materialism directly, so to speak, into enemy territory – into a 'culture' which was constructed as idealist in the first place, and which figures for its apologists as the last bastion of 'spirit' in a degraded world – it lends Marxist criticism a keener political edge. Nobody is much bothered by materialist readings of *Titus Andronicus*, or indeed by materialist theories of politics and economics, where one would expect such views to be relevant; but a materialist theory of culture – a theory of culture as production before it is expression – sounds, in the spontaneously idealist milieu of middle-class society, something of a category mistake or a contradiction in terms.

We may return, finally, to where we began – with the perilous future of Marxism itself. What would the 'death of Marxism' actually mean? For Marxism is as inseparable from modern civilization as Darwinism or Freudianism, as much part of our 'historical unconscious' as Newton was for the Enlightenment. One does not need to *agree* with all or even most of the doctrines of Newton or Freud to accept their utter centrality to modernity. So it is difficult to see how Marxism could simply 'die' without modernity dying too, which of course is what postmodernism exists to proclaim. If postmodernism is right – if modernity is effectively over – then Marxism is most certainly superannuated along with it. If, however, we are still struggling within the contradictions of modernity, and if it will not be over until we resolve them, and if its regular obituary notices have thus been greatly exaggerated, then Marxism remains as relevant as it ever was, which is not the same as claiming it as true. The 'end of modernity' is in any case a performative act masquerading as a constative proposition: who precisely wants to call off modernity, who has the title to do so, who is blowing the whistle on it for what purposes? Is the 'end of modernity' just a cryptic way of announcing that its contradictions have turned out to be insoluble, and that we therefore might as well move on to something else? Who precisely has the privilege to make this move, and who does not?

If postmodernism is right, then Marxism is wrong – *pace* those brands of postmodern Marxism which bear about the same relation to the classical tradition as guitar-toting vicars do to the Desert Fathers. But in another sense the proposition is misleading. For it is not as though one is being asked to choose between Marx and, say, Lyotard or Baudrillard. The very idea of such a choice involves, for a Marxist at least, a grotesque kind of category mistake, as though one were being asked to choose between a turkey sandwich and the concept of entropy. Marxism is not the body of work of an individual; it belongs to a much wider movement, that of socialism, which has in its time involved some millions of men and women across the nations and the centuries, a movement to which many have devoted themselves with impressive courage and for which some of them have been occasionally prepared to die. The practical transformations socialism envisages – the production of a new kind of human being who would find violence and exploitation abhorrent – would no doubt take several centuries to complete, though certain other vital changes would need to be carried through in a much shorter period. However much one might admire the ideas of Lyotard or Baudrillard, one is discussing an essentially different kind of reality, as only intellectuals could fail to realize.

It is surely not enough, however, that Marxism should survive only as part of our historical unconscious. For it is clear that capital is incapable of solving the human suffering it causes, and that its early emancipatory promise has long been exhausted. As more and more pre- or non-capitalist societies are drawn inexorably into its wake, the social devastation which ensues will make socialism more urgent and relevant a proposal than ever. The role that the specifically Marxist tradition might play in that broader project cannot be determined in advance. But the materials in this book alone reveal a wisdom, insight and imaginative flair which it is not only hard to see being simply written off, but which will surely play its part in any future change.

Notes

1 Francis Mulhern (ed.), *Contemporary Marxist Literary Criticism* (London: Longman, 1992), p. 22.
2 See Perry Anderson, *Considerations on Western Marxism* (London: Verso, 1979).

18 Marxism without Marxism: Jacques Derrida and *Specters of Marx*

There is no doubt that Derridean deconstruction was a political project from the outset, or that Jacques Derrida himself, in some suitably indeterminate sense, has always been a man of the Left. Nobody aware of the rigidly hierarchical nature of the French academic system could miss the political force of deconstruction's having originally germinated in its unwelcoming bosom, as the joker in the high-rationalist pack. In, but also out, since Derrida himself is a Sephardic-Jewish Algerian (post-)colonial, whose early encounters with a glacial Parisian high culture were, so one gathers, of an uncomfortably estranging kind. The Algerian connection, among other things, brought him close to Louis Althusser's celebrated circle in the rue d'Ulm, and so to a Marxism appealing in its anti-humanism while in other ways still too metaphysical for his taste. But Derrida has often been found insisting on the institutional rather than merely textual nature of deconstruction, so that it is not wholly surprising that the encounter with Marxism which, some decades back in *Positions*, he wryly announced as 'still to come', has finally, in some sense, arrived. He has, as the actress said to the bishop, been an unconscionably long time coming, and it is, as he is himself well aware, a mighty odd time to come; but the obvious point for a disgruntled Marxist to make – that Derrida has turned to Marxism just when it has become marginal, and so, in his post-structuralist reckoning, rather more alluring – is indeed too obvious to labour, if not to mention. If it is hard to resist asking, plaintively, where was Jacques Derrida when we needed him, in the long dark night of Reagan–Thatcher, it is also the case that Marxist fellow-travellers are thin enough on the ground these days to forbid one the privilege of looking a gift horse in the mouth, if not exactly of killing the fatted calf.

Even so, there is something pretty rich, as well as movingly sincere, about this sudden dramatic somersault onto a stalled bandwagon. For *Specters of Marx* doesn't just want to catch up with Marxism; it wants to outleft it by claiming that deconstruction was all along a radicalized version of the creed. 'Deconstruction', Derrida remarks, 'has never had any sense or interest, in my view at least, except as a radicalization, which is to say also *in the tradition* of a certain Marxism, in a certain *spirit of Marxism.*' This would certainly come as unpleasant news to Geoffrey Hartman, J. Hillis Miller or the late Paul de Man, who would no doubt read it for what, in part, it is: a handy piece of retrospective revisionism which hardly tallies with the historical phenomenon known in Cornell or California as deconstruction, however much it may reflect the (current) intentions of its founder. Perhaps de Man and the Californians got it wrong, in which case it is strange that Derrida did not chide them for such an egregious blunder. Whatever Derrida himself may now like to think, deconstruction – he must surely know it – has in truth operated as nothing in the least like a radicalized Marxism, but rather as an ersatz form of textual politics in an era when, socialism being on the run, academic leftists were grateful for a displaced brand of dissent which seemed to offer the twin benefits of at once outflanking Marxism in its audacious avant-gardism, and generating a sceptical sensibility which pulled the rug out from under anything as drearily undeconstructed as solidarity, organization or calculated political action. It was thus something of a godsend to North American oppositionalists whose outlets for political action were dismally few, ratifying a historically imposed inertia in glamorously ultra-libertarian terms.

Deconstruction has always shown the world two faces, the one prudently reformist, the other ecstatically ultra-leftist. Its problem has been that the former style of thought is acceptable but unspectacular; the latter exhilarating, but implausible. If its stance towards orthodox Marxism is not much more than a kind of anti-dogmatic *caveat*, then there is little to distinguish it from a host of familiar anti-Stalinisms. Such is the trouble with a work like, say, the American deconstructionist Michael Ryan's *Marxism and Deconstruction*, which argues for dynamic, open-ended, unmetaphysical, anti-foundational, multilevelled, non-mechanistic Marxism in a style that only a paid-up member of the Khmer Rouge might find mildly scandalous. How is a deconstructed Marxism different from, say, what the later Raymond Williams taught? If, on the other hand, deconstruction is to be more than some familiar *marxisant* revisionism or boring brand of left-liberalism, then it has to press its anti-metaphysical, anti-systemic, anti-rationalist claims to flamboyantly anarchic extremes, thus gaining a certain brio and panache at the risk of a drastic loss of intellectual credibility. The callower sort of epigones, who haven't all that much politically to lose, generally go in for the latter style of argument; the *maître* himself, who really *is* politically earnest and engaged, whose relevant contexts are Auschwitz and Algeria, Althusser, the ANC and Eastern Europe rather than Ithaca or Irvine, veers from one style to the other, rigorous philosophizing to portentous poeticizing, as it suits his purpose. The portentousness is ingrained in the very letter of this book, as one theatrically inflected rhetorical question tumbles hard on the heels of another in a tiresomely mannered syntax which lays itself wide open to parody. What is it, now, to chew carrots? Why this plural? Could there ever be more than one of them? Could this question even have meaning? Could one even speak of the 'chewing' of a carrot, and if so how, why, to whom, with what onto-teleo-theological animus?

The high humourlessness of Derrida's literary style – French 'playfulness' is a notoriously high-toned affair – reflects a residual debt to the academic world he has so courageously challenged. But there is no doubting the political passion at work in this book. If Marxism has become more attractive to Derrida on account of its marginality, it is also more appealing in the light of the unsavoury political alternatives to it. He is stirred to unwonted anger by the smug triumphalism of the New World Order, and relentlessly pursues the hapless Fukuyama through a series of admirably irate pages. If his critique is considerably less original than, say, Perry Anderson's essay on the subject, it is eloquent testimony to its author's enduring radicalism. Yet the truth is that Derrida – witness his embarrassingly disingenuous apologias for the collaborationist de Man – has never been at his most impressive when at his most politically explicit. His vague portmanteau talk here of 'tele-techno-medio-economic and scientifico-military forces', a kind of slipshod late-Frankfurt swearing, contrasts tellingly with the precision of his philosophical excursions elsewhere. Elsewhere rather than here – for what we have in this text, by and large, is a political discourse of an averagely-intelligent-layperson kind, and a philosophical rhetoric, of spectrality and the messianic, which is at once considerably more subtle and a good deal less convincing. The two registers subsist cheek-by-jowl without ever adequately interacting; the former committed yet rather crude, the latter exciting yet evanescent. They represent the two faces of Derrida, *émigré* and *éminence grise*, which have so far – but how could he wish it? – failed to merge into a persuasively coherent voice.

There is an exasperating kind of believer who holds what he does until he meets someone else who holds the same. At this point, confronted with the bugbear of an 'orthodoxy', he starts nervously to retract, or at least to qualify. There is more than a touch of this adolescent perversity in Derrida, who like many a postmodernist appears to feel (it is a matter of sensibility rather than reasoned conviction) that the dominant is *ipso facto* demonic and the marginal precious *per se*. One condition of the unthinking postmodern equation of the marginal with the creative, apart from a convenient obliviousness to such marginal groups as fascists, is the rolling back of political movements which are at once mass and oppositional. The mark of a genuine radical is a hearty desire to stop having to be so obdurately oppositional, a sentiment one can hardly imagine as dear to the heart of a deconstructionist. If one takes the point of James Joyce's retort to an invitation to return to a newly independent Irish republic – 'So as to be its first critic?' – one also registers the self-indulgence.

Derrida has now taken Marxism on board, or at least dragged it half-way up the gangplank, because he is properly enraged by liberal-capitalist complacency; but there is also something unavoidably opportunist about his political pact, which wants to exploit Marxism as critique, dissent, conveniently belabouring instrument, but is far less willing to engage with its positivity. What he wants, in effect, is a Marxism without Marxism, which is to say a Marxism on his own coolly appropriative terms. 'We would be tempted to distinguish this *spirit* of the Marxist critique . . . at once from Marxism as ontology, philosophical or metaphysical system, as "dialectical materialism", from Marxism as historical materialism or method, and from Marxism incorporated in the apparatuses of party, State, or workers' International.' It would not be difficult to translate this into the tones of a (suitably caricatured) liberal Anglicanism: we must distinguish the *spirit* of Christianity from such metaphysical baggage as the existence of God, the divinity of Christ, organized religion, the doctrine of the resurrection, the superstition of the Eucharist and the rest. Or: one would wish to distinguish the *spirit* of deconstruction from the dreary intellectual paraphernalia of 'writing', 'difference', 'trace', organized journals and conventions, formal reading groups, movements to install the teaching of philosophy in French schools and so on. It is entirely possible to approve of the spirit of the Huns, with all its admirable robustness, while deploring what they actually got up to. If Derrida thinks, as he appears to do, that there can be any effective socialism without organization, apparatuses and reasonably well-formulated doctrines and programmes, then he is merely the victim of some academicist fantasy which he has somehow mistaken for an enlightened anti-Stalinism. (He has, in fact, no materialist or historical analysis of Stalinism whatsoever, as opposed to an ethical rejection of it, unlike many more orthodox currents of Marxism.) The truth is that he is hardly concerned with an *effective* socialism at all. Deconstruction, with its preoccupation with slippage, failure, aporia, incoherence, not-quiteness, its suspicion of the achieved, integral or controlling, is a kind of intellectual equivalent of a vaguely leftish commitment to the underdog, and like all such commitments is nonplussed when those it speaks up for come to power. Post-structuralism dislikes success, a stance which allows it some superbly illuminating insights into the pretensions of monolithic literary texts or ideological self-identities and leaves it a mite wrong-footed in the face of the African National Congress.

Derrida's indifference to almost all of the *actual* historical or theoretical manifestations of Marxism is a kind of empty transcendence – a typically deconstructive trumping of some alternative position which leaves one's own case invulnerable only in proportion to its contentlessness. Much the same can be said of his curiously empty, formalistic messianism, which voids this rich theological tradition of its content and retains its ghostly impulse only, somewhat akin to the Kafka who (as Walter Benjamin remarks) is left with nothing but the transmissible forms of a tradition which has dwindled to nothing. The critical, negative passion of his politics in this book is one which ought rightly to embarrass every academic radical for whom deconstruction is a sexy form of common-or-garden scepticism, or yet another way of keeping the literary canon alive by plodding through it yet again, this time with a scalpel in hand. 'Instead of singing the advent of the ideal of liberal democracy and of the capitalist market in the euphoria of the end of history, instead of celebrating the "end of ideologies" and the end of the great emancipatory discourses, let us never neglect this obvious macroscopic fact, made up of innumerable singular sites of suffering: no degree of progress allows one to ignore that never before, in absolute figures, have so many men, women, and children been subjugated, starved, or exterminated on the earth.' This is not the kind of thing that is likely to go down well in Ithaca or Irvine, where they learnt long ago that ideology had ended and the great emancipatory discourses run thankfully aground.

And what does Derrida counterpose, in the very next paragraph, to the dire condition he so magnificently denounces? A 'New International', one 'without status, without title, and without name . . . without party, without country, without national community . . .' And, of course, as one gathers elsewhere in the book, without organization, without ontology, without method, without apparatus. It is the ultimate post-structuralist fantasy: an opposition without anything as distastefully systemic or drably 'orthodox' as an opposition, a dissent beyond all formulable discourse, a promise which would betray itself in the act of fulfilment, a perpetual excited openness to the Messiah who had better not let us down by doing anything as determinate as coming. Spectres of Marxism indeed.

Part IV Modernism and Postmodernism

Introduction

'The End of English' (Chapter 19) returns to the subtle intertwining of English-ness, modernism and colonialism that characterized *Exiles and Émigrés*, but it resolutely pursues its arguments all the way through to the postmodern, post-colonial present. The essay rehearses a familiar script in which modernist writers such as Conrad and Eliot are regarded as émigrés for whom English tradition is an object to be approached and reconfigured rather than respectfully preserved. A similar attitude to English culture is seen to emerge in Ireland, where colonial dispossession induces an art that revels in parodic and subversive techniques. Irish modernism issues, in part, from a severely shaken sense of linguistic and cultural identity at a time when realist, imperialist Britain is still confidently afloat.

The principal concern of the essay, however, is what happens to that national cultural formation known as 'English' when it encounters the shock waves of internationalism, not only in modernist cosmopolitanism but in the rapid growth of monopoly capitalism and the frenzied climax of the First World War. One indica-tion of what happens can be found in the contradictory response of F. R. Leavis and the *Scrutiny* formation in Cambridge, caught between a zealous campaigning on behalf of modern culture and a reactionary turning back to an idealized English past. Englishness survives, to some extent, by defusing and domesticating modern-ism, as the Anglican tone and sensibility of the later T. S. Eliot would seem to attest. Buttressed by an empire, 'English' and 'Englishness' resist the modernist onslaught, only to confront the more severe threat of the dissolution of empire itself.

The breakdown of a previously stable antithesis between colonial margin and metropolitan centre is a determining factor in the shift from modernism to postmodernism. What was previously displaced to the margins returns to haunt the centre. Like Fredric Jameson, for whom postmodernism is 'the cultural logic of late capitalism', Eagleton sees postmodernism emerging in a late phase of global con-sumer capitalism. The modernism that preceded it was driven by a dynamic phase of capitalist technology, of which futurism and constructivism were the logical cultural forms. The celebratory utopian spirit that accompanies the international circulation of commodities had its counterpart in the modernist circulation of 'tongues, myths and identities'. Postmodernism, by contrast, seems devoid of this positive euphoria; it makes its appearance at that moment when the ideology of Englishness seems finally discredited, and when the turn from 'English' to 'cultural studies' seems inevitable.

The coincidence of modernism with a dynamic, technological phase of capitalist production is investigated further in 'Modernism, Myth, and Monopoly Capitalism' (Chapter 20), a lecture delivered at the Politics of Modernism conference in Oxford in 1988. Once again, modernism and capitalism are presented as distinctively international phases of cultural and economic development. Modernism is seen as a movement that 'cuts indifferently across cities, societies, art-forms, languages, national traditions'; it belongs to 'the new, rootless semiotic networks of monopoly-capitalist Europe, floating in and out of Berlin, Paris, Zurich, Vienna as easily as the pound'. This cosmopolitan sweep has a genuinely progressive force, but like international capitalism it can also manifest itself as blind indifference to particular times and places. The deep ambivalence within modernism is palpably evident in works by those writers who are simultaneously bohemian exiles and confirmed elitists. Literary criticism then confronts the problem of an intellectual current that is both culturally avant-garde and politically reactionary.

If, at one level, modernism is the crisis of bourgeois culture propelled by the shifting gears of international monopoly capitalism, it also entails a primitivist reaching back into the realms of myth and magic. This savage, atavistic modernism – the modernism of Nietzsche and Freud, of Jungian archetypes and Yeatsian gyres – is construed here as a violent unleashing of the unconscious at the moment when the rationalism of an older liberal capitalism is superseded. The legacy of modernism might seem to reside in the irrationality and political violence of the holocaust, but there remains a 'candidly utopian' dimension to modernism, prefiguring new modes of consciousness, new styles of art and language, that might still invigorate contemporary culture.

Eagleton's commitment to the more progressive elements in modernism – particularly those exemplified by its revolutionary avant-garde – persists throughout the 1980s and 1990s and forms the basis of a continuing critique of 'the postmodern condition'. Jean-François Lyotard, who published a book with that title in 1984, is the subject of a trenchant and forthright analysis of postmodern culture in a seminal essay, 'Capitalism, Modernism and Postmodernism' (1985). In that essay Eagleton finds in postmodernism a grotesque caricature of the revolutionary aims of the modernist avant-garde, one that simultaneously parodies its style and strips away its political content. The strenuous efforts of modernism to resist commodification seem to be mocked by a postmodernism that all too readily immerses itself in the surrounding commodity culture. By the same token, postmodernism relinquishes too hastily the search within modernism for new ways of representing 'truth' and 'subjectivity'.

The two essays that follow mark a development in Eagleton's work from a defence of the radical potential of modernism to a scathing attack on the dubious politics of postmodernism. Together, these essays rehearse some of the fundamental political and moral imperatives that were to form the basis of a brief but compelling critique, appropriately titled *The Illusions of Postmodernism* (1996). Written in the early 1990s, when post-Marxism was hastily being added to the vocabulary of contemporary theory, these essays assert the need for ethical responsibility and vigilance at a time of widespread social upheaval and transformation. 'Defending the Free World' (Chapter 21) is remarkable not just for its resilient political faith, but for its buoyant, lampooning style. With a relish for Swiftian satire, the essay considers the assumption behind a good deal of American pragmatism and postmodernism that difference, conflict, plurality, open-endedness and heterogeneity are unquestionably 'good'. Clearly, the African National Congress falls short of these ideals in its impressive drive for unity, and one can only conclude that Bishop Tutu has failed to read his Richard Rorty and J. Hillis Miller. 'Defending the Free World' is both a castigation of a proliferating postmodern theory divorced from any practical political context, and a reassertion of what radical politics might achieve despite the prevailing scepticism.

'The Right and the Good: Postmodernism and the Liberal State' (Chapter 22) reflects upon the notion of 'the good life' and the many and conflicting versions of how it might be attained and secured. The moment of 'modernity' was that moment of perception that different conceptions of 'the good life' could not be metaphysically grounded, and that common agreement might not be realized. The political corollary of this dawning of modernity is liberalism and its trust in the state as a disinterested agency. The essay considers both the standard Marxist critique of liberalism and the 'communitarian' critique proposed by Charles Taylor, Alasdair MacIntyre and others. The impulse behind the essay, however, is an exposure of the ethical and political deficiencies of postmodernism: 'If socialism combines the best of liberalism and communitarianism, postmodernism combines the worst of both worlds.' A wariness of 'the autonomous subject' leads postmodernism towards a moral relativism and an evacuation of the the long liberal tradition of justice, equality and human rights. Since 'the subject' in Western philosophy is already a deeply problematic issue – for Kant and Hegel, as much as for Marx – the postmodernist orthodoxy of the dispersed and divided self involves 'a lot of self-righteous banging at a door which was already half-open'. To withdraw from the rational critique afforded by the liberal state is merely to ensure that the state remains in place, unchallenged and unchanged.

19   The End of English

'It is my revolt against the English conventions, literary and otherwise, that is the main source of my talent,' James Joyce once told a friend.[1] In an old familiar paradox of English modernism, it is the colonized and dispossessed who shall inherit the literary earth. Sean Golden, in a brilliantly suggestive essay on this subject, sees the Irish and Americans who seized the commanding heights of 'English' literature earlier in the century as able to carry through this audacious feat of inverted imperialism precisely because they lacked those vested emotional interests in an English literary tradition which hamstrung the natives.[2] James, Conrad, Eliot, Pound, Yeats, Joyce and Beckett could approach indigenous English traditions from the outside, objectify and appropriate them for their own devious ends, estrange and inhabit English culture in a single act, as those reared within its settled pieties could not. Positioned as they were within essentially peripheral histories, such artists could view native English lineages less as a heritage to be protected than as an object to be problematized. A Joyce or an Eliot could ramble across the whole span of European literature, shameless *bricoleurs* liberated from the Oedipal constraints of a motherland.

When John Synge pulled off the improbable trick of seeming to write in English and Gaelic simultaneously, he was revealing the profoundly dialogical nature of all such modernism, which inflects its own interests in the tongue of another, inside and outside a hegemonic discourse at the same moment, the parasite which – as with the poker-faced conventionalism of Wilde and Shaw – merges into the very image of the host. The émigrés who turned themselves into Little Englanders (James, Conrad, Eliot) did so with all the studied self-consciousness of the *parvenu* anxiously seeking paternal approval, flamboyantly anglicized outsiders who became, self-parodically, more English than the English, hijacking their cultural baggage with all the insouciance of the circus clown who nips off with the suitcase the strong man has been struggling to lift. It was never easy to know whether Oscar Wilde, son (so they said) of the dirtiest man in Dublin, was flattering English high society with his effortless imitations or impudently sending them up.

The pact between modernism and colonialism in early twentieth-century England, today being repeated with a difference in Latin America, turns on a profound historical irony. If the Irish were partly liberated from the dead weight of English bourgeois tradition, free since the days of Laurence Sterne to parody, subvert and disrupt, this was possible only because England over the centuries had stripped *them* of their native culture, thrown their national identity into dramatic crisis in a familiarly modernist way. Ireland became a devastated terrain in which everything had to be invented from scratch – in which, as with the brazenly opportunist narrators of Samuel Beckett's fiction, you made it up as you went along, turning political oppression to artistic advantage. Hence the later Yeats's solemn fiction of a homogeneous Anglo-Irish lineage, scooping the ill-assorted Swift, Goldsmith, Berkeley and Burke into portentous mythical continuity. Hence Eliot's habit of knocking off what seemed convenient from the European past, then piously consecrating this eclectic *mélange* of scraps and leavings with all the dignity of Tradition. 'Nothing is stable in this country,' wrote Joyce's brother Stanislaus; and it was exactly this sense of slippage and erasure, this chronic colonial incapacity to say who one was, which helped to nurture an Irish modernism at just the point where the realist, imperialist British were able to name themselves all too well. The effects of the empire striking back can still be felt today, in a British Isles whose finest poet is Irish, and whose major radical critic is Welsh.

'English literature' was the product of a Victorian imperial middle class, anxious to crystallize its spiritual identity in a material corpus of writing. No sooner had this discourse been refined to a point of maturity, however, than it was violently assailed by three structurally interrelated phenomena: the First World War, the explosion of modernism, and the mutation of the capitalist mode of production. All three phenomena are marked by an internationalism deeply at odds with the fostering of a national cultural formation. The First World War rocked those national securities to their foundation, at the same time as it lent increased impetus to the task of reinventing them as a refuge from ideological catastrophe. It is no accident that 'English', as moral discipline and spiritual balm, developed apace in post-war Cambridge, as a whole alternative identity for an exhausted imperial nation in accelerated decline. But, if English literary *criticism* takes root in this period, English *literature* does not. Major literary production shifts in large measure from the imperialist heartlands to the colonial or post-colonial periphery, leaving metropolitan criticism bereft of an appropriate contemporary object and bending it inexorably backwards, away from a despised and alien modernism to an imaginary native past. Modern English criticism, in other words, was *structurally* regressive from the outset, even as it sought to occupy the progressive role left open by its dismissal of the avant-garde. Hence the notorious ambiguities of *Scrutiny*, at once spiritual vanguard and reactionary rump, urgently responsive to the exigencies of the present at precisely the moment it pressed back into an idealized past.

In this contradictory situation, criticism confronts the unenviable destiny of becoming its own avant-garde, doubly estranged from its contemporary cultural moment in that the past it pits against the present is itself an idealized construct. *Scrutiny* became a displaced, distorted 'modernity', catching up in its vibrant, polemical, programmatic forms of cultural campaigning something of the pathbreaking zeal of the European avant-garde, while stoutly repelling most of the products of modernist Europe in its critical content. Caught precariously between imperialist hegemony and modernist revolt, English criticism was forced to counter the rebarbative realities of late capitalist culture with an *earlier* phase of bourgeois ideology: that of a liberal humanism already in the process of being historically superseded, on the defensive even in Matthew Arnold's day, a residual trace from a more buoyant, sanguine myth of bourgeois man. That this is still the major subjacent ideology of English studies half a century later is testimony both to the astonishing tenacity of that ideology, and to the increasing irrelevance of the entire project.

Scrutiny shared with modernism a certain marginal location, a resistance to the dominant metropolitan culture. If Ireland and New England were peripheral enclaves, then so in a different sense was Leavis's East Anglia. From both vantage-points, one could try to revaluate and reconstruct the dominant culture from the inside. The difference lay in the fact that what *Scrutiny* (and Bloomsbury) attempted – to oppose to both middle-class philistinism and upper-class frivolity the humane face of a liberal, non-conformist Englishness – was never a plausible tactic from the standpoint of the colonies. Joyce's *Ulysses* opens with the figure of the well-meaning English liberal Haines, who from Stephen Dedalus's viewpoint is of course no more than the acceptable face of Dublin Castle. H. G. Wells, recommending in a review that Joyce's *Portrait of the Artist as a Young Man* should be bought, read and locked up, whined that

> There is no discrimination in [its] hatred [of the British], there is no gleam of recognition that a considerable number of Englishmen have displayed a very earnest disposition to put matters right with Ireland . . . it is just hate, a cant cultivated to the pitch of monomania, an ungenerous violent direction of the mind.[3]

Joyce, of course, knew the stink of that Gladstonian earnestness about Ireland well enough – the well-meaning disposition of those who carried through the executions in Easter 1916.

From *Scrutiny*'s provincial standpoint, modernism and monopoly capitalism were akin in their cosmopolitan rootlessness, comrades in crime. It is a savage irony that its cult hero D. H. Lawrence spent his life tearing restlessly from one bit of the globe to another, a deracinated 'modern' if ever there was one. And *Scrutiny* was not, of course, wrong to discern a collusion between modernism and monopoly capitalism. For modernism's bold dissolution of national formations, that heady transgression of frontiers between both art forms and political states which led Philippe Sollers to describe *Finnegans Wake* as the greatest of anti-fascist novels, was, of course, made possible in part by the chronic nation-blindness of modern capitalism, which has no more respect than *The Waste Land* or the *Cantos* for regional particularism. The contradiction of such a system is that, in order to secure the political and ideological conditions for the international circulation of commodities, it needs to exploit exactly the national allegiances and identities which its economic activities constantly undermine.

In this sense, one can appreciate just what a desperate wager modernism must seem from a native nonconformist viewpoint: in seeking to challenge the oppressiveness of bourgeois nationhood, it must surrender itself inexorably to the rhythms of monopoly-capitalist internationalism, beginning, as Brecht said, from the 'bad new things' rather than the good old ones, permitting history to progress (as Marx said) by its bad side. For Leavis, there was a choice between being at home in your own language and being exiled in another's. But such a choice was not open to Joyce or Beckett, for whom one might as well be homeless in all languages as dispossessed in one's own. It is because the modernist colonials are exiled in their own speech, the tongue of the oppressor, that they can cast a cold eye on the notion of 'rootedness' – which is not to say that they did not have to pay, sometimes dearly, the price of a certain deeper deracination, as well as the cost of political isolation and aesthetic élitism. For Joyce and Beckett, as for Conrad before them, the paradigm case of the problematical nature of all discourse is to be disinherited in and by one's 'mother tongue'. Modernist cosmopolitanism, so to speak, merely universalizes the pain. One can trace this difficulty today in the poetry of Seamus Heaney, where a stubbornly specific regionalism (that of Catholic Derry) strives to articulate itself in a deftly cosmopolitan medium, in a linguistic pact constantly threatened with infidelity on both sides.

Since nobody actually lives absolved from all local allegiance, not even Joyce in Trieste or Pound in Rapallo, there is always an inevitably utopian moment in all such modernism – an assertive wager that one can be at home everywhere, in an equitable circulation of tongues, myths and identities of which the *Wake* is prototypical. And this, of course, is often enough compensation for the actual pains of exile. Those contemporary theories which would have us kick the referent and live euphorically on the inside of some great intertextual tangle of signs are, whether they know it or not, the appropriate coding of this real historical situation, and too often repress its actual misery. The utopic euphoria of such modernism corresponds in fact to an earlier moment of the twentieth-century capitalist mode of production, one which, despite Sollers's comment on the *Wake*, pre-dates the century's most virulent outbreak of nationalism, as well as the post-war consolidation of an international monopoly capitalism about which there seems little that is exhilarating. The cosmopolitan confidence of the early modernists has a different historical root: not only in the apparent promise of a more dynamic phase of capitalist technology, but in the more assertive international presence of its historical antagonist, the working class, which like the modernist artist knows no homeland. If art for the modernist writer was the name of that other, geographically unlocatable space where national identities crumbled, exploitation was its name for the world proletariat, and oppression for its subjugated groups and peoples.

British capitalism, however, had none of the restless dynamism which might have plausibly thrown up a futurism or constructivism. What attracted the 'Little Englander' literary émigrés to these shores, from James and Conrad to T. S. Eliot, was precisely the relatively settled nature of bourgeois hegemony, fruit of several centuries of imperialist domination abroad and class-collaborationism at home. Inertly traditionalist, replete with literary realism and liberal empiricism, English culture proved peculiarly resistant to the modernist experiment, just as for exactly the same reasons it inspired it by reaction in such writers as Joyce and Lawrence. England's closedness to modernism, which it 'exported' to the margins, meant on the one hand a welcome exclusion of subversive cultural forms. But it was at the same time a sign of capitalist stagnation and decline, and the ideology of 'Englishness' thrived on this backwardness. Shaken though it is in the early modernist period by severe class struggle, it is still at this point far from clear that England is finished – far from obvious that some refurbished 'nativism' à la Scrutiny, for all its regressive aspects, may not play some role in national reconsolidation. In such a context, modernism could be defused and domesticated, judiciously blended as in the later Eliot with a suitably Anglican tone and sensibility. Eliot could be aligned with Donne and Hopkins rather than with Mallarmé and Valéry; and it was the role of English criticism to effect such an alignment.

Besides, England still had at this point one powerful internationalist response to modernist cosmopolitanism: empire. If empire proved a breeding ground for modernism, as in the case of Ireland, it could also act as a bulwark for the mother country against it. English was a language in which one could be internationally at home, subsuming all regional particularities from Kerry to Kuala Lumpur, and thus resolving at a stroke the painful antithesis between parochialism on the one hand and global rootlessness on the other. Empire was England's secret weapon against a promiscuous modernism: the mere fact of the global reach of the English language was enough to buttress an indigenous culture otherwise grievously threatened with decline.

Englishness thus survived the modernist onslaught, which not long after the death of Lawrence had come to seem like a minor foreign aberration; but it then had to confront the much graver threat of the loss of empire itself. In the very enclave of Cambridge English in the critically crucial 1920s, *A Passage to India* was already presaging this catastrophe, ominously marking the limits of realist and liberal empiricist discourse, while quite unable itself to venture beyond them. The regional particularism so favoured by the Leavises returns with a vengeance in the middle decades of the century, rearing its head in the unpleasantly unfamiliar form of the various national liberation movements which detach one colonial society after another from British hegemony. The response of 'English' to this development would be the pathetic farce of 'Commonwealth literature'. 'English' begins to lose its global guarantee, and plunges its liberal humanist guardians into a severe dilemma. For, if that liberalism is restless with ruling-class imperial arrogance, its own belief in the centrality of the native was historically supported by just such an imperial system. The demise of *Scrutiny*, and the opening up of the major period of struggle against British imperialism, are historically coincident.

It is characteristic of what might loosely be called the modernist sensibility, from Baudelaire to T. S. Eliot, that the archaic and the innovative, the primeval and the modern, begin to enter into what Walter Benjamin would call 'shocking constellations' with one another, so that in the very act of 'making it new' one finds oneself excavating in recycled forms the eternally recurrent genealogies of a buried past. This uncanny convergence of the old and the new is nowhere more striking than in the curious parallelisms between colonialism and late capitalism, the pre- and post-industrial. What liberal humanism speaks up for, against the aesthetics of modernism, is the unitary subject, linear history, the self as agent, the world as knowable and totalizable – all ideological notions thrown into instant disorder by the colonial experience. A chronically backward colony like Joyce's Ireland lends itself to modernism as well as it does precisely because such notions are phenomenologically unworkable. In such conditions, the subject is less the strenuously self-mastering agent of its historical destiny than empty, powerless, without a name. Linear time, which is always, so to speak, on the side of Caesar, becomes cyclical, repetitive, untotalizable, denuded of tradition and teleology. The great unities of subject and object beloved of bourgeois idealist epistemology are inoperative from the outset, the object a blank, fragmented materiality sunk in the nausea of the quotidian, the subject a mere function of its circumstances, depthless and dispossessed. Meanwhile, altogether elsewhere, a classical bourgeois narrative of unified subjects, 'total' history and instantly intelligible signs conducts its triumphal existence, as the metropolitan fullness which drains the colonies dry.

What will be steadily eroded in the development of late capitalism, however, is precisely this apparently stable antithesis between colonial margin and metropolitan centre. For, as capitalism evolves beyond its great liberal-progressive epoch, it will come to seem as though the literature of modernist colonialism acted all along as the secret negative truth of the hegemony which produced it, prefiguring the final destiny of metropolitan society itself. As liberal capitalism yields ground to consumerism, it is as though a whole society undergoes the spiritual depletion and disinheritance previously reserved, with particular violence, for its meanest colonials. The margin shifts to the centre: now it is as though the very subjects of metropolitan capitalism are empty, dwindled, decentred, effects rather than agents, linear history struck vacuous by the ceaseless return of the commodity, cultural tradition brutally extirpated by the fetish of the Now. 'Primitive' mythology, repressed by the Enlightenment, returns with a vengeance: human life seems once more determined by great constant forces invisible to the naked eye, which shuffle around the contingent bits and pieces of reality in those gratuitous kaleidoscopic patterns we call 'change'. And just as the colonies seemed particularly hospitable to fantasy, to the dissolution of any stable reality in the great fracturings of repressed desire, so fantasy in the form of consumerism and the media now becomes structural to metropolitan society. Much of this, of course, was already evident in 'classical' modernism: what happens in the postmodern period is, first, that with the spread of consumerist capitalism these phenomena cease to be the artistic vision of an élite and penetrate more deeply into everyday life; and, second, that they become dissociated from the more positive, subversive, exhilarating impulses which earlier attended them. That positivity is once more 'exported': as all of this occurs within metropolitan society, the previously inert colonies gather strength in a striking historical inversion, begin to assert agency and fashion an intelligible history, translate dreams of freedom into political reality.

In the so-called postmodern condition, then, what was previously displaced to the margins returns to haunt the very centre: it is now not just Joyce's spiritually paralytic Dublin, but the stalely over-familiar global village of international monopoly capitalism, which revolves endlessly in the closed circuits of its mythologies. In this situation, 'English' begins to shed the last of its tattered credentials as any kind of ideologically plausible discourse. That discourse, I have argued, was seriously jeopardized by the First World War, but paradoxically consolidated by it. It was besieged almost instantly by modernism, but managed successfully to repel the alien invader. It had then to endure the loss of its global guarantee in the collapse of empire, but could still always turn back to a native tradition, constructing a literary lineage for itself from Hardy to Larkin in the manner of the young fogies of *PN Review*. What threatens it today is nothing less than the dissolution of its own subjacent ideology of liberal humanism, increasingly discredited by the later development of the very capitalism for which it was once so eloquent an apologist. The experiences of both modernism and colonialism were kept at bay, but in the latest historical irony now offer to repossess the metropolitan culture from inside in the shape of postmodernism. The fact that Donald Davie, one of the most vociferous spokespersons for post-imperial Little Englandism, actually emigrated to the USA some time ago is a nice irony: *actual* England is now, culturally speaking, pretty much like North America, and where you happen to be to launch your jeremiad is in that sense neither here nor there.

Perhaps the most minatory aspect of postmodernism for the ideology of English is its audio-visual character. This is not to espouse some glib mythology of the 'death of the novel', all of whose ritually issued obituary notices have proved remarkably premature. Those who regard writing as some charmingly archaic form no doubt have George Meredith rather than Robert Maxwell in mind. Nevertheless, it is a telling irony that contemporary literary theory has never been so obsessed with writing (admittedly in a suitably expanded sense of the term) in a cultural world where Rambo is only for a dwindling rump of us a French poet. The call for cultural studies, against some narrowly conceived literariness, is thus no more than a recognition of the inevitable. The mighty battles between parochial nativeness and modernist cosmopolitanism are being repeated in our own time, but this time as theory, which begins at Calais.

The terms of the conflict, however, are not quite the same as they were in the age of Joyce. At that time, as I have argued, it was still in some sense plausible for a native Englishness, buttressed by the reality of empire, to affirm itself, in a social order which had not yet witnessed the discrediting of liberal humanism as thoroughly as in our own. That ideology is still by no means to be underestimated: it remains powerfully entrenched in the academic institutions, and in the wider society still corresponds to some, though by no means all, of the imperatives of late capitalism. But it is significant that in a period of capitalist crisis the guardians of English are now in danger of erasing the 'liberal' from the phrase 'liberal humanist'; and it is also significant that they are today quite incapable of anything like the robust, aggressive campaigning of *Scrutiny*, falling back instead on chauvinist gut reactions dressed up as spiritual intuitions. If Leavis did not see the need to tangle with 'theory', this in part reflected a certain confidence as well as a certain nervousness – the sense of a tangible cultural tradition being 'richly present', concretely demonstrable, and capable of enthusing a good number of acolytes. Today, the paucity of that intuitionism is painfully obvious, a clumsy, transparently rearguard action with nothing of the Leavisian *élan*. It is 'theory' that nowadays recruits the kind of committed, zealous young disciples that Leavis did in his day.

The end of empire, in short, has taken its toll: in a post-imperial, postmodernist culture, 'English', which for some time now has been living on like a headless chicken, has proved to be an increasingly unworkable discourse, if not in the cloistered universities, then most certainly in the inner-city schools. The struggle between that and 'theory' in some ways re-enacts the battles of modernism, but does so at a more explicitly political level. Some of the most vital arguments *within* contemporary literary theory, like the dissensions between 'high' modernism and the revolutionary avant-garde, concern the relative merits of a 'negative' and a 'positive' politics. It is possible to see Derrida, or even Paul de Man, as 'negatively' political in something like the way Adorno saw Beckett, or as Joyce saw his own writing. The modernist artists, however, were forced to devote too much time and energy to their own painful extrication from untenable cultural situations to address these political questions at all directly. Today, because we have less of such writing, or because much of it has been absorbed and defused, we have discovered a new terrain – theory, criticism – from which such questions can be launched. The current deconstruction of the very opposition between 'criticism' and 'creativity' is perhaps in one sense a reluctance to acknowledge the passing of 'high' modernism: they had the *Cantos*, we have Jonathan Culler. On the other hand, it involves a recognition that the subversive impulses of modernism can indeed migrate from domain to domain, are indeed portable across styles of discourse as across political frontiers. Whatever the historical losses, it is 'theory' which today attracts something of the virulent hostility once reserved for Eliot or Pound. The final discrediting of 'native Englishness' in a postmodernist epoch at least clarifies the issues at stake: as the material conditions which historically supported the ideology of 'English' have been gradually eroded, it is clearer than ever that the only conflict

which finally matters is between the internationalism of late capitalist consumerism, and the internationalism of its political antagonist.

Notes

1   Ulrick O'Connor (ed.), *The James Joyce We Knew* (Cork: Mercier Press, 1967), p. 143.
2   Sean Golden, 'Post-Traditional English Literature: A Polemic', *The Crane Bag Book of Irish Studies* (Dublin: Blackwater Press, 1982), pp. 427–38.
3   Quoted in ibid., p. 429.

20 Modernism, Myth, and Monopoly Capitalism

The birth of language as an autonomous object of study, back in the early beginnings of European philology, brings with it the alarming recognition that we speak according to laws which can't by definition be present to consciousness in the act of utterance. The euphoric moment when we come to master language as an object, then, is also the dispirited moment in which we lose ourselves as subjects, come to acknowledge that language will always elude our practical grasp. And this moment, you might say, is the first theoretical opening of the unconscious. Language as such becomes a purely virtual system of formal possibilities, located now on a quite different terrain from our daily speech. It's the condition of possibility of all our representations, which can't itself be represented there. Or at least, it can be represented there only by a new and peculiar piece of acrobatics known as *reflexivity*. At the height of its historical confidence, in the period of German Idealism and the French Revolution, the bourgeoisie clings to the faith that men and women can indeed somehow turn round upon themselves in empty space, grasp in a giddy moment the very outer horizon or inner structure of their being. Yet to leap from our representations to their underlying conditions of possibility is already to recognise the existence of some fatal slippage or abyss between the two, to render human beings eccentric to themselves in the very act of seeking to close their fists over some transcendental truth. By the act of self-reflexivity, we can recover for subjective experience its unconscious determinants, that which made it possible in the first place; but those determinants have all the ambiguity of the borderline of a field, which is at once part of the field and not part of it at all.

While the philologists are seeking to recover the very grounds and possibility of meaning, Kant is seeking to do the same for the mind in general. He too takes the transcendental turn, unearthing the very categories which set our experience in place in the first place. But what kind of subject is it that can do *this*? Where must this subject be standing, in order to treat itself as an object of knowledge? In the very act of knowing the transcendental conditions of our possibility, the subject itself threatens to slip over the horizon of our knowledge and figure as no more than a cypher or cryptic silence, some extreme vanishing-point of our discourse. The subject might be able to know itself as an object – but that, precisely, is what subjects are not, is indeed the last thing they are.

The birth of what will come to be called the 'human sciences', then, fissures us right down the middle. Strung out between our empirical representations and their transcendental conditions of possibility, we need some bridge which will allow us to cross regularly from one to the other – and the name of the bridge is hermeneutics. With the birth of the human sciences comes the age of Interpretation. But this ceaseless event of interpretation is only necessary because *mis*interpretation is now thought to be chronic. No-one thought this particularly in early eighteenth-century England or fifth-century Athens; misinterpretations were just occasional blunders you cleared up by applying the correct rhetorical techniques. Now, however, the human animal has been born, as a creature who needs a science of itself because its fate is everywhere to misunderstand itself.

The thinking of Marx is entirely in line with this current of thought. Marx gives the name 'ideology' to our chronic, necessary self-misprisions, and believes that science is only essential because phenomena don't coincide with their essences. So far, then, we remain with the epoch of modernity. What will try to shatter that epoch into tiny pieces is Friedrich Nietzsche, who seeks to put an end to modernity and open up instead something called modernism. Nietzsche's chief tactic in this iconoclasm is the denial of reflexivity. How absurd to imagine that this puny, desirous, power-driven creature humanity could ever be able to lift itself up by its own bootstraps and examine, unthinkably, the very motives which drive it to think in the first place! How could we even find a *ground* to our thinking, without simply itching to slide yet another ground beneath that one? As Wittgenstein once remarked, it's difficult to think of an origin without feeling you can go back beyond it. Thought will from here on just have to make do with its fictional character, and reflexivity will plunge into abysmal irony. But for Nietzsche you shouldn't worry too much about the fact that all thought is fictional, arbitrary, gratuitous – because that's just the way the world is too. Our falsifications, would you believe it, are actually true to that enormous lie which is the universe, or more strictly for Nietzsche, Will to Power. Nietzsche will close the gap between phenomena and essence, empirical representations and their transcendental conditions, but do it in the most impudent way imaginable – by denying that there's anything *but* phenomena, empirical image, lived experience, violently collapsing this duality rather than seeking patiently to span it.

One whole current of twentieth-century modernism follows Nietzsche in this bold faith. The shift from realism to modernism is among other things a shift from reality to experience, from that solid stuff out there to these fragmentary sensations tracking their path through this body here. Another whole current of modernism turns its back on this irrationalist immediacy and remains true to the invisible – to the great, abstract, formal, purely virtual systems which speak and act through us but never directly reveal their hand. Whether one names such implacable powers Language or Being, Capital or the Unconscious, Tradition or the *élan vital*, Archetypes or the Destiny of the West, their effect is to underscore the gap opened up in the nineteenth century between the old befeathered ego and the true determinants of its identity.

Put these two currents together and what do you get? One answer might be James Joyce. *Ulysses* and the *Wake*, on the surface at least, are fragmentary, chaotic, sensational, a set of fortuitous conjunctures for which the typical modernist image is the two-second random encounter at some busy urban cross-roads. Yet we know of course that this whole apparently contingent experience is in fact coded to its roots, secretly regulated by some underlying subtext invisible to the naked eye, but capable of rigorously regulating the whole of this phenomenal world. The point, however, is that those determining structures now seem to stand an immense way off from the realm of sensuous immediacy, so formal and abstract are they, superbly autonomous of the chance combinations of matter they throw up, so that to bring subjective experience and its determining structures together in some simple act of self-reflexivity now seems increasingly implausible. This is surely true of the *Wake*, a text which seems to offer a minimum of mediation between its perverse units of signification and the mighty Viconian cycles which generate and enclose them. (Though what you lose on the semiotic swings, you make up on the Viconian roundabouts . . .) It isn't difficult to perceive a similar dislocation between Saussure's *langue* – the purely virtual system of language itself – and the apparently random, unformalisable nature of *parole*. And it's not hard to relate this duality either to the extraordinary resurgence of mythology in modernist culture – for myth too, if we believe Lévi-Strauss, operates by some rigorously abstract logic to which any particular concrete permutation is purely contingent.

Mythology is usually thought to belong to pre-industrial society; and with modernism we're moving very definitely into a higher stage of capitalism – international monopoly capitalism. Modernism, you might claim, is the crisis of bourgeois culture induced by that traumatic transition. So ironically, at this higher stage, capitalist society would seem to regress to the pre-industrial, a closed, cyclical, naturalised sphere of relentless fatality where historicity is suspended, where all is chaos and contingency on the surface but rigidly policed and impersonal beneath. This is surely the historical secret of that most recurrent of modernist formulas, the shocking conjunction of the very old and the very new, the archaic and the avant garde, of finding yourself, like Baudelaire or Freud, re-excavating the archaeological past in the very act of jettisoning tradition and making it New. At the very moment of a fresh technological dynamism, of Futurism and Constructivism, of an unprecedented expansion of the world capitalist economy in the early years of modernism, the present is sucked inexorably back into the past, gathered up once more into its sealed, cyclical, ever-changing/never-changing structures. The same returns, with a difference – the name for which, as Walter Benjamin knew, is fashion.

Or, if you like, more generally, the curious time of the commodity. The commodity indeed has a history – namely, the eternal repetition of its acts of exchange.

The commodity gets absolutely nowhere very fast indeed, which isn't perhaps a bad description of a lot of modernism. And the commodity, even more to the point, is itself a kind of incongruous embodiment of that disjuncture between the abstract and the sensuously particular I've been talking about. It has, as Marx commented, absolutely no *body*, lives only in the formal act of exchange; but what on the other hand could be more fetishistically sensuous, material, incarnate?

Under the sway of exchange-value, Georg Lukács argues in *History and Class Consciousness*, 'reality disintegrates into a multitude of irrational facts and over these a network of purely formal laws emptied of content is cast'. It's not a bad description of *Ulysses*, or for that matter of much modernist art, of which Theodor Adorno commented that its relations were as abstract as the real relations between human beings in the late bourgeois world. The story I've been telling at a philosophical level, in other words, has a material underside: the narrative of the commodity, which by the period of high modernism – let's say, 1900 to 1920 – has culminated in a now decisively internationalist system. Within this system, human subjects are on the one hand held fast in the mire of immediacy, atomised and decimated by the commodity's operations, and on the other hand dimly aware of themselves as subjected to the dominion of global iron laws with all the naturalised fatality of the world of myth. A world, you might say, where *both* chance and necessity seem equally apt accounts of what's going on.

What traditionally sought to bring together these antinomies – particular and general, content and form, sensuous and spiritual, contingency and necessity – was – wouldn't you have guessed it? – the work of art. And the name for *that* kind of artwork is realism. But realism belongs with an earlier, more classical phase of capitalism – liberal capitalism, if you like – which from the *fin-de-siècle* onwards is being superseded. It belongs, for example, with the ideologies of liberal humanism, which served the bourgeoisie superbly in their day and shouldn't ever, I think, be used as a mere glib swear-word by those who have just stumbled across the *New Accents* series. But the ways that liberal humanism defined the human subject (entirely appropriately for its historical time) just aren't working any more, correspond less and less to what it actually feels like to be around in the arena of a later, more systematised and administrative capitalism. Fewer and fewer people in *that* world can see themselves as the autonomous, sharply separate, strenuously self-regulating agents of their own historical destiny, whatever might have been possible for Walter Scott. Fewer people, too, can trust in the essential readability and intelligibility of the object, which is now typified by the opaque, fragmentary, impenetrable commodity. And nobody can muster much faith any more in progress and historicity – modernism belongs with an epochal shift in our notions of temporality, with a refusal to believe that the world is any longer story-shaped, that it has an immanent causal logic which art has then only to represent.

The places where you never did believe all this much anyway are on the colonised peripheries. Linear time, there, was always perceived as being, so to speak, on the side of Caesar; and nobody there was likely to find lucid and readable a history which was always someone else's, that of the victors. Nobody there either was habitually aware of themselves as centred, autonomous, vigorously self-determining. Hence the remarkable upsurge of an Irish modernism, with which Britain has nothing to compare (I take Ireland to have been part of the so-called Third World, until perhaps the middle decade of the century.) Hence too the resurgence of this strange alliance between modernism and colonialism in Latin America today.

If capitalism was now distinctively international, so, of course, was modernism. Modernism as a movement cuts indifferently across cities, societies, art forms, languages, national traditions. Released from the Oedipal constraints of a mother-land, it was able, from the vantage-point of some polyglot metropolis, to cast a cold estranging eye on all such national heritages. Instead, it sought like Joyce or Eliot to isolate the deep structures of all such parochial experience, to sweep them up in the great global mythological cycles. It belonged in this way to the new, rootless semiotic networks of monopoly-capitalist Europe, floating in and out of Berlin, Paris, Zurich, Vienna as easily as the pound. Raymond Williams has, I think, very shrewdly assessed the losses and gains of this cosmopolitan perspective: on the one hand, a bracing, freezing demystification of all parochial pieties; on the other hand, all of this performed from some empty, formal, transcendental vantage-point some-where round the corner from Saint Germain des Près. In dissociating itself from increasingly exhausted national traditions, modernism was in many respects genu-inely progressive; but it also, as Williams points out, cut itself off from what was still potentially alive and politically subversive in those lineages; and in exiling itself from them it couldn't avoid miming the habits of international capitalism itself, which is quite as blindly indifferent to particular times and places as *The Waste Land* or the *Cantos*.

What I'm claiming, in other words, is that the gap or slippage I began by speaking about – that between sensuous particularity and abstract enabling condi-tions of possibility – finally comes to a head in the very *topographical* conditions of modernism. But this topography has another implication too. The literally exilic status of many of the modernists, their existence as bohemian coteries or deracinated sub-cultures, can't of course be divorced from what was often their vicious, virulent right-wingism, their puerile elitism, raging contempt for liberal-ism, democracy, socialism, science, the so-called 'masses'. Taken together, the political attitudes of many of the most prominent modernists, from Gottfried Benn to Wyndham Lewis, from Filippo Marinetti to D. H. Lawrence, can only be characterised as squalid in the extreme. (There is, of course, quite another story, if you include within modernism what's sometimes called the avant-garde – if you include the links between Dada and Sparticism, the Surrealists and Trotskyism, Futurism and Bolshevism.) And so we have the puzzle of a current at once cultur-ally avant-garde and politically reactionary. The secret of *that* apparent paradox surely isn't hard to find: what unites both tendencies is an opposition to liberal-bourgeois democracy. The modernists may have been reactionaries, but they sure detested the middle class.

You could, then, take a simple line on the politics of modernism, as Bertrand Russell did: it leads straight to the death camps. Modernism, in this perspective, is part of that frenzied outburst of unreason which sweeps through Europe from the 1880s onwards, as the rationalism of a now superseded form of liberal capitalism gradually loses its credibility. Nietzsche and Freud, myth and magic and obscurantism, Jungian archetypes and the gyrating gyres, the dark gods, the rites of spring and the Fisher King: all of this – savage, atavistic, primitivist – you can see as the return of the repressed, the violent disfigurement of an apparently clapped-out Enlightenment reason by all that it's had to stamp hard on. And certainly that wouldn't be among other things a bad description of the Nazis. But the story surely isn't that simple. An explosion of unreason maybe, sometimes in the ugliest political forms; but at the same time the attempted subversion of a reified rationality, an attempt to lift oneself up by one's bootstraps, give the slip to the straitjacket of Enlightenment reason and think it all through again. For we are surely still not sufficiently distanced from modernism to be able very clearly to discriminate between these trends – between what might have led to the death camps on the one hand, and what might on the other hand prefigure new modes of subjectivity, new styles of relationship, new versions of language and art. If one side of modernism was pretty ugly, the other was candidly utopian, if often in a negative mode. Like Walter Benjamin, then, we have to grub patiently among the ruins, sift the rubble, and collect what might come in handy.

21   Defending the Free World

Towards the end of his essay entitled 'Solidarity', Richard Rorty, having just argued that those who helped Jews in the last world war probably did so less because they were fellow human beings than because they belonged to the same city, profession or other social grouping as themselves, asks us to consider why contemporary American liberals should help miserable young American blacks. 'Do we say that these people must be helped because they are our fellow human beings? We may, but it is much more persuasive, morally as well as politically, to describe them as our fellow *Americans* – to insist that it is outrageous that an *American* should live without hope'.[1]

Rorty's case here seems to me unworkably global. There are, after all, rather a lot of Americans, of various shapes and sizes, and there is surely something rebarbatively abstract about basing one's compassion on such grandiosely general grounds. It is almost as though 'Americanness' operates here as some sort of meta-discourse or metaphysical essence, conflating into some unitary phenomenon the vast variety of creeds, life-styles, skin-colours and so on which go to compose the United States. Better, surely, to found one's ethics on a *genuine* localism, such as, for example, the city block. This is still perhaps a little on the homogenising side, since your average city block does of course contain a fair sprinkling of different sorts of people; but it is surely a more manageable basis for justice and compassion than an abstraction like 'America'. One could demonstrate compassion towards those in the next apartment, for example, while withholding it from those a mile down the street. Personally, I only ever manifest compassion to fellow graduates of the University of Cambridge. It's true that such credentials aren't always easy to establish; indeed I have occasionally tossed a coin towards some tramp whom I thought I dimly recognised as a member of the class of '64, only to retrieve it again furtively when I recognised my mistake. But it suffices, whatever the practical difficulties, as a rule of thumb, and the implications of any alternative moral strategy are fairly dire. Once one begins extending one's compassionate reach to graduates of Oxford too, there seems no reason not to go on to the universities of London, Warwick and Wolverhampton, and before one knows it one is on the slippery slope to Habermas, universalism, foundationalism and the rest.

Incidentally, I haven't as yet withdrawn from the Campaign for Nuclear Disarmament, merely adjusted my reasons for membership. I now object to nuclear war not because it would blow up some metaphysical abstraction called the human race but because it would introduce a certain unpleasantness into the lives of my Oxford neighbours. The benefit of this adjustment is that my commitment as an anti-nuclear campaigner is no longer the anaemic, aridly intellectualist affair it was when I used to think in terms of theoretically disreputable universals like 'humanity', but lived sensuously on the pulses, brought home to me as richly concrete experience. If Oxford survives a nuclear catastrophe, I really couldn't give a damn about the University of Virginia. I have, however, resigned my membership of the Christian church, as there is clearly something theoretically dubious about the Good Samaritan.

Rorty is quite correct to believe that what is at stake in these issues is something called America, though not at all in the sense he thinks. We professional America-watchers, perched in our European fastness, are accustomed to witnessing the inhabitants of the Land of the Free engaging from time to time in spasms of smug self-congratulation. It is just that we were a little slow to appreciate, being at something of a distance, that the name of such narcissism had shifted so rapidly from Reaganism to neo-pragmatism. Another version of the case can be found in Barbara Hernstein Smith's *Contingencies of Value*, which argues at one point that 'it is perhaps just as well for "our society" that its norms are a "melange", that they constantly multiply, collide, and transform each other, that conflicts of judgement are negotiated ad hoc, and that normative authority itself is multiple and recurrently changes hands, variously strengthening and becoming diffuse.'[2] I don't quite know what those scare-quotes are doing nervously shielding the phrase 'our society', but Hernstein Smith's formulation inspires the dreadful suspicion, surely unworthy, that she actually takes herself here to be giving a thumbnail sketch of a country known as the United States. I can't believe that this is true, but the suspicion, for all one's charitable disposition, stubbornly lingers. It would be intriguing to know what Allende would have made of that multiple, recurrently changing authority, or whether the Nicaraguans have got round to savouring the pluralist, humbly ad hoc nature of US political judgements. That probably doesn't matter, since if Rorty is anything to go by they can be more or less written off anyway. One doesn't get too strong a sense that Rorty's 'American' stretches to Peruvian peasants or El Salvador guerilla fighters. In any case, it is relieving to know that, let's say, the CIA manifests a rich melange of ceaselessly variable norms, even if it's a little hard to appreciate when they have just been busy suborning your democratically elected government.

Rorty and Hernstein Smith, along with most other liberal or radical American critics, would appear united in their faith that difference, conflict, plurality, open-endedness and heterogeneity are 'absolute', unquestionable goods in themselves.

(I place the term 'absolute' in charitable scare-quotes, since these critics seem to have one or two problems with it.) It is a position I have long shared myself. It has always struck me as unduly impoverishing of British social life, for example, that we can only muster a mere two or three fascist parties. Instead of a ceaselessly varied, robustly proliferating, infinitely differentiated fascistic scene, with energising conflicts and ad hoc negotiations between its various currents, we are stuck with the dreary monism of the National Front and the British Movement. The postmodernist imperative to multiply small narratives at all costs has certainly not caught on among our local Nazis, who seem not to have read their Lyotard. If they really took literally what many American pragmatists, postmodernists and deconstructionists have been insisting on so 'absolutely' – that difference and plurality are good in themselves regardless of their political substance – then they would surely begin to spawn into eighty-three or so different movements rather than a mere boring two or three. The political left would then be kept energetically engaged in chasing them around the country, identifying their latest shifting positions in order to combat them, spreading its forces thin as fascists popped up in the most unpredictable places.

A similar lack of internal conflictiveness and multiplicity characterises such organisations as the African National Congress. Instead of learning from American postmodernists that unity is *ipso facto* a negative phenomenon – 'closure', 'essentialism', 'terroristic totalisation' and so on – they obtusely continue to strive to achieve the maximum degree of agreement and solidarity among the people of the townships in order to bring the apartheid regime to its knees. Bishop Tutu can't possibly have read his Smith, Rorty, Hartman, Hillis Miller, Felmann, Weber, or indeed hardly any left-leaning American critic at all. He certainly cannot have been reading most American feminist critics. There is now, among all such critics, an impressive degree of consensus that consensus is inherently oppressive.

Much the same goes for the current political struggles in Northern Ireland. The trouble with Sinn Fein is its disastrous abandonment of indeterminacy, even if it has the cheek to dub itself 'Provisional'. It actually seems to believe that it is an unquestionably bad thing that British soldiers kill indiscriminately on the streets of West Belfast; that it is 'true' (things go from bad to worse) that no lasting solution to the Irish question can be achieved without the withdrawal of these troops; and that in this process the 'closure' of unified, determinate political goals on its own part may prove productive. Whether or not Sinn Fein ever achieves those goals, it can certainly kiss goodbye to contributing to *Diacritics*. Far better, surely, to breed a republican movement with stimulating internal divisions, so that they could wrangle all day among themselves while men of the second paratroop regiment smashed up their furniture while pretending to hunt for arms. Such a transformed republicanism would find itself exhilaratedly unsure of exactly what it was doing when it found itself up against British guns; and though this exhilaration would have only a brief time-span, it would surely provide a more theoretically sophisticated way to die for a number of Irishmen and women currently trapped in the metaphysical delusion that the foreign occupation of their soil is unequivocally to be denounced.

An American feminist critic wrote recently about the need to multiply different idioms – idioms of gender, of race, and – so she added – of class. It is indeed another impoverishment of British society, whatever may be true of the United States, that we have *far too few social classes*, even if there are a few monistic metaphysicians around the place who suspect that we might have one or two too many. What we should strive to do is to generate as many social classes as possible, perhaps two or three new bourgeoisies and a fresh clutch of aristocracies. It all adds to the rich variety of social life. 'The more classes, the merrier' might then act as an appropriate slogan for radical pluralism. There is surely still room towards the bottom end of the social scale for a range of new sub-classes: there is already a kind of lumpen intelligentsia in Britain, given the shortage of academic jobs, and any pluralist sufficiently committed to the absolute value of heterogeneity would no doubt be able to dream up a few more ways of skilfully variegating our current somewhat restricted categories of oppression.

Social class tends nowadays to crop up as one item in the celebrated triptych of 'class, race and gender', a formula which has rapidly assumed for the left the kind of authority which the Holy Trinity exerts for the right. The logic of this triple linkage is surely obvious. Racism is a bad thing, and so is sexism, and so therefore is something called 'classism'. (I haven't encountered this feeble concept anywhere outside North America; its European meaning – roughly, 'class-reductionism' – is quite different). Marxists, however, churlishly refuse to subscribe to the fashionable orthodoxy that social class is a Bad Thing. Indeed they find it difficult to imagine how anyone regarding themselves as even vaguely politically radical could bring themselves to credit such an absurdity. For Marxism, the working class is an excellent thing, since without it we would never be able to expropriate the bourgeoisie. The bourgeoisie may be by and large a bad thing today, but it was an exceedingly good thing in its heyday, not least when it courageously resisted the brutalities of feudalist absolutism and bequeathed to us a precious liberal tradition. We might even go the whole hog and hand one or two accolades to that fine class of feudalist exploiters who did so much to end the slave mode of production. The pluralists and postmodernists who speak up for heterogeneous styles of thought are on the whole unaccustomed to such nuanced historical distinctions, which once upon a time went under the name of the dialectic. It is not that one is requesting such theorists to *agree* with these propositions; one is merely asking them to recognise that such, in effect, is what Marxism has traditionally held, and that this is a rather different theory from the abstract moralism which holds that class, like salt and smoking, is not very nice. Marxists have never been quite arrogant enough to believe that the whole of the Enlightenment was up a gum tree, and that suddenly, perhaps around 1972, we all began to read Saussure and get our act together. The crass triumphalism of this case, which like any other caricature has more than its kernel of truth, makes Georg Lukács look like Arthur Schopenhauer.

It has been Marxism, not liberal pluralism, which has regularly accorded admiration and respect to its historical antagonists.

Viewed in this light, then, the 'class, race and gender' formula comes near to involving what the philosophers might call a category mistake. But this is true in other senses too. On the surface, the triplet appears convincing enough: some people are oppressed because of their race, some on account of their gender, and some in accordance with their class. But this is of course grossly misleading. For it is not that some individuals manifest certain characteristics known as 'class', which then result in their oppression; on the contrary, to be a member of a social class just *is* to be oppressed, or to be an oppressor. Class is in this sense a wholly social category, as being black or female is not. To be black or female is a matter of Nature as well as culture. This, of course, is hardly the most acceptable pronouncement to the ears of that rampant left culturalism which has held sway over recent years – a culturalism which lays rhetorical claim to the title of 'materialist' and then proceeds to suppress the most obviously materialist bits of human beings, their biological make-up. Somewhere around the early 1970s, it was as though all attention to biology became 'biologistic' overnight, just as all concern with history became 'historicist' and all preoccupation with the empirical 'empiricist'. The social oppression of women is a matter of gender, which is entirely a social construct; but women are oppressed *as women*, which involves the kind of body one biologically has. Being a proletarian, by contrast, is not a question of biology, though it is true that we working-class North-of-Englanders tend to be small, dark and stunted. There will be no proletarians in an emancipated society, though there will certainly be women and Chinese. There can be liberated women, in the sense of people who are at once women and liberated, but there cannot be liberated serfs or workers in the sense of individuals who are at once both. Moreover, the *fact* that one is black or female is not because there are males or whites around, as the fact that one is proletarian is entirely because there is a bourgeoisie. The *social* constitution of categories like black and female is, like social class, a wholly relational affair; but nobody is black because someone else is white, in the sense that some people are only landless labourers because there are gentlemen farmers around the place. This distinction may not be of great political importance, but sloppy thinking about such crucial issues is always perilous.

In any case, Marxism is not definitively to do with social class at all. As Marx himself once commented, the distinctiveness of his and Engels's discovery was not the existence of a phenomenon known as social class, which had been as salient as Mont Blanc for quite a long time. It was, Marx claimed, the much more challenging and specific thesis that the genesis, evolution and demise of social classes is closely bound up with the development of historical modes of production. It is this which demarcates Marxism from those forms of so-called 'classism' which simply attend to the more visible effects of class oppression in the present. Once again, pragmatists and postmodernists may not *agree* with this hypothesis, but they have a responsibility to attend a little more closely to what exactly it is that Marxists have been arguing for the last century or so. Marxism is not just some high-sounding theoretical way of finding it somewhat distasteful or 'privileged' that some people belong to one social class and some to another, as it might be thought objectionable that some people get to attend cocktail parties while others have to make do with a can of beer from the ice-box. Marxism is a theory of the role played by the struggle between social classes in a much wider process of historical change, or it is nothing. And on this theory, social class cannot be said to be unequivocally a bad thing, as opposed to racism and sexism, about which there was never a good word to say.

There is another possible political error encouraged by the class, race and gender triplet. What these social groupings have in common is of course the fact that they are variously oppressed, denied their full humanity; but Marxism's interest in the working class is not at all in the first place to do with the fact that they are denied their full humanity. The proletariat is not a potential agent of revolutionary change because it suffers a good deal. As far as suffering goes, there are many better candidates for revolutionary agency than the working class: vagrants, perhaps, or impoverished students or prisoners or senior citizens. Many of these individuals suffer more than your average worker who drives a Renault and holidays annually in Greece. I do not wish to be misunderstood here: some of my best friends are vagrants, impoverished students, prisoners and senior citizens, and I have no personal grudge whatsoever against any of these groupings. But none of them is even potentially an agent of socialist transformation, as the working class is. Unlike the latter, these groups are not so objectively located within the capitalist mode of production, trained, organised and unified by that very system, as to be able to take it over. It is not Marxism which selects the proletariat as a potential revolutionary instrument, but capitalism, which as Marx wryly commented gives birth to its own gravedigger. Radical politics is not just a matter of looking around the place, determining who is most needy or desperate, and backing them against the system. Historical materialists can leave such a strategy to guilt-stricken middle-class liberals.

Marxists have always held to a belief in the unity of theory and practice, sometimes rather piously so. Some years ago I used to sell political newspapers with a comrade who once told me, in solemnly self-righteous terms, that he 'derived his theory from his practice'. No doubt this meant that he had arrived at his judgement that Luxemburg's theory of imperialism had the edge over Hilferding's by selling newspapers outside the Oxford branch of Woolworth. Piety apart, however, it is a traditional tenet of Marxism that radical theory, bereft of any practical political context, will tend to fray at the edges and sag in the middle. This seems to me exactly what is now happening in some areas of radical American thought, given the apparently intractable practical problems which the political opposition in that society faces. When one stumbles across a formulation as fatuous as Rorty's comments on Americanism, one can be reasonably sure that there is more at stake here than a simple lapse of individual sensitivity. 'Dig here', such comments signal, and you are likely to find a deeper historical deadlock and disorientation. The reverence lavished on the work of Michel Foucault by the new historicism is a similar case in point. Viewed from eight thousand miles off, that enthusiasm for Foucault has a good deal to do with a peculiarly American left defeatism, guilt-stricken relativism and ignorance of socialism – a syndrome which is understandable in Berkeley but, as I write, unintelligible in Beijing. The unconscious ethnocentrism of much of the US appropriation of such theory is very striking, at least to an outsider. What seems on the surface like a glamorous theory of the Renaissance keeps turning out to be about the dilemmas of ageing 1960s radicals in the epoch of Danforth Quayle. I write this article while the Chinese students and workers are still massing outside the Great Hall of the People; and I find it rather hard to understand why the neo-Stalinist bureaucrats have not, so far anyway, moved among the people distributing copies of Derrida, Foucault and Ernesto Laclau. For the Chinese students and workers to learn that their actions are aimed at a 'social totality' which is, theoretically speaking, non-existent would surely disperse them more rapidly than water cannons or bullets.

Given the fact that there is at present little thriving socialist culture in the United States, it seems at times to pass there as quite unexceptionable that some (if by no means all) theorists engaged with particular emancipatory struggles – ethnic or gender-based, let us say – appear as ignorant of or insouciant about socialism as Mr Quayle himself. Another disabling effect of this relative paucity of socialist theory and practice is that a good many American theorists who don't much like Marxism do not need, or are perhaps unable, to confront it head-on. It only takes a faint whiff of leftist paranoia to see much current American postmodernist and post-structuralist theory as a splendid strategy for trying to undermine Marxism without actually suffering the embarrassment of politically engaging with it. We hear very little about why exactly Stanley Fish has not rushed to espouse the theory of surplus value, or what Richard Rorty thinks of neo-colonialism, or the precise nature of Jonathan Culler's views of feudal absolutism. We do not hear this, because there is in fact no need. You can save yourself the trouble of a detailed involvement with these issues, which does after all require rather a developed knowledge of Marxist traditions and quite technical bodies of thought, simply by trying to pull the ontological and epistemological carpet out from under radical thinking as such. Why bother to debate whether this or that Marxist concept does its job when you can argue instead, much more grandiosely, that all social analysis is blinded and indeterminate, that the 'real' is undecidable, that all action beyond a timorous reformism will proliferate perilously beyond one's control, that there are no subjects sufficiently coherent to undertake such actions in the first place, that there is no 'total' system to be changed anyway, or that there is such totality but it is always terroristic, that any apparently oppositional stance has always already been included within what it resists, and that the way the world is is no particular way at all, if indeed we can know enough about it in the first place even to assert that?

One of the benefits of trying to scupper a radical politics in this way is that it doesn't make you appear quite such a red-neck reactionary as you might otherwise look. You can seem to be talking about the ineluctability of belief systems or the fact that institutionality goes all the way down whereas in fact you are talking about preserving the possibility of turning a fast buck. Richard Rorty is at least honest enough to admit that he is strenuously defending the Free World, which is more than can be said for most of his apparently avant-garde colleagues. Most of the positions I have just enumerated above suffer from the embarrassment of differing hardly at all from good old-fashioned liberal humanism; most of them, in fact, can be found lurking around as far back as *A Passage to India*. But they have now been dressed up in rather flashier theoretical guise. It would appear, in fact, that not all that much has changed since the good old post-war days of the End of Ideologies, when American sociologists were prone to argue that the Soviet Union was in the grip of a fanatical metaphysical ideology whereas the United States saw things more or less as they actually were. Sending your tanks into Czechoslovakia is an effect of logocentric delusion; bringing down the elected government of Chile is a piece of modest, pragmatic social engineering. It is true that not many American theorists these days are much enamoured of the concept of seeing things as they actually are; but the current distinction between the ideologico-metaphysical and the micropolitical (which sometimes seems to mean a politics so tiny as to be invisible) is among other things a variant on the end-of-ideologies epoch. To call your micropolitical pragmatism Foucaulteanism separates you less than you might think from the post-war intellectual wing of the CIA.

One of the problems, however, with this ontological and epistemological under-cutting is that it leaves political radicals with far too much elbow room, and so fails to achieve its purpose. We are extremely happy to admit that there is no transcendental vantage-point outside particular belief systems from which to launch a critique of Western society; in fact some of us hold that Marxism had been tediously insisting upon this fact long before the pragmatists got round to mentioning it. We do not mind in the least being informed that what we are doing is merely carrying on the conversation that is Western civilisation, a set of moves within an existing language game, as long as we can be allowed to get on and do it. If we in Britain are permitted to pull out of NATO, scrap our so-called independent nuclear deterrent, socialise industrial production under workers' self-management, dismantle the structures of patriarchy, return the Malvinas to the Argentinians and recall the troops from Northern Ireland, then it is really neither here nor there in our view whether what we are doing remains dismally imprisoned within a metaphysical problematic. Our theoretical opponents must either tell us that this means that we cannot really do it, a case which has a somewhat implausible ring to it, or that we *should* not really do it, in which case they are going to have to engage in a little more detailed political argument than they customarily do. They will have to come out from behind the cover of general theories of belief or anti-foundationalism or anti-logocentrism or the ontological ineluctability of micropolitics and let us know a little more clearly why they would like us to remain in NATO.

Somewhere in the later nineteenth century, the capitalist system found itself confronted by an awkward choice. Either it could continue to try to justify its activities by an appeal to metaphysical foundations, or it could simply abandon this whole project as a bad job. Neither alternative was very appealing. The problem with the former strategy, then as now, is that if such a society appeals to metaphysical values as part of its ideological self-legitimation, it will only succeed in exposing the farcical gap between such high-toned ethical or religious imperatives and the squalid nature of its actual marketplace practices. This is so because those practices belong to a rationalising, secularising current which tends continually to erode and discredit the very metaphysical discourses which are still necessary to it as a form of self-validation. Caught in this rather painful cleft stick, nineteenth-century bourgeois society was offered by Friedrich Nietzsche an alluring way out: don't bother trying to justify your practices at all. Forget about God, truth, morality, History, the state: let your activities become their own splendid, self-grounding justification, as marvellously self-born and self-generative as the work of art. It was, in fact, an aestheticising solution, and present-day American spokespersons for the death of meta-narrative and the collapse of ultimate legitimations are its aestheticising inheritors. Bourgeois society, however, was prudent enough to reject Nietzsche's audacious suggestion, and continues to do so today: it is canny enough to appreciate that without some perfunctory talk of God, Freedom and this Great Country of Ours, the marketplace is going to look rather a shaky, discreditable answer to the Meaning of Life. The seductive dream of throwing up the business of justification altogether, however, never quite receded, and in the midst of a sharp rightward-turn of the capitalist system is now once more back on the theoretical agenda. What Richard Rorty and his kind are saying to us is that there is no ultimate justification for the Western way of life. And this is exactly what we Marxists have been saying for a rather longer time.

Notes

1   Richard Rorty, *Contingency, Irony, and Solidarity* (Cambridge, 1989), p. 191.
2   Barbara Hernstein Smith, *Contingencies of Value* (Cambridge, Mass., and London, 1988), p. 94.

22 The Right and the Good: Postmodernism and the Liberal State

Nobody is in any doubt about what it is that all men and women want, only about what it means. What everyone wants is happiness, despite Marx's withering comment that only the English ever desired *that*. But this was a smack at the peculiarly anaemic notion of happiness espoused by the Utilitarians, for whom happiness is an essentially unproblematic concept, reducible in effect to pleasure. But to attain happiness I must sometimes pass up on short-term pleasures; and if happiness were not as opaque and bedevilled a notion as it is, we would not have landed ourselves with those convoluted discourses known as moral thought, whose task is precisely to examine what human happiness consists in and how it might be achieved.

The dawning of modernity was the moment when we began to realize that there are many conflicting ideas of the good life; that none of these ideas could be metaphysically grounded; and that, strangely enough, we were no longer able to agree on the most fundamental issues in this field. (I say 'strangely enough', since one might have thought that we could have agreed on the basics and then diverged on particulars. But though almost everybody agrees that torturing babies is wrong, we do not agree on our reasons for agreeing on this.) With the onset of the modern, humanity enters for the first time on that extraordinary condition (now thoroughly naturalized in our heads) in which we fail to see eye to eye on all the most vital matters – a condition which would have been mind-bendingly unimaginable to the ancients, and which seems to forestall all possibility of constructing a life in common.

The political upshot of this condition is liberalism. If there are many different conceptions of the good, then the state must be so constructed as to accommodate them all. The just state is one neutral in respect of any particular conception of the good life, limiting its jurisdiction to furnishing those conditions in which individuals may discover it for themselves. It does this by guaranteeing each individual the primary goods necessary for such exploration, and protecting them from being unjustly constrained in this enterprise by the actions of others. There is a contention between libertarian and welfarist liberals about how far this political initiative should extend: does it stretch, as the welfarist believes, to helping people to keep alive, since their pursuit of the good life would otherwise be gravely impeded, or would this (as one kind of libertarian holds) be an undue infringement of their liberty? Whatever this dispute, everyone must receive equal consideration in this respect, for everyone has as much right to the good life as everyone else. But the good life cannot be predefined, partly because there are many different versions of it around, partly because the process of creating or discovering it for oneself may precisely be part of it. For modernity, any good which I have not personally authenticated is necessarily incomplete.

In a move which antiquity would have found astonishing, then, the good life has now become a private affair, while the business of enabling it remains public. For the theorists of antiquity, no such distinction between the ethical and the political was imaginable. The ideology of civic or republican humanism views each in terms of the other: for me to exercise virtue, to realize my powers and capacities as a self-determining being, just is for me to participate with others in the running of the *polis*. There can be no such thing as private virtue, or a conception of the good life which is mine alone.

The liberal idea of the state, as its more astute apologists acknowledge, is clearly paradoxical. For to claim that the state should be neutral in respect of the good is inevitably to assert a certain conception of the good, and thus not to be neutral at all. It is also to imply a certain definition of the bad: namely, any individually or collectively pursued 'good' whose consequences would prove inimical to the state's ethical *apatheia*. It belongs to the integrity of the liberal state that it accommodates socialists and conservatives; but it cannot look indifferently on their projects, since if realized they would undermine its own indifference. And to this extent the liberal state is a sort of subject with desires and aversions of its own, even if it occasionally understands itself as the mere subjectless preconditions of subjectivity. Because its very structures necessarily allow for the engendering of interests hostile to them, it is not so much neutral as tolerant, and tolerance is a virtue only subjects can practise. But this point should not be mistaken for the usual reach-me-down leftist case that disinterestedness speciously masks a set of interests. The disinterestedness of the liberal state is *obviously* an interest in itself, and there is no reason why a liberal should be coy about this. My indifference to your moral torment doesn't mask my real attitude to you; it *is* an attitude to you, and not one I am bothered to dissemble. I am indifferent to your torment because I regard it as in your best interests for me to be so; there have been enough meddling do-gooders around here already. The interest of the liberal state is to be, within certain stringent limits, genuinely disinterested – not to care what kind of goods people come up with, because it believes that it has no rights in the matter and that this is the morally correct stance to adopt. That disinterestedness is a form of interest may be paradoxical, but it is not necessarily hypocritical or self-contradictory. From a communitarian stand-point, the liberal state is not to be criticized because it pretends not to care when it secretly does, but because it really doesn't care and it ought to. The communitarian claims that the state ought to concern itself more actively in the definition of the good life; but he or she recognizes that the liberal state does care a great deal about creating the preconditions for it – cares because it values individual flourishing, and believes passionately that disinterestedness – i.e. privileging no one of these individuals in their conception of what counts as such flourishing – is the most effective way to foster it all round.

In this respect, if not in certain others, liberalism is a paradoxical rather than self-contradictory doctrine, and some commonplace radical upbraiding of it thus falls to the ground. So do many of the now tediously familiar criticisms of its individualism. Liberalism is indeed a species of individualism, but the left commonly misrecognizes the level at which it entertains this belief. In a convenient piece of straw-targeting, all liberalism is seen as promoting some primitive Hobbesian notion of the self as a naked natural atom radically anterior to its social conditions, linked to other such antisocial atoms by a set of purely contractual relations extrinsic to its inner substance. The history of Western philosophy, so we are asked to believe, is by and large the narrative of this starkly autonomous subject, in contrast to the dispersed, divided, culturally constructed subject of a current left orthodoxy. This ignorant and dogmatic travesty of Western philosophy should not persist unchallenged. For Spinoza, the subject is the mere effect of an implacable determinism, its 'freedom' no more than the knowledge of iron necessity. The self for David Hume is a convenient fiction, a bundle of ideas and sense-data whose unity we hypothesize rather than experience. Kant's moral subject is indeed autonomous and self-determining, but in an ultimately inexplicable way quite at odds with its empirical determining. For Hegel, Schelling and the other Idealists, the subject is relational to its roots, as it is of course for Marx; for Kierkegaard and Sartre the self is agonizedly non-self-identical, and for Nietzsche a mere spin-off of the ubiquitous will to power. So much, then, for the naïve liberal idealism of Western thought. But even liberalism proper can cheerfully dispense with *ontological* individualism. Any reasonably sophisticated liberal will agree that the subject is culturally constructed, historically contextualized and radically relational; what he or she is urging is less a philosophical anthropology than a *political* doctrine concerning that subject's rights in the face of state power. And there is no reason why such rights should be conceived in some implausibly naturalistic, Rousseau-like sense. 'Rights' just means those needs and capacities which are so vital to our thriving and well-being that the state feels constrained to single them out for particular protection.

For all that, however, the fact remains that liberalism *is* individualist in an objectionable sense, as its political theory attests. What is wrong with the disinterestedness of the liberal state is not that it covertly masks some interest but that it quite explicitly enshrines one: the all-important interest of individual choice. It is not flawed because it has a notion of the good it furtively conceals, but because it has a drastically one-sided notion of the good to which other goods are unduly subordinated. And here it really does border on conceptual incoherence. For as Charles Taylor has demonstrated, assigning a right implies that the capacity protected by it should be positively nurtured, since it would be odd to protect a capacity and then be blithely indifferent as to whether or not it flourished. But this in turn implies actively fostering, through one's political participation, the kind of social order which would allow this to happen, which then challenges the liberal assumption that what is primary in political life is human rights.[1] What Taylor does here, in effect, is deconstruct the mighty opposition between deontologists and teleologists, Kantians and Utilitarians, the apologists for rights and justice and the devotees of virtue and happiness. Deontological theorists, like Kant or the great contemporary liberal John Rawls, give priority to the right over the good, justice over happiness, whereas teleological moralists like Marxists, Utilitarians and communitarians think that it is happiness or the good life which should be at the centre of our moral attention, and that talk of rights is meaningful only in relation to this. A full-blooded deontologist like Kant believes that actions are right or wrong quite independently of whether they happen to maximize human happiness, whereas a Utilitarian typically holds that right action just is such maximization. For the deontologist, the good is essentially our own individual business; for the teleologist, it vitally concerns political society as a whole. In Kantian theory, to ponder the socially beneficial results of my action is already to have contaminated its moral purity; for one rather vulgar brand of Utilitarianism, what matters is the promotion of the general well-being even if this rides roughshod over the freedom or well-being of particular individuals. All sorts of trade-offs between the two cases are of course possible: most of us would agree that the deontologists are right to claim that there are constraints on what can be demanded of one individual for the common good – that, as Rawls would put it, each person's good matters equally in a way that constrains the pursuit of the good as a whole; but many of us would also find persuasive the teleological claim that moral discourse ought to be about more than the preconditions of the good life – the equal distribution of freedom, for example – but should also examine in the manner of classical antiquity what the good life might consist in and how best to secure it.[2] It has been plausibly argued, for instance, that Marx is a 'mixed deontologist' who sees the moral good as the promotion of general well-being but not, say, at the expense of the deontological imperative that all men and women have an equal right to participate in this process.[3] What Taylor shows is that a liberal preoccupation with individual rights actually entails, despite itself, a positive concern with the political good – that having rights in the first place involves a moral obligation to participate in sustaining the institutions within which the powers and needs they guarantee may be fulfilled.

There is a standard Marxist critique of liberalism, which it is worth briefly rehearsing here before passing on to some rather less well-thumbed criticisms of the doctrine. This is the case that from one viewpoint liberalism really is self-contradictory, since the very political conditions which are meant to secure the good life in fact succeed only in undermining it. As long as individual rights centrally include property rights (though this, interestingly, is not the case for John

Rawls), the liberal state will engender precisely the kinds of inequality and exploitation which subvert the pursuit of the good life it was meant to promote. Everyone
will not in fact be in possession of the primary goods to carve their own path to
happiness. Some of them will be deprived of the necessary material and spiritual
resources, along with that esteem of others which is a vital component of human
well-being. Since this seems to me an unanswerable criticism, I shall not dwell on
it here; suffice it to note that Rawls, in his magisterial *Theory of Justice*, has a single
reference to exploitation, and that in a footnote. A different kind of critique of
liberalism has sprung over recent years from communitarian thinkers like Charles
Taylor and Alasdair MacIntyre, the former a lapsed Catholic, the latter, in a
pleasing symmetry, a recent convert. This case, an intriguing compound of
Wittgenstein, Aristotle and Aquinas, attends to the cultural and historical roots of
the self, its embeddedness in tradition and community, and from this vantage-point
denounces what it sees as the abstract Enlightenment atomism of the liberal subject, with its ahistorical, speciously universalist ethics.[4]

I have suggested already that there is no reason for the canny liberal to deny the
culturalist case. But there is no reason either why he or she should refuse the value
of community, since this is clearly one good which many individuals seek and
which the liberal state must therefore accommodate. As far as the liberal is
concerned, men and women are perfectly free to pursue communitarian ends, if
this happens to be the form of good life they choose; it is just that such
communitarianism must not be *built into* the state, for this would constitute an
undue infringement of the rights of those who wish to achieve happiness by sitting
in a darkened room with a paper bag over their head. If political arrangements are
such that I am compelled to take part much of the time in collective decision-
making, I have less time to spend the whole of my waking life trying on one leather
costume after another in the privacy of my bedroom; and if this happens to
constitute the good life for me, then it behoves the state not to discriminate against
me in this flagrantly prejudicial fashion. The state itself, in short, must not rank
goods hierarchically; but from a socialist point of view it has of course already done
so. For it has ruled out all forms of communitarianism beyond associations of a
local kind, and so censured any move to socialize industry under workers' self-
management. But if the liberal can agree that such communitarian forms represent
at least part of the good life for many individuals, why not make them as widely
available as possible? The answer is that they would interfere with other conceptions of the good, and with the possibilities of practising them. But what decides,
in this apparent conflict of goods, that it is the communitarian form that gives way?
Not, in one sense, the state, since the state is not in the business of adjudicating
between rival notions of happiness. It has no view on the question of whether
prancing around in a leather apron is in principle more or less valuable than the
democratic management of the economy. Its only concern is that no particular
conception of the good life should be actually built into its structures. But we have
seen already that such a conception is indeed implicit in it, namely the primacy of

individual choice, which only appears not to be a positive vision of the good because it is just a way of negatively licensing a plurality of such positive visions. So the liberal state's opposition to socialism cannot be because it thinks it lacks value in itself (it has no opinion on the matter), or because it would involve incorporating into itself a particular ideology (it does so already). It must rather be that socialism, or some other communitarian form, would limit the plurality of goods available, or violate the freedom of individuals by coercing them into this particular project. But this can be shown to be empirically not the case. First of all, socialism would greatly increase the primary goods accessible to each individual for his or her pursuit of happiness, and would do so with much greater equity than liberal states in practice allow; so that in this sense socialism is the consummation of liberalism, not its antithesis. Secondly, democratic socialism would extend what the liberal may well acknowledge as the major human good of community without any necessary detriment to other, more personally selected goods; indeed by developing the productive forces and shortening the working day it would considerably expand that personal arena. By extending the material means of community and, *by virtue of this*, increasing the time, leisure, material and spiritual resources essential for the pursuit of other goods, socialism overcomes the duality between public and private on which the liberal ideology rests. It can accommodate everything the liberal wants, but more so; and if the liberal has no effective arguments against it, it is because there are none.

Marxism has always understood itself as the sublation of the great liberal tradition, in contrast to those contemporary radicals for whom this magnificent emancipatory heritage can be vulgarly reduced to the bugbear of the 'autonomous subject'. Marx himself is a Kantian and an individualist: he believes that human beings should be treated as ends, not means, and that the moral good lies in the fullest development of their individual powers and capacities. But Marxism is just a name for what happens to this ethic in a social order in which material conditions necessarily constrain us into complex forms of co-operation. If everyone must be allowed to realize their unique capacities, and if everyone is ineluctably bound up with everyone else, then the only way in which my unique self-realization can be achieved is through and in terms of yours. This is a normative claim; but it also follows from the constraints placed upon liberal values by certain material and historical conditions. For both liberal and Marxist, freedom consists in determining as far as possible one's conditions of life; it is just that the liberal is historically unrealistic to believe that this can be confined to the private sphere alone. For the interpenetration of private and public realms in complex modern societies is such that I cannot be free personally unless I am allowed to shape my collective destiny too; and it is just this that the liberal state's refusal to build forms of solidarity into itself prohibits. Liberalism has traditionally assigned a rather low value to political participation, as opposed to the ancient and Marxist doctrine that participating in the state is a major way in which we exercise freedom and therefore a value in itself. I exercise virtue in the very process of helping to shape the communal structures which allow virtue to flourish. The liberal concern with democracy, by contrast, is a matter of rights rather than virtues: it is a question of everyone being given equal consideration (i.e. a question of justice), rather than a question of freedom and happiness consisting to some degree in the very practice of collective self-determination itself. Socialist democracy thus deconstructs the opposition between the deontological and the teleological; for here the maintenance of the political structures which will allow the good life to thrive is also a part of that life, the form part of the content. Ironically, then, it is the socialist rather than the liberal who sets the highest value on freedom. Freedom for the liberal is essentially instrumental, an absence of constraint which allows him to do what he wants; freedom for the socialist, grasped as the virtue of self-determination, is also instrumental, since our political decisions are about something other than themselves; but it is also a value in itself, which could not, for example, be traded off for a greater increase of other goods all round. If these decisions are not *our* decisions, so modernity rightly perceives, they are diminished in value however brilliant they are.

The liberal objects to socialism because he or she fears that everyone would end up believing the same thing, sharing the same notion of the good, and so fatally impoverishing the plurality of possible goods. The communitarian objects to liberalism exactly because everyone *doesn't* share a common life-form, and is therefore rootless, atomized, disinherited. Socialism, however, combines the best of liberalism and communitarianism in this way too. It shares with the communitarian a belief in the collective determination of meanings and values; but it holds that this will result not in a homogeneous society, but in precisely the kind of plurality that the liberal admires. This fact is only not seen because of a crucial ambiguity in the term 'common culture'. A common culture can mean one commonly shared, or one commonly made; and the communitarian is wrong to think that the latter implies the former. For the truth is that if everyone is able to participate fully in the definition of that culture, then it is likely to end up a good deal more heterogeneous than it is if its values are formulated by an elite. We would expect a common culture to share certain values which arise precisely from the fact of its collective democratic fashioning; but within this common view there would be ceaseless conflict and negotiation between the interests which these structures then enabled to be voiced. By suppressing these interests through its relative indifference to the virtue of participation, liberal society is less genuinely pluralist than its socialist antagonist.

If socialism combines the best of liberalism and communitarianism, postmodernism combines the worst of both worlds. It has, to begin with, an embarrassing amount in common with communitarianism – 'embarrassing', because neither Alasdair MacIntyre nor Richard Rorty would be much complimented by being told that they are mirror-images of each other. Like communitarianism, postmodernism finds nothing but error in the Enlightenment, and emphasizes the cultural and historical construction of the self to the point where submitting the traditions which shape it to fundamental critique would involve some hubristic leap into metaphysical outer space. Both creeds are forms of culturalism – a doctrine every bit as reductive as the naturalism and biologism it seeks to oppose. Both are brands of conventionalism, holding that right action or the good life cannot be defined apart from the particular cultural practices we have inherited. The self for both doctrines is embedded in a purely parochial history, and moral judgements thus cannot be universal. Moral judgements for Rorty and his ilk really say 'We don't do that kind of thing around here', appeal to a provisional consensus grounded only in contingent cultural practices; whereas as Will Kymlicka points out, when a Muslim woman in Egypt says 'Sexual discrimination is wrong', she means precisely that we *do* do that kind of thing around here but we shouldn't.[5] There are, of course, key differences between the two currents: the cultural tradition Rorty frankly espouses – bourgeois liberalism – has nothing much in common with MacIntyre's Aristotelian Thomism, and the former is prepared to be a good deal more ironic about his allegiances than the latter. But this difference of content conceals an identity of form: for both viewpoints, the self is at its best when belonging to a set of local cultural practices, and the liberal Enlightenment notion of fundamental critique would mean detaching oneself from this context in pursuit of some metaphysical fantasy. The fact that Rorty, as a bourgeois liberal, is relativistically ready to tolerate all sorts of local cultures, whereas MacIntyre as a holistic communitarian is not, makes no difference to this essential point.

Postmodernism, then, takes from the communitarian tradition its lopsided culturalism, moral relativism and hostility to critique, in contrast to a socialism which plucks from the same heritage its more positive values of community, historicity, relationality and the rest. But postmodernism then proceeds to combine all this with the worst aspects of the liberalism which the communitarians see as their enemy. It has almost nothing of interest to say about the great liberal motifs of justice, equality and human rights, since these sit uncomfortably with its nervousness of the 'autonomous subject' and fetishism of difference. And since, for similar reasons, it is wary of the ancient or positive conception of liberty as self-determination, it has to fall back on the modern or negative notion of freedom as doing your own thing, a kind of libertarianism without the liberal subject. At its extreme, then, the postmodernist subject is a strikingly paradoxical one, at once more and less free than the unified subject which preceded it. On the one hand, the culturalist bias of postmodernism can press to the point of determinism: we just are ineluctably shaped by power or conventions or interpretive communities into particular behaviours and beliefs. On the other hand, the subject is contingent, aleatory, incoherent, a caricatured version of the negative liberty of classical liberalism. Heterogeneity is then what pins these antithetical doctrines precariously together: the subject is mobile, free-floating, provisional because it is the product of many determining codes, lives at the juncture of clashing cultural frames. It is 'free' because it shares in the random, unstructured, open-ended nature of reality itself; but since all this structures it to its roots it is inexorably determined in its very freedom, which now has little or nothing in common with the positive liberty of self-determination.

There is much of the Nietzschean will to power in this vision; but it also corresponds pretty well to the experience of advanced capitalist societies. For where else do you feel at once moulded by implacably determining forces and absolutely adrift? This subject is as much the creature of the market-place as the very different subject of classical liberalism, which also had a problem in reconciling its freedom with its determination. The Kantian duality of the noumenal and phenomenal selves was in this respect no more than a confession of philosophical defeat. But the classical liberal subject was at least able to preserve its truth and autonomy along with its plurality. Now, in a drastic declension of that process, the subject of a more advanced capitalism is compelled to sacrifice its truth and autonomy to its heterogeneity – a logical impasse indeed, since who exactly experiences that alluring dance of differentiation? Or, to put it another way, the strenuously productive subject of liberal capitalism has yielded ground to the consumerist self of a later stage of that history. The freedom of the classical liberal subject was always constrained by its proper respect for the autonomy of others; now it is as though that freedom, at least in postmodernist fantasy, has come bursting through the very juridico-political frame which enabled it. It is able to do this because (again in fantasy) there are no longer any autonomous subjects out there to constrain it; but this is a Pyrrhic victory at best, since there is also no longer any autonomous subject in here to whom this euphoric freedom may be attached. And if there are no longer autonomous subjects, then there can be no talk of justice. All the vital questions over which classical political philosophy has agonized – your rights against mine, my struggle for emancipation against yours – can be simply dissolved away.

Nobody, of course, believes this for a moment. Even postmodernists deserve justice and esteem: even they are in this reasonable sense of the term autonomous subjects, as they would recognize if only they could relinquish a shoddy caricature of the notion that few people ever credited in the first place. It is tiresomely dogmatic to hold that autonomous, self-determining subjects need be atomistic, non-relational, unconstructed, dehistoricized, metaphysically grounded and the rest – a lot of self-righteous banging at a door which was already half-open. There are indeed such extreme ideologies around, and some strains of postmodernism have been valuably radical in their efforts to dislodge them. But to do so they have often enough fled straight into the arms of a culturalism and historicism which belong as much with the political right as the political left. You do not need to tell the Burkes and the Oakeshotts that the self is culturally shaped and locally instantiated. There is nothing in the least inherently radical about historicizing. Moreover, in selling the pass to the right-culturalists, postmodernism has paid scant attention to that mainstream radical tradition – call it Marxism or socialism – for which self-determination and decentrement are sides of the same political coin. Collective self-determination – socialist democracy – just means that the free subject is always extrinsic to itself, never self-identical, always receives its desire from the place of the Other. And in meticulously setting up its straw targets of Enlightenment, postmodernism forgets the moment where we came in – the moment of modernity, in which illumination dawns that versions of the good life do not in fact come ready-equipped with metaphysical seals of approval, and in which instead we have to argue the toss over them. Seeing this, and doing it, was liberalism's splendid achievement; and postmodernist pluralism is its heir. But the activity of arguing the toss over what we are unsure of is known as reason, for which postmodernism has in general a somewhat low regard. The liberal state provided a space of limited plurality in which interests could be bred which then rationally challenged, in the name of justice or the good life, that state itself. But if it is merely a space of incommensurable interests, between which there can be no rational negotiation, then there can be no question of any particular set of these interests submitting the others, and the very structures which enable them, to rational critique. And this, need one say, is exceedingly good news for the liberal state.

Notes

1 See Charles Taylor, 'Atomism', in *Philosophy and the Human Sciences: Philosophical Papers*, vol. 2 (Cambridge, 1985), pp. 188–210.
2 On the quarrel between deontology and teleology, see Will Kymlicka, *Liberalism, Community and Culture* (Oxford, 1989), ch. 3.
3 See R. G. Peffer, *Marxism, Morality, and Social Justice* (Princeton, 1990) Part 1.
4 See Charles Taylor, 'Atomism', and Alasdair MacIntyre, *After Virtue: A Study in Moral Theory* (London, 1981).
5 Kymlicka, p. 66.

Part V Friends and Philosophers

Introduction

The opening essay in this section (Chapter 23) was written as a memorial lecture for Raymond Williams shortly after his death on 26 January 1988. It was later adopted as the introduction to *Raymond Williams: Critical Perspectives* (1989). It presents a vivid and moving account of the life and work of a fellow socialist and cultural critic, tracing with warmth and admiration the diverse enthusiasms that Williams pursued, and charting his transformation of Cambridge English from the 1960s onwards. Terry Eagleton arrived in Cambridge as an undergraduate in the same year that Williams was appointed to a lectureship in the Faculty of English. As essays such as 'The Idea of a Common Culture' suggest, Eagleton's early cultural politics came to consciousness under Williams's tutelage, and a good deal of his later cultural criticism is nourished by a creative and sustaining dialogue with Williams's related endeavours.

In 1976 Eagleton published a controversial article in *New Left Review* (the article alluded to in 'The Ballad of Marxist Criticism' at the end of this volume), surveying the critical and fictional writings of Raymond Williams. The article formed a substantial part of the strategic opening of *Criticism and Ideology*, published in the same year. While acknowledging Williams's *Culture and Society 1780–1950* as 'the most suggestive and intricate body of socialist criticism in English history',[1] Eagleton was sharply critical of the idealist epistemology, organicist aesthetics and political gradualism of Williams's work. Several critics were surprised by the astringent nature of Eagleton's comments, and viewed them as an indication of a decisive, and in some ways inevitable, break with Williams. David Lodge, for instance, referred to Eagleton's 'somewhat Oedipal intellectual relationship' with Williams.[2]

What might appear as a harsh assessment of Williams's achievements needs to be read in the spirit of comradeship and good faith with which it is offered. The turn which Williams's work was to take after 1976 suggests that he responded positively to criticism. In any case, as the essay reprinted here suggests, Williams had an uncanny way of anticipating theoretical debate and of eventually emerging several steps ahead. The early critique of Williams also needs to be read alongside a revealing passage in *The Function of Criticism* (1984), in which Eagleton pays homage to Williams as 'the single most important critic of post-war Britain' and goes on to confess that 'while other materialists, including myself, diverted into structuralist Marxism, Williams sustained his historicist humanism only to find such theoreticians returning under changed political conditions to examine the case less cavalierly, if not to endorse it uncritically'.[3]

In the memorial lecture printed here Eagleton acknowledges the 'fertile conjuncture' in which Williams brought together two distinctive currents of Cambridge English – close textual analysis and 'life and thought' – transmuting these into his own distinctive preoccupation with historical linguistics and cultural politics. He provides an illuminating account of how Williams shifted beyond this 'first-stage radicalism' to the revolutionary politics of *Modern Tragedy* (1966) and a concern with the ownership and control of communications media in *Communications* (1962). He notes that a striking feature of Williams's career is that he moved steadily further to the political left 'in a welcome reversal of the usual clichéd trek from youthful radical to middle-aged reactionary'. He pays tribute to the grace and dignity with which Williams responded to the class prejudice and academic snobbery of Cambridge, and to the determination and resilience with which he cut across conventional academic disciplines and helped to establish cultural studies as a rich and resourceful body of work.

The relationship between the Welsh socialist Raymond Williams and the German metaphysician Arthur Schopenhauer might seem at best tangential, yet the book in which Eagleton writes so entertainingly about Schopenhauer, *The Ideology of the Aesthetic* (1990), might be regarded as the culmination of a cultural project initiated by Williams. The introduction to the book regards the 'Culture and Society' tradition which Williams articulated and expanded as part of a broader German intellectual legacy. Just as Williams considers the changing semantic history of 'art' and 'culture' as part of a shifting constellation that includes such words as 'class' and 'industry' and 'democracy', so Eagleton fastens upon the aesthetic as a category whose changing values and meanings are subtly implicated in the struggle of the European bourgeoisie for political dominance. While it seems to be a neutral concept, the aesthetic plays a crucial role in giving ideological coherence to the needs and interests of modern class society; it softens and sublimates the crude operations of class power and legitimizes the new forms of subjectivity on which that power depends. Like culture, however, the aesthetic is a contradictory phenomenon: if at one level it functions as an evasive strategy for the operations of class society, it can also effect a powerful critique of that society by inducing new and alternative modes of thinking and feeling.

The technique employed throughout *The Ideology of the Aesthetic* is the shamelessly eclectic one that draws conveniently on whatever theoretical materials happen to be at hand. If Williams is occasionally invoked for some illuminating remark on culture or modernity, so too are Benjamin, Bakhtin and Brecht. The notion of 'desire' that informs the essay on Schopenhauer (reprinted here as Chapter 24) is one that bears the imprint of the writings of Julia Kristeva, Gilles Deleuze, and at least a dozen other 'continental' theorists. It is a measure of the impact of Bakhtin and Brecht on Eagleton's work at this time that he should so studiously dispel the mental gloom popularly associated with Schopenhauer, and commence the essay with a seemingly incongruous comic account of the functions of the body in Schopenhauer's writings.

Yet there is, in Schopenhauer's meditations on the Will, a carnivalesque display of the yawning, sneezing, twitching, jerking and vomiting activities of the body, which is where the Will – 'that blindly persistent desire at the root of all phenomena' – is frequently detected. The spectacle of humanity going about its futile endeavours is, for Schopenhauer, cause enough for hysterical laughter, and in some respects his work has the potential for a full-blown theory of comedy: 'If humour and hopelessness lie so close together', Eagleton suggests, 'it is because human existence for Schopenhauer is less grand tragedy than squalid farce.' Then comes the sharp and sudden dialectical turn: what if the experience of the great majority of men and women throughout history has, indeed, been one of suffering and oppression?

Schopenhauer's conception of the Will might seem obsessive and outrageous, but it has a plausible and significant motive for appearing when it does. Eagleton claims that Schopenhauer is one of the first modern thinkers to give the abstract category of desire a central force and meaning: 'With Schopenhauer, desire has become the protagonist of the human theatre, and human subjects themselves its mere obedient bearers or underlings.' This coincides with the emergence of a social order in which 'appetite' is becoming a ruling ideology and dominant social practice, and in which the seemingly endless process of accumulation stimulates an *infinity* of desire. It is here that aesthetic experience comes into play, offering a temporary release from desire in a realm of contemplative ease. At one level, the Schopenhauerian aesthetic contains a glimpse of utopia, promising an alternative to a society powered by appetite, but it also presents an insurmountable paradox, since there is little in Schopenhauer's theory – preoccupied as it is with the delusion of the intellect and the tyranny of the Will – to suggest how a pure, disinterested aesthetic condition might ever come about. If Schopenhauer's aesthetic theory founders on its own contradictions, it also demolishes with them a long tradition of bourgeois ideology in which aesthetic ideals provide the perfect model of harmonious conduct.

Ludwig Wittgenstein was, as Eagleton points out, a devoted disciple of Schopenhauer, and his work is cited several times in *The Ideology of the Aesthetic*. Wittgenstein and Marx are notable companions in Eagleton's early work on language and belief, especially in *Directions: Pointers for the Post-Conciliar Church* (1968) and *The Body as Language* (1970), and Wittgenstein plays a considerable role in the much later (1986) critique of deconstruction in *Against the Grain* (see 'Wittgenstein's Friends', pp. 99–130). 'My Wittgenstein' (Chapter 25) belongs to a much more specific project and one that held immense significance for Eagleton in breaking down the distinction between theoretical and creative work. That project began in 1990 with Tariq Ali's idea for a series of Channel 4 television programmes on philosophy. What was intended as a programme on Wittgenstein, with a script by Terry Eagleton, became a film by Derek Jarman. As Colin MacCabe points out in his introduction to *Wittgenstein: The Terry Eagleton Script / The Derek Jarman Film* (1993), the changes wrought upon the script by Jarman and then by Ken Butler were extensive, yet 'the final film is unthinkable without the original screenplay' and 'draws much of its strength from it'. In Eagleton's opinion, the composite script, with its clash of styles and emotional tones, 'interestingly dramatises the conflicts and disjunctions in Wittgenstein's life and work'.[4]

'My Wittgenstein' is a version of the 'Introduction to Wittgenstein' which prefaces the screenplay published by the British Film Institute in 1993 (quoted above). As its title suggests, the essay is a personal reflection on Wittgenstein's significance, but it is also a candid narrative of the making of Jarman's film. For Eagleton, Wittgenstein's bold attempt to sketch the frontiers of language from within language itself places him in the modernist company of Joyce, Schoenberg, Picasso, and 'all those self-ironising avant-gardists who sought in their own fashion to represent and point to their representing at a stroke'. He sees the *Tractatus* as the first great work of philosophical modernism, marking that point where the modernist impulse migrates from film and poetry and sculpture, to take up residence within philosophy. With all the self-reflexiveness of modern art, the *Tractatus* shows philosophy bending back on itself and interrogating its own linguistic medium.

Trying to film Wittgenstein's ideas in terms of his life is, as Eagleton confesses, 'a hopeless enterprise', but there is clearly much in the life that he finds compelling, if sometimes exasperating. His Wittgenstein is 'an arresting mixture of monk, mystic and mechanic', fleeing from Vienna to Manchester, Cambridge, Norway, Austria, the Soviet Union and – to Eagleton's undisguised delight – Ireland. This Irish sojourn is the subject of Eagleton's 1987 novel *Saints and Scholars*, in which Wittgenstein encounters James Connolly and Nikolai Bakhtin (the elder brother of Mikhail Bakhtin) in a cottage in Galway. 'My Wittgenstein' recalls the visit Eagleton made to Killary harbour, where Wittgenstein arrived from Cambridge in 1948, and so paves the way for the section on Ireland that follows.

Notes

1   *Criticism and Ideology*, p. 24.
2   David Lodge (ed.), *Modern Criticism and Theory: A Reader* (London and New York: Longman, 1988), pp. 384–5.
3   *The Function of Criticism*, p. 109.
4   *Wittgenstein: The Terry Eagleton Script / The Derek Jarman Film* (London: British Film Institute, 1993), p. 2.

23   Resources for a Journey of Hope: Raymond Williams

Raymond Williams and I arrived in Cambridge simultaneously in 1961, he from a long stint in adult education to a college Fellowship, I from a year's teaching in a northern secondary modern school to an undergraduate place. It was hard to say which of us was more alienated. Williams had made the long trek from a rural working-class community in Wales to a college which seemed to judge people (as I was to find out later to my cost) by how often they dined at High Table. He looked and spoke more like a countryman than a don, and had a warmth and simplicity of manner which contrasted sharply with the suave, off-hand style of the upper-middle-class establishment. He never got used to the casual malice of the Senior Combination Room, and was to write years later, in a fine obituary of F. R. Leavis, that Cambridge was 'one of the rudest places on earth . . . shot through with cold, nasty and bloody-minded talk'. I found myself marooned within a student body where everyone seemed to be well over six foot, brayed rather than spoke, stamped their feet in cinemas at the feeblest joke and addressed each other like public meetings in intimate cafés. It was a toss-up which of us was going to make it.

I knew of Williams's work then only vaguely, mainly through association with Richard Hoggart and the so-called Angry Young Men of the 1950s, now mostly dyspeptic old Tories. Hearing him lecture was an extraordinary personal liberation: it was like seeing someone stand up in the most improbable place, formal and begowned, and articulate with enviable ease and eloquence all the struggling, smouldering political feelings you had yourself, but which were not so to speak official or academic, and which one had simply not expected to hear given voice in such an environment. It was as if a dispirited juvenile offender in a remand home (an experience not far removed from that of an early 1960s Cambridge college) was suddenly to realize to his astonishment that the Governor speaking up there at the front was sending out oblique but unmistakable messages that he was an offender too, a kind of fifth columnist in the prison service. Part of the delight of this, of course, was to hear one's own values and instincts argued far more subtly and beautifully than one could ever have done oneself – converted to a marvellously intricate intellectual case without any diminution of personal conviction. Williams was a man of remarkable grace and dignity; and through the medium of this authority I felt somehow authorized to speak myself, and through me all those relatives and friends who could never speak properly, who had never been given the means to say what they meant, whom nobody ever bothered to ask what they meant. It was as though one's most spontaneous gut reactions, which one wouldn't really have been able to defend, were suddenly out there in the public arena, dignified and justified at the level of tenacious argument. And all this seemed to be less a matter of academic debate than to spring directly from the slow personal ruminations of Williams himself, as though the ideas were just the more public, audible bits of an unusually rich and deep identity. I think everyone who met Williams was struck by what I can only call his deep inward ease of being, the sense of a man somehow centred and rooted and secure in himself at a level far beyond simple egoism. I wondered then where this inner balance and resilience came from, and how I might get hold of a bit. I was to learn as I got to know him that it came essentially from his class background – indeed that the whole of his lifelong political project was secretly nurtured by a formative early experience of working-class solidarity and mutual support which had left him unusually trusting and fearless. But I couldn't understand this quiet authority at the time, or the way he seemed at once so gentle and so rugged, and put it down, I suppose, to middle age, though in fact he was only forty. I asked myself where this man was coming from, and how he could speak out on behalf of the powerless in this place, with that degree of shrewdness and sureness. I understood about a third of what he said, and resolved to get to understand the rest.

Leavis was still lecturing across the road, just on the point of retirement. 'Queenie did it all in the Thirties' was his comment on Williams's work, conveyed to me by Williams himself with his customary dry amusement. George Steiner was at Churchill College, telling his students that the trouble with Williams was that he didn't appreciate the chastening power of human tragedy. Most of the rest of the English Faculty seemed to see him as some kind of sociologist who had strayed through the wrong departmental door and inadvertently got caught up in the Metaphysical poets. They, of course, dealt with the essentially human; Williams was distracting himself with historical red herrings, with class and industry and politics and all of that, and even worse with film and advertising and the popular press. I think this was probably the deepest irony of all, because the most evident difference between Williams and most of his colleagues was indeed a matter of humanity, but as it happened the other way round. Williams's discourse rose straight from a human depth which seemed to put almost everyone else, oneself included, in the shade; it was the *level* at which he spoke, not just what he said, that marked the real distinction. You couldn't separate what he said from the sense of a whole rich hinterland of experience informing his words. Long before the slogan 'the personal is political' became fashionable, Williams was living it, in the complex, intimate relations between his life and work. He never seemed to credit anything he hadn't personally assimilated, absorbed gradually into his own being; and he lived in a kind of slow, steady, meditative way, again very like a certain kind of countryman, taking the whole of his experience with an intense, unwavering seriousness quite removed from the portentous. This seemed quaint, amusingly archaic, to some of the hard-boiled cynics around him, to the young men on the take and on the make whose depth of experience seemed from the outside about that of a Disney cartoon. There were the predictable friendly-malicious comments about the flat cap and the farmer's boots, the kind of talk which Williams himself always rightly saw as a kind of sickness. Even one of the obituaries, tenacious to the last, managed to drag out the word 'nostalgia' to characterize a man who wrote a major work entitled *Towards 2000*. Quite unwittingly – for he was the kind of man you had to work very hard on to make him feel negatively about someone – Williams made people feel uneasy about their own glibness and stylish political scepticism, and they were sometimes not slow to strike back in their anxiety.

Williams's own Cambridge experience had not been primarily one of stamping, braying six-footers. It had been the experience of war: the interrupted English course, the armed struggle in Europe (he was a tank commander in France), then the young servicemen, those who had survived, back on King's Parade to take up their studies again, as a Labour government moved into power. It had also been for Williams the experience of the Communist party, of which he was briefly a member. When he returned to Cambridge in 1961, after years of teaching adults in village halls around the south of England, he found it hard to get used to the supervision system, to teaching the children of the privileged, and kept a wary distance from the system. Yet it was the outsider, in a familiar paradox, who upheld the most creative traditions of the place. I mean the best traditions of the Cambridge English Faculty, which Williams personally incarnated for years, among Faculty colleagues who often hardly knew what he was talking about. Williams brought together in a new conjuncture the two distinctive currents of Cambridge English: close textual analysis on the one hand, 'life and thought' on the other. But what they called 'close reading' or 'attention to language' he called historical linguistics, and what they called 'life and thought' he called 'society' or 'cultural history'.

If this was a fertile conjuncture, it was not without severe tensions. The close analysis, he well knew, was by no means ideologically innocent: it was the learnt habit of a specialized, separated intelligence, deeply dependent on unconscious ideological consensus and radically dissociated from how most people actually had to live. To bring that to bear on so-called 'life and thought', on a whole social and cultural formation, was thus to risk becoming caught in an immediate political contradiction. How do you analyze your own people from the outside? Doesn't the very form of that cognition run somehow counter to the content, as Matthew Price of *Border Country* suspects, and Peter Owen of *Second Generation* fears? It is a duality which crops up in Williams's work in all kinds of guises, and one I dismissed with the brisk impatience of relative youth in *Criticism and Ideology* (1976).

It is there in the running battle between 'common' and 'educated', between the 'knowable community' and the harsh world of capitalist production, between country and city, Milton and Donne, isolated civilized subtlety and a general common humanity. Williams picks up just this conflict in the work of Leavis, in his obituary – Leavis who 'committed himself heavily to . . . one form of the discontinuities, the detachments, the cold wit of Eliot, yet was seized, always, with especially strong feelings of continuity, of commitment, of the everyday substance of English provincial life'. Williams is surely here speaking obliquely about himself as well; he had a lifelong fascination with modernism, despite the 'realist' label I and some others too facilely stuck on him, and saw just how modernism's radical estrangement of the ordinary was at once a creative political experiment and a disabling deracination. Unlike some others, he wasn't going to come down too quickly on either side of that particular fence. If he came in effect to abandon the lineage of 'close analysis' in his later work, it was not because he was not good at it (he was very good at it) but because the political price came to seem to him too high. *Culture and Society* is a courageous, breathtakingly original attempt to bring that current of trained textual analysis to bear on a common social history; but it is therefore an acute instance of the conflict in question, and for all the acclaim it received as a radical text it was written in political isolation in the Cold War years, the book of one still having to negotiate the tension between Leavisism and socialism. 'First-stage radicalism' was how Williams would later characterize this most seminal work, in a calculated self-distancing.

He was always haunted by the border he had crossed from the 'knowable community' to the life of educated intelligence, and lived in border country the whole of his life. When he moved from Hastings to a brief spell in Oxford he homed in unerringly on just the same dilemma: *Second Generation* opens on Oxford's conveniently named Between Towns Road, where you can look one way to the spires of the university and the other way to the roofs of the Cowley car factory. Williams never of course believed for a moment that this contradiction, embedded as it is in a class-divided society, could be somehow intellectually resolved, and never in any case viewed it as a simple opposition. One of his earliest essays is entitled 'Culture is ordinary', in which he argues that nobody who understands the Welsh working-class respect for learning and literature could imagine that it was a sheer break to cross the border from Abergavenny to Cambridge. He also remarked in an interview I did with him towards the end of his life that one of the things his Welsh comrades valued most about him, when he came back to Wales, was exactly the fact that he had crossed the frontier and made his way in the metropolitan institutions. It wasn't just a case of 'culture' on one side of the border and 'society' on the other: what Williams grew up in, what nourished him, was a culture if anything was, and like Hardy's Jude in Oxford it didn't take him long to perceive that it was in all sorts of ways more precious than the nasty, cold-hearted talk he was to encounter in so-called civilized Cambridge. Williams helped to bring the very concept of culture to Cambridge, often enough to have it thrown back in his face by the cultivated. It wasn't a question of some nostalgic backward glance to the valleys and the hillsides: *The Country and the City* takes the 'organic society' illusion and undoes it with deadly, devastating insistence. He once said disparagingly of Nye Bevan that it took one Welshman to know another. I never knew anyone who had a deeper respect for rational enquiry than Williams, and that from a man who knew as well as anybody that reason is not, in the end, where it is at. He never underestimated the value of the intellectual tools of which his own people had been deliberately deprived; it was just that he took the instruments which he had been handed and turned them against the educators. He used them instead to create the finest body of cultural work of twentieth-century Britain, on behalf of those who had not enjoyed the privilege of arriving in Cambridge to be told by E. M. W. Tillyard that his boots were rather large.

Williams was not only ungrateful enough to bite the hand that fed him; he was truculent enough to do it more and more as he grew older. Those liberal critics who had welcomed *Culture and Society* with open arms were rather less enthused by his later talk of Third World insurrection and the brutalities of capitalism. A striking feature of Williams's career is that he moves steadily further to the political left, in a welcome reversal of the usual clichéd trek from youthful radical to middle-aged reactionary. The left reformism or left Leavisism of the very early Williams of the journal *Politics and Letters*, when he was out in the political cold of post-war Britain, yields to the quickening solidarity of the early New Left and CND, where he could find friends and supporters. The little book *Communications* of 1962 proposes with casual boldness and in some practical detail the social ownership and control of the communications media, and by the time of *Modern Tragedy* in 1966 the gradualist discourse of *The Long Revolution* has turned, five years on, into the long tragedy of armed struggle against imperialism. Around this time Williams began to turn backwards so that he could keep moving forwards, re-exploring his Welsh heritage in a deliberate distancing from both 'English' literature and the brave new world of a Labour government whose idea of culture was C. P. Snow. Like many an exile, he had to discover, reinvent almost, his own social history, fight his way gradually past the English and Eng. Lit. identity he had partly adopted, in order to find out who he was. He had purged some of the pain of leaving Wales in *Border Country*, and could now return. That whole dimension enters into *The Country and the City*, a work which he had more trouble in getting finished than probably any other, since its themes touched him to the quick. A new tone, almost a new sensibility or structure of feeling, emerges in that strange, profound, unclassifiable work, which takes a long steady look at the English country estate and reads in its ceremony and elegance one long history of fraud, crime and violence perpetrated against working people. This is a Williams who has now lived through Vietnam and the student movement and the crass utilitarianism of the Labour government, and the change is there in his voice: less courteous, gently reasonable and cautiously circumspect, more dry, steely and sardonic. His writing becomes coldly angry and implacable in those politically turbulent years, and as far as his liberal supporters are concerned he has clearly gone over the edge. 'Sullen' was Frank Kermode's revealing class-epithet for *Modern Tragedy*.

The formal rapprochement with Marxism arrived four years later with *Marxism and Literature*, and the formulation of the doctrine of 'cultural materialism'. But this is done in a way which suggests less that he has finally been appropriated by Marxism than that he has coolly appropriated it. ('Cultural materialism', he declared cautiously, was 'compatible' with Marxism.) He will out-Marxize the Marxists by going the whole hog, extending materialism full-bloodedly to cultural practices too; but in thus pressing Marxist logic to an extreme, he will by the same stroke undo the 'base'/'superstructure' distinction and so retain a certain critical distance. That was always Williams's way: he was not only deeply suspicious of orthodoxies, but rarely even quoted another thinker or paused to note an influence. The work was somehow as much all *his* as the life; he gave off a rock-like sense of self-sufficiency which sometimes merged into solitariness, though he was paradoxically the most social and public figure one could imagine. It was not the quirky introspection of one shut out so much as the arresting originality of one out in front; you had a sense of having struggled through to some theoretical position only to find that Williams had quietly pre-empted you, arriving there by his own personal, meditative route. He was a kind of 'Bakhtinian' social linguist when the Bakhtin industry was still only a gleam in the eye of Slavicist semioticians; he anticipated by several years some of Jürgen Habermas's major theses on communicative action. He wasn't what one would think of as a particularly feminist writer, yet *Second Generation* is as searching a study of the relations between work, politics, sexuality and the family as one could envisage. As early as *The Long Revolution*, well before the emergence of the women's movement, Williams was speaking of the centrality of what he then termed the 'system of generation and nurture', ranking it on a level with the political, economic and cultural spheres. He refused to be distracted by the wilder flights of Althusserian or post-structuralist theory and was still there, ready and waiting for us, when some of us younger theorists, sadder and wiser, finally re-emerged from one or two cul-de-sacs to rejoin him where we had left off. He had seen the 'Road Up' signs, but didn't believe in barracading a route.[1] I don't think I ever heard him use the word 'theory' in the sense current now in left cultural circles, and though he had a large, devoted following throughout the world he never made the slightest attempt to form a 'school'. I have had American left critics beg me to persuade him to visit the United States, where his work has widespread, enthusiastic support, but he refused to do so during the Vietnam war and made only one or two visits there afterwards. He wasn't interested in academic stardom, he had little or no sense of himself as part of a 'profession', and preferred to get on with his work at home.

I think there were limits as well as strengths to this independence. It led him at times into a certain magisterial isolation, imposed the odd Olympian tone or over-defensive gambit on his writing, and frustrated some of his supporters who wished him to launch a more trenchant, collective project. Perhaps he had grown too used to working on his own in the years of adult education; or perhaps he was wary of what had happened at Cambridge to the Scrutineers. Sectarianism bored him, and he had a way of combining the most pluralist, unsectarian approach to politics with a socialist commitment so deep and unyielding that you sometimes felt he literally could not imagine how anyone could believe otherwise. If a contained sardonic anger was one aspect of his work, the other was a trust in human potential so generous and steadfast that he could be almost physically shocked by the political right's routine cynical disparagement of people. This was not some sentimental optimism: there was a hard cool streak of realism about Williams, which came out in some unlikely ways – in his impressive abilities, for example, as an administrator and political coordinator. It was just that he knew from his own experience what ordinary unheroic people were capable of, and it drove him to smouldering fury to hear them slighted and demeaned. Tragedy for him was not the death of princes but the death of his railway signalman father, whom nobody would ever have heard of had it not been for his devoted son. It was not of course that he believed that these fundamental values, of love and compassion and solidarity, would inevitably politically prevail; how could such an astute political analyst in a dark period have credited such a view? It was rather that he refused to be shifted, whatever the immediate loss or set-back, from the faith that these values were in the end the only ones that mattered, that they might not win out but they were what it was all about, that if you abandoned this then you abandoned everything. He had known what community could be, and would not rest until it was recreated on an international scale. He had a remarkably quick sense of how easy it is to blaspheme against humanity, and the best of what he inherited from Leavis could be summarized simply as reverence. He knew from his study of Welsh history what unbelievable fortitude and resilience an oppressed people can manifest in the cruellest condi- tions; and this is one reason why it would not have been possible for him to do what so many have now done, scale down his hopes and trim his political sails, face reality. What he faced *was* for him reality; and his deep personal patience allowed him always to take the long perspective, to avoid, as he once dryly commented, 'making long-term adjustments to short-term problems'.

Some of the borders which Williams respected least were those which ran between conventional academic disciplines. In the end it was impossible to give his project a name: it was not quite sociology or philosophy or literary criticism or political theory, and it was quite as much 'creative' and 'imaginative' writing as academic work. In a list of his own keywords, 'connecting' could come high in the ranks, along with 'active', 'complex', 'difficult', 'changing'. He was a librarian's nightmare, and had been practising the current fashionable deconstruction of the 'creative' and 'theoretical' for a good thirty years. Language was one of his intellec- tual passions from beginning to end, from *Culture and Society* to *Keywords*, but his sense of what it signified ran so deep, shaded off in so many directions, that one hesitated to call him a linguist. Words for him were condensed social practices, sites of historical struggle, repositories of political wisdom or domination; he had a

Celtic feel for them, for their rich texture and density, and he himself spoke pretty much as he wrote, weightily, rhetorically, constructing and composing his speech rather than slinging it provisionally together. If he was a political theorist it was less in the sense of a short-term analyst (though he could organize sharp political interventions on particular issues) than in the manner of the figures from Blake to Morris of his own Culture and Society tradition, prophetically discerning the forms and movements of a whole culture. In this sense he belonged to the lineage of the classical intellectuals, those who eschew a single 'discipline' for a sense of intellectual responsibility to a whole social order; but if he avoided the myopia of the specialist he also sidestepped for the most part the amateur moralism of the traditional sage, if only by virtue of his literary sensitivity to the concrete and particular. Whereas Leavis had accommodated certain social and cultural issues by a literary colonizing of them, Williams came steadily to reverse this logic and 'decentre' literary studies into a wider field of cultural practices; but he never apologized for the fact that his first and persistent interest lay in writing – he simply transfigured the meaning of the category. It was ironic that some colleagues should view him as a reductive 'contents analyst' of literary works, for to him what brought everything together was form. His criticism rescued cultural forms from the formalists and discovered in them structures of social relations, histories of technological possibility, precipitations of whole socially determined ways of seeing. He could trace a change of ideological perception in a shift in stage technique, or detect the rhythms of urbanization in the very syntax of a Victorian novel.

Williams had, I think, an unusually strong sense of himself as an historical figure. If he could be aware of the massive importance of his own work without the least personal vanity, it was in part because he had a curious ability to look on himself from the outside, to see his own life as in a Lukácsian sense 'typical' rather than just individual. He lived everything he did from the inside, saturating his thought with personal experience; yet he also seemed able to place himself impersonally, judiciously, as 'an ordinary life, spanning the middle years of the twentieth century' (*Modern Tragedy*, p. 13). That he was at once ordinary and exceptional was one of the many paradoxes about him. Though he was personally the most generous and humble of men, with a warmth so radiant as to be almost tangible, it was perhaps this 'historicity' which helped more than anything to divide him from his colleagues. They were individual dons, working on this or that; his work was an historic project, of an intensely personal yet strangely impersonal kind. He had a quite extraordinary sense of the overall consistency of that work, and of the life in which it was rooted. He lived his life deliberately, vigilantly, as a committed act or coherent task. Others may write a book or two or even twenty, but Williams was engaged on a different sort of enterprise altogether. You had the strong sense that it would have got done somehow whether he was an academic or not; what some left academics sometimes like to feign – that they are merely passing through the system, dipping in and out, fundamentally detached – was in his case oddly true, even though he spent most of his working life as a Cambridge Fellow. He didn't need to apologize for being a don, in some excess of radical guilt, because it was palpably obvious that that was not at all the centre from which he lived. As far as the dons went, he was quite evidently not their kind of man, which sometimes bemused the well-intentioned and estranged the politically hostile even further. He assumed his place in Cambridge naturally, with dignity, as though he had a right to it, which of course he did; it was somewhere to carry on the work, and he didn't waste time complaining about the incongruities which that brought in its wake. He had the well-nigh universal respect of his colleagues, but not their collaboration; his collaborator from first to last was Joy Williams, 'virtual co-author' of *Culture and Society* as he writes in the preface to that book. The most intense intellectual partnership, and the deepest sharing of personal life and love, would for Williams naturally go together.

Almost single-handedly, he transformed cultural studies from the relative crudity in which he found them to a marvellously rich, resourceful body of work. In doing so, he altered irreversibly the intellectual and political map of Britain, and put hundreds of thousands of students and colleagues and readers enduringly in his debt. He could do this because he never relinquished his belief in the utter centrality of what he liked to call 'meanings and values'. He fought all his life against various left-wing reductions or displacements of these things, and believed that language and communication were where we lived, not just what we used to live. In this sense, he had held all along what some others on the left came gradually to discover sometime later, through Gramsci or discourse theory or psychoanalysis or the 'politics of the subject'. And then, just when everyone else had caught up with him and was busy pressing this case to an idealist extreme, he turned on his heel and began to speak of material modes of cultural production, of the social institutions of writing, of – in a word – cultural materialism. He had got there before us again, as he would no doubt have done several times more, if his premature death had not taken him from us and left us impoverished and bereft.

Note

1   A fuller word of explanation is perhaps in order here. I do not mean to suggest that all of the theoretical developments of this period were by any means cul-de-sacs; and Williams himself, while sharply critical of some of them, drew valuably on others. That his own work benefited from the flowering of a Marxist culture in the 1970s, even when it found itself at odds with some of those currents, is, I think, indisputable. My own critique of Williams's work in *Criticism and Ideology* grew out of those new trends, and was felt by some to be unjust or even faintly scandalous. This was not, for the record, Williams's own view. While dissenting from some of my criticisms, he concurred with others – a logical response from a thinker whose work was in continual evolution, who could himself be astringently critical of some of his own earlier positions, and who welcomed vigorous argument rather than obedient discipleship. Some of those who

generously leapt to his defence at the time, or who still do so, are thus perhaps not entirely at one with his own more shaded, self-critical attitude. I would still defend many of the criticisms I made of Williams's work in *Criticism and Ideology*, though I would advance them today in a more nuanced style, and in a different tone. Some of my formulations, in the struggle to distance myself critically from a body of work which had meant more to me than almost any other, were unacceptably acerbic and ungenerous, and for these I apologize.

24 The Death of Desire: Arthur Schopenhauer

Though Schopenhauer is undoubtedly one of the gloomiest philosophers who ever wrote, there is an unwitting comedy about his work which has to do with the presence of the body within it. Schopenhauer studied physiology at university, and is impressively learned about the lungs and pancreas; indeed it is a striking thought that his choice of university subjects might have reshaped the whole course of Western philosophy right up to the fashionable neo-Nietzscheanisms of our own time. For it is from Schopenhauer's coarsely materialist meditations on the pharynx and the larynx, on cramps, convulsions, epilepsy, tetanus and hydrophobia, that Nietzsche will derive much of his own ruthless physiological reductionism; and all that solemn, archaic nineteenth-century discourse on Man in terms of the ganglia and lumbar regions, which survives at least as long as Lawrence, thus forms a shady hinterland to that resurgence of theoretical interest in the body which has also, in our own epoch, rather more positive and political dimensions.

Schopenahuer is quite unembarrassed to detect his celebrated Will, that blindly persistent desire at the root of all phenomena, in yawning, sneezing and vomiting, in jerkings and twitchings of various kinds, and seems wholly oblivious of the bathos with which his language can veer without warning in the course of a page or so from high-flown reflections on free will to the structure of the spinal cord or the excrescences of the caterpillar. There is a kind of Bakhtinian bathos or Brechtian *plumpes Denken* about this sudden swooping from *Geist* to genitalia, from the oracular to the orificial, which in Bakhtin's hands at least is a political weapon against ruling-class idealism's paranoid fear of the flesh. With Schopenhauer it is less a question of political revolt than of a kind of cracker-barrel crassness, as when he solemnly illustrates the conflict between body and intellect by pointing out that people find it hard to walk and talk at the same time: 'For as soon as their brain has to link a few ideas together, it no longer has as much force left over as is required to keep the legs in motion through the motor nerves.'[1] Elsewhere he speculates that the boundless, infinite objective world 'is really only a certain movement or affection of the pulpy mass in the skull' (2, 273), or suggests that a short stature and neck are especially favourable to genius, 'because on the shorter path the blood reaches the brain with more energy' (2, 393). All of this vulgar literalism is a kind of theoretical posture in itself, a sardonic smack at high-toned Hegelianism from one who, though a full-blooded metaphysician himself, regards Hegel as a supreme charlatan and most philosophy except Plato, Kant and himself as a lot of hot air. Crotchety, arrogant and cantankerous, a scathing Juvenilian satirist who professes to believe that the Germans need their long words because it gives their slow minds more time to think, Schopenhauer's work reveals a carnivalesque coupling of the imposing and the commonplace evident in his very name.

Indeed incongruity becomes in Schopenhauer's hands the basis for a full-blown theory of comedy. The ludicrous, so he argues, springs from the paradoxical subsumption of an object under a concept in other ways heterogeneous to it, so that an Adorno-like insistence on the non-identity of object and concept can come to explain why animals cannot laugh. Humour, in this speciously generalizing view, is by and large high words and low meanings, and so like Schopenhauer's own philosophy has an ironic or dialogical structure. This is itself profoundly ironic, since the discrepancy between percept and concept which occasions the release of laughter is exactly that disjuncture between experience and intellect, or will and representation, which lies at the very core of Schopenhauer's disgusted view of humanity. The inner structure of this bleakest of visions is thus the structure of a joke. Reason, that crude, blundering servant of the imperious will, is always pathetic false consciousness, a mere reflex of desire which believes itself absurdly to present the world just as it is. Concepts, in a familiar brand of nineteenth-century irrationalism, cannot cling to the rich intricacies of experience, but appear maladroit and crudely reductive. But if this fissures the very being of humanity into illusion, so that merely to think is to be self-deceived, it also provides the elements of a Freudian theory of humour:

> [Perception] is the medium of the present, of enjoyment and cheerfulness; moreover it is not associated with any exertion. With thinking the opposite holds good; it is the second power of knowledge, whose exercise always requires some, often considerable, exertion; and it is the concepts of thinking that are so often opposed to the satisfaction of our immediate desires, since, as the medium of the past, of the future, and of what is serious, they act as the vehicle of our fears, our regrets, and all our cares. It must therefore be delightful for us to see this strict, untiring, and most troublesome governess, our faculty of reason, for once convicted of inadequacy. Therefore on this account the mien or appearance of laughter is very closely related to that of joy. (2, 98)

Comedy is the will's mocking revenge on the representation, the malicious strike of the Schopenhaurian id against the Hegelian superego; and this source of hilarity is also, curiously, the root of our utter hopelessness.[2]

If humour and hopelessness lie so close together, it is because human existence for Schopenhauer is less grand tragedy than squalid farce. Writhing in the toils of the voracious will, driven on by an implacable appetite they relentlessly idealize, men and women are less tragic protagonists than pitiably obtuse. The most fitting emblem of the human enterprise is the shovel-pawed mole: 'to dig strenuously with its enormous shovel-paws is the business of its whole life; permanent night surrounds it . . . what does it attain by this course of life that is full of trouble and devoid of pleasure? Nourishment and procreation, that is, only the means for continuing and beginning again in the new individual the same melancholy course' (2, 353–4). Nothing could be more obvious to Schopenhauer than the fact that it would be infinitely preferable if the world did not exist at all, that the whole project is a ghastly mistake which should long ago have been called off, and that only some crazed idealism could possibly believe the pleasures of existence to outweigh its pains. Only the most blatant self-delusion – ideas, values, the rest of that pointless paraphernalia – could blind individuals to this laughably self-evident truth. Sunk in its gross stupidity, humanity insists upon regarding as valuable a history which is so plainly the record of carnage, misery and wretchedness that our capacity to think it in the least tolerable must itself be explicable only as a ruse of the will, the low cunning with which it shields itself from our knowledge of its own futility. It is hard for Schopenhauer to restrain a burst of hysterical laughter at the sight of this pompously self-important race, gripped by a remorseless will-to-live which is secretly quite indifferent to any of them, piously convinced of their own supreme value, scrambling over each other in pursuit of some earnest goal which will turn instantly to ashes in their mouths. The world is one enormous market place, 'this world of constantly needy creatures who continue for a time merely by devouring one another, pass their existence in anxiety and want, and often endure terrible afflictions, until they fall at last into the arms of death' (2, 349). There is no grand *telos* to this 'battle-ground of tormented and agonized beings' (2, 581), only 'momentary gratification, fleeting pleasure conditioned by wants, much and long suffering, constant struggle, *bellum omnium*, everything a hunter and everything hunted, pressure, want, need and anxiety, shrieking and howling; and this goes on *in saecula saeculorum* or until once again the crust of the planet breaks' (2, 354). If human beings were capable of contemplating objectively for one moment this perverse attachment of theirs to unhappiness, they would necessarily abhor it. The whole race is like a diseased beggar who appeals to us for help to prolong his miserable existence, even though from an objective viewpoint his death would be altogether desirable. Only some sentimental humanism could see such a judgement as callous rather than coolly reasonable. The most fortunate life is that with endurable want and comparative painlessness, though the result of this is boredom. Boredom for Schopenhauer is the chief motive for sociality, since it is to avoid it that we seek out each other's loveless company. All of this sets the scene for high tragedy, yet even that we bungle: 'our life must contain all the woes of tragedy, and yet we cannot even assert the dignity of tragic characters, but, in the broad detail of life, are inevitably the foolish characters of a comedy' (1, 322). History is low burlesque rather than Attic solemnity: 'no-one has the remotest idea why the whole tragi-comedy exists, for it has no spectators, and the actors themselves undergo

endless worry with little and merely negative enjoyment' (2, 357). Life is a grotesquely bad absurdist drama full of farcical repetition, a set of trivial variations on
a shoddy script.

There is something amusing about the very relentless consistency of this
Schopenhauerian gloom, a perpetual grousing with all the monotonous, mechanical
repetition of the condition it denounces. If comedy for Schopenhauer involves
subsuming objects to inappropriate concepts, then this is ironically true of his own
pessimism, which stamps everything with its own inexorable colour and so has the
funniness of all monomania. Any such obsessive conversion of difference to identity is bound to be comic, however tragic the actual outlook. To see no difference
between roasting a leg of lamb and roasting a baby, to view both as mere indifferent
expressions of the metaphysical will, is as risible as mistaking one's left foot for the
notion of natural justice. Part of our laughter at such remorseless tunnel vision is no
doubt relief at the wanton parade of a monstrous egoism we ourselves have had
to camouflage – though in the case of a pervasively pessimistic vision like
Schopenhauer's such laughter may contain a nervously defensive quality too. His
perverse ignoring of what we feel to be the more positive aspects of life is outrageous enough to be amusing, as we would smile at someone whose only interest in
great painters was in how many of them had halitosis.

Schopenhauer's intense pessimism, however, is in one sense not in the least
outrageous – is, indeed, no more than the sober realism he himself considers it to
be. One-sided though this viewpoint may be, it is a fact that throughout class
history the fate of the great majority of men and women has been one of suffering
and fruitless toil. Schopenhauer may not have all of the truth; but he has a larger
share of it than the romantic humanists he is out to discredit. Any more hopeful
view of humanity which has not reckoned his particular narrative into account is
bound to be enfeebled. The dominant tale of history to date has indeed been one of
carnage, misery and oppression. Moral virtue has never flourished as the decisive
force in any political culture. Where such values have taken precarious root, they
have been largely confined to the private realm. The monotonous driving forces of
history have been enmity, appetite and dominion; and the scandal of that sordid
heritage is that it is indeed possible to ask of the lives of innumerable individuals
whether they would not have been better off dead. Any degree of freedom, dignity
and comfort has been confined to a tiny minority, while indigence, unhappiness and
hard labour have been the lot of the vast majority. 'To enter at the age of five a
cotton-spinning or other factory', Schopenhauer remarks, 'and from then on to sit
there every day first ten, then twelve, and finally fourteen hours, and perform the
same mechanical work, is to purchase dearly the pleasure of drawing breath' (2,
578). The dramatic mutations of human history, its epochal ruptures and upheavals, have been in one sense mere variations on a consistent theme of exploitation and
oppression. Nor could any future transformation, however radical, affect this
record in any substantial way. For all Walter Benjamin's efforts to raise the dead
themselves with the clarion call of his eloquence, for all his urgent attempts to

muster around the frail band of the living the fertilizing shades of the unjustly quelled, it remains the harsh truth that the dead can be raised only in revolutionary imagination.[3] There is no literal way in which we can compensate them for the sufferings they received at the hands of the ruling order. We cannot recall the crushed medieval peasantry or the wage-slaves of early industrial capitalism, the children who died afraid and unloved in the wretched hovels of class society, the women who broke their backs for regimes which used them with arrogance and contempt, the colonized nations which collapsed under an oppressor who found them at once sinister and charming. There is no literal way in which the shades of these dead can be summoned to claim justice from those who abused them. The pastness of the past is the simple truth that, rewrite and recuperate them as we may, the wretched of history have passed away, and will not share in any more compassionate social order we may be able to create. For all its homespun eccentricity and obdurate monomania, Schopenhauer's appalling vision is accurate in many of its essentials. He is mistaken to think that the destructive will is all there is; but there is a sense in which he is correct to see it as the *essence* of all history to date. This is not a truth particularly palatable to political radicals, even if it is in one sense the very motivation of their practice. That this intolerable narrative cannot continue is the belief which inspires their struggle, even as the crippling burden of that history would seem to bear mute witness against the feasibility of such a faith. The source of energy of a radical politics is thus always the potential source of its enervation.

Schopenhauer is perhaps the first major modern thinker to place at the centre of his work the abstract category of *desire itself*, irrespective of this or that particular hankering. It is this powerful abstraction which psychoanalysis will later inherit, though it is probable that Freud, who was said to consider Schopenhauer one of the half-dozen greatest individuals who had ever lived, came to know his work only after his own theories were already formed. Just as capitalist society is in this period evolving to the point where it will be possible for Marx to extract from it the key concept of abstract labour, a conceptual operation only possible on the basis of certain material conditions, so the determinant role and regular repetition of appetite in bourgeois society now permits a dramatic theoretical shift: the construction of desire as a thing in itself, a momentous metaphysical event or self-identical force, as against some earlier social order in which desire is still too narrowly particularistic, too intimately bound up with local or traditional obligation, to be reified in quite this way. With Schopenhauer, desire has become the protagonist of the human theatre, and human subjects themselves its mere obedient bearers or underlings. This is not only because of the emergence of a social order in which, in the form of commonplace possessive individualism, appetite is now becoming the order of the day, the ruling ideology and dominant social practice; it is more specifically because of the perceived *infinity* of desire in a social order where the only end of accumulation is to accumulate afresh. In a traumatic collapse of teleology, desire comes to seem independent of any particular ends, or at least as grotesquely disproportionate to them; and once it thus ceases to be (in the phenomenological sense) intentional, it begins monstrously to obtrude itself as a *Ding-an-sich*, an opaque, unfathomable, self-propelling power utterly without purpose or reason, like some grisly caricature of the deity. The Schopenhauerian will, as a form of purposiveness without purpose, is in this sense a savage travesty of the Kantian aesthetic, a shoddy, inferior artefact we could all well do without.

Once desire is for the first time homogenized as a singular entity, it can become the object of moral judgement as such – a move which would have seemed quite unintelligible to those moralists for whom there is no such phenomenon as 'desire', simply this or that particular appetency on which a particular judgement may be passed. If desire becomes hypostasized in this way, then it is possible, in a long Romantic-libertarian lineage from William Blake to Gilles Deleuze, to view it as supremely positive; but the preconditions of such Romantic affirmation are also the preconditions of the Schopenhauerian denunciation of desire *tout court*, accepting the categories of Romantic humanism but impudently inverting the valuations. Like Schopenhauer, you can retain the whole totalizing apparatus of bourgeois humanism at its most affirmative – the singular central principle informing the whole of reality, the integrated cosmic whole, the stable relations of phenomena and essence – while mischievously emptying these forms of their idealized content. You can drain off the ideological substance of the system – freedom, justice, reason, progress – and fill that system, still intact, with the actual degraded materials of everyday bourgeois existence. This, precisely, is what Schopenhauer's notion of the will achieves, which structurally speaking serves just the function of the Hegelian Idea or Romantic life-force, but is now nothing more than the uncouth rapacity of the average bourgeois, elevated to cosmic status and transformed to the prime metaphysical mover of the entire universe. It is as though one retained the whole paraphernalia of the Platonic Ideas but called them Profit, Philistinism, Self-Interest and so on.

The result of this move is ambivalent. On the one hand, it naturalizes and universalizes bourgeois behaviour: everything from the forces of gravity to the blind stirrings of the polyp or rumblings of the gut is invested with futile craving, the whole world recast in the image of the market place. On the other hand, this grandly generalizing gesture serves to discredit bourgeois Man all the more thoroughly, write him repellently large, project his sordid appetites as the very stuff of the cosmos. To reduce Man to the polyp is at once to exculpate him as a helpless puppet of the will, and to insult him. This debunking shakes bourgeois ideology to the root, at the same time as its naturalizing effect removes the hope of any historical alternative. Schopenhauer's system thus stands at the cusp of bourgeois historical fortunes, still confident enough in its *forms* to unify, essentialize, universalize, but precisely through these gestures inflating to intolerable proportions the meagre *contents* of social life. Those contents are thus discredited by the very move which grants them metaphysical status. The forms of the Hegelian system are turned against that philosophy with a vengeance; totalization is still possible, but now of a purely negative kind.

This is also true in another sense. For Hegel, the free subject articulates a universal dimension of consciousness (*Geist*) which is nevertheless at the very core of its identity, that which makes it uniquely what it is. And this transcendental principle, in order to be itself, stands in need of such individuation. Schopenhauer preserves this conceptual structure but lends it a malevolent twist. What makes me what I am, the will of which I am simply a materialization, is utterly indifferent to my individual identity, which it uses merely for its own pointless self-reproduction. At the very root of the human subject lies that which is implacably alien to it, so that in a devastating irony this will which is the very pith of my being, which I can feel from the inside of my body with incomparably greater immediacy than I can know anything else, is absolutely unlike me at all, without consciousness or motive, as blankly unfeeling and anonymous as the force which stirs the waves. No more powerful image of alienation could be imagined than this malicious parody of idealist humanism, in which the Kantian *Ding-an-sich* is brought nearer to knowledge as the directly intuitable interior of the subject, but nevertheless retains all the impenetrability to reason of that Kantian realm. This impenetrability is no longer a simple epistemological fact but an inert, intolerable weight of meaninglessness that we bear inside ourselves as the very principle of our being, as though permanently pregnant with monsters. Alienation lies now not in some oppressive mechanism out there in the world, which confiscates our products and identities, but in the mildest motions of our limbs and language, in the faintest flicker of curiosity or compassion, in all that makes us living, breathing, desiring creatures. What is now irreparably flawed is nothing less than the whole category of subjectivity itself, not just some perversion or estrangement of it. It is this which touches on the guilty secret or impossible paradox of bourgeois society, that it is exactly in their freedom that men and women are most inexorably enchained, that we live immured in our bodies like lifers in a cell. Subjectivity is that which we can least call our own. There was a time when our desires, however destructive, could at least be called ours; now desire breeds in us an illusion known as reason, in order to con us that its goals are ours too.

It is not that Schopenhauer ignores the will's more creative aspects. If yawning or yodelling are expressions of the will, so are all our nobler aspirations; but since they are thus caught up with desire they are part of the problem rather than the solution. To fight injustice is to desire, and so to be complicit with that deeper injustice which is human life. Only by somehow breaking absolutely with this chain of causality, the terrible sway of teleology, could true emancipation be achieved. Every bit of the world, from doorknobs and doctoral dissertations to modes of production and the law of the excluded middle, is the fruit of some stray appetite locked into the great empire of intentions and effects; human beings themselves are just walking materializations of their parents' copulatory instincts. The world is one vast externalization of a useless passion, and that alone is real. Since all desire is founded in lack, all desire is suffering: 'All *willing* springs from lack, from deficiency, and thus from suffering' (1, 196). Riddled by the will, the human race is creased over some central absence like a man doubled up over his ulcer; and

Schopenhauer is well aware of how, in modern psychoanalytical idiom, desire outstrips need. 'For one wish that is fulfilled there remain at least ten that are denied. Further, desiring lasts a long time, demands and requests go on to infinity; fulfilment is short and meted out sparingly' (1, 196). It is not therefore for the more creative impulses that we should be searching – not a matter, as with traditional morality, of ranging our desires on an evaluative scale and pitting the more positive against the more destructive. Only the quiescence of impulse itself would save us; yet to *seek* such quiescence, in a familiar Buddhist paradox, would be self-defeating.

Where then can we turn for a momentary staunching of this insatiable urge which builds the very stuff of our blood-stream and intestines? The answer for Schopenhauer is to the aesthetic, which signifies less a preoccupation with art than a transfigured attitude to reality. The intolerable tedium of existence is that we can never burst out of our own skins, never shuck off the straitjacket of our petty subjective interests. We drag our egos with us in everything we do, like some bar-room bore intruding his dreary obsessions into the most casual conversation. Desire denotes our inability to see anything straight, the compulsive referring of all objects to our own sectarian interests. Passion 'tinges the objects of knowledge with its colour' (2, 141), falsifying the given through hope, anxiety, expectation; and Schopenhauer gives us a home-spun little instance of this victory of will over intellect by gravely pointing out how, when we do our financial accounts, the unconscious slips we make are almost always to our own advantage. The aesthetic is a temporary escape from this prison-house of subjectivity, in which all desire drops away from us and we are able for a change to see the phenomenon as it really is. As we relinquish our heated claims over it, we dissolve contentedly into a pure, will-less subject of knowledge. But to become a pure subject of knowledge is paradoxically to cease to be a subject at all, to know oneself utterly decentred into the objects of one's contemplation. The gift of genius, Schopenhauer writes, is nothing more or less than the most complete objectivity. The aesthetic is what ruptures for a blessed moment the terrible sway of teleology, the tangled chain of functions and effects into which all things are locked, plucking an object for an instant out of the clammy grip of the will and savouring it purely as spectacle. (Dutch interiors, Schopenhauer argues, are flawed aesthetic objects, since their portrayal of oysters, herrings, crabs, wine and so on makes us hungry.) The world can be released from desire only by being aestheticized; and in this process the desiring subject will dwindle to a vanishing point of pure disinterestedness. But such disinterestedness has little in common with an Arnoldian large-mindedness, impartially weighing competing interests with an eye to the affirmative whole; on the contrary, it demands nothing less than a complete self-abandonment, a kind of serene self-immolation on the subject's part.

It is really rather too easy, however, to regard this doctrine as mere escapism. For the Buddhist tradition to which Schopenhauer is here indebted, nothing could be more bafflingly elusive than this apparently straightforward matter of seeing something as it is, a naive realism or (as Heidegger might say) a 'letting of things be' which is never really within our power, and which can occur only spontaneously in a stray moment of mystical illumination. Nor is such realism for Schopenhauer any mere positivism: on the contrary, he is a full-blooded Platonist on that score, holding that to see things as they are is to grasp them in their eternal essences or species-being. It is this well-nigh impossible realism we can attain in the blessed indifference of the aesthetic – that state in which the world is transmuted to theatrical charade, its shrieking and howling stilled to so much idle stage chatter for the unmoved spectator's delighted contemplation. The aesthetic is in this sense a kind of psychical defence mechanism by which the mind, threatened with an overload of pain, converts the cause of its agony into innocuous illusion. The sublime is therefore the most typical of all aesthetic moods, allowing us as it does to contemplate hostile objects with absolute equanimity, serene in the knowledge that they can no longer harm us. In the sublime, the paranoid ego fantasizes some state of triumphal invulnerability, wreaking Olympian vengeance on the sinister forces which would hound it to death. But this ultimate mastery, in which a predatory world is disarmed to a kind of fiction, is itself, as Freud taught us, the condition of death, towards which the battered, pitiable ego is driven for its ultimate self-preservation. The Schopenhauerian subject thus masters its own murder by suicide, outwits its predators through the premature self-abnegation of the aesthetic. The Schopenhauerian aesthetic is the death drive in action, though this death is secretly a kind of life, *Eros* disguised as *Thanatos*: the subject cannot be entirely negated as long as it still delights, even if what it takes pleasure in is the process of its own dissolution. The aesthetic condition thus presents an unsurmountable paradox, as Keats knew in contemplating the nightingale: there is no way in which one can savour one's own extinction. The more exultantly the aesthetic subject experiences its own nullity before the object the more, by that very token, the experience must have failed.

Indifference for Schopenhauer is a political as well as an aesthetic state of being; and to this extent he sustains, while also subverting, the classical Schillerian concept of art as social paradigm. For Schopenhauer as for his predecessors, the aesthetic is important because it speaks of more than itself. The detachment or ataraxia we attain for a precious moment in contemplating the artefact is an implicit alternative to appetitive egoism; art is no mere antithesis to society, but the most graphic instance of an ethical existence beyond the understanding of the state. Only by somehow piercing the veil of *Maya* and recognizing the fictional status of the individual ego can one behave to others with true indifference – which is to say, make no significant distinction between them and oneself. Satiric detachment is thus at the same time loving compassion, a state in which, the *principium individuationis* once unmasked for the ideological fraud it is, selves may be empathetically exchanged. Just as all true knowledge springs from the death of the subject, so too does all moral value; to act morally is not to act from a positive standpoint, but to act from no standpoint at all. The only good subject is a dead one, or at least one which can project itself by empathetic indifference into the place of every other. It is not a question of one individual behaving considerately towards the next, but of bursting beyond the whole wretched delusion of 'individuality', in a flash of what Walter Benjamin would call 'profane illumination', to some non-place unutterably far beyond it. Schopenhauer is thus led beyond the apparatus of bourgeois legality, of rights and responsibilities and obligations, since he rejects its prime datum of the individual subject. Unlike the fetishists of difference of our own day, he believes that what human beings share in common is ultimately of more substance than what distinguishes them.

Moral action, like aesthetic knowledge, would thus appear an unthinkable paradox. For there can be no practice without a subject; and with subjects come domination and desire. To speak of a compassionate subject would seem oxymoronic: even if a purely contemplative benevolence were possible, it could only realize itself in action at the cost of falling prey to the voracious will. Knowledge and practice would appear as ironically at odds for Schopenhauer as 'theory' and 'ideology' for some contemporary thought: if there can be no truth without a subject, there can be none with it either. All practice for Schopenhauer inhabits the domain of illusion: to prosecute my pity for you is in that moment to dispel it, to find myself writhing instead in the toils of self-interest. Only by transcending the diseased category of subjecthood altogether could one individual feel for another; but this very proposition cancels itself out. As William Blake knew, pity and sorrow are signs that the catastrophe has already happened, and would be unnecessary if it had not. In a society powered by appetite, where all action appears irredeemably contaminated, compassion must be banished to the realm of 'aesthetic' contemplation. In one sense, the aesthetic offers us a whole new form of social life: in its very dispassionate amorality, it teaches us to shed our disruptive desires and live humbly, ungreedily, with the simplicity of the saint. It is thus the first faint glimmerings of utopia, bearing with it a perfect, virulently misanthropic happiness. But this is not a happiness which could ever be actively realized: like the aesthetic state of a Schiller, it betrays and undoes itself as soon as it enters upon material existence.

It is in any case difficult to know how this state of disinterestedness could ever come about. It can obviously not be a product of the will, since it involves the will's momentary suspension; but it is hard to see how it can be the work of the alienated intellect either, and in Schopenhauer's drastically reduced universe there are really no other agents available. He himself writes obscurely of the intellect achieving in these moments a certain 'temporary preponderance' over the will; but the sources of this unwonted reversal remain significantly vague. There *is* positive value in bourgeois society, but its origins are deeply mysterious. As with the early Wittgenstein, himself a devoted disciple of Schopenhauer, value cannot really be *in* the world at all, but must be transcendental of it.[4] There is, it would seem, no way of shifting from fact to value; and Schopenhauer consequently manoeuvres himself into an inexplicable duality between the torture chamber of history on the one hand, and some vaguely Humean notion of intuitive affection on the other. In such compassion for others, he writes, we recognize our 'true and innermost self'; yet we have been told time and again that this innermost self is nothing but the ravenous will.

Schopenhauer is adamant that philosophy is quite incapable of altering human conduct, and disowns all prescriptive intent in his writing. There can be no truck between the cognitive and the ethical, which partake in the eternal enmity of the representation and the will. Yet his whole philosophy can be read as an implicit disproval of this claim, suggesting against its own conscious intentions how fact and value, description and prescription may indeed be mutually articulated. In fact his indebtedness to oriental thought betrays just how ethnocentric the fact/value dichotomy is – how deeply the consequence of a technological history from which it is admittedly impossible to derive value, since its facts have been constituted from the outset as value's very negation. The Buddhist critique of the principle of individuation, by contrast, is at once descriptive and prescriptive – an account of the way the world is, as well as, indissociably, the recommendation of a certain style of moral behaviour. It is hard to see how a genuine conviction of the relative insignificance of distinctions between selves could not affect one's practical conduct. Schopenhauer would seem to agree that a recognition of the fictional nature of identity will show up in one's actions, while refusing to acknowledge that his own discourse, which speaks of these matters, might produce such ethical effects.

To do otherwise would be to concede, contrary to one of his major tenets, that reason can influence the will. On such a remorselessly instrumentalist version of reason as Schopenhauer's, this would be clearly impossible. Reason is no more than a clumsy calculative device for the realization of desires which are themselves quite insulated from rational debate. The lineage from Schopenhauer and Nietzsche to contemporary pragmatism in this sense reduplicates the bourgeois model of appetitive man of Hobbes, Hume and Bentham. Reason is the mere tool of interest and slave of desire – interests and desires over which there can be fighting but no arguing. But if what Schopenhauer asserts on this score were true, his own work would be strictly speaking impossible. If he really credited his own doctrines, Schopenhauer would be unable to write. If his theory is able to dissect the insidious workings of the will, then reason must be to that extent capable of curving back on itself, scrutinizing the drives of which it proclaims itself the obedient servant. Either he has somehow given the will the slip in his theorizing, or that theorizing is just another of its futile expressions and so quite valueless.

Schopenhauer's comparison of philosophy with music suggests that he believes the former possibility to be the true one. Of all the arts, music is the most direct presentation of the will; indeed it is the will made audible, a kind of delicate, impalpable diagram of the inner life of desire, a revelation in non-conceptual discourse of the pure essence of the world. Any true philosophy is thus no more than a translation into conceptual terms of what speaks in music, performing rationally what music achieves intuitively. A theory which knew the world as it is would thus be characterized by a kind of aesthetic completion, would be an artefact all in itself, resisting discursive divisions and deferments so as to represent in its synchronic unity the cohesion of all things in the will. Philosophy must thus be transcendental; yet the only transcendental reality it seems to identify is the will itself. It cannot be that philosophy looks at the world from the vantage point of the will, for then it would be unable to pass any true comment on it; so it would appear to be inspecting the will and all its works from some other transcendental view-point. But since there is no such viewpoint acknowledged in Schopenhauer's writing, philosophy must be standing in a non-place, speaking from some location not included within itself. There is indeed such a non-place identified in the theory itself – the aesthetic – but this is not conceptual; and it is hard to see how it can be conceptually translated without falling instantly foul of the delusions of the intel-lect. In short, truth would appear to be possible, but we are quite at a loss to account for how this can be so. It can only be that the intellect, in rare, mysterious moments, seizes a precarious hold on the will of which it is no more than a manipulated plaything. These are epistemological dilemmas which Schopenhauer will bequeath to his most famous successor, Friedrich Nietzsche.

Bourgeois thought tends to construct a recurrent binary opposition between knowledge as the sheer determined reflex of desire, and knowledge as a form of sublime disinterestedness. If the former caricatures the true state of affairs of bourgeois civil society, where no reflection would seem innocent of self-interest, the latter is no more than its fantastic negation. Only a demonic desire could dream such an angelic antithesis. As an increasingly reified, fragmented social order comes gradually to discredit the idea of its own intelligibility, sublime disinterestedness must be progressively surrendered to pragmatist disenchantment. The price of this, however, is that any more ambitious ideological defence of the society as a whole, uncoupled as it is from particular interests, steadily loses its hold upon social practice. Schopenhauer and Nietzsche are transitional figures in this respect, full-blooded totalizers in one sense yet disenchanted pragmatists in another. Caught in this contradiction, Schopenhauer ends up with a kind of transcendentalism without a subject: the place of absolute knowledge is preserved, but it lacks all determinate identity. There can be no subject to fill it, for to be a subject is to desire, and to desire is to be deluded. An idealist philosophy which once dreamt of finding salvation through the subject is now forced to contemplate the unspeakable pros-pect that no salvation is possible without the wholesale immolation of the subject itself, the most privileged category of the entire system.

In one sense, of course, such an abject surrender of the subject is no more than a routine feature of the bourgeois social order. Schopenhauer's empathetic ethics serialize all individuals to equal exchangeability in much the same manner as the market place, if at a somewhat loftier level. In this most rampantly individualist of cultures, the individual is indeed little more than a fiction, given the blank indiffer-ence to it of the capitalist economy. It is simply that this prosaic levelling of individual specificity must now be sublated to a form of spiritual communion, disdainfully turned (as in the Kantian aesthetic) against the practical egoism which is in truth its material foundation. It is as though the cool disregard for specific identities displayed by the capitalist mode of production must be dignified to a spiritual discipline, elevated to a tender mutuality of souls. Yet if this desperate strategy mimes the problem to which it is a solution, its radicalism is at least equally striking. Once the actual bourgeois subject, rather than its high-minded idealist representation, is placed *à la* Schopenhauer at the nub of theory, there seems no way of avoiding the conclusion that it must be liquidated. There can be no question any longer of judicious reform: nothing short of that revolution of the subject which is its mystical obliteration will serve to liberate it from itself. The philosophy of subjectivity accordingly self-destructs, leaving in its wake a numinous aura of absolute value which is, precisely, nothing.

Enthusiastic Kantian though he is, the aesthetic for Schopenhauer signifies in one sense the exact opposite of what it means for his mentor. For Kant, as we have seen, the disinterested gaze which reads the world purely as form is a way of eliciting the object's enigmatic purposiveness, lifting it out of the web of practical functions in which it is enmeshed so as to endow it with something of the self-determining autonomy of a subject. It is by virtue of this crypto-subjectivity that Kant's aesthetic object 'hails' individuals, speaks meaningfully to them, assures them that Nature is not after all entirely alien to their preoccupations. For Schopenhauer, things are quite otherwise: what we glimpse in the aesthetic realm is not yet another image of our own intolerable subjectivity, but a reality benignly indifferent to our longings. If for Kant the aesthetic works within the register of the imaginary, it involves for his successor a gratifying shift to the symbolic, where we can come finally to accept that the object turns its back upon us, has no need of us, and is all the better for that. It is as though, having himself relentlessly anthropo-morphized the whole of reality, discerning analogies of human appetite in the falling of a stone or the blowing of a rose, Schopenhauer's nausea with that whole monstrously humanized world compels him to imagine how delightful it would be to look at things as though we were not there. Yet this, of course, is beyond our reach: the dissolution of the grasping ego, as we have seen, is also, unavoidably, the ego's exultant fantasy of securing an eternal, uninjured existence for itself. Perhaps, then, the aesthetic is no more than the last reckless card the will to live has to play, just as for Schopenhauer suicide is simply a sick joke by which the will craftily affirms itself through the individual's self-annihilation.

The dream of transcending one's own petty subjecthood is a familiar enough idealist fantasy; but it generally turns out to involve a flight into some higher, deeper form of subjectivity, with a corresponding gain of omnipotent mastery. One does not give the slip to the subject simply by collectivizing or universalizing it. Schopenhauer, however, sees that since the subject *is* its particular perspective, all that can be left behind when this has been surmounted is a kind of nothing: the nirvana of aesthetic contemplation. Even this nothing turns out to be a kind of something, a negative form of knowledge; but at least one has now shed the illusion of a positive mode of transcendence. All that is left to us is to take pity on the objects of the world, infected as they are by our own contagious yearnings, and save them from ourselves by some miraculous vanishing trick. What is from one viewpoint an irresponsible escapism is thus from another viewpoint the last word in moral heroism.

It is in the body, above all, that for Schopenhauer the impossible dilemmas of existence take on flesh. For it is in the body that we are most starkly confronted with the clash between the two utterly incompatible worlds in which we live simultaneously. In a rewriting of Kant's celebrated dualism, the body which we live from the inside is will, whereas the body as an object among others is representation. The human subject, that is, lives a unique double relation to its own body as at once noumenal and phenomenal; the flesh is the shadowy frontier where will and representation, inside and outside, come mysteriously, unthinkably together, converting human beings to a kind of walking philosophical conundrum. There is an unspannable gulf between our immediate presence to ourselves, and our indirect representational knowledge of everything else. This, of course, is the most banal of Romantic dichotomies; but Schopenhauer lends it an original inflection. If he privileges the inward in Romantic style, he nevertheless refuses to valorize it. This swift, unmediated knowledge of ourselves, far from signifying some ideal truth, is nothing other than our anguished apprehension of the appetitive will. There is indeed a style of cognition which by-passes the uncertain labours of the concept, but it delivers no value whatsoever. My intuitive presence to myself is the site of a problem, not of some logocentric solution; and in any case I can know the will at work within my body only phenomenally, never in itself. But if the spontaneous and immediate are thus brusquely uncoupled from creativity, one of the central aestheticizing strategies of bourgeois idealism is cancelled at a stroke. It is not, for Schopenhauer, a question of elevating a valued form of cognition over a valueless one, but of suspending the whole question of value itself, inextricably bound up as it is with the terrorism of desire. The only true value would be to abolish value altogether. This, indeed, is the valueless value of the aesthetic state – the insight that things just are eternally what they are, the mind-bending drama of an object's sheer identity with itself. To acknowledge this entails a kind of intuition; but it is intuition to the second power, a will-less overcoming of the spontaneous movement of will, which allows us to gaze unmoved for a moment into the very heart of darkness as the objects around us grow more luminously replete, more satisfyingly pointless, and we ourselves dwindle gradually away to nothing.

Despite its dispassionateness, the aesthetic would seem best figured by either weeping or laughing. If it signifies an infinite fellow-feeling for others, it is also the incredulous cackle of one who has extricated himself from the whole squalid melodrama and surveys it from an Olympian height. These antithetical responses are deeply interrelated, in the tragicomedy of the Schopenhauerian vision: I suffer with you because I know that your inner stuff, the cruel will, is also my own; but since everything is built from this lethal substance, I scorn its futility in a burst of blasphemous laughter. The aesthetic is the noblest form of cognitive and ethical truth; but what it tells us is that reason is useless and emancipation inconceivable. As an aporetic state in which one is simultaneously alive and dead, moved and unmoved, fulfilled and erased, it is a condition which has gone beyond all conditions, a solution which testifies in its very contradictoriness to the impossibility of a solution. Schopenhauer's work is thus the ruin of all those high hopes which bourgeois idealism has invested in the idea of the aesthetic, even though it remains faithful to the aesthetic as some ultimate redemption. A discourse which began as an idiom of the body has now become a flight from corporeal existence; a disinterestedness which promised the possibility of an alternative social order is now an alternative to history itself. By some curious logic, the aesthetic has ended up demolishing the very category of subjectivity it was intended to foster. The embarrassing rift in a Kant or Schiller between the actual and the ideal, civil society and aesthetic *Gemeinschaft*, has now been pressed to a destructive extreme, as any practical connection between the two spheres is summarily rejected. Schopenhauer tells in his own dourly universalizing way the plain, unvarnished tale of bourgeois civil society, in fine disregard for the affirmative ideological glosses; and he is clear-eyed and courageous enough to pursue the grim implications of this narrative to their scandalous, insupportable conclusions.

Notes

1   Arthur Schopenhauer, *The World as Will and Representation*, trans. E. F. J. Payne (New York, 1969), vol. 2, p. 284. All subsequent references to this work are given after quotations in the text.

2   See also, for one of numerous anticipations of Freud, Schopenhauer's comment that 'the intellect remains so much excluded from the real resolutions and secret decisions of its own will that sometimes it can only get to know them, like those of a stranger, by spying out and taking unawares; and it must surprise the will in the act of expressing itself, in order merely to discover its real intentions' (2, 209).

3   See Walter Benjamim, 'Theses on the Philosophy of History', in Hannah Arendt (ed.), *Illuminations* (London, 1970).

4   For the influence of Schopenhauer on Wittgenstein, see Patrick Gardiner, *Schopenhauer* (Harmondsworth, 1963), pp. 275–82, and Brian Magee, *The Philosophy of Schopenhauer* (Oxford, 1983), pp. 286–315. A somewhat threadbare account of Schopenhauer's aesthetics is to be found in I. Knox, *The Aesthetic Theories of Kant, Hegel, and Schopenhauer* (New York, 1958).

25   My Wittgenstein

How do you photograph ideas? What colour and texture are concepts? If these are relevant queries for a film about Ludwig Wittgenstein, it is not least because the early Wittgenstein was himself much preoccupied with the gap between showing and saying. Language could manifest in its inmost structure something of its relation to the world; but it could not state it, since this would involve having another language to gauge the distance between reality and our discourse about it. This would be like laying a ruler alongside an object to measure its length, and then trying with that very same ruler to calculate the distance between it and the object. Whatever the appropriate image, some utterly self-defeating piece of acrobatics is at stake here, some self-reflexive flip or mind-bending double take whereby we could jump on our own shadows or see ourselves seeing something; and though for the early Wittgenstein any such hauling of ourselves up by our linguistic bootstraps is quite out of the question, since our language can get a handle on itself no more than a tin-opener can slice itself open, it was a goal towards which the great wave of European modernism, to which the *Tractatus* secretly belongs, never ceased to strive. For the true coordinates of that astonishing mystical text are surely not Russell or Frege, but Joyce, Schoenberg, Picasso, all those self-ironising avant-gardists who sought in their own fashion to represent and point to their representing at a stroke. And just as there is something peculiarly self-deconstructive about any such enterprise, so the *Tractatus Logico–Philosophicus* secretes within itself a self-destruct device, since it strives absurdly to accomplish precisely what it has itself placed under censure – to speak of the relation of language to the world – and so, having absolutely no title to exist, must finally blow itself up. The reader who understands these propositions, Wittgenstein remarks cryptically at the conclusion, will grasp that they are nonsense; only by using them like ladders, kicked away as soon as mounted, will he or she see the world aright. The *Tractatus* thus cancels itself out in a gesture of modernist self-irony, illuminates the truth only by the dim glare created by its sudden implosion.

Wittgenstein puzzled his military headquarters during the First World War by constantly demanding to be transferred to more dangerous postings in the field.

The nearness of death, he hoped, might shed some faint light on his radically unfulfilled existence. With the drafts of the *Tractatus* in his pocket, he crouched in the trenches on the extreme limit of language, with the darkness of death at his back, and was struck dumb. You could show what you meant, like waving or smiling, but you could not say it; and this was no shambling existential inarticulacy or phonily portentous 'If I could tell you, I would let you know', but the most rigorous demonstration from the inside of the limits of representation. So it was that he would set out, in a classic gesture of critique, to sketch the frontiers of language from within language itself, sharply demarcating what philosophy could say – all those not terribly important things – from the host of vital topics about which it had better stay silent, and to which Dostoevsky and detective thrillers, Tolstoy and bad American movies, St. John and Mendelssohn might yield us the odd clue. The later Wittgenstein would come to discard this whole misleading metaphor of language 'picturing' the world as just another trope that holds us prisoner: language is not at a distance from reality, which is not to say that it is eyeball to eyeball with it either. But he retained his nostalgia for the extreme frontier, and pursued it, among other places, to an outer limit of Europe known as Killary harbour, which is where I first decided, years ago, to write about him.

Killary harbour is, technically speaking, the only fiord in Ireland, a sweep of stunning natural beauty in a Gaeltacht (Irish-speaking) region of northern Connemara; and it was here, to a cluster of four or five cottages known as Ross Roe, hardly even a village, that Wittgenstein fled from Cambridge in 1948. Local legend has it that he tamed the birds and scribbled much of what we now know as the *Philosophical Investigations*, some early drafts of which a local fisherman called Tom Mulkerrins was ordered to burn in the tiny outhouse of Wittgenstein's cottage. Tom was Wittgenstein's domestic help during his stay in Ross Roe; and when I first encountered him, many years later, I had with me a copy of Norman Malcolm's *Memoir* of Wittgenstein, which includes an approving reference to Tom in a letter from Wittgenstein to Russell. I showed Mulkerrins his name enshrined among the great and am delighted to record that he wasn't impressed in the least. Some time ago I returned to Ross Roe for a ceremony in which Her Excellency the President of Ireland unveiled a plaque to Wittgenstein at his cottage, which is now a youth hostel. Tom had died a year before; but I talked to some of the older fishermen about the imperious foreign scholar who had descended abruptly on them in his final years of life, and noted that their memories of him were not entirely favourable. I wanted to know, among other things, how tall he was, whether he spoke with a German accent or an English one, points that would be useful in making a film. His accent, as I had suspected, was impeccably upper-class English.

Frege is a philosopher's philosopher, Sartre the media's idea of an intellectual, and Bertrand Russell every shopkeeper's notion of the sage. 'Wot's it all about then, guv?' a London taxi driver is reputed to have asked Russell, when he recognised him in the back of his cab. But Wittgenstein is the philosopher of poets and

composers, playwrights and novelists, and snatches of his mighty *Tractatus* have
even been set to music. There is a Dutch cassette on which you can hear lines from
the work croaked and warbled in a hilarious German stage accent. Perhaps this is
because there is a fabular or mythological quality to Wittgenstein's riches-to-rags
career, a case of life outdoing art, which makes it easily available for artistic
representation. I wrote a novel about Ireland in 1987 (*Saints and Scholars*) in which
the republican leader James Connolly, the philosopher Nikolai Bakhtin, and
Wittgenstein have a bizarre encounter in Wittgenstein's Galway cottage; but even
here reality outstrips fiction, since Bakhtin, elder brother of the more celebrated
Mikhail and first professor of linguistics at Birmingham University, was indeed one
of Wittgenstein's closest friends, and the man to whom he first read the *Investigations* aloud. Bakhtin's own work bears a remarkable resemblance to his younger
brother's, even though the two had lost touch with each other in the aftermath of
Soviet revolutionary turbulence, and Nikolai had no knowledge even that Mikhail
had survived until he stumbled by chance on a copy of his book on Dostoevsky in
a Paris bookshop.

No doubt it was because of my novel that I was asked a couple of years ago to
write the screenplay for a film about Wittgenstein to be shown on Channel 4
television as part of a series of such plays called *The Philosophers*.[1] The series is
produced by Tariq Ali (Britain's answer to Daniel Cohn-Bendit during the 1960's),
whose Bandung Company produces excellent documentaries on the so-called
Third World for Channel 4. The brief, impossibly enough, was to assume an
almost wholly ignorant audience and communicate the main outlines of the
philosopher's ideas by dramatising his life. The director was Derek Jarman, one of
the most radical and controversial of English film-makers, who read my script and
asked why I had set it in Cambridge. 'Because that's where he mostly lived', I
replied. 'We're not filming in Cambridge', Jarman told me. 'First of all, everybody
films in bloody Cambridge. And secondly, the colleges charge the earth.' So we set
the piece instead in a disused studio in Waterloo, and shot it in two weeks for only
£300,000, with some financial help from the British Film Institute.

I shall omit the usual self-regarding narrative of how my screenplay was ripped
to shreds by the director. Suffice it to say that at one point my agent instructed me
to remove my name from the credits, whereupon the British Film Institute took
fright and persuaded me to keep it on. Jarman is a film-maker of rare brilliance and
astonishing audacity, but in the manner of brilliant film-makers he has little interest
in any idea that cannot be instantly translated into a breathtaking visual image. And
no doubt he himself would say, quite properly, that my script was (as befits an
Irishman) too verbose. Film, as they say, is not a verbal medium, even one about a
thinker whose preoccupation from beginning to end was language. The resulting
film has some splendid moments, and some deeply embarrassing ones, too. Hunky
young men in black leather jackets, for whom Spinoza is probably some kind of
pasta, shamble around thinly disguised as philosophers. They indulge in occasional
contrasts of the futility of philosophy with the excitement of scrambling into bed
with each other, which is not quite, I think, what Ludwig had in mind. A little

green man crops up from time to time apropos of nothing whatsoever and utters wads of meaningless whimsy. But Karl Johnson, a veritable Ludwig look-alike, is magnificent as the philosopher himself, and there is much else in the movie to admire. Anyway, experience of having my plays produced in Ireland and London had taught me that, as far as theatre and cinema go, the author is indeed dead – or if not quite dead, then sitting humbly at the back of the rehearsal room with the tea boy. Writers must discipline themselves to keep silent, whatever hideous massacring of their sacred text is currently in train, otherwise the actors will receive conflicting messages; and they must remember that their mere presence is likely to intimidate the cast and crew, who are not intellectuals and have the person-in-the-street's proper wariness of the breed. There are occasional gratifying deviations from this scenario: during the tour of my last play in Ireland, the actors requested a seminar with me on some of the more esoteric aspects of the script, and sat around scratching their heads and taking the odd bemused note as I expatiated sonorously and unintelligibly on the meaning of life.

To film Wittgenstein's ideas in terms of his life is finally a hopeless enterprise, since nothing is quite so striking as the contrast between the two. The early Wittgenstein is nostalgic for the pure ice of philosophical precision, for those countless gleaming metaphysical acres stretching silently to the horizon. It is a beautiful vision; but he came to see that if you tried to walk in that world, you would fall flat on your face. What we need to walk is friction, the roughness and inexactness of our common human practices. Do we need to measure our distance from the sun down to the nearest millimetre? Is an indistinct photograph of someone not a photograph at all? Is a field not a field simply because it lacks a precise boundary? Protesting that language isn't an exact instrument would be like complaining that you can't play a tune on a carrot. And so we have the later Wittgenstein of the *Investigations*, who has abandoned the crystalline purity of his ascetic youth and seeks to return us to the rough ground of our mixed, ambiguous, commonplace speech. But nothing could provide a greater contrast with the open-ended, pluralistic, demotic enquiries of this later period than the man himself: autocratic, haughtily patrician, driven by a fatiguing zeal for moral perfection, and well practised in brusquely casting off any friend who seemed to stand in the way. The fishermen of Ross Roe remembered wryly how he had kept his distance from them, and Tom Mulkerrins had a hard time keeping the barking dogs out of his irritable master's earshot. Wittgenstein was a lovable, utterly impossible character; the last thing he was was a Wittgensteinian, with the philosophical resonance the term now holds for us. He was an arresting mixture of monk, mystic, and mechanic: a high European intellectual with a yearning for Tolstoyan *simplicitas*, an irascible authoritarian with an unslakeable thirst for holiness. Something of all this, I hope, comes through in the film; but it is curiously at odds with the humble, workaday tolerance of his later thought – with the man who, on first hearing the idiomatic English phrase 'It takes all kinds to make a world', was deeply moved and commented with caught breath that it was a most beautiful and kindly saying.

'Nothing is hidden', writes Wittgenstein. 'Everything is open to view.' Of nothing was this less true than his own life, with its secretly pursued homosexual encounters. If Wittgenstein's thought is radical, it is because he restores to our speech and practice their true sociality, overthrowing that long-entrenched image of the self as a solitary substance brooding over its private, ineffable sensations. Can there be a private language? Well, this would be rather like a man who passes money from one of his hands to the other and thinks he has made a financial transaction. Or like a man who cries 'But I know how tall I am!' and places his hand on top of his own head. Wittgenstein was impatient with inwardness, with the fetish of 'personal experience', with all that self-righteous Cartesian jargon and the rampantly individualist politics that flowed from it. Is the difference between my pain and yours the fact that I *know* when I am in pain but can only speculate or infer that you are? Nonsense: it makes no sense at all to claim that I know that I am in pain, since the verb 'to know' has force only in a context of conceivable doubt, and that cannot be in question here. But it makes sense for me to say, sometimes at least, that I know with certainty what *you* are feeling. How do I have access to myself? – in much the same ways that I have access to you. And so on: there is no need to labour his marvellous demystifications of a long heritage of empiricist atomism or romantic individualism, simply to note that all this was carried through by a soul in solitary torment. So people think I behave eccentrically? he once asked. It is as though they are staring through a window at the strange motions of a man outside. They do not know that there is a storm raging out there, and that the man is keeping his feet only with the utmost difficulty. Wittgenstein kept his feet with immense labour, and the least gust of dishonesty would have been enough to blow him over for ever. And so he was grotesquely, absurdly ethical, plagued by that strange mania known as Protestantism for which everything is potentially a sign of salvation or damnation; and if only he had learnt to be a little less moral, he might have been more confident of salvation. In the end, he was marooned between the ice and the rough ground, at home in neither; and as Keynes remarks in the film, this was the source of all his sorrow.

He was, of course, socially disadvantaged. I mean by that he stemmed from a ludicrously wealthy family, and though he struggled hard against this signal disability – he gave all his money away – he could never quite eradicate its lethal traces. The Vienna from which he hailed was glutted, obese, overheated, a cockpit of subtle lusts and artistic kitsch, as the middle classes grew fat and shiny but shrivelled on the inside. All over the city, limbs were seizing up, vaginas drying out, and penises drooping. The population coughed and stuttered compulsively, afflicted by phantom cancers and false pregnancies, awaiting the ministrations of Sigmund Freud. For the logical positivists, mathematics would cure the terrible flatulence of Vienna. Everything was to be stark and singular, pure and integral in this Habsburg empire of cream cakes and swollen bodies. A monkish generation of sons struck Oedipally against their overbred fathers. A rash of them, worsted in the struggle, committed suicide, including two of Wittgenstein's brothers. The new austere philosophy was chaste, disciplined, and utterly integral; it was everything that Vienna was not. The film begins with this background, then tracks young Ludwig to Manchester (where he invented a new type of aeronautical engine), and finally to Cambridge, that toytown from which he never ceased trying to escape. He fled to Ireland, to a lonely Norwegian fiord (another extreme edge), to a monastery in Austria where he worked as an assistant gardener until hauled back kicking and screaming to academia. He even took flight to the Soviet Union in the darkest days of Stalinism, refused a couple of chairs in philosophy, and demanded instead to work there as a manual labourer. As perhaps the greatest philosopher of our century, he thought philosophy largely useless and urged his acolytes to give it up, just as he once stepped up to F. R. Leavis on King's Parade and impudently instructed him to give up literary criticism. He wrote only one book, and belonged to that heretical subcurrent of philosophy that works by joke, aphorism, anecdote, distilling a whole complex argument in some earthy dictum or casual epiphany. One thinks of the various jokers in the philosophical pack, from Kierkegaard and Nietzsche to Adorno and Derrida, who could say what they meant only by inventing a new genre of philosophical writing. The *Investigations* reads like an assemblage of images or scraps of narrative, wonders aloud, asks us questions that may or may not be on the level. Like the Freudian analyst, we suspect that the author has a few answers but is keeping them up his sleeve, forcing us into the work of self-demystification, genially engaging our participation, but running the odd ring around us at the same time. Philosophy for Wittgenstein was a sort of therapy; and if he was deeply sceptical of Freud, it was because (as he remarks in the film) it takes one Viennese to know another. If he attracts the admiration of artists, it is partly because he is of course a supremely fine one himself, his thought inseparable from the literary style of a man effortlessly at home in the world, which was the very last thing he was.

The film, in any case, is now on release, and there are young men and women walking around London wearing Wittgenstein T-shirts. The critics are hotly debating the significance of the little green man, and I am awaiting the phone call from Hollywood. In the meantime, the Irish theatre company for which I write is planning a Christmas pantomime in Belfast with Stephen Rea, who played Oscar Wilde in my play *Saint Oscar*. The IRA, however, have just blown up the venue. There are critics who believe that art is one thing and politics another. But not in Ireland.

Note

1   Now published as *Wittgenstein: The Terry Eagleton Script/The Derek Jarman Film*, with introductions by Colin MacCabe, Terry Eagleton and Derek Jarman (London: British Film Institute, 1993).

Part VI   Ireland's Own

Introduction

'History and Myth in Yeats's "Easter 1916"' (Chapter 26) is one of Terry
Eagleton's earliest encounters with modern Irish culture, and it shows the rigorous
techniques of practical criticism in the service of a formidable political intelligence.
Dutifully observing the presence of 'ambiguity' and 'paradox' in the syntactical
structure of Yeats's 'Easter 1916', the essay proceeds to show how ambiguity and
paradox are not just stylistic flourishes but powerful indicators of the political and
historical complexities out of which the poem is born. If the essay is an exercise in
'close reading', it is also a relentless theoretical enquiry into the workings of history
and myth in modern poetry. At one level, 'Easter 1916' seems confidently affirmative and rhetorically assured; at another level, it functions as a candid confession of
unresolved doubts and dilemmas. The short period of time between the Easter
Rebellion and the composition of the poem is such that no clear historical conclusion can be drawn within its scope of reference. At the time of writing, the event is
still too immediate for it to be represented as fixed and final. Even so, the poem
adopts a set of formal procedures which allow it to engage with the event while
strategically evading any further historical analysis. In adopting a decorous, elegiac
form of address, Yeats is able to affirm the tragic role of the rebels and at the same
time retain a measure of uncertainty about the historical circumstances in which
they died.

What the essay brings into focus is the tension between the poem's readiness to
create a myth and its lingering historical uneasiness. The characteristic duality of
Yeats's vision is evident in the vague and ambiguous relationship between the
image of the stone and the image of the stream in stanza three of the poem. By
likening the political action of 1916 to a stone in a stream, the poem naturalizes
disruptive rebellion but also distances and depersonalizes it. The stone appears to
have interrupted the natural process, but is itself part of nature. It remains unclear
whether the imagery is positing a contrast between the organic flow of nature
and the turmoil of politics or depicting the integration of politics into nature.
The ballad-like refrain of the poem similarly embodies a contradictory attitude:
it both celebrates heroic achievement and recognizes desultory failure; it holds

in tension the permanent stillness of myth and the blurred, unfinished business of history.

'Nationalism: Irony and Commitment' (Chapter 27) was originally published as a Field Day pamphlet in 1988, along with 'Modernism and Imperialism' by Fredric Jameson and 'Yeats and Decolonization' by Edward Said. The three pamphlets were reprinted in a single volume, *Nationalism, Colonialism and Literature* (University of Minnesota Press, 1990), with an introduction by Seamus Deane. The Field Day Theatre Company was founded in 1980 in the context of the continuing political crisis in Northern Ireland. Its main preoccupation has been the forging of a new sense of cultural identity for Ireland, and it was to enable a deeper exploration of the nature of 'the Irish problem' that Field Day embarked upon the publication of a series of pamphlets in 1983. The first six pamphlets of the series were collected under the title *Ireland's Field Day* and published in 1985. In the preface to that collection, the Field Day directors declared their belief that 'Field Day could and should contribute to the solution of the present crisis by producing analyses of the established opinions, myths and stereotypes which had become both a symptom and a cause of the current situation'.[1]

Eagleton's pamphlet notes that terms such as 'nationalism' are often the symptoms of alienation and separation, even when they function simultaneously as a source of comfort and consolation. Any sustained analysis of nationalism is likely to run up against irony and contradiction. Adopting a line from Raymond Williams, the pamphlet suggests that nationalism is like class: 'To have it, and to feel it, is the only way to end it'. In one sense, class and nationalism are untrustworthy essences, yet they continue to exert an implacable political force; to wish them away is to play straight into the hands of the oppressor. Somehow, we must 'go right through those estranging definitions to emerge somewhere on the other side'. The major difficulty is in trying to envisage what a desirable future might be like within the limited terms and restrictive categories of the present. Here we encounter a further irony in that emancipatory politics seem to function in a self-cancelling, self-abnegating way, to bring about those material conditions under which opposition and transformative action will no longer be necessary. In this context, ideas of 'class' or 'nation' have only a tenuous existence, since they look forward to a political formation under which such categories will cease to be known.

That other elusive term 'identity' also generates a good deal of irony, for it can be simultaneously regarded both as the construct of the oppressor and as an authentic sign of selfhood. Identity, it would seem, is often founded on antagonism, with any secure sense of definition relying upon continued opposition. Catholic and Protestant might be regarded as mutually dependent categories, since 'each term can always be shown to inhere parasitically within the other'. The pamphlet has enough self-irony to realize that explaining these sophistries on the Falls and Shankhill roads in Belfast would not be an easy business. With a Wildean flair reminiscent of 'The Soul of Man Under Socialism', the pamphlet sets about interrogating the very concept of Irishness. 'Are the Irish oppressed as Irish?', it asks. Initially the answer would seem to be 'no', since 'it is not their ethnic peculiarity but their territory and labour power which have entranced the British.' In another sense, however, it would be irresponsible to deny that there are forms of oppression and exploitation which are clearly directed at 'the Irish' as a particular group of people. The crucial paradox that emerges from this is that nationalist politics are not so much a declaration of difference as of sameness. The freedom in question is not the freedom to be Irish, but 'simply the freedom now enjoyed by certain other groups to determine their identity as they may wish.'

Oscar Wilde is a prominent figure in the pamphlet, not least because its publication coincided with preparations for the Field Day production of *Saint Oscar*. The play was first performed by Field Day Theatre Company in the Guildhall, Derry, on 25 September 1989, with Stephen Rea as Oscar Wilde. As the Foreword to *Saint Oscar* (Chapter 28) explains, the play emerged from Eagleton's meditation on two intriguingly related aspects of Wilde's career: his complex, protean sense of cultural identity (typically upper-class English *and* distinctively Irish) and the extent to which his work prefigures the insights of contemporary critical theory. In his endless delight in word play and his preoccupation with the contradictory nature of the human subject, Wilde is an Irish Roland Barthes. Wilde's predicament illustrates how colonial subjectivity induces a distrust of stable, representational forms such as literary realism and a preference for fantasy and imaginative extravagance. A crisis of identity manifests itself in ways that are fluid, diffuse and provisional, and brings with it an ironic response to existing social forms and conventions. In Wilde, then, can be found a startling connection between colonial experience and artistic experimentation. But the Irish Oxfordian socialist proto-deconstructionist who takes the stage here is Terry Eagleton as much as Oscar Wilde, and the Foreword to *Saint Oscar* is the most candid statement to date of his own fraught exploration of identity, commitment and style. With *Saint Oscar* the critic as artist makes the leap from so-called theoretical writing to so-called creative writing.

Saint Oscar involves a shrewd rethinking of the link between comedy and radical politics in the context of a political left not usually associated with fun and laughter. Oscar Wilde is now brought into the company of Mikhail Bakhtin and Bertolt Brecht, as the essay turns to contemplate the subversive potential of comedy and the politics of pleasure. Wilde's aestheticism is not merely a matter of self-gratification but 'a radical rejection of mean-spirited utility and a devotion to human self-realization as an end in itself which is very close to the writings of Karl Marx.' His style of writing is perverse in more than a merely formal sense, and it offers to an English intellectual a model that strongly counters conventional academic prose. Wilde is celebrated here – both in the foreword and in the play – in a style that is, itself, flamboyantly and audaciously Wildean, with all the customary inversions and subversions of Saint Oscar himself. At the same time, the play unravels its 'dark, sobering subtext' and finds in Wilde's confrontation with Sir Edward Carson a tragic anticipation of contemporary events in Ulster. As so often, it is Walter Benjamin who reveals how history might be rubbed against the grain so that ghosts from the past might teach us how to redeem the present.

The work of Field Day comes into focus once again in 'Unionism and Utopia' (Chapter 29), a review of Seamus Heaney's play *The Cure at Troy*, which was first performed in 1990. Heaney is seen to have produced from a loose translation of the Sophoclean tragedy *Philoctetes* an oblique but powerful allegory of 'the Troubles'. His play renders the parallels between ancient Athens and contemporary Ulster explicitly and effectively, and the glimpse of utopia in the Epilogue is seen as a bold and moving gesture. Even so, that utopian hope is enshrined in miracles and epiphanies, which are regarded in the review with profound scepticism. Eagleton's method is to push the political allegory as far as it can go, and in the process make it say more than it wants to. The burden of the allegory falls on Philoctetes, whose festering wound and painful immobility might seem an apt image of sectarian Northern Ireland. The resolution of historical conflict would seem, then, to accompany the healing of Philoctetes, but the triumphant role that Philoctetes has in Greek myth is not easily translated into the terms of contemporary political conflict. The play concentrates on the personal regeneration of Philoctetes rather than the eventual conquest of Troy, which might, if the allegory were pursued, suggest an obvious confrontation between Ireland and Britain. In this respect, the play's allegorical use of classical myth perhaps releases an unintended meaning.

This section closes with what might appear an unlikely juxtaposition: Heathcliff and the Great Hunger. Eagleton's determination to write about *Wuthering Heights* within an Irish cultural context, however, is evident as early as 1988, in the introduction to the second edition of *Myths of Power: A Marxist Study of the Brontës*: 'The Brontë sisters have entered the canon of English literature, but their background was not English at all; they were Irish by descent, as Heathcliff may well be too.'[2] The essay reprinted here (Chapter 30) is part of a much larger endeavour to bring contemporary cultural theory and Irish social and political history into a close and mutually illuminating relationship. What results is a mode of critical exegesis quite unlike anything Eagleton has previously written. 'Heathcliff and the Great Hunger' is neither literary criticism nor social history, but a cultural discourse altogether more fertile and provocative than those conventional categories habitually suggest. The method owes much to Walter Benjamin's explosive rupturing of settled historical narratives. The shock technique of moving unexpectedly and often abruptly between the text of *Wuthering Heights* and historical accounts of the Irish famine is a way of making both narratives yield a previously hidden significance.

Although the essay presents itself as an 'allegorical' reading of *Wuthering Heights*, there is nothing so conventional or consistent in its method. We are reminded that in August 1845, 'on the very eve of the Great Famine', Branwell Brontë visited Liverpool, a city 'soon to be thronged with its starving victims'. A few months later, Emily Brontë began writing *Wuthering Heights*, in which 'a dirty, ragged, black-haired child' is found starving on the streets of Liverpool. Undeterred by this slender evidence of Heathcliff's lineage and the uncertain chronology of events, Eagleton declares with sly insouciance that 'in this essay Heathcliff is Irish and the chronology is not awry'. What the essay presents is not a single, uniform reading of *Wuthering Heights* but a dazzling constellation of possibilities, in which Heathcliff is both oppressor and oppressed, 'condensing in his own person the various stages of the Irish revolution'. The essay fastens on the problematic relationship between nature and culture in *Wuthering Heights*, exploring through these terms some of the familiar nineteenth-century paradigms of Irish and British political relations. What begins as a biographical sketch of Branwell Brontë closes with a vigorous response to the current historiographical problems occluding a fuller understanding of the causes and consequences of the Famine.

Notes

1   Seamus Deane (ed.), *Ireland's Field Day* (London: Hutchinson, 1985), p. vii.
2   *Myths of Power: A Marxist Study of the Brontës*, 2nd edn (London: Macmillan, 1988), p. xix.

26 History and Myth in Yeats's 'Easter 1916'

Yeats wrote his 'Easter 1916' in the September of that year, over three months after the execution of the leaders of the uprising; and this time-interval – long enough for the event's implications to be deeply pondered, too brief for any hard historical conclusions to be drawn – is crucial for the poem's emotional structure. Like many mature Yeats poems, 'Easter 1916' combines confidently affirmative statement with a candid confession of painfully unresolved ambiguities; the point of the ballad-refrain is to create a framework within which a rhetorical firmness can be played off against the terse, shifting notations of conflicting, even contradictory, attitudes:

> What is it but nightfall?
> No, no, not night but death;
> Was it needless death after all?
> For England may keep faith
> For all that is done and said.
> We know their dream; enough
> To know they dreamed and are dead . . .

Like other Yeats poems also, the business of the poetic language is to separate, clarify and define, rather than cryptically conflate, the ambiguous feelings it handles. The ambiguities belong to the historical experience, as it were, rather than to the language which records it; and to this extent the purity of the poem's diction (as often in Yeats) suggests its capacity to stand over against, and take the measure of, the fluctuating complexities of the recorded event and its confused aftermath. This is not to suggest that there aren't points at which the confusion infiltrates the poem's own language, as I hope to show; rather that the decisive tone of the poem is established by its strategy of admitting the presence of complexities while simultaneously fending them off, either muting them to a disturbing resonance just beneath the poem's surface or gathering them into the affirmative statement.

This tension between the achieved poise of the poetic act, and the blurred, unfinished business it presents, is central to the poem's meaning. 'Easter 1916' is, evidently enough, the creation of a myth: its aim is less to comment analytically on the dead rebels than to 'write [them] out in a verse', so that what matters is the ritualising act of the art itself, defining its own limits and setting its own terms. In this sense, a refusal to pursue critical analysis which might undermine the myth can emerge as decorous – proper to the *genre* – rather than as cautiously evasive; Yeats can turn his own political reservations to poetic use, inserting qualifications which make their point but leave the elegiac balance undisturbed, since the death of the rebels has in any case rendered them irrelevant. Since the executions have prepared the ground for transmuting history into myth, replacing unresolved complexity with distanced finality, the English themselves have conveniently rendered further questioning redundant. The poem's language is thus not forced to be more uncomfortably specific in its moral criticism of the rebels, since there is properly nothing to be specific about – nothing, after the deaths, left to analyse:

> We know their dream; enough
> To know they dreamed and are dead;
> And what if excess of love
> Bewildered them till they died?
> I write it out in a verse –
> MacDonagh and MacBride
> And Connolly and Pearse
> Now and in time to be,
> Wherever green is worn,
> Are changed, changed utterly:
> A terrible beauty is born.

The urgent question raised in the third and fourth lines is neither answered nor evaded; the possibility needs to be entertained, but the movement of the poetry, intent on passing beyond shifting historical uncertainty to the permanent stillness of myth, can take it easily in its stride, neither over-emphasising nor underplaying its significance. It is important for Yeats's *general* doubts about the reliability of revolutionary emotion, and the relation of these doubts to his total attitude to the Irish situation, that the issue should be raised; but in the particular case of the executed rebels it can be courteously waived, if only because the answers are quite literally no longer important. This tension between a general attitude, and one particular to the dead leaders, is central to the poem: for if the affirmative feelings are directed on the whole towards the dead, the hesitations relate to the general historical context they have abandoned. In this sense, by separating the rebels from those historical doubts – or, more exactly, by exploiting the fact that the English have severed that connection by executing them – an affirmation of the rebels is possible which is in in fact more limited in its general application than the poem's tone would in part suggest.

As a piece of myth-creation, then, the poem is able to create its own reality, gathering and distancing the dead into the artifice of mythology; yet it does so with an uneasily analytic eye on the course of an objective history external to itself: the loose ends and incalculable effects of the uprising itself, still too contemporary an occurrence to be controlled and finalised within the poems's own art. From one viewpoint, the poignancy of 'Easter 1916' lies in its bold decision to mythologise the dead before the objective validity of that action – the assurance that it is more than subjective – can be historically confirmed, and to do so in full awareness of the risks and exposures involved: risks and exposures which, by courting the possibility of a rash prematureness, reflect the problematical character of the uprising itself. Yeats, bitterly certain that he had lived where motley is worn, has already been badly caught out once, forced into a humiliating *volte face*; the courage of the poem lies not merely in admitting a reversal, but in risking another. From another viewpoint, though, that exposure is by no means unmitigated: there are senses (more subtle than the striking oxymoron of 'terrible beauty') in which the poem covers itself defensively from the pitfalls of premature commitment:

> I write it out in a verse –
> MacDonagh and MacBride
> And Connolly and Pearse
> Now and in time to be,
> Wherever green is worn,
> Are changed, changed utterly . . .

The gathering crescendo of that first line promises a pregnant insight; yet the subsequent statement says much less than it appears to. What it actually says is that the heroes are changed and will be so for all time – but only, as the lines stand, in the platitudinous sense that every historical truth is true for all time. It is only the crucial reference to the wearing of green (ringing a change on the first stanza's 'motley') which implies that the transformation will be *fertilising*: received and lived out in the future. And this meaning, which the rhetorical resonance invites one to read in while simultaneously withdrawing any substantial evidence, must be played off against the literal sense of the lines, which promises and prophesises much less. That local ambiguity draws its force from one of the poem's more comprehensive paradoxes: the fact that what it asserts as utterly permanent is, ironically, a change. Death, in a fruitful ambivalence, is both transformation and finality; and a 'permanent change' can mean either one which brings you to a finalised, unalterable condition, or one which will be perpetually re-created in its effects. The lines quoted above say the first while hinting at the second: in this way the poem covers its losses under the shield of its rhetorical tone. 'History' and 'myth' – the real, unpredictable upshot of the events and the urge to draw them in the present, despite that worrying aftermath, into an achieved permanence – stand in uneasy interrelation; a sharp historical consciousness is retained, but also played off against the moral imperative which motivates the poet to mythologise the event now, in generous inattention to historical contingency. In its combination of a shrewd historical sense with a boldly affirmative impulse which cuts self-sufficiently through history's mere complexities, the poem reveals a characteristic duality in

Yeats's general sensibility. Moreover, both 'historical' and 'mythical' perspectives share a similar quality: both in their different ways distance the recorded event, the first by hinting at its relativity and therefore qualifying any over-eager claim for its centrality, the second by removing it from the realm of temporal contingency into the shadowy dimension of eternal achievement. In this sense, there is a quality of essential detachment inherent in the mythical treatment itself, carried over, as it were, from Yeats's prudent historical hesitations; and in this way a glorification of the dead can be achieved without an unreserved commitment to their *historical* importance.

This two-fold tendency – the mythical affirmation and the counterpointing historical uneasiness – emerges most clearly in the subtle changes rung, just beneath the poem's surface, on a set of key-notes: dream, drama, art, illusion, reality. The poem's opening lines juxtapose the heroic mythology of 'vivid faces' with the familiar realities of 'counter and desk'; yet the issue refuses to resolve itself to a simple counterposing of former illusion and present truth:

> I have passed with a nod of the head
> Or polite meaningless words,
> Or have lingered awhile and said
> Polite meaningless words,
> And thought before I had done
> Of a mocking tale or a gibe
> To please a companion
> Around the fire at the club,
> Being certain that they and I
> But lived where motley is worn . . .

'They' in that ninth line may refer either to the rebels with whom the poet has spoken, or to the club-companions; in either case, the interchanges of artifice and reality are interestingly complex. If 'they' refers to the companions, then the 'motley', it would seem, is a gesture outwards to the rebels: their posturing theatricality, the sceptical Yeats believed, shared in, as well as reacted against, the brittle unrealities of the clubmen's blandness, in a counterpointing of neurosis and complacency. Yet if the rebels pose histrionically behind assumed masks, so does the less-than-candid Yeats who exchanges polite conversation with them while conscious of his jeers (in an equally artificial club setting) behind their backs. Again, if 'they' refers to the rebels, then the motley perhaps attaches more closely to the clubmen themselves: the implication then may be that it is the shallowness of Ireland, rather than the rebels' own ideals, which renders them ludicrous. Both meanings seem present: it is, at any rate, not clear who wears the motley, and Yeats, through the ambivalence of that 'they', is stranded at a confused point between a common (if critical) front with the rebels against pervasive foolery and a contemptuous alliance with the clubmen against them.

The *certainty* that motley is worn has now, of course, been radically undermined, as utopian dream converts in part to historical reality; yet the poem's language still insists on the elements of illusion within the new creation:

> This other man I had dreamed
> A drunken, vainglorious lout.
> He had done most bitter wrong
> To some who are near my heart,
> Yet I number him in the song;
> He too has resigned his part
> In the casual comedy;
> He too has been changed in his turn,
> Transformed utterly . . .

The previous judgment on John MacBride is both formally retracted (*'dreamed'*) and restated: the old assumptions were – *must* have been – delusions, yet the fact of the 'most bitter wrong' still stands, to qualify the thoroughness of the transition. The new events have revised previous history, but not so much by showing it in a different light as by breaking to a new level which both leaves it intact and renders it redundant; and in this sense history seems both cancelled and preserved by what has happened, in a disorientating merging of perspectives. Thus, no such similar confession of former misapprehension is extended to the case of Constance Markiewicz, whose previous image ('What voice more sweet than hers/ When, young and beautiful,/ She rode to harriers?') still resists the necessary revision; and MacBride, in any case, seems to have resigned from the casual comedy, disengaged from artifice and illusion, only to assume the alternative dramatic role-playing of revolutionary heroism. He is 'changed *in his turn*', ritually exchanging one mask for another ('motley' for 'green'); and the passive verb distances and qualifies the personal character of the transformation, allowing him the objective glory of martyrdom while staying quiet, uncommittedly neutral, about the personal change which he may have actively achieved, as a moral agent, in the process.

The upshot of this sense that events have passed not only from illusion to reality but also, confusingly, from one dramatic artifice to another, is that reality itself seems dissolved rather than consolidated by what has occurred. The relations between dream, history, myth and drama are deeply obscured: if pre-uprising history was dream and complacent artifice, present history seems at once more and less 'real' than what went before – the concrete enactment of a vague utopian vision, an intersection of dream and reality which seems to have had the disturbing effect of disembodying both. Isolated from their historical consequences, the deaths of the leaders are indubitably substantial: the only substantial fact, indeed, on which Yeats can go to work. Yet they are also, in their way, a 'disembodying', a dissolution and negation; and this, even more sharply, is how they appear when they are returned to their historical context. If the events in question have the undeniable solidity of stone, it is stone grasped in terms of its blurring, dissipating, de-realising effect on the living stream of history:

> Hearts with one purpose alone
> Through summer and winter seem
> Enchanted to a stone
> To trouble the living stream.
> The horse that comes from the road,
> The rider, the birds that range
> From cloud to tumbling cloud,
> Minute by minute they change;
> A shadow of cloud on the stream
> Changes minute by minute;
> A horse-hoof slides on the brim,
> And a horse plashes within it . . .

The subjective illusion of 'enchanted' is fused with the hard objectivity of 'stone': the event is at once irreducibly concrete and vapidly elusive. What the stone symbolises is human *hearts*, a living historical action; but, at least by the end of this stanza, 'stone' stands in a similar relation to 'heart' as myth stands to history, emerging from it organically, yet also, in its transmuting of turbulent feeling to impersonal stillness, opaque and remote, difficult to dissolve back into human realities:

> The long-legged moor-hens dive,
> And hens to moor-cocks call;
> Minute by minute they live:
> The stone's in the midst of all.

The stone's symbolic reference to human agency ('hearts') has now been muted, leaving it a disconnected, autonomous, impenetrably mysterious object within the stream. It is the sheer, uninterpretable fact of its inert, depersonalised presence, its immovable, bruise-like insistence within the living flesh of Ireland which these lines stress, dislocating it from the human reference with which it was introduced. By the end of the stanza, the stone can be related back only with an effort to the hearts it symbolises, as the new image of MacBride is both a growth out of, and radically discontinuous with, his former state.

The point of the overall metaphor of the stanza is to sustain this duality of vision: to urge at once the living process of the event ('history') and its strange, stone-like inscrutability ('myth'). Thus, the imagery of stone and stream 'naturalises' the disruptive rebellion, transmuting it effortlessly to an organic disturbance within the texture of a known landscape; but by the same token it distances and depersonalises what has occurred to an elusively obscure process which can be registered rather than understood. The metaphor, that is, dignifies but also withdraws the historical experience, gracing and stylising the bloody events while holding them simultaneously at arm's length. It achieves simple definition at the cost of a calculated externalisation; and to this extent it evokes feelings of alienness and naturalness together. Both qualities fuse in the word 'stone', but they co-exist less satisfactorily in the stanza as a whole. Thus, reality has been dissolved and perhaps re-ordered by the new events, yet the precise relationship between 'stone' and 'stream' is surely vague. The stone 'troubles' the stream, but also lies inertly at its heart: it acts *on* the stream, stirring and disintegrating its waters, yet the end of the stanza ('The stone's in the midst of all') also insists on imaging it as a reality in itself, bluntly present but stolidly inactive. That there is a real ambiguity here is evident enough in the verbal shift from 'Minute by minute they (horses, rider, birds) *change*' to 'Minute by minute they (moor-hens) *live*': the first image envisages a landscape pervasively altered by the stone-created ripples, whereas the second seems to point up the mysteriousness of living processes which *persist* in their usual modes of being despite an 'objective' change of context. The ambiguities of real history – has the event changed anything or not? – here infiltrate the poem's own language: the simple nature images, which seemed a way of controlling, perhaps 'domesticating' the experience by rooting it in a familiar landscape, turn out to be ways of suggesting, but not adequately tackling, the complexity of what is at stake. The stone seems both to have metamorphosed the natural process and left it curiously intact, in a way which evokes the previous ambiguous relation between history before and after the uprising; and the joint effect of these two perspectives is to hint at a real change which is nevertheless too deep-seated and all-embracing to be concretely localised. The poem's own imagery is certainly unable to do more than feel after it, deploying 'objective' metaphor which promises, but fails, to 'objectify'. The change is pervasive enough to be insubstantial; and the persistence of the moor-hens' calls places an implicit question-mark over that substantiality, intimating a *contrast* between enduring natural reality and short-lived political turmoil which directly reverses the main tendency of the stanza's general metaphor: its *integration* of 'politics' into 'nature'. A stone which disturbs running water is in one sense 'natural' (part of the landscape), in another sense an interference with nature; and the inherent ambiguity of the image reflects Yeats's conflicting attitudes. Similarly, the stone's coldness and hardness is vividly evoked, but also softened by the appealing implications of 'enchanted'; and if the image of hearts turned to stone criticises the 'fanaticism' of the rebellion, it also suggests, more sympathetically, the stilled hearts of the executed leaders.

This set of ambiguities relates to a more general hesitation in the stanza: the question of whether the transformations at issue are 'subjective' or 'objective'. If the changes in horse and rider are subjective, part of a troubling inner disorientation projected onto the scene, the shifting of birds, clouds and shadows are objective enough; and the difficulty is to grasp the point of their close juxtaposition. The relation, in fact, is not successfully clarified: the stanza moves cryptically from images which suggest disintegrating illusion to a sense of routine objective flux, thus presenting that flux as both alien disturbance and organic continuity. Thus, the anxious sense of a dissolving reality is checked by an emphasis on change as natural and cyclical; but equally, that natural cycle is caught up into, and by implication made to share in, the dissolutions of the first, 'subjective' set of images. The poem, in other words, is radically uncertain in its choice between seeing a subjective loss of stability as no more alarming, and no less organically inevitable, than objective natural change, and, more gloomily, implying that natural reality is itself damagingly undermined by the human alterations which have taken place. So the absorption of history into nature cuts both ways: it graces and naturalises the unfamiliar, but only at the cost of rendering nature itself alien.

If the relation between the 'subjective' and 'objective' is imprecisely achieved here, however, it is put to powerful effect elsewhere, in the poem's 'Are changed, changed utterly' refrain. The phrase is, of course, grimly ironic: it refers at once to the mythical transformation which the rebels have undergone in the eyes of the Irish, and to the historical fact that the English have converted them into corpses. Here 'subjective' and 'objective' meanings forcefully interlock, defining a single event. Yet the poem's characteristic tension persists within this unity: for if its objective aspect points to failure, its subjective meaning suggests heroic achieve-ment. 'Utterly' evokes in the same breath the tragic finality of the rebels' death and the gloriously unalterable completeness of their new significance. The passive verb 'are changed' both qualifies and celebrates: it deprives the rebels of personal, self-creating autonomy by insisting (with an echo of the poem's general imagery of dramatic artifice and role-playing) on the thoroughness with which they have been reduced to the manipulated puppets of uncontrollable historical forces; yet it simultaneously exploits this victimised depersonalisation for the mysterious imper-sonality of heroic myth. In this way, it can transplant the dead from the contingen-cies of history to the inviolable security of myth without allowing the central historical fact of their failure to be lost sight of.

The dialectic of history and myth in 'Easter 1916' has a peculiar relevance to Yeats's own complex relation to the events he records, and it is worth adding a final comment on this. One major element of that relation is guilt; yet the guilt is not simple. To have been *certain* that motley was worn was, after all, to have had at one's disposal an evaluative perspective which went beyond the blindnesses of others, and out of which the confident judgment on the 'motley' could be made; and in that sense Yeats can defend himself from a charge of *mindless* complacency, in a way which both provides a precarious bridge to his present, revised attitude and saves him, if not from guilt, then at least from accusations of opportunism. The guilt, then, springs from seeing one's own jettisoned idealism tragically revived by others; and to that extent the poet is both external to what has occurred and yet has a title to participate, recognising the relation between the rebels' motives and his own discarded hopes. Yeats's own participation in the event is, of course, the poem itself: his 'part' in the drama is to transform it to permanence by ritually invoking the names of its protagonists:

> O when may it suffice?
> That is Heaven's part, our part
> To murmur name on name,
> As a mother names her child
> When sleep at last has come
> On limbs that had run wild . . .

The mother's naming is both purposeless (the child sleeps, unconscious of her presence) and yet an intimate benediction; she is excluded by the child's sleep, reduced to a merely external presence, yet the child is of her flesh. Through this image, then, Yeats confesses his own guilty estrangement from contemporary history at the same time as he obliquely claims a kind of maternity, acknowledging the uprising and its aftermath as the alien children of his own idealism. In a parallel way, the 'myth' of the poem both creates, and yet is subservient to, the historical material with which it deals. The naming (a murmuring, in any case, rather than an affirmative chant) must follow on the real history, when the wildness has wound itself out into deathly sleep; yet although in this sense myth merely revives and re-creates a history already finished and done with, the contrary implication – that event *becomes* history by the power of art and myth – is also active, providing the artist with a self-consciously restricted yet centrally significant role. The act of naming is both a passive recording of objective reality and a way of having it on one's own, creative and subjective terms; and this interaction between terse transcription and assured personal declaration sets the poem's tone. Thus, the weighty rhetorical confidence, in the case of MacBride, of 'Yet I number him in the song' (a confidence firm enough to imply that the possibility of actually *rejecting* MacBride from the poem lies within the poet's own free choice) co-exists with the modest, limited artistic purpose which the line actually defines. Myth, art and illusion grow out of historical reality and conform to its pressures; yet reciprocally, a dream has created an event: and with this assurance behind it, the poem can generate its own myth with genuine, if qualified, confidence in its efficacy.

27 Nationalism: Irony and Commitment

'Nationalism', remarks an African character in Raymond Williams's novel *Second Generation* (London, 1964), 'is in this sense like class. To have it, and to feel it, is the only way to end it. If you fail to claim it, or give it up too soon, you will merely be cheated, by other classes and other nations.' Nationalism, like class, would thus seem to involve an impossible irony. It is sometimes forgotten that social class, for Karl Marx at least, is itself a form of alienation, cancelling the particularity of an individual life into collective anonymity. Where Marx differs from the commonplace liberal view of such matters is in his belief that to undo this alienation you had to go, not around class, but somehow all the way through it and out the other side. To wish class or nation away, to seek to live sheer irreducible difference *now* in the manner of some contemporary post-structuralist theory, is to play straight into the hands of the oppressor. In a similar way, the philosopher Julia Kristeva has argued that the whole concept of gender is 'metaphysical' – a violent stabilising of the sheer precariousness and ambiguity of sexual identity to some spuriously self-identical essence.[1] The goal of a feminist politics would therefore be not an affirmation of some 'female identity', but a troubling and subverting of all such sexual straitjacketing. Yet the grim truth remains that women are oppressed *as women* – that such sexual categories, ontologically empty though they may be, continue to exert an implacable political force. It would thus be the worst form of premature utopianism for women to strive now merely to circumvent their sexual identities, celebrating only the particular and polymorphous, rather than – once again – try somehow to go right through those estranging definitions to emerge somewhere on the other side. Women are not so much fighting for the freedom to be women – as though we all understood exactly what that meant – as for the freedom to be fully human; but that inevitably abstract humanity can be articulated in the here and now only through their womanhood, since this is the place where their humanity is wounded and refused. Sexual politics, like class or nationalist struggle, will thus necessarily be caught up in the very metaphysical categories it hopes finally to abolish; and any such movement will demand a difficult, perhaps ultimately impossible, double optic, at once fighting on a terrain already mapped out by its antagonists and seeking even now to prefigure within that mundane strategy styles of being and identity for which we have as yet no proper names.

If the binary opposition between 'man' and 'woman' can always be deconstructed – if each term can always be shown to inhere parasitically within the other – then just the same is true of the opposition between those other virulently metaphysical forms of identity, Catholic and Protestant. Catholic, of course, means universal; so there is something curious in using it to define a particular kind of national identity. There is a good Joycean irony involved in establishing one's Irish identity by reference to a European capital. But the claim of the Roman Catholic church to universality is in any case only necessary once that status has been challenged by Protestantism, and so is no sooner raised than refuted, denying itself in the very act of assertion. Protestantism, on the other hand, is in one sense an aberration from such universal identity, an affirmation of national difference; yet it takes the historical form of a return to the pure universal essence of Christianity, which the Church of Rome has supposedly contaminated. This heretical deviancy is thus more orthodox than orthodoxy itself, the very metaphysical truth or essence of that which it denounces. Catholicism itself already contains a certain Protestantism – *ecclesia semper reformanda* – without which constant deviating from itself it would not be truly itself; and Protestantism cannot exist as such without its historical antagonist. All that remains is now to explain this on the Falls and Shankill roads. Even those who had the insolence to do so would no doubt soon be brought to realise that their assertion of the metaphysical emptiness of Catholic and Protestant identities was itself metaphysically empty.

What one might call the 'subjunctive mood' of 'bad' or premature utopianism grabs instantly for a future, projecting itself by an act of will or imagination beyond the compromised political structures of the present. By failing to attend to those forces or fault-lines *within* the present which, developed or prised open in particular ways, might induce that condition to surpass itself into a future, such utopianism is in danger of persuading us to desire uselessly rather than feasibly, and so, like the neurotic, to fall ill of unstaunchable longing. A desirable but unfeasible future, one which fails to found itself in the present in order to bridge us beyond it, is in this sense the reverse of the future offered us by some brands of social determinism, which is inevitable but not thereby necessarily desirable. (The inevitable, indeed, is usually pretty unpleasant.) A utopian thought which does not risk simply making us ill is one able to trace within the present that secret lack of identity with itself which is the spot where a feasible future might germinate – the place where the future overshadows and hollows out the present's spurious repleteness. To 'know the future' can only mean to grasp the present under the sign in its internal contradictions, in the alienations of its desire, in its persistent inability ever quite to coincide with itself.

Just as the pious Jews, so Walter Benjamin reminds us,[2] were forbidden on pain of idolatry to fashion graven images of the God of the future, so political radicals are prohibited under pain of fetishism from blueprinting their ultimate desire. Marx himself, who began his political career in contention with the 'wouldn't it be nice if' kind of revolutionary, is symptomatically silent for the most part about what a desirable future would look like, since the task of socialism is simply to identify and unlock those contradictions which are currently impeding its construction. The true soothsayers and clairvoyants are the technical experts hired by international capitalism to peer into the entrails of the system and assure its rulers that their profits are safe for another twenty years. Socialism belongs to the capitalist epoch as much as does the stock exchange, and like any emancipatory theory is preoccupied with putting itself progressively out of business. Emancipatory politics exist to bring about the material conditions which will spell their own demise, and so always have some peculiar self-destruct device built into them. If there are still political radicals on the scene in ten years' time, it will be a grim prospect. There will be no temple in the New Jerusalem, so the New Testament informs us, since ecclesial apparatuses belong to a history in conflict, not to the realm of freedom beyond that history's extreme horizon. All oppositional politics thus move under the sign of irony, knowing themselves ineluctably parasitic on their antagonists. Our grudge against the ruling order is not only that it has oppressed us in our social, sexual or racial identities, but that it has thereby forced us to lavish an extraordinary amount of attention on these things, which are not in the long run all that important. Those of us who happen to be British, yet who object to what has been done historically to other peoples in our name, would far prefer a situation in which we could take being British for granted and think about something more interesting for a change.

When Michel Foucault scathingly remarks that Marxism belongs entirely to the nineteenth century, the only bemusement for a Marxist is why he should assume that this constitutes a *criticism* of the creed. For the past is of course what we are made of; and the impasse of any transformative politics is that it can unravel what Marx and Stephen Dedalus call the nightmare of history only with the poor, contaminated instruments which that history has handed it. If Marxism belongs in a way to the museum, it is because capitalism has not yet awakened to its own drearily anachronistic nature, to the fact that it has long overstayed its welcome. Unable to remember the past, capitalism is bound compulsively to repeat it in that ceaseless sameness-within-difference which is commodity exchange; whereas for Marx the only truly memorable or historic event would be that by which we were able to leap from what he terms 'pre-history' – the eternal recurrence of new variants on persistent forms of exploitation – to 'history' proper: the kingdom of use-value, sensuous particularity and an endless productivity of difference. But all of that – what Marx enigmatically calls in *The Eighteenth Brumaire of Louis Bonaparte* 'the poetry of the future' – is a content which, as he says, 'goes beyond the phrase' of the present, and so can be figured only in silence, exile and cunning. It is necessary, even so, to 'remember' that future, about which nothing very positive can be said, in order to remember that as political radicals our identity stands and falls with those we oppose. It is in this sense, above all, that they have the upper hand.

Nationalism, Irish or otherwise, has never been particularly notable for its self-irony. Michael Collins never looked much like a man intent on doing himself out of business, a task which as it happened was left to others. And though irony may be a favoured trope of the literary intellectual, it is hard to summon much of it when you have been blinded by a British army rubber bullet. How is such irony not simply to defuse our anger? It is hard for us today to reinvent the boldness with which a Leon Trotsky could polemicise against the whole concept of 'proletarian culture' in his *Literature and Revolution*, since for Trotsky the proletariat was no more than a point of transition to a fully classless society. For Trotsky, the *proletkultists* have forgotten that social class, like colonialism, is a *relation*, and that a class or nation cannot live on as some corporate self-identical entity once those political relations have been dismantled. The whole concept of a 'nationalist culture' must surely fall under a similar political judgement; yet if Trotsky could speak out on such a topic it was of course because he had won his authority to be heard, as architect of the Red Army and veteran of Bolshevik class struggle, He had, that is to say, been right the way through and come out somewhere on the other side – which could hardly be said of those who would now dismiss the notion of an Irish nationalist culture from the tap rooms of Tottenham or the senior common rooms of Oxbridge. Besides, Trotsky's negative assessment of a proletarian culture is not easily dissociable from his chronically over-sanguine political temperament; and the whole concept, like that of a nationalist culture, is arguably too multiple and ambiguous in meaning to be simply spurned or celebrated.

The metaphysics of nationalism speak of the entry into full self-realisation of a unitary subject known as the people. As with all such philosophies of the subject from Hegel to the present, this monadic subject must somehow curiously pre-exist its own process of materialisation – must be equipped, even now, with certain highly determinate needs and desires, on the model of the autonomous human personality.[3] The problem is not so much one of discriminating among this subject's needs and desires – of determining, for example, which of them fore-shadow a desirable future and which are merely the reflexes of an oppressive present – but rather the sheer fact that these desires are repressed. The model, in other words, is an expression/blockage one, of a familiar Romantic kind; and as with any model of such historical tenacity there is undoubtedly much to be said for it. Subjects, national or otherwise, do indeed experience needs which are repressed but demand realisation; it is just that one ironic effect of such repression is to render us radically uncertain of what our needs really are. The very repressive conditions which make it necessary for the subject to express itself freely also tend to render it partially opaque to itself. If subjects have needs, then we already know what one at least of these needs must be, namely the need to know what one's needs are. The metaphysics of nationalism tend to obscure this point, by assuming a subject somehow intuitively present to itself; in privileging the concept of self-realisation, it elevates a subject–object relation over a subject–subject one, forgetting that the expression and formulation of needs is always a dialogical affair, that needs and desires are always in some sense received back from an 'other'. On the other hand, those contemporary thinkers, like Jürgen Habermas, who recall us to this truth tend to forget in their turn about the political necessities of lifting the repression, so that such dialogism can actually take place. A radical politics can prescribe what must be done for this to occur; but it cannot prescribe the content of what will then be lived, for the content, as Marx says, goes beyond the phrase. All radical politics are thus in a profound sense formalistic. As long as we can now adequately describe the transformations our political actions intend, we have failed by that token to advance beyond reformism.

If women are oppressed as women, are the Irish oppressed as Irish? In one sense, surely not: it was never of much interest to British imperialism whether the Irish were Irish or Eskimo, white or black, whether they worshipped tree gods or the Trinity. It is not their ethnic peculiarity but their territory and labour-power which have entranced the British. The Irish are simply denizens of a convenient neighbouring island; as long as they are *other* than the British they do not, like women, require certain specific innate characteristics to be ruled over. (The oppression of women is not of course reducible to such innate characteristics, but it is not independent of them either.) In another sense, however, it is clearly abstract cavilling to maintain that the Irish people has not been oppressed *as* Irish. However fundamentally indifferent colonialism may be to the nature of the peoples it does down, the fact remains that a particular people is in effect done down *as such*. And it is this fact that the truth of nationalism illuminates. As with the case of women, then, to attempt to by-pass the specificity of one's identity in the name of freedom will always be perilously abstract, even once one has recognised that such an identity is as much a construct of the oppressor as one's 'authentic' sense of oneself. Any emancipatory politics must begin with the specific, then, but must in the same gesture leave it behind. For the freedom in question is not the freedom to 'be Irish' or 'be a woman', whatever that might mean, but simply the freedom now enjoyed by certain other groups to determine their identity as they may wish. Ironically, then, a politics of difference or specificity is in the first place in the cause of sameness and universal identity – the right of a group victimised in its particularity to be on equal terms with others as far as their self-determination is concerned. This is the kernel of truth of bourgeois Enlightenment: the abstract universal right of all to be free, the shared essence or identity of all human subjects to be autonomous. In a further dialectical twist, however, this truth itself must be left behind as soon as seized; for the only point of enjoying such universal abstract equality is to discover and live one's own particular difference. The *telos* of the entire process is not, as the Enlightenment believed, universal truth, right and identity, but concrete particularity. It is just that such particularity has to pass through that abstract equality and come out somewhere on the other side, somewhere quite different from where it happens to be standing now. The most sterile form of nationalism, to continue the Hegelian idiom, is one which merely elevates a 'bad' or given particularity to the universal. The release of concrete, sensuously particular use-value – to put the matter in Marxist terms – cannot come about by circumventing the abstract universal equalisations of exchange value, but only, somehow, by entering into that alienated logic in order to turn it against itself. As Oscar Wilde well understood, socialism is essential for genuine individualism; and if Wilde's own outrageous individualism prefigures that in one sense, it also testifies in its very flamboyant artifice to the way in which any individualism of the present is bound to be a strained, fictive, parodic travesty of the real thing.

It is part of the embarrassment of bourgeois ideology that it has never really been able to reconcile difference and identity, the particular and the universal, and this for excellent historical reasons. The sensuous particularity of human needs and desires belongs in classical bourgeois thought to the degraded sphere of 'civil society', the essentially private realms of family and economic production. The ethical and political spheres, by contrast, are where men and women encounter one another as abstractly equalised universal subjects. And one of the tasks of bourgeois ideology is to square the grotesque discrepancy between these two worlds as brazenly as it can. The most effective critique of bourgeois society is accordingly one which like Marxism is 'immanent', installing itself within the very logic of that order's own most cherished values in order to unmask the necessary disconnection of this ideal universal realm from the sordidly particularistic appetites it serves to mystify. Other kinds of radical critique are also possible, however, which seize upon one pole of this particular/universal opposition in order to turn it against the other. In the manner of Enlightenment radicalism, you can press for the revolutionary *extension* of universal rights, embarrassing such ideals by reminding them forcibly of the groups and peoples they exclude; or, like Romantic radicalism, you can embrace the local, sensuously specific and irreducibly individual and seek to shipwreck an abstract idealism on the rock of the concretely real. These strategies are not actually as antithetical as they seem, since nothing could be more abstract than so-called Romantic 'immediacy'; but they constitute between them a kind of pincer movement to aggravate the contradictions of the bourgeois social order.

If Enlightenment radicalism means, in the context of Ireland, Wolfe Tone and the United Irishmen, the pieties of sensuous particularity mean the aestheticised politics of Young Ireland and much that has flowed from them. Particularity is either suppressed in the totality of universal Reason, the concrete Irish subject sublated to a citizen of the world, or celebrated as a unique, irreducible state of being impenetrable to all alien Enlightenment rationality. In modern European thought, however, the 'aesthetic' signifies less sensuous particularity in itself, than the very ideological model of how this contradiction between specific and universal may be harmoniously resolved. The work of art is itself governed by a total law, but a law which appears mysteriously, spontaneously at one with the very self-determining autonomy of each of its component parts. Behind this aesthetic model stands a new kind of bourgeois polity, in which – since the centralised law of feudal absolutism has been overthrown – each individual must somehow give the law to himself, work all by herself, discover the law inscribed in her very affections, sensations and bodily impulses. What is in question here, in short, is that historically new form of power which Antonio Gramsci has termed 'hegemony' – that process whereby the particular subject so introjects a universal law as to consent to its imperatives in the form of consenting to his own deepest being.

Any such hegemony is far more difficult to construct in colonial conditions. For the law in such conditions will appear visibly alien, heteronomous to the individual rather than the secret inner structure of her identity. It is the embarrassment of colonial ruling classes, as it is not so much of the metropolitan governing elites, that they figure as perceptibly 'other' to their subordinates, perhaps speaking a foreign language or having a different colour of skin. The law of political power always works best when it is invisible, as Edmund Burke well understood; for the law to be salient is for it to risk becoming itself an object of contestation. It is therefore perhaps not surprising that in Ireland the 'aesthetic' as totalising solution to the conflict of universal and particular is rather less in evidence. Instead, the aesthetic tends to emerge as one side of the dilemma – as expressive of the lived specificity of a unique people in the teeth of that abstract universalism which is taken to be the very mark of modernity. This is not to say, on the other hand, that the aesthetic as 'disinterested' mythic solution to real contradicitions is not in evidence in Ireland at all. There are Irish critics and commentators who deploy the term today as a privileged mark of that decency, civility and cultivation of which an uncouth nationalism is fatally bereft. In the stalest of Arnoldian clichés, the poetic is still being counterposed to the political – which is only to say that the 'poetic' as we have it today was, among other things, historically constructed to carry out just that business of suppressing political conflict. Imagination and enlightened liberal reason are still being offered to us in Ireland today as the antithesis of sectarianism; and like all such idealised values they forget their own roots in a social class and history not unnoted for its own virulent sectarianism, then and now. This bankrupt Irish Arnoldianism is particularly ironic when one considers that the title of Arnold's own major work, *Culture and Anarchy*, might well have been rewritten as *Britain and Ireland*. The liberal humanist notion of Culture was constituted, among other things, to marginalise such peoples as the Irish, so that it is particularly intriguing to find this sectarian gesture being rehearsed by a few of the Irish themselves.

If the rift between sensuous particularity and idealist abstraction has proved a constant source of unease for bourgeois society, it has proved something of the same for that society's political antagonists. For it is hard to see how the left can simply 'dialectically mediate' such oppositions without merely rehearsing the mystificatory gestures of the right. Somewhere around the turn of the nineteenth century, the left fatally surrendered the aesthetic to the right. Tom Paine's plain-minded scoffing at Burke's extravagantly metaphorical diction, or Mary Wollstonecraft's scathing dismissal of his 'pampered sensibility', are cases in point.

Feeling, imagination, the priority of local affections and unarguable allegiances, a subliminally nurturing cultural tradition: these things, from Burke and Coleridge to Yeats and T. S. Eliot, are effectively confiscated by political reaction, which is shrewd enough not to attempt to rule by the naked light of reason or utility alone. The political left is then doubly disabled: if it seeks to evolve its own discourse of place, body, inheritance, sensuous need, it will find itself miming the cultural forms of its opponents; if it does not do so it will appear bereft of a body, marooned with a purely rationalist politics which has cut loose from the intimate affective depths of the poetic. The feminist analogy is exact: if women speak the discourse of the body, the unconscious, the dark underside of formal speech – in a word, the Gothic – they merely confirm their aberrant status; if they appropriate like Wollstonecraft the language of radical rationalism, they are no different from men. Left political theory in Europe today is consequently divided between the rationalism of a Habermas, with his 'ideal speech communities' of universal, abstractly equal subjects from whom all bodily inclination has been drained, and the anarchic particularism of the post-structuralists, with their heady celebrations of delirium, pure difference, the fragment, flashes of libidinal intensity, against a rational totality now denounced as brutally totalitarian.

I have suggested that the aesthetic as a totalisation of particular and universal is in general absent in Ireland; but then what else, you might claim, is *Ulysses*? Where could one discover a more triumphant unity of the two than in that text, in which every particular opens cunningly out into the cosmic, every time, place or identity is secretly pregnant with every other? The aesthetics of *Ulysses* are in this sense pretty standard Hegelian stuff, and among other things fit compensation for the pains of exile. If anywhere is everywhere, then you can scribble away in Trieste without ever having left Dublin. But it would surely be obtuse to overlook the enormous irony with which the novel manages this remorseless totalisation, which gestures to its own flagrant arbitrariness in its very pokerfaced exhaustiveness. The form of *Ulysses* is indeed in one sense an aesthetic resolution of historical contradicitons – not least of the conflict between the new international circuits of capitalism, with their correlative cosmopolitan centres of culture in Paris, London, Berlin and New York, and the older national formations or cultural traditions which are being increasingly outmoded. Modernism is at once, contradictorily, an exhilarating estrangement of such clapped-out national lineages from the powerfully distancing perspectives of exile, and an expression of the rootless conditions of an international monopoly capitalism, whose abstractly universalist forms are mimed by modernism's own progressively abstract techniques.[4] If, like Joyce, you have little enough of a rich national lineage to begin with, then you become paradigmatic in your very colonial dispossession of the destiny of even advanced national formations in the era of international capital. For entirely different reasons, neither colonial backwardness nor the inbred provincialism of the imperial nations can produce the art which the age demands. Since Ireland, from the standpoint of the advanced societies, is already a kind of non-place and non-identity, it can lend itself peculiarly well to a cosmopolitan modernism for which all places and identities are becoming progressively interchangeable.

If *Ulysses* 'resolves' contradicitons, however, the sweated Flaubertian labor with which this is accomplished points to the effective impossibility of the whole project. The textual totality which lends a particular time and place fresh centrality does so in order to betray simultaneously just how radically contingent any such place or time has now become. Joyce's compliment to Ireland, in inscribing it on the cosmopolitan map, is in this sense distinctly backhanded. The novel celebrates and undermines the Irish national formation at a stroke, deploying the full battery of cosmopolitan modernist techniques to recreate it, while suggesting with its every breath just how easily it could have done the same for Bradford or the Bronx. Something of the same ambiguity haunts *Finnegans Wake*, a work which, as its radical apologists have pointed out, confounds and commingles all distinct identities in a manner scandalous to the rigorous hierarchies of orthodox bourgeois culture. Yet it is not only that this free play of difference and desire is arguably still contained within a *Ulysses*-like structure of eternal recurrence – that what you lose on the semiotic swings you make up on the Viconian roundabouts. It is also that what is turned disruptively against bourgeois *culture* is in a sense bourgeois *economy*: the levelling, equalising, indifferent operations of the commodity form itself, which respects no unique identity, transgresses all frontiers, melts solidity into air and profanes the holy. The *Wake*'s anarchic differencing is possible only on the basis of a secret homogenising of reality, a prior equalising of all items which then enables them to enter into the most shockingly idiosyncratic permutations.[5] There comes a point, as Hegel was well aware, at which 'pure' difference merely collapses back into 'pure' identity, united as they are in their utter indeterminacy.

Joyce, then, poses the problem of totalisation, rather than providing us with any very adequate solution. The ironic overtotalisation of *Ulysses* is a pedantic travesty of modern European aesthetics, whereas the *Wake* displays an enormous, disabling distance between its abstract 'deep structure' and its textual particulars. Either way, dialectical mediation is disrupted: immediate and universal are either too comically close for comfort or riven apart. Such ironic, impossible or aporetic relations between the two are perhaps still necessarily the case today, in the relations between particular political struggles and the goal of universal emancipation. What any oppressed group has most vitally in common is just the shared fact of their oppression. Their collective identity is in this sense importantly negative, defined less by shared positive characteristics than by a common antagonism to some political order. That negative collective identity, however, is bound over a period of time to generate a positive particular culture, without which political emancipation is probably impossible. Nobody can live in perpetual deferment of their sense of selfhood, or free themselves from bondage without a strongly affirmative consciousness of who they are. Without such self-consciousness, one would not even know what one lacked; and a subject which thinks itself complete feels no need to revolt. In this sense, the 'negativity' of an oppressed people – its sense of itself as dislocated and depleted – already implies a more positive style of being. The true triumph of alienation would be not to know that one was alienated at all. But since any such positive identity evolves *within* oppressive conditions, partly as compensatory for them, it can never be an unambiguous political gain, and will always be to some extent collusive with its antagonists. The paradox or aporia of any transformative politics is that it demands, to be successful, a 'centred', resolute, self-confident agent, but would not be necessary in the first place if such self-confidence were genuinely possible. Radical change is thus rendered highly vulnerable by what makes it necessary in the first place. The ideal revolutionary subject has broken with an imposed political identity into a kind of nameless, subversive negativity, yet has a sense of his or her own autonomous powers and capacities which far outstrips that hazy, indeterminate awareness of ourselves as agents which we derive from routine social life. This is not the kind of conundrum which any discourse of dialectical mediation will readily clarify.

Where human subjects politically begin, in all their sensuous specificity, is with certain needs and desires. Yet need and desire are also what render us non-identical with ourselves, opening us up to some broader social dimension; and what is posed within this dimension is the question of what *general* conditions would be necessary for our particular needs and desires to be fulfilled. Mediated through the general in this way, particular demands cease to be self-identical and return to themselves transformed by a discourse of the other. The feminist, nationalist or trade unionist might now come to recognise that in the long run none of their desires is realisable without the fulfilment of the others'. Where the anti-dialecticians are right is that such a recognition cannot be *lived* as simple, seamless unity. Indeed the fact that the Hegelian totality cannot be lived was Kierkegaard's recurrent complaint against it. It is only ambiguously, precariously, that any of us can experience at once the necessary absolutism of a particular demand – to be freed, for example, from an immediate, intolerable oppression – and the more general truth that no one such demand, however just and urgent, can finally exhaust or pre-programme a political future in which the content will have gone beyond the phrase. As Kierkegaard might have said, it is a matter of trying to live that dialectic passionately, ironically, in all of its elusive impossibility, rather than merely providing an elegant theoretical formulation of it.

Notes

1   See Julia Kristeva, 'La femme, ce n'est jamais ça', *Tel Quel* 59 (Autumn 1974).
2   See Walter Benjamin, 'Theses on the Philosophy of History', in H. Arendt (ed.), *Illuminations* (London: Jonathan Cape, 1970), p. 266.
3   For a valuable critique of this ideology, see Seyla Benhabib, *Critique, Norm, and Utopia* (New York: Columbia University Press, 1986).

4   For an excellent account of modernism in these terms, see Raymond Williams, 'Beyond Cambridge English', in *Writing in Society* (London: Verso, 1983).

5   'The pluralism of [Joyce's] styles and languages, the absorbent nature of his controlling myths and systems, finally gives a certain harmony to varied experience. But, it could be argued, it is the harmony of indifference, one in which everything is a version of something else, where sameness rules over diversity, where contradiction is finally and disquietingly written out' (Seamus Deane, *Heroic Styles: the tradition of an idea*. Field Day pamphlet no. 4, (Derry, 1984), p. 16).

28 Saint Oscar

I first thought of writing about Oscar Wilde when I discovered that hardly any of the Oxford students who asked to study him with me realized that he was Irish. Since Wilde himself realized this only fitfully, this is hardly a grievous crime, though it might be said to be evidence of one. English students of literature would know of course that Yeats and Joyce were Irish, and probably – thinking of those tasty babies of *A Modest Proposal* – Jonathan Swift; but it is more doubtful that they could name the nationality of Sterne, Sheridan, Goldsmith and Burke, and they might even hesitate over Bernard Shaw. British cultural imperialism has long annexed these gifted offshore islanders to its own literary canon, and of course Wilde himself was in many ways glad enough to be recruited. Yet several of the characteristics that make him appear most typically upper-class English – the scorn for bourgeois normality, the flamboyant self-display, the verbal *brio* and iconoclasm – are also, interestingly enough, where one might claim he is most distinctively Irish; and pondering this odd paradox was one point of origin of this play.

Another such point was my sense of how astonishingly Wilde's work prefigures the insights of contemporary cultural theory. Or perhaps it would be more accurate to say that such theory, for all its excited air of novelty, represents in some ways little advance on the *fin de siècle*. Language as self-referential, truth as a convenient fiction, the human subject as contradictory and 'deconstructed', criticism as a form of 'creative' writing, the body and its pleasures pitted against a pharisaical ideology: in these and several other ways, Oscar Wilde looms up for us more and more as the Irish Roland Barthes. The parallel is not fortuitous: somewhere behind Wilde, as somewhere behind modern literary theory, lurks the gigantic shadow of Friedrich Nietzsche. But for me personally this was more than just an intriguing intellectual conjuncture. I have been professionally engaged with radical cultural theory for some years; but during part of that time I have also been struggling to make sense of my own ambiguous, contradictory identity, as one of Irish working-class provenance now teaching in the very belly of the beast at Oxford. In the end, this combination of factors proved irresistible. Writing about the Irish Oxfordian socialist proto-deconstructionist Oscar Wilde came after a time to feel more like a necessity than a possibility; and the only problem then was to find an appropriate form. I flirted briefly with the idea of a long critical essay, then decided that it would have to be a play. As Wilde had hijacked the artistic forms of the English for his own devious ends, so I would try to turn his own dramatic parodies back on himself, finding some way of reinventing him without, as far as possible, actually quoting him.

As I moved more deeply into this work, I began to discover that the two factors that had triggered my fascination with Wilde – his Irishness, and his remarkable anticipation of some present-day theory – were in fact closely interrelated. I had argued in some previous work that the ideas of several of the leading avant-garde theorists of our own time had to be seen in the context of their socially marginal status, whether as ex-colonials (Jacques Derrida), women (Julia Kristeva) or homosexuals (Barthes, Foucault). It wasn't difficult to see just how this might illuminate Wilde, and to begin to fumble for some of the connections between modernism and colonialism. If, like Wilde, your history has been one of colonial oppression, you are less likely to be enamoured of stable representational forms, which are usually, so to speak, on the side of Caesar. You will find yourself a parodist and parasite, bereft of any imposingly continuous cultural tradition, cobbling one together as you go along. Your writing will tend to set up home with anti-realist fantasy and imaginative extravagance, forced often enough into these modes as poor compensation for a harsh social reality. If the language in which you write is, like Wilde's, the tongue of the colonial oppressor, then it is unlikely that you will avoid an intense verbal self-consciousness; and language will seem to you the one surviving space where you might momentarily be free, wresting a pyrrhic victory over an inexorably determining history. The colonial subject, pitched into a permanent crisis of identity, will not be overimpressed by the solid, well-rounded characters of classical literary realism, but will feel itself fluid, diffuse, provisional; and the same sense of provisionality will apply to social forms and conventions, breeding an ironic awareness of their fictive, ungrounded nature. In these as in other ways, there is a secret compact between artistic or theoretical experiment and the experience of colonialism, one still much in evidence today; and Wilde was for me one vital place where this could be explored, more for the sake of my own identity and allegiances than as a purely intellectual problem. He inherits a form of Anglo-Irish writing which is ironic about realism, sportive, satirical and fantastic, ecstatically comic with a dark, sobering subtext, and, in its contradictions and subversive wit, deeply perverse. It is a style of writing to which I find myself spontaneously attracted, whatever inferior version of it I may turn out; and it runs completely against the grain of my intellectual formation as an English academic. I think that my theoretical work over recent years has represented a long, painful effort to rediscover something of my own voice in this respect, to turn back to forms of writing bred, so to speak, in the bone; and it is one measure of the awesome power of conventional academic *genres* that in order to be faithful to this impulse I have had to make a break from theoretical to so-called 'creative' writing. What is at one level a question of style is at another level a matter of commitment and identity, a question of slowly discovering that which was 'Irish' in myself but had been suppressed by my formal English education. Examining the doubleness of Oscar Wilde, Oxford dandy and son of the dirtiest man in Dublin, then felt like an unavoidable stage in this self-exploration.

If Wilde is not usually thought of in England as Irish, neither is he seen as a particularly political figure. But Wilde is political in all the most fundamental senses of the term, political in ways that far outstrip the impoverished categories of parliamentary democracy. He was actually politically minded in some rather sharper, more specific meanings of the word too: he wrote finely about socialism, spoke up for Irish republicanism when the British sneered at it, and despite his carefully nurtured flippancy displayed throughout his life a tenderness and compassion towards the dispossessed. But he is also political in some more elusive senses of the term – political, for example, because he is very funny, a remorseless debunker of the high-toned *gravitas* of bourgeois Victorian England. He is a radical because he takes nothing seriously, cares only for form, appearance and pleasure, and is religiously devoted to his own self-gratification. In Victorian society, such a man did not need to bed the son of the Marquess of Queensberry to become an enemy of the state. I have tried to look in some of my own previous work[1] at the complex relations between comedy and radical politics, in the context of a political left not exactly celebrated for its uproarious good humour. The names of Mikhail Bakhtin and Bertolt Brecht signify something of this conjuncture in our time, but so also does that of Oscar Wilde. One of the many paradoxes of a transformative politics is that it is in the end all about pleasure, fulfilment, ease and serenity of being, but is forced, sometimes tragically, to forgo some of these precious qualities in the essential rigour and seriousness of its practice. This contradiction in turn conceals another: that values such as pleasure, style and serenity are always politically double-edged, always weapons in the armoury of the rulers as well as potential instruments of their subversion. Wilde lived these contradictions to the full, and was conscious enough of them in his own way. If he sometimes has the offensive irresponsibility of the aesthete, he also restores to us something of the full political force of that term, as a radical rejection of mean-spirited utility and a devotion to human self-realization as an end in itself which is very close to the writings of Karl Marx. If his concern with rhetoric, humour, self-irony, the mask, theatrical self-display are at one level the fruits of an Irish lineage at odds with middle-class English moralism, they are also preoccupations that can play straight into the hands of the English aristocracy. The line between a politically scandalous obsession with surfaces and a callow aestheticism the upper class could recognize as its own is always with him fascinatingly difficult to draw.

Wilde hailed from the city Joyce spelt as 'Doublin', and everything about him – his nationality, sexual identity, social status, politics – is precarious, unstable, double-edged. Much previous work on Wilde has centred on his homosexuality, and this is on any account at the heart of what he was; but if I have tried to avoid writing a 'gay' play about him, this is not only because as a heterosexual I am inevitably something of an outsider in such matters, but because it seems to me vital to put that particular ambiguity or doubleness back in the context of a much wider span of ambivalences. Wilde was perverse in much more than a sexual sense, and his sexual, social and artistic perversities are deeply interrelated. His fetish, from beginning to end, was language; and *Saint Oscar* joins a long line of Anglo-Irish plays that are, for many an English ear, a good deal too verbal. Unlike the life of its subject, it could hardly be said to be crammed with exhilarating dramatic action. This may well be to do with my own limitations as a dramatist; but it is also part of a deliberate attempt to reintroduce that artistic form which has always made the genetically empiricist English most deeply uneasy, the 'theatre of ideas'. If it manages to be entertaining at the same time, as I hope it is, then this may help to dissuade the English of their complacent dogma that the intellect is one thing and a sense of humour another, a division disabling to both faculties. The Irish have on the whole found it less trouble to be funny and tragic at one and the same time; and nowhere could this duality be more graphically figured than in the life of Oscar Wilde, clown and victim, scapegoat and entertainer.

Nobody can write now of Britain and Ireland in Wilde's day without bringing to mind the tragic events that have afflicted Ireland in the past two decades. Reflections on the past are always at some level meditations on the present; and in this play I seize on the fact that one of Wilde's prosecutors was Edward Carson, later to spearhead the Unionist opposition to Home Rule, to bring the trial of Wilde to bear on the politics of the present. The Irish, so they say, have to keep remembering their own history because the English keep forgetting it; and it was Sigmund Freud who reminded us that what we do not truly remember we are doomed to repeat. Oscar Wilde's treatment at the hands of a brutal, arrogant British Establishment is being acted out once more in Ireland today, with brutality of a different kind. The significant past, Walter Benjamin remarked, is that frail image which flashes up to us at a moment of extreme danger; and Benjamin's practice of revolutionary nostalgia was to summon into the present the shades of the unjustly quelled of history, so that they might lend us something of their power. I try in this play, then, to summon the shade of Oscar Wilde back to our side when we are in urgent need of him, confident in the knowledge that whatever indignities a dispossessed people may have to endure, small nations will not rest until they are free.

Note

1   See in particular my *Walter Benjamin, or Towards a Revolutionary Criticism* (London, 1981), and my novel *Saints and Scholars* (London, 1987).

29 Unionism and Utopia: *The Cure at Troy* by Seamus Heaney

One evening last November, the city of Belfast witnessed a mildly epochal moment of theatrical history. A couple of hundred men and women from Andersonstown, a working-class, strongly republican area of the city, crowded into a parish hall to watch a Sophoclean tragedy. For more than a few of the audience it would have been their first experience of theatre, let alone of classical drama; not many Andersonstown folk are habitués of the Lyric, Belfast's 'serious' theatre. What was the connection between audience and play?

The play in question was *The Cure at Troy*, Seamus Heaney's translation of *Philoctetes*. It was presented by Field Day theatre company, which each year tours a new play to about twenty-five venues both north and south of the border. Irish people come to watch Field Day because they can expect a play of relevance to their own concerns, and despite its Chorus and Attic costumes *The Cure at Troy* is no exception. For it isn't hard to read the piece as an oblique allegory of the 'Troubles', and Heaney's explicit allusions to hunger strikers and police widows in an appended Epilogue are meant to leave no-one in doubt about the bearing of ancient Athens on contemporary Ulster. Philoctetes, you may remember, was the Greek warrior involved in the siege of Troy who was unceremoniously dumped on the island of Lemnos by his disgusted comrades because he stank to high heaven as the result of a snake bite to his foot. But the Homeric heroes have to lever him off the island again, because without his unerring bow Troy will not fall to them. When the play opens, its ulcerated protagonist has dragged out a lonely decade as a castaway, trailing pus and blood behind him and bellowing with agony at every step; but the wily Odysseus puts into shore with a typically duplicitous scheme for inveigling his erstwhile comrade back into battle. This isn't going to be easy, given Philoctetes' understandable hatred for his treacherous colleagues; but Odysseus sets on his impressionable junior Neoptolemus to sweet-talk the pathetic old cripple out of his magical weapon.

Sullen, rancorous, inwardly gnawed by hatred and paralysed by memories of past injustice, Philoctetes is Heaney's unlovely image of the sectarian North of

Ireland. The dramatic trick is to keep the reality of his sense of hurt, and the sterile pathology of his response to it, in subtle equilibrium; and Des McAlteer, the gaunt, grizzled actor who played the part for Field Day, managed magnificently to combine the pathos of this betrayed warrior with his curmudgeonliness. Philoctetes is at once the very image of suffering humanity and sectarian stereotype; in a strikingly overdetermined image, he thus incarnates and transcends the Troubles at a stroke, nurturing historic wrongs while providing the play's touchstone of a common humanity at once more durable and more fundamental than such political divisions.

There's more than a whiff here of the cosmopolitan liberal-humanist Heaney at odds with the Derry republican; but it isn't a clear-cut case of the 'human' versus the 'political'. Moved by Philoctetes's plight, the vacillating Neoptolemus casts off the shady political role Odysseus has smooth-talked him into, offering instead to lift Philoctetes off the island. But this is to turn his back on the devious *realpolitik* of his senior colleague, the Charlie Haughey of Lemnos, rather than to abandon the political as such. If the humanity of Philoctetes finds an answerable impulse in himself, it is because he rejects a parochial Greek self-interest for an enlightened universal concept of political justice: 'The jurisdiction I am under here/Is justice herself. She isn't only Greek'. If there is a justice for Ireland, there is no distinctively Irish justice. The difference at stake is one between good and bad politics, sound principle and squalid pragmatism, not between the political and the personal, which would have been unintelligible to the ancient Greeks. Neoptolemus responds as he does because he is bound by a properly global law of comradeship, not because of some errant lapse into personal sentiment. Moreover, if Philoctetes symbolises the poor forked creature humanity itself, it is in the shape of a raw, recalcitrant, sheerly biological torment with which nothing in itself, politically speaking, can be done. He can figure, to be sure, as an *object* of pity, an index of the compassion (or lack of it) of others; and in this sense he's a negative sort of utopian figure, the recipient of a justice and fellow-feeling which surpasses Odyssean wheeler-dealing. But this humanity is impotent until he himself has shifted from object to subject, relinquished his self-lacerating misanthropy and re-entered the maelstrom of political history by assuming his position once more as a political agent before the walls of Troy. To do so involves strategic compromise, re-embracing the very Greeks who sold him down the river; and the dramatic problem is to distinguish such essential flexibility from the crafty dodges of an Odysseus, superficially alike as they seem. But if Odysseus's hard-nosed utility stands at one pole of the play, the simple intransigence of an historically fixated 'principle' stands at the other; and it's up to Neoptolemus, himself pitched between the two alternatives, to remind the surly Philoctetes that 'The danger is you'll break if you don't bend'. How, in the North of Ireland context, do you demarcate a resourceful open-endedness from shopping all you believe in? Philoctetes has to make the transition from the wound to the bow – from a festering contempt for political humanity to an active role in the resolution of historical conflict. He must do so, moreover, by his own free choice: it's a neat irony that his *decision* to re-enter the military fray is itself part of the gods' predetermined programme.

Humanity is an imperative which must be enacted *now*, as the befuddled Neoptolemus finally appreciates and the pragmatist Odysseus doesn't. For utopia to be conceivable at all it must, in Habermasian terms, be somewhere prefigurable in the flesh-and-blood of the present, in the shape of an instinctive creaturely response to another's needs. But the fullest realisation of this humanity is equally, ineluctably *deferred* to the just city of the future, which only political practice can bring about. For Heaney, this means deferring it not beyond the threshold of history, but (in terms of the myth) to the conquest of Troy and the final transcendence of all the old sectarian strife. It is on this glimpse of utopia that the play's Epilogue boldly, beautifully touches:

> Human beings suffer.
> They torture one another.
> They get hurt and get hard.
> No poem or play or song
> Can fully right a wrong
> Inflicted and endured . . .
>
> History says: *Don't hope*
> *On this side of the grave.*
> But then, once in a lifetime
> The longed-for tidal wave
> Of justice can rise up,
> And hope and history rhyme.
>
> So hope for a great sea change
> On the far side of revenge.
> Believe that a further shore
> Is reachable from here.
> Believe in miracles
> And cures and healing wells.

If there's a moving utopian hope here, there's also some notable confusion at the level of allegory. Is it really going to take a *miracle* to dislodge the British from Ireland? That was well enough for the Greeks, who had a magic bow conveniently at their disposal, whereas we just have Seamus Mallon, Sinn Fein and the Secretary of State for Northern Ireland. The myth, in other words, covertly determines its own kind of contemporary political stance, which amounts to an openness to the utterly inconceivable as nebulous as it is courageous. Resolution, as Heaney's naturalising imagery intimates ('tidal wave', 'sea-change'), arrives as miraculous gift rather than as political construct, inarticulable epiphany rather than political strategy.

No poem or play or song, so the Epilogue avers, can fully right a wrong. But in *The Cure at Troy* one allegory is struggling to get out of another, and this is the figure of Philoctetes as *poète maudit*. The trope of the doomed, marooned, mysteriously emasculated artist has of course a complex Romantic history behind it; and there's no doubt that in meditating on the ironies of principle and pragmatism, obduracy and flexibility, political engagement and utopic prefiguration, Heaney is casting a lateral glance at the fraught status of the North of Ireland poet, unsure whether to speak out or keep silent, take sides or just keep warm in his verse a tenderness and sensuousness which might be read as either political, meta-political or depoliticising. Unlike the resolutely *dégagé* Jocyean finale of *Station Island*, *The Cure at Troy* plumps for political commitment of a kind; if you stay on the island, whether in the Aegean or Loch Derg, you fester and rankle, grow self-involved and self-tormenting. But here the Greek myth serves Heaney less adroitly, granting the artist Philoctetes far too central, salvific a status. If it's possible in Homer for such a man to help end a war with his literal or rhetorical shafts, it's hardly on the cards in the six counties. The ignominy of the wound can't be so glibly reversed into the hubris of the visionary bow. In the play's concluding moments, the resolution of historical conflict and the healing of Philoctetes himself merge gracefully into a single compelling image; and in a general sense this may also be true of the North of Ireland poet, who will find imaginative peace only when the political wounds of his people have been salved and bound. But that poet won't heal himself by spearheading the troops, which is mere idealist compensation for actual ineffectiveness; and if the myth subtly falsifies here, it does so too in its proleptic celebration of the overthrow of Troy. For on any literal translation into modern terms, this can only suggest that the agonies of Ulster will be soothed when the political enemy is brought to its knees. The play pronounces this truth; but it doesn't, as it were, *mean* to pronounce it, since such a scenario is far removed from the mildly reconciliationist politics of a Heaney. Right at the play's end, then, the allegorical use of the myth releases an *unintended meaning*, which is only possible because the conquest of Troy has been distanced and stylised to a sort of metaphor of Philoctetes's own personal regeneration. The play thus 'unwittingly' inserts into its reconciliationist (Catholic–Protestant) mode the very confrontationist (Ireland–Britain) model which a good many Northern writers, including Heaney himself, would rush to disown. Pardoxically, in displacing the focus from the political to the personal, from outward to inward warfare, *The Cure at Troy* breeds a political implication which outruns its author's personal mastery.

30 Heathcliff and the Great Hunger

The fourth of the Brontë children, Patrick Branwell, has not been enshrined among the immortals. Being the brother of those sisters can't have been easy, but Branwell made a more spectacular hash of it than was strictly necessary. Drug addict and alcoholic, flushed with dreams of literary grandeur, he ended up as an embezzling ticket clerk on a Yorkshire railway station, scrawled his final document (a begging note for gin) in September 1848 and expired soon after, wasted and bronchitic, in his father's arms. Quaintly enough, he was for a brief period secretary of the local Temperance Society. He also taught in Sunday school, where he savaged his pupils in befuddled vengeance for his misfortunes. Chronically unemployable, he spent much of his time engaged in raffish carousals with louche artists in the George Hotel, Bradford, and with characteristic ill luck took up portrait painting just at the point where the industry was being killed off by the daguerreotype. Packed off to London as an art student of promise, he wandered around the capital in a dream, realized how shabby and provincial he appeared among the metropolitan crowd, and kept his letters of introduction to famous artists firmly in his pocket. He washed up instead in an East End pub, where he drank away his money and returned to Haworth with a pathetic tale of having been mugged. London had confirmed what he had already suspected: that he had ambitions of megalomaniac proportions and no interest whatsoever in realizing them. When he was not busy cadging gin money or chalking up an alarming slate at Haworth's Black Bull pub, he passed much of his time scribbling second-rate prose, experimenting with exotic pseudonyms and drawing pen portraits of himself hanged, stabbed or licked by the flames of eternal perdition.

Branwell lived, in short, a flamboyant stage-Irish existence, obediently conforming to the English stereotype of the feckless Mick. When his Tory father Patrick took to the Haworth hustings, Branwell, enraged at hearing him howled down by the crowd, intervened loyally on his behalf. The local populace demonstrated their displeasure by burning Branwell in effigy, a potato in one hand and a herring in the other.[1] The Brontës may have effaced their Irish origin, but the good people of Haworth evidently kept it well in mind.[2] Not that Branwell was consistently loyal to his father. His Angrian myth 'The Life of Northangerland' is a murderous Oedipal fantasy, understandably enough for anyone acquainted with the character of Patrick Brontë Senior.[3] Its dissolute, self-destructive protagonist Alexander Percy, anarchist and aristocrat, is Branwell himself shorn of the dope, spinelessness and pen-pushing in a railway station. Percy is in hock to the tune of £300,000, a suitably glamorized version of his author's slate at the Black Bull, and is egged on by his rebel comrades to commit parricide to relieve his debts. Prominent in this persuasion is a certain Mr R. P. King, otherwise known as S'Death, or occasionally – a nice touch, this – R. P. S'Death, a revoltingly evil old retainer who speaks the Yorkshire dialect despite the fact that the tale is set in Africa, and who is clearly the prototype of old Joseph in *Wuthering Heights*. Percy spearheads a political coup against the Angrian government, flanked by his trusty companions Naughty and Lawless. He and his men have bound themselves to atheism and revolution by a sacred oath, though the rationalist Percy, a stickler for political correctness, concludes the oath with the words 'So help me, my mind.' Branwell's chronicles – he wrote more than his sisters' work put together – are awash with political dissidence, and several of Percy's rebellious comrades are given Irish names. One of his closest confidants, formerly a lawyer, is the son of one William Daniel Henry Montmorency of Derrinane Abbey. Derrynane was the seat of the barrister Daniel O'Connell, who was victoriously concluding his campaign for Catholic Emancipation just as Branwell was in the process of launching his 'Branwell's Blackwood's Magazine' at the age of twelve. Alexander Percy is a supremely well-practised demagogue, and so of course was Daniel O'Connell. When the people of Haworth, stung by Branwell's defence of a father he loved and hated, burnt him in effigy as a truculent Irish peasant, they may not have been quite as off-target as it might appear.

In August 1845, Branwell took a trip from Haworth to Liverpool. It was on the very eve of the Great Famine, and the city was soon to be thronged with its starving victims. By June 1847, according to one historian, three hundred thousand destitute Irish had landed in the port.[4] As Emily Brontë's biographer comments: 'Their image, and especially those of the children, were unforgettably depicted in the *Illustrated London News* – starving scarecrows with a few rags on them and an animal growth of black hair almost obscuring their features'.[5] Many of these children were no doubt Irish speakers. A few months after Branwell's visit to Liverpool, Emily began writing *Wuthering Heights* – a novel whose male protagonist, Heathcliff, is picked up starving off the streets of Liverpool by old Earnshaw. Earnshaw unwraps his greatcoat to reveal to his family a 'dirty, ragged, black-haired child' who speaks a kind of 'gibberish', and who will later be variously labelled beast, savage, lunatic and demon. It is clear that this little Caliban has a nature on which nurture will never stick; and that is simply an English way of saying that he is quite possibly Irish.

Possibly, but by no means certainly. Heathcliff may be a gypsy, or (like Bertha Mason in *Jane Eyre*) a Creole, or any kind of alien. It is hard to know how black he is, or rather how much of the blackness is pigmentation and how much of it grime and bile. As for the Famine, the dates don't quite fit: the potato blight *phythopthera infestans* struck in the autumn of 1845, about the time that Emily Brontë was beginning her novel, so that August, the month of Branwell's visit to Liverpool, would be too early for him to have encountered Famine refugees. But there would no doubt have been a good many impoverished Irish immigrants hanging around the city; and it is tempting to speculate that Branwell ran into some of them and relayed the tale to his sister. There would be something symbolically apt in Branwell, the Luciferian rebel of the outfit, presenting Emily with the disruptive element of her work, and there is certainly a strong kinship between the brother and the novel's Byronic villain.

Wuthering Heights is much preoccupied with the relations between Nature and Culture; and Heathcliff, described by Catherine Earnshaw as an 'unreclaimed creature, without refinement, without cultivation: an arid wilderness of furze and whinstone', is about as natural as you can get without actually trailing your knuckles along the ground. (That, remember, is his *lover* speaking.) Thrushcross Grange, home of the landed gentry in the novel, stands roughly speaking for culture – for Nature worked up, cultivated and thus concealed. The Grange survives by Nature – the Lintons are the biggest landowners in the district – but like much class culture it occludes its own disreputable roots. Culture is the offspring of labour but, like the Oedipal child, denies its own lowly parentage and fantasizes that it was self-born. Culture is either self-parenting, or the offspring of previous culture. The Grange's relation to the land is a good deal more mediated than that of the Heights; the Earnshaws at the Heights are gentlefolk, but they are a remnant of the peculiarly English class of yeomen, and yeomen, unlike squires, work their own soil. J. C. Beckett points to the rarity of this sort of class, owning substantial acres of land and employing a number of labourers, in small-tenant Ireland.[6]

The reverse of the cultivation of Nature is the naturalization of culture, or, in a word, ideology. From Burke and Coleridge to Arnold and Eliot, a dominant ideological device in Britain is to transmute history itself into a seamless evolutionary continuum, endowing social institutions with all the stolid inevitability of a boulder. Society itself, in this view, becomes a marvellous aesthetic organism, self-generating and self-contained. This is a much rarer sort of discourse in Ireland. In Ireland, the land is of course an economic and political category, and an ethical one too ('racy of the soil'); it is also, more frequently than in Britain, a sexual subject, as the torn victim of imperial penetration. But it is, by and large, much less of an *aestheticized* concept – whereas in England, as John Barrell points out in his study of John Clare, it is hard to think of a word for an extensive tract of land, synchronically surveyed, other than the revealingly painterly term 'landscape'.[7] The English tend to think of paintings first and farms second – just as Jane Austen tends to look at a piece of land and see its price and proprietor but nobody actually working there. Ellen Wood has pointed to the close connection in English culture between the aesthetic appreciation of landscape and economic improvement, in the form of 'a new rural aesthetic which deliberately joined beauty with productivity and profit'.[8] The fact that rural improvement in Ireland was considerably less in evidence may then inspire a different way of perceiving the countryside.

The one place in Irish society where the land *is* aestheticized in this manner is the demesne, which is more artefact than agriculture despite the fact that demesne land traditionally represented a sizeable percentage of the worked soil. But this, of course, is essentially an English import. Nature in Ireland would often seem more a working environment than an object to be contemplated, which is in any case a typically urban way of relating to it. Stopford Brooke and T. W. Rolleston comment in the Preface to their *Treasury of Irish Poetry* that Nature as a theme has not been adequately treated by Irish poets,[9] while John Wilson Foster speculates that responses to Nature in ancient Irish writing may come from taking a spontaneous relation to it for granted.[10] But it may also reflect a certain native humanism. Yeats speaks in 'The Symbolism of Poetry' of the need for 'a casting out of descriptions of nature for the sake of nature',[11] and was certainly true to his own injunction. His natural descriptions have little of the sensuous nuance or close-wrought intricacy of a Keats or a Hopkins, though neither, one might add, do Wordsworth's. It is hard to imagine Wordsworth writing animal poetry, given the bodiless idealism of his feeling for Nature. Terence Brown remarks on the scant attention bestowed by Anglo-Irish poetry on 'features of topography or locale,' and considers the suggestion that this may have to do with a certain instability of settlement.[12] Tom Moore's lyric 'The Meeting of the Waters' has no sooner praised Nature than it qualifies the compliment by claiming that the intimate presence of friends intensifies its enchantment. Aubrey De Vere's poem 'The Year of Sorrow', written during the Famine, turns from a burgeoning Nature to the brute facts of starvation, then offers this natural vitality as a last consolation to the dying. James Clarence Mangan detested Nature, which crops up in his work only as part of a *paysage moralisé*.[13] John Nowlan, hero of John Banim's novel *The Nowlans*, is puzzled by a gentlewoman's enquiry about which part of his native landscape would be most worth sketching; for him, the scenery is too familiar to be picturesque.

Irish literary landscapes are often enough decipherable texts rather than aesthetic objects, places made precious or melancholic by the resonance of the human. It is the inscription of historical or contemporary meaning within their material appearance which tends to engage the poet's attention. Perhaps it was this intrusion of the human into the landscape which Hartley Coleridge had in mind when he remarked that Ireland would be a paradisal place were it not for the Catholics and Protestants. In response to J. C. Beckett's unpleasantly patronizing comment that 'we have in Ireland an element of stability – the land, and an element of instability – the people', John Wilson Foster remarks that 'in [Irish] literature – and I suspect in history . . . landscape is a cultural code that perpetuates instead of belying [these] instabilities and ruptures . . .'[14] The great Irish antiquarian George Petrie professed himself unconcerned with merely copying Nature in his paintings: 'my aim was something beyond that of the ordinary class of portrait painting . . . It was my wish to produce an Irish picture somewhat historical in its object, and poetical in its sentiment . . .'[15] One is tempted, somewhat fancifully, to find a parallel for this in the idealist thought of the greatest Irish philosopher, for whom Nature as thing-in-itself must yield to Nature as mind-related and subject-centred, a text or language which comes alive only in its transactions with human consciousness. In Berkeley's humanist perspective, matter itself is a mere fetish – a useless abstraction which distracts us from our practical business in the world, and which, like Kant's cryptic noumenon, cancels all the way through to leave everything exactly as it was. Berkeley is quite as hostile as Oscar Wilde to the appearance/reality dichotomy, if for entirely different reasons. But it may also be, as E. Estyn Evans suggests, that the Christian faith may have played its part here early on, with its devaluing of the sensuous and natural.[16] And it would seem probable that a landscape traced through with the historical scars of famine, deprivation and dispossession can never present itself to human perception with quite the rococo charm of a Keats, the sublimity of a Wordsworth or the assured sense of proprietorship of an Austen.

The word 'land' in England has Romantic connotations, as befits a largely urbanized society, and Nature is often enough the antithesis of the social. Ireland also witnesses a romanticizing of the countryside, in contrast to the morally corrupt, English-oriented metropolis; but this is more of an ethical than an aesthetic matter, and the English Romantic opposition of Nature and society is less easy to sustain in a country where the land is visibly a question of social relations and the town more continuous with its rural surroundings. Edna Longley discerns a tension in the imagination of Patrick Kavanagh between 'country poet' and 'nature poet'.[17] 'Land' in Ireland is a political rallying cry as well as a badge of cultural belonging, a question of rents as well as roots. It is not, need one say, that Irish writing reveals no sense of natural beauty; it is rather the absence of a particular ideology of that beauty which is peculiarly marked in Britain. Thomas MacDonagh, in his *Literature in Ireland*, praises early Irish literature for its delicate natural observation, but agrees with Kuno Meyer that such description is usually more impressionistic than elaborated.[18] This is not Nature poetry in the sense of writing self-consciously about landscape as a value in itself.

Whatever the cause, it would seem that the naturalizing strategies of English ideology don't stick so well in Ireland. To claim that the Ascendancy ruled, but was never entirely able to hegemonize that rule, is to suggest that it could never properly naturalize it. 'Whilst a new system has been given to the country,' remarks the distinguished surgeon and literary scholar George Sigerson, 'little trouble has been taken to naturalise it.'[19] Irish history is too palpably ruptured and discontinuous for the tropes of a sedate English evolutionism to take hold, and the latent triumphalism of such metaphors is flagrantly inappropriate to it. Nor is it very plausible to imagine a social order so fissured by social conflict as a mysteriously self-renewing organic entity, though a certain line of Romantic nationalist discourse did its best. Nature may figure in Ireland as an ethico-political category as well as an economic one; it may even be seen as a kind of subject; but this is not quite the transcendental-vitalist subject which informs English speculations on the natural world from Coleridge to Lawrence. It is hard to imagine an Irish Ruskin, apart perhaps from George Petrie, though there are even today in Ireland a few Constructive Unionists thinly masquerading as Hibernian Arnolds. Nature in Ireland is moralized and sexualized; and in so far as it is alive with mythic forces it is also transcendentalized. But it would appear on the whole less an object of aesthetic perception than in England, and one reason for this is not hard to find. It is that Nature in Ireland is too stubbornly social and material a category, too much a matter of rent, conacre, pigs and potatoes for it to be distanced, stylized and subjectivated in quite this way. Jim Daly, a character in Charles Lever's novel *The O'Donoghue* (1845), makes the point after conducting some dewy-eyed English visitors around his district:

> 'They've ways of their own, the English', interrupted Jim ... 'for whenever we passed a little potato-garden it was always, "God be good to us! but they're mighty poor hereabouts!" but when we got into the raal wild part of the glen, with divil a house nor a human being near us, sorrow word out of their mouths but "fine! beautiful! elegant!" till we came to Keim-an-eigh, and then ye'd think it was fifty acres of wheat they were looking at, wid all the praises they had for the big rocks and black cliffs over our heads.' (Ch. 2)

The embarrassment of Irish society in this respect is that it gives the vulgar Marxist far too easy a ride.[20] When material history bulks so blatantly large, when the connections between acreage, soil fertility, human fertility, sexual mores, social relations and modes of perception are so visibly on show, who needs to engage in elaborate theoretical defences of the model of base and superstructure?

But British society presents a somewhat parallel embarrassment. For throughout the British nineteenth century, a chronically idealizing, aestheticizing discourse of both Nature and society was secretly at loggerheads with an altogether more gross, materialist language, heavy with biological ballast and grotesquely bereft of 'culture'. This was the language of bourgeois political economy, which speaks of men and women as labouring instruments and fertilizing mechanisms in a kind of savage Swiftian reduction utterly out of key with the legitimating idiom of cultural idealism. The problem for the ruling British order was that this brutally practical discourse threatened to demystify its own idealizations; and this, in part, reflects a conflict between a kind of language organic to the industrial middle class, and one largely inherited by it from its patrician predecessors. Ireland, in this as in other ways, then comes to figure as the monstrous unconscious of the metropolitan society, the secret materialist history of endemically idealist England. It incarnates, for Carlyle, Froude and others, the Tennysonian nightmare of a Nature red in tooth and claw, obdurately resistant to refinement. For Carlyle, Ireland is 'the breaking point of the huge suppuration which all British and European society now is',[21] the neuralgic spot or open secret of a more general malaise. Such an existence seemed hardly worth sustaining: '[The Irish]', commented Chief Secretary Balfour in 1892, 'ought to have been exterminated long ago . . . but it is too late now.'[22] The unconscious, however, is a site of ambivalence: if Ireland is raw, turbulent, destructive, it is also a locus of play, pleasure, fantasy, a blessed release from the tyranny of the English reality principle. Ireland is the biological time-bomb which can be heard ticking softly away beneath the civilized superstructures of the Pall Mall clubs; and its history offers to lay bare the murky material roots of that civility as pitilessly as does Heathcliff. When the child Heathcliff trespasses on the Grange, the neurasthenically cultivated Lintons set the dogs on him, forced for a moment to expose the veiled violence which helps to prop them up.

There is another sense in which Ireland figured as Britain's unconscious. Just as we indulge in the world of the id in actions which the ego would find intolerable, so nineteenth-century Ireland became the place where the British were forced to betray their own principles, in a kind of negation or inversion of their conscious beliefs. It was the scene of an intensive state intervention which mocked its own *laissez faire* doctrines; it was the place where it was forced to make grudging political concessions to physical-force movements; it was the country whose custom-bound, unwritten sense of rights on the land it had finally to respect, against the grain of its own contractualist ideology; and it was an island ruled by a landowning oligarchy which it was forced in the end to expropriate. Ireland represented a rebarbative world which threatened to unmask Britain's own civility; and no doubt some excessively ingenious critic could uncover an allegory for this in *The Picture of Dorian Gray*.

Ireland as Nature to England's Culture, then; but the terms can be just as easily reversed. For Ireland is also tradition and spirituality in contrast to its rulers' crass materialism, aristocracy to their bourgeoisie. Indeed in so far as the Irish are *natural* aristocrats they offer to deconstruct the entire opposition and win themselves the best of both worlds. Irish nationalism, one might venture, begins with Nature (the rights of man) and ends up as culture; when John Kells Ingram, Isaac Butt, John Elliot Cairnes or Thomas Kettle question the applicability to Irish conditions of the natural operation of market forces, they are countering naturalism with the language of culturalism.[23] In his *The Character and Logical Method of Political Economy*, Cairnes claims that political economy is a science rather than an art; but what he seems to mean by this is that it should be disinterested rather than ideological, a question of principles rather than a defence of the economic status quo. There are indeed certain immutable economic laws, derived from human nature and psychology; but these laws, so Cairnes claims, are 'hypothetical' only, meaning that they are continually moulded by custom and circumstance.[24] T. E. Cliffe Leslie, another distinguished nineteenth-century Irish economist, boldly relativizes Adam Smith's economics as the product of a particular social history, stresses the uncertainty of scientific knowledge and the importance of culturally variable sentiment, and seeks to relocate political economy within the whole moral and intellectual context of social life. He also casts doubt on a 'science of man' which disregards the other (female) half of the human race, and highlights the economic importance of the domestic sphere.[25] John Kells Ingram, a Comtean of sorts, views political economy as an integral branch of sociology, and condemns Adam Smith both for his unhistorical method and for failing to regard wealth as 'a means to the higher ends of life'.[26] In Ruskinian style, the so-called Dublin school of political economists moralized and historicized the laws which their British counterparts regarded as amoral and immutable. Behind their emphasis on the complex interweaving of law and custom, sentiment and sociology, the tones of Edmund Burke are dimly detectable.

Heathcliff is a fragment of the Famine,[27] and goes on a sort of hunger strike towards the end of his life, as indeed does Catherine Earnshaw. Raymond Williams speaks of the Brontës' fiction in terms of the English 1840s: 'a world of desire and hunger, of rebellion and pallid convention, the terms of desire and fulfilment and the terms of oppression and deprivation profoundly connected in a single dimension of experience'.[28] The hunger in *Wuthering Heights* is called Heathcliff – 'a creature not of my species', as Nelly Dean frostily remarks, with his 'half-civilised ferocity'. But the hunger in Ireland was rather more literal. On the very threshold of modernity, Ireland experienced in the Famine all the blind, primeval force of the pre-modern, of a history as apparently remorseless as Nature itself, a history not *naturalized* but natural, a matter of blight and typhus and men and women crawling into the churchyard so as to die on sacred soil. In one sense, there was nothing very natural about this pre-eminently political catastrophe; but whereas in the British context history becomes Nature, in Ireland Nature becomes history. And this both in the sense that, in a largely pre-industrial society, the land is the prime determinant of human life, and in the sense that in the Famine history appears with all the brute, aleatory power of a seismic upheaval, thus writing large the course of much Irish history. The British have naturalized their own social relations as providential; and the effects of Nature in this sense will then appear over the water as Nature in its most Schopenhauerian guise. This in turn will feed back to the metropolitan nation as an image of the very Darwinism which is just about to shake them to their ideological foundations: Nature as random and purposeless, as a shattered landscape lurking as a terrifying possibility at the root of their own civility. Ireland and *Wuthering Heights* are names for that civility's sickening precariousness; for it too had in its time to be wrested inch by inch from the soil, and is thus permanently capable of sliding back into it.

Wherever you find meaning, so Freud taught us, you are bound to uncover non-meaning at its root. The Famine is the threatened death of the signifier in just this sense, the fear of history collapsing inertly under its own excess weight into sheer material process. Other European societies endured their crises and conflagrations in the late 1840s, but these, at least, were a matter of heroic action and revolutionary rhetoric. The Young Irelander Fintan Lalor viewed the Famine as a kind of negative revolution – as the dissolution of society, and thus as 'a deeper social disorganisation than the French Revolution – greater waste of life – wider loss of property – more than the horrors, with none of the hopes'.[29] Ireland's disaster was a kind of inverted image of European turmoil, one which you suffer rather than create, which strips culture to the poor forked Beckettian creature and which, in threatening to slip below the level of meaning itself, offers to deny you even the meagre consolations of tragedy. What lingers on, in such contaminated remnants of the epoch as the language itself, would seem less tragedy than the very different culture of shame. During the Famine, starving families boarded themselves into their cabins, so that their deaths might go decently unviewed. After the event, there were villages which could still speak Irish but didn't; it was considered bad luck. And to touch on the language question is to consider a death of the signifier of a rather different order. The Famine as apparently non-signifying, then, not only because it figures ideologically speaking as a brute act of Nature, but also because it threatens to burst through the bounds of representation as surely as Auschwitz did for Theodor Adorno. (Though at least, so some thought about the Holocaust, you could ascribe it to a subject of some kind, a transcendentally evil one; whereas a blankly indifferent Nature is not even enough of a subject to be malevolent.) Cormac Ó Gráda has remarked on the striking paucity of Irish historical writing on the Famine, a project which has been largely delegated to non-Irish scholars;[30] and this wary silence had already been noted by James Connolly in his *Labour in Irish History*.[31] But a parallel repression or evasion would seem to be at work in Irish literary culture, which is hardly rife with allusions to the event.

There is indeed a literature of the Famine, which has been valuably explored and anthologized by Christopher Morash.[32] But it is in neither sense of the word a major literature. There is a handful of novels and a body of poems, but few truly distinguished works. Where is the Famine in the literature of the Revival? Where is it in Joyce?[33] There is a question here, when it comes to the Revival, of the politics of form: much of that writing is programmatically non-representational, and thus no fit medium for historical realism,[34] if indeed any fit medium for such subject matter is conceivable. Wilde, Moore and Yeats are in full flight from Nature, towards whatever style, pose, mask or persona might seem its antithesis; and the more Joyce recuperates this naturalistic region for the ends of art, the more obtrusively artificial that redemption becomes. If the Famine stirred some to angry rhetoric, it would seem to have traumatized others into muteness.[35] The event strains at the limits of the articulable, and is truly in this sense the Irish Auschwitz. In both cases, there would seem something trivializing or dangerously familiarizing about the very act of representation itself. Liam O'Flaherty published a magnificent novel, *Famine*, in 1937, and the playwright Tom Murphy has bravely tackled the subject on stage; but there are a number of curious literary near-misses. William Carleton's novel *The Black Prophet*, published during the Famine, concerns a previous such disaster; Yeats's play *The Countess Cathleen* treats of famine, but of no specific one; Patrick Kavanagh's poem *The Great Hunger*, which shares the title of Cecil Woodham-Smith's celebrated study of the subject, uses famine as a metaphor for sexual and spiritual hungering.

It is not quite that the Famine strikes narrative cohesion out of Irish history. There are central continuities across it, and many developments which were once thought to postdate the event – mass emigration, language decline, late marriage, impartible inheritance, land consolidation, the so-called devotional revolution – were perhaps already in train before its occurrence.[36] It is rather that the Famine offers to reduce that history to what Walter Benjamin might have called the sheer empty homogeneous time of the body[37] – to insert, rather like Heathcliff, the disruptive temporality of Nature itself into the shapely schemas of historical chronology. In one sense, Nature has reared up and wreaked its terrible vengeance upon history; in another sense it images how that history had always in part appeared, ousting it at one level while miming it at another. The mediations between Nature and Culture are such things as food, labour, reproduction, the body – and all of these vital links have now been literally sundered. Culture is the surplus we have over stark need, and a social order shorn of that creative surplus can no longer *make* history at all, if indeed it ever properly could. History, like Nature, is now just an unmasterable exteriority, forever outrunning your control. This, interestingly enough, is also implicit in the naturalizing imagery of England – the sense that history is less something you strenuously fashion than spontaneously transmit, a lineage powered by its own inscrutably autonomous laws. The English and the Irish both have history in their bones, in entirely different senses. But we are talking here of teleology; and with the Famine such teleology can only ever be retrospective, constructed backwards after the unspeakable has already happened. Irish history would appear to have all the necessity of that teleological drive, but to absolutely no beneficent end. A necessity, in short, without a telos, implacable but distinctly unprovidential. The historical narrative, like the Chinese-box structure of *Wuthering Heights*, is strangely scrambled: the modern period in Ireland flows from an origin which is also an end, an abyss into which one quarter of the population disappears.

Because of the Famine, Irish society undergoes a surreal speed-up of its entry upon modernity; but what spurs that process on is, contradictorily, a thoroughly traditional calamity. Part of the horror of the Famine is its atavistic nature – the mind-shaking fact that an event with all the premodern character of a medieval pestilence happened in Ireland with frightening recentness. This deathly origin then shatters space as well as time, unmaking the nation and scattering Irish history across the globe. That history will of course continue; but as in Emily Brontë's novel there is something recalcitrant at its core which defeats articulation, some 'real' which stubbornly refuses to be symbolized. In both cases, this 'real' is a voracious desire which was beaten back and defeated, which could find no place in the symbolic order of social time and was expunged from it, but which like the shades of Catherine and Heathcliff will return to haunt a history now in the process of regathering its stalled momentum and moving onwards and upwards. Some primordial trauma has taken place, which fixates your development at one level even as you continue to unfold at another, so that time in Irish history and

Wuthering Heights would seem to move backwards and forwards simultaneously. Something, anyway, for good or ill, has been irrevocably lost; and in both Ireland and the novel it takes up its home on the alternative terrain of myth.

Wuthering Heights tells its story back to front, gazing back on the tragic storm from the vantage point of calm, fashioning a retrospective teleology of sorts. The uncouth Hareton has now been levered into the Grange, and the love of a good woman will ensure that whatever was energizing about Heathcliff will live on in him, in tamed and civilized form. The gentry have reached out to the stout yeomanry and infused their own overbred civility with something of that racy vigour. Or, to put the matter differently, the British are once more busily appropriating the more admirable qualities of the Celt; we are teetering here on the very brink of Matthew Arnold's *On the Study of Celtic Literature*, which will engage in precisely such an ideological manoeuvre. Even the Famine will yield a retrospective teleology of sorts, to those of a Malthusian frame of mind, and there were plenty in Victorian London who saw it as providential. 'When man has failed to rule the world rightly,' comments Anthony Trollope in *The Landleaguers*, 'God will step in, and will cause famine, and plague, and pestilence – even poverty itself – with His own Right Arm' (Ch. 41). The moral crassness of this is as unoriginal as most of Trollope's pronouncements: the position is lifted wholesale from Malthus's *Essay on Population*, which sees famine as a last-ditch divine corrective to human vice.[38] For the Trollope of *Castle Richmond*, the Famine is the consequence of God's mercy rather than his wrath, undoing the results of human folly and converting Ireland into a pleasant and prosperous land.

'Nothing but the successive failures of the potato', wrote Lord Lansdowne's agent W. S. Trench, 'could have produced the emigration which will, I trust, give us room to become civilised.'[39] In the Famine, Charles Trevelyan remarked, an all-merciful providence and 'Supreme Wisdom has educed permanent good out of transient evil,'[40] a moral obscenity which might have mattered rather less had Trevelyan not been in charge of the relief operation. Trevelyan held that the effects of the Famine should not be too thoroughly mitigated by British aid, so that its improvident victims might learn their lesson; he also considered death by starvation a lesser evil than bankruptcy, and was restrained in his abuse of the Irish only by his belief that as a Cornishman he stemmed from the same race.[41] The disaster in Trevelyan's view had miraculously resolved most of the country's problems, forcing its warring sects into cooperative action, fostering self-reliance, quelling agrarian militancy and modernizing the economy. The only problem for Nassau Senior, one of Britain's most influential economists, was whether the President of the Immortals would accomplish his work thoroughly enough: a million deaths, he confided to the Master of Balliol, 'would scarcely be enough to do much good'.[42] Even Robert Peel, generally applauded for his judicious response to the onset of hunger, shared this providentialist perspective.[43]

For some British officials, the Famine was a sign of divine displeasure with the potato, and a golden opportunity for the Irish to shift to a less barbarous form of nourishment.[44] In a kind of dietary determinism, a less lowly food would produce a more civilized, and hence less politically belligerent, people. What scandalized these commentators was the apparent bovine contentment of the Irish with their humdrum, socially unaspiring existence; and since growing potatoes involved little labour, it confirmed them in their endemic indolence. It is small wonder that some nationalists were stirred, however misguidedly, to speak of genocide; even as sober a commentator as George Sigerson is writing as late as 1868 of a 'policy of extermination' for Ireland in which men and women will give way to cattle.[45] One can, if one is so inclined, trace the providential pattern all the way from death, eviction and emigration to clearances, the consequent consolidating of land for pasturage, and the resulting emergence of a relatively prosperous rural middle class who would then form the material base for political independence.[46] And if the Famine helped to lay the economic ground for independence, it also dealt the single most lethal blow to whatever frail legitimacy the Irish ruling class could still muster. Even the meaningless will prove finally meaningful, as what is absolute loss for particular men and women becomes grist to the Hegelian mill. It is a process of which one can find a microcosm in the ancient Irish practice of hunger striking, which seeks to retrieve historical meaning from pure biological passivity, wrest significance from sheer facticity. But even the most dedicated dialectician is bound to baulk a little at this sanguine vista. If there *is* some providence stealthily afoot here, it would seem to have had to cancel itself out in order to realize itself, things having grown so extreme that only from some catastrophic engulfment of the present could new life begin to stir. Nature has thrown off the dead – as, in a casual afterthought, it threw off the living in the first place. In fact, things didn't have to happen that way – as *Wuthering Heights*, in this allegorical reading of it, can be persuaded to testify.

Nature, for English pastoral ideology, is plenitude and bountiful resource. In Irish culture and Brontë's novel it may occasionally be that too, but it also figures as harsh, niggardly, mean-spirited, and so as peasant rather than aristocrat. The Heights is more imposing than many an Irish farm, but what governs interpersonal relations in both cases is a tight material economy of labour, kinship and inheritance. For all the critical blather about transcendence and Romantic love, few more tenaciously materialist fictions have flowed from an English pen than this genealogically obsessed work, in which law, property and inheritance are the very stuff of the plot and kinship the very structure of the narrative. Personal relationships can be left to the Lintons, who have enough money to go in for them. One can scarcely speak of whatever it is that binds Catherine and Heathcliff together as a relationship, since the word implies an alterity they refuse. When the middle-class Lockwood first stumbles into the Heights, he is farcically incapable of deciphering the characters' relationships, since they are little more than a grisly parody of a conventional family. It is history, property and power which have thrown them together, not connubial love or filial affection. Heathcliff is adopted into the Earnshaw *ménage*, and ends up by biting the hand that feeds him. Show kindness to these savages and they will kick you in the teeth. In fact, Heathcliff revolts, rather like Ireland against Britain, because of the barbarous way he is treated; only Catherine will grant him the recognition he demands, and even she, perfidious little Albion that she is, sells him out for Edgar Linton. In the end, even the liberals will rally to the landowners. The Heathcliff–Catherine relationship is a classic case of the Lacanian 'imaginary', an utter merging of identities in which the existence of each is wholly dependent on the existence of the other, to the exclusion of the world about them. But young Catherine must assume her allotted place in the symbolic order, leaving her anguished companion historically arrested in the imaginary register. Catherine and Heathcliff – an oppressed woman and an exploited farm labourer – have a chance, so it would seem, to inaugurate a form of relationship at odds with the instrumental economy of the Heights; but Catherine's renegacy prevents that relationship from entering upon material existence, just as it compels Heathcliff to run off, turn himself into a gentleman and appropriate the weapons of the ruling class in order to bring them low.

Unlike Oscar Wilde, the 'traitor' William Joyce (Lord Haw-Haw), or Winston Churchill's Irish secretary Brendan Bracken, Heathcliff doesn't make too good a job of turning himself into an English gentleman. You can take Heathcliff out of the Heights, but you can't take the Heights out of Heathcliff.[47] Emily's father suc-ceeded rather better: born to a poor Irish peasant family, he Frenchified his surname and made it to Cambridge, right-wing Toryism and Anglican orders.[48] Heathcliff, by contrast, is a notoriously split subject: if he goes through the motions of undermining the ruling order from within, his soul remains arrested and fixated in the imaginary relation with Catherine. Indeed he engages in the former kind of activity precisely to avenge himself for the unavailability of the latter. Heathcliff starts out as an image of the famished Irish immigrant, becomes a landless labourer set to work in the Heights, and ends up as a symbol of the constitutional national-ism of the Irish parliamentary party. It is certainly a remarkably prescient novel – rather in the manner of Balzac's *Les Paysans*, which George Moore thought ex-traordinarily clairvoyant about later agrarian developments in Ireland.[49] Like those Redmondites who were both ranchers and rebels, Heathcliff is oppressor and oppressed in one body, condensing in his own person the various stages of the Irish revolution. As a child he is a kind of Defender or Ribbonman, chased out of the Grange in a minor rural outrage because the landlord thinks he is after his rents. He then shifts from rural proletarian – a dying breed in post-Famine Ireland – to rural bourgeois, cheating Hindley out of his possession of the Heights; and in this, one might claim, he recapitulates the drift of the Land League, which originated with the labourers, cottiers and smallholders of Connaught only to end up in the pockets of the conservative rural middle class. Once installed in the Heights, Heathcliff becomes a 'pitiless landlord' himself, and sets about dispossessing the local land-owner and taking over the Grange.

This, indeed, is just what the Irish farmers will eventually do, or at least what the British state will do on their behalf. But there is a significant difference here between British and Irish class history. The English squirearchy, the oldest landed capitalist class in Europe, will finally oust the superannuated yeomanry; and in this sense, at the end of *Wuthering Heights*, the Grange wins out over the Heights. Heathcliff dies in enigmatic ecstasy, the middle-class challenge to the landowners is accordingly beaten off, and young Catherine will reassume her proper place as heiress of the Grange, taking the *farouche* Hareton with her to inject a dose of earthy vigour into the place. The anarchic irruption of Nature into Culture has been fended off; that moment – the transgressive moment of Heathcliff and Catherine Earnshaw – is then distanced into mythology, and an evolutionary history all but blown to bits by it can now resume its stately upward trek. Heathcliff dramatizes among other things a ruling-class fear of revolution from below; but his furious insurrectionary energy now lies quiet in the grave, and by the close of the novel the stormy liaison with Catherine seems a long way off. One can't, however, banish from one's mind what just *might* have happened: the dreadful possibility that this raging *ressentiment* might finally come to usurp the gentry themselves. This is what will happen in Ireland, half a century on from the novel; and it is what very nearly happens in the novel too, since Heathcliff does in fact get his hands on the Grange but dies before he can enjoy his victory.

If Heathcliff is the rural revolution, however, he is that revolution gone sour. Indeed he represents its betrayal as well as its near-triumph, its right as well as its left wing. As the Irish parliamentarians were often enough warned, you can't play the enemy's game, assume his political persona and steal his cultural clothes, and hope to remain unscathed in your radical idealism. (It is worth recalling, however, that before women and the working class achieved a presence in the House of Commons, the Irish parliamentary party was the one representative there of an oppressed people.) Heathcliff is forced to nurture his idealism – his love for Catherine – in some quite separate inward sphere, in the realms of myth, the imaginary and cherished childhood memory, while behaving externally like any predatory English landlord; and this destructive non-congruence of myth and reality has a long history in Ireland. Heathcliff, like Marx's petty bourgeoisie, is contradiction incarnate, forced to inflect his desire in terms which can only alienate it; and in the end that contradiction will tear him apart. He has tried to outmanoeuvre the enemy at his own game, but his heart isn't in it, and he dies of unappeasable longing. He was a foreign brat who grew too big for his boots, and the English have long experience of how to take care of that. He is a landlord who eats in the kitchen, without grace or civility, brutal in his personal dealings; and to this extent he resembles a stereotypically uncouth minor Ascendancy figure more than he does anything out of Jane Austen. Indeed if one wanted a direct Irish comparison one might do worse than place him alongside the scheming, hardfaced, aggressive Charlotte Mullen of Somerville and Ross's *The Real Charlotte*, another exploiter whose monstrous violence is fuelled by disappointment in love.

One can, of course, try on a suitably revisionist reading of the whole affair. Like many Irish nationalists, Catherine and Heathcliff are in this view regressively fixated in some romanticized past, and would never have made it into the symbolic order of modern historical time. It is hard to imagine Heathcliff doing the dishes or wheeling the pram.[50] Catherine, on such a reading, is no kind of renegade: she is an unprotected woman who is unlikely to find the security she needs with such a disreputable partner. Edgar Linton, the Irish revisionist historian would be delighted to note, is not a bad sort of landlord; he may be something of a sap, but his love for Catherine is tender and steadfast, whatever Heathcliff's macho contempt for it. Like all of the Irish in a certain colonial view of them, Heathcliff is the eternal child, and his adult wheeler-dealing is ironically driven by this implacable infantile demand. Unable to deal 'maturely' with his rejection, he ends up with all the smouldering, self-lacerating hatred of a John Mitchel, or the blustering desperation of Parnell in his last days. There is an archaic weight of history with which English society has become entangled, and which is threatening to drag it down, and its name is Heathcliff, or Ireland. Better surely to shuck it off and face the future. But Heathcliff, like the Irish revolution itself, is archaic and modern together – a mournful remembrance of past wrongs which then unleashes a frenetically transformative drive to the future. That drive is in both cases thwarted, goes awry; but behind it lurks the memory of a bungled utopian moment, a subjunctive mood which still haunts the hills and refuses to lie quiet in its grave. From the gentry's standpoint, the novel recounts the tale of a catastrophe just averted; from a radical viewpoint it records the loss of revolutionary hopes, now projected into a mythologized past but, like the ghosts of Catherine and Heathcliff, still capable of infiltrating and disturbing the present. For their doomed relationship, despite its grotesque violence and perhaps because of its curiously genderless quality, involved an equality, solidarity and full mutual recognition which, had it been to the fore as a political ethic in the Land League, might have made a considerable difference to the subsequent course of Irish history. Meanwhile, the Lockwoods and Deans of the present, who as usual can't even hear the question, let alone provide an answer, continue to worry away at the hermeneutical riddle which haunts every page of *Wuthering Heights*: Who is Heathcliff? What is he? What does he want?

The naturalizing discourse of English culture may be less native to Ireland, but it has certainly been powerfully to the fore in much Irish discussion of the Famine. The typical gesture of Irish historiography on the subject has been to take the property relations of nineteenth-century Ireland for granted as some unquestionable context, and then to argue the toss within these constricted terms. In this, Irish historians re-enact the mental habits of the Victorian political economists, who similarly assumed that the frame of capitalist relations in Ireland fell beyond the bounds of criticism. Much historical debate over the Famine is thus loaded from the outset, secretly governed by what it dogmatically excludes as a legitimate topic of enquiry. Given those property relations, the Famine was arguably inevitable once the potato crop failed; but there was nothing inevitable about the relations themselves. Irish historians who are quick to pounce on the taken-for-grantedness of nationalist mythology are curiously blind to their own naturalizing habits of mind. Most historians are unwitting positivists, wary of what Hegel called the power of the negative, reluctant to grasp what happened in the light of what did not. They are also, commonly enough, ethical relativists in practice if not in theory, given to exculpating some piece of historical inhumanity on the grounds that one could have expected nothing more high-minded of the age in which it occurred. They contrast in this way with most Marxists, who are apt to claim that, say, slavery was a gross human injustice even if it is hard to see how, in a particular historical situation, anything different could have been imagined. In a typical comment, Mary Daly writes of the British government's handling of famine relief that 'it does not appear appropriate to pronounce in an unduly critical fashion on the limitations of previous generations'.[51] Why not? Does that also apply to witch burning, lunatic baiting and child labour? More to the point, does it apply to agrarian outrages, dynamiting, the assassination of Chief Secretaries or the slaying of unpopular landlords? It is the social worker theory of morality: Caligula was just the victim of social circumstance. We should seek to understand the headhunters rather than condemn them. It is just that the revisionist historian's admirable broadmindedness seems to stop mysteriously short of John Mitchel or Patrick Pearse.

'The Irish landlords', writes E. R. R. Green of the Famine, 'held the ultimate responsibility, but on the whole they were as much involved in disaster as their tenantry.'[52] It would be intriguing to know Dr Green's statistics for the number of landlords dead of hunger oedema in the workhouses or shipped off typhus-ridden to Canada. But at least he attributes a degree of responsibility to them, however abstractly 'ultimate', which for some other Irish historians is fighting talk. The treatment of the Famine in L. M. Cullen's *An Economic History of Ireland since 1600* is extraordinarily cursory – unsurprisingly, perhaps, for a historian who can write elsewhere that 'the land system and economic behaviour of the landlords as a class were not reprehensible.'[53] It is worth pointing out that if this complacency is warranted, then an immense proportion of the *literary* evidence about the land in Ireland can be written off as worthless. Literary testimony is not, to be sure, hard historical evidence; but it is an odd historical judgement which can run clean counter to such a major body of writing. Perhaps everyone from Edgeworth and Banim to Carleton and Moore was simply cursed with too lurid an imagination. Some modern Irish historians, including L. M. Cullen, are not quite so quick to set aside literary evidence when it comes to arguing that, say, early modern Ireland was not in general nationalistic. As far as the Famine goes, we are dealing with the most important episode of modern Irish history and the greatest social disaster of nineteeth-century Europe – an event with something of the characteristics of a low-level nuclear attack. The zealous sanitizing of the subject in R. D. Edwards and T. D. Williams's collection of essays *The Great Famine* is as tendentious as any nationalist polemic. Mary Daly's judicious, informative account, one by no means uncritical of Westminster, half-excuses the *laissez faire* dogmatism of the Whig government by remarking that the Society of Friends entertained similar beliefs about private property.[54] It is doubtful that Daly would exculpate the Ribbonmen on the grounds that the Defenders believed in shooting bailiffs too. R. F. Foster briefly allows that the Whigs' relief policies were 'generally ill-founded', in a narrative that is otherwise scrupulous to avoid assigning blame.[55] It has been fashionable among Irish historians to scorn Cecil Woodham-Smith's *The Great Hunger* as a popular tear-jerker; but although the book has its crop of errors and exaggerations, it is remarkable how much of its account is confirmed by the recent findings of James S. Donnelly, Jr, whom nobody could accuse of either amateurism or Anglophobia.[56]

There was no question of calculated genocide; and food imports, contrary to nationalist mythology, far outstripped exports in the Famine years.[57] But neither was the Famine an act of God. Peel's government moved quickly and effectively; the apparatus of public works and soup kitchens was extended with commendable efficiency into the remotest reaches of the island; and some landlords devoted themselves selflessly to the parlous condition of their tenants, bankrupting themselves in the process.[58] Taken as a whole, however, the landowners were precious little use, when their actions were not positively damaging. As for the government's record, the failure to stop the grain harvest of 1846 from being exported, before foreign aid arrived in early '47, had lethal consequences. The hiatus in the 1847 relief operation between the closure of public works and the opening of the soup kitchens sent many to their graves. The government denial of an emergency after 1847, along with its decision to abandon famine relief, was criminal. The ideological refusal to distribute free food until thousands had perished; the dumping of Famine costs on Ireland alone and on a ramshackle poor-law system; the Whig abandonment of the food depot project; the limiting of public works for fear of inhibiting private charity; the notorious Gregory clause which drove thousands off their land into fever-ridden workhouses; the mass evictions and subsidized emigration for the purpose of land consolidation; the niggardly sum spent on relief work (less than £10 million, in contrast to almost £70 million spent on the Crimean adventure): by all of these measures, half-measures and non-measures, the British government despatched hundreds of thousands to their needless deaths. It is these baneful policies that a certain species of modern historian would ask us to judge tolerantly, relativistically, in the light of the wisdom of their day.

But there is more to British responsibility than that. In his bold, brilliant study *Why Ireland Starved*, Joel Mokyr advances a series of controversial theses: that Ireland was not overpopulated, that its relative lack of raw materials was no adequate reason for its non-industrialized condition, that insecurity of land tenure played no major role in low agricultural productivity, that agrarian agitation proved no significant factor in deterring investment. Mokyr adds for good measure that Britain could most certainly have saved Ireland from the Famine had it possessed the will to do so – a judgement reinforced by Christine Kinealy's *This Great Calamity*. The country's plight, so Mokyr considers, sprang chiefly from lack of capital investment, rendering its economy peculiarly vulnerable to 'exogamous shocks' such as the failure of the potato crop. And the primary cause of that low investment was the poverty of its people. But Mokyr does not press this question in turn to its root cause; instead he veers into a critique of the largely discredited case that union with Britain was the source of Ireland's economic ills. But why was Ireland so poor? The answer is doubtless complex; but it must surely include the face of a vastly inequitable system of agrarian capitalism which was implanted by the British, run by their political clients, and conducted largely for their economic benefit.[59] Had that exploitative system been transformed – rent abolished, the graziers and strong farmers expropriated and their land equitably redistributed – a million men and women would surely not have perished. The empiricist historian would scoff at the idle utopianism of such a suggestion, and would be perfectly correct to do so. Such a revolution could not have conceivably happened at the time; neither the political will nor the political muscle for it were available. But the point of such subjunctive or counterfactual speculation is to place the ultimate responsibility for the disaster where it belongs – which is to say, not with 'the landlords' or 'the British,' but with the system they sustained.

Amartya Sen has persuasively advanced the counter-intuitive case that famines are not primarily caused by food shortage; they are caused chiefly by lack of 'entitlements' – the incapacity of the people to buy what food is available.[60] Three million people perished in Bengal in the 1940s, though arithmetically speaking there was enough food for everyone. The application of this case to the Irish Famine is problematical. Certainly rents were an important factor in preventing the bringing of the people and the food together. Cormac Ó Gráda has argued that there was, strictly speaking, enough grain in the country to feed all of its people, but that this, among other things, ignores the negative effects of crop requisitioning on subsequent production.[61] But if, so Ó Gráda argues, one considers the relevant food area as the United Kingdom rather than Ireland alone, then the Sen thesis is a forceful one. In this sense it can be reasonably claimed that the Irish did not die simply for lack of food, but because they largely lacked the funds to purchase food which was present in abundance in the kingdom as a whole, but which was not sufficiently available to them. In this sense, the Famine was the most lethal consequence of Britain's tendency to ignore, when it suited it, the union which it had oiled so many palms to achieve. As far as this particular castastrophe goes, it was not the union which contributed to Ireland's ills, but Britain's self-interested decision to set it aside. And the ultimate cause of this, whatever Trollope might have considered, was a matter of politics and property relations rather than of an all-merciful providence.

Notes

1   See Winifred Gerin, *Branwell Brontë* (London, 1961), p. 90.

2   A review of Elizabeth Gaskell's biography of Charlotte Brontë in the *Revue des Deux Mondes* (no. 4, 1857) by Emile Montégut speaks of Patrick Brontë as having 'la violente impétuosité du sang celtique'. The French too were evidently not fooled.

3   The text is now reprinted in Robert Collins (ed.), *The Hand of the Arch-Sinner: Two Angrian Chronicles of Branwell Brontë* (Oxford, 1993).

4   E. R. R. Green, 'The Great Famine (1845–1850)', in T. W. Moody and F. X. Martin (eds), *The Course of Irish History* (Cork, 1987), p. 272. There is a powerful depiction of the Liverpool Irish of the time in Herman Melville's novel *Redburn*. See also, for Liverpool in the Famine years, Robert Scally's *The End of Hidden Ireland* (Oxford, 1995), Part 2, Ch. 9.

5   Winifred Gerin, *Emily Brontë* (Oxford, 1971), pp. 225–6.

6   J. C. Beckett, 'Eighteenth-Century Ireland', in T. W. Moody and W. E. Vaughan (eds), *A New History of Ireland*: vol. 4: *Eighteenth-Century Ireland, 1691–1800* (Oxford, 1986), p. lvii.

7   See John Barrell, *The Idea of Landscape and the Sense of Place* (Cambridge, 1972), p. 1.

8   Ellen Meiksins Wood, *The Pristine Culture of Capitalism* (London, 1991), p. 111.

9   A. Stopford Brooke and T. W. Rolleston (eds), *A Treasury of Irish Poetry in the English Tongue* (London, 1900), p. xxxiii.

10 John Wilson Foster, *Fictions of the Irish Literary Revival* (Syracuse, 1987), p. 17.

11 W. B. Yeats, 'The Symbolism of Poetry', in *Essays and Introductions* (London, 1961), p. 163.

12 Terence Brown, *Northern Voices* (Dublin, 1975), p. 16.

13 'I hate scenery and suns. I see nothing in Creation but what is fallen and ruined' (James Kilroy (ed.), *The Autobiography of James Clarence Mangan* (London, 1968), p. 33). For some comments on Nature in Ireland as non-aesthetic, see Fintan O'Toole, 'Tourists in Our Own Land', in *Black Hole, Green Card* (Dublin, 1994). Part of what 'de-aestheticized' Nature in Ireland was of course the blot on the landscape represented by poverty and squalor.

14 John Wilson Foster, *Colonial Consequences* (Dublin, 1991), p. 149.

15 Quoted by William Stokes, *The Life and Labours in Art and Archaeology of George Petrie* (London, 1868), p. 15.

16 E. Estyn Evans, *The Personality of Ireland* (Dublin, 1992), p. 69.

17 Edna Longley, *The Living Stream: Literature and Revisionism in Ireland* (Newcastle upon Tyne, 1994), p. 204.

18 Thomas MacDonagh, *Literature in Ireland* (Dublin, 1916), pp. 127–8.

19 George Sigerson, *Modern Ireland* (London, 1868), p. 15.

20 For vulgar Marxism, see W. B. Yeats's assertion of a direct relation between the rise of allegory and the rise of the merchant class, in *Essays and Introductions* (London, 1961), p. 367.

21 Thomas Carlyle, *Reminiscences of My Irish Journey in 1849* (London, 1882), p. 1.

22 Quoted by Andrew Gailey, *Ireland and the Death of Kindness* (Cork, 1987), p. 30.

23 For a discussion of this topic, see Thomas A. Boylan and Timothy P. Foley, *Political Economy and Colonial Ireland* (London and New York, 1992). See also Isaac Butt,

Introductory Lecture delivered before the University of Dublin (Dublin, 1837), in which Butt, taking up his Chair of Political Economy, extends the concept of wealth to 'immaterial' goods. See also his *Land Tenure in Ireland: A Plea for the Celtic Race* (Dublin, 1866); and *The Irish People and the Irish Land* (Dublin, 1867). For Mill's tempering of his radical views on Irish land tenure, see E. D. Steele, 'John Stuart Mill and the Irish Question', *Historical Journal* 13/2 (1970).

24   See John E. Cairnes, *The Character and Logical Method of Political Economy* (London, 1857), Ch. 1. In an essay elsewhere, entitled 'Colonial Government', Cairnes argues that the original motivations for colonialism have now exhausted themselves, and ends by strikingly anticipating the shift from British Empire to British Commonwealth. Though much of what he says is of close relevance to Ireland, Ireland, intriguingly, is never mentioned. Perhaps Cairnes considered that to mention his own country might remind his English readership of his national origin, thus reducing the objective force of his case to a piece of special pleading. The essay can be found in his *Political Essays* (London, 1873).

25   T. E. Cliffe Leslie, *Essays in Political and Moral Philosophy* (Dublin, 1888), chs 2 and 16.

26   John Kells Ingram, *A History of Political Economy* (Edinburgh, 1888), p. 104.

27   I have indicated already that Heathcliff may not of course be Irish, and that even if he is the chronology is awry as far as the Famine goes. But in this essay Heathcliff is Irish, and the chronology is not awry.

28   Raymond Williams, *The English Novel from Dickens to Lawrence* (London, 1970), p. 60.

29   J. F. Lalor, *Collected Writings* (Dublin, 1918), p. 9.

30   Cormac Ó Gráda, *Ireland before and after the Famine* (Manchester, 1988), p. 78. Ó Gráda has developed his remarks in *Ireland: A New Economic History 1780–1939* (Oxford, 1994), Part 3, Ch. 8. Brendan Bradshaw notes that only one academic study of the Famine appeared in Ireland between the 1930s and 1980s ('Nationalism and Historical Scholarship', *Irish Historical Studies* 26 (Nov 1989), pp. 340–41).

31   James Connolly, *Labour in Irish History* (Dublin, 1910; repr. 1987), p. 41. The point is also noted by Patrick O'Farrell, 'Whose Reality? The Irish Famine in History and Literature', *Historical Studies of Australia and New Zealand* 20 (April 1982).

32   See Christopher A. Morash, ed., *The Hungry Voice: The Poetry of the Irish Famine* (Dublin, 1989), and his 'Imagining the Famine: Literary Representations of the Great Irish Famine' (PhD thesis, Trinity College, Dublin, 1990). I have also profited from Cormac Ó Gráda's 'The Great Famine in Folk Memory and in Song' (unpublished MS).

33   For Joyce, however, see Mary Lowe-Evans's remarkably original *Crimes against Fecundity: James Joyce and Population Control* (Syracuse, 1989), Ch. 1, which among other things usefully assembles Joycean allusions to the Famine.

34   Though the Dublin theatre of the day could suffer from an excess of realism too. Count Casimir Markiewicz, directing Galsworthy's proletarian drama *Strife* at the Gaiety Theatre, insisted on hiring real labourers off the docks but made the mistake of paying them in advance, so that by the time the big fight scene arrived on stage their 'blood was up'. See Sean O'Faolain, *Constance Markiewicz* (London, 1935, repr. 1968), p. 57.

35   Malcolm Brown comments on how frequently the Famine was said by eyewitnesses to defeat language and beggar description (*The Politics of Irish Literature*, London, 1972, p. 95).

36 A view held by some historians, but called into question by Cormac Ó Gráda in his *Ireland: A New Economic History*, p. 208.

37 See Walter Benjamin, 'Theses on the Philosophy of History', in *Illuminations*, ed. Hannah Arendt (London, 1970).

38 The view that the Famine was a divine punishment was widespread among the Irish people. See Roger J. McHugh's vivid piece of popular history 'The Famine in Irish Oral Tradition', in R. D. Edwards and T. D. Williams (eds), *The Great Famine* (London, 1956), p. 395. For a recent treatment of this theme, see D. Boyd Hilton, *The Age of Atonement* (Oxford, 1991). For the religious and moral dimension of the Famine see Donal A. Kerr, *A Nation of Beggars?* (Oxford, 1994).

39 Quoted by James S. Donnelly, Jr, 'The Great Famine: Its Interpreters, Old and New', *History Ireland* (August 1993), p. 33.

40 Charles Trevelyan, *The Irish Crisis* (London, 1848), p. 1. Trevelyan, pleased enough with his book, sent a copy to the Pope.

41 See Jennifer Hart, 'Sir Charles Trevelyan at the Treasury', *English Historical Review* 75 (1960).

42 Quoted by Cormac Ó Gráda, *Ireland before and after the Famine*, p. 112. For Senior's disgruntled comments on Ireland, see his *Journals, Conversations and Essays Relating to Ireland*, 2 vols. (London, 1868).

43 See Peter Gray, 'Potatoes and Providence: British Government's Responses to the Great Famine', *Bullán* 1 (spring 1994).

44 For some excellent research into the potato, see Austin Bourke, *The Visitation of God? The Potato and the Great Irish Famine* (Dublin, 1993).

45 Sigerson, *Modern Ireland*, p. 4. As late as 1967, Frank O'Connor writes of 'the deliberate destruction and scattering of a whole people' in *The Backward Look* (London, 1967), pp. 154–5.

46 In 1841, more than one-third of all Irish houses were one-roomed cabins; in 1861 they constituted less than 10 per cent of the housing stock. See Mary Daly, *The Famine in Ireland* (Dublin, 1986), p. 121. Oliver MacDonagh considers that without the Famine the density of the Irish population would have been too great for a viable peasant proprietorship. See his *Ireland: The Union and its Aftermath* (London, 1977), p. 23.

47 'You can take Paddy out of the bog, but you can't take the bog out of Paddy.'

48 For a somewhat Romantic biography, see John Lock and W. T. Dixon, *A Man of Sorrows: The Life, Letters and Times of the Rev. Patrick Brontë, 1777–1861* (London, 1979). For a sample of Brontë's own writings, including *Cottage Poems*, which urges the poor to reconcile themselves to their lowly state, and his abysmal Irish novella *The Maid of Killarney*, see *Brontëana: The Rev. Patrick Brontë, AB, His Collected Works and Life* (Bingley, 1898).

49 See Joseph Hone, *The Life of George Moore* (London, 1936), p. 86.

50 One of the first men to be seen wheeling a pram in the streets of Dublin was Thomas MacDonagh, lecturer in English at University College and one of the executed rebels of the Easter Rising. MacDonagh compounded this effeminacy by also, as a good Irish Irelander, wearing a kilt.

51 Daly, *The Famine in Ireland*, p. 113.

52 'The Great Famine (1845–1850)', p. 273.

53 L. M. Cullen, 'The Social Basis of Irish Cultural Nationalism', in Rosalind Mitchison (ed.), *The Roots of Nationalism* (Edinburgh, 1980), p. 93.

54 Daly, *The Famine in Ireland*, p. 113.

55 R. F. Foster, *Modern Ireland, 1600–1972* (London, 1988), p. 327.

56 See Donnelly's series of essays on the Famine in W. E. Vaughan, ed., *A New History of Ireland*, vol. 5: *Ireland Under the Union 1, 1801–70* (Oxford, 1989). See also his 'The Great Famine: Its Interpreters Old and New', *History Ireland* (autumn 1993), a rather more judicious assessment of the Young Irelander John Mitchel's views than R. F. Foster's calculatedly casual dismissal of him as a 'well-known American slaver'. For John Mitchel's celebrated charge of genocide, see Graham Davis, 'John Mitchel and the Great Famine', in Paul Hyland and Neil Sammels (eds), *Irish Writing: Exile and Subversion* (London, 1991).

57 In 1846 and '47 Ireland imported five times more grain than it exported. See Gearoid Ó Tuathaigh, *Ireland before the Famine* (London, 1991), p. 220.

58 See, for example, David Thompson and Moyra McGusty (eds), *The Irish Journals of Elizabeth Smith, 1840–50* (Oxford, 1980), for a fascinating record of one landowner's wife's mixture of compassionate concern and ferocious anti-Irish prejudice during the Famine years.

59 See Peter Gibbon, 'Colonialism and the Great Starvation in Ireland, 1845–9', *Race and Class* 17 (autumn 1975). See also Michael Hechter, *Internal Colonialism* (London, 1975).

60 Amartya Sen, *Poverty and Famines* (Oxford, 1981).

61 See Cormac Ó Gráda, *The Great Irish Famine* (London, 1989), p. 62, and *Ireland before and after the Famine*, pp. 108–10. See also his *Ireland: A New Economic History*, pp. 199–200.

The Ballad of Marxist Criticism (to the tune of 'Something Stupid' by Nancy and Frank Sinatra)

The day I found my Tutor was a populist reformist sentimentalist
Nostalgic petty-bourgeois social democrat subjectivist empiricist
I saw the light of day, I turned to Ray, my structure of feeling it was born anew
Until I went and spoiled it all by writing something stupid in New Left Review.

Well then I read some Lukács that was fine I toed the line about totality
And since I was a prole it stirred my soul to know my consciousness could set men
   free
I was ignorant of Scott but who was not it didn't matter Georgy was my man
That dirty low-down formalistic Stalinist historicist Hegelian.

Well things were getting schlecht I turned to Brecht and Piscator and Walter
   Benjamin
Productive forces shock Verfremdung contradiction, baby it was just my scene
Though Benjamin was swell well what the hell who could admire as his main
   theorist
An adjacentist eclectic individualist technologistic humanist?

You may talk of Adorno but I don't know it's pretty tortuous and gloomy stuff
And Jameson is fine but to imbibe it after wine just leaves you feeling rough

Well I was in a spin I couldn't win so I waxed slightly semiological
Till digging out deep structures was denounced by Macherey as metaphysical
Though Althusser is smart his views on art and ideology don't ring quite true
So hello Helen Gardner Donald Davie Denis Donoghue, I love you . . .

Bibliography

References within each section of the bibliography appear in chronological order of publication. The bibliography is arranged as follows:

1 Books and pamphlets
2 Plays and prose fiction
3 Chapters in books
4 Articles and reviews
5 Interviews and debates
6 Editorial work
7 Works about Terry Eagleton.

1 Books and Pamphlets

The New Left Church (London and Melbourne: Sheed & Ward, 1966).

Shakespeare and Society: Critical Studies in Shakespearean Drama (London: Chatto & Windus, 1967).

Directions: Pointers for the Post-Conciliar Church (ed.) (London and Sydney: Sheed & Ward, 1968).

From Culture to Revolution (ed. with Brian Wicker) (London and Sydney: Sheed & Ward, 1968).

The Body as Language (London and Sydney: Sheed & Ward, 1970).

Exiles and Émigrés: Studies in Modern Literature (London: Chatto & Windus, 1970).

Jude the Obscure by Thomas Hardy (introduced by Terry Eagleton), New Wessex Edition (London: Macmillan, 1974).

Myths of Power: A Marxist Study of the Brontës (London: Macmillan, 1975).

Criticism and Ideology: A Study in Marxist Literary Theory (London: New Left Books, 1976).

Marxism and Literary Criticism (London: Methuen, 1976).

Walter Benjamin, or Towards a Revolutionary Criticism (London and New York: Verso, 1981).

The Rape of Clarissa: Writing, Sexuality, and the Class-Struggle in Samuel Richardson (Oxford: Blackwell, 1982).

Literary Theory: An Introduction (Oxford: Blackwell, 1983).

The Function of Criticism: From the Spectator to Post-Structuralism (London and New York: Verso, 1984).

Against the Grain: Essays 1975–1985 (London and New York: Verso, 1986).

William Shakespeare, Rereading Literature Series (Oxford: Blackwell, 1986).

Hard Times by Charles Dickens (ed. and introduced by Terry Eagleton) (London: Methuen, 1987).

Myths of Power: A Marxist Study of the Brontës, 2nd edn (London: Macmillan, 1988).

Nationalism: Irony and Commitment, Field Day Pamphlet (Derry: Field Day, 1988).

Raymond Williams: Critical Perspectives (ed.) (Oxford: Polity Press with Blackwell, 1989).

The Ideology of the Aesthetic (Oxford: Blackwell, 1990).

The Significance of Theory, ed. and introduced by Michael Payne and M. A. R. Habib (Oxford: Blackwell, 1990).

Ideology: An Introduction (London and New York: Verso, 1991).

Plays, Prose Writings and Poems by Oscar Wilde (introduced by Terry Eagleton) (London: Everyman, 1991).

The Crisis of Contemporary Culture: An Inaugural Lecture delivered before the University of Oxford on 27 November 1992 (Oxford: Clarendon Press, 1993).

Ideology (ed.), Longman Critical Readers Series (London and New York: Longman, 1994).

Heathcliff and the Great Hunger: Studies in Irish Culture (London and New York: Verso, 1995).

Marxist Literary Theory (ed. with Drew Milne) (Oxford: Blackwell, 1995).

Literary Theory: An Introduction, 2nd edn (Oxford: Blackwell, 1996).

The Illusions of Postmodernism (Oxford: Blackwell, 1996).

2   Plays and Prose Fiction

Saints and Scholars (London and New York: Verso, 1987).

Saint Oscar (Derry: Field Day, 1989).

Saint Oscar and Other Plays (Oxford: Blackwell, 1997).

3   Chapters in Books

'Eliot and a Common Culture', in Graham Martin (ed.), *Eliot in Perspective: A Symposium* (London: Macmillan, 1970), pp. 279–95.

'Myth and History in Recent Poetry', in Michael Schmidt and Grevel Lindop (eds), *British Poetry Since 1960* (Oxford: Carcanet, 1972), pp. 233–9.

'Tennyson: Politics and Sexuality in *The Princess* and *In Memoriam*', in Francis Barker et al., *1848: The Sociology of Literature* (Colchester: Essex University Press, 1978), pp. 97–106. Repr. in Rebecca Stott (ed.), *Tennyson*. Longman Critical Readers Series. (London and New York: Longman, 1996), pp. 76–86.

'Text, Ideology, Realism', in Edward W. Said (ed.), *Literature and Society* (Baltimore: Johns Hopkins University Press, 1980), pp. 149–73.

'Psychoanalysis, the Kabbala and the Seventeenth Century', in Francis Barker et al. (eds),

1642: Literature and Power in the Seventeenth Century (Colchester: University of Essex Press, 1981), pp. 201–6.

'Macherey and Marxist Literary Theory', in G. H. R. Parkinson (ed.), *Marx and Marxisms* (Cambridge: Cambridge University Press, 1982), pp. 145–55. Repr. in *Against the Grain* (1986).

'Ideology and Scholarship', in Jerome J. McGann (ed.), *Historical Studies and Literary Criticism* (Madison: University of Wisconsin Press, 1985), pp. 114–25.

'Political Criticism', in Mary Ann Caws (ed.), *Textual Analysis: Some Readers Reading* (New York: Modern Language Association, 1986), pp. 257–71.

'The God That Failed', in Mary Nyquist and Margaret Ferguson (eds), *Remembering Milton: Essays on the Texts and Traditions* (New York: Methuen, 1987), pp. 342–9.

Introduction to Daniel Cotton, *Social Figures: George Eliot, Social History and Literary Representation* (Minneapolis: University of Minnesota Press, 1987).

Afterword to Graham Holderness (ed.), *The Shakespeare Myth* (Manchester: Manchester University Press, 1988), pp. 203–8.

Foreword to Malcolm Evans, *Signifying Nothing: Truth's True Contents in Shakespeare's Text*, 2nd edn (Hemel Hempstead: Harvester Wheatsheaf; Athens: University of Georgia Press, 1989), pp. ix–x.

'History, Narrative and Marxism', in James Phelan (ed.), *Reading Narrative: Form, Ethics, Ideology* (Columbus: Ohio State University Press, 1989), pp. 272–81.

'Joyce and Mythology', in Susan Dick (ed.), *Omnium Gatherum: Essays for Richard Ellmann* (Gerrards Cross: Smythe, 1989), pp. 310–19.

'Marxism and the Future of Criticism', in David Wood (ed.), Emmanuel Levinas (foreword) and David Allison (trans. of foreword), *Writing the Future* (London: Routledge, 1990), pp. 177–80.

'Nationalism: Irony and Commitment', in Seamus Deane (ed.), *Nationalism, Colonialism and Literature*, with Fredric Jameson and Edward W. Said (Minneapolis: University of Minnesota Press, 1990), pp. 23–39.

'The Politics of Postmodernism', in Danuta Zadworna-Fjellestad and Lennart Bjork (eds), *Criticism in the Twilight Zone: Postmodern Perspectives on Literature* (Stockholm: Almqvist & Wiksell, 1990), pp. 21–33.

'Aesthetics and Politics in Edmund Burke', in Michael Kenneally (ed.), *Irish Literature and Culture* (Gerrards Cross: Smythe, 1992), pp. 25–34.

'Free Particulars: The Rise of the Aesthetic', in Francis Mulhern (ed.), *Contemporary Marxist Literary Criticism* (London: Longman, 1992), pp. 55–70.

'The Ideology of the Aesthetic', in Stephen Regan (ed.), *The Politics of Pleasure: Aesthetics and Cultural Theory* (Buckingham: Open University Press, 1992), pp. 17–32.

'Deconstruction and Human Rights', in Barbara Johnson (ed.), *Freedom and Interpretation* (New York: Basic Books, 1993), pp. 122–45 [Oxford Amnesty Lectures 1992].

'Introduction to Wittgenstein', in *'Wittgenstein': The Terry Eagleton Script/The Derek Jarman Film* (with Colin MacCabe, Tariq Ali and Derek Jarman) (London: British Film Institute Publications, 1993), pp. 5–13.

'Self-Authoring Subjects', in Maurice Biriotti and Nicola Miller (eds), *What is an Author?* (Manchester: Manchester University Press, 1993), pp. 42–50.

'The Flight to the Real', in Sally Ledger and Scott McCracken (eds), *Cultural Politics at the 'Fin de Siècle'* (Cambridge: Cambridge University Press, 1995), pp. 11–21.

4 Articles and Reviews

1964
'Labour in the Vineyard', *Slant* 1: 1 (1964), 15–20.
'Mass and Media', *Slant* 1: 2 (1964), 12–14.
'The Morality of Capitalism', *Slant* 1: 3 (1964), 25–8.

1965
'The Bending of a Twig', *Slant* 1: 4 (1965), 4–9.
'Parish and Politics', *Slant* 1: 5 (1965), 12–14.
'Towards Socialism', *Slant* 1: 6 (1965), 23–5.

1966
'Politics and Benediction', *Slant* 9 (1966), 16–20.
'Politics and Benediction': Attack and Defences, *Slant* 10 (1966), 21–5.
'Language and Reality in *Twelfth Night*', *Critical Quarterly* 9: 3 (1966), 217–28.

1967
'Why We are Still in the Church', *Slant* 14 (1967), 25–8.
'*Slant* and its Critics: a Comment', *Slant* 16 (1967), 8–10.
'The *Slant* Symposium', *Slant* 17 (1967), 8–9.
Review of *The Churches and the Labour Movement* by Stephen Mayor, *Slant* 17 (1967), 27.

1968
'Politics and the Sacred', *Slant* 20 (1968), 18–23.
'Language, Reality and the Eucharist', *Slant* 21 (1968), 18–23.
'Language, Reality and the Eucharist (2)', *Slant* 22 (1968), 26–31.

1969
'Reluctant Heroes: the Novels of Graham Greene', *Slant* 25 (1969), 25–31.
'Reluctant Heroes: the Novels of Graham Greene (2)', *Slant* 26 (1969), 28–31.
'Priesthood and Leninism', *Slant* 27 (1969), 12–17.

1970
'Sector and Society: Problems of *Slant* Strategy', *Slant* 30 (1970), 17–21.

1971
'Faith and Revolution', *New Blackfriars* 52 (April 1971), 158–63.
'History and Myth in Yeats's "Easter 1916" ', *Essays in Criticism* 21: 3 (1971), 248–60.
'Modern Literary Criticism', *The Spectator* (30 Jan 1971), pp. 159–60.
'Thomas Hardy: Nature as Language', *Critical Quarterly* 13: 2 (1971), 155–62.

1972
'Alice and Anarchy', *New Blackfriars* 53 (Oct 1972), 447–55.
'Class, Power and Charlotte Brontë', *Critical Quarterly* 14: 3 (1972), 225–35.
'Criticism and Politics: A Rejoinder', *New Blackfriars* 53 (April 1972), 163–5.

1973

'Nature and the Fall in Hopkins: A Reading of "God's Grandeur" ', *Essays in Criticism* 23: 1 (1973), 68–75.

'William Hazlitt: An Empiricist Radical', *New Blackfriars* 54 (March 1973), 108–17.

1974

'The Form of His Fiction', *New Blackfriars* 55 (Oct 1974), 477–81

1975

'Ideology and Literary Form', *New Left Review* 90 (1975), 81–109.

'Marxists and Christians: Answers for Brian Wicker', *New Blackfriars* 56 (Oct 1975), 465–70.

'The Poetry of Peter Dale', *Agenda* 13: 3 (1975), 85–91.

1976

'Criticism and Politics: The Work of Raymond Williams', *New Left Review* 95 (1976), 3–23; repr. in *Criticism and Ideology*.

' "Decentring" God', *New Blackfriars* 57 (April 1976), 148–51.

'First-Class Fellow Travelling: The Poetry of W. H. Auden', *New Blackfriars* 57 (Dec 1976), 562–6.

'Sylvia's Lovers and Legality', *Essays in Criticism* 26: 1 (1976), 17–27.

'What is Fascism?', *New Blackfriars* 57 (March 1976), 100–6.

1977

'Marx, Freud and Morality', *New Blackfriars* 58 (Jan 1977), 21–9.

'Marxist Literary Criticism', in Hilda Schiff (ed.), *Contemporary Approaches to English Studies* (London: Heinemann), 94–103; repr. in *Sociological Review*, Monograph 25 (1977), 85–91.

'Raymond Williams e il populismo', *Calibano1* (1977), 159–84.

Review of *Aztec Calendar and other Poems* by A. Bartusek, *From Rivers* by J. Bodrowski, *Shema* by Peter Levi, *Dark Gate* by D. Vogel, *Selected Poems* by L. Goldberg, and *Names of Lost* by P. Levine, *Stand Magazine* 18: 3 (1977), 68–73.

Review of *Collected Poems* by Richard Eberhart, *Jack Straw's Castle* by Thom Gunn, and *Time Enough* by John Hewitt, *Stand Magazine* 18: 3 (1977), 75–8.

Review of *Karl Marx and World Literature* by S. S. Prawer, *Criticism* 19: 3 (1977), 260–2.

1978

'Aesthetics and Politics', *New Left Review* 107 (Jan/Feb 1978), 21–34.

'Form, Ideology, and *The Secret Agent*', *Sociological Review*, Monograph 26 (1978), 55–63; repr. in *Against the Grain* (1986).

'Liberality and Order: The Criticism of John Bayley', *New Left Review* 110 (July/Aug 1978), 29–40; repr. in *Against the Grain*.

'Literature and Politics Now', *Critical Quarterly* 20: 3 (1978), 65–9.

'*Marxism and Literary Criticism*: A Reply', *CLIO* 7: 2 (1978), 322–7.

Review of *Collected Poems* by Basil Bunting, *Complete Poems* by Keith Douglas, *Old Maps and New* by Norman MacCaig, *Or Where a Young Penguin Lies Screaming* by Gavin Ewart,

Purbeck Ingrained Island, by Paul Hyland, and *Art History and Class Struggle* by N. Hadjinicolaou, *Stand Magazine* 19: 4 (1978), 74–9.

Review of *Marxist Models of Literary Realism* by G. Bisztray, *Times Literary Supplement* 3977 (1978), 718.

Review of *Matthew Arnold* (Writers and their Background) by Kenneth Allott, *Notes and Queries* 25: 3 (1978), 267–8.

Review of *One Another* by Peter Dale, *Great Cloak* by John Montague, *Hearts Desire* by Jeffrey Wainwright, *Buying a Heart* by George Macbeth, *Selected James Simmons*, ed. Edna Longley, *Socialist Poems of Hugh MacDiarmid*, ed. T. S. Law and T. Berwick, *Stand Magazine* 20: 1 (1978), 74–9.

Review of *Selected Poems* by Osip Mandelstam, *Pataxanadu* by Christopher Middleton, *Gaudete* by Ted Hughes, *From Every Chink of Ark* by Peter Redgrove, and *Mules* by Paul Muldoon, *Stand Magazine* 19: 2 (1978), 76–80.

Review of *Serena* and *Collected Poems* by Samuel Beckett, *Translating Poetry* and *Selected Poems* by Zbigniew Herbert, *German Poetry* by Michael Hamburger, and *Poems* by Herman Hesse, *Stand Magazine* 19: 3 (1978), 72–7.

Review of *Shaw and the Play of Ideas* by R. F. Whiteman, *CLIO* 7: 3 (1978), 498–500.

Review of *Truth and Ideology* by H. Barth, *Notes and Queries* 25: 4 (1978), 361–2.

1979

'Irony and Commitment', *Stand Magazine* 20: 3 (1979), 24–7.

'The Poetry of E. P. Thompson', *Literature and History* 5: 2 (1979), 139–45.

'Radical Orthodoxies', *Oxford Literary Review* 3: 3 (1979), 99–103.

Review of *Bernard Shaw. Practical Politics: Twentieth-Century Views on Politics and Economics* by L. J. Hubenka, *Modern Language Review* 74: 1 (1979), 183–4.

Review of *Critical Twilight: Explorations in the Ideology of Anglo-American Literary Theory from Eliot to McLuhan* by John Fekete, *Journal of American Studies* 13: 2 (1979), 304–5.

Review of *Literary Sociology and Practical Criticism* by J. L. Sammons, *Modern Language Review* 74 (1979), 651–2.

Review of *Lough Derg* by Patrick Kavanagh, *Rain Dance* by John Hewitt, *Selected Poems* by Richard Murphy, *No Man's Land* by Wes Magee, *Heartwood* by R. Kell, and *My Shame in Crowds* by R. Wathen, *Stand Magazine* 20: 1 (1979), 70–4.

Review of *Modes of Modern Writing* by David Lodge, *Literature and History* 5: 2 (1979), 232–3.

Review of *New Directions in Literary History* by R. Cohen (ed.), *Language and Style* 11: 2 (1979), 129–30.

Review of *Solitude in Society: Sociological Study in French Literature* by R. Sayre, *Literature and History* 5: 2 (1979), 269.

Review of *Tenebrae* by Geoffrey Hill, *Collected Poems 1943–76* by V. Popa, *Sheltering Places* by G. Dawe, *Change of Affairs* by Michael Schmidt, *Camp One* and *31 Poems* by G. F. Dutton, *Rough Passage* by R. Parthasarathy, and *Jefuri* by A. Kolatkar, *Stand Magazine* 20: 3 (1979), 75–9.

1980

'How the Critical Revolution Started Rolling', *Times Higher Education Supplement* (19 Sept 1980), 9.

'Reconciliation With Reality', *New Statesman* (25 Jan 1980), 129–30.

Review of *Fictions and Ceremonies* by D. Chaney, and *Ideology and Cultural Production* by M. Barrett, P. Corrigan, A. Kuhn and J. Wolff, *Literature and History* 6: 2 (1980), 255–6.

Review of *Field Work* by S. Heaney, *Forced March* by M. Radnoti, *Moortown* by T. Hughes, *Poets from the North of Ireland* by F. Ormsby, and *Selected Poems 1950–1975* by T. Gunn, *Stand Magazine* 21: 3 (1980), 76–80.

Review of *Political Fictions* by M. Wilding, *Meanjin* 39: 3 (1980), 383–8.

Review of *Semiotics of Poetry* by Michael Riffaterre, and *Textual Strategies: Perspectives in Post-Structural Criticism* by J. V. Harari, *Literature and History* 6: 2 (1980), 255–7.

Review of *Socialist Propaganda in the 20th-Century British Novel* by D. Smith, *Review of English Studies* 31: 121 (1980), 106–7.

Review of *Tragic Realism and Modern Society* by J. Orr, *Literature and History* 6: 1 (1980), 117–18.

Review of *Tropics of Discourse: Essays in Cultural Criticism* by Hayden White, *Notes and Queries* 27: 5 (1980), 478.

1981

'The End of Criticism', *Southern Review* (Adelaide) 14: 2 (1981), 99–106.

'The Idealism of American Criticism', *New Left Review* 127 (1981), 53–65; repr. in *Against the Grain* (1986). Also as 'El idealismo de la critica norteamericana', *Escritura: Revista de Teoria y Critica Literarias* (Caracas), 6: 2 (1981), 247–61.

'Marxism and Deconstruction', *Contemporary Literature* 22: 4 (1981), 477–88.

Review of *Carminalenia* by C. Middleton, *Decadal: 10 Years of Sceptre Press* by M. Booth, *Gravities* by Seamus Heaney and Noel Connor, *The Sea of Fire* by R. Brennan, *Selected Poems* by P. Beer, *The Traveler Hears the Strange Machine* by D. Stanford, and *A Watching Brief* by R. McFadden, *Stand Magazine* 22: 2 (1981), 73–7.

Review of *The Collected Ewart, 1933–1980*, *Extractions* by C. H. Sisson, *The Man I Killed* by L. Lerner, *New Collected Poems* by V. Scannell, *Poems of Love and Death* by G. Macbeth, *Stand Magazine* 22: 4 (1981), 74–8.

Review of *Critical Assumptions* by K. K. Ruthven, and *Narrative and Structure: Exploratory Essays* by J. Holloway, *Review of English Studies* 32: 128 (1981), 498–9.

Review of *Interpretation: An Essay in the Philosophy of Literary Criticism* by P. D. Juhl, *Literature and History* 7: 2 (1981), 242–4.

Review of *One-Dimensional Marxism: Althusser and the Politics of Culture* by S. Clarke, T. Lovell, K. McDonnell, K. Robins and V. Jeleniewskiseidler, *French Studies* 35: 3 (1981), 369–70.

Review of *Working with Structuralism* by David Lodge, *New Society* 56: 971 (1981), 535–6.

1982

'Fredric Jameson: The Politics of Style', *Diacritics* 12: 3 (1982), 14–22; repr. in *Against the Grain* (1986).

'The Revolt of the Reader', *New Literary History* 13: 3 (1982), 449–452; repr. in *Against the Grain* (1986).

'Pierre Macherey and Marxist Literary Theory', *Philosophy* 14 (1982), 145–55; repr. in *Against the Grain* (1986).

'Wittgenstein's Friends', *New Left Review* 135 (1982), 64–90; repr. in *Against the Grain* (1986).

Review of *After the Dream* by A. Rudolf, *Collected Poems* by J. K. Baxter, *Danta Gradha* by

A. Young, *English Subtitles* by P. Porter, *The Flood* by C. Tomlinson, *Poems 1913–1956* by Bertolt Brecht, ed. J. Willett and R. Manheim, *Sea to the West* by N. Nicholson, *The Loveless Letters* by R. Pybus, *Tree* by R. Burns, and *XXI Poems* by G. Squires, *Stand Magazine* 23: 2 (1982), 62–8.

Review of *The Book of Jupiter* by Tom Paulin and Noel Connor, *The Butchers of Hull* by Peter Didsbury, *Fox Running* by Ken Smith, *The Go Situation* by M. Foley, *Night Cries* by John Cassidy, *A Rumoured City – New Poets from Hull* by Douglas Dunn, *The Sorrow Garden* by T. McCarthy, and *The Younger Irish Poets* by G. Dawe, *Stand Magazine* 24: 2 (1982), 66–72.

Review of *The Fortunate Traveller* by Derek Walcott, *Out of the Elements* by Andrew Waterman, *The Selected John Hewitt*, ed. A. Warner, *An Unofficial Rilke* by Michael Hamburger, and *Variations* by M. Hamburger, *Stand Magazine* 24: 1 (1982), 68–72.

Review of *Lucien Goldmann: An Introduction* by M. Evans, *French Studies* 36: 3 (1982), 363.

Review of *Romanticism and Ideology* by D. Aers, J. Cook and D. Punter, and *The Social Production of Art* by J. Wolff, *Literature and History* 8: 2 (1982), 255–6.

'Fiction with Conviction': Review of *The Socialist Novel in Britain* by H. Gustav Klaus (ed.), *New Statesman* (19 March 1982), 24–5.

'Total Interaction': Review of *The Sociology of Art* by A. Hauser, *Times Literary Supplement* (22 Oct 1982), 1168.

Review of *Writers of Wales: Raymond Williams* by J. P. Ward, *Poetry Wales* 17: 4 (1982), 87–9.

1983

'The Critic's New Clothes': Review of *Beautiful Theories: The Spectacle of Discourse in Contemporary Criticism* by Elizabeth W. Bruss, *Times Literary Supplement* (27 May 1983), 546.

'Power and Knowledge in "The Lifted Veil" ', *Literature and History* 9: 1 (1983), 52–61.

'The Task of the Cultural Critic (Politics and Culture)', *Meanjin* 42: 4 (1983), 445–8.

Review of *The Cornish Dancer* by Geoffrey Grigson, *The Flower Master* by Medbh McGuckian, *New and Selected Poems* by A. Cronin, *The Occasions of Poetry* and *The Passages of Joy* by Thom Gunn, *Selected Poems* by John Montague, and *The Sunflower of Hope: Poems from the Mozambican Revolution* by C. Searle, *Stand Magazine* 24: 3 (1983), 77–80.

Review of *Deconstruction: Theory and Practice* by C. Norris, and *Inventions: Writing, Textuality and Understanding in Literary History* by G. L. Burns, *Literature and History* 9: 2 (1983), 260–2.

Review of *Devotions* by C. Wilmer, *The Hunt By Night* by Derek Mahon, *A Late Harvest* by J. Ward, *Making Arrangements* by M. Simpson, *A Second Life* by W. Scammell, and *The Selected Paul Durcan*, ed. E. Longley, *Stand Magazine* 25: 1 (1983), 77–80.

Review of *The Institution of Criticism* by P. U. Hohendahl, *Literature and History* 9: 1 (1983), 97–101.

1984

'Naturally Unhoused': Review of *Collected Poems 1941–1983* by Michael Hamburger, and *Poems and Epigraphs* by J. M. v. Goethe, ed. Michael Hamburger, *Times Literary Supplement* (27 April 1984), 454.

'Nature and Violence: The Prefaces of Edward Bond', *Critical Quarterly* 26: 1/2 (1984), 127–35.

'One Country, Two Systems', *New Statesman* (30 Nov 1984), 26–8.

'Pious Heroines': Review of *Sex and Enlightenment: Women in Richardson and Diderot* by R. Goldberg, *Times Literary Supplement* (12 Oct 1984), 1170.

'Plenty of Life': Review of *Human Rites: Selected Poems 1970–1982* by E. A. Markham, and *Midsummer* by Derek Walcott, *Times Literary Supplement* (9 Nov 1984), 1290.

Review of *Black Literature and Literary Theory*, ed. H. L. Gates, *New York Times Book Review* 8 (1984), 45.

Review of *Interrelations of Literature* by J. P. Barricelli and J. Gibaldi, and *Literary Criticism and the Structures of History. Eric Auerbach and Leo Spitzer* by G. Green, *Modern Language Review* 79: 8 (1984), 385–6.

Review of *Inviolable Voice: History and 20th-Century Poetry* by Stan Smith, *Stand Magazine* 25: 2 (1984), 47–9.

Review of *Liberty Tree* by Tom Paulin, *111 Poems* by C. Middleton, *Quoof* by Paul Muldoon, *A Round House* by M. Sweeney, and *Selected Poems* by F. Adcock, *Stand Magazine* 25: 3 (1984), 76–80.

Review of *Marxism and Modernism: An Historical Study of Lukács, Brecht, Benjamin and Adorno* by E. Lunn, *Journal of Modern History* 56: 1 (1984), 124–5.

Review of *Modern French Marxism* by M. Kelly, *French Studies* 38: 1 (1984), 112.

Review of *News for Babylon: The Chatto Book of West Indian – British Poetry* by James Berry, *Poetry Review* 74: 2 (1984), 57–9.

Review of *Poetry and the Sociological Idea* by J. P. Ward, *Review of English Studies* 35: 139 (1984), 427–8.

Review of *Sexuality in 18th-Century Britain* by P. G. Bouce, *Notes and Queries* 31: 1 (1984), 129–30.

Review of *W. H. Auden: The Critical Heritage* by J. Haffenden, and *Auden: A Carnival of Intellect* by E. Callan, *Poetry Review* 73: 4 (1984), 60–1.

Review of *Writing and Sexual Difference* by E. Abel, *Modern Language Review* 79: 4 (1984), 879–80.

1985

'Brecht and Rhetoric', *New Literary History* 16: 3 (1985), 633–8; repr. in *Against the Grain* (1986).

'Capitalism, Modernism and Postmodernism,' *New Left Review* 152 (1985), 60–73; repr. in *Against the Grain* (1986).

'Literature and History', *Critical Quarterly* 27: 4 (1985), 23–6.

'Marxism and the Past', *Salmagundi* 68: 6 (1985), 271–90.

'Marxism, Structuralism, and Post-Structuralism', *Diacritics* 15: 4 (1985), 2–12; repr. in *Against the Grain* (1986).

'New Poetry' (H. D., H. Guest, E. Milne, S. Barry, G. Ewart and J. O'Callaghan), *Stand Magazine* 26: 1 (1985), 68–72.

'Politics and Sexuality in W. B. Yeats', *Crane Bag* 9: 2 (1985), 138–42.

Review of *By the Fisheries* by J. Reed, *Caribbean Poetry Now* by S. Brown, *Collected Poems* by C. H. Sisson, *The Dead Kingdom* by John Montague, and *Shadow Lands* by J. Bobrowski, *Stand Magazine* 26: 2 (1985), 66–70.

Review of *Collected Poems*, Volume 1, by M. Hartnett, *From The Irish* by J. Simmons, *The Price of Stone* by R. Murphy, and *The Rhetorical Town* by S. Barry, *Poetry Review* 75: 2 (1985), 64–5.

Review of *Dark Glasses* by Blake Morrison, *Minding Ruth* by A. C. Mathews, *The Non-Aligned Storyteller* by T. McCarthy, *Poems 1963–1983* by Michael Longley, and *Rich* by Craig Raine, *Stand Magazine* 26: 4 (1985), 69–72.

Review of *The Literary Labyrinth* by Bernard Sharratt, *Poetics Today* 6: 4 (1985), 780–2.

Review of *Reading for the Plot* by P. Brooks, *Literature and History* 11: 2 (1985), 295–6.

Review of *The Rise and Fall of Structural Marxism: Althusser and His Influence* by T. Benton, *French Studies* 39: 2 (1985), 239–40.

'The Subject of Literature', *English Magazine* 15 (1985), 2.

1986

'Meaning and Material': Review of *L'Aventure Semiologique* by Roland Barthes, and *The Responsibility of Forms: Critical Essays on Music, Art, and Representation* by Roland Barthes, *Times Literary Supplement* (2 May 1986), 477.

'The Poetry of Radical Republicanism', *New Left Review* 158 (1986), 123–8.

Review of *Collected Poems* by D. Egan, *Family Matters* by E. A. Markham, *The Fat Black Woman's Poems* by Grace Nichols, *Long Road to Nowhere* by Amryl Johnson, *Third World Poems* by E. K. Brathwaite, and *Trio 4* by A. Elliott, L. McAuley and C. O'Driscoll, *Stand Magazine* 27: 4 (1986), 76–9.

Review of *The Definition of Literature and Other Essays* by W. W. Robson, *Modern Language Review* 81: 2 (1986), 428.

Review of *Freud and the Culture of Psychoanalysis* by S. Marcus, *History Workshop Journal* 22 (1986), 193–4.

Review of *A Reader's Guide to Contemporary Literary Theory* by R. Selden, *Modern Language Review* 81: 4 (1986), 959–60.

Review of *Reading Althusser: An Essay on Structural Marxism* by S. G. Smith, *Journal of Modern History* 58: 1 (1986), 258–9.

Review of *v.* by Tony Harrison, *Poetry Review* 76: 1/2 (1986), 20–2.

1987

'The Art of the State', *Music Review* (20 March 1987), 8–11.

'Awakening from Modernity': Review of *Le Postmoderne Expliqué aux Enfants* by Jean-François Lyotard, and *Just Gaming* by Jean-François Lyotard and Jean-Loup Thebaud, *Times Literary Supplement* (20 Feb 1987), 194.

'The End of English', *Texual Practice* 1: 1 (1987), 1–9; repr. in *Central Institute of English and Foreign Languages Bulletin* 1: 1 (1987), 1–10.

'Estrangement and Irony in the Fiction of Milan Kundera', *Salmagundi* 73 (1987), 25–32.

'Frère Jacques: The Politics of Deconstruction', *Semiotica* 63: 3/4 (1987), 3–4; repr. in *Against the Grain* (1986).

Review of *Cuts* by M. Bradbury, and *No, Not Bloomsbury* by M. Bradbury, *Times Literary Supplement* (12 June 1987), 627.

Review of *A Furnace* by R. Fisher, *The Lame Waltzer* by Matthew Sweeney, *A New Primer for Irish Schools* by D. Bolger and M. O'Loughlin, *Letter to an Englishman* by A. Cronin, *A Northern Spring* by F. Ormsby, *The Berlin Wall Cafe* by Paul Durcan, *Antarctica* by Derek Mahon, and *Standing Female Nude* by Carol Ann Duffy, *Stand Magazine* 28: 2 (1987), 68–72.

Review of *Fragments of Modernity* by D. Frisby, *Sociological Review* 35: 1 (1987), 178–80.
Review of *Theories of Discourse: An Introduction* by D. MacDonell, *Literature and History* 13: 1 (1987), 137–8.

1988

'From Swiss Cottage to the Sandinistas': Review of *The Captain and the Enemy* by Graham Greene, *Graham Greene: On the Frontier: Politics and Religion in the Novels* by Mario Couto, *A Reader's Guide to Graham Greene* by Paul O'Prey, and *An Underground Fate: The Idiom of Romance in the Later Novels of Graham Greene* by Brian Thomas, *Times Literary Supplement* (16 Sept 1988), 1013.

'The Ideology of the Aesthetic', *Poetics Today* 9: 2 (1988), 327–38; repr. in Stephen Regan (ed.), *The Politics of Pleasure: Aesthetics and Cultural Theory* (Buckingham: Open University Press, 1992), 17–31.

'The Ideology of the Aesthetic', *Times Literary Supplement* (22 Jan 1988), 84, 94.

'J. L. Austin and Jonah', *New Blackfriars* 69: 815 (1988), 164–8.

'Poetry Chronicle', *Stand Magazine* 29: 3 (1988), 67–70.

'Posturing in the Gutter': Review of *Between Heaven and Charing Cross: The Life of Francis Thompson* by Brigid M. Boardman, and *God and Two Poets: Arthur Hugh Clough and Gerard Manley Hopkins* by Anthony Kenny, *Times Literary Supplement* (1 July 1988), 725.

'Rereading Literature: or Inside Leviathan', *Antithesis* 1: 1 (1988), 11–14.

'Resources for a Journey of Hope: The Significance of Raymond Williams', *New Left Review* (March/April 1988), 3–11.

Review of *Collected Writings* by John Cornford, *Collected Poems* by Christopher Caudwell, *Living in Disguise* by E. A. Markham, *Leaseholder* by D. Weissbort, *Collected Poems* by Derek Walcott, and *The Faber Book of Contemporary Irish Poetry*, ed. Paul Muldoon, *Stand Magazine* 29: 1 (1988), 65–7.

'The Silences of David Lodge', *New Left Review* (Nov/Dec 1988), 93–102.

'Stop Taking the Tablets', *New Statesman and Society* (23 Sept 1988), 24–6.

'Two Approaches in the Sociology of Literature', *Critical Inquiry* 14: 3 (1988), 469–76.

'Where there's a Will': Review of *The Life and Times of William Shakespeare* by Peter Levi, *The Observer* (30 Oct 1988).

1989

'Aesthetics and Politics in Edmund Burke', *History Workshop Journal* 28 (1989), 53–62.

'The Emptying of a Former Self': Review of *Wartime Journalism, 1939–1943* by Paul de Man, *Responses on Paul de Man's Wartime Journalism* by Werner Hamacher, Neil Hertz and Thomas Keenan (eds), *Paul de Man: Deconstruction and the Critique of Aesthetic Ideology* by Christopher Norris, *Paul de Man: Critical Writings, 1953–1978* by Lindsay Waters (ed.), and *Reading Paul de Man Reading* by Lindsay Waters and Wlad Godzich (eds), *Times Literary Supplement* (26 May 1989), 573–4.

'Escape into the Ineffable': Review of *Reading Modern Poetry* by Michael Schmidt, *Under Briggflatts: A History of Poetry in Great Britain, 1960–1988* by Donald Davie, *Instabilities in Contemporary British Poetry* by Alan Robinson, *Literary Theory and Poetry: Extending the Canon* by David Murray (ed.), and *Passing Judgements: Poetry in the Eighties* by John Mole, *Times Literary Supplement* (24 Nov 1989), 1291–2.

'Modernism, Myth and Monopoly Capitalism', *News from Nowhere* 7 (1989), pp. 19–24.

'Post–Modern Tristesse': Review of *A Sinking Island: The Modern English Writers* by Hugh Kenner, *Poetry Review* 79: 2 (1989), 6–7.

'Recent English Poetry', *Poetry Review* 79: 4 (1989), 46–7.

Review of *Lipstick Traces: A Secret History of the Twentieth Century* by G. Marcus, *New York Times Book Review* (1989), 12.

'Saint Oscar: A Foreword', *New Left Review* (Sept/Oct 1989), 125–8.

'Schopenhauer and the Aesthetic', *Signature* 1 (1989), 3–22.

'Turning Towards Europe': Review of *Transitions: Narratives in Modern Irish Culture* and *The Wake of Imagination: Ideas of Creativity in Western Culture* by Richard Kearney, *Times Literary Supplement* (10 Feb 1989), 132.

1990

'Back to the Future', *New Statesman and Society* (5 Jan 1990), 42–3.

'Defending the Free World', *Socialist Register* (1990), 85–94.

'English in Crisis', *English Review* (1 Sept 1990), 25–6.

'Masks of the Saboteur': Review of *Oscar Wilde* by Isobel Murray (ed.), *Oscar Wilde* by Peter Raby, and *Oscar Wilde: The Works of a Conformist Rebel* by Norbert Kohl, *Times Literary Supplement* (2 Feb 1990), 124.

'Poetry Chronicle', *Stand Magazine* 31: 2 (1990), 27–31.

'Poetry Chronicle', *Stand Magazine* 31: 4 (1990), 18–21.

Review of *Reclaiming Reality* by R. Bhaskar, *Textual Practice* 4: 3 (1990), 469.

Review of *Selected Poems 1990* by D. J. Enright, and *Life by Other Means: Essays on D. J. Enright* by J. Sims (ed.), *Poetry Review* 80: 3 (1990) 71.

'Rituals of Reconciliation': Review of *Prospecting: From Reader Response to Literary Anthropology* by W. Iser, *Times Literary Supplement* (16 March 1990), 294.

'Schools for Scandal': Review of *Ancient Cultures of Conceit: British University Fiction in the Post-War Years* by Ian Carter, *New Statesman and Society* (20 April 1990), 31–2.

'Shakespeare and the Class Struggle', *International Socialism* 49 (1990), 115–21.

1991

'Bleaker Discomforts': Review of *Love in a Life* by Andrew Motion, *Times Literary Supplement* (12 April 1991), 21.

'Booze and Belligerence': Review of Sean O'Casey's *The Plough and the Stars* (The Young Vic, London), *Times Literary Supplement* (17 May 1991), 16.

'Death of the Authors': Review of *French Philosophers in Conversation: Levinas, Schneider, Serres, Irigaray, Le Doeuff, Derrida* by Raoul Mortley, and *Comments on the Society of the Spectacle* by Guy Debord, *New Statesman and Society* (11 Jan 1991), 35–6.

'The Historian as Body-Snatcher': Review of *Learning to Curse: Essays in Early Modern Culture* by Stephen Greenblatt, *Times Literary Supplement* (18 Jan 1991), 7.

'Hitler the Hood': Review of Bertolt Brecht's *Resistible Rise of Arturo Ui* (Olivier Theatre, London), *Times Literary Supplement* (16 Aug 1991), 19.

'Out of the Closet': Review of Harold Pinter's *Party Time* (Almeida Theatre, London), *Times Literary Supplement* (15 Nov 1991), 20.

Review of *Belfast Confetti* by Ciaran Carson, *Poetry Review* 81: 2 (1991), 20–1.

Review of John Le Carré's *A Murder of Quality* [TV review], *Times Literary Supplement* (12 April 1991), 16.

'Rewriting Ireland': Review of *The Field Day Anthology of Irish Writing, Independent on Sunday* (24 Nov 1991), 36–7.

'Unionism and Utopia: *The Cure at Troy* by Seamus Heaney', *News from Nowhere* 9 (1991), 93–5.

1992

'The Crisis of Contemporary Culture', *New Left Review* 196 (1992), 29–41.

'A Culture in Crisis', *The Guardian* (27 Nov 1992), Review, 4, 6.

'Emily Brontë and the Great Hunger', *Irish Review* 12 (1992), 107–19.

'Native Tongues, Native Eyes': Review of *Black Robe* [film review], *Times Literary Supplement* (31 Jan 1992), 20.

'Proust, Punk or Both: How Ought We to Value Popular Culture?': Review of *Theory and Cultural Value* by Steven Connor, *Cultural Populism* by J. McGuigan, *Cultural Studies* by L. Grossberg et al., and *Cultural Studies as Critical Theory* by B. Agger, *Times Literary Supplement* (18 Dec 1992), 5–6.

Review of *The Culture Industry: Selected Essays on Mass Culture* by Theodor Adorno, *Sociology* 26: 1 (1992), 126.

Review of *Freud and Fiction* by S. Kofman, and *Psychoanalysis and Cultural Theory* by J. Donald, *Literature and History* (3rd series) 1: 2 (1992), 97–8.

'Seeking Sfax Appeal': Review of *The Death of the Author* by Gilbert Adair, *Times Literary Supplement* (21 Aug 1992), 18.

'Superior Persons: The Modernist Avant-Garde and the Rank and File': Review of *The Intellectuals and the Masses: Pride and Prejudice Among the Literary Intelligentsia, 1880–1939* by John Carey, *Times Literary Supplement* (17 July 1992), 5.

'Will and Ted's Bogus Journey': Review of *Shakespeare and the Goddess of Complete Being* by Ted Hughes, *The Guardian* (2 April 1992), Review, 26.

1993

'It is Not Quite True that I Have a Body, and Not Quite True that I am One Either': Review of *Body Work* by Peter Brooks, *London Review of Books* (27 May 1993), 7–8.

'The Moustache that Roared', *The Guardian* (10 Sept 1993), Supplement, 4–5.

'Radical Roots': Review of *Witness Against the Beast: William Blake and the Moral Law* by E. P. Thompson, *New Statesman and Society* (26 Nov 1993), 39–40.

Review of *The Gaze of the Gorgon* by Tony Harrison, *Poetry Review* 82: 4 (1993), 53–4.

Review of *The New Historicism and Other Old-Fashioned Topics* by B. Thomas, *Literature and History* (3rd series) 2: 1 (1993), 95–6.

Review of *William Empson: Essays on Renaissance Literature*, ed. John Haffenden, and *William Empson: The Critical Achievement*, ed. Christopher Norris and Nigel Mapp, *The Guardian* (8 June 1993), Review, 10.

'Vulgar, Vain and Venal': Review of *No Exit* by Julie Burchill, *The Man Who Made Husbands Jealous* by Jilly Cooper, *American Star* by Jackie Collins, and *Scruples Two: Fifteen Years Later* by Judith Krantz, *Times Literary Supplement* (28 May 1993), 7–8.

1994

'Deadly Fetishes': Review of *East, West* by Salman Rushdie, *London Review of Books* (6 Oct 1994), 20.

'Discourse and Discos: Theory in the Space between Culture and Capitalism', *Times Literary Supplement* (15 July 1994), 3–4.

'Feeding Off History', *The Observer* (20 Feb 1994), Magazine, pp 42–4 [the famine museum in Strokestown, Roscommon].

'My Wittgenstein', *Common Knowledge* 3: 1 (1994), 152–7.

'Oscar and George', *Nineteenth-Century Contexts* 18: 3 (1994), 205–23 [on Wilde and Shaw].

'A Postmodern Punch', *Irish Studies Review* 6 (1994), 2–3.

'The Right and the Good: Postmodernism and the Liberal State', *Textual Practice* 8: 1 (1994), 1–10.

'Spooky': Review of *The Collected Letters of W. B. Yeats. Vol. III: 1901–1904*, ed. John Kelly and Ronald Schuchard, and *Modern Irish Literature: Sources and Founders* by Vivian Mercier, *London Review of Books* (7 July 1994), 8–9.

'Texts in Time': Review of *The Wager of Lucien Goldmann: Tragedy, Dialectics and a Hidden God* by Mitchell Cohen, *New Statesman and Society* (30 Sept 1994), 56–7.

1995

'Biogspeak': Review of *George Eliot: A Biography* by Frederick Karl, *London Review of Books* (21 Sept 1995), 26–7.

'The Death of Self-Criticism': Review of *Professional Correctness: Literary Studies and Political Change* by Stanley Fish, *Times Literary Supplement* (24 Nov 1995), 6–7.

'Indigestible Truths', *New Statesman and Society* (2 June 1995), 22–3.

'Ireland's Obdurate Nationalisms', *New Left Review* 213 (1995), 130–6.

'The Lone Revolutionary': Review of *Raymond Williams: The Life* by Fred Inglis, *New Statesman and Society* (13 Oct 1995), 31–2.

'Love thy Neighbourhood': Review of *The Curious Enlightenment of Professor Caritat* by Steven Lukes, *London Review of Books* (16 Nov 1995), 12.

'Marxism without Marxism': Review of *Specters of Marx* by Jacques Derrida, *Radical Philosophy* 73 (1995), 35–7.

Review of *Explaining Northern Ireland* by Jon McGarry and Brendan O'Leary, *New Left Review* 213 (1995), 130–6.

Review of *Politics and Value in English Studies* by J. M. Guy and I. Small, *Literature and History* (3rd series) 4: 1 (1995), 91–4.

'Wallpaper and Barricades': Review of *William Morris: A Life for Our Time* by Fiona MacCarthy, *London Review of Books* (23 Feb 1995), 8.

'Where Do Postmodernists Come From?', *Monthly Review* 47: 3 (1995), 59–70.

1996

'Cork and the Carnivalesque: Francis Sylvester Mahony (Fr. Prout)', *Irish Studies Review* 16 (1996), 2–7.

'Getting Mad and Getting Even': Review of *Revenge Tragedy: Aeschylus to Armageddon* by John Kerrigan, *Times Literary Supplement* (2 Aug 1996), 4.

'The Hippest': Review of *Stuart Hall: Critical Dialogues*, ed. David Morley and Kuan-Hsing Chen, *London Review of Books* (7 March 1996), 3, 5.

'Homelessness': Review of *States of Fantasy* by Jacqueline Rose, *London Review of Books* (20 June 1996), 9.

'The Irish Sublime', *Religion and Literature* 28: 2/3 (1996), 25–32.

'Mixed Baggy Monsters': Review of *Modern Epic: The World System from Goethe to García*

Márquez by Franco Moretti, *Times Literary Supplement* (21 June 1996), 26.

'Priesthood and Paradox', *New Blackfriars* 77: 906 (1996), 316–19 [special issue for Herbert McCabe OP on his seventieth birthday, edited by Fergus Kerr OP].

1997

'In the same boat': Review of *After Marxism* by Ronald Aronson, *Marx at the Millenium* by Cyril Smith, *The Politics of Marxism* by Jules Townsend, *Marxism in the Postmodern Age* by Antonio Callari, Stephen Cullenberg and Carole Biewener (eds), and *Marxism, Mysticism and Modern Theory* by Suke Walton (ed.), *Radical Philosophy* 82 (1997), 37–40.

Review of *After the End of Art: Contemporary Art and the Pale of History* by A. C. Danto, *New York Times Book Review* (16 Feb 1997), 21.

Review of *Justice, Nature and the Geography of Difference* by David Harvey, *London Review of Books* (24 April 1997), 22–3.

'The Contradictions of Postmodernism', *New Literary History* 28:1 (1997), 1–6.

'Imperfect Strangers': Review of *Postmodernity and its Discontents* by Zygmunt Bauman, *Times Literary Supplement* (23 May 1997), 22.

5   Interviews and Debates

'Oxford's Great English Literature Debate: "That the Oxford English Course is Inadequate" ' (with Carl Schmidt, Daniel Baron Cohen and Terry Eagleton), *Times Higher Education Supplement* (21 March 1980), 10–11.

'Terry Eagleton', an interview with James H. Kavanagh and Thomas E. Lewis, *Diacritics* 12: 1 (1982), 53–64.

'Literary Theory in the University – a Survey' (with D. Bleich et al.), *New Literary History*, 14: 2 (1983), 411–51.

'The Question of Value – a Discussion' (with Peter Fuller), *New Left Review* 142 (1983), 76–90.

'The Rise of English Studies: An Interview with Terry Eagleton', *Southern Review* (Adelaide) 17: 1 (1984), 18–32.

'The "Text in Itself": A Symposium' (with Tony Bennett, Noel King, Ian Hunter, Catherine Belsey and John Frow), *Southern Review* (Adelaide) 17: 2 (1984), 115–46.

'Interview with Terry Eagleton' (with Patrice Petro and Andrew Martin), *Iowa Journal of Literary Studies* 6 (1985), 1–17.

'The Practice of Possibility' (Raymond Williams interviewed by Terry Eagleton), *New Statesman* (7 Aug 1987), 19–21.

'International Books of the Year', *Times Literary Supplement* (2 Dec 1988), 1342.

'A Cry from the Citadel', an interview with Catherine Bennett, *The Guardian* (15 Aug 1991), 21–2.

'Entrevista con Terry Eagleton' (with Ana Gabriela Macedo, Joan Ferreira Duarte, and Maria Filomena Louro), *Vertice* 43 (1991), 97–101.

'Aesthetic Value', an interview with Stuart Sim for the Open University course AA301, *Philosophy of the Arts*, 1992. Recorded on audio-cassette.

'Conversation with Terry Eagleton' (interview with James Wood), *Poetry Review* 82: 1 (1992), 4–7.

'Doxa and Common Life' (transcript of discussion with Pierre Bourdieu), *New Left Review* (1992), 111–21.

'International Books of the Year: 34 Writers Select the Books that Most Impressed Them in 1992', *Times Literary Supplement* (4 Dec 1992), 9–13.

'One Hundred Years After: 12 Writers Reflect on Tennyson's Achievement', *Times Literary Supplement* (2 Oct 1992), 8–9.

'International Books of the Year', *Times Literary Supplement* (3 Dec 1993), 10

'Is English Literature Worth Teaching?' (with Matthew D'Ancona) *The Times* (19 April 1993), 14.

'International Books of the Year: 33 Writers Select the Books that Impressed Them Most in 1994', *Times Literary Supplement* (2 Dec 1994), pp. 8–12.

'Meet Professor Playwright', an interview with Paul Taylor and a review of the play *Disappearances, The Independent* (5 July 1997), 5.

6   Editorial Work

General editor of Rereading Literature Series, published by Basil Blackwell, Oxford. Volumes published to date (with prefaces by Terry Eagleton):

W. H. Auden by Stan Smith (1985), *William Blake* by Edward Larrissy (1985), *Emily Brontë* by James H. Kavanagh (1985),*Charles Dickens* by Steven Connor (1985), *Alexander Pope* by Laura Brown (1985), *Geoffrey Chaucer* by Stephen Knight (1986), *William Shakespeare* by Terry Eagleton (1986), *Alfred Tennyson* by Alan Sinfield (1986), *Ben Jonson* by Peter Womack (1987), *Virginia Woolf* by Rachel Bowlby (1988), *John Milton* by Catherine Belsey (1988) and *Thomas Hardy* by John Goode (1988).

7   Works about Terry Eagleton

1968

Kernan, Alvin B., *Yale Review* 57 (1968), 294. Review of *Shakespeare and Society*.

Lazarescu, Dan A., *Viata Romaneasca* [Bucharest] 9 (1968), 150–3. Review of *Shakespeare and Society*.

1975

Hook, Judith, *Victorian Studies* 19 (1975), 284–6. Review of *Myths of Power*.

Mulhern, Francis, ' "Ideology and Literary Form": A comment', *New Left Review* 91 (1975), 80–7.

1976

Allott, Miriam, *Nineteenth Century Fiction* 31 (1976), 225–30. Review of *Myths of Power*.

Barnett, Anthony, 'Raymond Williams and Marxism: A Rejoinder to Terry Eagleton', *New Left Review* 99 (1976), 47–64.

Conrad, Peter, *The Spectator* (21 Aug 1976), 25. Review of *Marxism and Literary Criticism*.

Dusinberre, Juliet, *Notes and Queries* 23 (1976), 420–1. Review of *Myths of Power*.

Watson, Melvin R., *CLIO* 5 (1976), 265–9. Review of *Myths of Power*.

Wicker, Brian, *Month* 9 (1976), 391–2. Review of *Marxism and Literary Criticism*.

Worth, George J., *CEA Critic* 39: 1 (1976), 29–34. Review of *Myths of Power*.

1977

Casey, John, *Times Literary Supplement* (20 May 1977), 606–7. Review of *Criticism and Ideology*.

Keith, W. J., *University of Toronto Quarterly* 47 (1977), 86–9. Review of *Myths of Power*.

Mitchell, Stanley, *Times Literary Supplement* (21 Jan 1977), 76. Review of *Marxism and Literary Criticism*.

1978

Harvey, J. R., 'Criticism, Ideology, Raymond Williams and Terry Eagleton', *Cambridge Quarterly* 8· 1 (1978), 56–65.

Huyssen, Andreas, *CLIO* 7 (1978), 315–22. Review of *Marxism and Literary Criticism*.

1979

Behrend, Hanna, *Zeitschrift für Anglistik und Amerikanistik* [Leipzig] 27 (1979), 87–9. Review of *Marxism and Literary Criticism*.

Wilding, Michael, *Modern Language Review* 74 (1979), 151–3. Review of *Marxism and Literary Criticism*.

1981

Craib, Ian, 'Criticism and Ideology: Theory and Experience', *Contemporary Literature* 22: 4 (1981), 489–509.

1982

Bullock, M., *Minnesota Review* 18 (1982), 156–8. Review of *Walter Benjamin or Towards a Revolutionary Criticism*.

Butler, Marilyn, *Times Literary Supplement* (12 Nov 1982), 1241–2. Review of *The Rape of Clarissa*.

Frow, John, 'Structuralist Marxism', *Southern Review* (Adelaide), 15: 2 (1982), 208–17.

Womack, Peter, *Cencrastus* 8 (1982), 47–8. Review of *Walter Benjamin or Towards a Revolutionary Criticism*.

1983

Allentuch, H. R., *Gradiva* 3: 1 (1983), 73–6 Review of *Literary Theory*.

Barton, A., *New York Review of Books* 30: 12 (1983), 30–2. Review of *The Rape of Clarissa*.

Bayley, John: 'The Uncommon Pursuit', *Times Literary Supplement* (10 June 1983), 587–8. Review of *Literary Theory*.

Davis, Lennard J., *Nation* 238 (1983), 59–60. Review of *Literary Theory*.

Donoghue, Denis, *New York Review of Books* 30: 19 (1983), 43–5. Review of *Literary Theory*.

Forgacs, David, *Poetics Today* 4: 1 (1983), 183–6. Review of *Walter Benjamin or Towards a Revolutionary Criticism*.

Gibson, Andrew, *English* 32: 143 (1983), 166–76. Review of *The Rape of Clarissa*.

Hutcheon, Linda, *Diacritics* 13: 4 (1983), 33–42. Review of *Literary Theory*.

Kendrick, W., *New York Times Book Review* 88: 36 (1983), 9. Review of *Literary Theory*.

Norris, Christopher, *London Review of Books* 5: 12 (1983), 21–4. Review of *Literary Theory*.

Rosen, Michael, *Times Literary Supplement* (4 Feb 1983), 109–10. Review of *Walter Benjamin or Towards a Revolutionary Criticism*.

Scobie, Stephen, *Malahat Review* 66 (1983), 170–1. Review of *The Rape of Clarissa* and *Literary Theory*.

Servotte, H., *Spiegel der Letteren* 25: 4 (1983), 318–19. Review of *Literary Theory*.

Showalter, Elaine, *Raritan* 3: 2 (1983), 130–49. Review of *The Rape of Clarissa* and *Literary Theory*.

Wagner, Peter, *Eighteenth-Century Life* 8: 3 (1983), 108–15. Review of *The Rape of Clarissa*.

Warner, W. B., *Diacritics* 13: 4 (1983), 12–32. Review of *The Rape of Clarissa*.

Wood, Michael, *London Review of Books* 5: 8 (1983), 18–19. Review of *The Rape of Clarissa*.

1984

Aikins, J. E., *University of Toronto Quarterly* 54: 1 (1984), 106–19. Review of *The Rape of Clarissa*.

Baldick, Chris, *Times Literary Supplement* (23 Nov 1984), 1339. Review of *The Function of Criticism*.

Burns, Wayne, 'Marxism, Criticism and the Disappearing Individual', *Recovering Literature: A Journal of Contextualist Criticism* 12 (1984), 7–28.

Cronk, Nicholas, *Notes and Queries* 31: 1 (1984), 133–5. Review of *The Rape of Clarissa*.

Culler, Jonathan, *Poetics Today* 5: 1 (1984), 149–56. Review of *Literary Theory*.

Davis, Lennard J., *Review* 6 (1984), 237–49. Review of *The Rape of Clarissa*.

Dussinger, John A., *Eighteenth-Century Studies* 17: 3 (1984), 350–4. Review of *The Rape of Clarissa*.

Forgacs, David, *Poetics Today* 5: 2 (1984), 429–33. Review of *Literary Theory*.

Frow, John, 'Marxism after Structuralism', *Southern Review* 17: 1 (1984), 33–50.

Fry, P. H., *Yale Review* 73: 4 (1984), 603–16. Review of *Literary Theory*.

Grundy, Isobel, *Scriblerian and the Kit-Cats* 16: 2 (1984), 153–5. Review of *The Rape of Clarissa*.

Guetti, J., *Raritan* 3: 4 (1984), 124–37. Review of *Literary Theory*.

Kellman, S. G., *Modern Fiction Studies* 30: 2 (1984), 399–403. Review of *Literary Theory*.

King. R., *Kenyon Review* 6: 4 (1984), 114–18. Review of *Literary Theory*.

Martínez-Victorio, J., *Atlantis* 6: 1/2 (1984), 105–6. Review of *Literary Theory*.

Moseley, M., *Sewanee Review* 92: 2 (1984), 47–8. Review of *The Rape of Clarissa*.

Murphy, J. W., *Studies in Soviet Thought* 27: 2 (1984), 179–81. Review of *Walter Benjamin or Towards a Revolutionary Criticism*.

Murphy, M., *Radical History Review* 31 (1984), 33–8. Review of *Literary Theory*.

Rogers, Pat, *Literature and History* 10: 1 (1984), 124–5. Review of *The Rape of Clarissa*.

Ryan, Michael, *Sub-Stance* 44: 4 (1984), 134–6. Review of *Literary Theory*.

Ryan, Michael, 'The Marxism-Deconstruction Debate in Literary Theory', *New Orleans Review* 11: 1 (1984), 29–35.

Sprinker, Michael, *Minnesota Review* 22 (1984), 152–6. Review of *Literary Theory*.

Swingewood, Alan, *Sociological Review* 32: 1 (1984), 169–72. Review of *Literary Theory*.

Todd, D. D., *Philosophy and Literature* 8: 1 (1984), 129–30. Review of *Literary Theory*.

Todd, Janet, *British Journal for Eighteenth Century Studies* 7 (1984), 127–8. Review of *The Rape of Clarissa*.

Vanleer, D., *American Quarterly* 36: 2 (1984), 291–6. Review of *Literary Theory*.

1985

Aczel, Richard: 'Eagleton and English', *New Left Review* 154 (1985), 113–23.

Bennett, J. R., *Journal of Literary Semantics* 14: 1 (1985), 76–9. Review of *Literary Theory*.

Boak, D., *AUMLA: Journal of the Australasian Universities Language and Literature Association* 64 (1985), 269–73. Review of *Literary Theory*.

Bouce, P. G., *Review of English Studies* 36: 141 (1985), 94–5. Review of *The Rape of Clarissa*.

Boumelha, Penny, *AUMLA: Journal of the Australasian Universities Language and Literature Association* 64 (1985), 273–5. Review of *Literary Theory*.

Cusin, Michael, *Études Anglaises* 38: 3 (1985), 295–6. Review of *Literary Theory*.

Hansford, H. J., *Review of English Studies* 36: 144 (1985), 615–16. Review of *Literary Theory*.

Holub, Robert C., *German Quarterly* 58: 3 (1985), 440–2. Review of *Literary Theory*.

Jackson, Wallace, *South Atlantic Quarterly* 84: 3 (1985), 328–30. Review of *Literary Theory*.

Johnston, K., *College English* 47: 4 (1985), 407–19. Review of *Literary Theory*.

Neetens, W., *Revue belge de philologie et d'histoire* [Brussels] 63: 3 (1985), 605–7. Review of *The Function of Criticism*.

Norris, Christopher, *Southern Humanities Review* 19: 3 (1985), 286–7. Review of *The Function of Criticism*.

Parrinder, Patrick, *London Review of Books* (7 Feb 1985), 16–17. Review of *The Function of Criticism*. Reprinted in *The Failure of Theory* (1987).

Paul, Anthony, *Dutch Quarterly Review* 15: 2 (1985), 126–36. Review of *Literary Theory*.

Poole, Roger, 'Generating Believable Entities: Post-Marxism as a Theological Enterprise', *Comparative Criticism: A Yearbook* 7 (1985), 49–71.

Rooney, Ellen and Caraher, Brian: 'Going Farther: Literary Theory and the Passage to Cultural Criticism', *Works and Days* 3: 1 (1985), 51–77.

Selden, Raman, *Modern Language Review* 80: 2 (1985), 396–8. Review of *Literary Theory*.

Shumway, David R., 'Transforming Literary Studies into Cultural Criticism: The Role of Interpretation and Theory', *Works and Days* 3: 1 (1985), 79–89.

Stivale, C. J., *French Review* 58: 4 (1985), 572–3. Review of *Literary Theory*.

Sugnet, C., *American Book Review* 7: 4 (1985), 5–6. Review of *Literary Theory*.

Thomas, Ronald R., *Modern Philology* 83: 1 (1985), 104–8. Review of *Literary Theory*.

Tompkins, P. K., *Quarterly Journal of Speech* 71: 1 (1985), 119–31. Review of *Literary Theory*.

Wess, R., *Minnesota Review* 25 (1985), 139–41. Review of *The Rape of Clarissa* and *The Function of Criticism*.

1986

Adams, R. M., *New York Review of Books* 33: 17 (1986), 50–4. Review of *William Shakespeare*.

Bialostosky, Don, *Novel* 19: 2 (1986), 168–9. Review of *Literary Theory*.

Cain, W. E., *Comparative Literature* 38: 4 (1986), 362–6. Review of *Literary Theory*.

Corngold, S., *Modern Language Studies* 16: 3 (1986), 367–72. Review of *Walter Benjamin or Towards a Revolutionary Criticism*.

Donaldson, Ian, *Yearbook of English Studies* 16 (1986), 262–4. Review of *The Rape of Clarissa*.

Godden, Richard, *Poetics Today* 7: 1 (1986), 147–56. Review of *The Function of Criticism*.

Lucas, John, *Times Literary Supplement* (4 July 1986), 731. Review of *Against the Grain*.

MacDonald, R. R., *Shakespeare Quarterly* 37: 4 (1986), 532–4. Review of *William Shakespeare*.

Michaud, G., *Liberté* 28: 3 (1986), 142–7. Review of *The Function of Criticism*.

Neuman, Shirley, *Canadian Review of Comparative Literature* 13: 4 (1986), 641–4. Review of *Literary Theory*.

Rissik, Andrew, *New Statesman* (21 March 1986), 26–7. Review of *William Shakespeare*.

Speirs, Logan, 'Terry Eagleton and *The Function of Criticism*', *Cambridge Quarterly* 15 (1986), 57–63. Review of *The Function of Criticism*.

Venuti, L., *Scriblerian and the Kit-Cats* 18: 2 (1986), 209–10. Review of *The Function of Criticism*.

Weis, René, *Times Higher Education Supplement* 698 (1986), 168–9. Review of *William Shakespeare*.

Wihl, G., *South Atlantic Quarterly* 85: 2 (1986), 199–202. Review of *The Function of Criticism*.

1987

Bennington, Geoff, 'Demanding History', in Derek Attridge, Robert Young and Geoff Bennington (eds), *Post-Structuralism and the Question of History* (Cambridge: Cambridge University Press, 1987), 15–29.

Bialostosky, D., *Minnesota Review* 28 (1987), 140–2. Review of *Against the Grain*.

Breslow, Maurice, *Queen's Quarterly* 94: 2 (1987), 596–601. Review of *The Function of Criticism*.

Flamm, M., *New York Times Book Review* (Oct 1987), 30. Review of *Saints and Scholars*.

Foster, Roy, *Times Literary Supplement* (4 Sept 1987), 947. Review of *Saints and Scholars*.

Heath, Stephen, *Comparative Criticism* 9 (1987), 281–326. Review of *Literary Theory*.

Kamps, Ivo, *Minnesota Review* 28 (1987), 127–9. Review of *William Shakespeare*.

Nakano, Yukito, 'Terry Eagleton as Critic', *Studies in English Language and Literature* 37 (1987), 27–51.

Parrinder, Patrick, 'The Myth of Terry Eagleton', in *The Failure of Theory: Essays in Criticism and Contemporary Fiction* (Hemel Hempstead: Harvester Wheatsheaf, 1987), 30–8.

Patrick, Julian, *University of Toronto Quarterly* 56: 2 (1986/7), 352–6. Review of *Literary Theory*.

1988

Coyle, Martin, *Notes and Queries* 35: 1 (1988), 80. Review of *William Shakespeare*.

Freadman, Richard and Miller, S. R., 'Three Views of Literary Theory', *Poetics* 17: 1/2 (1988), 9–24.

Frey, K., *Minnesota Review* 30: 3 (1988), 208–9. Review of *Saints and Scholars*.

Jackson, Russell, *Cahiers Elisabethains* 34 (1988), 127–31. Review of *William Shakespeare*.

Kastan, David Scott, *College English* 50: 6 (1988), 697. Review of *William Shakespeare*.

Palmer, R. Barton, 'Philology and the Material, Dialogical Word: Bakhtin, Eagleton, and Medieval Historicism', *Envoi* 1: 1 (1988), 41–57.

Simpson, D., *American Book Review* 10: 5 (1988), 12. Review of *Saints and Scholars*.

Strier, Richard, *Modern Philology* 86: 1 (1988), 72–6. Review of *William Shakespeare*.

Wilson, Richard, *Literature and History* 14: 2 (1988), 210–18. Review of *William Shakespeare*.

1989

Cronin, Richard, 'Politicizing Literature', *Modern Age* 32: 4 (1988), 311–17.

Ellis, D., *Cambridge Quarterly* 18: 1 (1989), 86–97. Review of *William Shakespeare*.

Leighton, Angela, *Times Literary Supplement* (1 Sept 1989), 950. Review of *Myths of Power: A Marxist Study of the Brontës* (2nd edn).

Monod, S., *Etudes Anglaises* 42: 2 (1989), 222–3. Review of *Hard Times* by Charles Dickens (ed. Terry Eagleton).

Pollard, Arthur, *Brontë Society Transactions* 19: 8 (1989), 378. Review of *Myths of Power* (2nd edn).

Strickland, R., *Poetics Today* 10: 3 (1989), 635–7. Review of *Against the Grain*.

Thompson, Ann, *Modern Language Review* 84: 3 (1989), 713–16. Review of *William Shakespeare*.

Tóibín, Colm, *Fortnight* 271 (1989), 21. Review of 'Nationalism: Irony and Commitment' [Field Day Pamphlet].

1990

Banville, John, *The Observer* (4 March 1990), 42. Review of *The Ideology of the Aesthetic*.

Bonhert, C., *German Studies Review* 13: 2 (1990), 368–70. Review of *Literary Theory*.

Dantanus, Ulf, *Irish University Review* 19: 2 (1990), 368–70. Review of 'Nationalism: Irony and Commitment' [Field Day Pamphlet].

Gardner, S., *Times Literary Supplement* (30 March 1990), 337. Review of *The Significance of Theory* and *The Ideology of the Aesthetic*.

Kermode, Frank, *London Review of Books* (5 April 1990), 14–15. Review of *The Ideology of the Aesthetic*.

Kimball, Roger, 'The Contradictions of Terry Eagleton', *New Criterion* 9: 1 (1990), 17–23.

Smallwood, Philip, 'Terry Eagleton', in *Modern Critics in Practice: Critical Portraits of British Literary Critics* (Hemel Hempstead: Harvester Wheatsheaf, 1990), 7–40.

Watson, D., *Literature and History* (3rd series) 1: 2 (1990), 116–17. Review of *The Ideology of the Aesthetic*.

Widdowson, Peter, *Literature and History* (3rd series) 1: 2 (1990), 82–5. Review of *Raymond Williams: Critical Perspectives*.

1991

Anon., 'Oxford gets a Marxist', *The Observer* (21 April 1991) [profile].

Bate, Jonathan, *London Review of Books* (23 May 1991), 14–15. Review of *Ideology: An Introduction*.

Classen, A., *Studia Neophilogica* 63: 2 (1991), 239–41. Review of *Literary Theory*.

Connor, Steven, 'The Poetry of the Meantime: Terry Eagleton and the Politics of Style', *The Year's Work in Critical and Cultural Theory* 1 (1991), 243–64.

Cunningham, Adrian, 'The December Group: Terry Eagleton and the New Left Church', *The Year's Work in Critical and Cultural Theory* 1 (1991), 210–15.

Dasenbrock, R. W., *World Literature Today* 65: 2 (1991), 371–2. Review of *Nationalism, Colonialism, and Literature*, ed. Seamus Deane (with Terry Eagleton, Fredric Jameson and Edward Said).

Easthope, Antony, 'Iron on the Shoulder: For Young Terry at 50', *The Year's Work in Critical and Cultural Theory* 1 (1991), 288–93.

Eden, Frank, 'The Ballad of Terry Eagleton', *The Year's Work in Critical and Cultural Theory* 1 (1991), 208–9.

Gardiner, M., *Sociology: The Journal of the British Sociological Association* 25: 4 (1991), 748–9. Review of *Ideology: An Introduction.*

Giddens, Anthony, *Times Higher Education Supplement* (21 June 1991), 18–19. Review of *Ideology: An Introduction.*

Goode, John, 'For a Pilgrim of Hope', *The Year's Work in Critical and Cultural Theory* 1 (1991), 294–301.

Griffiths, E., *Times Literary Supplement* (28 June 1991), 6–7. Review of *Ideology: An Introduction.*

Griffiths, Sian, 'Marxist Elevated at Oxford', *Times Higher Education Supplement* (22 March 1991), 2.

Griffiths, Sian, 'In the Belly of the Beast', *Times Higher Education Supplement* (21 June 1991), 16.

Gross, D. S., *World Literature Today* 65: 1 (1991), 198–9. Review of *The Significance of Theory.*

Kelly, D., *James Joyce Quarterly* 28: 3 (1991), 705–8. Review of *Nationalism, Colonialism, and Literature*, ed. Seamus Deane (with Terry Eagleton, Fredric Jameson and Edward Said).

Knoenagel, A., *International Fiction Review* 18: 1 (1991), 63–4. Review of *Nationalism, Colonialism, and Literature*, ed. Seamus Deane (with Terry Eagleton, Fredric Jameson and Edward Said).

Larrissy, Edward, 'The Sign of Value: Reflections on Eagleton and Aesthetic Value', *The Year's Work in Critical and Cultural Theory* 1 (1991), 230–42.

Lloyd, D., *Art History* 14: 4 (1991), 620–4. Review of *The Ideology of the Aesthetic.*

Lyas, C., *British Journal of Aesthetics* 31: 2 (1991), 169–71. Review of *The Ideology of the Aesthetic.*

Maley, Willy, 'Brother Tel: The Politics of Eagletonism', *The Year's Work in Critical and Cultural Theory* 1 (1991), 270–87.

Mitchell, S., *Oxford Art Journal* 14: 1 (1991), 92–4. Review of *The Ideology of the Aesthetic.*

Norris, Christopher, '*Ideology*: A Review', *The Year's Work in Critical and Cultural Theory* 1 (1991), 265–9.

O'Flinn, Paul, 'Memories of Underdevelopment: Teaching Shakespeare in 1969', *The Year's Work in Critical and Cultural Theory* 1 (1991), 216–18.

Redhead, S., *Theory, Culture and Society* 8: 4 (1991), 123. Review of *Raymond Williams: Critical Perspectives.*

Regan, Stephen, et al., 'Barbarian at the Gate: Essays for Terry Eagleton', *The Year's Work in Critical and Cultural Theory* 1 (1991), 207–301.

Roberts, David, *Studies in English Literature* (1991), 69–74. Review of *The Ideology of the Aesthetic.*

Rolleston, J., *Diacritics* 21: 4 (1991), 87–100. Review of *The Ideology of the Aesthetic.*

Sands, Sarah, 'Return of the History Man', *Evening Standard* (11 April 1991), 25 [profile].

Seamon, R., *Canadian Literature* 130 (1991), 161–2. Review of *Saints and Scholars.*

Schusterman, R., *Journal of Aesthetics and Art Criticism* 49: 3 (1991), 259–61. Review of *The Ideology of the Aesthetic.*

Sprinker, M., *Contemporary Literature* 32: 4 (1991), 573–9. Review of *The Ideology of the Aesthetic.*

Wade, Geoff, 'Changes: A Critical Survey of Terry Eagleton's Work', *The Year's Work in Critical and Cultural Theory* 1 (1991), 219–29.

Wade, Jean-Philippe, ' "The Humanity of the Senses": Terry Eagleton's Political Journey to *The Ideology of the Aesthetic*', *Theoria* 77 (1991), 39–57.

Vice, Sue, *Notes and Queries* 38: 2 (1991), 274–5. Review of *The Significance of Theory*.

Wright, E., *Modern Language Review* 86: 3 (1991), 653–4. Review of *The Ideology of the Aesthetic*.

Zmijewski, N., *Australian and New Zealand Journal of Sociology* 27: 3 (1991), 415–16. Review of *The Ideology of the Aesthetic*.

1992

Barker, M., *Media, Culture and Society* 14: 1 (1992), 152. Review of *Ideology: An Introduction*.

Blumenbach, U., *Zeitschrift für Anglistik und Amerikanistik* 40: 3 (1992), 275–6. Review of *Nationalism, Colonialism, and Literature*, ed. Seamus Deane (with Terry Eagleton, Fredric Jameson and Edward Said).

Elderkin, S. H., *Labour/Le Travail* 30 (1992), 327–30. Review of *Ideology: An Introduction*.

Franke, A., *Argument* 34: 1 (1992), 136–8. Review of *Ideology: An Introduction*.

Henderson, G., *University of Toronto Quarterly* 61: 2 (1992), 28–88. Review of *Ideology: An Introduction*.

Lechte, J., *Australian Journal of Political Science* 27: 2 (1992), 391–2. Review of *Ideology: An Introduction*.

Lord, T. C., *Philosophy and Literature* 16: 2 (1992), 374–6. Review of *The Ideology of the Aesthetic*.

Meynell, H., *Heythrop Journal: A Quarterly Review of Philosophy and Theology* 33: 1 (1992), 94–5. Review of *The Ideology of the Aesthetic*.

Pepper, W. T., *Minnesota Review* 38 (1992), 135–7. Review of *Ideology: An Introduction*.

Reiss, Timothy J., *American Literary History* 4: 4 (1992), 649–54. Review of *Nationalism, Colonialism and Literature*, ed. Seamus Deane (with Terry Eagleton, Fredric Jameson and Edward Said).

Reiss, Timothy J., *American Literary History* 4: 4 (1992), 657–61. Review of *Ideology: An Introduction*.

Regan, Stephen, 'Ireland's Field Day', *History Workshop Journal* 33 (1992), 25–37. Review of *Nationalism: Irony and Commitment*.

Segal, Alex, 'Language Games and Justice', *Textual Practice* 6 (1992), 210–24.

Soper, Kate, *New Left Review* (1992), 120–32. Review of *The Ideology of the Aesthetic*.

Swingewood, Alan, *British Journal of Sociology* 43: 4 (1992), 682. Review of *Ideology: An Introduction*.

Tyndall, P., *Canadian Literature* 134 (1992), 109–10. Review of *The Ideology of the Aesthetic*.

Vigouroux-Frey, Nicole, 'D'Oscar à Saint Oscar (Terry Eagleton, 1989), identité et/ou difference culturelle?', in Pierre Sahel (introd.), *Différence et Identité* (Provence: University of Provence Press, 1992), 165–76.

Watson, D., *Literature and History* (3rd series) 1: 1 (1992), 82–3. Review of *Ideology: An Introduction*.

Zmijewski, N., *Australian and New Zealand Journal of Sociology* 28: 3 (1992), 433–6. Review of *Ideology: An Introduction*.

1993

Armstrong, Isobel, 'So What's All This About the Mother's Body?: The Aesthetic, Gender and the Polis', in Judith Still and Michael Worton (eds), *Textuality and Sexuality: Reading Theories and Practices* (Manchester: Manchester University Press, 1993), 218–36.

Bjornson, R., *Comparative Literature* 45: 3 (1993), 300–3. Review of *Nationalism, Colonialism, and Literature*, ed. Seamus Deane (with Terry Eagleton, Fredric Jameson and Edward Said).

Connor, Steven, *Times Literary Supplement* (28 May 1993), 15–16. Review of *The Crisis of Contemporary Culture*.

Helmling, Steven, 'Marxist Pleasure: Jameson and Eagleton', *Postmodern Culture: An Electronic Journal of Interdisciplinary Criticism* 3: 3 (1993), 27.

Lord, Timothy C., 'A Paradigm Case of Polemical History: Terry Eagleton's *The Ideology of the Aesthetic*', *CLIO: A Journal of Literature, History, and the Philosophy of History* 22: 4 (1993), 337–56.

McGowan, J., *Southern Humanities Review* 27: 2 (1993), 166–9. Review of *Ideology: An Introduction*.

Mullins, W. A., *Canadian Journal of Political Science* 26 (1993), 829–31. Review of *Ideology: An Introduction*.

Murphy, J. W., *Studies in East European Thought* 45: 3 (1993), 229–30. Review of *Ideology: An Introduction*.

Rocktaschel, L., *Deutsche Zeitschrift für Philosophie* 41: 5 (1993), 936–9. Review of *Ideology: An Introduction*.

1994

Hadfield, A., *Anglia Zeitschrift für Englische Philologie* 112: 1/2 (1994), 260–2. Review of *Nationalism, Colonialism, and Literature*, ed. Seamus Deane (with Terry Eagleton, Fredric Jameson and Edward Said).

Hogan, P. C., *Philosophy of the Social Sciences* 24: 1 (1994), 84–92. Review of *Ideology: An Introduction*.

Morgan, Austen, 'Derrida, Derry and Terry', *Irish Studies Review* 7 (1994), 36–7.

Norris, Christopher, *Comparative Literature* 46: 4 (1994), 390–3. Review of *Ideology: An Introduction*.

1995

Bertens, H., 'Literary Criticism and Theory: An Introduction', *Revue de Littérature Comparée* 69: 4 (1995), 488–90.

Deane, Seamus, *London Review of Books* (19 Oct 1995), 28. Review of *Heathcliff and the Great Hunger*.

Donoghue, Denis, *New Republic* (21 Aug 1995), 42. Review of *Heathcliff and the Great Hunger*.

Easthope, Antony, *Irish Studies Review* 12 (1995), 38–41. Review of *Heathcliff and the Great Hunger*.

Hadfield, A., *Times Literary Supplement* (7 July 1995), 24. Review of *Heathcliff and the Great Hunger*.

Leerssen, J., *Irish Review* 17/18 (1995), 167–75. Review of *Heathcliff and the Great Hunger*.

Lenk, K., *Politische Vierteljahresschrift* 36: 3 (1995), 553–4. Review of *Ideologie: eine Einfuhrung* [*Ideology: An Introduction*].

'Used Books: *Literary Theory: An Introduction* by Terry Eagleton', *Critical Quarterly*, 37: 1 (1995), 95–101.

1996
Cooper, A. R., *Notes and Queries* 69: 5 (1996), 119–21. Review of *Ideology: An Introduction*.
Daly, Nicholas, *Novel: A Forum on Fiction* 29: 2 (1996), 248–9. Review of *Heathcliff and the Great Hunger*.
Dufays, J. L., 'Critique et théorie littéraires: une introduction', *Recherches Sociologiques* 27: 2 (1996), 147–8. Review article.
Hogan, P. C., *College Literature* 23: 3 (1996), 178–88. Review of *Heathcliff and the Great Hunger*.
Strumpte, M., 'Aesthetics; A History of its Ideology', *Zeitschrift für Religions und Geistesgeschichte* 48: 2 (1996), 186–7.
Sturm, E., 'Literary Criticism and Theory: An Introduction', *French Review* 69: 5 (1996), 795–7.
Waters, H., *Race and Class* 37: 3 (1996), 79–82. Review of *Heathcliff and the Great Hunger*.

Index

10; desire 362; dichotomies 334;
English landscape 382; humanism 171,
172, 177, 188–9, 193 n, 326; ideal
language 160; idealism 93–4, 151, 165,
182, 185; ideas of culture 100, 104–8;
individualism 166, 176–7, 179, 340,
364; Kundera 93–4; life-force 326;
Nature and society 382; *poéte maudit*
377; radicalism 364, 366; *Wuthering
Heights* 58; *see also* German
Romanticism
Rorty, Richard 269, 291, 292, 293, 300;
and Americanness 285–7, 290–1; as
bourgeois liberal 301; essay, 'Solidarity'
285; moral judgements 301
Ross, Martin, *The Real Charlotte* (with
Somerville) 391
Ross Roe, Wittgenstein in 337, 339
Rousseau, Jean-Jacques: and the body 160,
161; *La Nouvelle Héloise* 161; *Les
Confessions* 161; natural rights 296
ruling class: élite 111, 113, 155;
Heathcliff's appropriation 390; ideology
234, 235; Ireland 389; *see also* hegemony
rural society: George Eliot 177, 179–80,
182, 186; Ireland 389, 390
Ruskin, John 99, 102, 111, 383, 385; art
and society 106, 110; Romantic
humanism 171
Russell, Bertrand 284, 336, 337
Russian revolution 169, 249; culture 249,
254
Ryan, Michael, *Marxism and Deconstruction*
261

Said, Edward 167; 'Yeats and
Decolonization' 346
Saint Oscar (Eagleton) xiv, 341, 347–8,
370–3
Saints and Scholars (Eagleton) 310, 338
Sartre, Jean-Paul 337; attack on capitalist
and Soviet states 255; and the body
160; concept of the self 296; Western
Marxist lineage 254–5
Saussure, Ferdinand de 281, 288
Scargill, Arthur 89
Schelling, Friedrich von 296
Schiller, Friedrich von 217; aesthetic state
330; art as social paradigm 329; binary

oppostions in 335
Scholem, Gershom 210 n
Schopenhauer, Arthur 242, 288, 308–9,
385; aesthetic 328–9, 330, 332, 333, 335;
alienation 327; anticipations of Freud
325, 335 n; Bakhtinian aspects 321; the
body 309, 321–2, 327, 334, 335;
boredom 323; and bourgeois ideology
309, 326, 335; Brechtian aspects 321;
carnivalesque in 309, 322; comedy,
humour and laughter 321, 322, 324,
334–5; compassion and detachment
329–30, 331; concept of philosophy
331–2; desire 309, 322, 325–6, 327–8,
331; disinterestedness 328, 330–1, 335;
ethics 332; genius as objectivity 328;
German language 322; happiness as
unrealizable 330; Hegel 322; history
323–5; humour and hopelessness 309,
322–3; id against Hegelian superego
322; intellect 330, 332, 335 n; Kant 322;
knowledge and practice 330;
materialism 321; meaningless of being
327; moral value and action 329–30;
music and the will 331–2; nausea 333;
negative form of knowledge 333–4;
Nietzsche 242, 321, 331, 332; passion
328; pessimism 321, 324–5; on Plato
322, 329; realism 324, 329; reason 322,
327, 331; self-immolation 328–9, 332–3;
subjectivity and the subject 327, 328,
329–30, 332–3; sublime 329; tragedy of
human life 323–4; tragicomedy of vision
334–5; transcendentalism 330, 332,
333–4; value 334; the Will 242, 309,
321, 325, 327–8, 330, 332, 334;
Wittgenstein 309
science: and ideology 231; of text 165
script 167, 201; anonymity, *Tristram
Shandy* 204; puritan tradition 202;
Trauerspiel 197; and word 197
Scrutiny 154, 165, 267, 275, 277, 317;
Hardy 45, 46; modernism 271, 272,
274; modernity 272
Second World War 256, 285, 313
the self 85; communitarian view 301;
concepts 296; deconstructionist idea
167; Hobbesian idea 296; Hume 296;
postmodernist view 301; sexual identity